Different Field Types Behave in Different Parts of the Layout

Browse Mode - View as List

Field Type	Title Header / Header	Leading Grand Summary	Sub-summary (when sorted, above)	Body	Sub-summary (when sorted, below)	Trailing Grand Summary	Footer / Title Footer
Biggest in Found Set	Part Not Visible	Biggest in Found Set	Biggest in Found Set	Part Not Visible	Biggest in Found Set	Biggest in Found Set	Part Not Visible
Standard Deviation of Found Set	Part Not Visible	Standard Deviation of Found Set	Standard Deviation of Found Set	Part Not Visible	Standard Deviation of Found Set	Standard Deviation of Found Set	Part Not Visible
Fraction of Total of Found Set	Part Not Visible	100%	100%	Single Record Percentage of Found Set	100%	100%	Part Not Visible
Total of Found Set	Part Not Visible	Total of Found Set	Total of Found Set	Part Not Visible	Total of Found Set	Total of Found Set	Part Not Visible
Count of Found Set	Part Not Visible	Count of Found Set	Count of Found Set	Part Not Visible	Count of Found Set	Count of Found Set	Part Not Visible
Weighted Average of Found Set	Part Not Visible	Weighted Average of Found Set	Weighted Average of Found Set	Part Not Visible	Weighted Average of Found Set	Weighted Average of Found Set	Part Not Visible
Summary - Weighted Average	Part Not Visible	Part Visible	Part Visible	Part Not Visible	Part Visible	Part Visible	Part Not Visible
Summary - Running Count	Part Not Visible	Part Visible	Part Visible	Total of Records up to and Including Current Record	Part Visible	Part Visible	Part Not Visible
Summary - Fraction of Total when Subtotaled	Part Not Visible	Empty (when sorted)	Empty (when sorted)	Current Record Percentage of Subtotal Group (when sorted)	Empty (when sorted)	Empty (when sorted)	Part Not Visible

How Different Field Types Behave in Different Parts of the Layout

Browse Mode - View as List

Field Types	Title Header	Header	Leading Grand Summary	Leading Sub-summary	Body	Trailing Sub-summary	Trailing Grand Summary	Footer	Title Footer
Text	Part Not Visible	Value from Selected Record	Value from First Record in Found Set	Part Not Visible	Value from Multiple Records	Part Not Visible	Value from Last Record in Found Set	Value from Selected Record	Part Not Visible
Number	Part Not Visible	Value from Selected Record	Value from First Record in Found Set	Part Not Visible	Value from Multiple Records***	Part Not Visible	Value from Last Record in Found Set	Value from Selected Record	Part Not Visible
Date	Part Not Visible	Value from Selected Record	Value from First Record in Found Set	Part Not Visible	Value from Multiple Records***	Part Not Visible	Value from Last Record in Found Set	Value from Selected Record	Part Not Visible
Time	Part Not Visible	Value from Selected Record	Value from First Record in Found Set	Part Not Visible	Value from Multiple Records***	Part Not Visible	Value from Last Record in Found Set	Value from Selected Record	Part Not Visible
Container	Part Not Visible	Value from Selected Record	Value from First Record in Found Set	Part Not Visible	Value from Multiple Records***	Part Not Visible	Value from Last Record in Found Set	Value from Selected Record	Part Not Visible
Calculation	Part Not Visible	Value from Selected Record	Value from First Record in Found Set	Part Not Visible	Value from Multiple Records	Part Not Visible	Value from Last Record in Found Set	Value from Selected Record	Part Not Visible
Global	Part Not Visible	Global Field Value	Global Field Value	Part Not Visible	Global Field Value***	Part Not Visible	Global Field Value	Global Field Value	Part Not Visible
Summary - Total	Part Not Visible	Total of Found Set	Total of Found Set	Part Not Visible	Total of Found Set	Part Not Visible	Total of Found Set	Total of Found Set	Part Not Visible
Summary - Average	Part Not Visible	Average of Found Set	Average of Found Set	Part Not Visible	Average of Found Set	Part Not Visible	Average of Found Set	Average of Found Set	Part Not Visible
Summary - Count	Part Not Visible	Count of Found Set	Count of Found Set	Part Not Visible	Count of Found Set	Part Not Visible	Count of Found Set	Count of Found Set	Part Not Visible
Summary -	Part Not	Smallest in	Smallest in	Part Not	Smallest in	Part Not Visible	Smallest in	Smallest in	Part Not Visible

Special Edition Using FileMaker Pro 5

Rich Coulombre

Jonathan Price

Contents at a Glance

I Planning
1. Planning 21
2. Articulating Your Plans as They Evolve 33
3. Specifying Your Fields 55
4. Case Studies in Planning 83

II Building
5. Building Your Files 107
6. Maintaining Referential Integrity 133
7. Keeping Your Data in Good Shape 173
8. Crafting the User Interface 213
9. "Webifying" Your Database 249
10. Hot Calculations 273
11. Reporting 341
12. Dumb Portal Tricks 395
13. The Joys of Self-Joins and Other Interesting Relationships 421

III Scripting
14. Scripting 443
15. Troubleshooting a Script 481

IV Reaching Out
16. Integrating FileMaker, Expanding Its Reach 497
17. FileMaker Pro Multiuser Design and Deployment Considerations 519

Index 533

que

A Division of Macmillan Computer Publishing, USA
201 W. 103rd Street
Indianapolis, Indiana 46290

Special Edition Using FileMaker Pro 5

Copyright © 2000 by Que

All rights reserved. No part of this book shall be reproduced, stored in a retrieval system, or transmitted by any means, electronic, mechanical, photocopying, recording, or otherwise, without written permission from the publisher. No patent liability is assumed with respect to the use of the information contained herein. Although every precaution has been taken in the preparation of this book, the publisher and author assume no responsibility for errors or omissions. Nor is any liability assumed for damages resulting from the use of the information contained herein.

International Standard Book Number: 0-7897-2201-1

Library of Congress Catalog Card Number: 99-65685

Printed in the United States of America

First Printing: September, 2000

02   01   00   4   3   2   1

Trademarks

All terms mentioned in this book that are known to be trademarks or service marks have been appropriately capitalized. Que cannot attest to the accuracy of this information. Use of a term in this book should not be regarded as affecting the validity of any trademark or service mark.

Warning and Disclaimer

Every effort has been made to make this book as complete and as accurate as possible, but no warranty or fitness is implied. The information provided is on an "as is" basis. The author(s) and the publisher shall have neither liability nor responsibility to any person or entity with respect to any loss or damages arising from the information contained in this book or from the use of the CD or programs accompanying it.

Associate Publisher
Greg Wiegand

Acquisitions Editor
Stephanie J. McComb

Development Editor
Marta Justak

Managing Editor
Thomas F. Hayes

Technical Editor
Stephen Blackwell

Media Developer
Jay Payne

Indexer
Bill Meyers

Proofreader
Harvey Stanbrough

Layout Technician
Steve Geiselman

Contents

Introduction 1

A Developer Muses in Garden Supplies **2**

The Gist of the Relational Approach **4**

The Benefits of Going Relational **5**

The Problem with Lookups **7**

The Most Common Relationship: One to Many **10**

How We Keep Track of All the Children **14**

What's Next **17**

I Planning

1 Planning 21

Some Good Reasons to Plan Ahead **22**

What Goes into Planning **23**

Explore the Culture Like an Anthropologist **24**
    Encourage Griping, Day-Dreaming, and Brainstorming **25**
    Interview Managers First **26**
    Listen to the Staff for a Different Perspective **28**
    Ask the Staff What You Can Do to Make Their Life Easier **29**

Report on the Plan in a Preliminary Proposal **30**

2 Articulating Your Plans as They Evolve 33

Adopt the Client's Point of View **34**

What Goes into the Proposal **34**
    Articulate the Business Problem **35**
    Clarify the Purpose **36**
    Identity the Information **36**
    Estimate the Time and Money Needed for Developing the Database **37**
    Act as a Consultant to a Client **38**

Create an Entity Relationship Diagram **39**
    Deciding What an Entity Is **39**
    Turning Our Attention to Attributes **40**
    Make Up a List of Candidates **42**
    Start the Diagram at the Heart of the Database **43**
    Defining the Relationships Between Entities **44**
    Confirming That the Emerging Diagram Fulfills the System Requirements **48**
    Formalizing the Diagrams **49**
    Refining Your ER Diagram by Questioning Your Tables **51**
    Working Document: The Absolutely Positively Final ER Diagram **51**

Create a File Structure Diagram **52**

3 Specifying Your Fields 55

Creating a Field Specification List **56**

Naming the Field **59**

Defining the Field Type **62**
    Consider How You Want to Sort the Values in the Field **63**
    The Way You Want to Search Affects Your Choice of Field Type **64**
    Automatic Formatting Depends on Field Type **65**
    The Way You Can Calculate Depends on the Field Type **69**

Considering What Actually Will Be
Entered in the Field   70
   What to Put in a Text Field   70
   What to Put in a Number Field   71
   What to Put in a Date Field   71
   What to Put in a Time Field   72
   What to Put in a Container Field   73
   What to Put in a Calculation Field   74
   What to Put in a Summary Field   75
   What to Put in a Global Field   75

Changing the Order in Which FileMaker
Lists Fields   76

Deleting Fields   77

Changing Field Types   78

Changing Field Names   79

Anticipating the Layout for
Each Field   80

4 Case Studies in Planning   83

Why Case Studies   84

A Case Study of Old Willy's
Country Club   84
   Talking with Shirley   85
   Developing the Entities and Their
   Relationships   85
   Considering Some Business Rules   87
   Scores by Hole   87
   Entering Scores   88
   Field Definitions   88
   Fields in the Scores by Hole File   89

A Case Study of Klodner's Kar
Dealership   93
   Playing with Entities   94
   Developing the Field Definitions for
   the Kar Dealership   98

II Building

5 Building Your Files   107

Build Your Tables   108
   Naming Names   108
   The Naming of Entities   109

Create Your Fields   110

Create Relationships Between Files   112
   Name Those Relationships!   112
   Create Relationships   113
   Deciding What Kind of Relationship
   You Need   115
   How to Display Data from the Parent
   Side   117
   Implications for Searching and Sorting   120
   Creating a Relationship from a Parent
   to Children   120
   Choosing the Options for your
   Relationship   122
   Displaying Data from the
   Child Side   124
   Implications for Finding
   and Sorting   126
   Finding in a Portal   127
   Using Data from the Related Child
   Fields   127
   Using Data That Is More Than
   One File Away   128
   Special Focus: Using a File of
   Constants, or a Template File   130

6 Maintaining Referential Integrity   133

Why You Need Referential
Integrity   134

Problems with Referential Integrity   134

Following the Rules   136
   Implementing Rule #1: Primary
   Keys Must Be Unique   136
      Implementing Rule #2: Foreign
      Keys Must Be Valid   137

Creating a Child from a Parent
via a Portal 144
Another Way to Insert a Value into
the Foreign Key Field 146
Setting Two Foreign Keys 149
Filling the Foreign Key Field at the
Click of a Button 152

Dealing with Threats to Referential
Integrity 152
    Threat #1: User-Assigned or Editable
    Primary Keys 152
    Threat #2: Deletion of a Parent 153
    Collecting, Rather than Deleting,
    Contacts When Their Company
    Dies 156
    Using a Delete Table 161
    Threat #3: Users Messing with
    Menus 164
    Threat #4: Users Messing with Layouts
    They Shouldn't See or Use 165
    Threat #5: Users Creating Incomplete
    Parent Records from Within the
    Child 166
    Threat #6: Importing a Parent or
    Child Record 167

Maintaining a Unique Compound
Primary Key 169
    Weaknesses 170
    How You Create the Interface
    Can Help Validate 171
    Alternate Approach to
    Validation 171

Testing for Valid Referential
Integrity 172

7 Keeping Your Data in Good Shape 173

Keeping Your Data Healthy 174

Why Good Data Goes Bad 174

Enabling Accuracy 174

The Dream: Complete Accuracy 176

Offering Lists of Choices 176
    Pop-Up Lists 176
    Pop-Up Menus 177
    Radio Buttons 178
    Check Boxes 179
    Perfecting the Interface of Radio
    Buttons and Check Boxes 181

Conditional Value Lists 181

Having FileMaker Automatically
Enter Information 185

Lookups 189

Allowing or Preventing Entry
in Fields 192

Having FileMaker Check for
Accuracy 197
    Of Type 198
    Not Empty 198
    Unique 198
    Existing 199
    Member of a Value List 199
    In a Range 199
    By Calculation 199
    Validating Social Security
    Numbers 202
    Not Allowing Users to Override the
    Validation 204
    Displaying a Message if Validation
    Fails 205
    Validating Global Fields 205
    Conditional Validation 206

Preventing Users from Editing a Record
After It Has Been Created 208

Adjusting the Tab Order to Suit the
User's Habits 209

Extra Carefulness: Keeping Carriage
Returns Out of the Data 210

8 Crafting the User Interface 213

The Interface Is All There Is—
for Users 214

Let Users' Tasks Shape Your Design   214

Decide Which Layouts to Focus On   215

Use Tabs for Convenience and Clarity   217

Use Menus if You Must   218

Combine the Best of Both Approaches   220

Decide on Your Default Views   220

Fit Information into a Single Record View   222
  Unfold Minor Information Gradually   224

Distinguish Groups of Information by Their Functions   224
  The Main Idea   224
  Setting a Customer   225
  Add Text to Clarify the Purpose of Layouts and Areas   226
  Yes, You Should Include Lists   228
  Make Your Own Sort Buttons   228
  Use Color and Graphics to Indicate Functionality   229

Prepare for Consistency   230
  Make Your Layouts Look Stable   230
  Set the Default Formatting for Text and Graphics   230
  Let FileMaker Help You Keep Formats Consistent   232
  Make Objects Line Up Consistently   233

Make Data Entry Easy   237
  Never Have the Users Do What the Computer Can Do for Them   237
  Go With the User's Flow   238
  Signal Exactly Where to Enter Information   238

Design Meaningful Buttons   238

Arrange Buttons in Functional Areas   240

Print the Reports the Users Expect   241
  Describe Printing the Way Users Do   242

Test Prototypes and Get User Feedback   243

Use the Interface Prototyper   245
  Buttons and Tabs   246
  Tabs Within Tabs   247
  Main Menu   247

9 "Webifying" Your Database   249

Letting People Interact with Your Data   250

How FileMaker Came to the Web   251

Choosing Between Instant and Custom Web Publishing   254

Instant Web Publishing   255

Custom Web Publishing   260
  How Links Work   260
  How Links Differ from Forms   261
  How Forms Work   261
  Creating an Error Page   263

Understanding Security   264

How to Plan for Web Delivery   264

Putting Your Database Directly on the Internet   266

Exporting Data as HTML Pages with the Results of Calculations   267

Creating Detail Records   269

Using Lasso to Go Beyond the Web Companion   271

10 Hot Calculations   273

Why Calculations Can Get Hot   274

Welcome to the Formula   274

Mathematical and Financial
Calculations   275
   Using Rounding to Avoid Errors in
   Summaries   275
   Using the Int and Mod Functions to
   Get Whole Numbers   277
   Calculating Payments   278

Text Calculations   279
   Taking Apart a Text String to
   Reformat It   281
   Putting Together a Full Address   283
   Using Overlapping Fields to Simulate
   Typing in a Calculation Field   284
   Overlapping Fields to Mimic
   Conditional Text   287
   Using the PatternCount Function to
   Spot Values   289
   Extracting the Prefix to the Name,
   First, Middle Initial, Last Name, and
   Suffix to the Last Name   290

Date Calculations   294
   Calculating How Long It's Been Since
   the Last Contact   294
   Calculating the Next Appointment
   Date   295
   Breaking Apart a Date for
   Subtotals   301

Time Calculations   305
   Calculating the Total Amount
   of Time   305

Conditional Calculations   307
   Comparing IF, Case, and Choose
   Statements   307
   Using IF Statements for a Multi-
   Column Report   309
   Using IF Statements to Extract the
   Choices of Radio Buttons   310

Calculations with Container
Results   312
   Flagging Key Items for Management
   with Graphics   312

Creating a Fully Formatted Document
for Database Publishing   313

Calculating with Check Boxes   316
   Sorting Check Box Items and
   Converting Values to a Comma-
   Separated List   317
   Allowing the User to Modify
   Standard Text   320
   Doing a Mail Merge on a
   Text Field   321
   Doing a Search-and-Replace
   Within a Field   323

Generating Random Numbers   326

Creating a Bar Graph   329

Exporting or Importing Fixed-Length
Records   331
   Exporting to Fixed-Length
   Records   331
   Importing Fixed-Length
   Records   333
   Custom Delimiter   335

Handling Aggregate Functions   338

11 Reporting   341

Layouts at the Heart   342

Using the Report Wizard   342

How Layout Parts Work   343
   Sub-Summaries   344
   Title Header and Header   344
   Leading Grand Summary   344
   Leading Sub-Summary   345
   Body   345
   Trailing Sub-Summary   345
   Trailing Grand Summary   345
   Title Footer and Footer   345

How FileMaker Figures Out What to
Put Where   346

Creating Summary Reports   348
   Generating Reports with Subtotals
   by Month or Quarter   354

Putting Sub-summaries on Every Page   355

Using Sub-Summaries Without Summary Fields   357

Using the GetSummary Function in a Calculation Field   358

Where Should You Report From?   361
   Printing from the Parent   361
   Printing from the Child   363
   Many to Many   365

Interesting Reporting Techniques   366
   Providing the User with Editable Report Headers and Footers   366
   Creating a Script to Allow the User to Perform a Search as the Basis for a Report   367
   Taking Advantage of Fixed Page Margins for Multiple Printers   373
   Finding the Median in Subtotals and Grand Totals   374

Variations in Effect   378
   Print or Preview   379
   Browse Mode-View as Form   381
   Browse Mode-View as List   381

12 Dumb Portal Tricks   395

What Shows Up in a Portal— and How   396

Dumb Portal Trick #1: Lets You See in a Portal All Records from Another File   396

Dumb Portal Trick #2: Lets You Use Conditional Value Lists with Portals   398

Dumb Portal Trick #3: Highlights Selected Items in Portals   401

Dumb Portal Trick #4: Moves Records from One Portal to Another   403

Dumb Portal Trick #5: Uses Calculated Multivalued Keys to Filter Which Child Records Show Up in the Parent Record   405

Dumb Portal Trick #6: Moves Portal Rows and Inserts a Portal Row   406

Dumb Portal Trick #7: Allows the User to Choose the Sort Order in a Portal   412

Dumb Portal Trick #8: Makes the Portal Disappear!   414

Dumb Portal Trick #9: Uses a Portal to Control Access to Records in Another File   417
   Filtering the Records   418
   Allowing Users to Edit   419

13 The Joys of Self-Joins and Other Interesting Relationships   421

The Miracle of a Self-Join   422

Assembly-Subassembly, a.k.a. the Hamburger Example   426

Many to Many to Many   431

An Outer Join   435
   The Not-So-Hot Button   436
   A Hotter Button   437

III Scripting

14 Scripting   443

The Benefits of Scripting   444

Creating and Editing Scripts   444

Good Scripting Practices   448
   Naming Your Script   448
   Add Comments   450
   Modularize Your Scripts   450

Write Once, Run Many Ways   453

Startup Scripts 453
    Startup Part 1: Open All the Files and Maximize the Windows 454
    Startup Part 2: Decide What to Do with the Status Area 455
    Startup Part 3: Go to the Right Layout 455
    Startup Part #4: Show All and Unsort 456
    Startup Part #5: Initialize Those Variables 456
    Startup Part #6: Show a Welcome Screen, if You Have One 457
    Startup Part #7: Set Page Setup/Print Setup, if Users Can Select Print from the Menu 457
    Startup Part #8: Create a Log of Who Enters This System and When 458
    Startup Script 458

Shutdown Scripts 458
    Close All Files in the System 459
    A Shutdown Script 459

Scripts to Help Users Navigate Among Layouts 459
    1: Make Sure You Know What Mode You Are In 459
    2: Go to the Right Layout 460
    3: Initialize Any Variables You Need 460
    The show_data_entry_notes Script 460

Scripts for Navigating Among Parents and Children 461
    Child-to-Parent Navigation 461
    Parent-to-Child Navigation 463
    Parent-to-Parent Navigation in a Many-to-Many Relationship 464

Scripts That Delete 465
    Deleting a Parent 465
    Deleting a Child 466

Scripts for Creating New Records 468
    Easy Example of Creating New Records 468
    The new_invoice script in Invoices 468

Scripts for Sorting 468
    To Ascend or Descend 469
    Returning the User to the Original Record 469
    The sort_by_date_of_invoice Script 470

Scripts for Reporting 470
    The capture_id_of_found_set_of_customers Script 471
    Capturing the IDs of the Current Invoices 472
    Printing, at Last 472
    The print_ar_aging_by_customer Subscript in Invoices 472
    The print_ar_aging_by_customer Script in Customers 473

Scripts Asking Users What They Want to Print 473
    The print_invoice_button Script Behind the Print Button 474

Scripts for Preparing Canned Finds 474

Scripts That Duplicate Records 476

Handling Button Actions in Your Scripts 476

15 Troubleshooting a Script 481

Looking for Trouble 482
    Interrupting with Pause 482
    Interrupting and Showing Messages 482
    Halting the Script at Different Places to See Whether It Worked so Far 482
    Writing Script Results to a Log Field or File 483
    Beeping at Yourself 483

Using Analyzer—A Two Thumbs
Up Product   **483**
Printing the Scripts   **484**

Scripting Gotchas   **484**

IV Reaching Out

16 Integrating FileMaker, Expanding Its Reach   497

FileMaker at the Center   **498**

Examples of the New Connectivity   **499**
  Salespeople on the Road   **499**
  Furniture Inventories on the Hoof   **499**
  Upscale Furnishings   **500**
  Press Office   **500**

How FileMaker Connects   **500**

Different Ways of Connecting with FileMaker   **501**
  Platforms   **501**
  Wireless PDAs, PDAs, Pagers, and Cell Phones   **502**

Taking Advantage of Industry Standards for Data Exchange   **505**

Using ODBC, JDBC, and Java   **506**
  Making FileMaker Pro a Data Source for ODBC Applications   **506**
  Getting ODBC Data Out of FileMaker   **509**
  Importing ODBC Data   **511**
  JDBC and Java   **516**

Going from HTML to XML and WML   **517**

And Don't Forget Reports   **518**

17 FileMaker Pro Multiuser Design and Deployment Considerations   519

The Idea of Multiple Users   **520**

Designing Multiuser Files   **521**

Deploying Multiuser Files   **523**

FileMaker Server   **524**
  Defining Fields as Sole Guest   **527**
  Safe Hosting   **527**

Multiuser Deployment, Design, and Networking Tips and Pitfalls Checklist   **528**

Index   533

About the Authors

Rich Coulombre is co-owner of The Support Group, Inc., a database design, development, and training organization founded in 1985 and located in Natick, Massachusetts. The Support Group specializes in FileMaker Pro (http://www.supportgroup.com). The Support Group is a partner level member of the FileMaker Solutions Alliance as a consulting and training organization.

Rich is a frequent speaker at MacWorld, Seybold Conferences, and all FileMaker Pro Developer Conferences. He has trained literally thousands of users and developers in FileMaker Pro. He provides developer-level training at both Harvard University and MIT, and has frequently been hired by FileMaker, Inc. to teach their sales and sales engineering staff.

Rich is the only two-time winner of the FileMaker Pro Excellence Award. He won it in 1998 for delivering and developing outstanding training, and in 1999 for increasing awareness of the FileMaker Platform. He has also won the Mad Dog Mallon PR Achievement Award.

Rich is co-author with Jonathan Price of *FileMaker Pro 2.0 for Windows* and *FileMaker Pro 2.0 for Macintosh*. Author of numerous technical articles on FileMaker Pro published in a variety of magazines and technical journals, Rich has also produced a training video on behalf of Claris Corp called "FileMaker Pro 3.0 Relational Video."

Jonathan Price wrote *How to Write an Apple Manual*, which later became *How to Write a Computer Manual*. Its latest version, co-authored with Henry Korman, is called *How to Communicate Technical Information*.

Jonathan consults with writing groups and content providers, and creates manuals, help systems, and Web pages for companies such as America Online, Apple, Cadence, Canon, Casio, Claris, Epson, Fujitsu, Go, Hewlett-Packard, IBM, IDG, Informix, Kodak, Nikon, Oracle, Panasonic, Ricoh, Sony, and Sun. His articles have appeared in magazines such as *Esquire, Family PC, Harper's, Home Office Computing*, and *Reader's Digest*. He created *The Virtual Playhouse for the Macintosh* for Macmillan, and has published more than two dozen other books on subjects such as computing, television, and writing.

About the Technical Editor

Steven H. Blackwell is President & CEO of Management Counseling Services of Alexandria, Virginia and a Partner level member of the FileMaker Solutions Alliance. He has extensive background in communication strategy consulting, association management, and business consulting. He was the recipient in 1998 of the FileMaker Pro Excellence Award. Working with FileMaker Pro for over 14 years, he has extensive experience in the development and deployment of database management solutions for enterprise workgroups, associations, and small businesses. He has more information and FileMaker Pro reference materials available at http://www.FMP-Power.com.

Dedications

From Rich

The book is dedicated to the most important aspect of my life—my family:

My wife, Jean, my children Leigh, Stephanie, and Joseph, my mother, "Grammy" Coulombre, and my sister, "Auntie" Jeanne.

From Jonathan

A big hug to Lisa, Noah, and Ben, who've been so patient and supportive through many long phone calls and sessions at the computer. And a belly rub to Toby, our Welsh Corgi, for chasing away balloons and robins, and to Summer, our Beagle, for being so sweet.

Acknowledgements

From Rich

To my wife Jean and my children Joseph, Stephanie, and Leigh, I appreciate their understanding during this project. Most of the work on this book was done nights and weekends, during time generally reserved for my family. Now that it is done I promise to play more games in the backyard and to organize many more fun family outings.

To Steven Blackwell, Karl Pittenger, and Marc Norman—these guys went way beyond the call of duty in helping to make this a great product, and their gracious offers of assistance are deeply appreciated. To members of The Support Group, Inc. and the many current and former employees of FileMaker, Inc. and industry contacts, we also extend a heartfelt thank you. A work of this size and complexity requires a team effort, and these guys belong in the hall of fame.

And finally a personal note to a creative thinking team that I have co-coached with Karen Yetra for the past four years. The organizations we have worked with are called Odyssey of the Mind and Destination Imagination (www.dini.org). They provide children starting early in their education process with an opportunity to solve detailed problems by using highly creative thinking with a heavy emphasis on teamwork. I have had the privilege to work with the following team members over the past few years: Sarah Benesi, Matt Boole, Leigh Coulombre, Reba Cunningham, Alex Mercuri, Luke Parsons, Brett Pendleton, Courtney Soule, and Lauren Yetra.

I am constantly amazed at how bright, hard working, and creative these team members are and how well they work together. I thoroughly enjoy working with them, and have great respect for them. If our future is in their hands, we are in good shape!

Rich's Technical Hall of Fame:

Steven Blackwell: Not only did Steven act as our technical editor, he has been a constant cheerleader in getting this book done and promoted.

Marc Norman: Marc knows more about FileMaker Pro than anyone I know. While writing this book, I relied heavily on Marc's deep knowledge of the intricacies of FileMaker Pro and his outstanding user interface skills. Marc also spent countless hours reviewing and testing the sample files and making many recommendations on improvements.

Karl Pittenger: Karl is a systems engineer who volunteered to provide a technical review. His deep knowledge of FileMaker Pro provided us with excellent feedback on this book

Members of The Support Group, Inc: The following members of my company, The Support Group, Inc, gave constant feedback on the development of the sample files and text and overall assistance in the book's production: My business partner, Rick Kollmeyer; FileMaker developers extraordinaire Chad Novotny, Sheila Kleinrichert, Julien LaFleur, Monique Mikrut, Adam Klodner, and Jeff Fox; as well as John Phillips, a member of our enterprise development team; and our office manager Jean Todd.

Others who were also instrumental in helping this book:

Kevin Mallon and Steve Ruddock, PR guys from FileMaker, Inc.

Darren Terry, Delfina Daves and Judith Coley, members of the FSA team at FileMaker, Inc.

Eric Culver and Jay Welshofer, systems engineers for FileMaker, Inc.

Stephen Gallagher from FileMaker, Inc.

Tony Campitelli, Christian Thomas, and Geri Hyde formerly of FileMaker, Inc.

Ric Ford from www.macintouch.com

Jane Reeder from FileMaker, Inc.

Robert Munne and Dave Dumas formerly of FileMaker, Inc.

Debi Fuchs from Aptworks Consulting

Albert Harum-Alvarez from Small Company

Peter Baanen from TROI

Dave McKee from FileMaker, Inc.

Bill Schissler from FileMaker, Inc.

John Mark Osborne from Database Pro's

Danny Mack from New Millennium Communications

Vince Menanno from Waves in Motion

Bill Doerrfeld from Blue World Communications

Jeff Gagne from Apple Computer

And all of those who submitted the scripting "gotchas" (see Chapter 15)!

Tell Us What You Think!

As the reader of this book, *you* are our most important critic and commentator. We value your opinion and want to know what we're doing right, what we could do better, what areas you'd like to see us publish in, and any other words of wisdom you're willing to pass our way.

As an Associate Publisher for Que, I welcome your comments. You can fax, email, or write me directly to let me know what you did or didn't like about this book—as well as what we can do to make our books stronger.

Please note that I cannot help you with technical problems related to the topic of this book, and that due to the high volume of mail I receive, I might not be able to reply to every message.

When you write, please be sure to include this book's title and author as well as your name and phone or fax number. I will carefully review your comments and share them with the author and editors who worked on the book.

Fax: 317-581-4666

Email: `office_que@mcp.com`

Mail: Associate Publisher
Que
201 West 103rd Street
Indianapolis, IN 46290 USA

INTRODUCTION

WHAT MAKES A DATABASE RELATIONAL

In this introduction

A Developer Muses in Garden Supplies   2
The Gist of the Relational Approach   4
The Benefits of Going Relational   5
The Problem with Lookups   7
The Most Common Relationship: One to Many   10
How We Keep Track of All the Children   14
What's Next   17

A Developer Muses in Garden Supplies

If you know your way around relational databases, please skip this introduction. You might want to jump right to Chapter 1 to start planning your new database. In this preface, we'll provide an overview of some of the key ideas that make a database relational.

Think of a credit card. It's your passport to a relational database.

The other day I went into Sears to buy a new lawnmower, pruning saw, and soaker hose. I took these items over to the cashier, and when he rang them up I handed him a credit card. He swiped it through the little black box, and then the waiting began. As I settled in for the usual network delays, I asked myself, "What's going on here?"

Information, I imagined, is read off the credit card and sent to a computer acting as a clearinghouse that OKs or refuses to OK the card for that transaction. Then, I imagined, the clearinghouse goes back to the issuing bank and gets approval or not, the bank sends an OK to the clearinghouse, and from there the OK makes its way back to Sears. But, still waiting for that to happen, I wondered exactly what information is actually sent to the clearinghouse and bank, and what information does Sears get back?

Probably, I thought, the clearinghouse gets information such as the credit card number, name, amount of purchase, and perhaps the type of transaction (such as credit), date, and a vendor ID ("This is Sears Store 23 calling"), and perhaps a vendor transaction number, so a particular credit card transaction can be tied back to a particular sales slip. All that info gets sent off, and the clearinghouse figures out which bank to go to, gets approval, and then sends that info back to the store, saying, yes, go ahead and accept this credit card, with an approval number, which is probably also stored by the clearinghouse and the vendor, as shown in Figure I.1. The data is piling up!

Figure I.1
Information flows from the store to the clearinghouse, from there to the bank, and back.

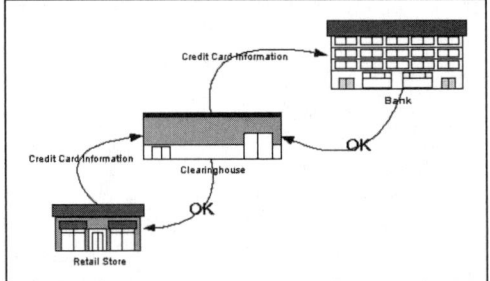

So what does the clearinghouse do with that transaction data? When Sears accepts a credit card as payment, their accounting staff knows that they are going to get reimbursed by the credit card company eventually, so the bank has to keep track of the transaction so Sears can get its money. And the bank must store all these transactions, because they have to pay Sears on my behalf, and in turn they are going to be eager to collect that money, plus interest, from me.

The bank may have a file with customer information organized by credit card number. That file has all the information about my account. Now the credit card company must have hundreds of thousands, even millions of accounts. So how does their billing software know which name and address to use? Well, it prints out the name and address for the customer that has the same account number as the transaction. The bank's database is drawing together data from two files (see Figure I.2).

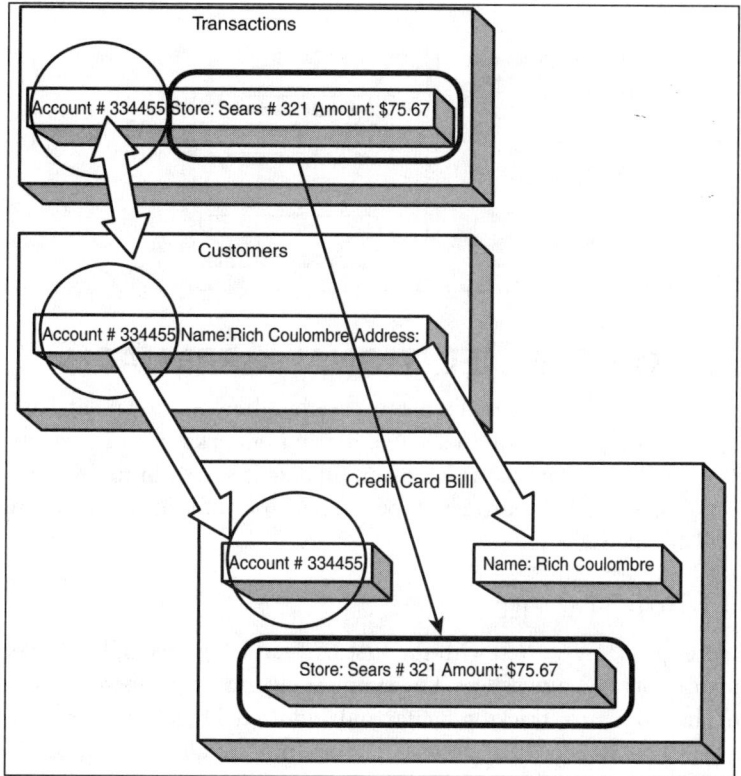

Figure I.2
The customer's bill is a report drawing on data from different files, such as the Customers file and the Transactions file.

And the description of the transaction itself, on the bill, will say Sears, and give a phone number. Now where does the vendor name and phone number come from? Maybe there is a Vendor table with a list of all vendors and associated vendor IDs and since each transaction record includes a vendor ID, and there is a matching vendor ID in the Vendor table, the software can put the two together, take a name and phone number from the Vendor table, and take my name and address from the Accounts table, plus detail lines from the Transactions table and print all of those on one report, as shown in Figure I.3. That efficient synthesis is what relational databases are all about.

So the software is smart enough to be able to use info from multiple files (or tables), and it can join records in one table to records in another table because they share a common piece of information. Those common pieces of matching information are called keys.

In a moment, the little black box clicked and started printing out the sales slip for me to sign. I was soon on my way home to clean up my lawn.

Figure I.3
The bill reports information from the Vendor table, the Accounts table, and the Transactions table.

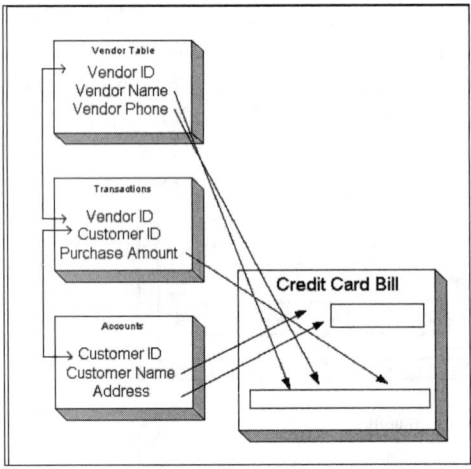

THE GIST OF THE RELATIONAL APPROACH

The moral of this story is that when we are building relational databases, we strive to keep a single type of information in a single file and other kinds of information in other files. Then we build a system by which common data is stored in those files to allow records from multiple files to be extracted for the purposes of reporting, viewing, searching, sorting, and calculating.

GOODBYE TO THE FLAT FILE

Databases probably started with the first list—an inventory of bricks perhaps, or a catalog of manuscripts in a monastery. The simplest electronic databases we deal with today grow out of that approach, tracking names and addresses in an imitation of the desktop Rolodex™—one record per person, and one tray for all the records. This approach, known as a flat-file database, works very well in a lot of circumstances, but when applied to a complex business, the flat file database tends to pile up lots of redundant data (as if each transaction record had to carry the customer's full address), and to freeze information as it was on the date of entry (so that the new address may not be shown on old records).

MINIMIZING REDUNDANT DATA

Historically, relational databases grew out of a need to minimize redundant data because storage was so expensive back in the 60s and 70s. Once businesses started to store data on tapes and giant platters, they realized that it would be cheaper to store a customer's data once and not over and over again, so programmers (using COBOL and RPG) started developing the standards, rules, and conventions of a relational approach.

Academics and consultants joined in, creating advice and rules for optimizing this kind of multifile database. The two main benefits of the relational approach are that it saves space by eliminating redundant data (such as putting the customer's address in the record of every transaction for that customer) and it allows hot links (so that the latest customer address can be put together with the latest transactions, and the bank doesn't happen to send a bill to Rich's old address). Let's ponder those benefits for a moment.

The Benefits of Going Relational

Going relational improves the efficiency, timeliness, and accuracy of your database. You can cut way back on redundancy in your data, ensure that your information stays up-to-date, and improve the speed and precision of sorting, searching, calculating, and preparing reports.

The critical difference between an old-fashioned flat-file database and a relational database like FileMaker Pro 5 lies in the way the two of them store information.

A flat-file database can track and manipulate only the data within the current file. It generally cannot take advantage of some form of hot link, where the data comes in on the fly from some other file. As a result, it must store data redundantly. Also, not having the capability to borrow the latest customer data from another file on the fly, the flat-file database must store that data with every transaction, which makes the database grow heavy and cumbersome.

A flat-file database, then, is a single table. There may be many columns for different types of information, such as name, address, area code, and phone number, as well as many rows with individual records, such as those for your pediatrician, gynecologist, therapist, and acupuncturist, but the database is still just one big table. In that sense it has no depth, no third dimension. It does not relate to, or rely on, any other tables. Hence, the information appears in only one file, and that file is, compared to a relational database with its big pile of files, a bit flat.

In a flat-file database, you can only display, edit, calculate, or report on data that exists in the current file. Of course, you can use a lookup to gather information from another file, but that information is then copied into your current file. Now you have the same info in two places. But if the other file should happen to get new information, your current file won't necessarily get the news. Gradually, the two files may slip out of sync, and at least one may become inaccurate, out-of-date, or just plain wrong.

In a relational database such as FileMaker Pro 5, on the other hand, you can store data in several different files as shown in Figure I.4, in which a layout in the People file borrows corporate information from the Company file, and a layout over in the Company file grabs information from the People file at the moment the user asks to see the information.

Figure I.4
In a relational database, data is stored in separate files and brought together on the fly.

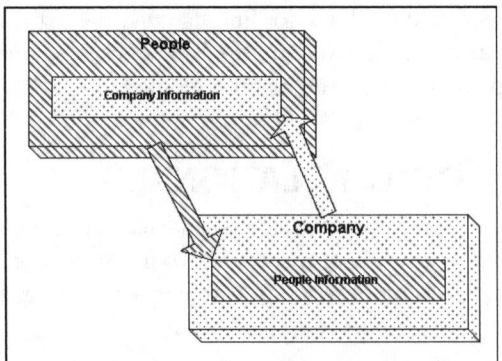

In a relational database, the file can use its own information and then flesh that out by borrowing the latest info from another, related file. To take another example, each individual invoice in an Invoice file contains some information unique to its file, such as an invoice total, and shipping and handling fees for that invoice, but the invoice also draws the latest customer address from an address file, so when a customer moves, you only have to correct one record in one file (see Figure I.5).

Figure I.5
The Invoice file has its own data, and supplements that with information drawn from the Address file.

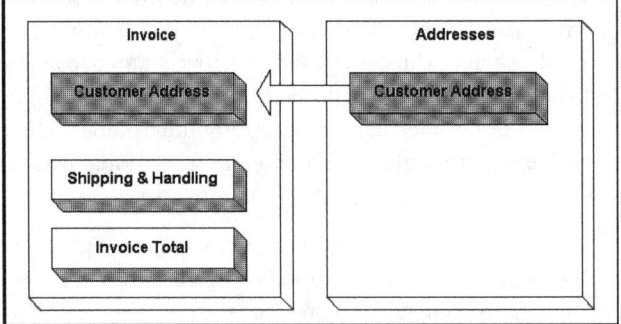

You have to build a relationship between the two files, but once you get those properly "related," you avoid the burden of redundant data and ensure that you're pulling in the most recent information, rather than working with something you copied months ago, such as an address that may or may not be current.

➔For a graphic analysis of the details of files in a relational database, **see** "Create a File Structure Diagram," **p. 52.**

Agreeing on Terms
To clarify our terms, we ought to point out that there are three different lingoes used for talking about databases.

- The simplest terms are those used by FileMaker most of the time: You have a file containing a set of records, and each record has a bunch of fields into which you can enter data.

- The Information Technology departments prefer to describe a file as a table, which has rows (or records) and columns (or fields).

- Database scientists call the file or table a relation, which has tuples (rows or records) and vectors or attributes(columns or fields). Don't ask us to justify the Computer Science jargon; if you never have to talk with an academic or a Ph.D. in Database Design, you can forget tuples and vectors.

The people who invented FileMaker adopted the simpler, more everyday terms, because they were writing an application for the rest of us.

TABLE I.1 TERMS FOR KEY COMPONENTS OF DATABASES

FileMaker	Information Technology Professionals	Computer Science Professors
File	Table	Relation
Record	Row	Tuple
Field	Column	Vector

THE PROBLEM WITH LOOKUPS

In a flat-file database, the Lookup function serves to bring data into one file from another. But the lookup occurs only once, copying the actual data in, and swells the file with this duplicated information. Each time you look up some information, your file expands. As shown in Figure I.6, a flat-file database of People can look up company information in another flat-file database called Company, but each time it does so, the actual data is brought in and gets stored with the record. As the staff adds people, all that company info gets looked up each time and incorporated into the new records, so instead of storing the information about the company once, you may end up storing it a hundred or more times.

Figure I.6
Each time a flat-file database performs a lookup, its record stores all the information it borrows, leading to bloat and data clog.

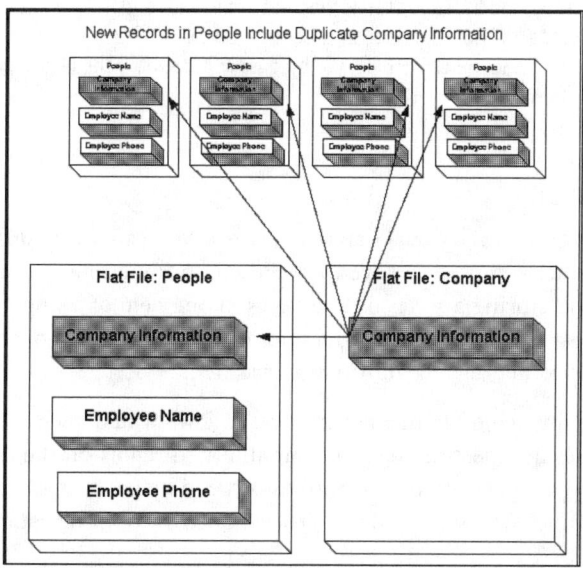

Let's say your group is using an invoicing system in an old-fashioned, flat-file database, and whenever a clerk enters a customer code, the invoicing file performs a lookup into the customer file and copies the name and address from that file, storing the information (redundantly) in the invoicing file. If the clerk happens to send a hundred invoices to a particular customer, then that customer's name and address gets stored 101 times, that is, 100 times in the invoice file and once in the source, or customer file. Not a pretty sight if you run a medium-size business.

And the situation gets worse if the customer moves. Over in the Customer file, you update the address. But with a lookup scenario, you do not get any automatic updating of the addresses in those 100 invoices. The accuracy of all those invoices is left up to the clerk's initiative, so updating is likely to be hit or miss.

(Yes, you could use a Relookup option or command to get the latest data from the source; it would tell the database, "For every record in the found set, go back to the source and bring over the latest name and address." But because this relookup only works on found sets, users might find it difficult to remember how to use the relookup correctly, and you have no guarantee that all records—not just the found sets—will get updated.)

In FileMaker Pro 5, with a relational link between the two files, the moment you update the Customer file, the latest information is available on every invoice for that customer. The actual data lives in the Customer file and is borrowed on the fly to be displayed or printed on the invoice. But the data is not stored in the Invoice file. So the relational approach cuts down on redundancy and makes sure you have the latest information whenever you need it.

> **Note**
> Of course, even in FileMaker Pro 5 there are times when you will probably want to use a lookup. For example, you probably want to look up today's price for a product and have that entered into a bill permanently. (Later, if the price changes in the Product file, you don't want that new price to update all of your existing invoices). A lookup, then, is great for capturing a historical snapshot. But in the days of flat-file databases we often had to resort to lookups and relookups because they were the only way we could grab some data from outside the current file. We used lookups to make the files look as if they were relational. A kludge!

Reporting Is Improved

Reports also go better in a relational database because you can set up different files to contain the extra data that you used to have to squeeze into something like a Repeating Field. Essentially, you were storing a series of line items in one field of a single record. When you wanted to generate a report, the items could not easily be separated out or evaluated individually. Hence, reporting on this information was hell.

For example, in an invoicing file in a flat-file database we would keep all the details of the customer's purchases in repeating fields, so our ability to report on the details was limited. Let's say we wanted a report on total quantities ordered by product. Because the information was in a repeating field, we could not process one row of information separately from another row; all the details of the customer's purchases were clumped together in one field. But in a relational database like FileMaker Pro 5, we can store the invoice-specific information in the Invoice file, and each line item can become a separate record in an Invoice Line Items file.

Now, because the details of the customer's purchases are separate records, we can add them up and produce a subsummary report that shows total quantities purchased by product. By putting the information in related fields, we make reporting far more flexible.

How Files Relate

One of the most important things to determine as you create a database is the nature of the relationship between the files. Although files relate to one another in many ways, the most common derive from the number of one file's records that relate to the number of records in the other file. Hence, there are three most common relationships, as shown in Figure I.7.

- One to many
- One to one
- Many to many

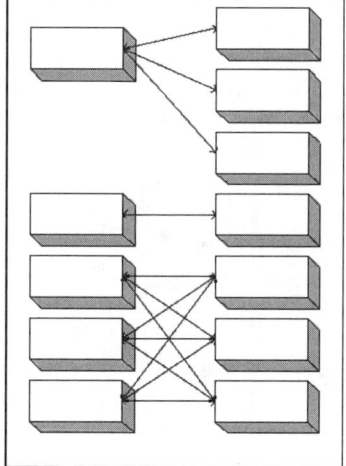

Figure I.7
Three common relationships: one to many, one to one, and many to many.

If we have an Invoice database, when we look at one customer, we realize that a customer can have many invoices. But when we look at a single invoice, it must belong to one and only one customer.

Tip from
Rich

People who are new to relational databases often are able to convince themselves that every relationship is many to many. Going back to the customers and invoices, they do not look at a single customer. Instead, they say, "Customers get many invoices, and invoices are sent to many customers. So we must have a many-to-many situation." The error here is that they are looking at the problem at the entity level (the class as a whole) rather than at the record level (an individual instance of the entity). At the record level, one customer has many invoices, and those invoices are not owned by any other customers.

The Most Common Relationship: One to Many

The most common way in which files are related to each other is one to many. For example, a birth mother may have many children, but any given baby belongs to only one birth mother; in that case, the Mom is the one, and the babies are many. Probably 90% to 95% of the relationships you create will be one to many.

In understanding one-to-many relationships, it's helpful to identify one file as containing parents and the other file as containing children. We don't mean that one spawns the other. We are more concerned with "belongingness." A single parent may have many children, but each child can have only one parent, in the database world. Thus, one customer may have many invoices, but each invoice goes to only one customer. So the Customer file earns the designation "parent," and the Invoices are "children" (see Figure I.8).

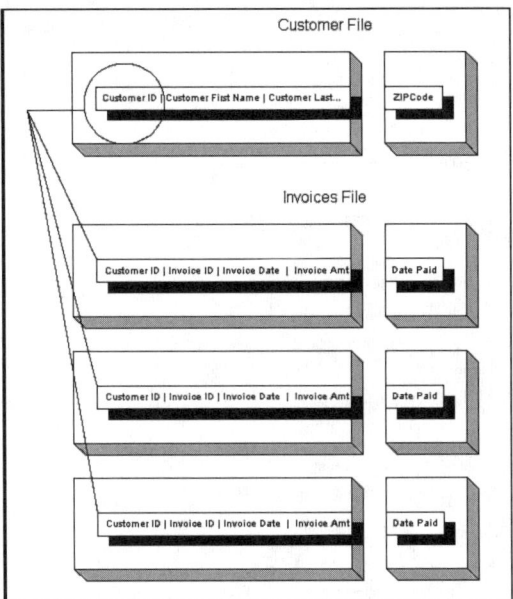

Figure I.8
For each customer, there may be many invoices, as children all belonging to the single parent.

The Other Popular Relationship: One-to-One

You are facing a one-to-one relationship when for every instance of entity A there is zero or one related instance of entity B and vice versa.

One-to-one relationships are not that common. If we look at an example, you'll understand why. Consider someone who creates a file with a Customer Code and a Customer Name, and a different file with the same Customer Code and a Customer Street address, and a different file with the same Customer Code and the Customer City, and another file with the same Customer code and the Customer state, and another file with the same Customer code, and the Customer ZIP code. In this situation all of these files have one-to-one relationships between them, because only one record in each file corresponds to one record in another. Would anyone really do this? Most people would recognize that you would probably prefer to collect all these records in a single file. In designing systems, whenever we see several one-to-one relationships, we try to collect them all in one place, in a single file. But there are still times and places where it will make sense to preserve a one-to-one relationship with two separate files.

Sometimes, you have to keep track of *temporary* information, and a one-to-one relationship takes care of that. Imagine you have a Customer file, and the company president decides to send a survey out to all customers, and asks that you add the survey (and all of its fields and layouts and scripts) to the busy Customer file. You ask, "How long do you want to track this information?" The president says it won't be valid beyond six months. So after six months you will have to delete all of those temporary fields, layouts, and scripts. It would be best in this case to create a separate survey file, and each survey has the ID of the customer it belongs to. That way, you have a one-to-one relationship between one customer and one survey as shown in Figure I.9; a customer will have zero or one surveys, and every survey will belong to one and only one customer. By putting the survey in a separate file, you can throw it away without damaging or marring the customer file.

Figure I.9
A valid one-to-one relationship.

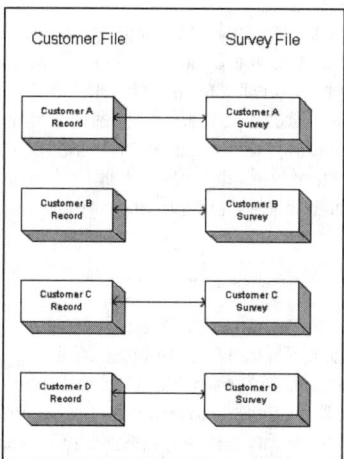

Tip from
Rich

Don't really throw away the survey file. Tell the boss you have discarded it, but store it on the hard disk, because you never know when the boss will want to run another survey, or take another look at the results.

Also, occasionally you may have data that is a *subset* of other data, and a one-to-one relationship lets you handle those subsets without cluttering up your main file. Let's say you have a Human Resources database, and it has fields you track for all employees, such as Name, Address, and Social Security Account Number, but there are certain groups of people within the company for whom you would like to track additional information.

For example, for all the VPs, there are a few dozen extra fields you don't need to track for anyone else, and for the scientists there are additional fields about their education, and then there are the members of the Board of Directors, and you have to track their industry experience.

Now, you could add all those fields to the HR database, burdening every record with a bunch of fields that do not apply to most people; frequently, these fields would be sitting there empty, cluttering up the form, and tempting idle clerks to enter information even when it doesn't belong there. To avoid the waste of space and the possibility of confusion, you could create a separate file for each group's special information. In this approach, you would end up with four files: the HR file tracking the HR attributes for everyone, a file to track the extra information specific to VPs, a file for extra information relating just to scientists, and a file for extra information relating just to members of the Board. So if your company has a thousand people of whom 20 are Vice Presidents, your HR database would have a thousand records, including those of the Board, VPs, and scientists, but the VP database would have only 20 records, one for each VP, each of which would be related to the VP's personal record back in the HR database via her Employee ID—one to one.

Tip from *Rich*	As a general rule, a field or a column must be something that can be used by every row or record in the database. For example, in a Contacts database you can be pretty sure that every person who deserves a record will have a Last Name. But applying this general rule is a matter of judgement. If a particular field only applies to half the records, you might decide to include it, because adding another table would increase the complexity of the system. But if you discover a lot of attributes, each of which applies only to a small number of records, think about splitting them out into one or more other files.
Tip from *Rich*	Emptiness, as in Zen, can be a legitimate value. You may have a field for a spouse, but not everyone is married. Does that mean you have to move all the spouse information to a separate file? Or you may have a field for a home telephone number, but a couple of people don't have home phones. Does that mean you can't put the field Home Telephone in? Common sense must prevail. An empty phone number may be a valid value, meaning, "There is no phone." Empty, then, would be an accurate value for that attribute. If a field describes a lot of records, it probably should be included, rather than getting too picky and forcing that information to live out in its own file.

BE SUSPICIOUS OF MANY-TO-MANY RELATIONSHIPS

When you first develop your database, you may encounter a relationship in which an instance of an entity on one side seems to relate to many different instances of an entity over on the other side and vice versa. For instance, any given invoice may include many products, and any given product may show up on many invoices. Or a student may take many classes, and each class may have many students. When you call a catalog company to order clothing, your invoice includes a shirt, a belt, and a pair of pants (in other words, several products); and in turn, the belt shows up on many other invoices for other customers. Abstractly, one record on one side is related to many records on the other side, and on the other side, one record relates back to many records on this side. In a many-to-many relationship, the question comes up: How do we track which group of records on one side are related to which group of records on the other side?

Good practice in the database world is to create a file in the middle to keep track of which records in one file are related to which records in the other file. Called variously a *bridge*, *composite*, *join*, or *link* file, this file postulates a new entity.

For example, in an invoicing system, you might create a file of line items whose main purpose would be to record the identity of the invoice and the identity of the product being ordered in that line. Each record would be another line item.

Similarly, with the students and classes, we could create a new entity called a registration; each record has a student ID and a class ID, indicating that this student has registered for this class. The join table may be quite simple, with only a few columns showing a simple link between items of information.

But when you think about it, you may decide that a registration record could contain a little more information about the actual registration, such as the amount paid for the class, the date paid, the number of days absent, and the final grade. As shown in Figure I.10, the linking file, then, keeps two pointers (or Foreign keys)—one is the Student ID, and the other is the Class ID—plus any additional information about the link.

Figure I.10
A linking file points in two directions.

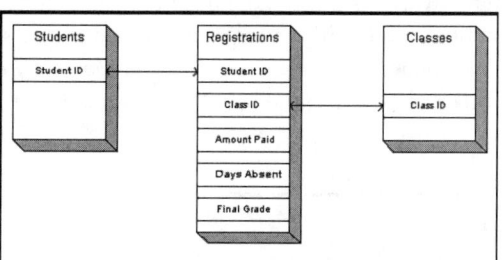

For example, with students and classes, we start out with a many-to-many relationship. On one side, we have a set of students with their Student IDs, and on the other side we have a list of classes, each with its Class ID. This school is a bit backward, though. The Registrar does not have a computer yet and still puts everything on paper. When a student signs up for a few classes, the Registrar draws a line from the student's name over on the left to a class over on the right. So there are multiple lines from each student to the student's various classes. You could follow the lines from the student name to find out which classes that student is taking, but you could also start at a class and trace lines back to names to find out who is enrolled in the class. Of course, the paper diagram is a mess. When the Registrar does computerize, the staff needs to convert each line as well as the two lists. Each line has a starting point and ending point. Can we identify the starting point and ending point as data? Yes, the starting point is the Student ID and the ending point is the Class ID. The middle file that converts a many-to-many relationship into two one-to-many relationships represents the lines. Each record is an instance of one student taking one class.

You may wonder how you add data in this situation. You can add data directly to the middle file, but often the data is added from the two original files in the relationship, and when it is added, that data pours into the middle file as well. Hence, data in that middle file can be added from either the Student file or the Classes file, through relationships. If you go to the Student file and sign the student up for a class, that adds a new record to the middle Registrations file. But if you go over to the Classes file and look at the class, that student is now listed as a participant, because the Classes file also shows records from the common Registrations database.

The question now arises: How does one file "know" which of its records relate to which records of another file? What keeps all of these relationships straight?

How We Keep Track of All the Children

As you design your database, you need to come up with a way the software itself can determine which records in one file are related to which records in another file. You need a device called a *key*. Before we get into details of the way your database will actually deal with keys, let's consider an example that is, sort of, from real life.

Imagine walking into an elementary school's playground that's full of teachers and children. Could you identify which child belongs to which teacher? No. Change the scenario. Let's say you walk around the schoolyard with the same teachers and children, but now the teachers are all wearing T-shirts, each with a unique color, and the students have hats matching the color of their teachers' T-shirts. Now can you identify which students belong to which teacher? Yes. In this case, color is the key. In Figure I.11, patterns represent different colors.

Figure I.11
Here we use patterns to match kids to teachers, so the pattern is the key.

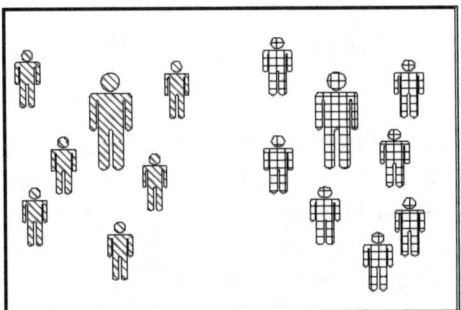

In this imaginary school, we are looking at one-to-many relationships. One teacher has many students, and any one student has only one teacher. The teacher, then, has a key color, and each student possesses a similar-looking key, but the function of the keys is different. Because the teacher is the Parent, the teacher has the Primary key, and in this case, the Primary key is the color. All the students wearing green hats form the Many gathering around that teacher. Each student is a Child file, and so each student's record contains a Foreign key (meaning it comes from outside)—in this case, the color of their hat, which matches the color of the Teacher's T-shirt.

Let's call the teacher's key (the colored T-shirt) a Primary key, because the teacher is the Parent here, and all the students in the teacher's class belong to that teacher—in database terms they are children. The students' hats, echoing the color of their teachers' T-shirt, are Foreign keys, because they are worn by people who "belong to" the teacher without themselves being teachers. Each teacher must have a unique Primary key, or else the whole system collapses, whereas many students carry the same echoing color, or Foreign key.

Here's why the Primary key must be unique. Usually, Teacher Sally wears red and Teacher Jim wears blue, but one day Jim gets confused and wears red. Now there are two problems: Students wearing red hats cannot tell who their teacher is; and in turn, any student wearing a blue hat is without a teacher because they are wearing the identity of a teacher who apparently no longer exists—not a good situation, as shown in Figure I.12.

Figure I.12
What happens when both teachers come wearing the same pattern?

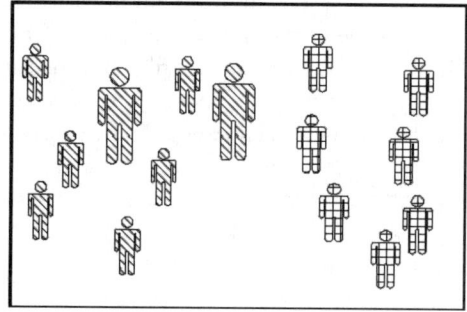

From this little scene, we can draw several conclusions:

- **A key lets us determine which records in one file are related to which records in another file.**
- **The parent file owns the Primary key.** The child files contain a field for the Foreign key, that is, a value that matches one record, and only one record, in the Parent file.
- **The Primary key must be unique.**
- **The Foreign key must be valid.** That is, the foreign key (the value in the Child file) must correspond to a matching value in the Parent file—one record, and only one record, in the Parent file must carry that identifier, or else all the children carrying that value in their Foreign key field will have no matching parent. They will be, in effect, orphaned. The effect would be that when we run reports from the Parent file and the Child file, we could get different results.

> **Caution**
>
> Because it carries the Foreign key with a unique identifier of the related Parent record, a child file's record carries a reminder of the parent, but the parent has no idea what children exist.

APPLYING THE IDEA OF KEYS IN A DATABASE

The relational world, for all its talk about relationships, prefers that parents be single. In this world of single parents, then, we need to make sure we know which children belong to each parent. In the Parent file, we have to set up a special field that will work as the Primary key, a unique identifier for each record. Because the Customer is the Parent, for instance, we need to create a field called Customer ID in the Customer file, containing a unique value for each customer.

Every time a child is born, for example, every time we start a new invoice, it carries the genes of a particular parent, or, in practical terms, a field containing the Customer ID of a particular customer. Because that key information comes from the parent file (outside of the child file), the field is called a Foreign key. The information in that field is "foreign" in the sense of "coming from outside"—outside of the Invoices file, that is. Figure I.13 shows a Primary key (the Customer ID) living in the Customers file, and the same field over in the Invoices file acting as a Foreign key on every record; when the value on a Customer record matches the value on an Invoice, the system understands the two records are related.

Figure I.13
The Primary key lives in the parent file, while the Foreign key shows up in the child files.

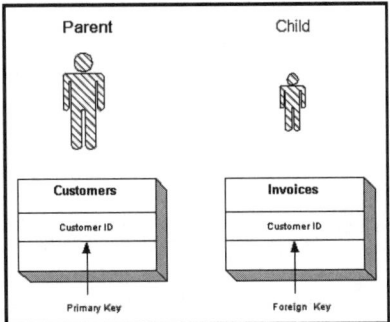

> **Tip from**
> *Rich*
>
> The first field in every file should be an auto-entered serial number that is nonmodifiable and never reused. That way, FileMaker automatically assigns each record a serial number that we can count on as being unique and that we know the users can never change. For example, my employee ID should never be reassigned after I leave the company, because Human Resources may need to look me up later, when I dispute my pension benefits.

Now you have a way of matching an invoice with a particular customer. So FileMaker Pro 5 can bring information about that customer, such as the name and address, into the Invoice file. That information pops up in the invoice right next to data that a clerk enters; when the clerk prints the invoice, the name and address appear along with the purchases, totals, and tax. As soon as the invoicing clerk types in the customer ID, or selects the customer ID from a value list, FileMaker Pro 5 borrows the name and address from the Customer file on the fly. From the clerk's point of view, that information "just appears."

Behind the scenes, though, you know that the data exists in two different files, both part of the same overarching relational system. For instance, if you were to look at the Define Fields list in the invoicing file, you would not find the Customer Name and Customer Address fields. Yet if you were to look at an Invoice layout, you would see the fields Customer Name and Customer Address, and you would see those because the Invoice file has a relationship established to the Customer file; through that relationship, you are permitted to use, or "borrow," values from fields in the Customer file.

There is, then, only one piece of information that is stored redundantly—the Customer ID field. You store that in both files so that FileMaker Pro 5 can determine which customer record is related to which invoices and vice versa. Of course, the Customer ID field, which might be 4 characters long, contains a lot less data than the whole name and address, which might average 75 characters. By storing that one ID redundantly, you avoid having to save all the other information in both files.

And if you send 100 invoices to one customer, the customer name and address information is still stored only one time (in a flat-file database it would be stored 101 times). The customer name and address is borrowed as required from the Customer file for viewing, calculating, finding, sorting, summarizing, and printing. So the *related* field can be used in virtually all situations as if it were really a field in the current file.

Of course, we are talking about only two files here, but in a large organization, the customer name and address may appear in dozens, even hundreds of other files throughout the corporation, so the saving on data storage becomes significant.

Now, imagine an update. In the relational invoicing system, if you change a customer's name and address in the customer file, you don't need a relookup process, because the Invoice file is using those very fields from the Customer file for its data, and it receives an instantaneous update of its values. If you happen to be looking at an invoice to that customer, the name and address will change immediately, on-screen.

So using keys guarantees that the right records in one file are matched up with the right records in another file, allowing for less-redundant information and more accurate updates.

→For the nitty gritty on setting up relationships and keys, **see** "Create Relationships Between Files" **p. 112.**

What's Next

To take advantage of these capabilities in your work, tune into the very first part of this book, where we discuss how to analyze the business problem, identify potential components of your database, work out their relationships, define the needed files, and turn out a blueprint for the construction of your relational database. What kind of relationships are you about to get into? Sometimes, relational databases make Dear Abby blush!

PART 1

PLANNING

1 Planning 21

2 Articulating Your Plans as They Evolve 33

3 Specifying Your Fields 55

4 Case Studies in Planning 83

Careful planning can save you hours of headaches during implementation. In this section, we'll walk through a reliable process for finding out what your clients' business needs are, developing a plan, and confirming it with them.

CHAPTER 1

PLANNING

In this chapter

Some Good Reasons to Plan Ahead   22
What Goes into Planning   23
Explore the Culture Like an Anthropologist   24
Report on the Plan in a Preliminary Proposal   30

Some Good Reasons to Plan Ahead

Planning can't eliminate all chances of chaos, but if you don't plan at all, or if you indulge in casual or haphazard planning, you can be *sure* you will encounter major changes late in a project, and your users may end up complaining that the database still doesn't meet their needs. To help you go to bed at a decent hour even during the last weeks of a project, and to help you make your users smile, we suggest taking the time to do significant planning—before you do the "real" work of creating your database.

In this chapter, you'll get a rationale for putting energy into planning, and then find out how to start by interviewing the boss and the workers who will use your new database.

If you've used FileMaker Pro for years, you may recall a more free-and-easy approach to planning. Back when all the information lived in a single file, a lot of us got in the habit of creating fields, files, reports, and even scripts without thinking too hard ahead of time about where they would go or how they would work together. In fact, in earlier days, we could usually get away with that kind of seat-of-the-pants planning because the software was so forgiving.

But in FileMaker Pro 5, where information is stored in several different files and you borrow that information as needed for calculating, displaying, or reporting, we need a good design from the get-go. With a relational database, careful planning helps ensure that every file (and script) knows where its related files are. If you happen to change one or two of these little details later, or need to add or remove files at some point, you may accidentally mess up scripts, clog the information flow, and end up spending hours hunting down myriad problems.

Think of asking an architect to design and build a home for you. Let's assume you just said, "Build me a Colonial." You had tremendous trust in the designer, and he built you a wonderful home, and after it was finished, you came in and said, "You've done a marvelous job, but there are some changes I'd like to make."

Now, "some" changes would be relatively easy to make. For example, "I'd like to change the color of this room, and I'd rather have a stainless steel sink," are easy changes.

But imagine walking into the new house and saying, "I'd like you to move the kitchen over there where the bathroom is now, and bring the bathroom over here, and, oh, while you're at it, could you change the size of the foundation?" Those changes would require demolition and reconstruction, not just a new coat of paint or a trip to the nearest Home-A-Rama store. Obviously, a homebuyer could avoid this extra expense and delay just by looking at the detailed plans before giving the go-ahead.

In building a database, you are in the role of an architect facing a similar situation. As the developer, if you do not start with detailed specifications that the client can mull over, tinker with, and buy into, you may build a wonderful database, but that system may not do what the client wants. And then, to get what the client really wants, you may have to put in a lot of time demolishing what you built and rebuilding it.

Tip from *Rich*

> The first step in the creation of any database is to turn the computer off. Break out your yellow pad, your pen or pencil, and an awfully big eraser, so you can set your ideas down on paper before you try to implement them on the computer. This restraint keeps you from plunging into the implementation too quickly.

EXAMPLE: PROBLEMS WITH NOT THINKING AHEAD

The boss said, "Could you just make a little database so we can turn out mailing labels to send invoices and newsletters to our customers?" Taking the boss at his word, the designer made up a single field for the customer's name. No need for a field for first name, another for middle initial, another for last name, another for an honorific, if any, and another for title. The designer told the staff to just type all that into the Name field, which became Line One of the mailing label. So the Name field collected entries like these:

- Ms. Cheryl M. Pinkerton
- Mrs. C. M. Pinkerton, CIO
- Reverend Billy Bob Herman
- Herr Professor Gustavus Nagler
- Herb Hanover, Manager
- Señor Alfredo Candelaria

But as the company expanded, its database grew to more than 10,000 records. Now, the boss was so excited that he wanted to send out form letters, beginning "Dear Cheryl" or "Dear Billy." But the designer had no sure way to pull out first names without risking gaffes like, "Dear Herr" or "Dear Mrs." And within the letter, when the boss hoped to be saying, "For all of you in the Nagler family," the database kept spitting out "For all of you in the Herr Professor Gustavus Nagler family," which didn't have quite the ring the boss hoped for. So the boss chewed out the designer, and the designer had to create new fields, and the company had to hire an office temp to re-enter everyone's information into the new First Name, Middle Initial, Last Name, Honorific, and Title fields. What a mess!

COMMON MISTAKE: PLANNING AS YOU GO

When your database grows like a tumbleweed in a wet month, you may discover you can't handle certain queries, calculations, or reports, because you didn't build the data structures right. Of course, if you are cooking up a little database for yourself, you won't mind the kludges, workarounds, and inconveniences. But users find poor design an annoyance, and tell you so, but worse, they make mistakes because they do not understand what is going on, and their group ends up with inconsistent, inaccurate, and useless data, while the finger points at you.

What Goes into Planning

Planning ahead helps ensure a system that will be easy for ordinary users to learn and use and reliable enough to use for real work. With that goal in mind, you should undertake the activities of analysis and design, developing a series of documents as shown in Figure 1.1.

- Figuring out what different users do on the job right now, what the database should make easier for them, and, if possible, what new tasks the database could perform to make their work better, faster, or easier
- Defining the business case for the new database and giving your "guesstimate" of time and money
- Working iteratively with your client to develop the preliminary proposal into a final specification for your new system
- Creating an Entity Relationship Diagram to capture the major elements of your database
- Making a File Structure Diagram to work out what goes into which tables, and where
- Planning what fields you need, of what type, and with what options, in your Field Definition Table
- Wrapping up all discussions in a final specification

➔For suggestions on ways to discover what needs to be done, **see** "Explore the Culture Like an Anthropologist," below.
➔For details of the document that describes all this, **see** "What Goes into the Proposal," **p. 34.**
➔For the ins and outs and ups and downs of this important tool, **see** "Create an Entity Relationship Diagram," **p. 39.**
➔To see how this diagram can help you plan your work, **see** "Create a File Structure Diagram," **p. 52.**
➔For details on creating a specification for your fields, **see** Chapter 3, "Specifying Your Fields," **p. 55.**

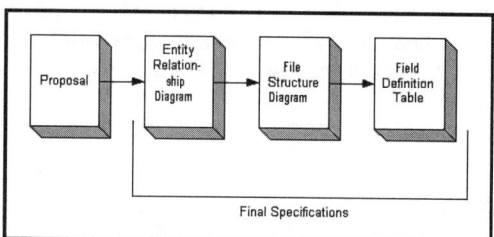

Figure 1.1
Planning involves creating an evolving document as a talking paper and then an agreement with your clients, followed by documents you can use as working plans.

In the rest of this chapter, and continuing in Chapters 2 through 4, you'll learn specific actions to take, questions to ask, and documents to produce during a thorough planning phase.

Explore the Culture Like an Anthropologist

In your role as a developer, you have to take a different point of view from that of an advanced user who is putting together a database for personal use. As a developer, you are creating databases for other folks to use. They are your clients, whether they work in some other company or within your own department, circle, or organization. You need to think through their needs, wishes, tastes, and even cultures, to ensure success for them and for you. And to make sure that you are creating a database that does what they need done the way they like it, you have to talk with them.

Tip from *Rich*
> Find out what kind of work these people do every day. We have developed databases for a number of architectural firms, tracking their clients and projects, and one of the things we learned very quickly was that architects are in a very visual business. We learned that when we presented them with prototypes. If all the fields were not perfectly lined up like bricks in a wall, they thought that the prototype must be broken. In order to get real feedback from these clients, we had to clean up the aesthetics; otherwise they could not get beyond the look.
>
> So, you have to know your audience and be aware of what really matters to them, what affects their judgement. Even when you say, "Don't pay attention to this or that." Your clients are always going to pay attention to whatever they work on and know best—and only later, after they get past those concerns, can they examine your work on the database. (This also means you have to adopt some of their attitudes, just to get your prototypes working for them.)

You have to talk with your future users over and over, like an anthropologist studying a tribe or small town. The first time you talk with the clients, they may tell you a dozen functions they want. And they may mention a few extras they'd like, if the cost doesn't run too high. But as you sketch out possibilities, and perhaps make a prototype, they begin to say things like, "Well, if you can do that, could you maybe also do this, and, well, like this, and that, too?"

As you discuss functionality, anticipate that your conversations with clients will demand regular and repeated feedback:

- Listen, and come up with ideas, get comments, revise your ideas, and try again.
- Don't count on getting all the requirements in one clean half-hour of chatting.
- Don't try to limit the talk to a single interview.

Think of this as an iterative process in which you can all refine your ideas together.

Tip from *Rich*
> For a small project, figure on spending a day interviewing your clients and a day writing up your notes. For a big, complicated project, the interviews may take place over the course of a week or more, and you may need two or three days to write up the results.

ENCOURAGE GRIPING, DAY-DREAMING, AND BRAINSTORMING

When you ask users to sketch out their ideal system, they are often constrained, unconsciously, by their mental models of the current system. They hesitate to tell you what they really want because, limited by their experience or by something they heard a few years ago, they may not believe such a wonderful database could be possible. And heck, it may not be possible. But you'll be able to build something closer to wonderful if you can find out what they really need by asking open-ended questions like those in Figure 1.2. So encourage them to open up with the following list of ideas to use as openers.

- Start with the work they have to get done using the database. What do they have to get out of the database, to do their jobs?
- Explore the problems they encounter with the current systems in the office, including the database.
- What would they like to accomplish, if they could?
- If people start apologizing, saying "I doubt that you can do this, but…" or "It would be impossible, I know, but what I would really like is…," then give them permission to fantasize.
- Resist laughing hysterically. If the users want something you have no way of providing, postpone the bad news until they have finished brainstorming so they do not get discouraged and clam up.
- Don't stress limits, either, because to be polite, users quickly limit their requests, anticipating an inefficient or crippled database just like their old one.

Figure 1.2
Questions like these elicit the context you need for design.

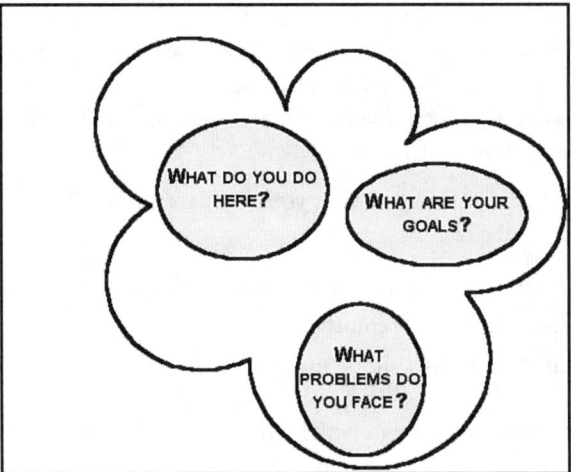

INTERVIEW MANAGERS FIRST

Managers are the folks who approve your invoices and sign the checks. So talk to them first, as shown in the timeline in Figure 1.3. If you don't understand their needs right off, you may not get that recommendation you're after, or, worst case, you may lose the job.

Plus, a manager can usually give you the big picture. A manager can tell you

- Where the database will fit into the flow of work.
- How the database will solve certain problems.
- How the database will improve the speed, accuracy, or efficiency of the work.

Figure 1.3
Your timeline for interviewing might look like this one.

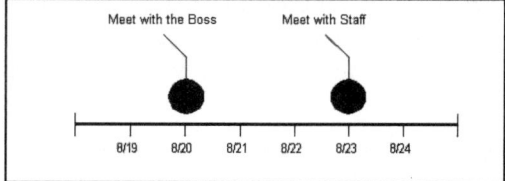

Try to find out what motivates the manager:

- What is driving the manager to look for a new database?
- Does the group need better access to information?
- Does the manager want better reports or reports that don't even exist now?
- Does the manager need to track and regulate the activities of the staff with more precision?

Usually, a manager has one key reason—at most two or three—for requesting a new database. What are the major business reasons justifying the expense and time you are about to put into developing this database? Of course, once a manager gets caught up in the excitement of brainstorming, he or she may begin to realize that the group could get other benefits from the new database—other reports, other searches, sorts, calculations. But your job is to keep your eye on the top priorities, so you can be very sure your design addresses those.

To get to the business reasons behind the decision to build a database, ask the manager questions like these:

- **What do you want this database to do?** What are you trying to accomplish, here? ("I'd like to automate the quoting system for our sales reps.")
- **How will you determine whether the database is succeeding?** ("I'll see a decline in the hours they spend doing their estimates. Right now, they spend three days a month. I'd be happy if we got that down to three hours a month.")
- **How do you carry out this task, or one like it, now?** In many situations, you discover that the staff is already keeping track of most of the necessary data on paper, but suffering from delays, inaccuracies, or inconsistencies, and the manager hopes that going electronic will improve the quality of the data and speed up the process of entering and reporting. ("We have one man who spends two weeks or more writing up a summary of what the department has done in the last quarter, working from paper forms. If all that data were in a database, he could get most of the reports he needs in a few minutes.")
- **What exactly is wrong with the current system?** Is it just that the old system ran on hardware they are yanking? Is the old system unable to move to the latest millenium?

Or is the interface a tangled mess? Does the old database just not do what they want? You have to be extremely thorough in probing what they like and what they hate with their current database. What problems must you avoid?

- **What data are you collecting, already, in electronic or paper forms?** Get copies of every form the staff uses now. These forms give you a leg up on your data dictionary.

- **Where is all this information coming from?** Do people call in? Do folks fax it in? Does some information come from your mainframe? The source of the information has an impact on how you design the file structure of the system as well as on the way data gets entered.

- **What reports do you issue?** These reports help you define the kind of data you'll need to include in the database. Often, managers hesitate to show you their current reports because they are not as fancy as they would like, and the whole point of having you develop a new database is to turn out better reports. But insist that you get a chance to go over these reports together, so you understand the data and the ways in which the manager hopes to improve the reports. Ask what the manager wants to keep, add, or delete.

- **Is there some new challenge you face that demands you have this database?** ("We never used to have to track this kind of data, but now the government requires we collect it right away. It's a new and immediate need.")

- **What special automation will be required?** For instance, is the data coming from a mainframe, so you need to build in some routines that allow FileMaker to import that data automatically? Or are they piping data up to the mainframe at times, so you have to plan the conversions? For example, you may have to post new data to the mainframe, and then get back a text file from the mainframe saying which data was valid and which was not. In that situation, you have to alert the users to the transactions that were accepted and the ones that were declined, along with error codes that let the user figure out what the problems were, such as the data being too long or too short for the field range. Then a user has to repair the transactions that were declined, flag those for resubmission, and you have to resubmit them.

LISTEN TO THE STAFF FOR A DIFFERENT PERSPECTIVE

Ask the manager's permission to talk to the users directly. Although some managers may say, "Why bother?" the users give you a lot of information that the manager simply doesn't know or doesn't care much about. These details may include issues that the workers deal with on a day-to-day basis, weirdo exceptions, or pathological problems that keep coming up. You get great inside dope from them. That's the first reason to bother talking with users.

The second reason is simply human nature. If you don't involve users in the design of your database, they won't use it.

The worst possible situation is a manager saying, "You build it the way I say," and when you do, he hands the database to the users saying, "Use this." That doesn't go over very well.

Users who feel left out of the process may drag their feet, cause subtle difficulties, deliberately misunderstand things, refuse to follow procedures, and generally sabotage the transition, resulting in so many complaints that the manager eventually comes to believe that the real problem is your database, not his autocratic style.

On the other hand, if you sincerely solicit advice and counsel from the users throughout the design and development of your database, the users will be chomping at the bit to use your database. They will have a vested interest in its success.

Ask the users the same questions you posed to the manager. Describe the ideas you heard from management and find out whether these proposals really make sense from a worker's point of view. Will these changes make their work easier, more efficient, and more accurate? Or is there some risk that the changes will screw up the data for years? How realistic are these ideas?

Ask the Staff What You Can Do to Make Their Life Easier

Staff people can tell you exactly the kind of details you will need to make your work easier. For example, they might cite the following things:

- Typical entries
- Exceptional entries
- Common searches (What facts do they regularly look up?)
- Common mistakes in data entry (Do you need to verify the entries in certain fields?)

In turn, you can make their lives easier if you probe to find out this information:

- What information they consider really important, and what is less important (so you can highlight the critical information on your layouts, and de-emphasize the less important stuff)
- What interface, data entry, search, calculations, or sort problems they would like cleared up, and similarly, what tasks they have trouble performing in these areas (and why), so you can pay particular attention to these aspects of the database
- What manual calculations, summaries, and write-ups they are currently performing (so you can offer to automate some of these tasks)
- The sequence in which they like to enter information or read it off the forms (so you can arrange the fields and the tab order that way)

Tip from
Rich

> Ask managers and users to draw you a picture of each report, showing what goes on top, what is on the left, and all the parts in-between, because they usually remember all the data elements in a report, but they tend to forget them if you just ask, "What are all your data elements?"

Get ready for strong emotions. Sometimes the staff members are the ones who have been demanding a new database, so they are giddy with relief that you are actually going to be working on it. That's great.

> **Tip from** *Rich*
>
> If you can't avoid working on a project that seems likely to become a battlefield, then insist that the staff and manager meet together with you and argue out their differences before you proceed. No matter how flexible you are, you cannot stretch far enough to please both sides in a civil war. You need at least a general agreement on the purposes of the database before you go on.

Rarely do the staff people completely agree with their managers. In most cases, what you hear from the managers and staff is reasonably consistent. But there are usually some issues, questions of interpretation, differences in emphasis, and downright disagreements that will surface. You should present those to the manager as decisions to make, because you need guidance on how to develop the database, and the manager may also need to consult with the team to thrash out their own consensus.

Sometimes, when the manager and the workers have not talked in detail about the project, and they come to it with very different experiences and perspectives, you may discover that their ideas are far apart. You need to present the areas of disagreement to the manager, diplomatically pointing out when these involve goals, methods, or results, not just a few aesthetic whims. Perhaps the manager needs to sit down with the staff to discuss what they are trying to accomplish as a team. Your job is not to judge what people want, or what would be best for them, if they only had the wisdom you have. Your job, in this situation, is to urge them to reach an agreement on what they want you to do.

> **Tip from** *Rich*
>
> We often think we know what is best for our clients, but we need to show respect for the people we deal with. It is okay to say that other clients have asked for these functions in similar systems. But the people you are dealing with are experts in their own business. We have to rely on and be respectful of their expertise, and our job is to create a tool that handles the business problems they describe. We can make suggestions based on our own experience, but we must never underestimate how smart these folks are.

REPORT ON THE PLAN IN A PRELIMINARY PROPOSAL

After the manager and the workers agree, you can move forward. When you see that a good consensus has emerged, and both managers and end users are in sync on the business purpose of the system, the major components, processing, and results, you can go back to your office, sit down, and write a report detailing what you believe they are asking for. This report usually fills two to five pages on a small project, and ten to fifteen pages on a larger project. It's not a detailed system specification, but a starting point. You might call it a preliminary proposal, a letter of understanding, or a mini system spec. In the next chapter, you'll learn how to create this planning document.

→To get an overview of the components of the preliminary proposal, **see** "What Goes into the Proposal," **p. 34.**

CASE STUDY: THE MANAGER WHO WAS TOO BUSY

Not long ago, we were asked to develop a new database for a group, and we talked extensively with the users, but the manager was always too busy to meet with us. The manager kept leaving phone messages saying he was excited and interested in the new system, but just couldn't get around to meeting with us yet. So, finally in discussion with the staff, we came to a general agreement about the scope and cost of the system, and when we visited the company to present our proposal, the manager finally met with us. He said, "I've read what you and my people agreed on, and I think it is a wonderful start… But to my way of thinking, the system must do all these other things as well." And these little extras were not trivial. They increased the scope of the system by a factor of six or eight. We learned our lesson: it's awfully important to talk to everyone involved, from the beginning—particularly the manager.

CHAPTER 2

ARTICULATING YOUR PLANS AS THEY EVOLVE

In this chapter

Adopt the Client's Point of View   34
What Goes into the Proposal   34
Create an Entity Relationship Diagram   39
Create a File Structure Diagram   52

Adopt the Client's Point of View

As you learn about the database the team needs, you gradually build up a document that will serve as an agreement between you and your clients—a letter for a short project, or a more detailed proposal for a complex project, describing the business problem and the database solution you envision. This document grows during several rounds of discussion as you hammer out details. Once you reach agreement on the way the system will help the clients carry on their business, you can proceed to sketch out the database, creating Entity Relationship Diagrams and File Structure Diagrams as working documents you can use when you actually create the database.

→For the ins and outs and ups and downs of an important tool for developers, please **see** "Create an Entity Relationship Diagram," **p. 39**.

→To see how an annotated diagram can help you plan your work, **see** "Create a File Structure Diagram," **p. 52**.

In your developing proposal or letter of understanding, you are describing the purpose, scope, and components of the database by using terms the manager and staff understand. To make sure you are on the same wavelength, you might use the following dialogue:

- "You're looking for a system that can do the following things."
- "Here are the reports you say you need."
- "Here is the special automation you've mentioned you want."
- "Here are the files I expect you will need."
- "Here are elements of a user interface you may want to consider using."

Make it clear that you are trying to record what you have learned from them, not prescribing some alien system because it would be good for them. You should invite discussion, comments, and participation with appeals like these:

- "Please tell me what's correct or incorrect here, what's missing, and what's in here that you don't need."
- "Please use this document as a starting point for getting on paper what you really want the system to do."

What Goes into the Proposal

Your write-up of the client's vision—and your response—can be thought of as a first draft of a document that evolves as your discussions continue. Here are some major components of this document, as shown in Figure 2.1.

Figure 2.1
These are the major components of your proposal or letter of understanding.

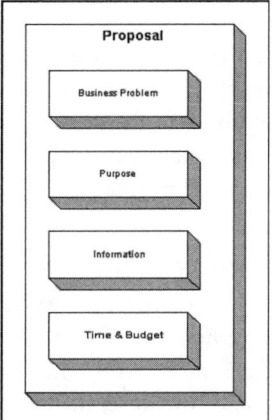

1. The **business problem** that needs to be addressed, along with its context (constraints, important goals, priorities).
2. The **purpose** of the system you are going to build.
3. What kind of **information** people are already entering, and what new information they will be able to track.
4. An estimate of **time and budget**, so the client can sign off on the project.

> **Note**
>
> Here are some of the entities you may want to track down:
> - The files you anticipate may be needed to store all that information
> - The reports the system should kick out.
> - Automation, such as sending email, faxes, having the software do some kind of file manipulation on the server, or ODBC connectivity. Perhaps you need to have FileMaker create HTML files and send them to a Web server.
> - Security required, with levels such as master (you), managerial, administrative, staff, and special (only Human Resources gets to see the salaries). Who gets to go where and do what?
> - Web access, if any, and what type.

Articulate the Business Problem

Start by spelling out the business case for the database as an executive overview because your proposal may accompany the manager's request for a budget, and someone upstairs, who is not nearly as involved with the project as the manager, may wonder why it is necessary. Make clear what the problem is, what the surrounding context is, and therefore why the database is needed.

Clarify the Purpose

To articulate the purpose of the system, review all your notes from the interview and try to create an image of what the clients are looking to do. At a gut level, understand the gist of what they are telling you. Identify what the main focus of the system is. What's the point? Is this primarily a workflow automation system, or is it mainly a company and contact communication system? Or is it a way of tracking employee performance? What is the heart and soul of this system?

Once you understand the core purpose of the system, you can determine which information is crucial and which is subordinate. For example, if you are being asked to create a contact management system, the person (the contact) is at the core, and although you are going to track all the phone calls, meetings, email exchanges, and letters with this contact person, that data is secondary. The focus of the system is not the different ways a user communicated with the contact person; the focus is the person.

After you have a handle on the primary focus, you can communicate better with your clients, even if they have not been explicit about the core of the system or have used ambiguous phrases to describe its essence. For instance, the customer may say, "We want to track projects." But when you ask about the projects, you find out that they really want to track who is working on the preliminary design, who is developing the artwork, who is handling typography and writing, how the work is going, what the deadlines are, and so on. The clients are not really tracking half a dozen different projects, or more; they just want to be able to monitor the progress of a particular project, as it moves across various people's desks. So although the clients use the term "Project-tracking," they are really tracking the flow of work through their group, and the main use of the system will be to look up the current status of the project. It's a workflow system, then, and your understanding of the database flows from this core.

Identity the Information

You need to spell out what kind of data will be recorded (much of this the client is already tracking, although perhaps on paper). The challenge here is to sketch out, roughly, what files and what functionality will be needed.

Describing the Files

Files reflect the major entities you envision as part of the system. Telling the client what files you expect to develop helps the client understand how you are thinking about the business problem. Also, this list gives the client a concrete list of deliverables to look forward to.

Describing Functionality

In discussing reports, automation, security, and Web issues, you need to be explicit about what the system does. Keep the focus on functions—what the system does, not just what information exists—because later, when you develop working plans by sketching various components of the system and their relationships, you will need to compare these functions with the structures you set up to ensure that the system will really perform the tasks the client expects it to do.

> **Tip from**
> *Rich*
>
> Include a paragraph pointing out that although you have tried your best to describe the system as the clients envision it, you want them to point out anything that needs to be added or fixed. Even though we call this document a spec, you and the team should view it as a talking paper.

> **Tip from**
> *Rich*
>
> Throughout this document, you want to make sure that the clients feel confident that you understand their needs. You are telling them what they told you. Never underestimate the impact of listening well. You are confirming that you have heard what the clients have said, appreciate their concerns, and see a way to solve some of their problems.

ESTIMATE THE TIME AND MONEY NEEDED FOR DEVELOPING THE DATABASE

During this period of analysis and planning, you should come up with a rough estimate of the cost, which goes with your developing system spec so the client can determine whether or not to proceed. Of course, you don't yet know exactly what is going to be involved, so you should not commit to a specific figure yet.

Talk in terms of a range of hours and dollars. For instance, you might estimate that a very small project will take between 40 and 60 hours, or a complicated project between 400 and 500 hours, at your usual rate. Multiply hours by dollars so they know about how much this database will cost.

In estimating a range of time and money, make your lowest figure reflect what could happen if everything goes perfectly, and the clients never change their minds. Most of us tend to underestimate, ignoring the many factors that could push up the hours, so even your lowest figure will probably be higher than your first hunch.

Make sure that the higher figure really takes into account the kinds of possibilities that drive project managers mad:

- The clients change their minds, going back and forth, dithering.
- The clients undergo three reorganizations, and the project bounces from one manager to another, each of whom has "a few suggestions."
- The guts of the project turn out to be tougher than you expected.
- The information the team promised doesn't show up on time. Exactly what is the format the mainframe expects?

The upper figure reflects the possibility that the clients may come back to you and say, "You've given us exactly what we asked for, but now we realize, this is not really what we want, and could you make all the following changes, without charging us another dime?" In a range of X to Y, the Y number is very important, because if you come in under Y, in general, your client is happy. If you come in over Y, no matter how many changes they made, the manager has to justify another Purchase Order or Budget Item and looks bad. So when you are quoting a project, make sure that the higher number has plenty of room for the unforeseen and undecided.

A range is enough for the organization to make a decision about whether they want to proceed. Another plus is that offering a range gives you some room to negotiate as the discussions continue.

ACT AS A CONSULTANT TO A CLIENT

As you discuss various drafts of the evolving proposal or letter of understanding, you are effectively acting as a consultant talking with a client, even if you and the "client" work for the same company or department. Once someone asks you to start planning a database, that person becomes your client, and you need to make an extra effort to spell out agreements on paper, rather than assuming that you are in accord.

As a consultant, you must also be the mentor or guide. One point you must get across is that during planning and development, the only constant is change. So with the best of intentions on all sides, all participants must check their egos at the door, recognizing that there are likely to be changes to the business process or model, as well as the database.

As a consultant, you also need to keep in mind that the audience you are talking to is not technically sophisticated. Your job is not to lay out the details you would tell a fellow developer, the neat tricks and turns you anticipate, or the special terms you use for precision when talking to a fellow expert. You have to communicate, first of all, about their business requirements, and only secondarily about the technical details of the solution you propose (even though these details are what probably interest you the most). Your job will be to take their business requirements—when you and your clients agree on them—and translate them into technical requirements, fleshing those out as elegant systems that solve the business problems. That's what you get paid to do.

> **Tip from Steven**
>
> This ability to see both sides of the table is what distinguishes the developer from the tinkerer and from the novice and even from the so-called "power user." To be successful, you must be able to communicate at a business level, but prepared to shift to the technical side later.

While you are working on this document, you are primarily focused on the business, describing several interrelated business problems and identifying ways you can automate solutions. You may say things like, "We need to track this kind of information, we need this kind of report, and we need to get information from these other databases or put it on the Web." But in this first draft, you do not spell out the technical side of the solution. You don't say "Here are the fields, and the files, and the application." In theory, your proposal is independent of any particular product and platform.

> **Tip from Rich**
>
> What you are trying to do here is paint a picture in the client's mind by showing what you intend to deliver. The document may not have the details you would expect in a full-blown technical spec. If you presented a real spec to most clients, they would be lost. You are, instead, trying to help the client understand, at a gut level, what you are going to produce for them. Done correctly, the document should increase their confidence in you and set expectations so they are not disappointed later.

You will expand on the details later, to produce the plans you work from or your internal specs. But this external version gives you and the client the first full picture of the system, so you can proceed to create an Entity Relationship Diagram, develop a File Structure Diagram, make up lists of tables and fields, and define the characteristics of those fields as shown in Figure 2.2.

Figure 2.2
Your proposal or letter of understanding describes the business problem and the database solution in the client's terms; once you have agreement on those ideas, you can proceed to create your own working documents, the Entity Relationship Diagram, and the File Structure Diagram.

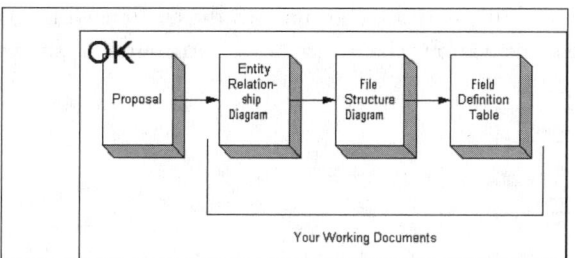

CREATE AN ENTITY RELATIONSHIP DIAGRAM

Creating an Entity Relationship Diagram is a way to put the proposed database structures into visual form, so you can analyze and improve them. You are going to represent all your entities and relationships, so the diagram represents a roadmap for your system. On a small system, the diagram may be fairly small, but on a big system, the diagram gets quite complex. Drawing up this diagram is a step toward defining the technical solution of the business problem you laid out in your proposal, minispec, or letter of understanding. But the ERD is for you, not the client; it is a working document.

DECIDING WHAT AN ENTITY IS

You have already begun to define the things you are going to keep track of, manipulate, and report on. What are these things? Entities. Not disembodied entities or sci-fi thingies. *Entity* is just a fancy name for a thing. But for you as a developer, an entity is anything about which a business needs to track information, as shown in Figure 2.3.

Figure 2.3
Entities are things (or information) that a business needs to track, such as customers, products, or invoices.

An entity might be a customer, a product, an invoice, or a student in a school. Entities tend to track objects, people, and events. So if you have an entity called Students, you anticipate having a series of instances of that entity—that is, individual examples (records), with names like Cheryl, Didi, Esmeralda, Fluffy, George, Harry, and Inez.

Turning Our Attention to Attributes

As soon as you start defining entities, you run into the challenge of attributes. The idea is simple: an entity can have various characteristics, or attributes, as shown in Figure 2.4.

Figure 2.4
An instance of an entity has its own particular values for various characteristics, or attributes.

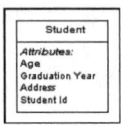

A student has attributes such as age, graduation year, and address. For the student George, the Age attribute has the value of 18, but for Harry, the value of the Age attribute is 23. So, an attribute can be thought of as a field on a record, with various values possible, whereas the entity is the subject of the record as a whole; or, in traditional database terms, an attribute is a column in a table devoted to a particular entity. But then, as you think about the matter, you begin to wonder whether grades form an entity on their own, or just form an attribute of the student, or even perhaps the class. How can you tell whether a thing is itself an entity or just an attribute of another entity? Ask yourself these questions:

- **How many instances of the proposed attribute relate to one entity?** If you have a book catalog, and each book entity has one ISBN number, then the ISBN number is just an attribute of a book. But if you happen to define a book as a single title, in hardbound and paperback, each with its own ISBN, then the ISBN becomes an entity, because a single title has multiple ISBNs.

> **Note**
> Of course, you might then decide that what was really important was the edition itself, so that the hardbound edition would be one entity, and the paperbound edition another entity; in that case, the ISBN would fall back to being an attribute of the entity Edition (see Figure 2.5).

- **Is this potential attribute really just a report?** If an item of information is derived from your data through a calculation or a summary operation, or if it is just a listing of the records, it is probably a calculation, summary, or report, and not an attribute. For instance, we once created an Entity Relationship Diagram with Orders and Invoices, but when we looked more closely, we realized that the invoice was not an entity by itself, but simply a report on the order (see Figure 2.6).

Figure 2.5
Sometimes the book number is an entity, and sometimes it is just an attribute.

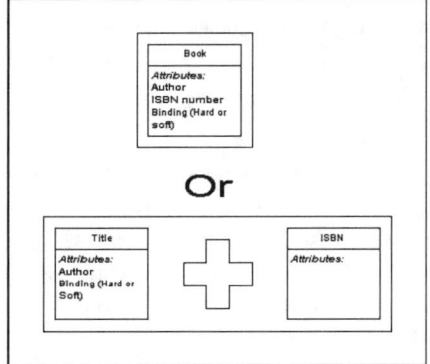

Figure 2.6
Sometimes what you thought would be an entity turns out to be a mere report.

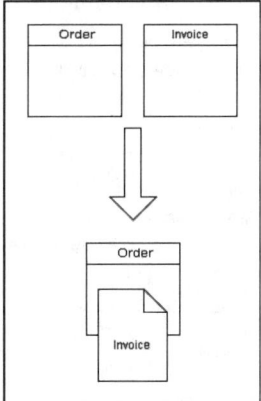

- **If I define this as an attribute of a particular entity, will I find a value for this attribute when I examine every single instance of the entity?** If an attribute doesn't seem to apply to every entity in the class, you may have discovered a separate entity. Of course, you may not have discovered an *important* entity. And you can go crazy with this analysis. For instance, if a few customers lack a fax machine, does that really disqualify Fax as an attribute of Customer, and do we really want to take the time to set up a new entity called Fax, just to handle a few exceptional cases? (Probably not.)

Hence, to qualify as an attribute, a candidate should usually have one and only one value per instance (or record). To sum up, an attribute has

- One value for each instance.
- No more than one value per instance.

Tip from
Rich

> *Empty* can be considered a valid value, in some cases. For instance, if a person has no home phone, then leaving that field empty is correct. What you have to watch out for are moments when empty is not a valid value, that is, when this instance will never have a hope of having a value. For example, a single person may not have a spouse now, but has hopes. You just want to make sure that the attribute applies to a reasonable number of records.

| **Tip from** Rich | Entity names are usually plural, and attribute names are usually singular. |

MAKE UP A LIST OF CANDIDATES

The best way to come up with a useful list of entities and attributes is to brainstorm with anyone else who is working on developing the database. Get together around a white board, read through the mini system spec a few times, and individually come up with lists of candidate entities. Put all the ideas up on the white board so you can be sure you have not missed any. At this stage there are no wrong answers. You just want to make sure you are including everything anyone can think of.

Then look at the board and weed out anything that is not genuinely an entity. Perhaps it is a report, a calculation, or an attribute, and not a full-fledged entity on its own. But perhaps it is a real entity, just one that was not anticipated in the mini system spec (so you have to check with the clients before including it).

| **Tip from** Rich | Beware of creeping elegance when identifying possible entities. Do not add entities that go beyond the customer's requests. Sometimes, you get an idea, and think the client will love it. Maybe so, but you have to give folks a chance to veto the idea before you include it in the database. Going back to our analogy of building a home, an architect might think that an extra room would be wonderful, but you would be upset if the architect just added the room—and the cost—without getting your OK. |

As you work to identify all the entities you need, you may want to work in two ways—from the **top down**, and from the **bottom up**, as shown in Figure 2.7. Working from the top down, you can identify all the entities you need to build the system; then you can add their attributes as extras, as discussed earlier. For example, if you were building a database to track training, you might decide that one important entity would be a class, and then ask yourself, "What are the attributes of a class?" You might decide that class attributes will include teacher name, student names, and workshop name.

Figure 2.7
You can work from the top down or the bottom up.

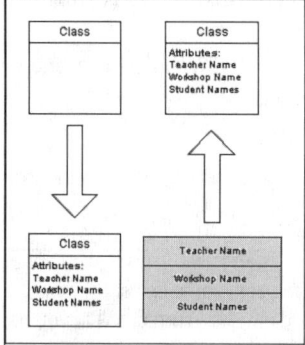

Working from the bottom up, you list every attribute you can think of, and then look around to spot a possible entity to hold all the related attributes. For instance, in the training database, we may need to issue reports that include the teacher's date of hire, student's graduation class year, student's final grade, and student's number of absences. While for other purposes, we may need to track the student's name and address, teacher's name and address, workshop titles, meeting times, meeting room, class number, teacher's employee ID, brief course description, required texts, and recommended texts. So when we look over all these factoids, we see that a lot of them relate to a student, so we probably need a student entity to contain that bunch. Other facts refer to an instructor or a workshop, so we probably also need entities called Teachers and Classes and Texts.

Often, when working from the bottom up, you get most of the attributes assigned, but have one or two left over. For example, what entity should own the grade that the student got in a workshop and the number of times the individual student was absent from that workshop? Is the grade an attribute of the student? Well, not really. Is it an attribute of the workshop itself? Well, not really. Is it a characteristic of the teacher, like an address? No.

So when a potential attribute does not easily characterize one of our entities, we may be facing the need to create a new entity, such as a student in a particular class, or registration. Then the grade and the number of days absent would be related to the student's participation in that class, so they become attributes of our new entity, Registration.

Start the Diagram at the Heart of the Database

Now, you have a sizeable list of entities, and you want to create a diagram of them all, but where do you begin? As you examine your entities, you see them drop into one of four major classes—data entities, code or validation entities, join entities involving many-to-many relationships, or subset tables in a one-to-one relationship. When you are looking at your system, the data entries are the ones that hold your most important information. If the system is a reasonable size, you should be able to pick out a few data entities and say, "These are the heart and soul of the system." And the rest of the entities, while important, are attached to and supporting those entities.

When you are beginning your Entity Relationship diagram, start with those two or three core entities and determine the relationship between them. After you have those relationships defined, you can more easily see where the other entities fit in.

> **Tip from**
> *Rich*
>
> You can use a simple rectangle to represent each entity. The term Entity Relationship Diagram sounds quite grand, but in fact you can sketch it on a napkin, as long as the napkin is large enough. We add lines indicating relationships, and crows feet indicating that a particular entity will probably have multiple instances relating to an individual instance of the other entity, as in Figure 2.8.

Figure 2.8
Here are the components of a simple Entity Relationship Diagram: entity, relationship, and indicator of one-to-many.

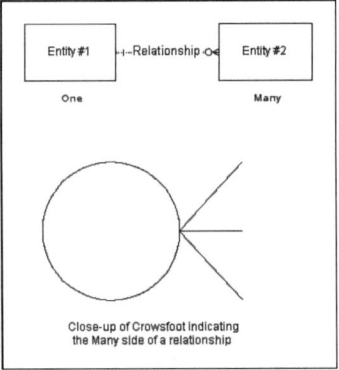

CASE STUDY: ARCHITECTURAL ENTITIES

At our company, the Support Group, we have done work with several architectural firms, and their systems all ended up being quite different, but at the heart of them all were three entities—customer companies, contacts within those companies, and projects performed for those customers, as shown in Figure 2.9. Those entities formed the central nervous system. And once we realized that, we could add supporting entities more easily, tracking lots of things about companies, contacts, and projects.

Figure 2.9
You can see the entities needed for an architectural firm's database.

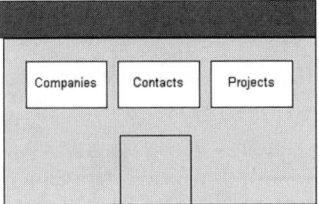

Defining the Relationships Between Entities

After you have identified various entities, you must figure out how they interact with each other in business terms, and, based on the rules of the particular business, how many of each kind of entity may (or must) participate in any given relationship. Are these one-to-one, one-to-many, or many-to-many? So you face several questions about each relationship:

- **If you have an instance of an entity, how many instances of some other kind of entity does it relate to?** For example, if you have a Customer entity, how many instances of the Invoice entity could that customer be related to? Quite a few, we hope. So you would call this a one-to-many relationship, looking at it from the customer side, because a customer may be sent many invoices, but any one invoice belongs to only one customer (see Figure 2.10).

Figure 2.10
One customer can be related to zero, one, or more invoices.

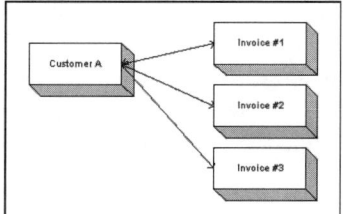

- **How many instances of one kind of entity must be, or may be, related to one instance of another kind of entity?** You could create a customer record before you bill that customer for anything. In that situation, you have an instance of the Customer entity relating to zero invoices. In business terms, that is acceptable. However, every invoice, by definition, must be related to a customer. You cannot have some independent invoices just sitting out there in the ether, waiting to be attached to a particular customer. This boundary situation does not invalidate the basic definition of the relationship between Customer and Invoices as one to many. You just refine your definition by saying that the Customer entity can be related to zero or more invoices, while the Invoice entity must be related to one Customer, as shown in Figure 2.11.

Figure 2.11
You should indicate boundary situations; here the same customer is created, and places one order, then many orders. But no invoice exists without a customer.

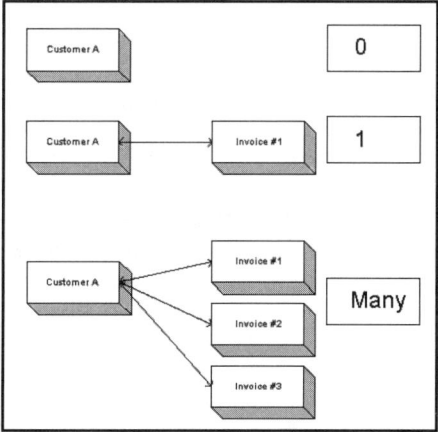

Tip from
Rich

Sometimes, children appear before parents. How could that be? Think of a situation in which a car dealership has an entity for Sales People and one for Cars Sold. There is a one-to-many relationship between a salesperson and cars sold. In this situation, a car is entered into the database before it is sold, and, although it will end up as a child to a particular sales person, you will not know which salesperson is the parent until a sale takes place. In this case, we have children who are orphans until, well, adopted. You might be able to develop a dummy sales person for unsold cars, to keep cars from being orphans until you can re-assign a child to a real parent after a sales transaction.

As a start, write the entity names on yellow stickies, put those on a white board, and draw lines between them, indicating whether the relationship is one to one, one to many, or many to many. A single line leading from an entity indicates one entity is involved, and a crows-foot, or set of lines at the other end indicates that there are likely to be multiple entities at that end. This simple approach makes it easy to move entities around, as you think through the system. Figure 2.12, for instance, shows how you might sketch one-to-one, one-to-many, and many-to-many relationships.

Figure 2.12
Sketch out various kinds of relationships.

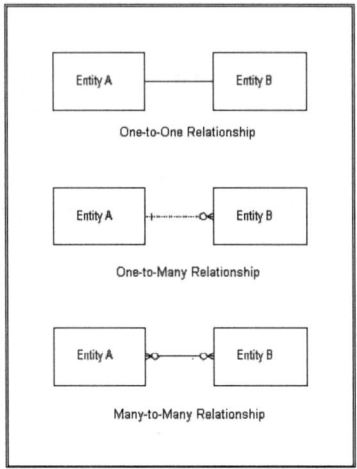

As you work, you may wonder about certain issues and debate certain questions:

- **Are these two perhaps the same entity, masquerading under different names?** For instance, you discover you have an entity named Client, and another named Customer, and their attributes seem to match; perhaps you can merge these two into a single entity (see Figure 2.13). Also, if the two names suggested different aspects of the entity, should you be adding an attribute to handle that difference?

Figure 2.13
Two entities turn out to be one.

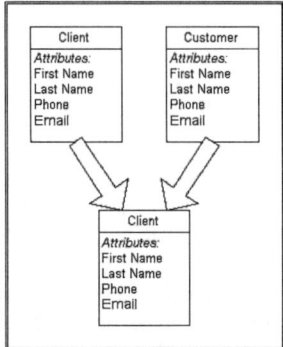

- **Is this potential entity really just an attribute of some other entity?** For example, you have a sticky showing an entity called Schedule, but as you examine it, you realize that this is just the date of delivery on the order, so it is more likely to be an attribute of the order—not a full-blown schedule of workflow. By renaming (as Order Delivery

Date, rather than Schedule), and by downgrading from entity to attribute, you place an order delivery date on the invoice, and can print out reports showing, by date, which orders are due (see Figure 2.14).

Figure 2.14
Here we turn the Schedule entity into a mere delivery date, an attribute of the Order entity.

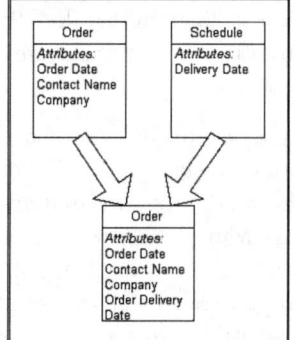

- **Does this entity really belong in the system?** Could we drop it without ruining anything?
- **If this candidate would make a nice addition to the database, is it worth the extra time and money?**

| Tip from Rich | Your first ER diagram is never right. It's normal to redo it many times. |

- **Do you have a lonely file, related to nothing else?** Perhaps it is irrelevant, and can be discarded.
- **Have you spotted a file with only one record?** The question becomes Do you really need it then? For example, in a large university, we might need a file tracking all the buildings, so we can associate classrooms with the different buildings. But in a different kind of organization, which has only one building, we no longer need a separate Building file, because it would have only one record; we can, for the moment, assume that all rooms exist within the one building. Goodbye, Building file!
- **Have you discovered a one-to-one relationship?** Perhaps you thought this relationship would turn out to be one to many, but now you realize it isn't. For instance, you thought there were big differences between a client and a customer, but as the project develops, you have learned that when you link them together, the relationship is actually one to one. A client represents one customer, and a customer represents one client. So they can be merged into a single entity, using whichever name means the most to the organization.

Confirming That the Emerging Diagram Fulfills the System Requirements

Now that you have a whiteboard covered with diagrams showing entities and their relationships, you need to confirm that this system will really do the job. Go through the functions mentioned in the mini system specs, one by one, to make sure that each is dealt with in your diagram. Most will be, but what if you have an ER diagram that does 95% of what the client wanted, but to handle one extra piece seems to offer a major challenge and threatens to take a lot of time and energy?

Well, first, you ought to make very sure that your clients insist on that functionality, particularly if you fear that inserting it now may cause you a lot of grief. Here's why. After you insert that item, you have to go back and recheck every other requirement that you confirmed earlier, because the changes you make now may affect whether you can still successfully perform those other tasks. For example, if you're moving along smoothly, checking off functional requirements, and run into a report you realize you cannot produce—at least not the way you have set things up so far—you may have to shift entities around a bit and change some relationships, or establish a relationship between two entities that used to have no connection. Alas, at that point you have to go back and re-examine everything you have already looked at, to make sure nothing has been affected by these changes.

> **Tip from**
> *Rich*
>
> It really is about cost. Does the client view a particularly difficult feature as worth the time and the cost involved? If so, you'll put it in.

CASE STUDY: DEFINING CONTACTS

You've been working on a database for an architectural firm tracking their client firms, contact people, and projects. At the heart of this system you have customer entities related to many projects, and customer entities related to many of their staff who serve as various contacts with the architectural firm. Everything has gone smoothly as you check your diagram against the functional requirements, until you realize that you need to report on which contacts work on which projects. The firm may work on five different projects for a client, with 12 different contact people. But until now, you have not established a way to relate contact people to particular projects. Time for revision.

Now you need to add a new table showing the relationship between a contact and a particular project, with a record being an instance of that contact working on that project. So this new table will show who worked on what project and what their roles were. Does adding this file mean you should cancel the relationship between client companies and their projects, because you could infer that information from a relationship between a contact person (who works for the client) and a project? But if you ax that relationship, how are you going to validate that the contacts a user assigns to a project really work for the correct client? You might have a user accidentally tying a project to the wrong company's contact person, and send updates to the wrong company (a competitor!).

In this case, then, having examined the impact, you would probably leave these relationships as they exist, while adding the new table (see Figure 2.15).

Figure 2.15
Sometimes adding a new entity resolves a problem.

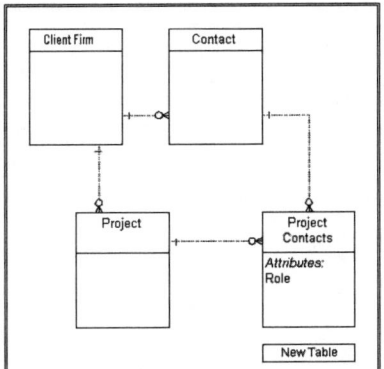

Formalizing the Diagrams

Now that you have pretty much settled on a group of entities, and their relationships, you can document the diagrams formally. Even if you are the only person working on this project, you will probably want to create nice, clean diagrams, using a ruler, template, or software like Vision, so you can consult the diagram over and over, without confusion.

There are many diagramming methods. In this book, for simplicity, we use Entity-Relationship diagrams to show whether an entity may or must have a relationship with zero, one, or more entities of some other class. An important part of an Entity-Relationship diagram is the crowsfoot line. The single line points to the one in the one-to-many relationship, and the splayed-out lines point to the many. Numbers indicate the minimum and maximum number of instances allowed—usually zero, one, or more than one. Figures 2.16 through 2.18 show some examples.

Figure 2.16
Customer to Invoice: One customer has a relationship with zero or more invoices; each invoice belongs to one and only one customer.

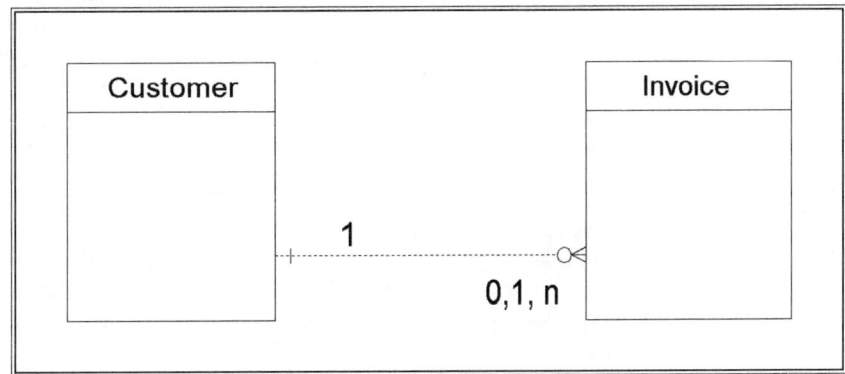

Figure 2.17
Invoice to line items: One invoice may have a relationship with one or more line items, but an invoice should not come into existence if it is going to have no line items.

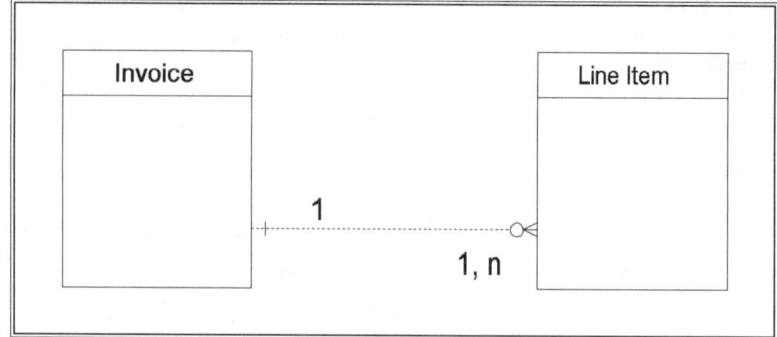

Figure 2.18
Department to Employees: One Department has a relationship with more than one Employee; each Employee works for one and only one Department.

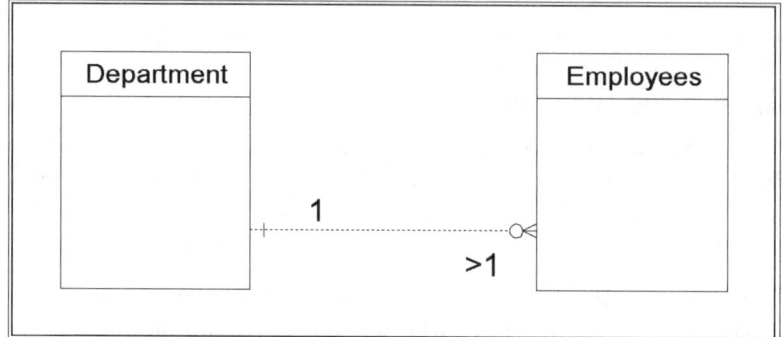

Tip from *Rich*	Make sure that you investigate the real situation on the ground, rather than making an assumption based on "what usually happens." For instance, in the old days, one employee really did work for only one department, but today, a single employee may be farmed out to several different departments, or work in shipping on Monday and Friday, and in maintenance in the middle of the week (a many-to-many relationship). Similarly, if you start off with Subscribers and Magazines you discover a many-to-many relationship because one subscriber may sign up for many magazines, and each magazine will have, we hope, many subscribers. You might resolve this relationship with a Subscription file in between (see Figure 2.19).

Tip from *Rich*	If you think there might be any doubt, use labels that make sense in business terms. For example, an employee "works for" a manager, and, looked at from the other direction, a manager "supervises" the employee. You are creating a data model that should reflect the business environment, so that even a manager on the client side can understand the diagrams.

Figure 2.19
Subscriber to Magazines: One Subscriber may subscribe to one or more Magazines; each Magazine has zero or more Subscribers.

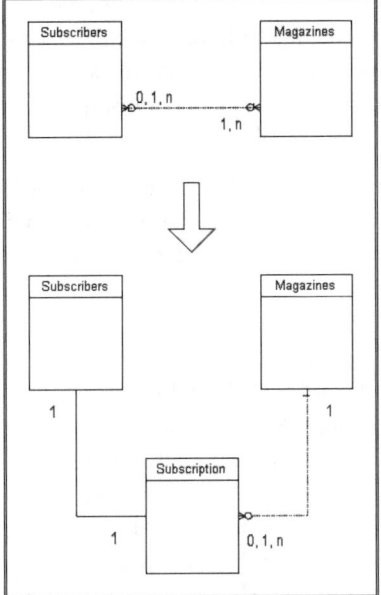

Tip from Rich

Make sure that your entity names and labels are in accord with your clients' own terminology. If you mention the term to any group, whether staff or managerial, they should know what you mean, and you should know what they mean, too. Do not try to alter your client's perceptions or definitions. If they call a customer a client, you call the customer a client.

REFINING YOUR ER DIAGRAM BY QUESTIONING YOUR TABLES

The diagram is a tool for thinking because it lays out relationships visually so you can analyze them, and, if necessary, make refinements and improvements to the overall structure. The first draft is never right. You improve it by comparing it with your spec and analyzing each aspect of the structure.

Even though you have already poked and probed every entity and relationship, you may find that your suspicions have been raised about this or that entity, so you may take this opportunity to review the whole diagram, looking for redundant entities, unnecessary entities, or dubious relationships. Although you may have been working on the design for quite a while, you may still discover interesting nuances at this stage; for instance, you may realize that you have been assuming that each customer is a single entity, but for your purposes, you have to know which of several locations to ship to, so you may have to create a new entity—the Shipping Locations.

WORKING DOCUMENT: THE ABSOLUTELY POSITIVELY FINAL ER DIAGRAM

After many passes through the ER Diagram, you emerge with a vastly improved version, which is primarily for your use as a developer, although you may want to share it with a technically sophisticated member of the client team. (This is not a document that will appeal to a nontechnical manager on the client side). You have now thought through the information from many angles, and your understanding has deepened as you continued to examine, tinker with, and polish the entities and their intricate relationships. By now, you are probably impatient to get to work developing the database.

The next step in that direction is to transform the ER Diagram into a File Structure Diagram. Where the ER Diagram focuses primarily on entities and their relationships, you will develop the File Structure Diagram to explore the details of attributes and keys, field by field, file by file.

Create a File Structure Diagram

Now that you have a map of the entities and their relationships, you can figure that each entity will get its own file. So you should now ask yourself, for each file "What kind of table will exist inside this file?" You know the entity the table describes, or you think you do, but now that you have a clean, new diagram, you can test your design as a set of tables. The Entity Relationship diagram shows entities and relationships in the abstract. The File Structure Diagram has a box for each entity, but shows its attributes, and therefore allows you to identify the Primary and Foreign keys, so you can identify the pieces of information common to various files.

As you develop the File Structure Diagram, you may ask questions such as

- **What kind of fields will you have in this table?** We are most interested in the kind of data that will go into each field. For instance, you should be on the lookout for multi-part or multivalue fields, where you try to put two different kinds of information into the same field. Example: An address field that contains name, company, street, city, state, and ZIP when you anticipate sorting by company, last name, city, state, and ZIP at different times. (Time to contemplate additional fields). Another example: In a contact's database, a repeating field as a place to list all the contact's children.

- **Have you by chance planned several fields that track the same kind of information, such as Contact 1, Contact 2, Contact 3, or a repeating field?** The problem here is that you will have trouble extracting information from all of these for calculations, summaries, or reports. You may succeed, with difficulty, but you face ticklish challenges. When searching for a contact, which field would you use? (You wouldn't know which contact field the person might be listed in).

> **Tip from**
> *Rich*
>
> If you have inadvertently assumed a series of fields dealing with the same information, the best solution is to create a child file devoted to that entity, so you can have a series of records instead of a series of values within similar (but distinct) fields.

- **Do you happen to have two or more files tracking the same information?** The ideal is to track data in one and only one place, and, when needed elsewhere, draw it in through a relationship between files. You don't want a clerk facing the dilemma: Should

I enter part of the information about the new product in the Inventory file, and the rest over in Products, or should I start in Manufacturing Output file? Multiple points at which a user can enter data may mean that you never capture all the info you need, or the same facts get entered differently at different times.

- **Is one table handling more than one kind of information?** We are probing for compound records, that is, two or more different types of information in the same record. For example, we might have a table that allows a single record to contain detailed information about an individual student as well as detailed information about a particular class that student is taking. The problem? We cannot enter a student into our system until the student registers for a class, but we cannot enter a class until a student registers for it. These tables raise metaphysical questions: At what moment does a class come to life? But the practical questions nag, as well. Staffers will ask: How can I set up a class before I have any students who might want to register? Also, if I delete a registration, and that was the only class a student had signed up for, I lose the only record for that student, and if that student was the only one to sign up so far, I also lose the class. And if a student registers for six classes, I have to store the student info six times; and if 20 students sign up for the class, I have class information repeated 20 times. Not good. In the database world, such situations are known as insertion and deletion anomalies.

> **Tip from**
> *Rich*
>
> An entity tracks only one kind of information. Or, to put this another way, each file should have a table that deals with only one category or class of information. Otherwise, you risk confusing yourself and your users.

> **Tip from**
> *Rich*
>
> Another way to think about this situation is to keep in mind that a file must have only one Primary key—is, the one that refers to its main subject, the entity around which the table revolves. Every attribute in the file should be a characteristic of a single Primary key. So, know you should smell danger if you recognize that a particular file has several Primary keys, such as Student ID, Class ID, and Registration ID because that suggests you are trying to store information about all three categories of information in a single table. It's time to divide the file into three files and define the relationships.

> **Tip from**
> *Rich*
>
> Sometimes, an entity is the child of several other entities. An order, for instance, may be the child of the Store's entity, the Customer's entity, and the Sales Person's entity, and as such, the order would contain Foreign keys pointing to all three of those entities. In such a situation, the file will contain multiple Foreign keys, but only one Primary key (its own).

> **Caution**
>
> You know you are in trouble if the staff starts putting workarounds on yellow stickies hung on their monitors. One problem that drives people to post these kludges is compound records. The staff explains, "Well, we can't put up a class until we have a student to take it, and no student signs up for a class that doesn't yet exist, so we have created a student named Anonymous, who signs up for every new class. Of course, that makes our student count wrong for every class. But we know, here in the office, to subtract one from every roster, to get the accurate count. Of course, Anonymous keeps getting notices from the system warning that she is taking too many courses at once."

> **Caution**
>
> You should ask yourself if you have inadvertently planned to include attributes of attributes? For example, if you have a file focused on individual students, you plan a record devoted to a particular student, and one attribute of that student is the name of the student's advisor. But what if you have innocently planned to add the advisor's phone number and office location? Now, part of the student's record deals with facts that are not characteristics of that student, but attributes of the advisor, whose name (on this record, or in this table) is just an attribute of the student. The problems that can arise in this situation are similar to those caused by a compound record (one that deals with two distinct entities): you may have trouble keeping information about the advisor up-to-date, you may lose information about an advisor if you delete a student, and you cannot add information about an advisor until the advisor is assigned to at least one student. So when you hire a new professor, there is no way to slip her into the system except as a set of details trailing along after one or more students. (The advisors may be fine people, worthy of a table of their own).

> **Tip from**
> *Rich*
>
> Each file should track a single entity and its attributes, but should not get into additional information about a particular attribute, which is like growing hair on hair. The table should contain only one Primary key, such as Student ID, and every attribute (or field) on a record should describe that entity. What you want to avoid is a situation in which the Primary key is A, and you have an attribute of A called B, and then you have several attributes of B called C, D, and E. If C, D, and E really have nothing to do with the main topic of the table, in this case, A, they should be banished to their own table, where they can gather around entity B.

If your File Structure Diagram passes all these tests, you are in good shape, and if you have corrected these problems, you have probably gotten rid of the worst contortions a real user might have to go through in order to make the database work. You may not yet have a database design that is as pure as a Computer Science professor would like, but you'll probably end up with a database that does not cause serious difficulty for an average user.

CHAPTER 3

SPECIFYING YOUR FIELDS

In this chapter

Creating a Field Specification List 56
Naming the Field 59
Defining the Field Type 62
Considering What Actually Will Be Entered in the Field 70
Changing the Order in Which FileMaker Lists Fields 76
Deleting Fields 77
Changing Field Types 78
Changing Field Names 79
Anticipating the Layout for Each Field 80

Creating a Field Specification List

With the File Structure Diagram in front of you and the Entity Relationship Diagram behind you, you can take the next big step in planning, considering each entity as a file, and each attribute as a field within its entity's file. And for each file, you have now identified the fields that will serve as Primary and Foreign keys.

In these ways, you are moving even farther from the original business problem toward an automated solution. You are sharpening your vision of the actual database, clarifying the gritty details. Creating a Field Specification List will take you even closer to the bits and bytes of the database you are about to create.

FileMaker always suggests creating fields as soon as you start a new database. In preparation for that moment, you are going to identify each file and its fields, its characteristics, and any business rules that apply to the fields. You'll identify the following items as identified in Figure 3.1, although you will probably find a tabular arrangement easier—with a row for each field, and a column for each category of information about that field.

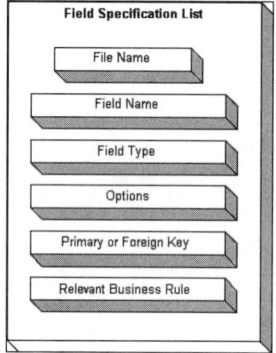

Figure 3.1
The Field Specification List brings together all the information you will need when creating the fields.

- A file for each entity. For instance, if you have an entity Customer, you plan to have a file named, well, Customer. Easy—you've already got this on your File Structure Diagram.
- A field for each attribute. In the Customer file, you may identify fields such as Customer First Name, Customer Last Name, Customer Honorific, Area Code, Work Phone, Home Phone, Email Address, Fax Number. Earlier, each of these facts was considered an attribute of the entity Customer. For each attribute, then, we are going to plan a field to track the values, as shown in Figure 3.2.
- The field type, which is not always as obvious as you might think at first glance.
- Options. For instance, if the field involves a calculation, we'll write the formula now.
- Indication of which fields are Primary keys and which are Foreign keys.
- Any business rules that put some constraint on the values in the field or require some form of validation of an entry. For example, if this is the State field, it must contain a two-digit code from a table of acceptable entries, or if the field is Gender, in our com-

pany we only accept a value of M or F. Or if the field Marital Status is set to Married, then the field Spouse's Name must not be left empty when the user moves to leave the record.

Figure 3.2
Attributes become fields.

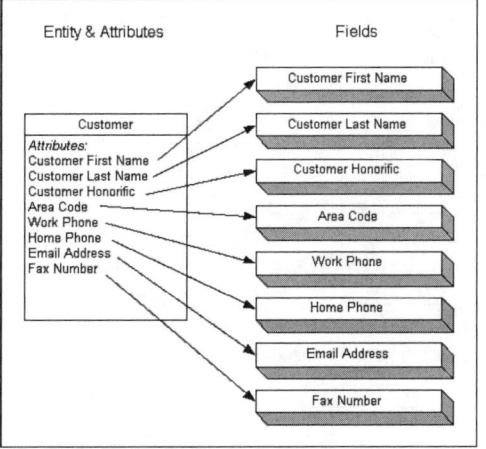

> **Tip from**
> *Rich*
>
> Business rules are not necessarily the kind of strategies talked about at the Harvard Business School. A business rule is just a requirement flowing from the way the organization does business, a constraint placed on the values in the field. Often, a business rule involves validating that entry or ensuring that other fields are also filled in. In some ways, business rules reflect assumptions that the client has always made, such as, "Well, we always have a customer before we record an order for the customer," or "We can't risk having an invoice without a valid customer to send it to." (Note that these rules are specifying a relationship: a Customer may have many invoices, but an Invoice must have one, and only one Customer, just to exist.)

Business rules emerge when you map the technology to the business challenge. People may have been performing the task for years without any automation, sharing the assumptions as they train a new employee, embedding the "obvious" in procedures in a manual, and passing along this lore as customary practice ("We never schedule Fred to operate on Wednesday afternoon, because that's his golf afternoon"). Lore is the accumulated knowledge of "how to do the job," and may involve quite complex considerations, such as the following example.

In part of a File Structure Diagram, illustrated in Figure 3.3, we show the Customer and Invoice files, each of which has a field devoted to the Customer ID (shown at the top of the diagram). The thin end of the line points to the Customer file's field for Customer ID, indicating one customer has a relationship with many invoices, and in turn the crowfoot points to the Customer ID field over in the Invoice file, indicating many invoices are related to the one customer. Hence, the thin end of the line points to the Primary key (parent), and the crowfoot points to the Foreign key (child). These facts are pulled out and placed in the Field Specification List.

Figure 3.3
Part of the File Structure Diagram shows how the Customer ID field acts as a key to the relationship.

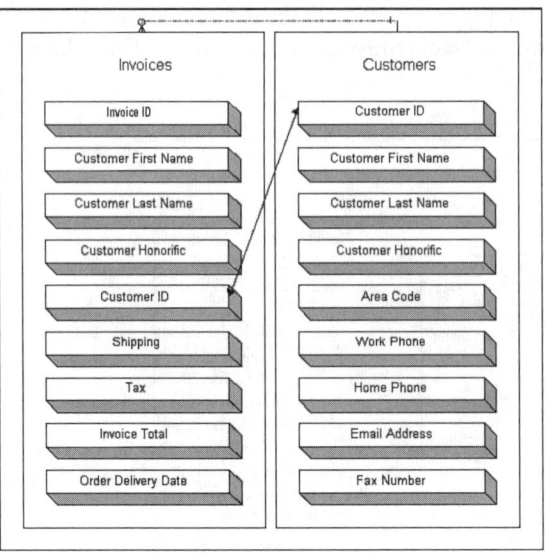

Using Visio to Create Diagrams

Visio Professional includes stencils (predesigned shapes) you can use to create your Entity Relationship and File Structure Diagrams. Now offered by Microsoft, the Visio products give you stencils (see Figure 3.4), which are really vector graphic objects you can easily manipulate, changing the size, adding fill patterns, garnishing with color, labeling, and arranging as you want. The results look professional, so you can show these diagrams to clients if you need to. But even if you are just developing the diagrams for your own use, the Visio software lets you clarify your structure visually so that you can refresh your memory quickly when you forget your plan, analyze relationships, and make changes as you go.

Figure 3.4
Visio offers you stencils following various diagramming systems, so you can quickly put together Entity Relationship and File Structure Diagrams without having to create them from scratch.

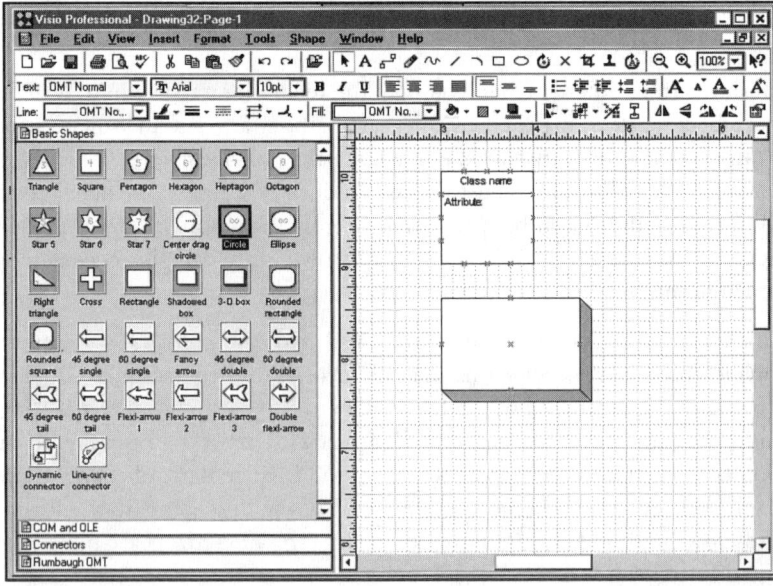

The table may be as formal as a spreadsheet, or as informal as Rich's Yellow Sheet of Paper—whatever is clear enough to use as you work and tough enough to survive for later use as a reminder of what you have done.

You've already thought quite a bit about most of your fields, from several different angles. Now's the time to jot down the critical details while you are still thinking analytically about the whole database—something that is not always possible when you get down to the actual process of creating an individual calculation field. In a little while you will get your hands on the software, and you'll start creating like crazy. But to ensure you don't accidentally screw up, you can use the Field Definition Table to come up with a logical plan for the whole database, at the level of fields.

The simple act of creating one field can have a tremendous impact on the system. To avoid "gotchas" later, and to get the results you want, take this opportunity to think through the following for each field:

- Naming the field
- Defining the field type
- Considering what will actually be entered in the field
- Ordering fields
- Deleting fields
- Changing field names or types
- Anticipating the layout for each field

Naming the Field

Field names are your tools. You're most aware of the field name at the moment of creation, when you have to enter the name in the Define Fields dialog box (see Figure 3.5). But you'll need to be able to recognize this field by its name, distinguishing it from others like it, whenever you set up a layout, develop a report, critique relationships, or troubleshoot. To avoid mistakes and confusion, you should probably adopt a method for creating names, so that even if you don't recall a particular field's name, you can anticipate what it should be, so you can find it more quickly in the list of fields, and, in turn, if you are wondering which field to pick from a set of similarly named ones, you can pick the one you want right away.

Even users rely on field names. And for users, the names must make sense to them, even if one of their number gave you the name. Rich once had to modify a database someone else had developed, and he found a field called SOB, containing an unpredictable mix of letters and numbers, sometimes with dollar signs, on different records. He asked the users, "What's this field for?" No, it was not a list of nasty jerks. But beyond that, the team could not agree. The staff in one office thought SOB stood for Success Oriented Behavior, but the people in another office thought it was Sign On Bonus. So, not knowing what the name meant, people were just entering anything they thought might fit there.

Figure 3.5
The Define Fields dialog box is where you give the field a name, a type, and any options you want.

Each field name, then, should reveal what is unique about a field (this field deals with license plate numbers) and perhaps what is common about it (this is another Number field). What convention you adopt to express the individuality of each field is entirely up to you, but if you work with others in development or hope to turn the database over to other developers for maintenance later, you should probably go beyond a private code system to a method that will make sense to everyone.

COMMON MISTAKE: USING RESERVED CHARACTERS IN A FIELD NAME

In the past, when naming a field, you may have received a warning like that shown in Figure 3.6, politely pointing out that the name you have proposed includes restricted characters. We recommend you cancel out of the dialog box and revise your name so you avoid these characters. Why? During calculations that involve field names, FileMaker may get confused, treating your illegitimate field name as if it were a logical expression or mathematical formula, resulting in very weird totals, averages, and invoices. The characters to avoid appear in Table 3.1. Also, be sure not to start with a period or a number, and be sure not to use a name that is already the name of a function, such as SUM or AVERAGE. For examples of illegal field names, please see Table 3.2.

Figure 3.6
This is a warning you should not ignore. No, no, no—don't proceed. Cancel out and come up with a new name.

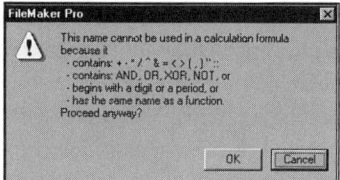

TABLE 3.1 DON'T USE THESE CHARACTERS IN A FIELD NAME

Mathematical Symbols	Punctuation	Logical Operators
+	,	AND
-	"	OR
*	.	NOT

Mathematical Symbols	Punctuation	Logical Operators
/		
^		
=		
<		
>		
[		
]		

TABLE 3.2 EXAMPLES OF ILLEGAL FIELD NAMES

Field Name	Troublesome Word or Character
A OR B	OR
OK(IF NEEDED)	IF and ( )
1st & Last Name	1, &
Initials/OK	/
Note	*

Tip from Rich

If you really like using a slash to divide a name into two parts, avoid the one for division (/). Instead, use the backward slash (\) or the vertical bar (|), neither of which is a reserved character or mathematical symbol for FileMaker.

Tip from Rich

Don't put space characters into a name. If you publish on the Web, some browsers may not recognize the entire name, so they will send the wrong field name back to FileMaker. Also, ODBC does not like spaces either. Basically, if you only work within FileMaker, a space character will be fine, but once you depend on other programs, the space may make them choke. Instead, use an underscore character Like_This.

CASE STUDY: SLASHING A DATABASE TO BITS

A customer called us in, claiming her database was psychotic. We went over and took a look, and indeed, the database was acting in a very bizarre fashion. We tried recovering the file, and that didn't work; we reinstalled the software, and that made no difference; we checked for viruses, reinstalled the operating system, and moved the database to another computer. Nothing helped. The client said, "I think I should call a priest." We went to Define Fields and noticed that several fields used the slash and dash in their names. When those field names were used in calculations, FileMaker was taking the slash as an indication that it ought to try to divide, and the hyphen as a minus sign; struggling to divide and subtract pieces of field names, FileMaker was producing very odd results. We renamed the fields, and the problems went away. It was like putting the database on St. John's Wort.

Tip from
Rich

> Most field types are obvious, once you know what the name means. A Last Name field is likely to contain text. But sometimes you need to be able to find all your globals, Primary keys, or Foreign keys. In these situations, use a prefix, such as starting the names of all global fields with *g_*, all Primary keys with *pk_*, and all Foreign keys with *fk_*. That way, even when you list fields by name, alphabetically, you can locate these three field types quickly, without having to read every name.

DEFINING THE FIELD TYPE

If you are an intermediate to experienced developer, you are already quite familiar with field types, but you may still want to browse through this section, because you may pick up a few new wrinkles, or reminders of times when choosing the wrong field type seriously messed up a database.

What kind of field is this going to be? FileMaker lets you characterize the information in your new field as one of eight types—Text, Number, Date, Time, Container, Calculation, Summary, or Global, as shown in Figure 3.7. Your decision about a field's type can have a wide-ranging impact. What you want to do with the data later will make at least as much difference in your decision as the nature of the data itself.

Figure 3.7
FileMaker lets you define the kind of data you will put into the field. Your choice affects what you can put in the field, and how you can sort, search, format, summarize, and calculate those values.

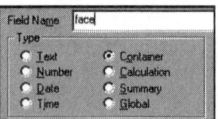

The way that FileMaker sorts, searches, formats, summarizes, and calculates is heavily dependent on the type of information the program expects in a field. That's because FileMaker has been designed to follow the conventions our culture itself has adopted when manipulating lists of numbers, dates, times, texts, or whatever.

- We expect that if the data is dates, the sort will be chronological or reverse chronological, whereas if the data is text, we think of alphabetical or the reverse, which in turn is different from a strictly numerical order.

- Indexes of the values in a field also tend to follow these conventions, so searching mechanisms must be built to take different sequences into account.

- Automatic formatting of a number in dollars and cents is one thing, but to force decimal points, commas, and dollar signs on a piece of innocent text would be horribly confusing.

- Calculations, too, depend on data types. For example, if we ask FileMaker to figure out how many days fall between two dates, we will be surprised if the fields are numeric in type, and the system subtracts 06/08/2006 from 06/08/2007, and seems to conclude that one day has elapsed between them, rather than 365, because the slashes are dropped, and the program subtracts 06082006 from 06082007.

Consider How You Want to Sort the Values in the Field

The way FileMaker sorts depends on the type of data it expects to find in the field—the field type. If you want to sort dates or times chronologically, you must use a Date or Time field type, and make sure that data is entered in the right format. If you expect to sort numbers, they have to be real numbers in a Number field. If, by chance, you place a date, time, or number in a Text field, that data will be sorted alphabetically, left to right, character by character, resulting in some very strange and unexpected sequences.

COMMON MISTAKE: PUTTING DATES INTO A TEXT FIELD

The impulse is understandable: you have users screaming that they want dates displayed in the format "Wednesday, March 18 2010," but when they encounter an official Date field, FileMaker demands that they enter the date in the Month-Day-Year order separated by a non-numeric character such as the slash or hyphen: M/D/YYYY (month/day/year) or M-D-YYYY (Month-day-year). Of course, once the dates have been entered in that format, you can use the Date Format command on the Format menu to transform the numbers into the text format. The real problem with putting a date in a text field appears when you sort, because the values are sorted alphabetically, not chronologically, resulting in this new calendar:

- April
- August
- December
- February
- January
- July
- June
- March
- May
- November
- October
- September

COMMON MISTAKE: SORTING NUMBERS IN A TEXT FIELD

Alphabetic sorts, like those in a Text field, sort by the first character, then the next, then the next, placing AA, standing for anti-aircraft, before Aardvark, the famous earth pig of Africa. But when you sort a bunch of numbers in this way, you come out with anomalies such as 1222 showing up before 123, which comes before 2, as shown in Table 3.3

TABLE # 3.3 NUMBERS GET SORTED DIFFERENTLY

Sorting in a Text Field	Sorting in a Number Field
11	2
1222	9
123	11
1456	123
2	1222
9	1456

THE WAY YOU WANT TO SEARCH AFFECTS YOUR CHOICE OF FIELD TYPE

The way FileMaker carries out a search varies by field type, so you need to know what you will be looking for in the field in order to pick the right type. If FileMaker just did a full, character-by-character search on every field, you would be sure to find whatever you needed, but the process would take a long time. To speed the process up, FileMaker's designers created an index (you will probably want to tell FileMaker to create this index ahead of time), and they organized the index in an order that's appropriate for the values they expect to find in a field of this type.

- In a Number field, FileMaker indexes only numeric values, because the index will be organized in numerical order; FileMaker's search, then, ignores any text as irrelevant. So if you search a Number field looking for text, you won't find it. But the payoff is that you can look for exact numbers—and a range of numbers.

> **Tip from**
> *Rich*
>
> True and False conditions form an exception to the general rule that FileMaker ignores text in numeric fields. If you begin a number field with a T or F, a Y or an N, then FileMaker interprets the T as True or Boolean 1, the Y as Yes or True or 1, and interprets the F and N as False or No or 0.

- In a Time or Date field, FileMaker only indexes correctly formatted times or dates, arranges those in chronological order, and allows you to look up a particular moment or range. Of course, for text or numbers, you are out of luck; they simply cannot be entered.
- In a Text field, you can find an exact match to a word or phrase, text that starts with a particular text string, or contains it. Hence, if your users are careful when they type, they will be able to locate a number, time, or date within a Text field because those show up in the alphabetical index as raw text. But users cannot look up a range of numbers, times, or dates in a Text field.

COMMON MISTAKE: SEARCHING FOR TEXT IN A NUMBER FIELD

Yes, a user can type ordinary text into a Number field (unless the developer has specifically prohibited this), and the text shows up, but when FileMaker makes up an index for that field, it only indexes numbers. You will not be able to locate the text using the ordinary Find or a Find with wildcards. And you cannot perform a literal (character-by-character) or full search in this field, because for efficiency the designers excluded that slow process, assuming that this field would really contain only numbers.

COMMON MISTAKE: SEARCHING FOR A RANGE OF DATES IN A TEXT FIELD

In a Date field, you can search for a range of dates, but not in a Text field. How come? Well, in a Text field, FileMaker indexes everything as text, so yes, the date 8/15/07 goes into the index alphabetically, but nothing about the item indicates it is a date. You can locate this particular string of characters by using an ordinary Find or a literal Find, but as soon as you type in a range of dates, FileMaker looks for that string, and, probably, announces that "No records match this request." Solution? Go through every entry to make sure that you have nothing but dates there, all entered correctly, and then change the field type to Date.

Tip from
Rich

Can't find anything in the field? Perhaps you accidentally assigned the wrong type to this field. We know someone who freaked out when she wasn't able to find anything in a field. Turns out she had made the field a Number rather than a Text field, and then entered text. Because FileMaker's standard Find turns up only numbers, there was nothing to find.

Tip from
Steven

In FileMaker Pro 5, you can assign strict date and time validations to fields so that dates must have 4-digit years and that times must be times of day. You can also prevent text from being entered into a number field. All these validations are triggered from the Validations Tab under the Options button in the Define Field dialog box.

AUTOMATIC FORMATTING DEPENDS ON FIELD TYPE

If you want to have FileMaker apply some kind of automatic formatting, make sure that you use the right field types. For example, if you happen to enter numbers, dates, or times in a Text field, you won't be able to get FileMaker to reformat them because it has no idea which text string is a date and which is a Fig Newton.

NUMBER FORMAT

FileMaker offers a wonderful collection of formats you can apply to numbers through the Number Format dialog box (see Figure 3.8). You can, for example, do the following things:

- Format the number as a decimal number
- Specify separators for thousands and decimals
- Say how to display negative numbers
- Turn the number into a percentage

- Add currency symbols of your choosing
- Treat the number as a Boolean expression
- Apply the usual text formats to the number (bold, italic, and so on)

But you can have this formatting applied only when the numbers appear inside a Number field, a Calculation field with a numeric result, a Summary field, or a Global Number field—or when the contents of one of these fields appears merged into a text block on the layout.

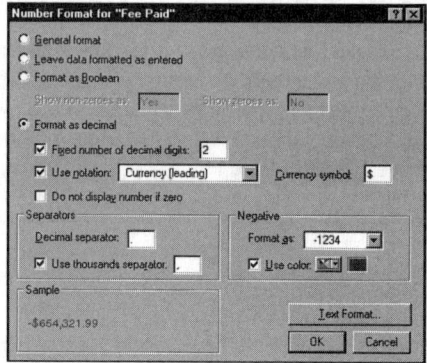

Figure 3.8
The Number Format dialog box lets you apply formatting to numbers in a Calculation field (with a numeric result), a Number field, a Summary field, a Global Number field, or any of these fields when they appear merged within a text block on the layout.

Date Format

FileMaker will apply many different formats to the way dates get displayed (not the same as the way they are entered and stored). Use the Date Format dialog box (see Figure 3.9). You can, for instance, do the following things:

- Insert a leading zero before a one-digit day or month
- Change the separator that goes between the day, month, and year
- Pick one of several complete formats for the date (such as October 31, 2008; Thu., Oct 31, 2008; Thu., 31 Oct., 2008; or Q4 2008)
- Set up a custom format
- Apply regular text formatting (fonts, sizes, styles, alignment) to whatever appears in the field

But you can apply these formats to dates only when they appear in a Date field, a Calculation field with a date result, a Global Date field, or when one of these fields appears merged into a text block on the layout or on the date symbol (//) on your layout.

Figure 3.9
The Date Format dialog box lets you apply formatting to dates.

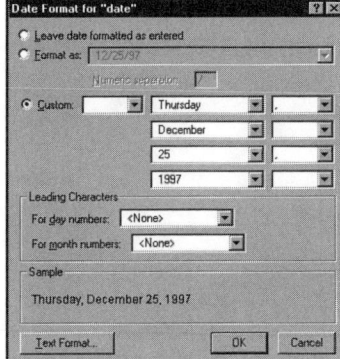

Time Format

FileMaker lets you format times through the Time Format dialog box, shown in Figure 3.10, with options like these:

- Show the time in 24-hour or 12-hour format with A.M. or P.M.
- Change the separator character between hours, minutes, and seconds
- Pick one of several formats for the entire time (such as 05:25:55)

But you can only have these formats applied automatically to times that appear in a Time field, a Calculation field with a time result, a Global Time field, one of these fields merged into a text block on the layout, or the time symbol (::) on your layout.

Figure 3.10
The Time Format dialog box lets you apply formatting to times.

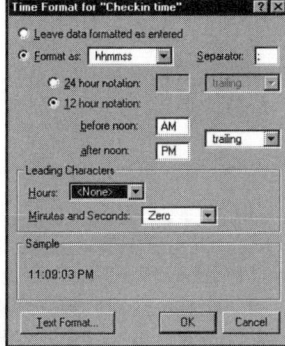

Container Format

The Container field acts as a box into which you can drop a picture, a sound, or a video. If you want to edit the picture, sound, or video, you must go back to the original applications. But you can apply a little formatting to pictures and movies—mostly having to do with placement within the box that frames the images—using the Graphic Format dialog box (see Figure 3.11):

- Aligning the picture horizontally or vertically within the box
- Reducing, enlarging, or doing whatever it takes to get the picture to fit within the box

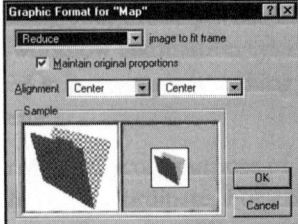

Figure 3.11
The Graphic Format dialog box lets you apply formatting to pictures and movies.

TEXT FORMAT

You can have FileMaker apply formatting to the font, size, style, alignment, line spacing, and color of any characters in any field except the Container. (What font could you possibly use for video?) Because these formats are so ubiquitous, you have several ways of applying them: the first command on the Format menu, the Text Format command, which brings up the Text Format dialog box shown in Figure 3.12, or the Text Format button on other format dialog boxes.

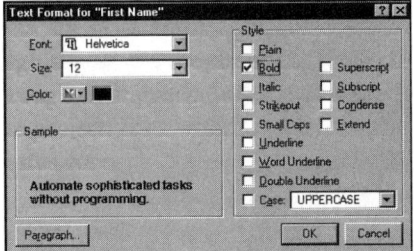

Figure 3.12
The Text Format dialog box lets you apply formatting to values.

Tip from
Rich

Keep in mind that whatever a user enters survives, no matter how he formats the data. FileMaker stores the exact data as entered. Of course, how that data looks on-screen or appears in a printout, depends on the formatting he applies. Just remember, though, that the entry survives, deep in FileMaker's mind, and all formatting is applied to that before displaying or printing. Formatting does not change the value; it only changes the way the value is displayed.

COMMON MISTAKE: FORMATTING ENTRIES SO THEY DISAPPEAR

If you have already entered some data and then change the formatting, you may accidentally make the entries extend beyond the edges of the field in your layout; at that point, you just see question marks! Like a cartoon character, you may wonder, "What happened to my data?" It's still there. Solution? Go back to Layout and increase the size of the field.

> **Tip from Jonathan**
>
> Take the shortcut to automatic formatting. If you are in Layout, hold down Alt on a Windows keyboard, or Option on a Mac keyboard, and then double-click the field. In a moment, you'll get the right formatting dialog box for that field type.

THE WAY YOU CAN CALCULATE DEPENDS ON THE FIELD TYPE

You can only perform addition on numbers. You knew that already? Well, then this constraint will make sense to you. You can run many calculations on numbers, but they won't work correctly if you try to apply them to data entered as a date (6/6/08) or time (01:05:07). Similarly, FileMaker offers many neat calculations you can perform on text, but only when that text appears in a Text field.

EXAMPLE: HOW OLD IS YOUR INVOICE?

In an invoicing database you may want to know the age of an invoice. Is it time to send a follow-up or a threatening notice? If the date of the invoice appears in a Date field, you can quickly subtract it from today's date to find out how many days old the invoice really is. But this trick won't work in a Number field, where the date of June 6th, 2008, entered as 6/6/08 would be interpreted as 6,608.

COMMON MISTAKE: CONFUSING A CALCULATION FIELD WITH A SUMMARY FIELD

Imagine a table of data: In the simplest form, Calculation fields do math only within a single row, and Summary fields do math within a single column. In the old days, this was a complete description of the difference between Calculation and Summary fields, but we have made progress, confusingly. As developers become more sophisticated, they soon discovered that a Calculation field could now perform math by referencing the following information:

- Fields in other records through relationships
- Global fields, which are not part of the record
- A field in a group of related records through an Aggregate function
- Summary fields using the Get Summary function

So the Calculation field can still be used as a simple device, but its power has been magnified.

So what the heck is the difference between a Calculation field and a Summary field? Comparing the two fields in their simplest forms, a Calculation does math on values within a record by using many fields, and a Summary does math on values in many records, using only one field. For example, if you want to multiply the Unit Price times the Quantity to get the Extended Price on an Invoice Line Item record, you do not need to leave that record to do the figuring, so you could make Extended Price a Calculation field. On the other hand, if you want to add up the total invoice amount on all your Invoice records to get a grand total for the month's invoices, you would be collecting values from multiple invoices, so you could use a Summary.

But we have to warn you that this distinction is oversimplified. We will go into more detail when we discuss relationships in Chapter 5, calculations in Chapter 10, and summary reports in Chapter 11.

➔For more information about the strategies behind relationships, **see** "Create Relationships Between Files," **p. 112**.
➔If you want to explore calculations in greater depth, **see** Chapter 10 "Hot Calculations," **p. 273**.
➔For details on Summary reports, **see** "Creating Summary Reports," **p. 348**.

Considering What Actually Will Be Entered in the Field

You've seen how your hopes for sorting, searching, formatting, and calculating can affect your choice of field type. The other strong influence on your choice is, well, the kind of data you are actually going to enter.

What to Put in a Text Field

Obviously, text. Up to 64,000 characters at a shot.

But you should also use a Text field any time your data contains alphabetic characters or special characters used as punctuation, *even if most of the other material is numeric.* Why? If the non-numeric data matters, you will probably want to search and sort on it, and if you were to place these entries in a Number field, FileMaker would not find those non-numeric characters there, so the results would be screwy.

For instance, if you set up a Number field to contain phone numbers, and a user types in 555-4912, FileMaker ignores the hyphen, and considers that number 5,554,912. No way you are going to find all phone numbers in the 555 area code, because FileMaker considers the actual phone numbers to be ten thousand times larger than your request. Even if you make up a separate field for Area Code (a good idea in a day when these change so often), your users will probably surround the three digits with opening and closing parentheses. In a Number field, the parentheses indicate a negative number. Text fields do just fine for phone numbers.

Tip from
Rich

> If you have large blocks of text, such as notes on books or product data, use Text fields. You can format individual words and characters so your reports are readable, and you can search the text in lots of different ways. If the material is already in electronic form, you can also copy and paste. What is not so easy is using some form of Optical Character Recognition (OCR) software to scan sheets of paper, soak up the text, and turn it into electronic form—too many errors per square inch.

COMMON MISTAKE: PUTTING ZIP CODES INTO A NUMBER FIELD

Put them in a Text field. If you put ZIP codes into a Number field, FileMaker ignores all non-numeric values when it makes up its index, treating whatever is left as a single number. Hence, if you are in ZIP code 87107-6414 like Jonathan, FileMaker drops the hyphen, and lists the number as 871076414. Mathematically, that is not at all the same thing as 87107. So if you look the five-digit code up, FileMaker finds no records with that value. Also, if you sort by numeric value, 87107 will not appear along with its subsets, 87107-6414. Solution? Make up a Text field for ZIP codes. Then when a user invokes a standard Find and enters the five-digit code, FileMaker will find that "beginning syllable" in the index, contained within the larger "word" of 87107-6414. (A standard Find does prefix word searching; that is, it looks for any word that begins with the text you entered, or exactly matches it.) Also, in sorting, the initial five digits all show up together, followed by the subsets, in order. Another reason to use a Text field for ZIP code would be if you happen to have foreign ZIP codes, which contain text.

> **Tip from**
> *Rich*
>
> If you have a set of form letters, or boilerplate texts, store them in different records in another database and use Lookup to fetch the one that your user wants. In this way, the standard text remains untouched, but the user can draw it into the current layout, modify the text, and send it out. For example, in an Estimating database, the sales people wanted a selection of two dozen different letters available so they could pick the one that seemed closest to the particular job they were bidding on. Putting those into individual records in a separate file allowed us to preserve their integrity, and yet serve them up to the sales people in a Text field for subsequent modification, so the letters could be tailored for the individual client.

WHAT TO PUT IN A NUMBER FIELD

Yes, numbers. But under rare circumstances, you may put in a little text, too. Use a Number field for the following information:

- Numbers you want to be able to use in calculations, format automatically, search, or sort numerically
- Numbers that are accurate up to 15 digits total (including everything before or after the decimal point). You can enter up to 120 digits, but when you calculate, be aware that the calculations will only be accurate to 15 digits.
- Text you want displayed next to the numbers, where you expect to calculate, search, or sort using only the numbers (because FileMaker will ignore the text when doing calculations, formatting, searching, and sorting).
- Text you want evaluated to True (1) or False (0).

> **Tip from**
> *Rich*
>
> Normally, FileMaker allows users to enter text in a Number field (for example, $4.99 per pound), but if the field is used in a calculation or is indexed, FileMaker just ignores the non-numeric characters and uses whatever number remains. If you want to prevent users from entering text, you have to specifically set that option when you create the field.

> **Tip from**
> *Rich*
>
> Feel free to use commas and dollar signs. FileMaker is easy. It accepts commas and dollar signs without freaking out, but does not demand them. Most users find commas and dollar signs help them enter a number accurately. No matter how the number is entered, though, you can force it to be displayed in a consistent format by using the Number Format command.

WHAT TO PUT IN A DATE FIELD

Dates, of course. If they matter to you as dates. Use a Date field if your entries are going to be

- Dates on which you have to perform calculations such as figuring the number of days a bill is overdue, or the years an employee has been with the company.

- Dates you need to format in different ways (because automatic formatting of dates is only available in a Date field).
- Dates you want to be able to search and sort correctly (as dates, not numbers or text).

If you type the field as Date, users must enter dates in a Month-Day-Year format, using any non-numeric character between the month, day, and year. If FileMaker detects any deviation from this standard, (except when you have created your own custom validation with your own error messages), the software warns the user, as shown in Figure 3.13.

Figure 3.13
FileMaker balks if a user tries to enter a date in a way that the system cannot interpret as a date.

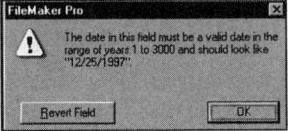

Tip from
Rich

Remember, what FileMaker stores is the date as entered, but you can have FileMaker format that date consistently for display or printing. Also, using the Custom Date format, you can develop almost any format you like.

Tip from
Rich

FileMaker lets you require that the year part of a date be entered as two digits or four digits. If your user enters a two-digit year, FileMaker interprets that as best it can. We recommend that you require users to enter four digits. At first, users may not like the extra typing, but they will appreciate not having their accounts fouled up later.

WHAT TO PUT IN A TIME FIELD

Create a Time field for the following information:

- Times you want to use in calculations of hours, minutes, or seconds
- Times you want to be able to look up or sort
- Times you want reformatted automatically for a consistent display

Remember that your users will have to enter times in one of these formats:

- xx:xx:xx (interpreted as HH:MM:SS)
- xx:xx (interpreted as HH:MM)
- xx (interpreted as HH:00)

> **Tip from**
> *Rich*
>
> You can make a record into a time card. Record the Time In and the Time Out, and then use a Calculation to determine the total time worked and multiply by the hourly rate to get the gross pay due for that day.

WHAT TO PUT IN A CONTAINER FIELD

Container fields hold pictures, sounds, or videos. You can create the material in another program, save it as a file, and then pick up the file as an entry in this field.

Pictures can come in a lot of formats, including the following:

- Adobe Photoshop (.psd) (Windows and Mac)
- Aldus/Window Metafile (.WMF) (Windows only)
- Autocad Slide (.SLD) (Windows only)
- Computer Graphics Metafile (.CGM) (Windows only)
- Encapsulated PostScript (.EPS) (Windows and Mac)
- Graphic Interchange Format GIF (.GIF) (not transparent or animated, though) (Windows and Mac)
- Joint Photographic Experts' Group (.JPG) (Windows and Mac)
- Lotus Picture (.PIC) (Windows only)
- Mac OS PICT (.PCT) (Windows and Mac)
- MacPaint (.MAC) (Windows and Mac)
- MicroGraphix Designer (.DRW) (Windows only)
- Portable Network Graphics (.png) (Windows and Mac)
- Tag Image File Format (.TIF) (Windows and Mac)
- Windows Bitmap Format (.BMP) (Windows only)
- Zsoft Paintbrush (.PCX) (Windows only)

Where FileMaker Puts Pictures

Because pictures take up so much space on a hard disk, FileMaker stores them in a special library and loads them only when the user actually switches to a layout that includes a Container field with images. This approach speeds up access to layouts without Container fields, but you can suffer a performance hit on the layouts with Container fields. Good news! If the same image shows up in different fields or different layouts, FileMaker only stores the picture once, placing pointers to it in all the other locations.

Also, each time a user puts a picture in a Container field, FileMaker consults its library to see whether another image of the same size and type already exists there. If so, FileMaker compares the new image with the stored image, bit by bit, to see if they are the same. If so, FileMaker just stores a pointer to the image that is already in the library.

> **Tip from Rich**
>
> If you add so much art, sound, and video that your database is approaching 2 Gigabytes, divide it into pieces. FileMaker can handle a database as large as 2 G, but two seconds of video often takes up 1 Meg of memory, so 33 minutes of uncompressed video would fill up your database. If you anticipate lots of color images, long sound bytes, or as much as a half hour of video, consider simply storing a reference to the file instead of importing the graphics or video. In that way, FileMaker will go and retrieve the graphic when needed, but the graphic itself is never imported into the FileMaker database.

> **Tip from Rich**
>
> If a database is storing a reference to its container field objects, in a multiuser environment, then all users must have access to the volume containing the directory where those graphics are stored.

You see sound clips on Web stores selling music, so customers can get a quick sample of a track or two before buying a CD. Some people make up rosters of conference participants and include recordings to show managers how to pronounce their names. You can paste a sound directly into the field from the clipboard. FileMaker accepts .AVI, .WAV, and QuickTime 3.0 (and later) files, and files such as Adobe Photoshop files (.psd) and Portable Network Graphics (.png) that have been converted to QuickTime format, but FileMaker does not play WAV files on the Macintosh, and cannot play sound on the Web.

Similarly, movie stores offer short video clips from their databases to tempt the customer into ordering. You can import movies because FileMaker accepts QuickTime files.

> **Tip from Steven**
>
> On the Macintosh platform, sometimes a particular sound format will not import into a FileMaker Pro container field, but it can be dragged from the desktop into the scrapbook. If so, you often can drag it from the scrapbook into a Container field if Drag and Drop is enabled. System 8 sound files, the ones with the loudspeaker icon, can be treated in this fashion. Or in other instances, the QuickTime Pro editor can convert sounds from one format to another. An example of this is a MIDI file converted to a QuickTime file.

What to Put in a Calculation Field

Use a Calculation field when you want to perform operations such as the following:

- Addition
- Aggregate functions, such as averaging, totaling, counting on repeating fields, or on groups of related records
- Comparison of two pictures bit by bit to see whether they are the same
- Calculations that yield a container result
- Date functions, such as figuring the number of days since January 1
- Design functions, such as listing the scripts defined for a particular file

- Division
- External functions, accessed through FileMaker's plug-in architecture, which we cover in Chapters 9 and 15
- Financial functions, such as Net Present Value
- Logical functions, such as testing a text string to see whether it is true or false
- Multiplication
- Status functions, such as returning the day's date, or the name of the field containing the insertion pointer
- Subtraction
- Summary functions, getting the results of a summary (not to be confused with a Summary field)
- Text functions, such as replacing one string of characters with another or transforming a date into a text equivalent
- Time functions, such as figuring the time elapsed
- Trigonometric functions such as sine, cosine, tangent
- Web functions, such as encoding the contents of a field in HTML

> **Tip from Jonathan**
> To avoid problems with some calculations, consider the option of having the calculation disabled if all of the referenced fields are empty.

You'll find an in-depth exploration of the subtleties of calculations in Chapter 10.

What to Put in a Summary Field

Whenever you want to perform a mathematical operation on data that appears across multiple records, use a Summary field. You might want to use one for the following information:

- Any summing up (such as a count or average) on a single field in multiple records
- Subtotals for some group of records, such as sales by one sales person
- Grand totals for all your found records

➔ If you want to create reports with summaries, **see** "Creating Summary Reports," **p. 348**.

> **Tip from Rich**
> Summary operations work only on the found set of records, whereas Calculations work on all related records, whether found or not.

What to Put in a Global Field

Global fields are designed to hold a value in a file that any record in the database can get, but the value lives at the file level, not at the record level, so there is one and only one value for that field in the whole file, and even though you see it on a layout within a single record, if you ever change it, the new value is immediately displayed in all the other records simultaneously. The value can be a container value, date, number, text, or time. Use a Global field to hold the following information:

- A fixed value you want to use in calculations in every record in the file
- A fixed value to be used as a variable in a script

Changing the Order in Which FileMaker Lists Fields

As a designer, you often go to the Define Fields dialog box to check the list of fields you've already created. By default, that list appears in the order you created the fields, which is, well, not always very useful. And if you allow users to look at this list when they want to sort or add fields, you risk confusion, because the sequence makes no particular sense to them.

To group the fields into a sequence that makes sense to you and your users, change the order as you work, and then, before delivering the database, set the order so it makes sense to your users. You can list the fields like this:

- In the order they were created
- Alphabetically by field name
- Grouped by field type (and alphabetical within the group)
- In a custom order that you devise by dragging field names up or down the list

To change the order, use the View By area of the Define Fields dialog box. To customize an order, drag the arrow to the left of a field name up or down, or press Control while using the Up or Down arrows.

Tip from
Rich

If you have a lot of fields, organize them by function or purpose. When you add a new field, it appears at the bottom of the list. Drag it up to live with its fellows, so you have groups devoted to, say, Primary keys, Foreign keys, or global values. This arrangement speeds your work.

Tip from
Rich

If you sort a few important fields over and over, use Custom order. Put those fields at the top of your list of fields, so they are immediately visible when the Sort dialog opens.

Caution

If you have to recover a file using the Recover command, you *may* lose your Custom field order. If the moons are aligned properly with Jupiter and there has not been a lot of damage, you might actually recover the Custom field order.

Deleting Fields

Deleting can be dangerous because the field you get rid of may still be referred to elsewhere within your own database, or out on a Web site, or over a connection using ODBC. When some other file looks for the field and fails to find it, your users get hit with an error message.

Remember, too, that if you have already populated the field with data, the data goes "bye bye" with the field. Undo will not save the data. After you delete the field, the data will never again be accessible. Also, if you care, deleting the field also eliminates any labels that match the field name, so your layouts may suffer unsightly gaps if you have carefully aligned a lot of fields and labels.

You have to be concerned about whether the field was used in a script or in a related file. You could get fewer results, or sometimes, skewed or unexpected results. As you contemplate deletion, ask yourself, "Have I used this field in any of my scripts or in any related files?"

Tip from
Rich

> You don't have to delete. Consider the alternative. Just remove the field from all layouts without deleting it from the database. In this way you preserve the field and all its information as a precaution. The storage overhead is not bad, and the payoff is enormous if you later find you need the field after all. You just plop it back on the layout. Warning: Over the years we have met multiple users who change their minds; this precaution comes from real-life experience.

If you decide to delete a field, it's easy. Too easy, in fact. You open Define Fields, select the field, and click Delete. Luckily, FileMaker refuses to let you delete a field if it is used in a calculation or summary, and displays the error message shown in Figure 3.14.

Figure 3.14
FileMaker saves you from disaster by preventing deletion of a field used in a calculation or summary.

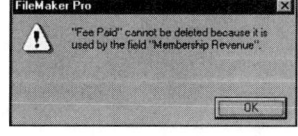

Even if the field is not used in a calculation or summary, FileMaker gives you the warning shown in Figure 3.15.

Figure 3.15.
FileMaker gives you a moment to rethink your decision.

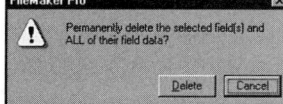

Tip from Rich	Double-check whenever you get the warning. Make absolutely sure you are deleting the right field. Think it through. Will you never need this data again?

Tip from Rich	Want to delete without warning? On a Mac, hold down Option and click Delete. On a PC, hold down Shift as you click Delete. (This technique is only for the very brave).

Tip from Rich	Always back up your database before making a significant—and non-undoable—change, such as deleting a field.

Changing Field Types

Changing the type of a field could foul up any searches or sorts that you have already set up to run on the field, because the indexes and sequences are predicated on a certain type of data, such as numbers, text, dates, or time. If someone has already entered data in the field, you also risk losing that.

Different field types contain different amounts of data. So if you switch the type from a large holder to a small one, some of the data may be thrown away in the process. Luckily, FileMaker issues a warning if it is about to dump data (see Figure 3.16). We recommend that you heed the warning and find some way to preserve the data before changing the field type.

Figure 3.16
If changing a field's type will throw away data, FileMaker issues this warning.

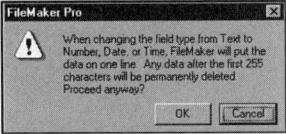

For example, if you were to transform a Text field, containing up to 64,000 characters, into a Number field, which can only hold 255 characters, you would lose all but the first 255 characters of your data on each record. FileMaker alerts you to this possibility. We recommend clicking Cancel to back out of the change and trying to find a way to preserve the data if it is important.

Also, if you are turning a Text, Number, Date, or Time field into a Calculation field, all your current entries will be replaced with the results of your new calculation. If you are turning one of these fields into a Container, Global, or Summary field, all entries are forever lost. Are you sure you want this to happen?

> **Caution**
>
> If the field is the target of an ODBC connection, changing the field type may result in confusion on that side as well.

> **Tip from Rich**
>
> Change the field type only after it's done its job. If you change a Calculation field to another type, FileMaker leaves the results of the last calculation in the field (if the calculation was stored).

CHANGING FIELD NAMES

FileMaker makes this operation safe. Go ahead! Change a field name.

Select the field name in the Define Fields dialog box (see Figure 3.17), edit it, or type in a new name; then click Change.

Figure 3.17
The Define Fields dialog box lets you quickly change a field name.

You won't lose any data, or screw up any scripts, calculations, or summaries. FileMaker goes through changing any references to the field name in calculations, summaries, layouts, and scripts. FileMaker even fixes the labels on layouts.

> **Tip from Steven**
>
> Changing a field name within FileMaker will not update any AppleScript, Web client, or ODBC clients, and so if you are using any of those technologies, the change may require that you update the field name in locations outside of FileMaker.

> **Tip from Rich**
>
> Deep down inside of FileMaker, FileMaker assigns a unique numeric ID to each field, and when you reference a field in a calculation, script, or summary, FileMaker actually references the field not by the name but by its unique ID. That is why when you change the name of the field, FileMaker doesn't require that you update your calculations, scripts, and summaries. The name is just a characteristic of that ID.

Anticipating the Layout for Each Field

Sometimes, you lose a field. You know it is in your database somewhere, but on which layout? The Analyzer, from Waves in Motion, comes to the rescue as shown in Figure 3.18, going through your database and emerging with a report on which layouts carry which fields. This tool is so useful we've put a demo copy on the CD.

Figure 3.18
Waves in Motion provides the Analyzer 2, showing you which fields show up on which layouts.

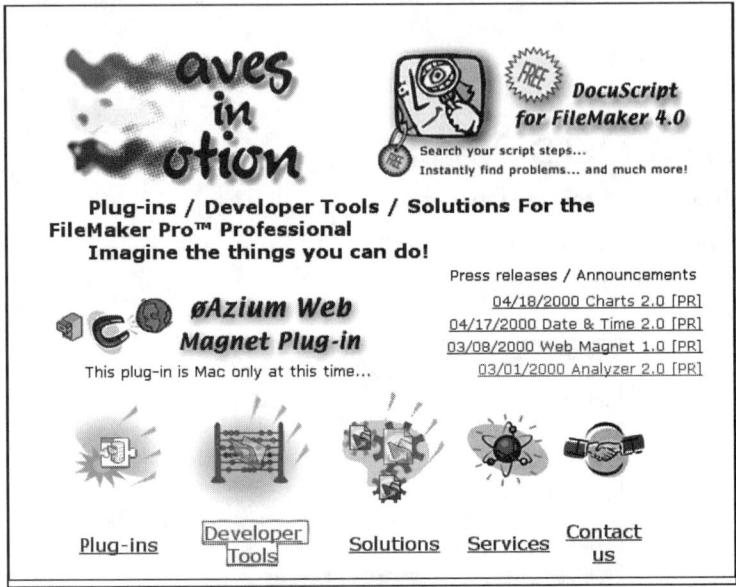

Tip from
Rich

Print out a list of fields. If you have a few dozen fields, you may not be able to recall the exact name of a field you created a month ago. Scrolling through the list in the Define Fields dialog box may not help, because you overscroll, drift up, and miss the thing going by at high speed. Instead, print out the list. Choose Print from the File menu, and in the Print dialog (see Figure 3.19), click Field Definitions to get the complete list with options.

Figure 3.19
Using the Print Fields option will give you a printed list of field definitions.

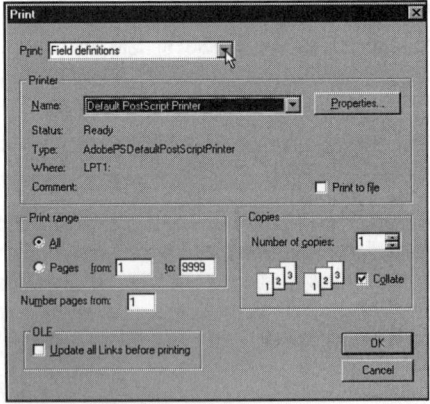

Tip from
Steven

In FileMaker Pro 5, if you have a tab-delimited file containing field names in the first row and sample data (comprised of Text, Number, Date, or Time) in the second row of tab-delimited sample data, FileMaker Pro can open that file and use the first row as a source of field names, and then, examining the data in the second row, determine the appropriate field types. The easiest way to do this is from an Excel spreadsheet where the first row across has the field names and the second row has sample data corresponding to the field names immediately above.

CHAPTER 4

CASE STUDIES IN PLANNING

In this chapter

Why Case Studies 84
A Case Study of Old Willy's Country Club 84
A Case Study of Klodner's Kar Dealership 93

Why Case Studies

In this chapter, we present two case studies of planning. One involves Old Willy's Country Club, an expanding golf course business, and the other deals with Klodner's Kar Dealership, which actually sells more than just kars. You'll hear the history, see the diagrams, and listen over our shoulders as real-life planning gets done.

We've found that we learn best from examples, and these two examples provide a sense of the complexities involved in developing a plan for a new database. The process ebbs and flows, moves forward and then returns as you dig deeper into the business and understand more about the requirements, the users, and the culture you are representing.

A Case Study of Old Willy's Country Club

Old Willy owned a country club with three eighteen-hole golf courses. As his golfers completed a round of golf, they had to submit their score cards so Old Willy could keep track of their scores and submit them to the Professional Golf Association (PGA) so their handicaps could be determined. But one day the PGA told Old Willy that the golf scores would have to be submitted electronically from now on.

When he told us that, we had an idea of the purpose and scope of the system. We asked, "How is it being done now?" By hand. They had a ledger card for each golfer and for each season, and as the golfers finished, their scores were entered on the ledger. Once every couple of weeks, someone sat down and calculated the golfers' scores and handicaps by hand and submitted them on a paper form provided by the PGA. As soon as we heard this, we asked for copies of the ledger form and the forms that went to the PGA.

Old Willy also said that if he was going to have to go through all the effort of putting this data into the computer, he wondered how easy it would be to give individual golfers summaries of their scores both by course and overall. He was also interested in having the system automatically calculate their handicaps.

But sometimes players play nine holes, and sometimes eighteen. And sometimes they walk off the course in the middle of a round because of rain. How would we handle those exceptional circumstances?

Another question we asked Old Willy was how long he wanted to keep this information. He said he wanted to keep it only for the current season, but he wanted a way at the end of the season to post the golfers' final handicaps as part of their records, so they could compare those with last year's handicaps and see how they were doing. (The final handicap of the year, then, would be posted to the golfer's record as Last Year's Handicap, but we would not have to save all the other information live, although Old Willy said he would archive it somewhere, in case he ever had to get at it.)

We asked Old Willy if there were any other people we ought to talk to about the system because they might be affected by it. He suggested talking to his business manager, Shirley.

TALKING WITH SHIRLEY

Shirley had some different ideas. She wanted to use the system to track revenue. So now we had to track information on every golfer, not just those who chose to have their handicaps figured and tracked. And Shirley was also interested in getting some reports out that would show activity by the day of the week (How many rounds were usually played on Tuesday) and by the hour of the day (Is 5 P.M. as busy as 9 A.M.?), and by month (what are the best months, year by year?) She also wanted to capture more information from the golfers for marketing: Which town do they live in? How did they hear about the course? Have they played here before? And finally, she said, "How easy would it be to have this database track what the golfers have done, but also do scheduling, as well?" We mentioned to Shirley that certainly this database could be used for scheduling, but that would add a real layer of complexity. Up to the schedule, everything she had mentioned was consistent with what Old Willy asked for. But this scheduling request would incur substantial extra expenses. Shirley said Old Willy was pretty tight, so we should just forget the scheduling.

DEVELOPING THE ENTITIES AND THEIR RELATIONSHIPS

In preparing a plan for old Willy, we examined potential entities and started to put together an initial Entity Relationship Diagram. Trying to pick the two major entities, we decided on Courses and Golfers. We then identified the relationship as many to many, because any one course is played by many golfers, and any one golfer may play many courses.

Whenever we have a many-to-many relationship, we know that we should try to resolve it with a middle file. In this case, that would be a Round of Golf. So we came up with one course, which offers many rounds of golf; and one golfer may be related to many rounds of golf, too. We made our first sketch of an Entity Relationship diagram, as shown in Figure 4.1.

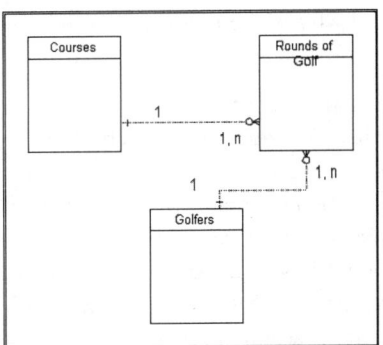

Figure 4.1
Here is our first sketch of an Entity Relationship diagram for Old Willy's Country Club.

When we asked about attributes, though, Old Willy allowed as how he would probably need to know what the par was for each hole on each course. One way to record that would be to come up with 18 separate fields for each course, Course A Hole 1 Par, Course A Hole 2 Par, and so on through Course C Hole 18 Par. Then, in the Rounds file, we would have fields for Course A Hole 1 Score, Course A Hole 2 Score, and so on, through Course C Hole 18 Score, because Old Willy and Shirley want to turn out one report showing a golfer how he or she performed by hole on a given course and another report showing how the golfer performed on Par 3 holes (on various courses), compared with his performance on Par 4 holes or Par 5 holes.

So when we looked more closely at the situation, we saw we were dealing with a field that had multiple values, somewhat like Product #1 Name, Product #2 Name, and so on and so there was a likelihood that these scores and pars all belonged in another file. If we put all 18 pars in each course record, or if we put all 18 scores in each round record, we knew we might end up with problems when we wanted to run certain queries or reports.

For example, Old Willy wanted to report a golfer's performance on a particular hole on a particular course. "How has this golfer done on Hole 7, historically?" The Hole 7 Score and the Hole 14 Score are different fields, so we would have to come up with a different report layout for each hole (18 holes on 3 courses, for 54 different layouts). Worse, Willy also mentioned in a phone conversation that he wanted, for any given round of golf, to know by hole a golfer's variance from par. In that case, we would need 18 calculations for each course, one for each hole, comparing the actual score with the par for that hole. If the golfer wanted to know, on average, what his variation was for each hole on a given course, or for a range of dates, then we were going to need another 18 summary fields showing those averages. And, from a query, we would have 18 fields showing different values by hole.

If the golfer would like to find all instances of his or her score exceeding par by three or more strokes, now there were 18 fields we would have to create for each course, with names like "Course A Hole 1 Difference From Par," and so on, and we would have to search in the Rounds file, saying, "Find all the records in which the variation on Hole 1 is greater than 3, and all the records in which the variation on Hole 2 is greater than 3," with new requests all the way up to Hole 18, but what we would recover would be records of the whole rounds, not individual records for each hole, so there would be even more work to be done with each record after it was discovered. And what if a golfer only played nine holes, although the record had 18 slots to fill?

To avoid such labor, with its rich potential for confusion and error, we invented two child files. One was called Holes. In the Holes file, which was the child of the Courses file, there would be 18 records, one for each hole on a given 18-hole course. One record in the Holes file described the attributes of a single hole on a given course, such as par. The other file was a child to the Rounds file, and we called it Scores by Hole. Each record here represented a particular score on one hole on one course during one round of golf. By creating those two child files, we did away with the Course A Hole 1 Par, Course A Hole 2 Par fields, all living within a single record, because those became individual records within a child file.

If we now tried to tie our system back together, we discovered that there was a many-to-many relationship between the Holes file and the Rounds file. Any given round of golf involved multiple holes. And any given hole was used in many rounds of golf. Luckily, this was resolved by the file dedicated to Scores by Hole.

So now we were at our final ER diagram (see Figure 4.2).

Figure 4.2
You can now see the final Entity Relationship diagram for Old Willy.

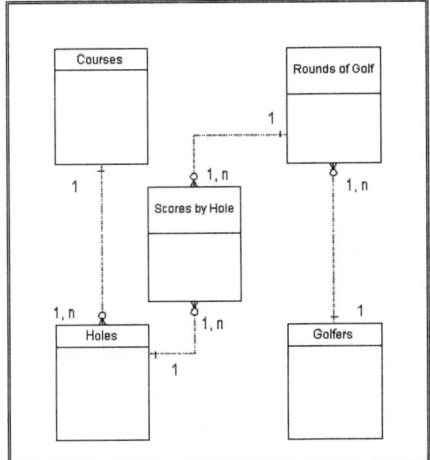

Considering Some Business Rules

Even at a country club there are some business rules—well, some sports rules—involved. In the Holes file we would need a single record for each hole on each course. Course A has holes 1 through 18. Ditto for Course B and Course C. We wanted to make sure that Old Willy was very precise in creating these records, and we wanted to make sure that nobody messed with them afterwards. Or we would have to create scripts in the Courses file, so that if Old Willy opened up a new course, as he was hoping to do in the acres he just bought out in Medfield, the user could press a button to create new records for the new holes, entering the par for each. In this way, we could reduce the potential for user error.

Scores by Hole

A similar issue appears with the Scores by Hole file. For any given round of golf, we wanted a record in the Scores by Hole file for each hole the golfer played, and we wanted to be sure we did not accidentally create duplicate records. (Golf rule: No one should play the same hole twice during the same round). So we thought we might add buttons running scripts in the Rounds file to create either 9 records in the Scores by Hole file for the front nine, or 9 records for the back nine, or perhaps all 18 holes for a full round. We wanted to avoid people accidentally entering the same score twice, or slipping from the first hole on the front nine to the second hole on the back nine. So we had FileMaker create the records automatically, to ensure referential integrity. The user, then, would see a portal in the Rounds file, and when the user pressed the button for Front Nine, FileMaker created nine records over in the Scores by Hole file for Holes 1 through 9, and it would do the same for the Back Nine, or create 18 records for a Full Round. The user, then, could not add new records by hand, but could have FileMaker add the records for each hole, performing any calculations automatically.

Old Willy reminded us of one other issue when we talked with him following up on these ideas: Sometimes people do not play the whole course, or even the first nine. Some folks walk off the course after the sixth hole, or they get rained out on the fourth. So we had to offer users a way to delete records of holes when the golfer never played those holes. We just wanted FileMaker to create the records to avoid errors and duplicate records.

ENTERING SCORES

One other issue emerged: When a user is entering the scores from a round of golf, FileMaker will be creating 9 or 18 records in the Scores by Hole file. In order to create those records, we needed to know which holes we were talking about—that is, which course the golfer was playing on. So, when creating a round of golf record, we would need to start by asking the user which course the golfer was on. When FileMaker created a record in the Scores by Hole file, then, we could determine which course that round of golf was played on just by looking at the holes played.

The course ID is a characteristic of that round of golf, so even though we could infer which course the golfer played from the particular holes, we would tend to capture the course name as part of the Rounds file. By doing that, we could, for instance, create a relationship from the Courses file to the Rounds file, so we could then show, for any given course, a list of all of the rounds played that day, week, or month. Also, this redundant data is not likely to change over time; we don't have to worry about someone changing the holes on which the golfer played later, so the redundant data is OK, and we do not have to worry about updates. The key is that we could relate the Courses file and the Rounds file, and produce reports on that relationship.

FIELD DEFINITIONS

The ER diagram shows how the files will be put together in a way that matches the way the business operates. But that diagram does not have any information about the business rules. So once we built the ER diagram, we had to think through the business rules very carefully. Some were very straightforward: the par of a course needs to be 3, 4, or 5. But sometimes the rules get more complicated. One of Willy's rules was that the combination of a Hole number and a Course ID must be unique, that is, each hole belonged to one course, and no more. We had to end up with a single record for each hole on any course.

To make sure that was the case, we could tinker with the interface: Any time we created a new record in the Courses file (as when Old Willy completes that new course designed by the pro), we would have a button that the user could press to create 18 child records in the Holes file, and we would make sure that if those records already existed, we did not add them again. Plus, we wanted to make sure that no one could delete those records, accidentally eliminating the fifth hole on Course B, for example. How did we do all this? Not through field validation, but through the buttons that ran scripts checking to see that no such records existed, and, if that was true, created the new records, and some password protection preventing users from deleting records in the Holes file. In this way, we did not rely on the user having to add those records by hand—a tedious and potentially error-prone process. All the user had to do was hit a button to create the records and then enter the par for each hole.

Fields in the Scores by Hole File

We faced a similar issue in the Scores by Hole file. We had to be sure we were adding the right number of records in that file. We wanted to avoid duplication or omission of a record. And we wanted to avoid having a record of a score for a hole the player never got around to playing. If someone played the front nine and went in because of a thunderstorm, we did not want to show records for the back nine. So we might have buttons for Front Nine, Back Nine, and All 18 Holes, which were the most common situations.

But sometimes players started a round and left in the middle, due to hailstorms, darkness, time constraints, or getting mad at the ball. We wanted to be able to enter records only for the holes played, but we also wanted to create an environment that gave the user a good chance for success. One scenario was to allow users to press a button for Front Nine, Back Nine, or All 18, but to add a button for Custom. When the user pressed Custom, a bunch of check boxes appeared, so the user could check off the holes a golfer had actually played during this round and then click OK; a script took care of adding those records to the Scores by Hole file, and presented them to the user to enter the actual scores. That script would need to be smart enough to make sure that the user was not adding the same hole more than once for any given round of golf. (The user must therefore start recording a golfer's scores by entering the round, which had attributes such as the day, golfer, and start time, as well as its Round ID.)

The user, then, would rarely see the Scores by Hole file directly. The user would enter those scores through a portal in the Rounds file. We would not give the user access to the Scores by Hole file itself. There was a similar situation in the Invoices file, where there was a file called Line Items. A majority of reports derived information from that file, and users entered a lot of data into line items, but they were not doing that directly in the Line Items file; they did so through a portal in the Invoices file. Of course, we allowed users to go and look at the Line Items directly if they really wanted to. (Choose the Advanced Line Items report in the Summary Reports drop-down list.) But even in that interface, the users could query and report on line item information, even though they could not directly change that information because that would make mistakes too easy.

In the golf club, the user could pick the holes for which records should be created. If we were stricter, any time a golfer had a new round of golf, we would create 18 holes in the Scores by Hole, and the user would enter the scores for any holes played, and then, through some searching and calculating, we would exclude the holes that were not played (that is, those with no value in the score field) before generating any reports. But one downside to this approach would be that we could not require a user to enter a score for every record, because it was perfectly possible for an empty value to be a valid score. Result: a casual user might forget to enter a score, and we would never know.

Another option might be to require the user to enter a score of zero or NA (not applicable) for any holes the golfer did not play. We could set validation to say, "Do not let the score on this record be empty; it must be an actual score, or a zero or an NA," which in our coding scheme meant a hole that was not played. In this way, we could positively identify which holes were not played (the ones with a score of zero or NA). So the field definition for Score said "Not Empty."

In this way, we developed a long set of field definitions, shown in Table 4.1. A lot of people will say, "I don't need to do this; I can start right off building fields," but you can see how many little twists and turns can catch up with you. It's much better to sit down with paper and plan the entities and the fields, because you are less likely to be caught up with actual creation and tinkering with the interface. You are putting a puzzle together. Also, doing it this way, you get some documentation so other folks can take your notes and do the actual building of the database, if you're fortunate enough to have help.

TABLE 4.1 FIELD DEFINITIONS

File Name	Field Name	Field Type	Field Options
Golfers			
	pk_golfer_id	T	Auto-entered serial # GLF10001, incremented by 1, non-modifiable.
	golfer_first_name	T	
	golfer_middle_name	T	
	golfer_last_name	T	
	golfer_casual_name	T	
	golfer_name_prefix	T	
	golfer_name_suffix	T	
	golfer_street	T	
	golfer_city	T	
	golfer_state	T	
	golfer_zip	T	
	golfer_home_phone	T	
	golfer_work_phone	T	
	last_year_handicap	N	
	method_heard_about_course	T	value list: radio buttons: value list: friend, newspaper, radio, Internet, other
	c_rounds_played	C/N	count (Rounds | fk_golfer_ ID::pk_rounds_ID)
	c_avg_score	C/N	Average (Rounds | fk_golfer_ ID::c_rounds_total)
	c_avg_strokes_from_par	C/N	Average (Rounds | fk_golfer_ID:: c_strokes_from_par)
	Note: have a record for "miscellaneous golfer" for those people who choose not to supply their names and addresses		

TABLE 4.1 CONTINUED

File Name	Field Name	Field Type	Field Options
	c_tot_cost_of_round	C/N	sum (Rounds I golfer_ID::cost-of-round)
Rounds			
	pk_round_id	T	Auto-enter serial # rnd10001, increment by 1, non-modifiable
	fk_golfer_id	T	Valid member of value list golfer ID
	date_of_round	D	not empty
	time_of_round	T	not empty
	c_day_of_week	C/T	DayOfWeek (date_of_round)
	c_first_of_month	C/D	DateMonth (date_of_round),1,year (date_of_round))
	c_day_of_time	C/T	case (Time_of_round<TextToTime (8:00:00),"Early morning",time_of_round<TextToTime(12:00:00),"Morning",Time_of_Round<TextToTime(16:00:00),"Afternoon",time_of_round>TextToTime(16:00:00),"Evening")
	fk_course_id	T	not empty
	c_round_total	C/N	sum (scoresbyhole I fk_round_ID::score)
	c_holes_played	C/N	count (scoresbyhole I fk_round_ID::score)
	c_roun d_eval	C/T	case (round_total<scoresbyhole I fk_round_ID::c_hole_par_pipeline,"Below PAR",round_total<scoresbyhole I fk_round_ID::c_hole_par_pipeline,"PAR",round_total>scoresbyhole I fk_round_ID::c_hole_par_pipeline,"Above PAR")
	c_cnt_holes	C/N	count (scoresbyhole I fk_round_ID::PK_scores_by_hole)score)
	c_strokes_from_par	C/N	C_round_total – courses I pic_course_ID::c_Par
	s_cnt_rounds	S	Count of pk_round_id
	s_tot_holes_played	S	Total of C_holes_played
	s_avg_round_total	S	Average of C_round_total
	s_avg_strokes_from_par	S	Average of c_strokes_from_par
	cost_of_round	N	
	s_tot_cost_of_round	S	Total of cost_of_round
	s_avg_cost_of_round	S	Average of cost_of_round

TABLE 4.1	CONTINUED		
File Name	**Field Name**	**Field Type**	**Field Options**
Holes			
	pk_hole_id	T	auto-enter serial # hle10001, increment by 1, non-modifiable
	fk_course_id	T	Valid member of value list, course ID
	hole_number	N	In the range of 1-18, pop-up menu
	hole_par	N	In range of 1-3, radio buttons, not empty: value list=1,2,3
	notes	T	
	c-avg_score	C/N	Average (scoresbyhole|fk_hole_ID::score)
Notes			
	Combination of hole_number and fk_course_id must be unique.		
	Create a button for users in the course file that will create 9 or 18 records in the Holes file automatically. Usersthen simply enter the par scores.		
ScoresByHole			
	pk_scores_by_hole_id	T	auto-enter serial #m SBH10001, increment by 1, non-modifiable
	fk_hole_id	T	valid member value list of hole_IDs
	fk_round_id	T	valid member of value list of round_ids
	c_hole_par_pipeline	C/N	holes|pk_hole_ID::hole_par
	score	N	not empty
	hole_eval	C/T	case (score<c_hole_par_pipeline,"Below Par",score=c_hole_par_pipeline,"par",score>c_hole_par_pipeline,"Above Par")
	s_tot_score	s	Total of score
	s_avg_score	S	Average of score
	s_cnt_score	S	Count of score
	s_tot_par	S	Total of c_hole_par_pipeline

TABLE 4.1 CONTINUED

File Name	Field Name	Field Type	Field Options
	s_avg_par	S	Average of Cc_hole_par_pipeline
	Note: When a user creates a new round, havea script create new records in this file automatically. Then the user only needs to enter the score.		
Courses			
	pk_course_id	T	auto-enter serial # CRS10001, increment by 1, non-modifiable
	course_name	T	unique, not empty
	notes	T	
	c_par	C/N	sum (holes|fk_course_ID::hole_par)
	c_cnt_holes	C/N	Count (holes|fk_course_ID::pk_hole_ID)

A Case Study of Klodner's Kar Dealership

The owner of a new and used car dealership was interested in getting a better handle on sales and inventory. In our meeting, he said that everything was paper-based. No one had a good idea of what cars were in stock and what cars were coming. That caused a lot of confusion.

He was price sensitive, but he wanted a system to track his inventory, sales, customers, profitability, and financing. When we talked with him about inventory, we found out that his inventory was just cars, used and new. He wanted his staff to be able to go to the computer and find out what they had in stock at that moment.

From a sales perspective, he wanted reports showing sales by sales people, and, rolling that up, sales by sales managers as well, since he had several different sales managers.

He also wanted to track customers because at that time they did not do a good job going back to customers saying, "Gee, you've had that car for a few years, and we have some new cars you might be interested in. Would you like to come in and take a test drive?" And he hoped to send out Christmas cards and to notify people of special incentive deals. The customer file, then, would be used as a sales and marketing tool. Over time, the file would also reveal which cars a particular customer had bought.

He wanted a secure area to track profitability, to see what each car cost him, how much money he had put into it for repair or maintenance, how long he had kept it on the lot (which affected his financing costs) so he could see on a car-by-car basis what the profits were. He could then extend that to see profitability by sales person or sales manager.

Finally, he wanted a screen on which he could track what kind of financing had been sold along with each car.

We then asked the owner to sketch out the reports he was after. We also asked whether there were other people in the organization we should talk to. He suggested we talk to the service and sales departments.

We spoke to the service department manager. He did not have much to do with car sales, except that he was sometimes asked to update or repair trade-ins and to prep cars for delivery. His group often had problems keeping a handle on what cars needed to be prepped and when they needed to be ready. The service manager wondered whether the system could help with those two issues.

Then we met with the sales reps and the sales managers. The first thing they were interested in was better commission reporting. At that time, it was all done by hand and things fell between the cracks. They also wanted to get a better idea of existing and incoming inventory, so they could answer a prospect's question about what cars were available on the lot, and where. Also, they wanted to be able to say, "Well, we don't have that model today, but we will be getting one in next week." The sales managers said that a lot of people were asking them whether they had any pictures of these cars on the Web. "Would it be possible to create a Web presence for these cars?" The sales manager thought they could get more people walking through the door if customers could see the cars online.

The good news was that what we had heard from everyone was reasonably consistent.

PLAYING WITH ENTITIES

In pondering the car dealership, we first thought that the entities would be sales managers, sales people, vehicles, and customers, as shown in Figure 4.3. (Remember, entity names are plural, usually). And in our first pass at the ER diagram, we figured that the two most important entities would be customers and vehicles. We put those at the heart of the business. But what did that mean?

At first we figured that one customer could buy several vehicles over time, but any one vehicle would be purchased by one and only one customer. But as we talked with folks at the dealership, we began to wonder whether that was really true. What if Fred came in and bought a car from the dealership today and then came back in a few years and traded that one in for a new car. Oops. The dealership might then sell that same car to someone else. So the same car might end up being sold to several different customers. Is this a many-to-many relationship, with many cars relating to many customers? If so, we would have to create a join table called something like Vehicle Sales, where some info about the car is in the Cars file and other info is in the Vehicle Sales record for each transaction; such added complexity would challenge a user, and us, as developers. We wanted to avoid that situation if we could.

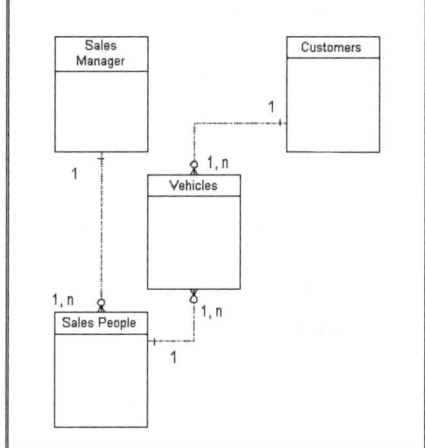

Figure 4.3
Here is the first pass at an entity-relationship diagram for the car dealership.

Changing Views of the Car

As we talked some more with the sales folks, we began to see that the car, when it came back to them, was not the same item it was. It had lost value. Those dings and dents had diminished its shine; the mileage was high; the bluebook value had gone way down. Because Fred may have added a CD player and a sunroof, what the dealership was selling was really different from the original car, with its new-car smell. The Vehicle Identification Number (VIN) would be the same, the year and make would be the same, but overall, it had probably become a different car. If so, we could make up a new record for the used car, and although it would carry some redundant info, such as the VIN, make, model, and year, that would be a small sacrifice to keep from having a many-to-many relationship and being forced to create an extra file for Vehicle Sales. Thus, as we dug deeper into what was really going on in the business, we returned to a simpler structure and easier interface.

Thinking of People

If we stuck with the idea that one steady customer might buy multiple vehicles, then all we had to add to the ER diagram were sales managers and sales people. We could attach sales people to the car records on the theory that a sales person might sell multiple cars, but any car was sold by one and only one sales person. Or we could attach a sales person to a customer (shocking idea!), so that any one customer got only one sales person, while a sales person had many customers. But couldn't a customer have dealings with more than one sales person? One way we thought about this was that any given customer dealt with one sales person at a time, so it would be possible to say that a sales person had many customers over time, but a customer had only one current sales person. And a customer could buy several cars, but any one car was bought by only one customer.

Here is the downside to this model. We would know which customer purchased a car, and we would know which sales person currently was responsible for that customer, but what if a customer bought a car from a different sales person a few years ago? In this model, we could never track down previous sales people. Yes, a workaround might be to track the sales rep ID as part of the Cars file, so that for any car we could tell who sold it. But then we would be tracking the sales rep ID as part of the Customer record and as part of the vehicle record. If a customer returned to the dealership, traded in her old car, and bought a new car from a new salesperson, someone would have to put that sales person ID into the customer record and into the record for the new car. Not likely to happen all the time, what with the turnover of clerks and the many distractions on the shop floor.

Here is an alternate perspective. Tracking the sales rep ID as part of the customer record was redundant. If each car record had the ID of the sales rep, we could have FileMaker look at the latest car record, grab the sales rep ID from that, and *presume* that the customer who bought that car belonged to that sales person. The Vehicles file has the ID of the customer and the ID of the sales person. So now if we entered a car sales transaction in the Vehicles file, we would assign that transaction to a particular sales rep, so we knew who made that sale (and who should get the commission), and concluded that that sales rep was currently responsible for that customer. (In this scenario, the Vehicles file had information about the car itself and about the sale). But perhaps that made each record a compound record because we were trying to track two different kinds of information in one file? Yes, partly—we had entered a gray area. We could create a sales transactions file, or we could just fudge along with the sales info in the Vehicles file.

But we decided that the same vehicle returning to the lot to be sold as used was a "different" car. Now, we had a one-to-one relationship between a car and a transaction. That means, a "car" had only one sale, so we did not need an extra file. (In general, we wanted to merge any one-to-one relationships into a single entity). So the Vehicles record had attributes of the vehicle and the sales transaction.

We transformed the Vehicles file into a Vehicle Sales file, which had descriptions of the car, and, when the car was sold, details of the transaction. So this file referred to cars on the lot, cars that were due to come in over the next month, and cars that had been sold. We had moved from focusing on the physical cars to their business role: things that were supposed to be sold. Also, early on, we discovered that the dealership sold more than cars: vans, trucks, and pickups. So the file we started off calling Cars got renamed Vehicles. But that was not descriptive enough because we needed those records to carry information about the sales transactions. We then refined the name to Vehicle Sales, and the characteristics of the vehicle sale included attributes of the vehicle, as well as attributes of the sale itself.

BUT WHAT ABOUT SALES MANAGERS?

Our first pass showed a sales manager having many salespeople, but a salesperson working for only one manager, with one salesperson responsible for each sale, and one customer buying, potentially, many cars. But as we talked some more to the folks at the dealership, we discovered that the sales managers themselves sometimes sold cars. In that situation, the sales manager acted as a sales person. So we had to look at the diagram, and ask, "How could a sales manager also be a salesperson?"

One way would be to have a record for the sales manager in the Sales Managers file *and* in the Sales People file. But we realized that the information we would be tracking for the sales manager was identical to the information we would be tracking for the sales person, so we decided that instead of having a separate entity for sales managers, we would just put sales people and sales managers all in the same file. Then the question became how do we know which sales people work for which sales managers? In a way, the Sales People file had a one-to-many relationship with itself. Thus, for each record in the Sales People file, we would have a sales person ID, and we would also have a field for the ID of the sales person's manager, which would be the sales manager's ID as a sales person. Now we had a way to link sales people to their managers, all within the same file. (This technique is known as a self-join).

➔ If you would like to explore the joys and benefits of self-joins, **see** Chapter 13, "The Joys of Self-Joins and Other Interesting Relationships," **p. 421**.

Most relationships are parent and child, where the parent records are in one file and the child records are in another. The only difference here was that both parent and child records were in the same file. We could now create a report summarized by the sales manager field, showing the results for each sales person who reported to each sales manager.

We know that for each vehicle sale we were capturing the ID of the sales person. So we could infer from that information which sales manager was responsible, because the sales manager's ID was a characteristic of the salesperson. The only problem with inferring that was that sometimes sales people change managers. In that situation, the sales person's new manager would get credit for all previous sales that the person made before being transferred. So in the Vehicle Sales file, we added an additional field for sales manager ID—at the time of that particular sale. The users did not have to enter anything here. They entered the sales person's ID, and we did a lookup of that person's manager. We did not want this manager "updated." We wanted to preserve the information as it was on the day of the sale so we had historically accurate information. On the ER diagram, then, we had two one-to-many relationships from the Sales People file to the Vehicle Sales file: one tracks the ID of the salesperson; the other tracks the ID of the sales manager.

When we started, we thought the two main entities would be customers and cars, and now we faced customers and vehicle sales. We added sales people and sales managers, but now we had melded them together in the sales people file. Originally, we had a one-to-one relationship between Sales People and customers, but we realized that this relationship could be many to many, because over time a single customer might deal with several different sales people, and each sales person would, we hoped, have more than one customer. Customers, then, should have a one-to-many relationship to vehicle sales, and salespeople should have a many-to-many relationship to customers, resolved through the Vehicle Sales file. Vehicle Sales now acted as a join file between sales people and customers, as shown in our final ER diagram in Figure 4.4.

Figure 4.4
This is the final Entity Relationship diagram for the car dealership.

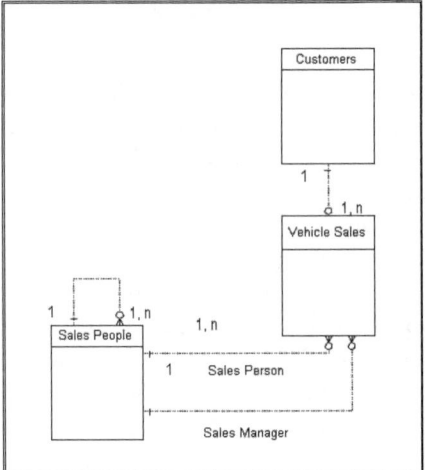

In the big scheme of things, these were relatively simple ER diagrams. Yet consider how many different ways we could have looked at them as we learned to take into account the way the entities interacted with each other in a business sense. As a developer, then, you are trying to create a structure that will track data in a way that mirrors the way the business actually operates. It is better for a database to work the way a business works than to force the business to change the way it works and bend its rules to accommodate the software.

When you are in the ER diagramming stage, you are not really being technical, and you should not be thinking too much about your tools. The ER diagram maps the data structures of the business, so the ER diagram is still more of a description of the way the business works rather than a plan for the database.

Now when you start building file structure diagrams and field descriptions, you can move toward the technical side. Every database tool handles these differently, so you have to start thinking in more detail about the way your tool works. You just hope you have defined your business correctly.

Developing the Field Definitions for the Kar Dealership

There are a whole lot more fields in the Vehicle Sales file, in part because of what we were tracking, but also because we needed calculations and summaries. If you looked at this file as the resolution of a many-to-many relationship between Customers and Sales People, you would find the greatest number of fields show up here because it is a join file. This build-up of fields often happens in a join file because it is where all the data comes together. (If you look at our Invoicing file, you will see that there are a majority of reports coming from the Line Items file, which acts to join the Invoices and Products files).

Table 4.2 Field Definitions for the Kar Dealership

File Name	Field Name	Field Type	Field Options
Customers			
	pk_cust_id	T	Auto-enter serial # cst10001, increment by 1, non-modifiable
	first_name	T	
	middle_name	T	
	last_name	T	
	name_prefix	T	value list: Mr. Reverend
	casual_name	T	
	street	T	
	city	T	
	state	T	
	zip	T	
	home_phone	T	
	work_phone	T	
	other_phone	T	
	other_phone_type	T	value list: cell phone
	gender	T	value list: male female
	c_recent_sales_rep	C/T	last (vehicle sales|fk_cust_id: fk_sales_id)
Sales People			
	pk_sales_id	T	auto-enter serial # sls10001, increment by 1, non-modifiable
	first_name	T	
	middle_name	T	
	last_name	T	
	casual_name	T	
	title	T	
	date_of_hire	D	
	fk_sales_mgr_id	T	valid member of value list of sales reps. If person is sales manager, may be left empty.
	notes	T	
Vehicle Sales			
	pk_vehicle_id	T	Auto-entered serial number car 10001, increment by 1, non-modifiable

Table 4.2 Continued

File Name	Field Name	Field Type	Field Options
	fk_sales_id	T	valid member of value list of sales IDs
	fk_cust_id	T	valid member of value list of customer IDs
	year	N	Range of 1950-current year + 1
	mfr	T	
	make	T	
	model	T	
	condition	T	Value list: poor, below average, average, above average, excellent in radio buttons
	mileage	N	
	body type	T	Value list: sedan, coupe, convertible, truck, mini-van, SUV, station wagon, in pop-up menu
	options	T	Value list: details to follow, in check boxes
	new_or_used	T	value list: new, used, demo, in radio buttons
	exterior color	T	
	interior color	T	
	status	T	value list: sold, available, sale pending
	front_view_picture	Container	
	side_view_picture	Container	
	rear_view_picture	Container	
	interior_picture	Container	
	delivery_date	D	
	notes	T	
	acquisition_cost	N	
	cost_of_repairs	N	
	c_cost_of_car	C/N	acquisition_cost+cost_of_repairs
	sales_price	N	
	trade_in_value	N	

Table 4.2 Continued

File Name	Field Name	Field Type	Field Options
	down_payment	N	
	amount_financed	C/N	sales_price – trade_in_value – down_payment - rebates
	rebates	N	
	interest_rate	N	
	term_of_loan	N	
	monthly_pmt	c/n	(formula to follow)
	commission_percent	n	auto-enter .25
	commission_adjust	N	
	c_commission	c/n	(commission_percent*c_profit) – commission_adjust
	c_profit	c/n	sales_price – c_cost_of_car
	c_profit_after_commission	c/n	c_profit – c_commission
	s_cnt_car	s	count of pk_car_id
	car_received+date	D	
	expected_car_receive_date	D	
	expected_car_delivery_date	D	
	date_of_sale	D	
	first_of_month_date_of_sale	C/D	DATE (month (date_of_sale), 1,year(Date_of_sale))
	first_of_quarter_date_of_sale	C/D	DATE (choose (month(date_of_sale),"",1,1,1,4,4,4,7,7,7,10,10,10),1,year(date_of_sale))
	s_tot_acquisition_cost	S	Total of acquisition_cost
	s_avg_acquisition_cost	S	Average of acquisition_cost
	s_tot_cost_of_car	S	Total of C_cost_of_car
	s_avg_cost_of_car	S	Average of c_cost_of_car
	s_tot_sales_price	S	Total of sales_price
	s_avg_sales_price	S	Average of sales_price
	s_tot_trade_in_value	S	Total of trade_in_value

Table 4.2 Continued

File Name	Field Name	Field Type	Field Options
	s_avg_trade_in_value	S	Average of trade_in_value
	s_tot_down_payment	S	Total of down_payment
	s-avg-down_payment	S	Average of down_payment
	s_tot_amount_financed	S	Total of amount_financed
	s-avg_amount_financed	S	Average of amount_financed
	s_avg_commission_percent	S	Average of commission_percent
	s_tot_commission_adjust	S	Total of commission_adjust
	s_avg_commission_adjust	S	Average of commission_adjust
	s_tot_commission	S	Total of c_commission
	s-avg_commission	S	Average of c_commission
	s_tot_profit	S	Total of c_profit
	s_avg_profit	S	Average of c_profit
	s_tot_profit_after_commission	S	Total of c_profit_after_commission
	s_avg_profit_after_commission	S	Average of c_profit_after_commission
	sales_mgr_id	T	Lookup of sales_mgr_ID from Sales People file
	c_sales_mgr_id	C/T	IF (is empty (sales_mgr_ID),fk_sales_ID, sales_mgr_ID)
Sales People			
	pk_sales_id	T	Auto-enter serial # SLS10001, increment by 1, non-modifiable
	first_name	T	
	middle_name	T	
	last_name	T	
	casual_name	T	
	title	T	
	date_of_hire	D	

Table 4.2 Continued

File Name	Field Name	Field Type	Field Options
	fk_sales_mgr_id	T	Valid member of value list of sales reps. If person is sales manager, may be left empty.
	notes	T	

PART II

BUILDING

5   Building Your Files   107

6   Maintaining Referential Integrity   133

7   Keeping Your Data in Good Shape   173

8   Crafting the User Interface   213

9   "Webifying" Your Database   249

10 Hot Calculations   273

11 Reporting   341

12 Dumb Portal Tricks   395

13 The Joys of Self-Joins and Other Interesting Relationships   421

Building your database around relationships expands its power, but makes new demands on you when you are building your files and fields. In this part, we'll explore ways you can maintain the integrity of your references, keep your data in good shape, and build an interface that users will enjoy and use even as you guide them to make accurate and consistent choices. We'll look at calculations, reporting, portals, and specialty relationships, such as self-joins. We'll also explore what's involved with mounting the database on the Web.

CHAPTER 5

BUILDING YOUR FILES

In this chapter

Build Your Tables 108
Create Your Fields 110
Create Relationships Between Files 112

Build Your Tables

So now you have mounds of paper in front of you, with table descriptions, definitions, sample reports, and sketches of your interface underneath the take-out menus. You may feel weighed down by all this preparation, but if you've done a thorough job creating the ER diagram, File Structure diagram, and Field Specification List, you are going to have a much easier time from here on.

Building your files means creating them and populating them with fields, carrying out these tasks:

- Creating a file for each entity
- Creating fields
- Creating relationships between files, relying on certain fields as Primary and Foreign keys, so you can use data from the related files
- Figuring out how to display the data from the related files

Tables form the foundation for the rest of your development, so your first step in creating the database you have planned is to create the raw tables. Basically, you create the file, give it a name, define the fields, and, perhaps, define field options, such as auto-entered values and validation.

Naming Names

Ain't it great? Now even a Windows document can have filenames longer than eight characters. But wait!

Even though the Macintosh has always allowed long filenames, and Windows has since 1995, we favor limiting filenames to eight characters as a general precaution. Long filenames may not survive untruncated in a Unix email or file-server environment. The names may get mangled as they move in and out of email systems, and although all current operating systems claim to handle the long filenames, not every component can. Even if you work in a sealed-off Mac world, you may eventually have to communicate by using email, or talk to PCs and Unix, so although we love long filenames because they are immediately meaningful, we restrain ourselves.

What difference does a broken filename make? Just try running a script or maintaining a relationship with a file that you thought would be called InventoryMaintenance.fp5, when some system or other has renamed it Invent~1.fp5. Your scripts skip a beat, and relationships fail. In fact, any activity that depends on getting in touch with the file will go haywire. Filenames are your golden threads, so don't let them get melted down by a small-thinking gatekeeper.

Tip from
Rich

> Whether you are writing for Mac or Windows, you should end all your filenames with .fp5, because you never know when your client will want to go cross platform. We know, we know; it's ugly. But if you ever have to venture off the Mac platform, the extension will save you a lot of work.

If you have to collaborate on a team with other developers, you'll definitely need to talk through your mutual approach to filenaming, so that everyone can parse everyone else's filenames. You know the group is in sync if everyone can anticipate exactly how someone else will make up a filename—even before the file has been created.

EXAMPLE: FILENAME FOUL-UPS

Here's an example of some filename foul-ups. We had sent some files to a customer via email, but when the customer got them, she said they did not work. We went out to visit, and after poking around, discovered that her email system could only handle attachments with names of eight characters, so it had truncated all our filenames. Once we reset the filenames, everything worked fine.

The Naming of Entities

Within every organization, certain words or phrases have a particular meaning, not the one in the dictionary but a specific interpretation local to that culture. For instance, different educational institutions attach different meanings to the terms *class*, *course*, *module*, *workshop*, and *seminar*. As you ponder assigning names to various entities, try to give them names that make sense to the users, or to the majority of the people in the organization. If you follow their naming system, they will understand immediately what the entities refer to, so they will flounder around less and make fewer mistakes.

Tip from
Rich

> For words like *companies* and *contacts*, use the first eight letters, as in contacts.fp5 or the singular, as in company.fp5. But if you have a lot of files that start with the same word or phrase, you may have to abbreviate. For this, you need a system, and you should plan to give users a crib sheet (ahem, documentation). For files such as Order Items and Order Invoices (where there are multiple invoices per order) or Product Information and Product Inventory, we abbreviate the first word in three letters, and the next in two or three letters, using SiliconValleyCapitalization, such as OrdItem.fp5 and OrdInvo.fp5, or ProdInfo.fp5 and ProdInve.fp5. You can see why users will need an explanation of these codes.

Tip from
Rich

> If your end users are going to need to know filenames, consider putting a button on the main layout or in a Help layout, offering to list all the files. For each file, you might also summarize the file's purpose in the system.

Make sure that your layout identifies the purpose of the file, in English, right up there at the top, so anyone who has to work on the file as a fellow developer, administrator, or tinkerer can find out what it does just by opening it. For instance, if your file name is ProdInfo.fp5, the window says Product Information. This term is probably the name of the entity, from your ER diagram. In this way, the filename appears in the title bar, and a translation appears right below.

You never want to let users change your filenames because your average user can be as innocently destructive as UNIX. But there may be "designated drivers" among the users, people who have to modify the files after you leave, and for them, your systematic approach to filenaming will be a big help.

Tip from
Rich

> You want to be careful when you are naming files, to make sure that you do not have multiple files with the same name on a computer or on the network, as you might have created during development, or when users get hold of your system and start playing. For instance, during operation, your users might have several files called Company.fp5 on their hard drives, and a couple of other instances open on the network. FileMaker tries to open the proper version, but it also tries to be helpful, and if it can't locate the file that it expects (as when a server goes down), it goes to look elsewhere, pawing through the current folder, the FileMaker Pro folder, and directories out on the network. Hence, if it cannot find the right version, FileMaker may discover another file with that name, such as your early draft. What a mess, if a customer enters data one day and cannot find it the next, and the person who actually owns the file discovers surprising new data.

CASE STUDY: MULTIUSER MAYHEM

A couple of users go to the fileserver and shut it down at the end of the day; then they bring the file back to their local machines to run off complex reports faster. The next day, FileMaker finds the correct file on the server, but it also discovers the copies out on the users' hard drives. The users were making copies and leaving them as multiuser. So FileMaker found two or three multiuser copies on the same zone, and kindly opened the first one it found, which might not be the master copy

This problem occurs frequently in Novell and AppleTalk networks. You cannot prevent the problem there, except by training users not to download a file while maintaining its status as multiuser. If you are using TCP/IP, you can identify the file by the IP address, which helps eliminate the problem.

CREATE YOUR FIELDS

As soon as you create a file, FileMaker asks you what fields to include. Now, working from the list you developed during planning, you enter the field name, field type, and field options.

To keep track of each record in the file, make the first field you create an auto-entered serial number, and make that field unmodifiable so you always have a unique identifier for each record, no matter what. If you consider a database as a table made up of rows and columns (corresponding to FileMaker's file made up of records with various fields on them), you can see that although the table itself has a name (the filename) and the columns have names (field names), rows (individual records) do *not* have names. You're creating a way to identify each row so you can work with it. You will use that serial number as the identifier for a parent record, and all the child records will carry the identifier of the parent's record as a Foreign key. You can now go on with confidence to use that number to identify that particular row in relationships.

> **Tip from**
> *Rich*
>
> I like to start the auto-entered serial numbers with one, two, or three letters. Let's say I have a customer file and an invoicing file. If I am using pure numbers, and I see a number in a file, I may have a customer number 101 and an invoice number 101, and I have to work harder to understand what the data means. But if I start all invoice numbers with INV and all customer numbers with CST, then as soon as I see that identifying prefix, I know what it refers to. Letters add meaning to the data.

> **Tip from**
> *Rich*
>
> If you have data you are importing from one system into another, you have to reset the auto-entered serial number. Say you have one version of the Customer file, and independent of that, you have been updating another version of the customer file. When you put the new module in, you move the data over and import their original customer IDs. But you don't want to change those, so inside the file, in the auto-entered field, you assign the next serial number. In the new file, you probably won't know where you left off in the old one with customer IDs and what the next one should be. So after the import, you have to find the biggest customer ID and reset the auto-enter section of Define Fields to the next number. (If you are interested in automating that, use a plug-in called Dialog Magic from New Millennium, which allows you to script this very reset.)

> **Tip from**
> *Rich*
>
> Primary keys should not convey too much meaning. How come? A lot of folks who are new to databases like to manually assign customer codes by grabbing the first few letters of the customer name and the last four digits of the customer phone number, and put all those together so they can look at the key and figure out who it refers to. But customer names and numbers change. Before long, your Primary keys, once so meaningful, convey the wrong meaning. How do you update them? If you do, you have to update every location where that value is used as a foreign key. That's confusing. If you do update it and you go back to an earlier version, you can no longer recognize the customer ID. So just make the customer ID a unique entry that never has to change.

Build all of a file's fields in one pass, defining names, types, and options, such as auto-entered data, validation, or storage. (Doing this in one pass lessens the risk of accidentally creating more or less the same field twice.)

Tip from Rich

Consider using prefixes for the names of fields of a particular type. Field names can be a real pain if you have a lot in the Define Fields list and are trying to find a particular one. Many names are self-evident, such as Date Modified, Time In, and Product Number. But other field names—such as those for many Calculation and Global fields—are harder to sum up in a few letters. We recommend using a prefix to make these fields stand out. You might start the name of all Calculation fields with C_, and you might start the name of every Global field with G_. In this way, even when you have the list arranged alphabetically, you get all the Calculation fields grouped together and all the Global fields grouped together. Also, when you are working on a layout, this trick alerts you to what kind of field you are dealing with, so you know, for instance, that because the field is a Calculation, users cannot enter their own values, so you need to shade the background. Other field types you may want to single out in this way are S_TOT for Summary Total, or S_AVG for Summary Average. To avoid misreading, we use an underscore rather than a space character. The point is not to have elaborate names, but to modify the names for your own convenience. For example, if you have two fields dealing with a customer's address, you might find it helpful to know which one is a calculation—the one that is named C_address.

Tip from Rich

Consider doing something similar to identify Primary keys and Foreign keys. So if you see a field that starts with PK, you know you are in the parent looking at the unique identifier, whereas if the field name begins with FK, you are in a child, pointing to a parent.

Create Relationships Between Files

You now have a bunch of tables, each of which will contain information about a single class or type of information, but the beauty of a relational database is that you can take information from multiple tables and pull it together to view, print, search, sort, and report. And the way we permit one file to use data from another file is through relationships.

The golden rule of relationships is this: You create a relationship to another file when you need to use information from that file. If you need to use information from another file, then, create a relationship to that other file.

You have now built tables so you have fields and can now create relationships. Nailing together a set of tables is like framing out the rooms of a house. Creating the relationships is like running the plumbing, wiring, air-conditioning ducts, and connecting all the rooms in the house. (Polishing the user interface might correspond to putting up drywall and trim, painting, and scraping the stickers off the windowglass. Security is, well, like adding child-proof gates and loud alarms.)

Name Those Relationships!

Before you start right into creating relationships, you may save yourself some time later on by pondering a systematic approach to relationship naming.

Tip from
Rich

> Name relationships so you can tell what file is being related to what other file. You might start with the name of the file you are relating to, then use a vertical bar or goalpost (|), and then put the name of the Foreign key field you will use. That way, if there are any problems with the relationship, you can figure out what the foreign file is and what field you are using as the key.
>
> Let's say you have a relationship between companies and contacts, and in the Companies file you have a field for the Company ID, and in the Contacts file you also have a field for Company ID. In the Companies file, when you want to show related contacts, you define the relationship in the name, saying, in essence, I am relating this file to Contacts, so the name reads: contacts|companyid. This kind of naming helps you keep relationships in order. For instance, when you go back three months later, having been out of touch with the system, or if someone else has to take over the project, the name makes clear that this relationship ties together this file and this field.
>
> Also, if you ever change the name of a file, and you have to repoint your relationship, you'll discover that FileMaker does not automatically remember the name of the field you are relating to, but if the name of that field is already embedded in the name of the relationship, you can figure it out.

CREATE RELATIONSHIPS

Relationships on the Entity Relationship diagram—such as that between Customers and Invoices—can now be brought to life in the database, using the files and fields you have just made up. But, as in the dating game, just because two entities are in a relationship does not mean that information will flow both ways, unless you purposely set things up that way.

When you are in one file and create a relationship to another, FileMaker allows the file you're in to view (and update) information from the other file. But the other file cannot borrow information that originates in this file until you go over to the other file and create a relationship back to your original file. Setting up one relationship in FileMaker, then, doesn't mean that the two entities can automatically swap information back and forth; one relationship just means that the information from another file will be available to the current file, the one in which you stand when you create the relationship in FileMaker.

So if you want to promote sharing and caring between entities, with information flowing in both directions, you have to enter each file and create a relationship with the other. Two actions to enable the information to flow both ways.

EXAMPLE: A CUSTOMER FILE AND AN INVOICE FILE

From the Customer file, we have a one-to-many relationship to the Invoices. If we look at one particular invoice record, we might want to see the customer name and address drawn from the parent's (Customer) file, so within the Invoice file we would have to create a relationship with the Customer file. If we were in the Customer file, it might be helpful to see all the customer's invoices. To bring that information into the Customer file, we would need to open the Customer file and define a new, and separate, relationship to bring information from the Invoice file (see Figure 5.1).

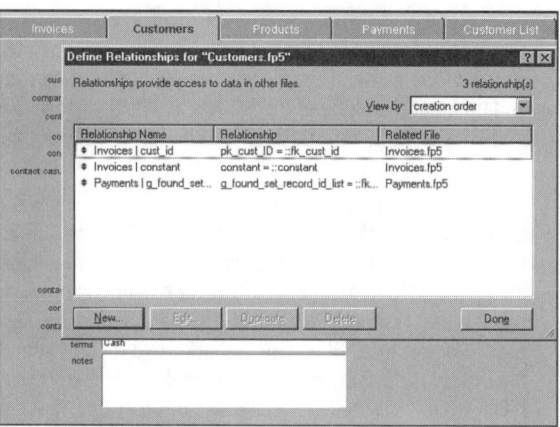

Figure 5.1
The Define Relationships dialog lets you create and modify relationships.

> **Caution**
>
> When you create a relationship from A to B, A can use or manipulate information in B, but B cannot get information that starts or originates in A. If my wife has a relationship with me, she can take money out of her purse and my wallet, but that doesn't mean I can take money out of her purse.
>
> When creating a child-to-parent relationship, the child can use information from the parent, but that relationship does not allow the parent access to the child's information.
>
> If the parent needs to use information from the child, you have to set up a relationship from the parent to the child.
>
> So you generally have to set up relationships in both directions.

In creating a relationship to draw some information out of another file, keep in mind that the information available depends on the nature of the relationship. Usually, if you have a pair of related tables, one is the parent and the other is a child. So if you are in a child file, looking at a particular child record, you may want to see information from the child's parent. But you normally won't see all the information from the parent file (such as information about parents who have nothing to do with this child). You can see just the information that is related to the child described in the current record.

> **Caution**
>
> Setting up a relationship from within a particular file gives that file access to all of the fields in the other file. You can only limit a user's access to the information in those fields via passwords or with interface and layout (for instance, by leaving certain fields from the related file out of a layout, making fields unmodifiable, defining fields to disallow entry, or using a Calculated field). But the relationship itself does not limit the fields you can use. Remember, if a user has restrictions on a particular field (such as View Only, or no access at all) due to passwords, those restrictions stay with the field, carrying over to any other file in which that field is used in a relationship.

Deciding What Kind of Relationship You Need

Related information can be used in almost all cases as if the field were part of the current file.

But if you are creating a relationship from a parent to a child, you'll use it one way, whereas if you are creating a relationship from a child to a parent, you'll use the information another way. In the following sections, we'll look at the issues you need to consider in each situation.

Creating a Relationship from a Child to a Parent

If you are in a child file and want to display data from the parent file, create the relationship from the child to the parent; once you have that relationship, add the related fields you want to use in one or more layouts in the child file.

1. Choose File, Define, Relationships. The Define Relationships dialog appears, as shown in Figure 5.2, with the names of any relationships you have already set up, along with cryptic codes indicating the nature of the relationships (more on this later) and the related files.

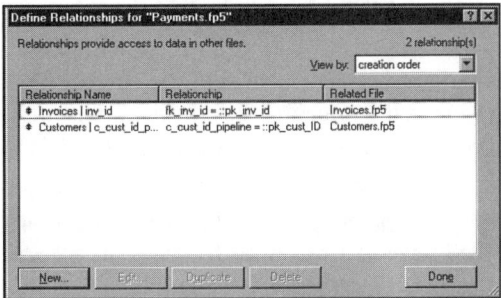

Figure 5.2
The Define Relationships dialog shows the names of existing relationships, and allows you to create new ones.

2. In the Define Relationships dialog, click New. In a moment, you see the Open File dialog (see Figure 5.3).

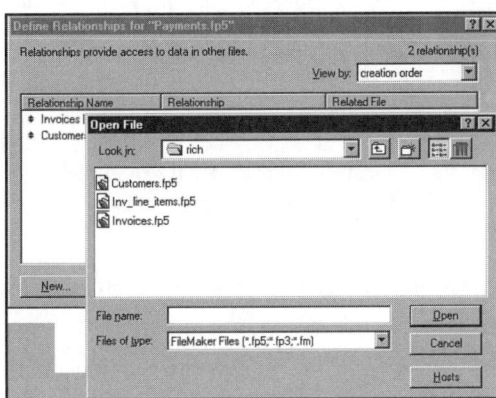

Figure 5.3
Use the Open File dialog to identify the file you want to establish a relationship with.

3. In the Open File dialog box, select the file you are going to establish a relationship with and click Open. You can see the Edit Relationship dialog (see Figure 5.4).

Tip from
Rich

Be very careful when picking the file you are relating to. As a conscientious developer, you should make backup copies of your files, so you end up with multiple versions on your hard disk. Be careful not to relate the current file to an out-of-date version of another file.

Figure 5.4
The Edit Relationship dialog lets you pick the key fields.

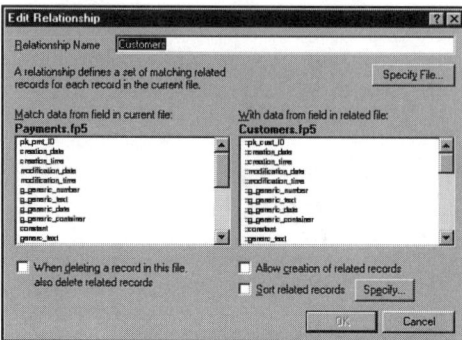

4. In the Edit Relationship dialog, select the field in the current file (on the left), with whose value you want to match a value in a field in the other file. Then pick the field in the other file. You are identifying the fields the relationship is based on.

Note

On the left side of the dialog are fields in the current file, and on the right are fields in the related file. FileMaker does not know which is the parent and which is the child; it just knows you want to set up a relationship.

But as you select fields here, you need to know which file is the child (the one you are in now, whose fields show up on the left), and which is the parent (the list on the right). When the value in a field in your child file, called the Foreign key, matches a value in the parent's field called the Primary key, the records will match, which means they are related. In the child file, the Foreign key often identifies the parent—the unique record number for a particular parent. (If you defined fields as we suggested, you could spot the Primary or Foreign key field names because they begin with PK or FK.)

Note

When two files are related, they are related at the record level. Zero or more records in the child file are related to one record in the parent file.

5. Leave the options unchecked, unless you have very special circumstances.
6. Click OK.
7. In the Define Relationships dialog, confirm that the relationship name is the way you want it and then click Done.

Why You Should Ignore the Options

Located at the bottom of the dialog, these three options apply to the relationship. And the reason we urge you to ignore the options is that they work best in the parent-to-child relationship. We rarely use them in a child-to-parent relationship.

- **When deleting a record in this file, delete related records.** Known as *cascading deletes*, this option sounds—and is—dangerous. Why would you want to do this? Essentially, this option says, "If I delete a child, please kill off the parent as well." Not a great idea, because, among other things, there may be lots of other children who survive, but they become orphans as soon as you delete one child. (This option is best used in a parent file, when establishing a relationship with a child file, where you don't want to leave homeless children lying around the file after you delete the parent). But because you are now creating a relationship from a child to a parent, you should probably leave this option unchecked.

- **Allow creation of related records.** You intend to have at least one layout in the child file with a mixture of fields from the current child and from that child's parent. If this option is checked, the user can enter information into the parent's fields and create a new parent. This ability to spawn new parents is not a great idea in most situations. Why not? Generally, when users look at a child they do not see all the fields from the parent, so they cannot fill out the parent record completely. Also, if you let the users just type the information in, how do the users know whether the parent already exists? Better if they go to the parent file, make sure the record does not exist, and then create it there and fill out the whole record—and only then create the child record. So leave this option unchecked, too.

- **Sort related records.** Sure, why not? You are in the child record, and a child has only one parent, so sorting one record is not going to take long. On second thought, leave this one unchecked, too. Why bother?

> **Note**
>
> The names of relationships have to be unique, meaningful, and helpful—to you. You may have several different relationships to the same file, so you cannot use the file name alone as the name of the relationship.

HOW TO DISPLAY DATA FROM THE PARENT SIDE

After you have the relationship set up, you can take fields from the related file and place them on a layout just as if they were fields in the current file. Because you are in a child file and a child only has one parent, you do not need a portal, which displays a list of related records.

1. Switch to Layout View.
2. Drag the Field button out onto the layout. The Specify Field dialog appears, with a list of fields from the current file and any related files (see Figure 5.5). At the top of the dialog, the drop-down menu shows you the current file, and below that, the relationships you have defined so far.
3. Specify the relationship you are counting on, at the top of the Specify Field dialog.
4. Pick a field from the parent file.

Figure 5.5
You can specify the relationship by using the Specify Field dialog.

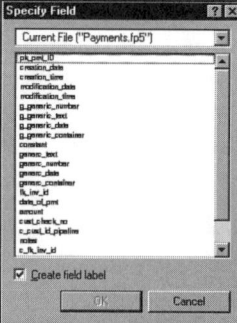

> **Caution**
>
> When users view this layout in Browse, FileMaker will display the data from the child record as well as the field data from that child's parent. Assuming that the field is enterable, and editable, and there are no password issues to restrain them, users will be able to enter and edit the data in the field that lives on the parent file.

> **Tip from**
> *Rich*
>
> When putting parent fields on a child layout, you may want to set those fields to prevent users from entering new information. Users, particularly new users, just see data on the screen and do not understand where it came from. They may try to change a value, such as a customer address, thinking the change would affect only this particular invoice, because they do not understand that through the miracle of relational databases, they are also changing this address for all other invoices to that customer. To clarify your interface, you might want to create a standard format for View Only fields, such as a light gray background, compared to a white box for fields allowing data entry.

  5. If you want to block entry into the field, select the field, choose Format, Field Format, and make sure that under Behavior, at the bottom of the Field Format dialog, the option Allow entry into field is unchecked (see Figure 5.6).

Figure 5.6
In the Field Format dialog, leave the option Allow entry into field unchecked, to block entry into the field.

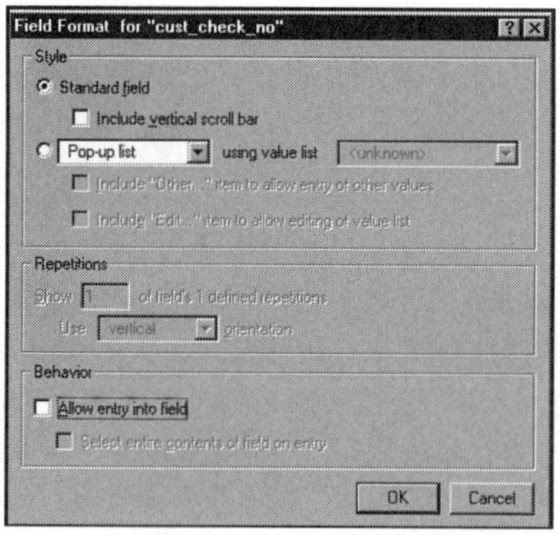

Tip from
Rich

When you set a field's format to block entry into the field, users cannot enter criteria into the field in Find mode either, so no one can do a search on that field. This may be a problem. In those instances, create a Calculation field with a value exactly equal to the value in the field into which the real data appears. Put that Calculation field on the layout. With this approach, the user can enter the field for a Find, but because the values are calculated, users cannot add or modify the values. This way, your data is safe, and the users can still find what they need.

Tip from
Rich

If you are going to restrict people's capability to change the data in a related field, you may want to have some sort of mechanism by which users can get back to the real data to edit it. You might offer users a button that takes them to the parent file to make that update. Write the button label to make clear it takes the users to a new location, and if your users are easily confused, add a warning before taking them to the other file.

Or create another layout that looks just like this one, but contains enterable fields. Then write a script so that when the user presses your Find button, you secretly take them to the other layout, where they can enter their Find criteria. When they click Find again, the script does the find, and takes them back to the original layout, the one in which they cannot enter data in those fields. In this script, use the command Allow User Abort [Off] to prevent the user from having a Cancel button because if they clicked it, the script would be canceled, and the user would be left in the layout, where they could go to Browse mode and start entering and editing data.

Tip from
Rich

Another technique: For every field you want to bring from the parent, go back to the parent file and create a Calculation field for each of those fields, so in addition to Customer Name you have CalcCustomerName, or C_CustomerName. Then, when you go back to the child file, grab those Calculation fields from the parent and drop them into the child layout. Benefits: A) Calculation fields cannot be typed into, so we remove the issue of accidental typeovers. B) If the users want to look something up by using a Find button, they can switch to Find and successfully enter a value to be searched for. To make this work efficiently, though, you must make sure that the Calculation fields are stored and indexed. Why? Because users will search on them. If you forget to store and index those fields, every time the user does a search from a child, the search will take a very, very long time. You may say, "But that is storing the information twice!" And the answer is, "Yes, that is correct." We are not requiring people to enter data twice, but it is being stored twice. Better to store that information twice than to jeopardize the integrity of the data or compromise the functionality by preventing searches. And don't worry about files getting too big, because they can swell to 2G each, and hard disk space is cheap. Would database scientists approve? No. But sometimes you have to make tradeoffs.

Parent fields in the child file behave, in 99% of the cases, just like a field that is part of the file, so users can't always tell the difference. For instance, users might want to find all invoices from a particular state, where the state information is stored in a customer file, or sort the invoices by customer name, and even though those fields are not in the invoice file, the user will never know and doesn't care.

IMPLICATIONS FOR SEARCHING AND SORTING

Users can only run searches on fields in the current layout, but sorts can be ordered around a field that is not on the current layout, even if it is in the related file. In sorting, when a user goes into the Sort dialog, the user can pick the source of the field—that is, the current file or a related file. FileMaker shows all the files to which a relationship has been established, but it knows no more than that. The point is that in order to sort on a parent's field, the field does not have to be on the layout.

> **EXAMPLE: SORTING**
>
> If you are in an Invoices file and want to sort on the parent company name, you are using information from the related file to perform the sort.

Speed is also affected by the location you choose to sort or search on. When you sort or find within the current file, the process is quicker because those fields belong to records in the current file, but when you go to the other file, FileMaker has to get the field and the proper records (that is, the ones that are related), so there are extra steps involved. If we are looking at invoices, and we choose to sort invoices by date, date is part of the Invoicee file, so FileMaker does not have to look any farther; but if we sort by customer name, well, the customer name field does not live in the Invoicee file, so FileMaker has to follow the relationship to get there, and that adds overhead to the sort. Both files are open, but whenever you do a find or sort on data that is not in the current file, that takes more work than to find or sort the current records.

CREATING A RELATIONSHIP FROM A PARENT TO CHILDREN

The actual process of creating a relationship from the parent to the child is the same as for creating any other relationship. But in general, the way you look at the options at the bottom are different.

1. Choose File, Define, Relationships.

   The Define Relationships dialog box shows the names of any relationships you have already set up (see Figure 5.7).

Figure 5.7
The Define Relationships dialog box shows existing relationships and allows you to create new ones

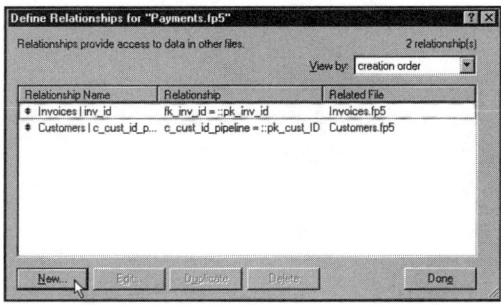

2. In the Define Relationships dialog box, click New.

   The Open File dialog box appears (see Figure 5.8).

Figure 5.8
The Open File dialog box lets you pick the file you are going to use in the relationship

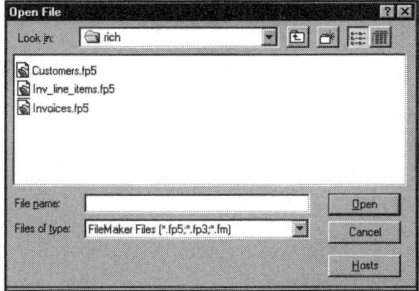

3. In the Open File dialog box, select the file you are going to establish a relationship with and click Open. The Edit Relationship dialog box appears, as shown in Figure 5.9.

Figure 5.9
In the Edit Relationship dialog box, the left side shows fields in the current file, and the right shows fields in the related file.

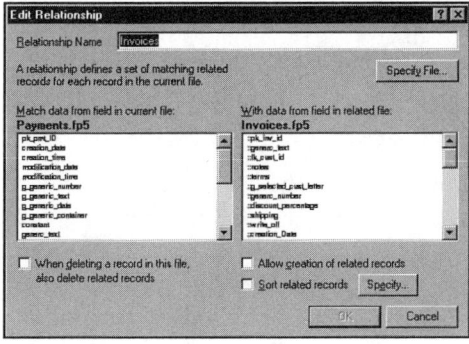

4. In the Edit Relationships dialog box, select the field in the current file (on the left), whose value you want to match a value in a field in the other file. Then pick the field in the other file.

As you select fields here, you need to know which file is the parent (the one you are in now, whose fields show up on the left), and which is the child (the list on the right). When the value in a field in your parent file, called the Primary key, matches a value in the child's field, called the Foreign key, the records will match—that is, they are related. (If you defined fields as we suggested, you can spot the Primary or Foreign key field names because they begin with PK or FK.)

5. At the bottom of the dialog, pick your options carefully, as described in the next section.
6. Click OK.
7. In the Define Relationships dialog, confirm that the relationship name is the way you want it; then click Done.

Choosing the Options for your Relationship

Be careful when choosing among the three options that apply to the relationship.

When Deleting a Record in This File, Also Delete Related Records

Essentially, this option says, "If I delete a parent, please kill off the related children as well." You should consider this option only when establishing a relationship with a child file where you don't want to leave orphaned records lying around the file after you delete a parent. Usually, a business rule applies. For instance, in an invoicing system, an invoice has multiple line items as children. It would be inappropriate to delete an invoice and leave the line items in existence, because then if a user in the invoicing file ran a report on total expected revenue, the value would not match the result of totaling line items. The invoicing report would only pick up line items that exist inside invoices. But if you ran a similar report on line items, you would get a different answer, collecting all line items, whether they appeared on an invoice or not. So business rules dictate that line items only exist on an invoice, to support that invoice. And if the invoice goes away, all its line items must disappear as well. (On the other hand, you would allow a user to delete a line item without destroying the rest of the invoice.)

Allow Creation of Related Records

You may plan to have at least one layout in the parent file with a mixture of fields from the current parent and from that parent's various children. If this option is checked, the user can enter information into a child's fields and create a new child. Unfortunately, when users look at a child's fields, they may not see *all* the fields from the child, so they may not fill out the child record completely. In this case, it's better if they go to the child file and fill out the whole record and then create the child record. So in this situation, leave this option unchecked.

In a parent-to-child relationship, we do sometimes use the option to allow creation of related records, although it is rarely used in a child-to-parent relationship. In the parent file, the list of child records appears in a portal, a user's window onto the related records. Allowing creation of related records just opens up one extra blank row at the end of the list inside the portal, so when a user enters data into a field in that row and tabs to the next field, FileMaker creates a brand new child record and automatically sets the Foreign key value of the child in this relationship. In essence, you are allowing users to create children from the parent.

This option works best when the fields that must be filled out can all fit into the portal. If a user can fill out the entire child record in three or four fields, fine. But if the child record has 47 fields, all of which must be filled out, create a button that takes users to the child file, creates a record, and lets the user fill it out there. Remember that behind this process there is probably a business rule: When a child record is created, you want to collect what?

> **Tip from**
> *Rich*
>
> Adoption is another solution to the problem posed by the death of a parent. Imagine a system with a teacher file and a student's file in elementary school, so each student has one and only one teacher. If a teacher were to resign, and the staff decided to delete that teacher's record, they would not want to delete all the records of students who had been in the teacher's class. Instead, you should bring in a new teacher, reassigning the students to another teacher before deleting the old teacher.

> **Tip from**
> *Rich*
>
> If you want to allow users to kill off a parent, but only when all the kids are already dead, use the technique called Restricted Delete. Through scripts and security, you can prevent a parent from being deleted if it has children. In this scenario, a user can only opt to kill a parent when all the children have already been removed.

SORT RELATED RECORDS

This option allows you to specify the order in which the children will be seen from within the parent file. If you do not specify a sort, the child records appear in the order they were entered. In general, you should specify a sort that will show the records to the users in an order that makes sense to them. Of course, if you really, really want to display the records in entry order for some reason, leave this option unchecked. If you choose to specify the order, you will see the Specify Sort dialog box (see Figure 5.10), in which you can move fields from the left to the right to form a sort order.

Figure 5.10
When using the Specify Sort dialog box, ask yourself, "Will this sort order make sense to users?"

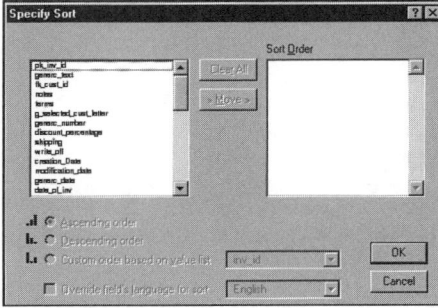

Note

Remember, records show up in a portal, but the sort order is specified when you create the relationship. If you want to allow users to switch between sort orders, going, say, from Customer Name to Order Date, turn to the chapter on portals for some tips.

Tip from
Rich

If your user calls in anxiety because he just entered a child record in a portal and it has disappeared, think sort order. Usually what has happened is that the user typed in some data and hit Enter or clicked out of the portal, so FileMaker decided to refresh the data in the portal, and followed the sort order you specified when you created the relationship itself. So although the data is there, it no longer appears in the bottom line. Suggestion: When using the portal as a data-entry device, warn users that the record may now seem to disappear because it is moved; train them to recognize that the record is still there, but has been put into its proper place following the sort order.

Tip from
Rich

If users object to the blank row at the end of the list in the portal, just go back to the Define Relationships dialog box and uncheck the option allowing users to create related records. You can always create a button and scripts to create the new record in the portal behind the user's back.

DISPLAYING DATA FROM THE CHILD SIDE

After you have established the relationship, you can display the information from various children on the parent's record. But because there may be numerous children, you need some way to let the user scroll through all the related child records. For that purpose (and others), you use a portal.

1. Switch to Layout view.
2. Choose the Portal tool, the broken rectangle in the lower right-hand corner of the toolbox at the top left of your FileMaker window (shown in Figure 5.11).

Figure 5.11
The Portal tool lets you draw a box to contain the portal.

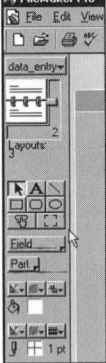

3. Use the Portal tool to draw a box on the layout, to be the area in which the portal will go.

   The Portal Setup dialog box (see Figure 5.12) asks which relationship your portal will be based on.

Figure 5.12
The Portal Setup dialog box lets you specify the relationship needed in the portal

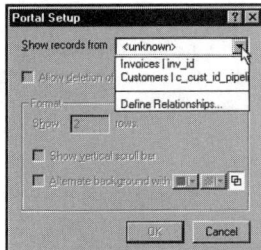

4. Pick the name of the relationship that this portal will handle from the drop-down list at the top of the dialog box.
5. Set options for the portal.
   - Allowing users to delete records through the portal (that is, in this case, to delete child records from within the parent). In general, users need a button such as a trash-can with which they can delete a record; otherwise, they may not realize that they can delete a record.
   - Defining the number of rows (or records) to display in the portal
   - Deciding whether to have a vertical scroll bar in the portal (Yes)
   - Deciding whether to have alternating color and patterns helps users differentiate one row from another (and picking the color and pattern)
6. Drag the Field tool into the portal, making sure that the upper left-hand corner of the field lands within the first row only, and does not poke outside the portal even a little bit.

   If your field touches anything outside the upper left-hand corner of the portal, FileMaker considers the field part of the surroundings, not the portal. In that case, it will pick up information from the first related record in the other file only.

   The way you set up the first row is the way all the other rows will appear.
7. When FileMaker asks what field to put in this position, pick a field from the current file or the related file.

> **Caution**
> The field you pick must match the relationship you chose for the portal.

Tip from
Rich

If you go back to the Browse view and the information that shows up in the portal is clearly wrong, and in fact you are seeing the same info repeated row after row, you have stumbled onto this problem: The relationship you specified for the portal is different from the relationship of the fields you chose to put inside the portal. Let's say you have an invoicing file and you create a portal to show the line items. So you have a relationship to a LineItems file. You start adding fields to that portal, but by accident you pick a field from a different file. You see bizarre results because the portal is based on the LineItems file, but the field comes from another file. In this situation, you often see a record from the other file repeated over and over.

Implications for Finding and Sorting

We are seeing the multiple related children within a portal. So when we talk about sorting, the first thing you have to understand is that you may be able to alter the order of the records within the portal by setting the sort specification of the relationship that is being used by the portal. When you go into the Define Relationships dialog box and double-click a relationship to edit it, near the bottom of the dialog box there are three options for specifying how the relationship will work. The third option allows the user to specify a sort order in which the child records will show up in the portal. Access to this dialog box, of course, depends on password security—that is, what permissions the user has. In general, keep users away from the nuts and bolts like the Define Relationships dialog box, via passwords so users cannot alter the sort order you set up.

Tip from
Rich

In the parent file, don't try to sort by a value in the child file. If you try, you face a difficult question. There may be multiple children, so which child's value will you use for this sort? If you say you want to sort a parent by a value in the child, FileMaker will just take the value from the first child record, which is likely to yield useless results. Not a good idea, then.

Wondering how to set the order in the portal? Ask users what makes sense to them. Sort orders are definitely a user issue.

Tip from
Rich

If you have a script that has to capture a value from the last record in the portal or work with that record in some way, do not define a sort order for the relationship. Then the records appear in the order they were entered, so when you go to the last row, you know that will be the most recently entered record. But if you were to apply a sort order to the portal (or let users apply one), the most recently created record will land, well, almost anywhere else. In that circumstance, even if you use a script to create a record in a portal, once that record is committed, it gets dropped into the list in the right position, and you have lost track of where it might be—unless you thought to capture the record ID before entering it.

Finding in a Portal

When you do a find in a portal, remember that the portal has multiple rows, so you don't have to worry about which row the data is in, because FileMaker will search every row. Imagine a parent file with company information and a child file of contacts. Let's say a user is in the company file and does a find in the portal, using the First Name field and typing in *Fred*. In one company, a Fred might appear in row 15, but in another company a different Fred might show up at row 76. Both companies who have Freds working there will be found, and even though you are doing a search on child data from the parent, you are actually finding the parents whose portals include that data. After the find, you see a found set of parent records. And then when you look at those parents, they will still have all their children, not just various Freds. So this turns out to be a way to find companies, not Freds.

Another implication for finding: If you enter multiple criteria within a row of the portal, FileMaker assumes ORs between them, not ANDs. So if you say "Find all companies where the first name is Fred and the last name is Smith," you get all companies that have anyone named Fred and anyone named Smith. That is not the standard find. In a normal find when you enter multiple criteria, FileMaker assumes an AND condition. In the portal, though, it assumes an OR. Why? We don't know.

When you do a find on a portal, it is critical to understand that you are trying to find the parents. Your find does not limit the children that come with those parents.

→If you want to limit the results, **see** "Dumb Portal Trick #5: Uses Calculated Multivalued Keys to Filter Which Child Records Show Up in the Parent Record," **p. 405**.

Using Data from the Related Child Fields

There are various reasons why we display child information in the parent. In the simplest form, we are using the portal to show a list of children, but not as a way to enter new ones or edit the current ones. This is just a look-see. For example, we might have a customer file and an invoicing file, and in the customer file we could have a portal showing a list of all invoices including their dates, paid status, and their total amounts. In this case, we would not be letting users enter new invoices through the portal. We would just be providing that limited invoice information to help users identify the individual invoices, and we might have a button that allows users to navigate directly to a particular invoice. But the list is just a presentation and navigation mechanism, not a data-entry and editing mechanism. The button, when pressed, captures the identification number for the current customer, and through script control, goes to the invoicing file, creates a new invoice, and assigns that new invoice to the customer ID. You are creating a child automatically, just not through the portal.

When we think about a portal, we also have to consider how much data we really want to put into the portal. In a database that is handling companies and the contacts within them, we might have a portal in the company file that shows contacts, and we might want to let users edit or add contacts from that position. But there is a lot more information we will want to capture about each contact. So we'd better have a way for users to navigate to the whole record, so they can capture all the information, rather than just the fields that show up in the portal. You might put an arrow at the right, so they can click and go to a record you now create over in the contact file. Here, a portal is being used for some limited data entry and editing, but in reality, you still have to go to the child file to fill out the whole record.

Sometimes, you have so little information to enter, you can enter it all within the portal. For example, in an invoice file, the portal shows invoice line items, and they have so few fields, they can be entered or edited directly through the portal. All you are likely to enter or edit is the product ID, description, quantity, and unit price. Relationships and field options can allow a lookup of the description and unit price based on the product ID. Then your users can edit as needed.

USING DATA THAT IS MORE THAN ONE FILE AWAY

Relationships can be set up between a parent and children, and vice versa, but what about grandparents and grandchildren? Let's say you have a parent file and a child file and a grandchild file, and maybe even a great-grandchild file. For instance, you have sales regions, and each region has multiple districts, and each district can have multiple sales managers, and each sales manager may have multiple sales people. Now we are looking at a sales person's record, and we would like to see some of the regional information, such as the regional manager's name and phone number on the same screen. The problem is that the region file is not directly related to the Sales Person file. Instead, the Sales Person file is directly related to the Sales Manager file, which is directly related to the District file, and that is directly related to the Region file. When you first build those files, you may wonder how to display data from a grandparent or great-grandparent file, when by definition they are not linked by a single piece of data.

There are several ways to handle that kind of borrowing from afar. One way is *pipelining*. In pipelining, you create several calculated fields in the District file that equal the same fields in the Region file. One would be the Regional Manager Name, and another would be the Regional Manager Phone Number. Then, in the Sales Manager file, you can create calculated fields that equal the Regional Manager Name in the District file and the Regional Manager Phone Number in the District file. Now that those fields are in the Sales Manager file, we can put them in a layout in the Sales Person file because there is a relationship between the Sales Manager file and the Sales Person file.

These calculations, of course, depend on the relationships because the only way you can get the Region data into the District file is because there is a relationship. So now those fields can be represented in the Sales Person file.

Tip from
Rich

> When you are pipelining, particularly with a field that goes across multiple links, be prepared to wait if you ever do a search or sort on that field. Because these calculations reference related fields in other files, they cannot be stored and indexed. FileMaker does not store the results of any calculation that references a global field, a summary field, a related field (as here), or another unstored calculation. Why not? That is just the way it works. It is a feature.

Tip from Rich

Pipelining works when the data is going from parent to child. Although it will appear to work with data moving from child to parent, it is, in most cases, pretty useless. Why? If you are in a child receiving data that has been pipelined from a parent, that child has only one parent, so you know exactly what data you will get. But if you create a pipeline calculation in a parent taking data from a child, you will get that related field value from the first child record but none of the others. If that first record has the data you want, fine; if not, you are in trouble. Example: As a father, Rich has three children, named Leigh, Stephanie, and Joseph. So in the child record, he could easily pipeline the name of their parent, which would be Richard, and since each one has one and only one father, there is no ambiguity. But if in the father database, we created a field to pipeline the child's name, we would get Leigh, who was born first, and therefore entered first, but nobody else.

Technique number two for moving data from noncontiguous files involves using the primary key of the great-grandparent. Imagine that there are 15 or 20 fields you want to see in the Sales Person file from the Regions file; it would be mighty tedious to pipeline that stuff down. In this case, pipeline the Primary key of the Region file to the District, and from there to the Sales Manager file, and from there to the Sales Person file. Then, using the Primary key for the region, create a relationship directly from the Sales Person to the Region based on that pipeline ID. Then using the pipelined Primary key for that region, you can directly add the Region fields to the layout in the Sales Person file. The Sales Person is the great-grandchild of the Region. If you have a lot of intervening files, you might try this instead of pipelining all the fields.

Caution

You might assume that since one field is in the Region file and in the Sales Person file, you could create a relationship of Region to Sales Person and have a portal in the Region showing all the sales reps from that region. But, surprise, you cannot. When you create a relationship from the Sales Person file to the Region file, you go into the Define Relationship dialog box and select the pipeline region ID in the Sales Person file on the left side of the dialog. On the right side, you select the Region ID from the Region file. So far, so good. That works because when you are creating a relationship, whatever field you select on the right side of the Define Relationship dialog box must be a field that can be indexed; relational links are based on field indexes. So this will work going from the great-grandchild to the great-grandparent, because the grandparent region ID field can be indexed. But if you attempt to set up a relationship from the great-grandparent to the great-grandchild, you would want to use the field Region ID Pipeline on the right side of the Define Relationship dialog box. But, alas, a pipeline field is, by definition, an unstored Calculation field, and therefore cannot be indexed. Why not? Well, that is just the way FMP indexing works.

Tip from Rich

Sometimes, people get upset seeing all these pipeline fields, assuming they are taking up a lot of space on the hard disk, but these are just pipes. These fields do not take up much space. Data flows through them, but never pools inside.

Lookups form another workaround for imitating grandparent-grandchild relationships. If you have tried pipelining, and discovered that people were searching frequently on those pipeline fields and complaining because the performance sagged, consider lookups. Lookups actually replicate the data from the other file. You end up with a field in the Sales Person file that contains the name of the regional manager, and another field with the regional manager's phone number. That works well enough, until the manager is fired, married, or divorced. You do not have automatic update of the lookup. The name change would go into the Region file, but would not automatically cascade to the lookup locations. (Yes, you could add a button prompting the user to do a relookup, but then you are relying on people to carry out the work for you. It's possible to have the relookup carried out automatically, but it's not easy.) The good news is that because the data is replicated, it can be indexed, and users can look up stuff quickly. But you need to make sure that whenever one of those pieces of data gets edited over in the Region file, you can force the relookup to take place in the Sales Person file.

Tip from *Rich*	Sometimes, you have to go with what works. Some people will argue, and correctly, that replicating data is not a good design. But we would argue back that in some cases, the tool you are using and the requirements of the user dictate that you digress from the proper path. And that is OK. You wouldn't want to present one of these workarounds in the final exam for a data structures course, but in real life there may be a rule telling you that you cannot do something, and then there is the way you get it done.

SPECIAL FOCUS: USING A FILE OF CONSTANTS, OR A TEMPLATE FILE

When you have values you want to share or make available in multiple files, you may want to create a constant file. Often this is a file with one record, with a few fields. And you create a constant relationship to that file.

Now any file can retrieve those constant values or update them through that constant relationship. But, you may ask, if the values change, how can they be called *constant*? Well, these are values that are the same, or constant, throughout the whole system at any given moment. For example, in a system that people use to take orders for products, whenever the clerks sell something, they have to apply sales tax to the total, so we would open a constant file containing the sales tax rate for the customer's state, so we could apply that percentage to the total to figure out the right sales tax. Naturally, when the legislature of our state ups the sales tax, we need to change the rate in our constant file, but from that moment on, the new sales tax will be applied equally everywhere, with no exceptions.

A constant field differs from a global field because although the global field may start with the same value for everyone, users can modify that value within their own systems, and those changes do not show up throughout the whole system. A global value is a suggestion, then, a default, a starting value, allowing every user to go off on his own, whereas, once established, the constant remains the same for everyone.

Sometimes, when a user changes a certain value, such as a unit price for the top-selling product, that new value must be available right away to all users. That's the kind of situation in which you need to create a constants file, containing a date, time, or text field, so that when a user changes the value, then all users have the new value available. In a constants file, then, the value is shared by all users, whereas the global field starts with the same value for everyone, but allows modifications to be made.

> **Tip from**
> *Rich*
>
> If you have a set of official codes, such as the correct abbreviation for each state or province, use a constants file. In this case, we call the file a code table.

CHAPTER

Maintaining Referential Integrity

In this chapter

Why You Need Referential Integrity 134

Problems with Referential Integrity 134

Following the Rules 136

Dealing with Threats to Referential Integrity 152

Maintaining a Unique Compound Primary Key 169

Testing for Valid Referential Integrity 172

Why You Need Referential Integrity

Because your relational database depends on references back and forth between files, those references must be accurate so that searches, calculations, scripts, and reports run smoothly. Problems with referential integrity can cause a database to go bad, losing touch with certain records, getting confused about which child records belong to which parent, fouling up searches, and rendering calculations, scripts, and reports incomplete, inconsistent, or just downright wrong. As you set up relationships, you need to anticipate what can go wrong, and create a force field around your references, so they can withstand a lot of users pounding on the system, inventive hackers poking holes in your defenses, and invasions by alien records.

To review relationships: In a relational database, each parent record has a Primary key field, with a value that uniquely identifies the record. A child of one of those parents has its own unique identifier, but it also has an additional attribute, called a Foreign key—a field with a value matching the identity of the parent, which should, of course, be the value in that parent's Primary key field. If a parent's Primary key is Bubba, then all of that parent's kids have a Foreign key value set to Bubba.

→ For a high-level overview of relationships, **see** the "Introduction," **p. 1**.

→ For the nitty-gritty on creating relationships, **see** "Create Relationships Between Files," **p. 112**.

If we want our data set to live in peace and harmony, we follow two rules:

1. Each Primary key value must be unique.
2. Foreign key values must be valid. (The value the child carries must have a matching value in the parent).

These rules seem obvious enough when stated baldly. But during the planning, creation, and use of your database, subtle confusions can creep in. We'll take a look at some potential problems and then consider ways you can preserve your references in good health.

→ For an overview of the importance of keys, **see** "How We Keep Track of All the Children," **p. 14**.

Problems with Referential Integrity

Think back to that weird schoolyard where the teachers wore colored hats and their students walked around with t-shirts tie-dyed the color of their teachers' hats.

Now imagine that one teacher has a blue hat and a class full of kids with blue t-shirts; one day, though, disaster strikes. The school merges with another one, and a second teacher shows up wearing a blue hat (violating Rule #1), with more kids wearing blue t-shirts. Now none of the kids know which teacher they ought to follow. (In database terms, this confusion can arise when a user imports a bunch of records with non-unique keys). Each kid has a perfectly valid Foreign key (blueness); the kids, then, are not orphans, but they cannot tell which of the blue-hatted teachers is their parent. As a result, if you did a search in the portal of a teacher file for a child's name, you would get two teacher records, and you could not tell which teacher was responsible for that student. If you were in the student file looking at a child's related teacher information, you would discover that since you have two teachers with blue hats, the data comes from whichever teacher was first entered into the database, which is wrong about half the time.

What if a student accidentally wore a sibling's t-shirt, and that t-shirt did not match the color of any teacher's hat? This dress-code violation would also be a violation of Rule #2, turning the kid into an orphan. In a database dealing with invoices, for instance, there is a one-to-many relationship between a customer and invoices, so each invoice carries the identity of its customer. If we were to allow users to type any old customer ID into the Invoices file without making sure the ID was valid, then we would face a situation in which referential integrity could easily break down, and we might end up with invoices that have no apparent customer, and similarly, with customers who are missing some of their invoices.

Now imagine that a teacher wears the wrong colored hat to school one day, a color that does not match that of any other teacher's hat or the t-shirts of any children. All of a sudden, that teacher's students are wearing the wrong colored t-shirts; our system is broken because Rule #2 has been violated. The students now have invalid Foreign keys, and therefore have nowhere to go. We call these child records orphans because they have no valid matching value in a parent. This situation, where referential integrity has collapsed, causes numerous problems:

- Reports go wrong. If you counted the students in the playground one by one, you would get a different value than if you counted them in individual teachers' classes, because some students don't show up as belonging to any particular teacher. Also, if you are in the student file and want to prepare a report including some matching teacher information, these orphan students will have no such information because they are not matched up with any teachers.

- Searches also go wrong. If we did a search through the teachers' files for a particular student, we might discover no teacher for that student, leading us to believe, wrongly, that there is no such student.

Wearing the wrong color hat, then, is like letting a user change the value of a Primary key in a parent after the children have been created (each carrying the original Primary key value in their Foreign key field). The new Primary key value may still be unique, but it no longer matches the value in the Foreign key field of the children, and those children become orphans.

Tip from
Rich

> Changing the Primary key value in the parent file does not automatically update the value in the children (although you could script this). The value in a Primary key field is a separate and distinct value from that in the child's Foreign key field. Yes, they are tied together by the relationship, but that relationship does not automatically update the Foreign key if the Primary key changes. Why not? Because the Foreign key does not live in the parent file; usually, it is entered into the child record at birth, and continues its life over in the child record. The data is taken once, at the creation of the child record, but from then on, it is just a value in the child record. Hence, if the teacher wears a new color hat, that doesn't automatically force the students to wear the new color, so, at least for a moment, they are lost. If you change the Primary key value in a parent, or worse, allow users to do so, you need to pour those updates to the children, or they become orphans. (This updating of the Foreign keys when the Primary key changes is often called *cascading updates*).

There is no heritage. FileMaker looks at the Foreign key as it stands, goes over to the parent file, and tries to find a match in the Primary key field. If it can't find a match, FileMaker is stumped. It does not remember how these child records used to belong to so-and-so, or have the same hairstyle, or genetic makeup. FileMaker just concludes these kids have no parent.

Here's another example. One day, a teacher accidentally wears a hat with the wrong color, but worse, it is the color of another teacher. Now we face two problems: one whole class is orphaned, and another class is left wondering which teacher to report to. In a real database, this situation occurs when you allow a user to enter and edit Primary key values at will, or when you import records without confirming that the Primary keys coming in are different from those in the existing database.

Following the Rules

Here's how to go about making sure that your database observes Rich's two rules of referential integrity. Generally, you want to make sure that you automate as much as you can and leave few decisions up to chance, or worse, to the users. The more effort you put into following the rules up front, the fewer headaches you'll have later when you have half-forgotten how you set the database up. Users tend not to discover problems caused by referential breakdown until months after they have been using the system, at which point their data may be seriously compromised.

Implementing Rule #1: Primary Keys Must Be Unique

If There are three optimum characteristics for Primary keys:

- They are machine-assigned.
- They are not editable.
- They are never reused.

Make a Primary key the first field you create in every file. The Primary key field should contain an auto-entered serial number that is non-modifiable and never reused, as shown in Figure 6.1. If you have FileMaker enter those serial numbers and you set the field so it cannot be edited, your only threat comes from imports; if you happen to bring in a record that has the same serial number, your data could get seriously confused. As long as you do not import data, you will be safe. If you do plan to import records, skip to the end of this chapter to find out how to do so safely.

Figure 6.1
Here is an example of a Primary key that is auto-entered and non-modifiable.

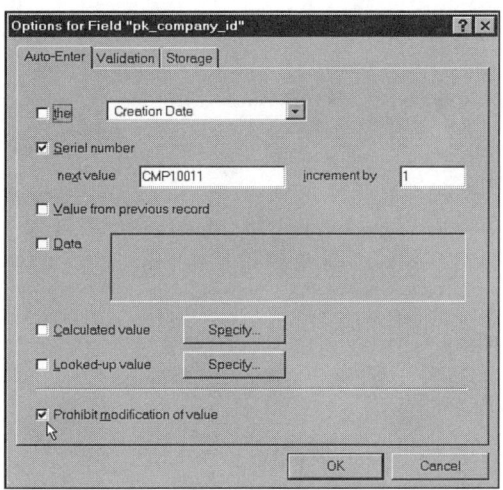

→ For more details on the whole process of specifying fields, **see** "Creating a File Specification List," p. 56.

Here's an example of reuse: The government reassigns a Social Security Number after the person dies. If you have historical data going back 20 years, some newly hired kid could end up with the historical records from a ghost. That's the danger of reusing a Primary key.

CASE STUDY: THE DANGERS OF DEMOCRATIC DATA ENTRY

The new guy wanted users to be able to type in their own Primary keys, and he wanted users to be able to modify them. He also wanted them to get into layouts and scripts. We suggested that this was asking for trouble. He looked at me funny. He said, "I don't want you to spend a lot of time on the project." We pointed out this wasn't an issue of time, but of doing it right or wrong. He deeply felt people ought to have their freedom. So after the boss and I had listened to this point of view, I told the boss that if he wanted to follow this advice, we would decline to bid on the project. Once your customers stop seeing the value of your advice, it is time to reevaluate whether you really want to keep the work. Don't be afraid to walk, if not run, from situations that are doomed to fail.

IMPLEMENTING RULE #2: FOREIGN KEYS MUST BE VALID

Every child must have a field that contains a pointer to its parent (the Foreign key).

- The child's Foreign key must equal the Primary key of its parent.
- If you make a typo, you have a child who is an orphan.
- On entry, validate that a Foreign key has a matching value in the parent file.

In practical terms, the Foreign key is just a field in the child file. The type must match the type of the field used to hold the parent's Primary key value. There are several ways to put the value in this field.

THE SIMPLE WAY—IF YOU VALIDATE

Technically, the simplest approach is to let users type in the Foreign key value. From a customer's point of view, though, this may be tough because the staff has to remember the Foreign keys. Now this approach sounds risky, but you can set up a validation on that Foreign key value, stating that "Whatever is entered here must be a valid member of a value list." The value list equals the Primary key values found in the parent file. FileMaker can find those on the fly. Here's how to set up this validation.

1. Choose File, Define Value Lists, click New, give the list a name, and choose the option to use values from a field.
2. Specify the Primary key field from the parent file. Click OK.
3. Choose File, Define Fields, and in the Define Fields dialog, double-click the Foreign key field.
4. Choose the tab for validation.
5. Select the checkbox Member of Value List, and on the pop-up list, choose the name of the value list, as shown in Figure 6.2.
6. Set validation to Strict, so that no user can override it.
7. Create a custom message explaining that the user has just typed an invalid ID, and should try again (see Figure 6.3). Then click OK.

Figure 6.2
Use a value list to validate from, in the Validation tab of the options in the Define Fields dialog.

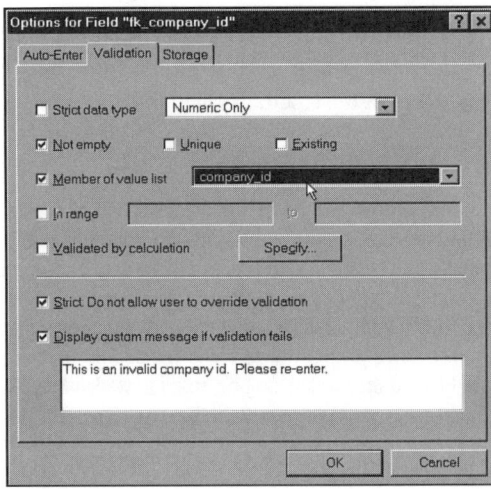

Figure 6.3
If users type in an invalid company ID, an error message suggests they go back and fix it or revert to the original ID.

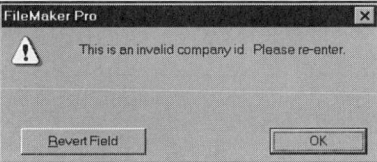

Now the value list contains all of the valid values for the Foreign key field in the child. FileMaker checks whatever the user enters against that list, and if what has been entered does not show up on that list, FileMaker refuses to accept the value and posts your message asking the user to try again.

Tip from
Rich

When you validate, you should always create your own error message, because the ones that FileMaker comes up with may mean more to developers than to users.

For examples of files that validate the Foreign key in a contacts file, see Contacts_F01 in folder f01-Simple Validation, in the Chapter 6 folder on the CD. The field fk_company_ID is strictly validated to be a valid member of a value list of all the company IDs in the Companies_F01 file, which exists in the same directory (see Figure 6.4, 6.5). This way, users can type whatever they want into the Company ID field, but before they leave the field, we make sure that they have entered a valid value.

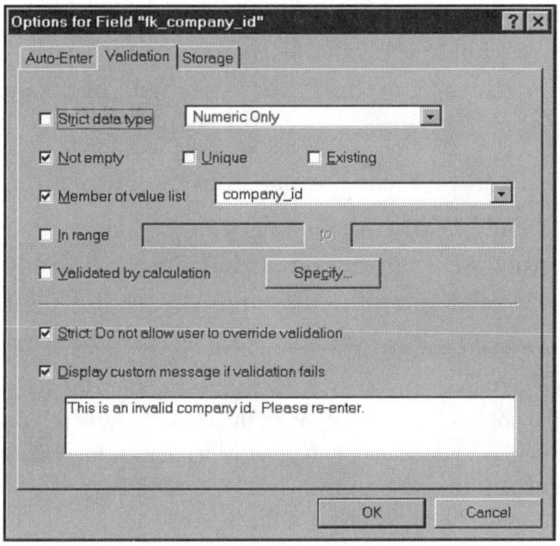

Figure 6.4
Validation is strict for the Foreign key field: fk_company_id in the Contacts_F01.

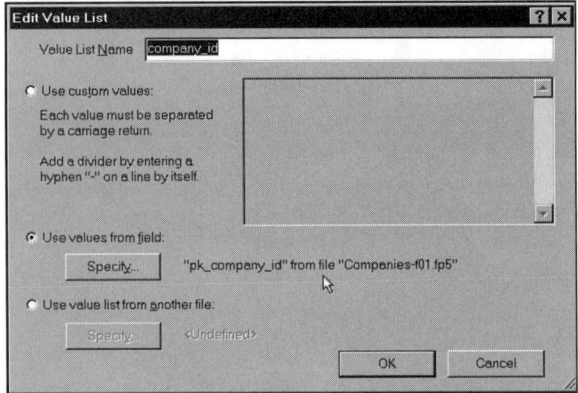

Figure 6.5
The value list is, essentially, all the values entered into the pk_companies_id field in the Companies-f01.fp5 file.

By the way, we would also like to set the Foreign key to be Not Empty, as well. But if we make the field be Not Empty, then the user cannot leave until it is filled in, so the user does not have the opportunity to go to the Companies file to look up the ID. This is not very elegant because the user must remember the Company ID, or go back to the Companies file to get the Company ID before even creating the contact record. And there are better ways to validate the Foreign key.

Pop-Ups or Radio Buttons

Another way to populate the Foreign key field is to create a pop-up list, pop-up menu, or radio buttons offering values for a user to choose (thus preventing typos and, uh, creative data entry). Here's one way to define the value lists. You use the Define Value Lists dialog to create a value list that draws values from the Primary key field in the parent, and then, when you are in Layout mode, do the following:

1. Select the field and then choose Field Format from the Format menu.
2. In the Style area of the Field Format dialog, click the second radio button and then choose pop-up list, pop-up menu, or radio button from the drop-down list. These items encourage users to pick a valid entry, but definitely do not restrict users to valid entries.

Tip from Rich

Lists do not guarantee correctness. If the field is a pop-up list, then users can click in the field while the pop-up list is visible, or hit the Escape key, which dismisses the list, and puts users in the field with the ability to type anything they want. With pop-up menus and radio buttons, users have to be more creative to enter something that is not on the list, but they can do so by a) tabbing or clicking into the field and pasting data in or b) holding the Shift key down to make multiple selections from the list. So, in reality, even though you are presenting the user with valid choices, a determined user can circumvent your plan and insert an invalid value.

Note

You really don't want two or three values in the Foreign key field or a made-up but wrong value leading to confusion about parents. Even though you offer the list of valid values, then, you will need to validate what the user enters.

3. In the drop-down list, pick the value list you created by drawing values from the Primary key field inside the parent file.

4. Click OK.

5. Validate the value entered, as in the previous procedure.

Essentially, you pick the Primary key field inside the parent file—FileMaker will collect all those values on the fly, whenever someone enters something in the Foreign key field, and check that value against the value list.

 In our example file Contacts-f02 (in the Chapter 6 folder, in the folder f06-FK Set by Value List), the users pick from a list of valid available Foreign keys. When users enter the field "fk_company_id" in the Contacts file, they are presented with a value list. So users get to pick a value rather than remember it—always a good idea. We should note that the value in the field "fk_company_id" is also validated to be a valid member of the field "pk_company_id" in the Companies file just in case some user gets creative and enters something not in the value list.

Also, we set up the value list definition to show the "pk_company_id" as the first field and Company Name as the second field, so users can tell which ID they really want (the ID by itself isn't that meaningful) (see Figures 6.6 and 6.7).

We set the value list to show the values sorted by the value in the second field. This puts the values in a logical order for the users, rather than sorting by the company ID. We figure most people will look up an ID by company. A limitation on this technique is the number of potential parents: if you have hundreds or thousands of companies, you may want to try another method for helping the user enter a valid ID and then validating the Foreign key.

Figure 6.6
When a user clicks into the company_id field within Contacts-f02.fp5, we show a value list containing all valid company IDs (followed by the company names, for clarity's sake).

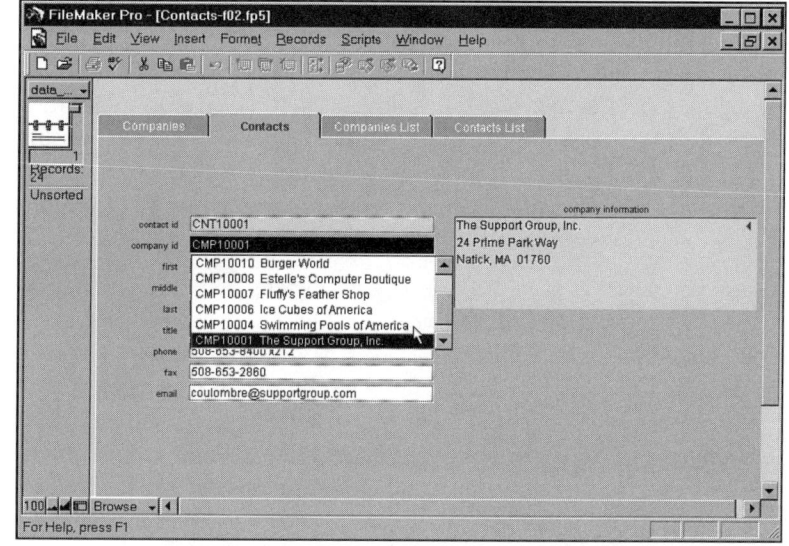

Figure 6.7
In the Contacts-f02.fp5 file, when we define the field for company_id, we pick a value list we made up, combining the actual ID with a company name, using the Specify Fields dialog.

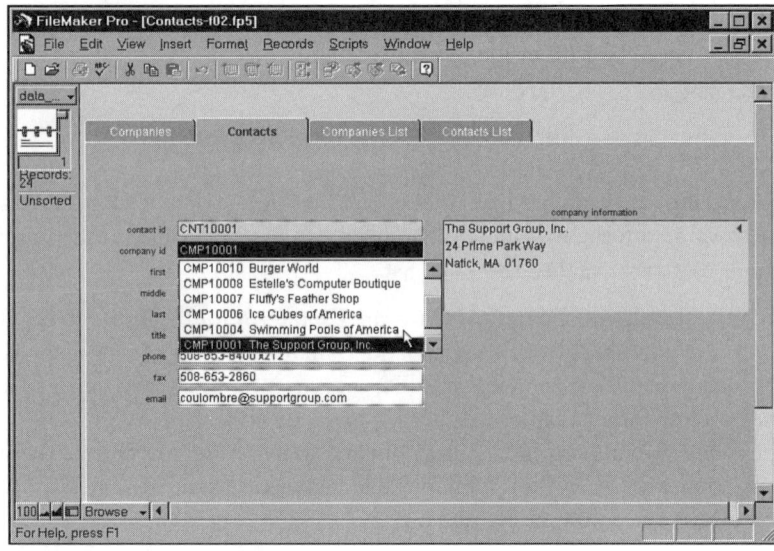

THE PORTAL APPROACH

The first two methods we have looked at involve creating child records in the child file. A third way to put values into a Foreign key field is to allow users to create child records in a portal within the parent file. That portal is already based on a relationship that says, "When the Primary key value of the parent matches the Foreign key value in the child, then those records should show up automatically within this portal." While creating that relationship, you can set the option to allow the creation of related records. If you do so, then a user can create a new record by typing data into a field in the first empty row in the portal, then pressing Tab or Enter, or clicking outside the field, and bingo, FileMaker creates the child record with that information. Because you are creating that record from within a portal in a parent record, FileMaker automatically fills in the Primary key value from that parent in the Foreign key field in the child. How does it know which field to put the value in? That was the field that you previously defined on the right side of the relationship box when you were creating the relationship. (If you want to see this in action, go to our Invoicing system, on the Invoices tab, and add a payment: the new payment record is automatically created, and that invoice's ID is automatically inserted into the Foreign key field on that payment record.)

Another approach is to add a button that creates a new contact line, as in sample files in the folder f03–Create Child from Parent via Button in the Chapter 6 folder on our CD. On the Companies tab in sample file Companies-f03, there is a New Contact button under the portal showing Contacts, as seen in Figure 6.8. Pressing this button runs a script (shown in Figure 6.9) in the Companies file that transfers the "pk_company_id" in the Companies file to a temporary Global field in the Contacts file, g_Temp_company_id. Then an external script is run (over in the Contacts file) to go to the data entry layout within Contacts, create a new record, set the field "fk_company_id" equal to the transferred "pk_company_id", and go to the field First Name (see Figure 6.10). This last step is a help to the data-entry person because we assume that the first name would be the next logical field to fill out.

Figure 6.8
The New Contact button helps a user set up a new contact from within the file Companies-f03.fp5.

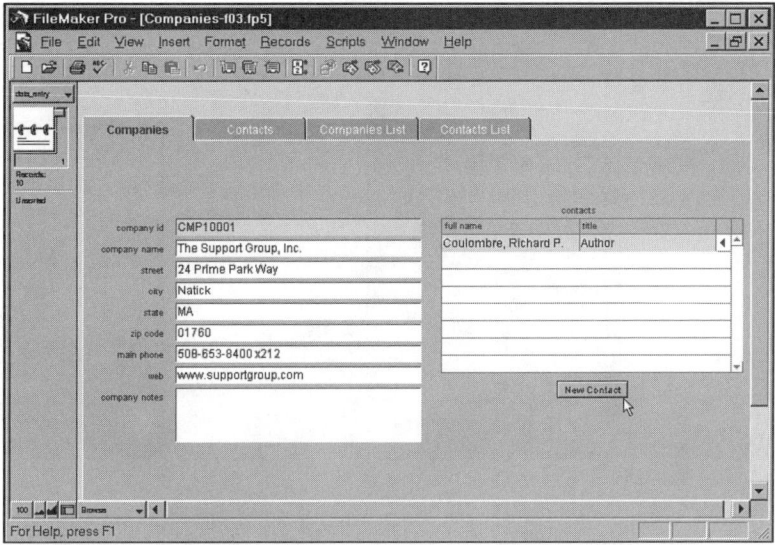

Figure 6.9
The New Contact button script in Companies-f03.fp5.

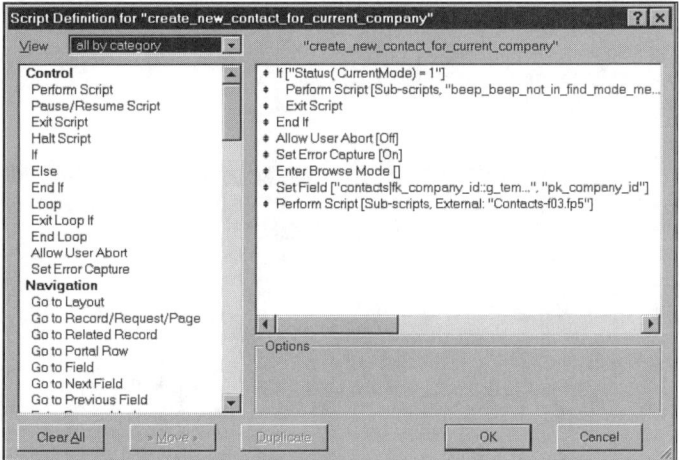

The script behind the New Contact button is called create_new_contact_for_current_company.

```
If ["Status( CurrentMode) = 1"]
        Perform Script [ "beep_beep_not_in_find_mode_message" ]
                [ Sub-scripts ]
        Exit Script
End If
Allow User Abort [ Off ]
Set Error Capture [ On ]
Enter Browse Mode
Set Field [ "contacts|fk_company_id::g_temp_company_id, "pk_company_id"]
Perform Script [ Filename: "Contacts-f03.fp5", "create_new_contact_from_companies"
]
            [ Sub-scripts ]
```

Figure 6.10
Here is the corresponding script in Contacts-f03.fp5.

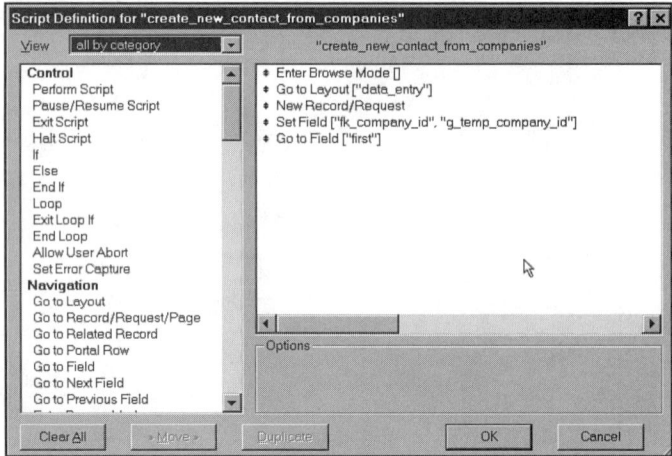

In the Contacts file, the script for creating a new contact is called create_new_contact_from_companies. Here is the script:

```
Enter Browse Mode
Go to Layout [ data_entry ]
New Record/Request
Set Field [ fk_company_id, g_temp_company_id ]
Go to Field [ first ]
```

Figure 6.11
When the user clicks the New Contact button, the screen shifts to the Contacts database and puts the blinking cursor into the First Name field.

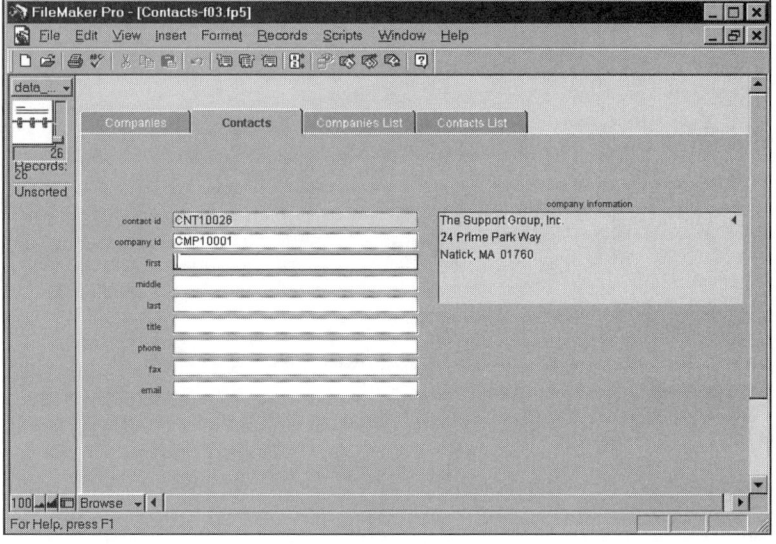

CREATING A CHILD FROM A PARENT VIA A PORTAL

You can create a child record from a parent via a portal, as you can see in our sample files Companies-f04.fp5 and Contacts-f04.fp5, in folder f04 in the Chapter 6 folder on the CD. When creating the relationship from Companies to Contacts, we checked "Allow Creation of Related Records," as shown in Figure 6.12. This option puts an extra blank row at the end of the portal (see Figure 6.13) so users can create a new child record and enter data, as shown in Figure 6.14. In this example, the user is only able to fill out the fields First, MI, Last, and Title—not the entire record. Therefore, the user will have to go the Contacts file anyway to fill out the rest of the record (see Figure 6.15). We could possibly make the portal wider to show other fields. Also we could make each portal row taller and put in multiple rows of fields so that all fields would fit, but that is not a very elegant way to ask users to enter data. Yes, you can use this method to create a new child, but you should only use this method in limited situations where small amounts of data are entered. Otherwise, just make users go to the child file to enter the record.

Figure 6.12
By defining the relationship, you can allow creation of related records.

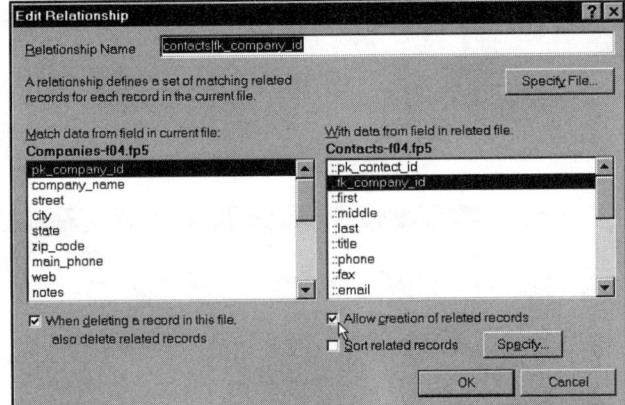

Figure 6.13
The portal has an extra row, just waiting for the user.

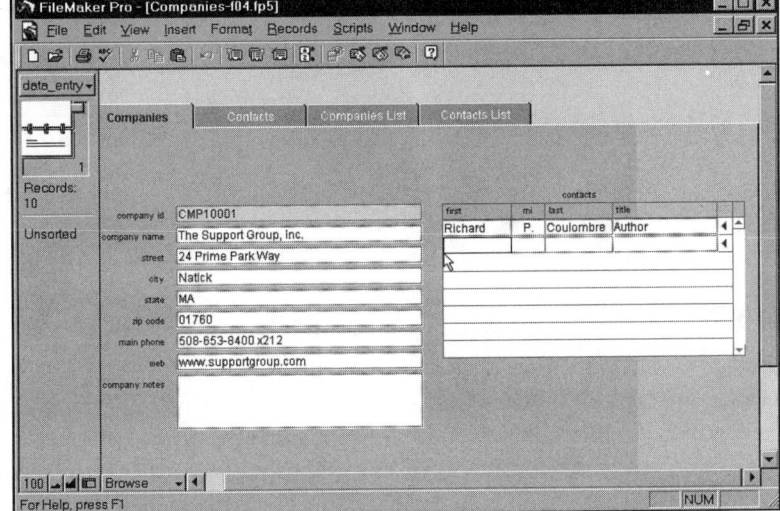

Figure 6.14
The user enters data into the extra row to create a new record over in Contacts.

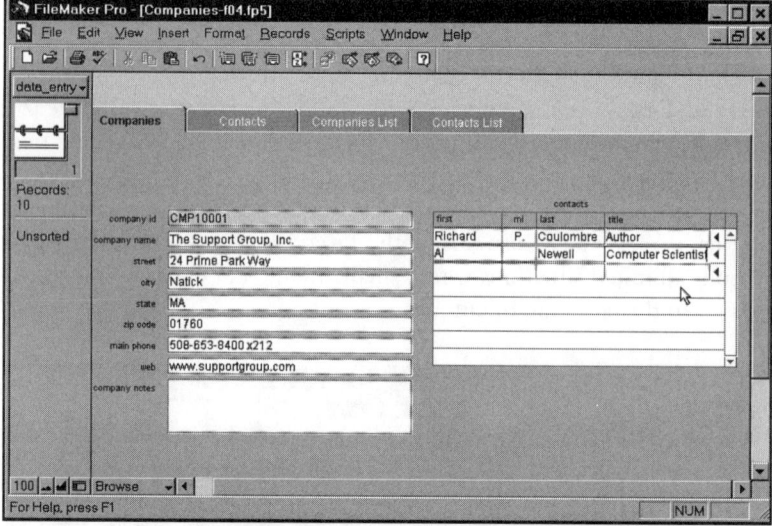

Figure 6.15
Having created the record through the portal over in Companies, the record now exists over in Contacts, with some fields still to be filled in.

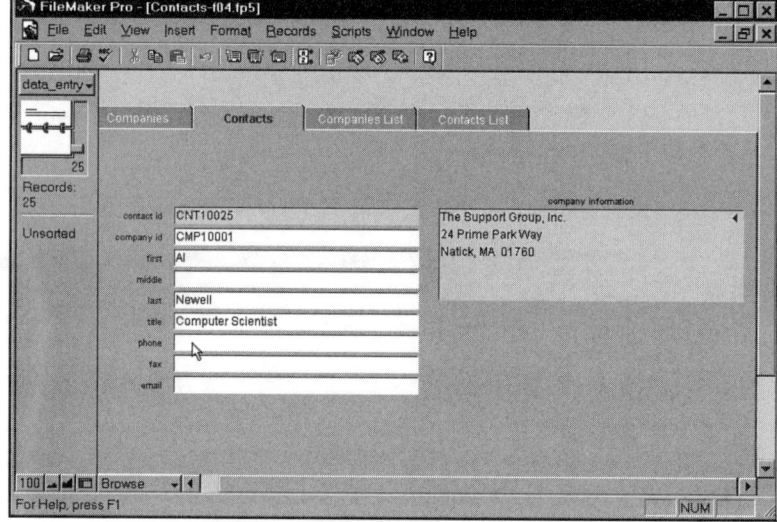

ANOTHER WAY TO INSERT A VALUE INTO THE FOREIGN KEY FIELD

Another method for inserting a value into the Foreign key field involves choosing a parent ID from a portal within the child, showing some or all available parents. In general, portals are designed to show a list of children from within the parent, but here the portal is used as part of the interface, not as a way of showing data that is truly related. An example of this appears in Contacts-f05.fp5, in the f05 folder for Chapter 6.

In the Contacts-f05 file, each record, including a New Record, has a portal that shows all possible parents, through a special kind of constant relationship, called a self-join, shown in Figure 6.16.

➔For more on such relationships, please **see** Chapter 13, "The Joys of Self-Joins and Other Interesting Relationships," **p. 421.**

The fields in the portal are defined as buttons (see Figure 6.17). When the user clicks on a parent's button, a script runs (see Figure 6.18), assigning that child to the selected parent by grabbing the pk_company_id value from the record of the parent within the row clicked on, and putting that value in the field fk_company_id in the Contacts file.

The script that does this magic also includes some error checking, because we have to figure that a user might accidentally click on the portal. What happens if that overwrites the company to whom that contact is currently assigned? The error checking says, "If the field fk_company_id is not empty, give the users an opportunity to change their minds." We post a message offering them the opportunity to cancel out.

Figure 6.16
We create the relationship between companies and the constant.

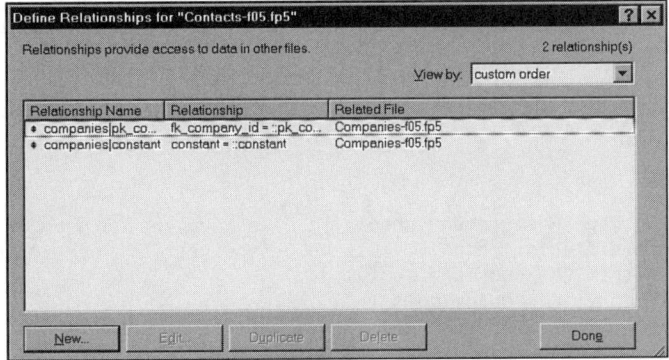

Figure 6.17
The Contacts screen has a portal showing all parents available for a new record.

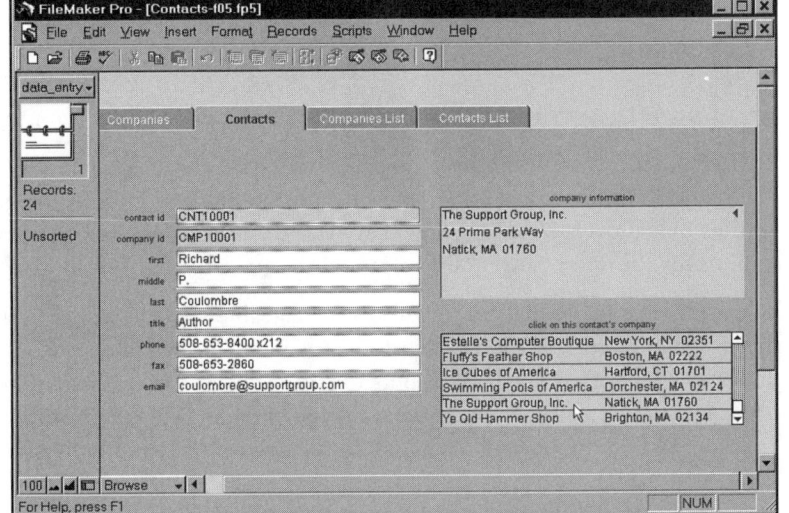

Figure 6.18
The script assigns that child to the selected parent.

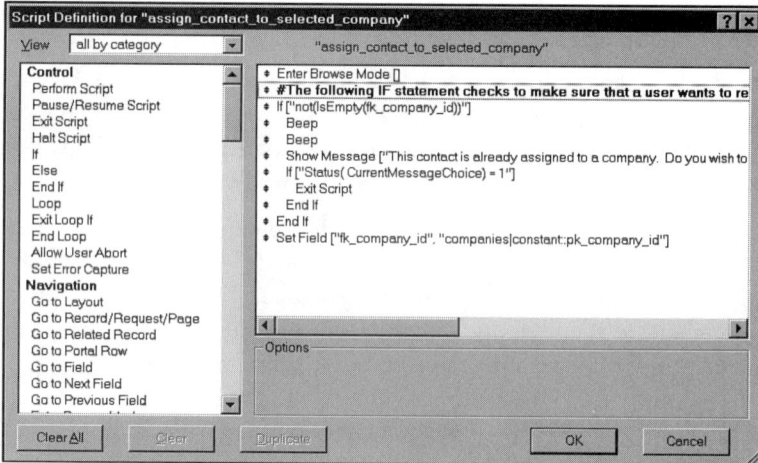

In the Contacts file, the assign_contact_to_selected_company script assigns the child to the selected parent:

```
Enter Browse Mode

# "The following IF statement checks to make sure that a user wants to reassign a
contact to a different company. This helps the user if they accidentally click on
a company within the constant portal."
If [ not(IsEmpty(fk_company_id)) ]
        Beep
        Beep
        Show Message [ Buttons: "Cancel", "OK", ""; Data: "This contact is already
assigned to a company. Do you wish to reassign it?" ]
If [ Status( CurrentMessageChoice) = 1 ]
        Exit Script
End If
End If
Set Field [ fk_company_id, companies|constant::pk_company_id ]
```

Another perspective: In the Invoicing file, when you are looking at Set Customers area of the Invoices tab, there is a portal showing a list of all customers (see Figure 6.19), and some buttons that allow the user to filter that list, because you have more customers than would comfortably fit into a pop-up list or radio buttons.

When the user filters that list down to a manageable size, the user can then find the customer. Then the user clicks on a customer, launching a script that takes the ID of that customer as a Primary key value and puts that into the customer ID field in the current invoice (the one that is visible). Even if you are reassigning an invoice, you end up with a valid Foreign key because only valid candidates for the role of parent will show up in that portal.

Figure 6.19
The Set Customers area of the Invoices tab offers a portal with a list of all customers, as well as buttons to filter that list.

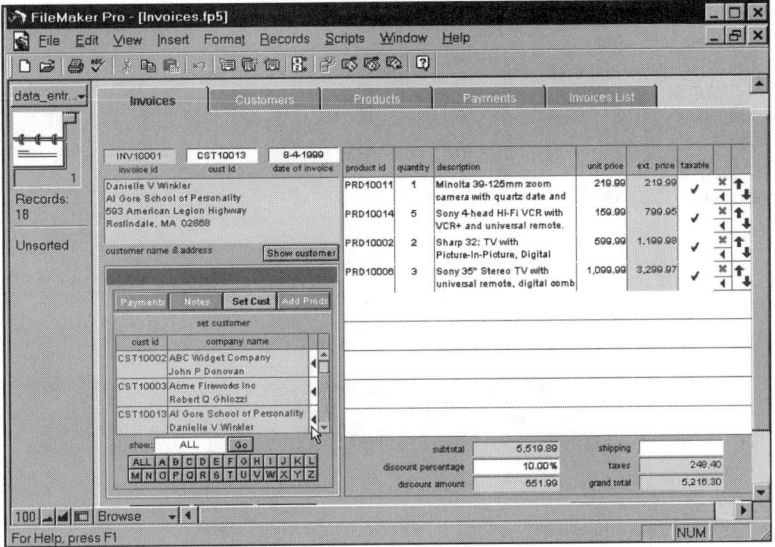

Setting Two Foreign Keys

In the Invoices tab in our Invoicing system, users can add products. In that case, we are creating child records in the Line Items file, but we have to set two Foreign keys there: one is the ID of the invoice, which is the one we are working on, and the other is the ID of the product for that line item. So on the Add Products tab, we have a portal that shows a list of product types. Users can pick a type and get a new list of products within that category (see Figure 6.20). When the user picks one of those products, scripts (see Figures 6.21 and 6.22) create a new record in the Line Items file, setting the ID of the current invoice as one Foreign key and setting the ID of the product as another Foreign key. So here we have a child with two parents. What makes this understandable is that each Foreign key points to a different file. The Line Item file is a join file in a many-to-many relationship between Invoices and Products, so it has pointers to both parents. In this case, we are creating the child record from within one of the parents, and making sure that the Foreign key fields are filled correctly.

Figure 6.20
In the Invoices tab, users can add products by using a portal to the Products file. First, they select a product category, such as Television, and then a product.

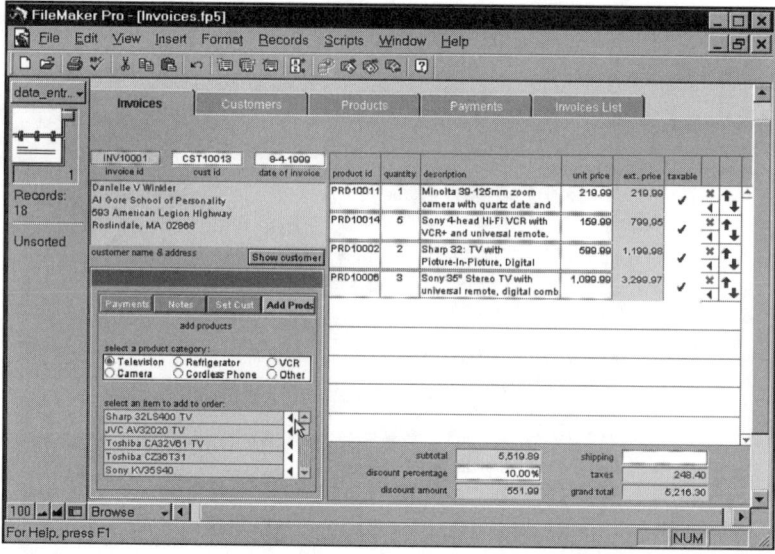

Figure 6.21
The create_new_line_item_record script in the Invoices file enables users to create new line item records.

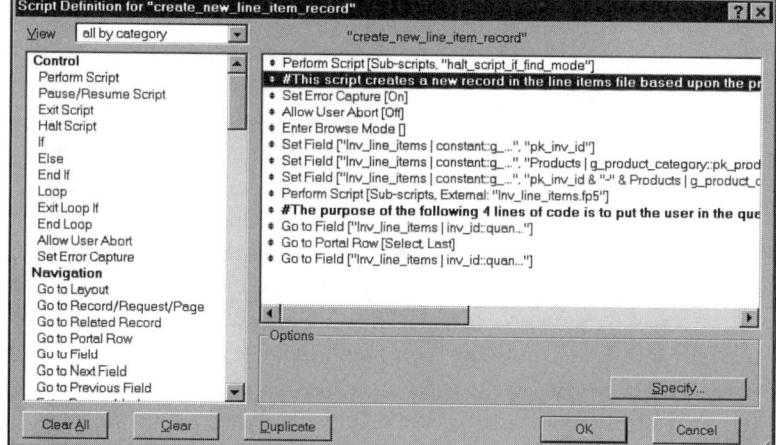

Here is the full create_new_line_item_record script:

```
Perform Script [ "halt_script_if_find_mode" ]
        [ Sub-scripts ]
# "This script creates a new record in the line items file based upon the product
selected from the "Add Prod" section."
Set Error Capture [ On ]
Allow User Abort [ Off ]
Enter Browse Mode
Set Field [ Inv_line_items | constant::g_temp_inv_id, pk_inv_id ]
Set Field [ Inv_line_items | constant::g_temp_prod_id, Products |
g_product_category::pk_prod_ID ]
Set Field [ Inv_line_items | constant::g_concatenated_key, pk_inv_id & "-" &
Products | g_product_category::pk_prod_ID ]
```

```
Perform Script [ Filename: "Inv_line_items.fp5",
"create_new_line_item_record_from_invoices" ]
            [ Sub-scripts ]
# "The purpose of the following 4 lines of code is to put the user in the quantity
field of the newly created record in the Line Items portal. Basically, it says to
go to a field in the line items portal, go to the last row of the portal, and then
go to the quantity field. I know, it does seem like a lot of work!"
Go to Field [ Inv_line_items | inv_id::quantity ]
Go to Portal Row
[ Last, Select entire contents ]
Go to Field [ Inv_line_items | inv_id::quantity ]
```

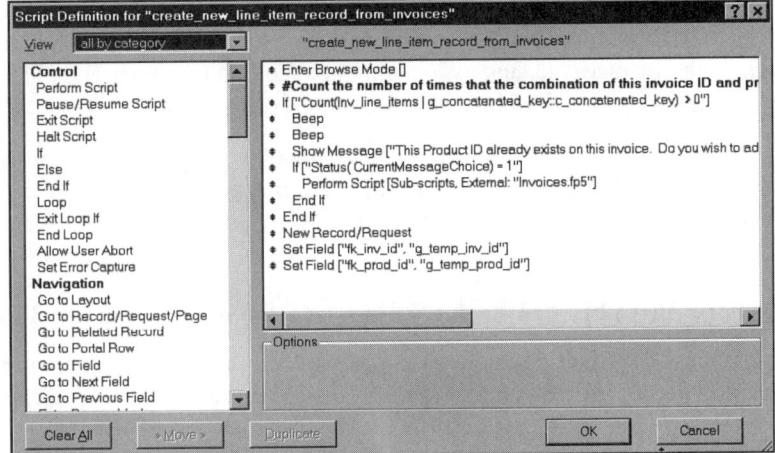

Figure 6.22
The script in Line Items allows users to create new line item records from over in the Invoices file.

The following create_new_line_item_record_from_invoices script does the job of creating new line item records in the Line Items file.

```
Enter Browse Mode
# "Count the number of times that the combination of this invoice ID and product
ID exist in this file. If the count is greater than 0, then tell the user that
this product ID already exists on this invoice, and ask if they really want to
create another? This is a good example of a self-join."
If [ Count(Inv_line_items | g_concatenated_key::c_concatenated_key) > 0 ]
        Beep
        Beep
        Show Message [ Buttons: "No", "Yes", ""; Data: "This Product ID already
exists on this invoice. Do you wish to add another?" ]
        If [ Status( CurrentMessageChoice) = 1 ]
             Perform Script [ Filename: "Invoices.fp5", "halt_script" ]
                    [ Sub-scripts ]
        End If
End If
New Record/Request
Set Field [ fk_inv_id, g_temp_inv_id ]
Set Field [ fk_prod_id, g_temp_prod_id ]
```

> **Tip from**
> *Jonathan*
>
> It is not unusual for one file to be the child of two, three, or four other files. Each file has its own Foreign key field within the child.

FILLING THE FOREIGN KEY FIELD AT THE CLICK OF A BUTTON

In this method, the user presses a button in the child file. For example, imagine we want to create a new invoice record, and need to assign a customer to the invoice because the invoice is the child of a customer. In the Invoices file, the user presses a button, goes to the Customer's file, where the user can search for the right customer, get a results list, and presses another button there, running a script that captures the customer's ID, takes the user back to the Invoices file, and assigns that invoice that customer ID. (That related customer information is then available for display within the invoice.)

There are literally dozens of ways to populate a Foreign key field. These are the most common, but don't feel limited to them. Just keep the user from 1) inventing IDs that don't correspond to any real parent, 2) creating duplicate IDs, 3) editing, or 4) erasing an ID.

DEALING WITH THREATS TO REFERENTIAL INTEGRITY

Now that you've built your database to ensure that the references between files will be accurate, you need to guard yourself against possible threats. The biggest threat is probably a user let loose to play with your Primary keys. The second biggest threat is you, if you build disaster into the design by not thinking through issues such as what will happen when you delete a parent or a child.

THREAT #1: USER-ASSIGNED OR EDITABLE PRIMARY KEYS

Avoid this at all costs, whenever possible! Make the Primary key auto-entered and non-modifiable.

CASE STUDY: THE CASE OF THE CHANGING COMPANY NAMES

A few years ago, we were hired to write a FileMaker system to replace an existing 4th Dimension database. Knowing that 4th Dimension could print file structure diagrams, we asked the client for a printout. They had a file for companies, and a file for contacts, and each contact as a child carried with it the identity of the company. We noticed that the Primary key in the Company file was the company name, so the Foreign key in the contacts was the company name, too. We asked the clients if they ever had companies whose names changed. "Sure." So we asked, "When you change the name of the company, does it cause problems?" They looked at us as if we were psychic. "Yes, but how could you know that? You haven't seen our 4th Dimension system." In fact, any time they changed the company name, all the related company information disappeared. That database had a user-enterable and editable Primary key, because the designer had just taken the company name as a key. That presented two issues: If users entered company names, they might not be unique or correctly typed. Also, if users edited a company name after it was initially entered, then unless you built in some special automation, that change of the Primary key value would not automatically cascade into the Foreign key fields in the children, so the existing children would no longer be tied to any company. In essence, the common piece of information that tied the children to the parent would have been changed on the parent side, but not on the child side, resulting in chaos.

That's why we recommended making the first field in every file an auto-entered serial number. And whenever they chose that option in Define Fields, they got to choose another option: *Prohibit Modification of Auto-entered Value*. We wanted *that v*alue to stay with the record forever and ever, so no children were ever orphaned.

Tip from
Rich
> You can clean up imported data by assigning your own serial numbers. Once in a while we encounter a situation where we cannot assign serial numbers at the creation of records, as when we have to collect mainframe data such as a product list or customer list, with ID numbers that are used throughout the organization. Those records, then, may come in with their own record IDs. We have to rely on the database administrator of the other system to be sure that the Primary key values are really unique. And we can still create an auto-entered serial number for each record behind the scenes, so we can use that for absolute certainty. There are lots of situations where you really want to be able to identify your own records, individually. You are not using up very much hard disk space, and you may be very happy, later, that you have done so.

THREAT #2: DELETION OF A PARENT

When a user deletes a parent, what are you going to do with the kids? They could be carrying around the identity of a parent who no longer exists. Here are a few ways to avoid this situation.

HONEY, I DELETED THE CHILDREN TOO (CASCADING DELETES)

In the Define Relationships dialog box, you can just select the relationship, click Edit, and check the checkbox that says, "When deleting a record in this file, also delete related records." The good news is that this option is easy to set; that's the bad news, too. You avoid complex scripting; you just build the cascading deletes into the relationship as you create it. But be careful. Sometimes, when people are new to FileMaker and new to relationships, they check this option just to see what will happen, and bingo, all their child records go out the window when the parent is deleted. Or they delete a child, and inadvertently wipe out a parent. We hear from customers that records are disappearing, and they do not know why. The designers have checked that check box, perhaps even in a relationship from a child to a parent, so later when a user is deleting one invoice, say, the customer gets blasted away. And if the option is set in a parent-to-child relationship, the death of one parent kills off all the children, too. So even though this option looks like some kind of minor after-thought, it is a very powerful tool, one that you have to think very carefully about before using.

154 Chapter 6 Maintaining Referential Integrity

In Companies-f06, when a user deletes a company, all of the contacts get deleted automatically. Why? When we set up the relationship from companies to contacts we set the check box for "When deleting a record in this file, also delete related records," as shown in Figure 6.23. In this way, as shown in Figures 6.24 and 6.25, when the user deletes a company that happened to have four contacts, the count of contacts goes down by four in response.

Figure 6.23
To clear out the contacts of a company when it is deleted, we set the relationship to delete related records.

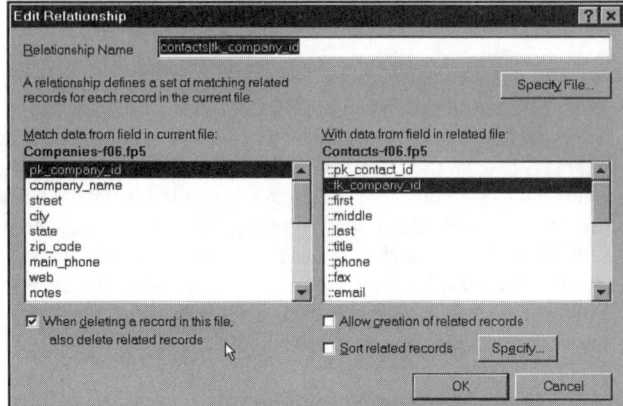

Figure 6.24
Before we delete the company Herb's Garden Shoppe, the Contacts file shows a total of 24 records, four of which belong to Herb and his employees.

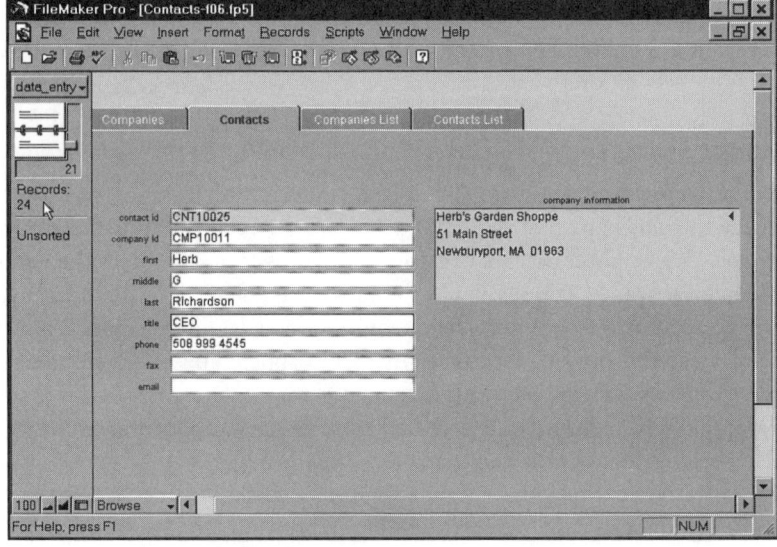

Figure 6.25
After Herb's Garden Shoppe is deleted from the Companies file, its contacts are also deleted, reducing the count of Contacts records from 24 to 20.

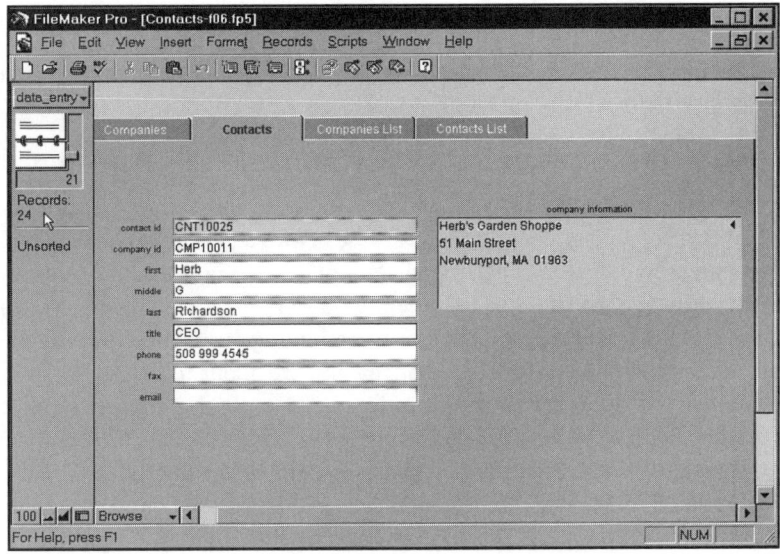

> **Caution**
>
> Never use this option in a relationship from a child to a parent.

You can occasionally use this option in a relationship from a parent to a child. How to handle the children when a parent goes away is not a technical decision, though. It's a business decision. The business may want to delete them, in which case, check the check box. But the business may prefer to reassign them to another parent through adoption. Or the business may prohibit the deletion of any parent who has children; that is called a *restricted delete*.

REASSIGNING THE CHILDREN (ADOPTION)

Think of our elementary school tracking teachers and students in separate files. If a particular teacher quits and the principal deletes the teacher's record, we would probably need to set up some automation that reassigns all that teacher's students to a new teacher. We would prompt the user to specify the new teacher before allowing the old one to be deleted from the database.

CASE STUDY: THE CASE OF THE CONTACTS IN LIMBO

We built a sales automation system for a customer who had client firms that went out of business, but the industry was small, so the individual contacts would soon show up at work at other client firms. So when our customer deleted a client company, he did not want to get rid of the contact records related to that company. He set up a client company called Unknown, and whenever he was about to delete a company, he reassigned all the contacts to the Unknown company. In the client file, when the user pressed a Delete button, a script was run, displaying a message asking for confirmation that the user really wanted to proceed with deletion. When that was OK'd, the script would go to the contacts file, find all the contacts from that client, and update the

Foreign key in that found set of records, linking those contacts with the Unknown company, and then, returning to the clients file, would delete the client company. So over time, the Unknown company had a lot of employees. But when our customer saw a person working for another company, he could change the company from Unknown to the new client firm's name.

COLLECTING, RATHER THAN DELETING, CONTACTS WHEN THEIR COMPANY DIES

Look at the files in f07 in the Chapter 6 folder for an example of preserving contacts even when their company goes away. Basically, before a parent is deleted, we take the children of that parent and have another parent "adopt" them via the delete_record script. In the Companies-f07.fp5 file, for instance, if you start to delete a company, this script does a little error checking, and then, in the last three lines, goes to the Contacts file and shows all of the contacts who work for the company you are about to delete, so all of these contacts form a found set. Then it runs a script in the Contacts-f07.fp5 file, changing the value in their Foreign key fk_company_ID to the company CMP10001. That company ID, over in the Companies file, corresponds to a made-up company called Unassigned Contacts (see Figures 6.26, 6.27, 6.28). In this way, we have taken the contacts, assigned them to a different parent, and prepared the way for deleting the original company. The script now deletes the company (see Figure 6.29).

Figure 6.26
The Unassigned Contacts record collects contacts who have lost their companies.

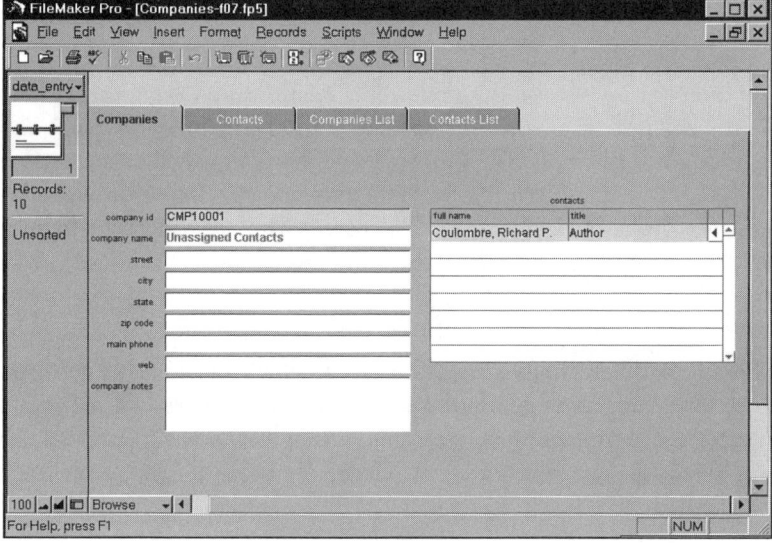

DEALING WITH THREATS TO REFERENTIAL INTEGRITY | 157

Figure 6.27
Here we are about to delete this company, but we do not want to orphan all its contacts or delete them.

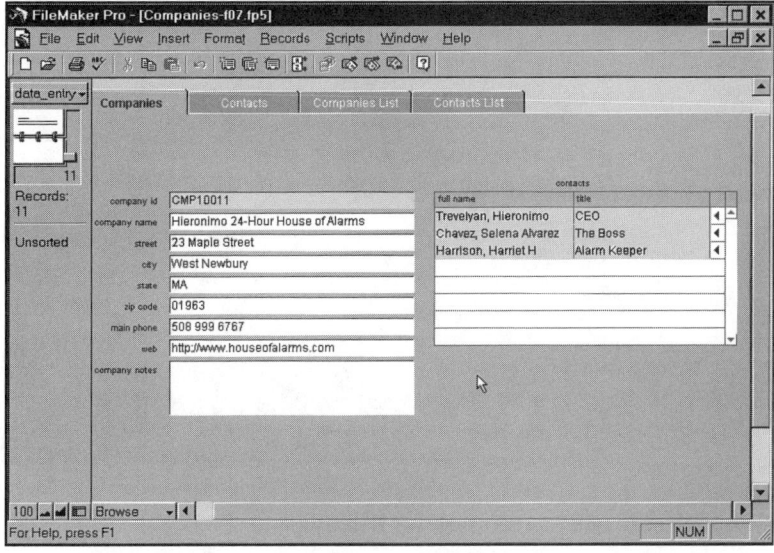

Figure 6.28
Now the contacts that once belonged to the company we deleted have landed in the Unassigned Contacts record.

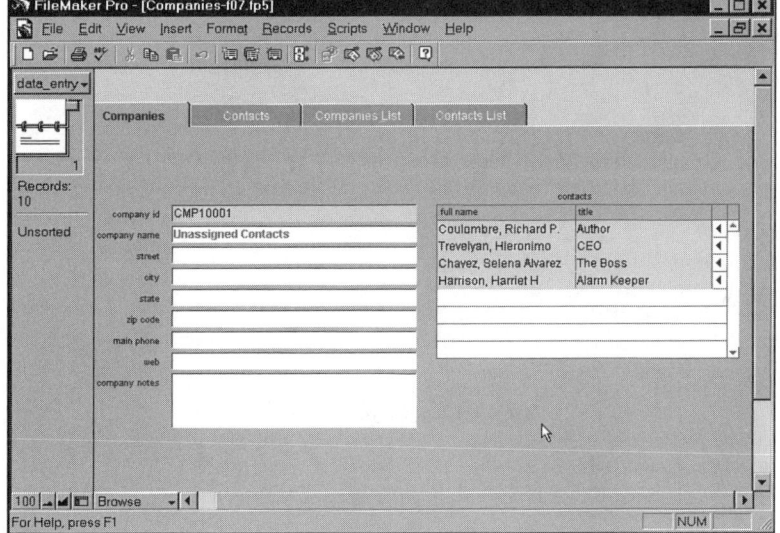

PART
II
CH
6

CHAPTER 6 MAINTAINING REFERENTIAL INTEGRITY

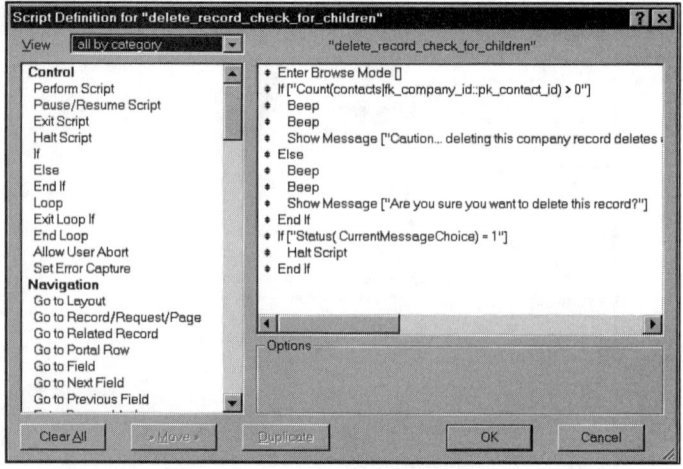

Figure 6.29
The delete_record script allows users to delete companies while secretly reassigning the contacts to the placeholder company Unassigned Contacts.

Here is the full delete_record script in Companies-f07:

```
If [ Status( CurrentMode) = 1 ]
        Perform Script [ "beep_beep_not_in_find_mode_message" ]
            [ Sub-scripts ]
        Exit Script
End If
If [ pk_company_id = "CMP10001" ]
        Beep
        Beep
        Show Message [ Buttons: "OK", "", ""; Data: "The "Unassigned Company"
record cannot be deleted." ]
        Exit Script
End If
Allow User Abort [ Off ]
Set Error Capture [ On ]
Enter Browse Mode
Perform Script [ "delete_record_check_for_children" ]
        [ Sub-scripts ]
Go to Related Record [ contacts|fk_company_id ]
        [ Show only related records ]
Perform Script [ Filename: "Contacts-f07.fp5",
"assign_found_set_to_unassigned_contacts_record" ]
        [ Sub-scripts ]
Delete Record/Request
        [ No dialog ]
```

Here is the Contacts script called assign_found_set_to_unassigned_contacts_record:

```
Enter Browse Mode
Replace [ fk_company_id, Replace data:Calculation: , "CMP10001" ]
        [ No dialog ]note indentation
Show All Records
```

Figure 6.30
The script in Contacts-f07.fp5 places the found set of contacts into the record that collects people who have had their company deleted out from under them.

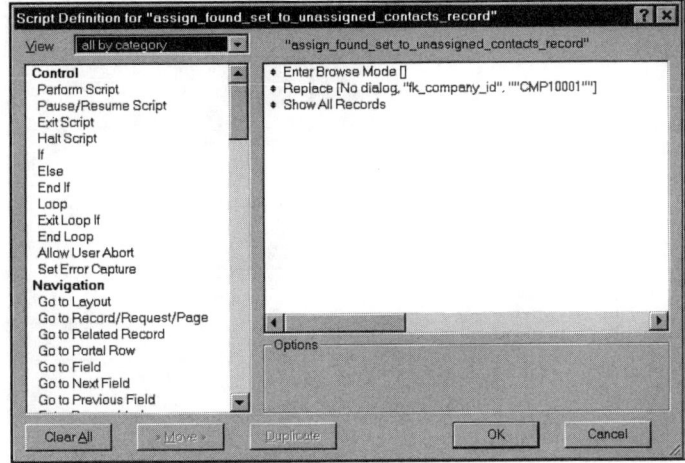

RESTRICTED DELETES

In restricting deletes, you want to prevent users from deleting a parent if that parent has any children. If you have a Customers file and an Invoices file, you might not mind a user deleting a customer who has no invoices, but if the customer has some invoices, you certainly don't want to delete the customer or the invoices. Method: put a Delete button in the Customers file, and when a user presses it, run a script that counts how many invoices are tied to that customer. If the invoice count equals zero, then go ahead and delete the customer. If the invoice count equals more than zero, beep a few times and display a message saying, "You can't delete this customer because the customer still has at least one invoice."

There is another wrinkle to iron out: Unless the users are prevented by password, they may go up to the Records menu and use the command Delete Record, and that command does not know about any of our scripts, so it just goes ahead and deletes the record. Oh my gosh! What you have to do to prevent this, then, is set up a password, and in the Define Passwords dialog under Available Commands, choose Editing Only so users can cut, copy, or paste, rather than the full range of Normal menus. The only person we typically give zero menu access (None) is the boss, the most dangerous person in the office.

When our client says that we should never delete a parent when it still has some children, we use this approach, shown in the files in the f08 folder in the folder for Chapter 6.

When the user clicks the Delete Record button in the Companies-f08.fp5 file, it runs the delete_record script, shown in Figure 6.32. This script basically counts the number of related contact children. If the count is greater than 0, then the script tells the users that they cannot delete the record because it has related records. The message appears in Figure 6.33. Otherwise, we offer the user the chance to delete it.

Figure 6.31
The boss's password gives no menu access.

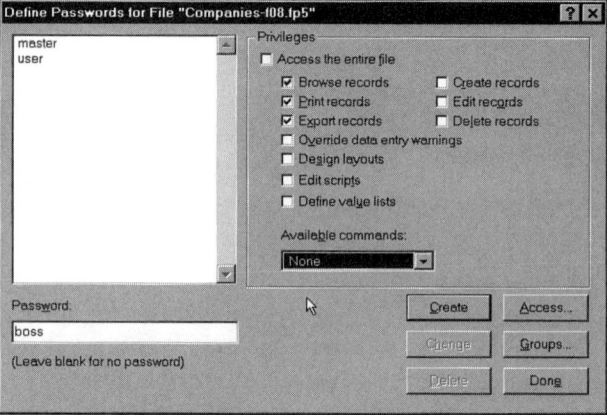

Figure 6.32
The script checks whether there are children, and it displays a warning message.

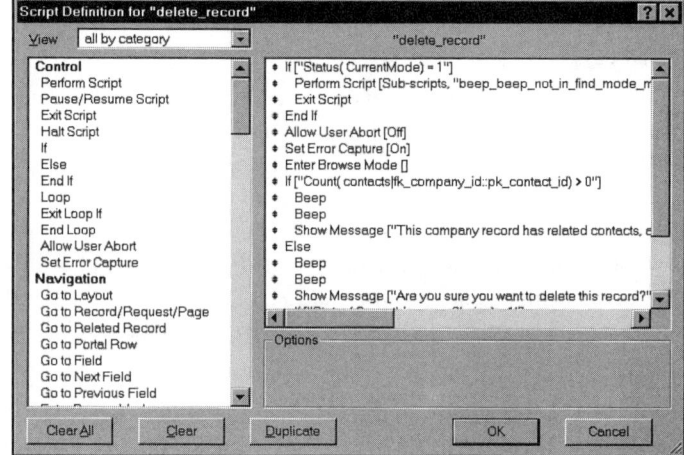

In the Companies-f08.fp5 file, the delete-record script checks whether there are children and warns the user:

```
If [ Status( CurrentMode) = 1 ]
        Perform Script [ "beep_beep_not_in_find_mode_message" ]
           [ Sub-scripts ]
        Exit Script
End If
Allow User Abort [ Off ]
Set Error Capture [ On ]
Enter Browse Mode
If [ Count( contacts|fk_company_id::pk_contact_id) > 0 ]
        Beep
        Beep
        Show Message [ Buttons: "OK", "", ""; Data: "This company record has
related contacts, and cannot be deleted." ]
Else
        Beep
```

```
                Beep
                Show Message [ Buttons: "No", "Yes", ""; Data: "Are you sure you want to
        delete this record?" ]
                If [ Status( CurrentMessageChoice) = 1 ]
                Exit Script
                End If
                Delete Record/Request
                    [ No dialog ]
        End If
```

Figure 6.33
The warning alerts users that they are trying to delete a company that still has some living children.

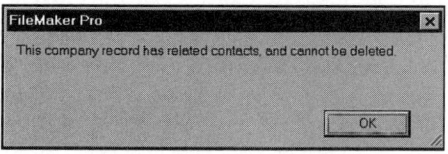

MOVING DELETED RECORDS TO DELETE TABLES

Another approach to deleting the children is to store them in another database, hidden from most users, but ready in case you need to recover the so-called "deleted" records.

CASE STUDY: THE CASE OF THE HIDDEN RECORDS

One of our clients is a very smart businessperson, and when he discovered that his users could delete records, he was shaken. His feeling was that if someone had gone to the trouble of entering that information, his company ought to preserve it. One solution was to prevent users from deleting records. But the users complained that their files were getting too large with unnecessary information. The compromise was to move the records the users wanted to "delete," behind the users' back, from the day-to-day operational files to a set of tables behind the scenes. These tables had the same fields, and provided a convenient place to park the information out of sight of the users. The records are truly deleted from the day-to-day files, but not thrown away. Whenever the owner needed to look up old data, he could open the delete tables. We even set up automation that would move records back, because every once and a while they discovered they *did* need this old information because of new business. So we would move the parent and all the children, via scripting, back into the day-to-day files and delete them from the delete tables.

USING A DELETE TABLE

If you turn to the files in the f09 folder for Chapter 6, you'll discover that the archive files open when a user clicks the Delete Record button, shown in Figure 6.34, and the user never sees them and may not understand that data is being transferred to them whenever the user performs a delete. When the user has a company record open and presses the Delete button, we run our delete_record script (see Figure 6.35), and it asks the user if he or she really wants to delete the record; then if that is OK, it checks the number of related children. If there are more than zero, the script says "Go to those related contacts in the Contacts file and put them in a found set, then send a message to the Archived_Contacts file, telling it to run a script." If the Archived_Contacts file isn't already open, the request to run a script will open it. There, the script import_found_set_of_contacts (see Figure 6.36, and displayed in full below) imports the found set of records from the Contacts file. Now the contacts from Contacts have been archived. The script in the Companies file comes back to life, takes the current company record, and makes sure that the current record is the only one in the found set (so we don't accidentally delete other records for this company).

Then the script goes to the Archived Companies file and runs a script there to import the record we are looking at, which is now the only record in the found set. The Companies script, then, says, "show all records," making every record part of the found set; then we say "omit record", which of course, means that the only record that is not found is the one we want, so we use the show omitted command that swaps out the current found set as the "not found" set and makes the "omitted" record the only record in the new found set. So when we import from Companies into Archived Companies, only that record will come across. (We want Delete to work only on the currently visible record, not others lying behind the scenes.) Now that the record has been brought over to Archived Companies, we say, "Go ahead and delete this record in Companies, then show all remaining records in Companies, and then close Archived Companies and Archived Contacts so the user doesn't accidentally wander into those." We hope the average user never knows the archives exist. The relationship is preset to delete related records, so when the parent goes away, the children do too (although we know they have actually just gone to the temporary heaven of the archives).

Note Over in the Archive Companies file, we have put a button called Move Back to Active Files to move an individual company and all its related contacts back to Companies and Contacts any time the system administrator decides to.

Figure 6.34
The Delete button beckons in the file for Companies-f09.fp5.

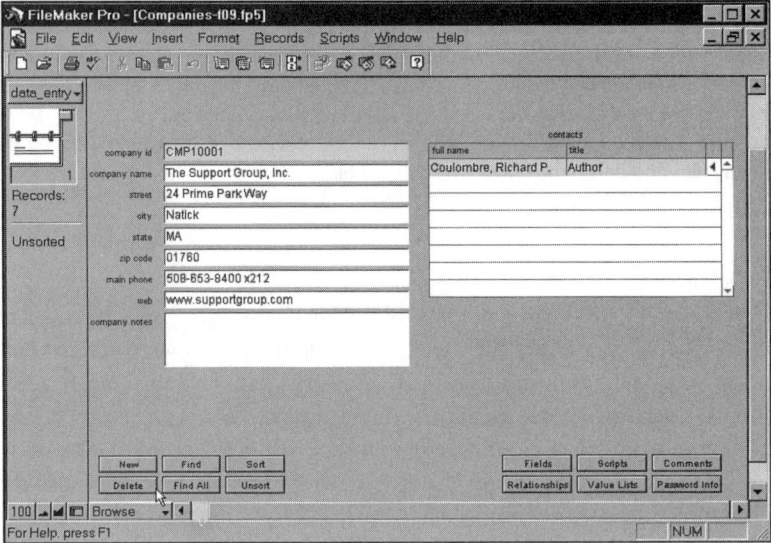

Dealing with Threats to Referential Integrity

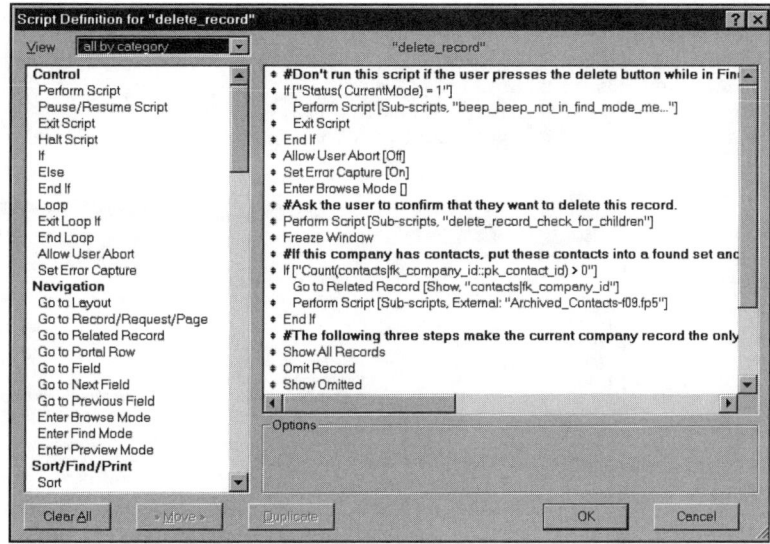

Figure 6.35
The Delete button triggers a script, which preserves the records in the secret table of deletes, and then deletes them from the Companies-f09.fp5 file.

Here is the entire delete_record script in Companies-f09.fp5:

```
# "Don't run this script if the user presses the Delete button while in Find
mode."
If [ Status( CurrentMode) = 1 ]
        Perform Script [ "beep_beep_not_in_find_mode_message" ]
            [ Sub-scripts ]
        Exit Script
End If
Allow User Abort [ Off ]
Set Error Capture [ On ]
Enter Browse Mode
# "Ask the user to confirm that they want to delete this record."
Perform Script [ "delete_record_check_for_children" ]
        [ Sub-scripts ]
Freeze Window
# "If this company has contacts, put these contacts into a found set and import
them into the Deleted_Contacts file."
If [ Count(contacts|fk_company_id::pk_contact_id) > 0 ]
        Go to Related Record [ contacts|fk_company_id ]
            [ Show only related records ]
        Perform Script [ Filename: "Archived_Contacts-f09.fp5",
"import_found_set_of_contacts" ]
            [ Sub-scripts ]
End If
# "The following three steps make the current company record the only record in a
found set."
Show All Records
Omit Record
Show Omitted
# "Import the current company record into the Deleted Companies file and delete
the record from this file."
Perform Script [ Filename: "Archived_Companies-f09.fp5",
"import_found_set_of_companies" ]
```

```
                [ Sub-scripts ]
Delete Record/Request
                [ No dialog ]
Show All Records
Close [ Filename: "Archived_Companies-f09.fp5" ]
Close [ Filename: "Archived_Contacts-f09.fp5" ]
```

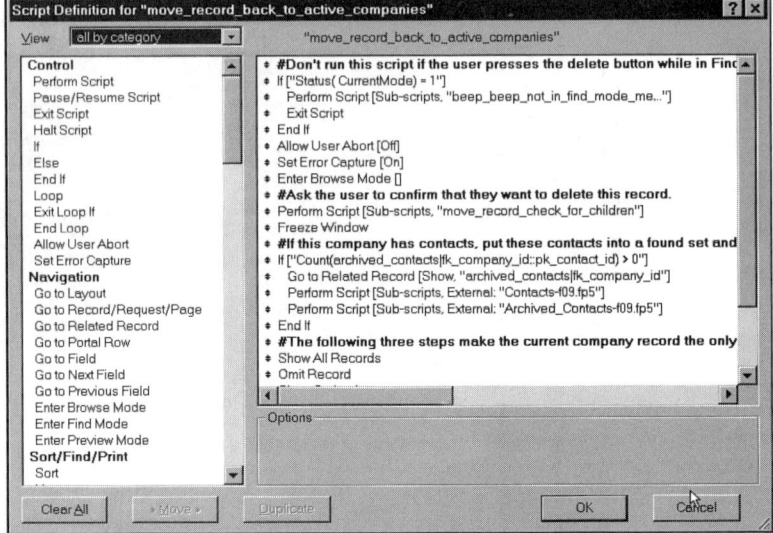

Figure 6.36
In the archival files for Companies and Contacts, scripts allow the boss to move records back to the regular files.

Here is the script called import_found_set_of_contacts from Archived_Contacts-f09.fp5.

```
Enter Browse Mode
Import Records [ Filename: "Contacts-f09.fp5"; Import Order: pk_contact_id(Text),
fk_company_id(Text), first(Text), middle(Text), last(Text),
title(Text), phone(Text), fax(Text), email(Text) ]
        [ Restore import order, No dialog ]
Show All Records
```

THREAT #3: USERS MESSING WITH MENUS

Keep users out of the menu system. *This is not subject to negotiation.*

Imagine that you have built a carefully planned, functional, attractive interface, but you work for a liberal organization that does not want to restrict users. The boss says, grandly, "We want users to have access to everything." Well, giving users access to everything means giving them access to more than data: it means giving access to relationships, fields, value lists, scripts, and layouts. So if the company has some highly motivated but unskilled users or some soreheads, they may peek under the hood and tweak the system just a little—resulting in wholesale destruction. They could easily and innocently screw up the system. In a single-user system they could go into Define Fields and change the field definitions, auto-enter, or validation options, resulting in problems such as orphaned children, violation of business rules, failed queries, incomplete reports, inaccurate calculations, summaries, and data. Imagine we have a validation insisting that users enter the year as a 4-digit date: if someone turns that off, all new dates may be inaccurate, and calculations involving years could go haywire.

EXAMPLE: AN INNOCENT LITTLE MISTAKE

One customer chose to give the master password to everybody. One user decided that she didn't like the customer IDs that the system was assigning, so she went into Define Fields and turned off the auto-enter option for the Primary key. Wow, were they surprised when the system didn't work, because child records no longer were connected to their parents.

We recommend using the Define Passwords dialog to set password protection to Edit Only so that most users can only edit the data (cut, copy, and paste), rather than using all the normal menus.

THREAT #4: USERS MESSING WITH LAYOUTS THEY SHOULDN'T SEE OR USE

Sometimes we create a script that contains a command that expects to find a particular field on a layout. If the user has access to Layout mode and removes that field from the layout, the script fails. So, in general, use passwords to prevent the user from editing a layout.

Tip from
Rich

Using passwords, generally, you want to prevent users from designing layouts, editing scripts, and defining value lists. By turning those options off, you are also turning off access to the entire file, so the users cannot edit the passwords or define fields, thank goodness.

HIDE CERTAIN LAYOUTS

When you are in Browse mode, there is a pop-up menu of layouts the user can go to. In most cases, you should not allow users to navigate by using that menu because you may have some layouts you never want them to get involved with. For instance, to allow them to perform a Find on a field that you do not want edited, you might make the field itself non-modifiable, and then set up a special Find button, transfer them to a layout that exactly duplicates the original, but allows entry into this field only in the Find mode, captures the value, runs the Find, and returns the user to the original layout with the results. In this situation, you never want users wandering into the layout in which the data is exposed to their editorial pencil.

To prevent access to a particular layout, go to the layout and choose Layout Setup. In the dialog box, deselect the option that says "Include in the Layouts Menu."

To turn off a whole batch of layouts, go to the Set Layout Order command on the Layouts menu, and in that dialog box, which provides a list of all your layouts, click and drag the layouts to change their order, and to the left of each layout, make sure there are no check marks, meaning that you do not want the layout included in the Layouts menu. If you want to turn off a whole bunch, click on a visible check mark, hold the mouse button down, and drag up and down through that column, turning off other layouts. As a result, the user only sees the name of the current layout in the Layout menu. You are not actually deleting the menu, just reducing its contents to the current layout, which shows up there even if you have said, "Please don't show it on the menu." (So the layout's appearance there is just a record of its being the current layout, nothing more.)

Another reason to keep the users from choosing to go from one layout to another is that we may want to run a script as they move from one record to another. In that case, we want users to use buttons on-screen to move from layout to layout so we can run scripts behind the scenes. (If they just choose another layout from the menu, no script gets run.)

Tip from *Rich*

You must make sure that the user cannot design layouts. If the password allows users into Layout mode, then when you are in Layout mode, that layout pop-up menu contains all the layouts, irrespective of the Include or Not Include buttons, because developers have to get to those layouts. Use password protection to keep users from designing layouts, as well as keeping them from seeing the layouts on the menu.

Don't Let Users Get into Scripts

If you let users get into ScriptMaker, any sort of automation will be at risk. Sometimes a user may just move one step below another, almost as an experiment, figuring the change won't make any difference, but that little change makes the whole script go wrong. In many scripts, the order of steps does not matter, but in some, the order is critical. Deleting a step is bad, but once they enter ScriptMaker, users can add their own steps, and, oh my gosh, delete a whole script. Bottom line: We just don't want users messing around with our scripts. In the Define Password dialog, under password privileges, set the option for Edit Scripts to Off.

→ For more detail on what to do, and what to avoid when scripting, **see** "Good Scripting Practices," **p. 448.**

Threat #5: Users Creating Incomplete Parent Records from Within the Child

Do not allow the creation of parent records from within the child.

If you are in a relationship from a child to a parent and you have chosen to allow the creation of related records, then FileMaker will allow users to create the parent at the same time as the child. But that can cause some difficulties. When a user is creating a child record, you have to have a way to assign that record to the proper parent. If you just let the user start typing in parent data, how can you be sure that the parent does not already exist? Users probably don't know for sure. When we assign a child to a parent, we want a valid Foreign key, but that means we have to make sure that the parent record's Primary key is unique, and in fact, that the parent record itself is unique (no duplicate parents, please). Rather than letting the user create a parent from within a child, we recommend that you force the user to go to the parent file, and in that file double-check to make sure there is no other record for that parent. In the invoices file, for example, when the user is assigning the invoice to a customer, the user can either click on a letter or type in a few letters, and get a list of matches; we want our users to do that kind of test before creating a brand new record. In our system if the user doesn't find a customer in the list, they have to switch to the customer, create that new record, and then come back to the invoices file to assign that invoice to the new customer. In this way, we can be protected against users inadvertently creating the same customer record many times.

THREAT #6: IMPORTING A PARENT OR CHILD RECORD

This can be a real problem. If you follow Rich's rule that the first field in every file should be an auto-entered serial number, which is non-modifiable, you are OK. But what happens if, along the way, you get data from another source, with no Primary keys? Or what if you get combinations of parent and child data with keys that match keys that are already in your file?

When you import the parent data with no keys, such as a mailing list, make sure that as each record comes in, you enable the option to auto-enter data, so our new records get serialized according to the Primary key we have already set up. When preparing the import, in the Import Records dialog, just check the option to Perform auto-enter options while importing. That brings in the data and assigns Primary keys to the records, continuing your previous serial numbers.

But you run into problems if you start using copies of the same database in various offices, if no one has taken care that the Primary keys in the offices do not overlap. In that situation, different groups send extracts from their database to the home office, and then the home office staff imports all that data, relying on the Primary keys already embedded in the records, so they often end up with three or four records with the same Primary key. Also, any new records generated in the home office database will probably have serial numbers that already exist in the Primary key field of the imported records. How to handle this? Create a field in the database for the old Primary key and then auto-enter the new Primary key on import. That way, if the satellite office calls and refers to something by their number, you can find it. But you also have the ability to assign a Primary key that is guaranteed to be unique. You could have a Primary key field in each home office record as well as a new field called satellite Primary key, and when importing, you could tell FileMaker to take data from the Satellite Records' Primary Key field and put that into the home office's Satellite Primary Key field.

For example, look at the files in folder f10 in the Chapter 6 folder. As shown in Figure 6.37, we have a field set up to capture the old Primary key, while we generate a new one for each record, to make sure there are no duplicates.

Figure 6.37
These are the existing records. To make sure that any new imported records will have unique Primary keys, our script will assign them new Primary keys, while preserving these old ones as "Old Company ID."

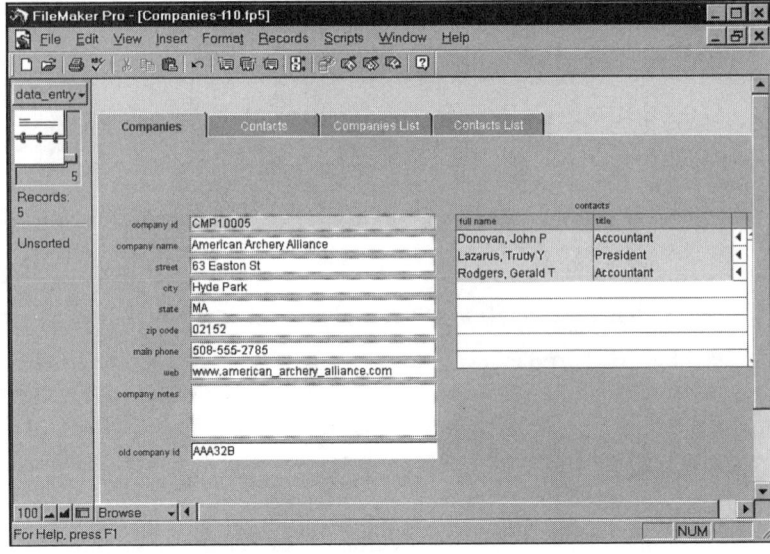

Tip from
Rich

Here is another technique worth considering for importing parents (only). After you import the records from a particular office, you could concatenate a letter to that primary field value, indicating what office it came from. That assures that each office's Primary key data will end up unique within the home office. (Of course, this would orphan any children, unless you also worked on their records). This is not an ideal solution because Primary keys should not have meaning, because the names of companies or offices change. But having said that, this is not too bad, because people do not change office names often. You will have old office records. Customer 1000A comes from the Amsterdam office, and customer 1000B comes from Boston, and customer 1000C comes from Carterette, and if that office moves to Newark, you have to just stick with C, and tell people, well, uh, that refers to the Newark office. When the meaning changes, it causes confusion for users, although the database itself is not confused because each record has a unique Primary key. Better idea: set up each database when you give it to an office, with an increment of A, B, C, or whatever. But if you forget to take this precaution before distributing your database, you are in trouble. This seems trivial, but if overlooked, can turn your database into a confused, trembling mess.

What if there are parents and children? Not only do you have to make sure that the Primary key values are unique, but also you have to make sure that the children's Foreign keys still match the Primary keys of their parents after importing. If you create unique Primary keys for each satellite office, then the children will already have that unique identification too. But if you are actually modifying the Primary key during consolidation, you must somehow cascade those changes through the children with some fancy scripting. On import, if you add B to the Boston records, and H to the Hartford records, then you have to do the same for all the child records' Foreign keys. If you script the import, you can say that all the imported records form a found set, and you can then run a script with a calculated Replace command, saying, "Take whatever is in this Primary key field of the parent, append an A to it, and put it back in the field."

Maintaining a Unique Compound Primary Key

Breaking down a many-to-many relationship into a series of one-to-many relationships, you produce a join file. In that join file, you may need to create a compound Primary key.

Imagine we have a pair of files for students and classes, and each student can attend many classes, and each class has many students. To resolve this many-to-many relationship, we insert a third file in the middle, and we call this one Registrations. (For sample files, see the f11 folder in the Chapter 6 folder on the C).

One of our business rules is that we do not enroll a student in a class more than once. We have to make sure that certain characteristics are unique in each record in the Registrations file. At a minimum, the record has a student ID and a class ID, and the question is "What needs to be unique?" It's not the student ID because the student registers for many classes. Similarly, the class ID is not unique within this file because it shows up every time a student signs up for the class. What has to be unique is the intersection—the point at which the student ID and the class ID come together. The easiest way to do this is to create a field in the Registrations file to contain a composite key—that is, a key made up of the student ID, a separator character that never appears in the student or class IDs, followed by the class ID. These IDs begin life as Primary keys in the Students file or the Classes file, as auto-entered serial numbers, and they appear in the Class Registrations file as Foreign keys.

In this way, we are sure that each part of the compound is unique to begin with, but that does not guarantee that the combination itself will also be unique, because staff might try to register a student twice. The Composite Key field, then, is a calculation that has to be validated so we can be absolutely sure the result is unique. For fields that are text, number, date, or time, we can set validation that says, "This value must be unique." But we cannot set that kind of validation when the field type is Calculation, as it is here. And we could validate either student ID or class ID, because those are both text, but we can't check the compound value. How, then, can we validate the composite key? We do it through a self-join.

We create a relationship between the Registrations file and itself, when the composite key matches the composite key. The value in this field will change whenever the student ID or the class ID changes because it is recalculated. Here's the really tricky part: we are going to set a validation in the student ID and class ID Fields, a validation that secretly is validating the composite key. We say that the count of the composite field, through this relationship, equals zero. You would think it would count itself. But, in fact, until the record is fully committed—that is, entered into the database—the record does not exist in the index. So when the self-relationship looks through the index, it does not find itself. Because the relationship is such that the composite key equals itself, when the validation is run, it takes the value in the current record and goes back through the self relationship looking for any other record with the same value. We hope it finds no other record with that value. If it does, this new record fails validation, and we give the user a warning, "You are trying to register this student in this class a second time. The student is already registered."

Whenever FileMaker looks for related records in a related file, it does so through the index. The relationship, then, forces FileMaker to use the index. We want to find no other records like the one we propose to enter. It isn't entered yet, and won't be until all its fields pass validation.

Practically speaking, you set this validation up by having the student ID and class ID available, create the composite key as a Calculation field, then create a relationship between the field and itself, where the composite key matches the composite key, and then go into validation options for student ID and class ID in the Registrations file, and set a calculated validation, which says, "The count through the self-join of composite key must equal zero." In essence, if a user tries to edit the student ID, the validation goes to check that the combination is unique.

Weaknesses

One of the weaknesses of this method is that for it to work, the related record in the portal must already have been created. What the user is doing is adding a new child record directly from the portal. The way FileMaker works, when you start entering data into any of those fields and press Enter or Tab, at that moment the new related record is created, even though the data the user typed is not put into the field until it passes validation. With strict validation turned on, the user could only commit and enter the record when the validation rules were passed.

Behind this strategy are two processes you need to understand:

- When a user types some data into a field and tabs to the next field, FileMaker creates a record, but the data is not committed to that record until the record itself, and all its data, has passed validation. Commitment in this sense means the record will be saved with its data.
- The data for a record is committed all at once, for the entire record, not field by field. At that time, any of the record's fields that have indexes will have their indexes updated.

Both of these keys are Foreign keys, so we must validate that both of them are valid members of their parent's Primary key fields.

Here is another potential problem with the composite key: If the user enters something that fails validation, even if the user goes back and wipes out the product ID, that record still exists. It has a Primary key, but no Foreign key, so you can end up with a catch-22 situation if you turn on strict validation, because a user will have to actively go in and delete the record, but the user cannot delete it because it has not been formally entered, and won't be until the user succeeds in entering the data correctly and passes validation.

How You Create the Interface Can Help Validate

If you build the interface in such a way that there is a portal in the Students file, and the relationship allows the creation of child records, then in the empty portal row, the user can enter a class ID and press Tab. At that point, the registration record is created, with the class ID already typed in by the user as well as the student ID of the current student.

Or you could do the same thing backward. Start on the classes side, and have the user type in a student ID.

Or you can have the user go to the Class Registrations file and create a record there. In that case, the user will have to enter both the student ID and the class ID, preferably from value lists or through some automation. Only use the composite key if you do not have some other scripted validation.

Which interface method you use for validation depends on the way the staff works that is, what they are familiar with. Technically, how much information do we need to fill out for each registration record? If it is as simple as a student ID, a class ID, and the date of registration, we can put all three fields into a portal. But if a registration requires a lot more info, we are going to have to go the Class Registrations file to create the record and enter the data.

Alternate Approach to Validation

Interfaces can validate without bothering with a composite key. If we look at the Invoices tab in our Invoicing database and go to the Add Products screen, there is a portal there showing a list of products from the selected category; when a user clicks on a product, that runs a script that performs a validation. (Note that we are using a script rather than relying on validation options in FileMaker.) The script captures the ID of the product the user clicked on, goes to the Line Items file where, through a self-relationship, we count the number of instances of that combination of invoice ID and product ID, and if that is greater than zero, warn the user that the product has already been ordered within this invoice. This is a soft validation technique. We just notify the user and let the user decide. In this business case, we allow a user to go ahead and add the same item to the invoice several times, if necessary.

This approach to validation works because in order to add a product to an invoice, the user must press our button. We do not let the user choose New Record from the Records menu. So we can intercept the user on the way to the new record. This causes a problem if we let the user change product ID, because the validation was done earlier through a script, and the change is not caught or validated because the script is no longer running and is not retriggered. If we really wanted to let users change the product ID itself, we would make users use a button that runs a script, goes to another layout, and runs validation when they enter the new ID, and then presents the users with a button to go back.

Testing for Valid Referential Integrity

Sometimes our existing database must pull in data from a mainframe or another client, and we need to check it.

In a pure parent-child relationship, where the child has only one Foreign key, we can create a field in the child file called Count of Parents, using the Count function through the relationship from the child to the parent, counting the number of matching parent records that exist (which should be just one). If we do a search on that field for every record that shows a count other than one in the child file, we would spot the orphans (with zero) and the children with too many parents (more than one) because the system could not uniquely identify the parent.

In a many-to-many situation, each record in the join file is a child with two parents. We certainly could use that same process for each of those Foreign keys—that is, have two separate Count fields—but if we want to validate the uniqueness of the composite key, we would create the Composite Key field and then use the Find Duplicates command, which involves putting an exclamation mark in the Composite Key field and doing a Find. That would surface all records that have duplicate combinations of student ID and class ID (multiple registrations).

In validating referential integrity we have just dealt with relationships, making sure that all the entities will live together in peace and harmony. In the next chapter we'll deal with validation of data so it follows the rules of the business.

CHAPTER 7

KEEPING YOUR DATA IN GOOD SHAPE

In this chapter

Keeping Your Data Healthy   174

Why Good Data Goes Bad   174

Enabling Accuracy   174

The Dream: Complete Accuracy   176

Conditional Value Lists   181

Having FileMaker Automatically Enter Information   185

Lookups   189

Allowing or Preventing Entry in Fields   192

Having FileMaker Check for Accuracy   197

Preventing Users from Editing a Record After It Has Been Created   208

Adjusting the Tab Order to Suit the User's Habits   209

Extra Carefulness: Keeping Carriage Returns Out of the Data   210

Keeping Your Data Healthy

Corrupt, inconsistent, or inaccurate data can make hash out of your calculations, reports, searches, sorts—and your reputation. You may have heard users complaining for the following reasons:

- When I looked up the product, I got only three invoices, but I know there are more invoices with that product.
- I asked the database to sort the records, but they came out all higgledy-piggledy.
- It won't let me enter the real number, so I just use a number that worked before.

Any data that violates the rules established by the business should be considered bad. Bad data may exist on index cards, on the back of a business card, or in your database. But the information is important enough for the staff to collect. Over the years, the company has worked out guidelines to define whether an individual fact, or a collection of data, is valid or not. For instance, a three-digit ZIP code is a no-no. Or if we enter information about an automobile, and the user enters GM as the manufacturer, then the auto make should not be a Lincoln or Mercury.

Why Good Data Goes Bad

Even earnest employees make mistakes because of the following reasons:

- Typing is not easy. Typing skills fall off when people only type occasionally or only send email. Errors increase when folks are under pressure.
- Typos are a snap. Users do not always realize they have made a mistake, and accept the results at face value. For instance, if a user were to type *Banc* instead of *Bank*, and then search for Bank, the record would not be discovered, and the user might never know it existed.
- Anger builds up. When users begin to resent a system, they just come up with tricks for outwitting any constraints you try to impose. Users can become experts at proving your database stinks, just because they resent the efforts to police their data.

Enabling Accuracy

The first line of defense against mistakes and bogus entries is ease of use. Make it convenient to enter the right data.

- Offer people a list of choices, so no one has to type.
- Have FileMaker enter some information automatically.
- Have FileMaker control whether or not a user can enter information in a field.
- Have FileMaker check the data for consistency and accuracy (validation).
- Arrange the tab order so it matches the sequence users expect, so they don't enter information into the wrong fields.

CASE STUDY: WHEN TIME STOOD STILL

We recently worked with an organization that used a time-clock application to track the hours that employees worked. In theory, employees were supposed to check in when they arrived in the morning and clock out when they left. Now the owner wanted to take the data from that system and move it into a FileMaker database so he could track and analyze the times. We built the FileMaker system and pipelined the data from this other application. But when their office manager started to provide reports on how many hours were worked on a given day, a whole lot of discrepancies showed up. The boss was convinced there were flaws in our FileMaker system.

When we started to look at the situation, though, we discovered that the erratic results stemmed from poor data. We observed that most employees punched in and out several times during the day, so there were multiple records for each day. Some punched in and forgot to punch out. Or they punched out without having punched in. The time-clock system did not keep track of AM or PM, so if someone came in at 7AM and left at 8PM, the old application would credit the person with one hour of work that day. We learned that the office manager had been correcting the data all along, but no one had ever fixed the old program. Based on her memory and knowledge of the employees, she knew enough to disbelieve the data when making up pay rosters, but FileMaker didn't have her at its elbow, telling it which values to ignore, which to modify, and which to accept. Thus, the business process (checking in and out) was not working the way the boss thought it was, and the inconsistent behavior, combined with an unwary time-clock application, generated lousy data. If that data had been used to generate pay stubs, there would have been a lot of upset employees! Moral: Double-check any incoming data, or you could take the blame for errors.

Tip from
Rich

> Create scripts or calculations to help users find invalid records. Sometimes you can place calculations to post a message telling the user what is wrong. Or you can run a script to find all the records that violate one rule or another to help users clean up their data. In this way, you are offering the power of the computer to spot problems before they get out of hand.

CASE STUDY: EVANGELIZING DATA ENTRY

An architectural firm had information all over the organization about customers, contacts, and projects, plus marketing. The company was growing quickly, and the staff realized that this information remained in people's heads, people's desk drawers, and private databases. To centralize the information and make it available throughout the organization, they hired us. Making the database was easy. But what was hard was persuading some people to release the legacy data, which they guarded very protectively, and, equally important, getting that information entered consistently. The system only worked because one woman made intense efforts to persuade people to give up their personal databanks and to combine them with others so that the data would have value and meaning for everyone.

Tip from
Rich

> If your client is using FileMaker for important information, identify someone who watches over the data as it goes in, so people know they can rely on it. What you don't want is people saying that the information in the database is flaky or inaccurate. Ask who is responsible for the success of the database. Who will collect the data? Who will clean up the data? Without a person tending the database, you cannot prevent flaky data. Overall, ensuring that people enter and update the information properly will cost the client more than the computers, the software, and the database put together. And if data validation is not done well, the damage can cost even more.

CASE STUDY: THE DANGER OF DEMOTING A DEGREE

A school's alumni office is sensitive to the honorifics on an address in their mailings because they don't want to offend potential donors. They also want to make sure that a donor is assigned to the right donor level. The database is not that challenging to create, but the data entry is critical. If some clerk types the wrong graduate degree, a potential donor can be insulted—permanently. Because data entry affects the success of the database, you may have to investigate the way a clerk's work is proofread, or double-checked, by another clerk, when FileMaker has no way of knowing, for instance, whether a person is really Dr. or Mr. The moral of the story is that computers can't be held entirely responsible for their data.

THE DREAM: COMPLETE ACCURACY

You'd like to make sure that your users enter complete, accurate information in the right places. And we'll describe some devices that encourage correct entry. But remember that a really determined user—or an angry one—can circumvent almost any trick you use and enter the wrong data. So you need to make doing the right thing easy, convenient, and appealing.

OFFERING LISTS OF CHOICES

One way to encourage consistency in data entry while helping someone who is keyboard impaired is to offer a prepared list of choices. When creating such lists, you take two steps.

1. Create the value list—the set of choices for the user (see Figure 7.1).

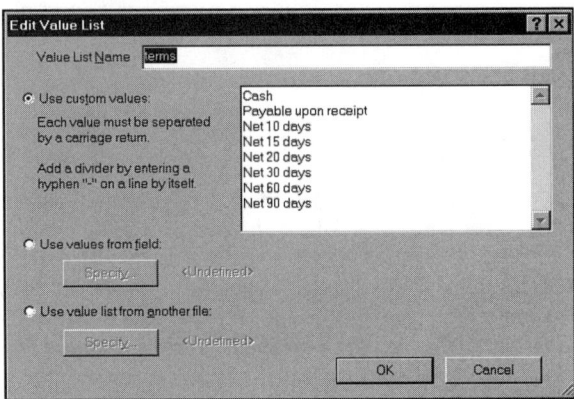

Figure 7.1
When you choose to define a value list, you enter the values in a list like this.

2. On a layout, put in the field and decide how it will be displayed—as a pop-up list, pop-up menu, set of radio buttons, or collection of check boxes.

As a developer, you have to decide which method works best in the context. Here are some of the reasons you might choose one approach over another.

POP-UP LISTS

With a pop-up list, you present the user with a set of choices as in Figure 7.2, and let the user make a selection with the mouse or the keyboard. Whatever item the user selects goes into the field as data. But the user is, by default, able to override the list, putting something else into the field. If the list is visible, the user can click in the field again (or press Escape), which dismisses the list, allowing the user to type a completely original entry into the field. So pop-up lists are most helpful when you want the user to pick something from the list most of the time, but need to allow the user to type something else in occasionally. You just hope that whatever they type in on their own will be innocuous.

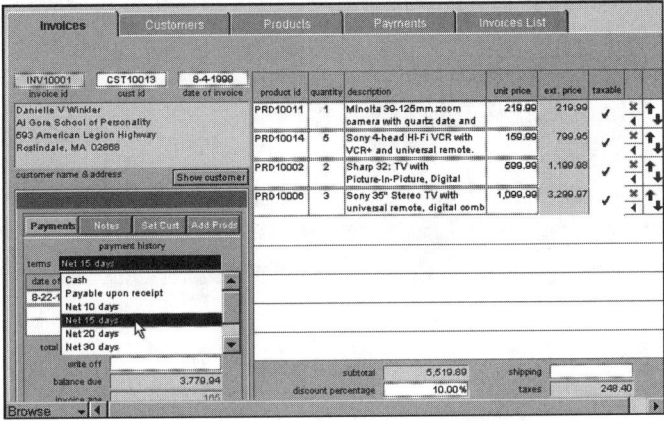

Figure 7.2
A pop-up list offers choices, in the hope that a user will select one rather than entering a typo.

Pop-Up Menus

The pop-up menu resembles the pop-up list in that as soon as the user enters the field, the list of choices shows up, and if a value has already been selected, that choice is highlighted on the list. (On a new record, where there is no value in the field, the first item on the list is highlighted.) The user can select another item or leave the original item selected; when the user leaves the field, the list disappears, and the selected value appears in the field. So both pop-up lists and pop-up menus are temporary, because they appear and then disappear. With a pop-up menu, though, the average user cannot enter a value that is not in the list—unless the user knows some very sophisticated tricks, or you offer an item such as Edit, which allows the user to edit values on the list. Hence, a pop-up menu like that shown in Figure 7.3 is a better way to nudge the average user into picking one item from the list.

Tip from
Rich

> Pop-up menus work differently under different versions of the operating system and on different platforms. It's best to test them in the user's own environment to make sure they are working the way you hope.

The workarounds: If the user holds down Shift while selecting a value, that value is added to the field, instead of replacing the earlier value in the field. A creative user can therefore make multiple choices. A user can even enter something brand new by tabbing or clicking into the field, and then doing a paste by using either keyboard combinations or the Paste command on the menu to insert some value you have never heard of.

So the pop-up menu is a way to guide most users, but not all. You'll soon find that you have some very clever users out there.

Figure 7.3
The pop-up menu guides users to select a correctly spelled value.

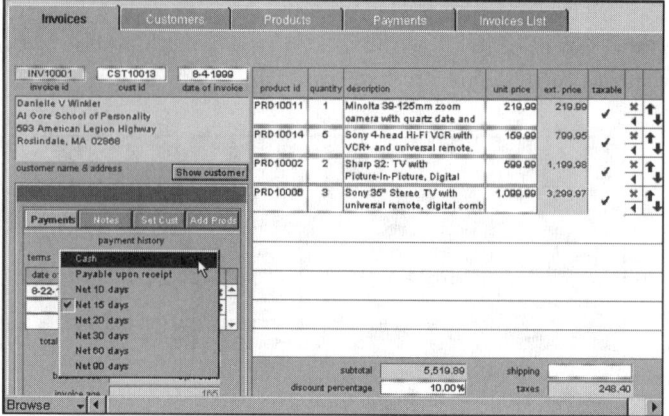

Radio Buttons

Radio buttons offer another way to guide the user to a single choice. The items are permanently visible. Users generally like this approach because they can compare all the options at once (see Figure 7.4), and even after they have selected one item, they can see what other options they might try if they change their mind. Most users believe that radio buttons represent all the available choices and accept the idea that they must make a choice between the items. But by holding down the Shift key, a sophisticated user can click several radio buttons in a row, making multiple selections, and FileMaker won't even beep. Even more insidious, if the clever user tabs into the field or clicks in it, the person can insert whatever is on the clipboard by pasting. The pasted item goes right into the field, but does not show up on-screen. In this case, no one radio button would be selected, even though there is data in the field, hidden from view. The user might think, later, there is no data in the field (because no option has been selected), when in fact there is an entry—and it may well be bad. Gauge your users: If most are law-abiding citizens, radio buttons limit the entries to ones you approve of. Course, if you have a lot of choices, you must surrender a lot of real estate.

> **Tip from**
> *Rich*
>
> User interface guidelines suggest that one radio button should always be selected because you want to make clear that one, and only one, choice can be made. Either you listen to the classical station or the World Pop station, but not both at once. When you create a new record, make sure that one button is selected, on creation. For instance, if you have a value list for gender, offering choices for Male, Female, and Unknown, you might make Unknown the default. To do this, in the auto-enter options for the field Gender, type the word *Unknown*. In this way, every time the user creates a new record, the Unknown radio button will be selected.

THE DREAM: COMPLETE ACCURACY | 179

Tip from
Rich

Be wary of changing value lists for radio buttons and check boxes. If users have already been using the database for a while and then you remove some choices or add some new ones, you do not change the data that was already entered by using those choices. In this situation, users could not find those records now, because those choices would no longer be offered by radio buttons or check boxes.

Figure 7.4
Radio buttons strongly suggest that a user should only pick one item. Here the user must choose only one product category.

CHECK BOXES

Letting users check this, that, and the other option means that users are less likely to type their own creative and wrong data—less likely, but not absolutely prevented. As shown in Figure 7.5, check boxes allow multiple choices. But they may cause problems with sorting and reporting. If you are making a database for your local pizzeria, you can offer multiple toppings through check boxes, with choices such as cheese, pepperoni, mushrooms, onions, green chiles, red chiles, and, ugh, anchovies. You could also design the database to auto-enter the choice of cheeses, because almost every pizza starts with cheese. So when you create a new pizza order record, the check box for cheese would already be selected, and the staff could enter the other toppings as the customer picked them. For instance, one customer might order pepperoni, mushrooms, and anchovies; as the order taker clicks the boxes, the values go into the field in the order in which they were selected, with carriage returns between them. So if you were to grab the values in that field and put them in a different layout showing the field values as text rather than check boxes, you would see each word on a separate line, as shown in sample file Check boxes example-g01.fp5, (see Figure 7.6).

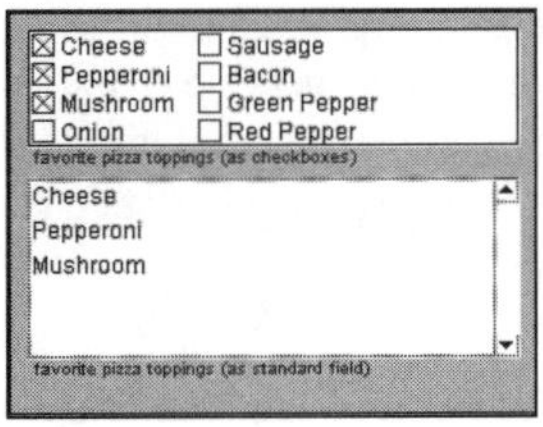

Figure 7.5
Check boxes mean that multiple choices are likely to be entered correctly, even in a pizza parlor. Note the same field repeated, in standard text format in the figure (sample file Checknospaceboxes example-g01.fp5).

PART
II
CH
7

Figure 7.6
The data collected via checkboxes is just text with returns between each value, as shown in the lower box. But the values appear in the order in which they were selected (sample file Checknospacehereinth efilenameboxes example-g01.fp5).

The good news is that because all those values are in a single field, you can successfully search on them. If you are looking for records of all pizzas that happened to have pepperoni as one of the toppings (or all the pizzas that had pepperoni, mushrooms, and cheese), you'll find them all.

But the bad news is that with multiple items entered in this way, you may not be able to sort records consistently or report on the different choices separately. When different customers order the same combination of options in different orders, you will have a hard time counting the number of pizzas with pepperoni, mushroom, and anchovies, because one customer ordered mushrooms, then anchovies, and then pepperoni, while another thought of anchovies first, then mushrooms, and added pepperoni as an afterthought, and so on. Also, when putting together these records in a list, the pizza made when the customer thought of anchovies first will appear at the beginning, even though that pizza is, to the taste, the same thing as the one described in the record that starts with pepperoni as a topping. If sorting and reporting are important, then, consider another approach, or, if you stick with check boxes, be alert to the potential problems.

➔For calculation tricks for counting radio buttons and check boxes, **see** Chapter 10, "Hot Calculations," **p. 273.**

> **Caution**
>
> Check-box data may need to be cleaned up before it is exported. If you copy data from a check-box field, the values are copied to the clipboard with carriage returns between them, but if you go to do an export in most export formats, the carriage return signals a new record, so FileMaker replaces the return with vertical tab character (the new line character, the backward facing arrow). That may cause problems at the other end, if the other program does not handle check boxes the same way, and most don't.

➔For a way to turn these choices into an understandable message, **see** Chapter 10, "Hot Calculations," **p. 273.**

Tip from Jonathan

Make values distinct when using radio buttons and check boxes. Let's say the value list of pizza toppings includes *cheese, pepper, onions, pepperoni,* and *mushrooms*. For months, the staff enters these options using check boxes. But later, the boss decides she wants to find all the records of pizzas that used pepper. Oops, she gets the *pepperoni* records as well as the *pepper* records. To avoid confusion, make sure that the values you put on the list are quite distinct. Instead of pepper, you might say green pepper. Here in New Mexico, we would put red pepper and green pepper, because the state question asked at every restaurant is, "Red or green?"

Perfecting the Interface of Radio Buttons and Check Boxes

Remember that the information you collect in one place through radio buttons and check boxes can be displayed elsewhere in a list or a text field without any buttons or boxes in evidence. If you take data from check boxes, make your field tall enough to show all choices, because each is followed by a carriage return.

Tip from Rich

Don't count on radio buttons always having one option selected. If a user clicks a button, then holds down Shift and clicks it again, the effect is to deselect that item without selecting anything else.

Caution

Beware of blotting out radio buttons or check boxes with borders that are too thick, dark patterns in the border, or a border pattern with too light colors. If the border around the buttons or boxes gets too thick, it may turn them into blobs. If you have no border, you get no buttons.

Conditional Value Lists

In earlier versions of FileMaker, a value list was a list of choices that the user could pick from, but the list was relatively static. The same list came up no matter what else the user had entered. But now FileMaker lets you offer different value lists depending on what the user has entered in another field. Imagine a database in which the user enters the manufacturer of an auto, and, after that, must enter the make. If the user entered General Motors, you would want only GM makes to appear as a value list. With conditional value lists, you can vary the values that are displayed, based on the user's entry in another field. This feature is done through relationships.

For instance, within the Conditional Values folder for this chapter, see the sample files Customer Interest-g02.fp5 and Products-g02.fp5. In the Customer Interest file we have the field Category, which shows a list of all the categories of products over in the Products file. The value list for Category equals the field Categories in the file Products.fp5.

Tip from
Rich

> Value lists based on a field look in the index. In this case, we have created a value list called Categories that equals the values in the field Categories in the Products file. If you were to look at the Products file, you would see some 27 records within 5 categories. So each category is mentioned more than once. But when we look at the value list in the Customer Interest file, a particular category only shows up once. How come? When creating a value list from a field, FileMaker uses the index, and since the item only appears once in the index, you only get one instance of it in the list.

When a user chooses a category, we display a list of manufacturers who sell products in that category (see Figure 7.7). For instance, if a user chooses Camera as a category, we display a list including Canon, Minolta, Olympus, and Samsung, but when a user chooses Refrigerator, the value list of manufacturers changes to Amana, Frigidaire, GE, HotPoint, Maytag, and Whirlpool. In this case, the conditional value list leads users to enter only valid combinations of Category and Product.

Figure 7.7
Having chosen a category, the user sees a list of manufacturers in that category.

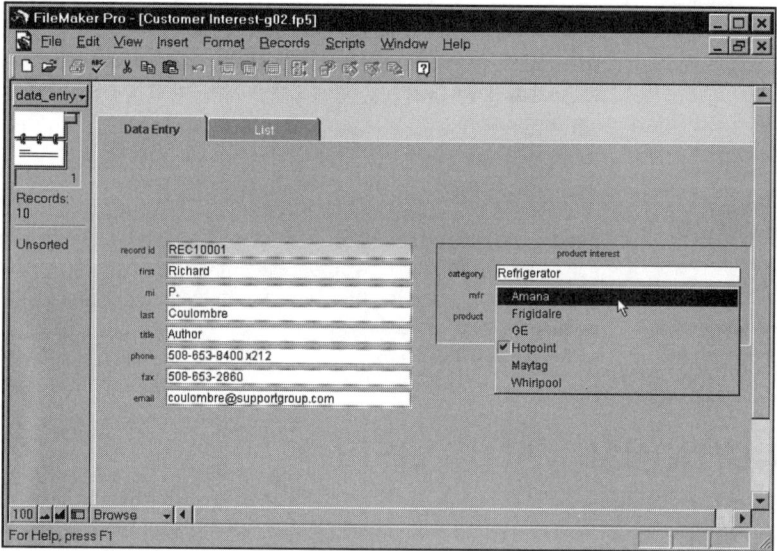

To get only the manufacturers within a product category, we have to create a relationship from the Customer Interest file to the Products file when the field Category in Customer Interest matches the field Category in the Products file. Then we create a value list, choosing to use values from a field, and instead of choosing to see All Values from the Field, we use the option Only Related Values based on the relationship. Thus, we only want manufacturers in whose records the value for Category matches the value the user has just entered into the Category field in the current record, over in Customer Interest. When a user chooses a manufacturer, we display a list of that manufacturer's products within the previously selected product category. To do this, we have to play a trick on FileMaker. What we want to see appear in the Products pop-up are those products that come from a particular manufacturer, and even there, just the products within the category. If we based the list just on Product, we would see all products irrespective of manufacturer, and if we based it on manufacturer, we would see all products, including those outside the category. We want values from records that have the manufacturer and the category. So we created a calculated key field in Customer Interests and Products, and that calculated key concatenates category and manufacturer, with a space between them, to give us a value representing both. (When a user creates a new record for something like an Amana refrigerator, the user would enter Refrigerator in the Category field and Amana in the manufacturer field; the calculated key field would then be filled with the results of the calculation, and ready for a match when the user goes to Customer Interest and picks the category and manufacturer). Then we created a relationship between the calculated key fields in the two files, and we derived the value list for Products from the calculated key field. The result is a pop-up menu with the doubly filtered product list, as shown in Figure 7.8.

Figure 7.8
Having chosen a category, and within that category, a manufacturer, the user sees a pop-up menu with products from that manufacturer, in that category.

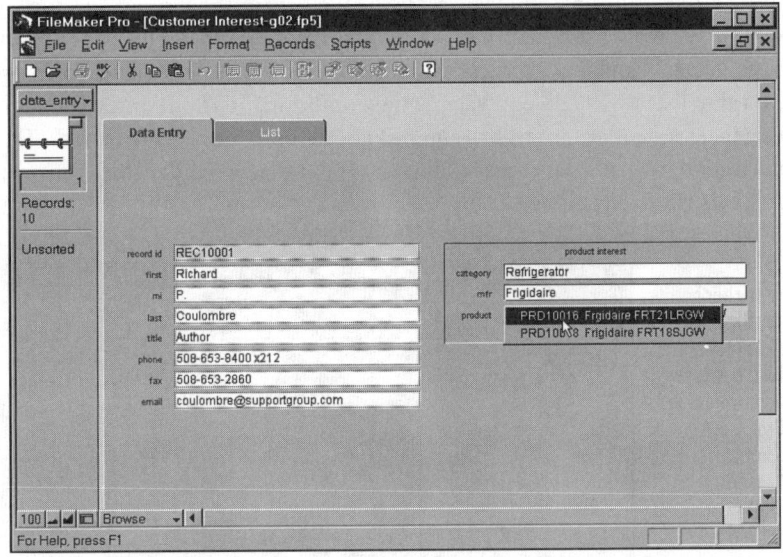

Tip from
Rich

Conditional value lists can also be used to validate data. For instance, in the fields Category and Manufacturer in the Products-g02.fp5 file, as we learned earlier, determined users can get around check boxes. Validation lets us make sure that the values being entered really do belong to that category or manufacturer.

Tip from
Rich

> In this example, we concatenated Category and Manufacturer to create a calculated key. This is a common technique. In this case, as part of the calculation, we put a space between the two values because of what FileMaker puts into a value. When creating an index on a Text field for relational purposes, FileMaker indexes the first 20 characters of each word or the first 60 characters of the key, so when you might be concatenating two (or more) words, you can easily exceed the 20 characters per word limit, but if you put spaces between the words, you are less likely to run into that problem and you will get each word in your index.

When you create a conditional value list in one file, that value list isn't automatically available in another file that shows that data through a portal. In FileMaker a value list lives in the file in which it was defined. To make the value list available for the same data in a related file, you can take advantage of a feature in FileMaker Pro 5 that allows the value list from one file to equal a value list in another. In Contacts-g02 we defined value lists for two fields—Gender and Salutation—and made the Salutation value list depend on whether the contact was Male or Female. To make those value lists available in the Contacts portal over in the Companies-g02 file, we created value lists in the Companies file, and in the Edit Value Lists dialog used the Use Value List from Another File option, and pointed those value lists to Contacts, so each was equal to the equivalent value list in the Contacts. Once the value lists are made equivalent, the conditionality flows into Companies, so that when a user picks a gender, the right value list shows up over in Salutations. (Try changing someone's gender to see the correct value list for the new gender drop down, thanks to the Tab order, as shown in Figure 7.9).

Figure 7.9
When a user changes the gender, the correct list of Salutations drops down, because that is the next field in the Tab Order, and we have changed the value list based on the choice of gender.

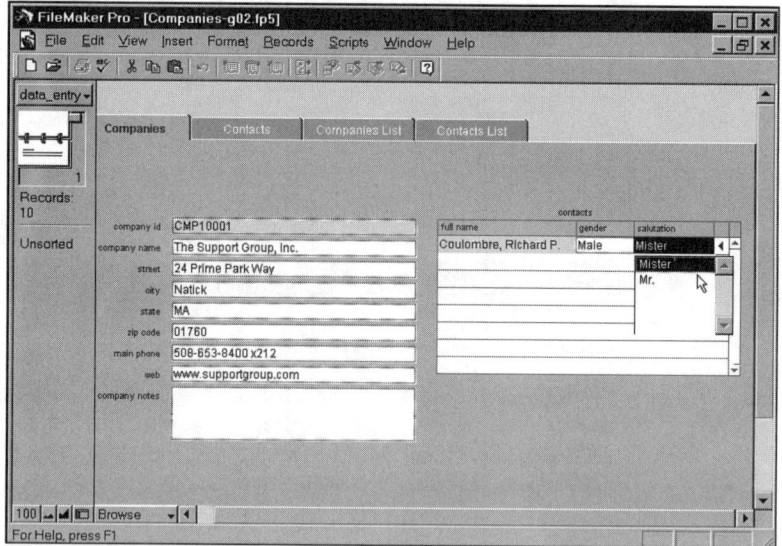

Having FileMaker Automatically Enter Information

Tip from
Rich

Define a value list for a field within the file in which you created the field. If you need to use that value list elsewhere, just point to it, using the option Use Value List from Another File, as shown in Figures 7.10 and 7.11. If you are consistent about this, then anyone who has to maintain your system can find out where to find the original value list. Also, if you change the original value list, all the others that point to it will be updated automatically.

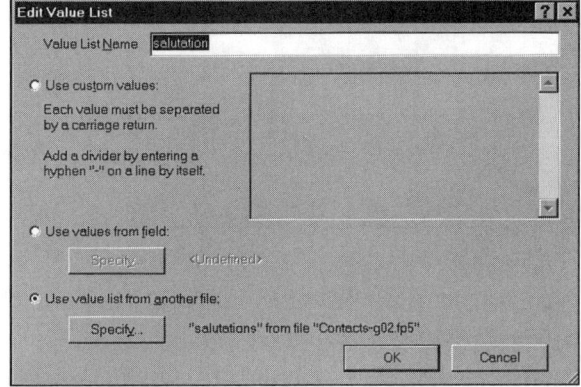

Figure 7.10
The Edit Value Lists dialog in the Companies-g02.fp5, shows a value list for the Salutation field taken from another file.

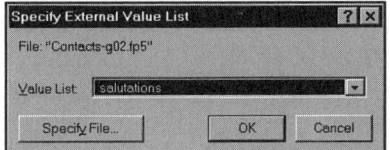

Figure 7.11
Then Specify External Value List dialog lets you pick the file from which to borrow the value list.

Having FileMaker Automatically Enter Information

Typically, you have FileMaker automatically enter text, date, time, or numeric information when a new record is being created (but not always). Usually, you do this when there is a reasonable likelihood that one particular value will be used most of the time, or at least frequently. For example, in an invoicing system, you might set the default invoice terms to Net 30 Days, because that is the most common option. In this situation, the automatic entry serves as a convenience for the user, a suggestion, but not a read-only value. The user can change the entry by picking an alternate value from a value list or just by entering something new.

1. Choose File, Define Fields.
2. Define or select a Date, Number, Text, or Time field.
3. Click Options or double-click the field name.
4. On the Options for the Field dialog, go to the Auto-Enter tab (see Figure 7.12).

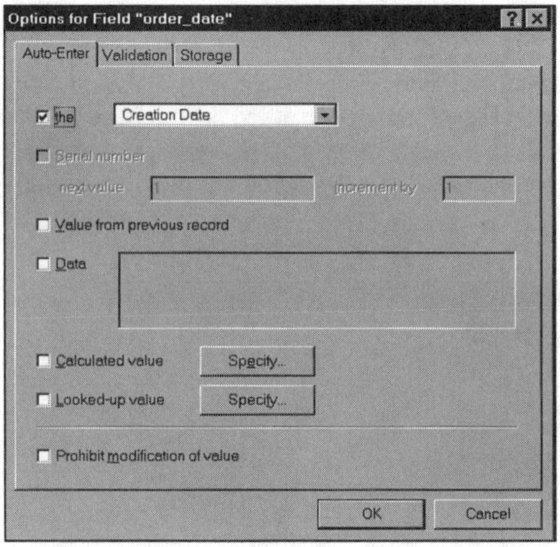

Figure 7.12
The Options for the Field dialog, open to the Auto-Enter tab.

The drop-down menu for the first option lets you auto-enter one of the following:

- The creation date or time
- The modification date or time
- The creator name
- The modifier name

If you look at the sample invoicing system we have included on the CD, you will notice that we have four fields in every file, one for the first four of these options, and each is automatically entered. In that way we create an audit trail through the records. Typically, we do not show these fields to ordinary users, but tuck them away in a layout for the use of developers only.

The next option is the one to auto-enter a serial number. We recommend starting off each file with a field for an auto-entered serial number as a way of ensuring you have a unique identifier for each record.

→ To learn more about the advantages of auto-entered serial numbers, **see** "Implementing Rule #1: Primary Keys Must Be Unique," **p. 136.**

> **Tip from**
> *Rich*
>
> You can include text in the auto-entered serial number, as we have in every sample file. For instance, you could start the serial number in Invoices with INV, and the serial number in Products with PRD. In this way, you could easily differentiate a Primary key that comes from the invoices file from a Primary key coming from the products file.

You probably won't find a lot of use for the option of entering a value from the previous record, because this just takes whatever was in this field in the last record the user worked on and moves that value into the same field in the new record. Good for repetitive entry, but not much else.

You can also have FileMaker automatically enter any data you choose. When you click the data option in the Options dialog, a box appears with a flashing insertion point. You can type alphanumeric information in there.

Tip from
Jonathan

> If you have a lot of text you want entered automatically, write it in a word processor; then copy and paste. You'll be able to use all the tools of word processing to get the text cut, copied, rearranged, and rewritten before moving it over.

You can also enter a calculated value, which is a very powerful function. Then, when the record is created, the calculation is evaluated and the result appears in the field. Imagine you are writing a database for a small store. Saturdays are the slowest days of the week. The owner decides to offer 10% off on all items on Saturdays to stimulate business. So what you could do is create an auto-entered calculation that says, "When a new invoice is created, figure out if the name of today is Saturday, and if it is, auto-enter a 0.10 into the discount field; otherwise, put a zero there."

 Here's an example: Using the sample file Orders-g03.fp5 within the folder g03-Auto Enter Calc, you'll see a field called Discount %. We create an auto-entered calculation for this field, saying,

```
If(DayName(order_date) = "Saturday", .10, 0)
```

Order Date is itself an auto-entered field, with today's date. If the name of the day within OrderDate happens to equal Saturday, FileMaker will go ahead and automatically enter the discount of .10 in the Discount% field; otherwise, enter 0. See Figure 7.13 for the way this appears to the user.

Figure 7.13
When the user identifies the date as Saturday, the special Saturday discount appears.

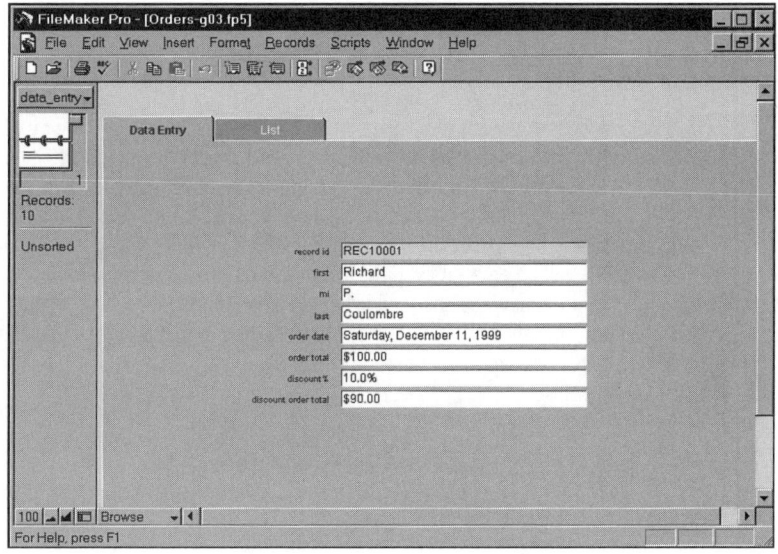

Most of the time auto-entering takes place when the record is created. But look deep inside the Specify Calculation dialog that appears when you choose a calculated value on the auto-entry dialog. At the bottom is a check box saying, "Do not evaluate if all referenced fields are empty." That is the default, so it is checked. If you leave that checked, then the auto-entry only occurs when the user has entered a value into any of the fields the auto-entered calculation is based on. You are saying evaluate even if some of the fields are empty, but you are also saying that the system ought to perform the calculation as soon as the user enters data into any of the referenced fields. If your calculation references several fields and the user only enters data into one, the calculation is immediately performed, but, alas, it is not recalculated even when the user fills in the data for the other fields. If your client needs instant recalculation when a user changes one of the values the calculation is based on, use a Calculation field.

Tip from
Rich

The auto-entry calculation can put data into a field that is not, itself, a Calculation field. The beauty, and danger, is that the user may then proceed to modify the entry, unless you say no. In a non-Calculation field, the user can normally select and replace the value. For instance, in the store that offers a 10% discount on Saturdays, if that field is simply a Number field, the clerk can select the 0.10 and replace it with 0.50 when his Mom comes through the checkout.

Tip from
Rich

When a record is duplicated, normally any auto-entered options on a field take precedence over the data from the record being duplicated. The auto-enter mechanism is triggered and overwrites what was in a field in the original record. This may or may not cause problems. And there is one exception: If you auto-enter a calculated value, the calculated value is not auto-entered over any existing data. When you have an auto-entered calculated value, if that field is empty in the original record, then the auto-entered calculated value gets entered, but if there is already data there, the calculation is not triggered, and the data just comes across as it was. There are times when you can use this twist to your benefit. Imagine you want to auto-enter the invoice term of Net 30 days, but in certain circumstances you want to allow users to change that. Now imagine you have an invoice where the user has changed the value to Net 60 days. When duplicating the record, you can decide whether you want to keep that value or retrigger the Net 30 days. It is a business decision: to keep the existing value or go back to the default. If you decide to keep the default one, check the data option in the auto-entry dialog and enter Net 30 days, and then that will be entered every time a new record is created (even during duplication). If you want to allow the changed value to remain during duplication, go to the auto-entry options and choose to have a calculated value; then in that Specify Calculation dialog, put Net 30 days in quotes.

Lookups

Another form of auto-entry is a lookup, which is triggered whenever there is a change in the key field, which exists in the file that does the lookup. But if the data is changed in the source file, it is not automatically changed in the destination file.

This is a good approach to automating the entry of data into fields if you want to preserve a snapshot of the information rather than to keep updating it. For example, in our sample invoicing database, in the Invoice Line Items file, reachable through the last item in the Summary Reports list at the bottom right of the Invoices tab, there are a lot of fields defined as lookups. The Unit Price, the Description, and Taxability (whether or not the product is taxable) shown in Figure 7.14 are all lookup fields. We want to know the current value, but we do not want to allow that value to be changed on this particular record in the future. When a product is included on the invoice, the lookup brings in the current values, and the user can then edit the price or product description on that record without affecting the values back in the field from which we looked up the information. In this way, the price remains unchanged and the invoice total remains the same, even if there is a price hike later in the year. We need each invoice to stay as it was, if we want to make sure we are billing and collecting accurately.

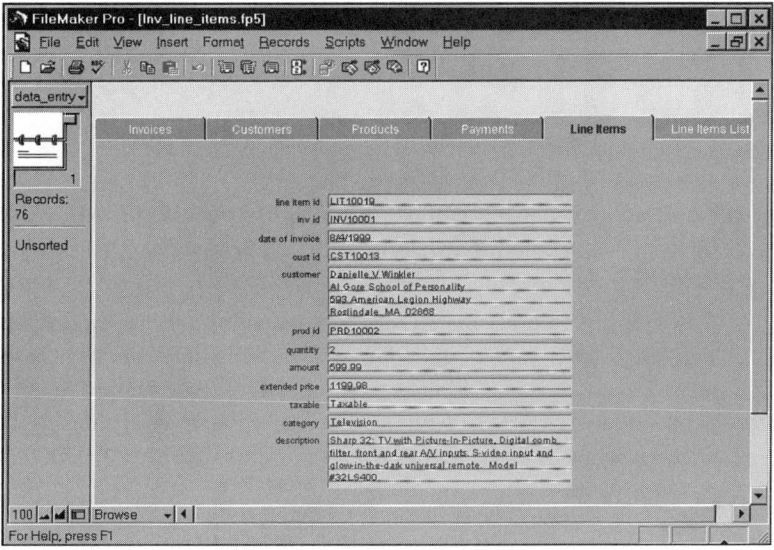

Figure 7.14
Lookup fields include Unit Price, Description, and Taxability.

Lookups use the same relationships used by related fields. The difference is that lookups are set as part of the field's auto-entry options, and the value is entered only once. To get a lookup to work, you can have the relationship all set up, or you can set it up while creating the lookup. Then do the following:

1. Choose Define, Fields.
2. In the dialog, double-click the field.
3. Choose the Auto-Enter tab
4. Check the item called Looked Up Value.
5. In the Lookup specification dialog (see Figure 7.15), select the name of the relationship that you are going to use. (If it doesn't exist, use the option to define the relationship).
6. In the list of fields from the related file, choose the field from which you want to get a value.
7. If you want, define the options.

Figure 7.15
The Lookup dialog asks you to start by specifying a relationship. Then you pick a field from which you want a value.

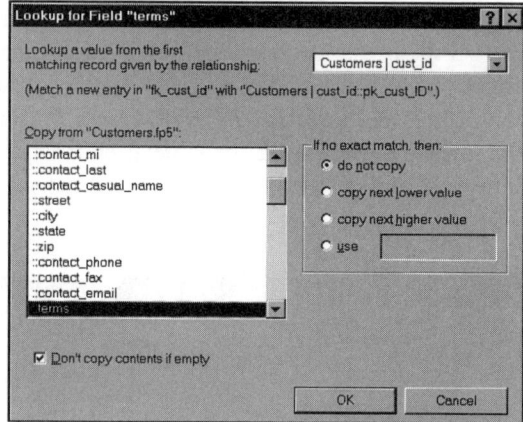

"Don't copy contents if empty." Sounds silly, doesn't it? You may already have a value in the field that is going to be auto-entered. Checking this, then, if a lookup or relookup is performed, and the other field is empty, blankness will not replace the current value.

If there is not an exact match for the key field, what do you do? "do not copy." Or "copy next lower value," or "copy next higher value," or "use" (and type in an all-purpose message, such as "There was no match.") (The sample file called Customer Orders within the folder g04: Lookup Lower Value shows a situation in which you would choose to copy the next higher value, as shown in Figure 7.16).

8. Click OK.
9. On the Auto-Enter screen, click OK to return to Define Fields.
10. Click Done.

Figure 7.16
After the user enters a product ID and a quantity, we look up a price break.

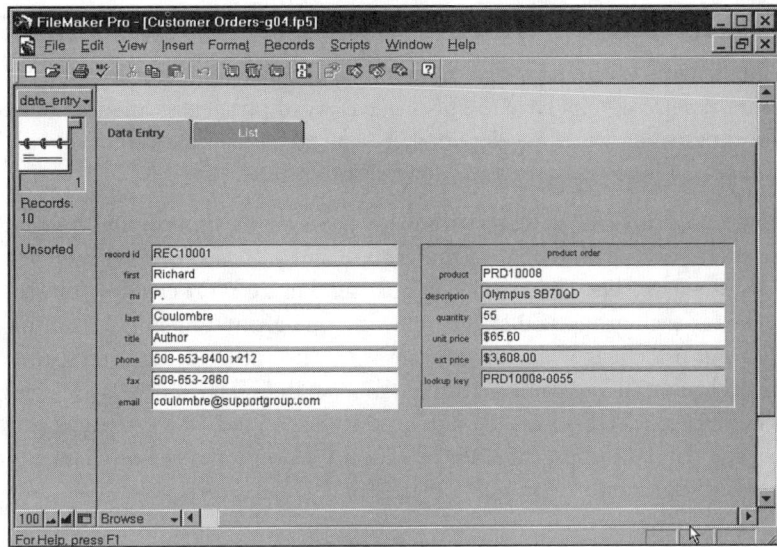

EXAMPLE: GIVING A BREAK FOR QUANTITY

In the sample file Customer Orders-g04.fp5 within folder g04-Lookup Lower Value, the user enters a product ID and a quantity. If the business has different price breaks depending on quantity (one price if you order up to 9 units, a different price for 10–24, another for 25–49, and another for 50–99, and a final one for 100 plus), how do we get FileMaker to look up the proper price for the product, in this quantity? We could create a Product Prices file that combines that product ID and the quantity, and lists a price for that. If we might sell up to 9,999 units of a product, we would need 9,999 different records in order to get an exact match on the product ID and quantity—probably not a great way to go.

But what if we just wanted to include the break points? You can create a field in both Customer Orders and Product Prices that combines the product ID and the quantity. We are calculating a field called Price_Lookup_Key. In the Customer Orders file we also have an IF statement: If the Product ID or Quantity is empty, then make this key empty. We do not want to do a lookup until someone has entered both the Product ID and the Quantity. If both values are entered, we put them together. Here we put a hyphen between the product and the quantity. Because the field contains the Product ID, the type is Text. To take advantage of the option to look up a value, and if there is no exact match, to go to the next lower value, we have to remember that numbers are evaluated numerically in a Number field, but in a text field, they are evaluated alphabetically.

So, to get around that, we have to make sure that all the quantities are of the same length, that is, have the same number of characters. So we said, "Take 4 zeroes, and concatenate with that the quantity, and take the right-most four digits of the result." Now if someone enters a 2, that becomes 0002, and if they enter 111, it becomes 0111. When all the quantities are the same length, our comparison for the next lower value will work, even though the numbers are in a text field. If we typed in 4, and we said "go to the next lower value," FileMaker would normally go to 25 next, because that is alphabetically lower, ignoring 1. By padding with zeroes, we ensure that FileMaker can go to the next lower number, even though it is sorting alphabetically.

Allowing or Preventing Entry in Fields

The default behavior for text, number, date, time, container, and Global fields is to allow the users, assuming they have the proper password privileges, to enter and edit values. But there are times when we as developers may want to control the extent to which users get to enter and edit. There are several ways to exert this control.

You can set up groups (each with its own password, or with multiple passwords, as when you have one for each member of the group), and you can specify which groups get to tinker with the data. The Groups dialog box (see Figure 7.17) enables you to define different privileges for each group you create, allowing one group to edit data, letting another view the data but not change it, while preventing a third group from even seeing the data on any given layout, in any particular field. You can define layout by layout, or field by field, whether values are accessible, not accessible, or read only. (*Accessibility* includes entering and editing data). Groups, then, let you specify who gets to see or change the data in particular fields. (See sample file in g08 Create Edit New Records.)

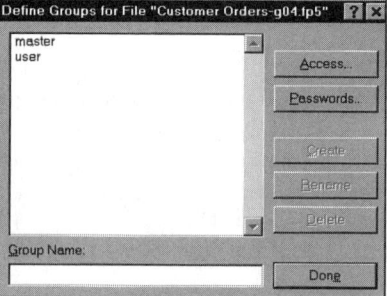

Figure 7.17
The Groups dialog lets you define a group and give it a particular kind of access. You can define the forms of access through password control.

Tip from
Rich

Groups have their limits. Yes, groups let you define access to a given layout or to a certain field, but sometimes you really want to control the level of access to a field on one layout versus the same field on another layout. To control access to a field, consider a Merge field. On a layout where you want to prevent someone modifying the data, instead of putting the actual field on the layout, use a Merge field. A Merge field shows the data on the layout, but the user cannot enter or edit anything in that field. Because a Merge field prevents users from entering a value even when they go into Find mode, the Merge field cannot be searched. For searching, you may need to shunt people over to the layout that includes the field itself or a Calculation field that equals the field.

Tip from
Rich

Restrain your passwords. You can assign a group multiple passwords, and you can assign one password to several different groups. In general, for the sake of clarity, you may want to have a password belong to one and only one person. Create one password for everyone to use, or a different password for each member of the group. If you create a different password for each person, that is more work, and you have to create a new password for each new hire. But if everyone in the group uses the same password, alas, if one s.o.b.

changes his password, everyone else is locked out, because they are trying to use the old password, but that no longer works. If someone moves to another department, that person needs a new password, and you have to change the password for the old group and notify everyone. Better to give each person a password, and when one person leaves, disable that password, because that has no impact on anyone else. Also, this means that you do the bulk of the work, and you are not relying on the group to take action or exercise discipline on all its members. Even if you assign each person a different password, they may all have the same group privileges, which is very handy.

Tip from
Steven

Changing a password in many files can be tedious. However, you can automate that process by using a product called DialogMagic from New Millennium Communications (http://www.newmillennium.com). This plug-in lets you change a password in all files at once.

Tip from
Rich

You can get the name of the current user as a value by using the function Status (CurrentGroups). This returns the name of the groups to which the current user belongs. When someone performs an action, you sometimes want to be able to identify that person. In some cases, you can use whatever name the user specified in the general application preferences, but who knows what name the person may have picked? And that name actually is tied to the computer, not the user.

What if we want to identify the individuals, but not the work station? You can use the Status (CurrentGroups) function, so that if the user logs in with a password, FileMaker knows what group (or groups) that person belongs to. Typically, groups don't generally identify the particular user, but if you give each password its own group, you can identify that particular user, through the Status (CurrentGroups) function. (This function forms part of a calculation, which can show up in a Calculation field, or as part of a script when you set up a field). Now you know whom you are talking to, and can put her name or job title in the field if you want. This could be useful if you need to identify who created each record. You could auto-enter a creator name (on the Mac, that would be the System name, or whatever the user types into the Preferences; in Windows, the creator name is whatever the user entered into the general application Preferences), but this is the computer's name, not the individual user. If you need to get more specific, you would create a field called Creator and auto-enter into it a calculated value that equals Status (CurrentGroups). (This lets you identify individuals, rather than computer owners, such as Valued Sony Customer).

Tip from
Rich

If you are using merge fields to protect data, avoid gigantic field names. When you look at a layout, you can identify Merge fields because they begin << symbols and end with >>. But what if the field name is very long? You might have two fields, one of which has the name <<contacts | fk_company_id:: first_name >> and another field with the name <<contacts| fk_company_id:: last name>>. Names like that will extend across your layout. In any merged field, the way you format the first less-than symbol in the field name is the way the data will be formatted. So, format those angle brackets correctly. Then select the rest of the name and set it in 6 points. This workaround lets you see other objects underneath and near the field, and saves space.

> **Caution**
>
> If you are using Merge fields inside a block of text, formatting can be a challenge. If you want to apply number, time, or date formatting to an element within the block, you have to apply it to the whole block of text, affecting the format of all fields of that type in the block. For instance, if you have a Merge field for the Number of Days Old, and another for the Amount Due, and both are in the same block of text (such as a letter to the customer), if you select the block as a whole and choose the Number option on the Format menu, and use the dialog to format numbers with dollar signs and two figures to the right of the decimal point, then the Amount Due would get that formatting, and so would the Age of Invoice, because it, too, is a Number field, or a Calculation field with a Number result. So you might end up talking about an invoice that is 60.00 days old. You cannot pick out one Number field and format it, say, for currency, and pick out another Number field and format it for scientific notation.

Another technique for protecting data from users is to format the field so that you completely prevent any user from entering data. In Layout view, select the field, and on the Format menu, choose Field Format, and in the Field Format dialog, block entry to the field by unchecking the option to Allow Entry into the Field (see Figure 7.18).

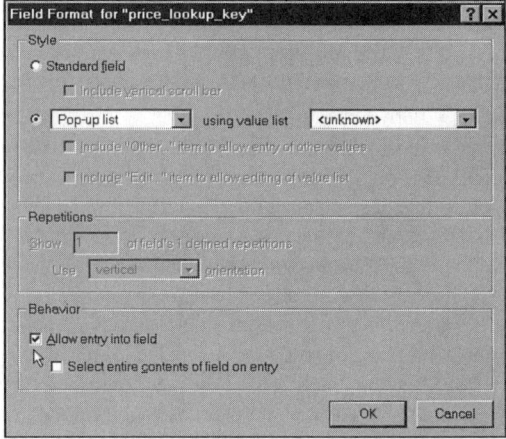

Figure 7.18
To block entry into the field, you deselect the option Allow Entry into the Field.

What is the difference between using a Merge field and formatting a field to prevent data entry? One difference is that Merge fields of the type Number, Time, or Date cannot be formatted individually within the same block of text. Another difference is that regular fields are more polite when you are working on a layout because their names do not grow as big as the Merge fields names often do. But Merge fields do one thing better than regular fields: By definition they slide data left and up, removing any blank space, even in the Browse mode. This approach certainly improves the look of the data. Merge fields are also a little easier to align because they just drop into the line of the text, within the edges of the text block.

Formatting the field to prevent data entry also lets you offer users a way to search the field, through a rather devious trick. With a merged field, finding is completely impossible. But with a regular field, when the user cannot enter the field, you can provide a button running a script that puts a cursor into the field for the user to use. Normally, you don't want the user in the field, but under special circumstances, you may choose to allow the user to get into the field under your script control. In this way, you can protect the data most of the time, while allowing an occasional override if you approve. But when does the script actually run?

EXAMPLE: ALLOWING FINDS WHEN DATA ENTRY IS BLOCKED

In the file called People-g05.fp5 within the folder g05 Entering the Field in Find Mode, we have a field called Notes, to which two business rules apply. After notes have been entered, we don't want the users to enter or edit them again. But users must be able to do Finds on those notes. Problem: If data entry is blocked, how can we allow the user to enter the criteria for the find? We create a script that checks what mode the user is in, and based on that, gives permission to edit. In the first test, we see if the user is in Browse mode; if so, we further test to see if the field Notes is empty, and if it is empty, we use the Go to Field command to put the cursor in that field. Even though the field Notes has been defined in Field Format dialog to not allow entry, all that does is prevent a user from tabbing into or clicking into the field; it does not prevent a script from putting a cursor into the field. If there is a value in the field, and the user is in Browse mode, we post a message saying, "Once notes have been entered, they cannot be changed." On the other hand, if the user is in Find mode, we say, go ahead and put the cursor into the field to do the search. Thus, we let the user into the field, but only in certain circumstances (that is, when the user has switched to Find mode).

```
People-g05.fp5 contains the script called enter_data_into_notes:
Allow User Abort [ Off ]
Set Error Capture [ On ]
# "If the user is in the Browse mode, and the field notes is empty, put the cursor
into the field notes. That way a user can enter notes when empty,
but will not be allowed to modify existing notes. This script is run when the user
clicks on the notes field."
If [ Status( CurrentMode) = 0 ]
        If [ IsEmpty(notes) ]
                Go to Field [ notes ]
        Else
                Halt Script
        End If
End If
# "If the user is in the find mode, enter the field notes when the user clicks on
the field."
If [ Status( CurrentMode) = 1 ]
        Go to Field [ notes ]
End If?
```

Figure 7.19
The script in People-g05.fp5 allows data entry on creation, and also when in Find mode, but blocks editing.

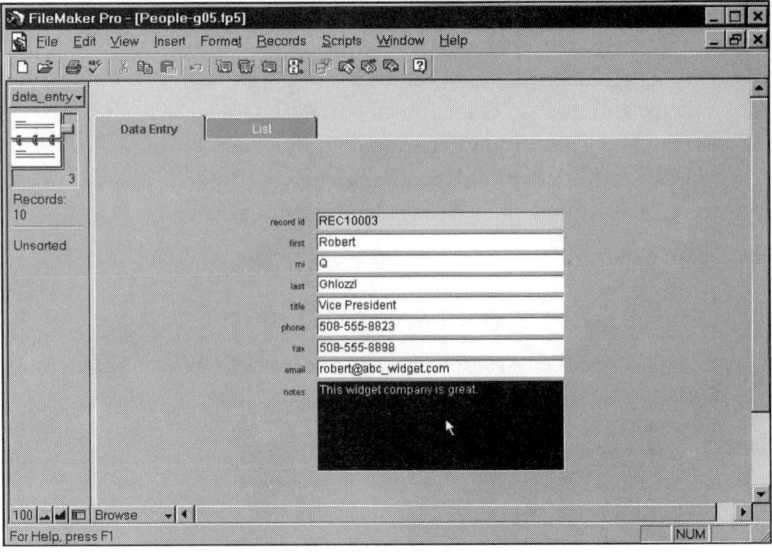

A third technique for protecting data from users looks wasteful but works well. We have used this technique quite often in our sample Invoicing system, because we decided to prevent users from editing data in list views, so we chose to put, in place of editable fields, Calculation fields that equaled those editable fields. (The light gray background cues users that this data cannot be changed.)

If you want the user to see the data and search on the data, but not edit it, create a calculation that happens to equal the value and put the Calculation field on the layout, while not putting the actual field on the layout. In this way, the user can see the information, copy a value, and run a find, but not edit the value. In this case, because you expect users to be running a find, you want to make sure the calculation results are stored and indexed. In the Define Fields dialog, create the Calculation field, and then, in the Calculation dialog, click the Storage Option button, and in the dialog shown in Figure 7.20, choose to have the calculation results stored and indexed.

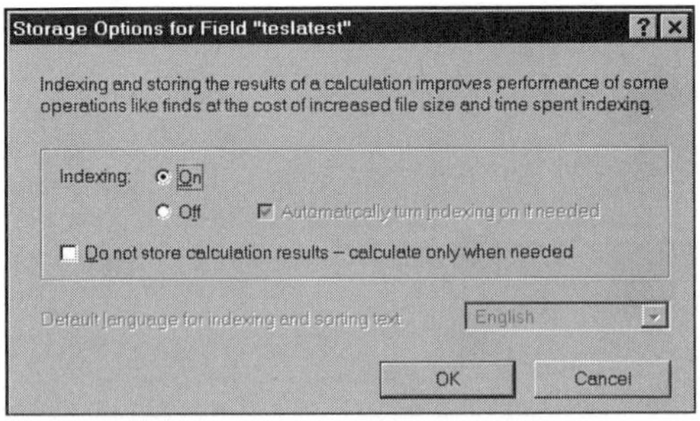

Figure 7.20
The Storage Option dialog allows you to ensure that calculation results are stored and indexed.

> **Tip from Rich**
>
> Remember that not all Calculation fields can be stored—and when they cannot be stored, they cannot be indexed. If a Calculation field references a Global field, a Summary field, a related field, or another unstored calculation, by definition its results cannot be stored. If your user quits and returns, the value is recalculated, but it is never stored on the hard disk. Hence, there is no index at hand.

Having FileMaker Check for Accuracy

If your users want to find and report on information without gaps and glitches, the data has to flow into the database with consistent accuracy. Inconsistent and inaccurate data entry can cost the business in ways that are not obvious, leading staff to make decisions based on flawed data, accidentally omitting live customers, abandoning invoices, or neglecting shipments. Validation helps alert users to inconsistent or unacceptable entries before they get stored in the database forever.

You may, for instance, need to test the validity of data within a single entry. In one insurance company we worked with, the policy number had to be a specific number of digits. The first three digits had to be within a certain range. Then some letters came along indicating the type of policy, from a list of valid policies. Then came a 9-digit unique policy identifier. Here, then, we had to look at three components of a single entry to make sure each was valid.

Validation is not an arbitrary quest for pure truth. Fundamentally, the question is "Does the information conform to the expectations of the business?"

> **Tip from Rich**
>
> Don't go too far. If you follow the wishes of a boss who has a tendency toward being a control freak, then the computer will interrupt the staff's work repeatedly to tell them they are wrong. Bad users! To avoid making users feel guilty and angry, you have to tell your client that although it is important to validate data, it is equally important to be judicious in applying validation. We have seen cases where the system validated everything, and the users got so frustrated that they stopped entering anything, or they entered only things that made the system happy, which, of course, circumvented the real purpose of the validation. People were entering valid data that was not actually correct, and chuckling.

CASE STUDY: WE FELT THEIR PAIN

"Terrible troubles!" the clients exclaimed. We asked them to describe their pain. "We know that data is in these fields, but we can't find it." We went to the actual records to look at the data. The database tracked a software library, and the users had to choose which platform a particular application ran on. We found that the data sometimes said *Mac* and sometimes *M* and sometimes *Macintosh*; for Windows, the values included *Win 95*, *DOS*, *W*, *w*, and *Windows*. Of course, the database interpreted these values as eight different platforms, not just two, and if someone looked up *Mac* or *Windows*, many records were ignored. We had to point out that the staff would have to learn to enter the data consistently, or they could pay us to redo the database to encourage consistency through validation and other techniques. But even if we persuaded users to achieve perfect data entry from this point on, someone would have to go through every existing record to regularize the terms for the operating system. No one had trained the staff or explained how badly a little careless data entry could damage their system.

When you define a field, you can set options for validation that the entry is the right type, that the user has not left the field empty, that the entry is unique, matches an existing entry, matches an item on a value list, fits within a specified range of values, or satisfies a calculation. You may want to set several of these options at once.

OF TYPE

Validating data for its type lets you make sure that only numbers are accepted in a Number field, that only strict four-digit dates appear in a Date field, and that only correctly formatted times of day show up in a Time field.

Normally, in a Number field, FileMaker allows you to enter anything you want; it just ignores non-numeric characters including punctuation and non-mathematical symbols when it creates the index and runs searches. FileMaker does consider a minus sign, the decimal point, commas for thousands, and parentheses as mathematical symbols, but oddly a plus sign is not; an asterisk, standing for multiplication, is not a mathematical symbol for these purposes, and neither is the slash (for division). So when you set the validation by type, insisting on numbers, FileMaker refuses to let a user type in a +, *, %, or currency symbols. Strict numeric validation, then, focuses on getting a single value. The plus seems to be assumed. The minus sign (and the pair of parentheses indicating a loss) indicates negative value, and is accepted. But FileMaker refuses to perform the calculations implied by multiplication or division.

> **Tip from**
> *Rich*
>
> If you have a Date field, use the strict four-digit date format and insist on this format. Look on the FileMaker site for information on the Y2k aftermath. This is not negotiable.

NOT EMPTY

If there is a key piece of information you can't live without, such as a Foreign key field in a child file (because every child must be attached to a parent), you might want to make sure that the field is not empty.

UNIQUE

If you need to make sure that what the user enters in this record does not appear in the same field in any other record, set this option. You don't need to set this when you auto-enter serial numbers, because those are unique. But if you are drawing the Primary keys from another system or people may manually enter the Primary keys, you might ensure uniqueness by this validation technique.

Existing

We've never used this kind of validation. Perhaps if you have a bunch of harried data entry clerks and you wanted to make sure they were entering values consistently, you could raise a flag if they happened to enter a value that didn't already exist somewhere in the file. Of course, that raises the question "How would you get the first instance in?" If you have a state field, and populated it with all the acceptable two-letter designations, you could let people type those into the field on a new record and the validation would check to make sure that what they typed matched something already existing in the field in another record, but if you already know what the valid values are, you might just as well give users a value list.

Member of a Value List

Basically, you are asking FileMaker to make sure that anything the user enters matches a value on a list you specify. This approach can be very helpful when you have multiple values all of which are acceptable.

> **Caution**
>
> If the field is left empty, it is not validated. When you validate by a value list, FileMaker does that validation on anything the user enters, but if the user leaves the field empty, FileMaker does not bother to perform the validation. Why? Because FileMaker validates when the value in the field gets changed; leaving the field blank doesn't change anything, so validation is not triggered. Therefore, if you choose to validate that a value is a member of a particular value list, you should also specify that the field must be Not Empty. For instance, if you say that the Foreign key must be a member of the value list, you should also insist that the Foreign key field not be left empty.

→If you would like to learn more about value lists as a way of securing your data, **see** "Having FileMaker Automatically Enter Information," **p. 185.**

In a Range

If the business rules insist that ages must be between 18 and 70, or dates must fall in the current or next year, or times must be limited to business hours, you can validate in a range, specifying the acceptable minimum and maximum number, date, or time. Remember that even if FileMaker doesn't beep at you when you fail to put in both values in the range choices within the Validation dialog, you must do so (or else you don't really have a range).

By Calculation

Validation by calculation is an extremely powerful technique. When you check this option in the Validation dialog, a dialog box appears, in which you can create an algebraic expression with a Boolean result, that is, one or zero. If the result is one, then the value is accepted. If the result is zero, the value is rejected and the user is presented with FileMaker's own error message, or yours.

In the algebraic expression, the variables are values in other fields. Note that the validation turns its gaze outward; you are making sure that whatever has been entered matches up correctly with other values in other fields.

Sometimes, a client wants to lock certain records so nobody can accidentally change them. You can manage this by creating a check box field with a name like Lock. If an administrator checks that box, then you could enter the word Lock in the field. Until the administrator consciously unlocks the record, then, any changes to other fields will be met with a validation by calculation, which goes out and checks the Lock field's value. If the value is Lock, then the user cannot change any field on that record, but if the value is empty, then the user can modify everything. You can then use the Lock field in the validation of every other field. You are saying "Only allow the user to change a value if the record itself is unlocked."

For example, in the folder g06 Locking Records, the file People-g06.fp5 has a field called Lock. This field appears as a check box, and a record is either locked or not. The way it is set up, the group privileges do not allow the User password to change the status of the field called Lock. But when you are logged in with the Master password, you can. To do this, we set a validation on every field; oddly, this has nothing to do with what the user entered. We are just checking that the field Lock_Record is not equal to "Lock." If it is not equal, the person can enter a value or edit one. If it is equal to Lock, the person is locked out. The field passes validation when the test is true, which is only concerned with the Lock field (not something the user entered).

Thus, for each enterable field, we are saying "Anything you enter is OK, as long as the record is not locked. If by chance the record is locked, then anything you enter will fail validation."

One of the ugly parts of this technique is that, even though the record is locked and the user should notice that it is locked, the user can still type in the field because the validation only takes place when she tries to leave the field: very annoying! The user may ask, "Why didn't you just prevent me from typing in the darn field in the first place?"

Another gotcha: The validation message that comes up has two buttons and Revert Field, as shown in Figure 7.21. What we hope is that the user will click Revert Field, which undoes the entry. But if the user clicks OK, he is returned to the field, with the edits he just made, even though those changes are unacceptable. Clicking OK does not solve the problem; in fact, it may put the user into a loop. So, as you write the message, prompt the user to click Revert Field to get out of Validation Hell. (This is a simple, low-maintenance way to lock records. For details on the way you can build this arrangement, see Figures 7.22, 7.23, and 7.24.)

Figure 7.21
This warning comes up if a user tries to modify a field when the record is locked.

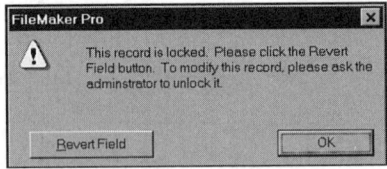

Figure 7.22
Many fields have strict validation by calculation turned on, with a message prepared as a warning.

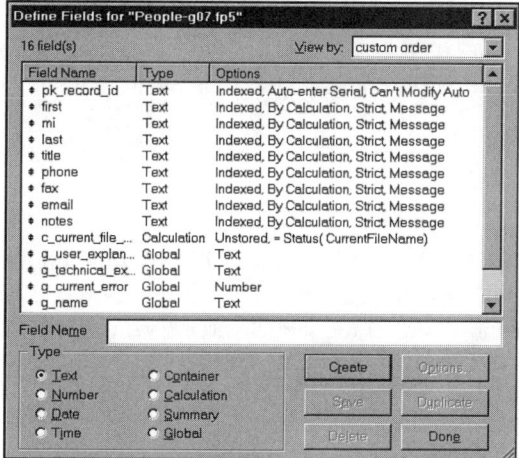

Figure 7.23
In the Groups dialog, the field Lock Records is set to Read Only for Users.

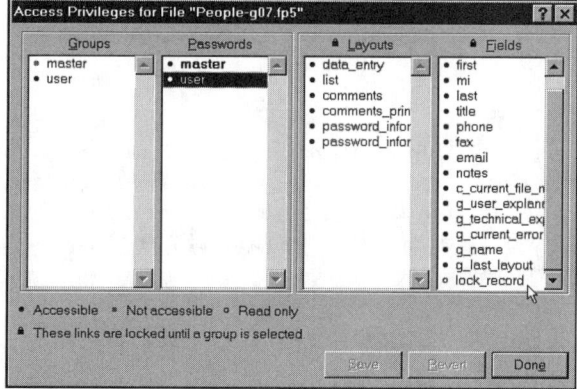

Figure 7.24
You can set validation by calculation.

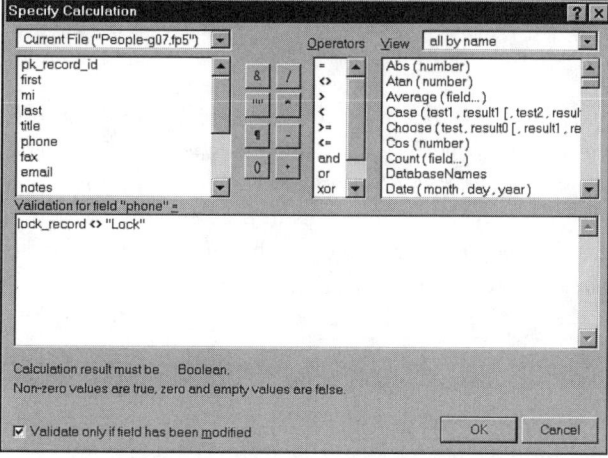

Validating Social Security Numbers

Depending on how strict you are, you can validate that the Social Security Number is eleven digits, and that the fourth and seventh characters are hyphens. You create a calculated validation, saying

```
Length(ssn)=11 and
Middle(ssn),4,1="-" and
Middle(ssm),7,1="-"
```

This calculation says, essentially, count the number of characters and make sure that they total 11. Then, in the middle of that entry, at the fourth position, grab one character and make sure that it is a hyphen. Then do the same for the seventh character.

There are a few holes in this method, though. If the user does not know his or her Social Security number, he or she will still have to enter a bogus number here, just to be able to leave the record (if you are using strict validation), or to recover from an error message (if you are feeling kind). The workaround is to append a little something saying, after two more carriage returns,

```
Or
Length(ssn)=0
```

> **Tip from Rich**
>
> In a calculated validation, there may be several different ways to satisfy the validation. For instance, a local phone number would be different from the long distance number, which in turn would be different from the international number; so it is OK in a calculated validation to have multiple satisfactory conditions just separated by OR. This is a plain old OR. Any one of these conditions will do.

> **Tip from Rich**
>
> If you are using calculated validation, you should always consider whether you want to allow users to leave the field blank. Is nothing or empty a valid value? Are there times when a user may legitimately have nothing to put here, and you would rather have nothing instead of some bogus placeholder, which would look like real data, but be wrong?

Another hole in our simple validation for Social Security Numbers is that the user could enter an alphabetical value—that is, use something other than numbers. To plug this loophole, you might want to make this a Number field, but the problem is that although FileMaker remembers you typed the hyphens in the field, the hyphens are not used to evaluate the number, and if the field is indexed, the hyphens do not show up in the index. Generally, we make Social Security a Text field, even though it is mostly numbers. So how do you make sure the user enters only numbers (and hyphens)?

Some folks use a Number field, and then grab the first three characters and make sure they form a number from 0 to 1,000. But there are lots of other characters that can be validly entered into a Number field, such as the minus sign. The best way to validate a Number or Text field is to check digit by digit. Grab the first character and make sure it is a member of the set of digits 0 through 9. You also can do that with characters 2, 3, 5, 6, 8, 9, 10, and 11.

This seems like a lengthy way to validate, but compared with other tricks folks have used, this turns out to be dumb, but straightforward. It is also easy for someone later to understand.

> **Tip from**
> *Rich*
>
> When building a system, sometimes the tried-and-true, low-and-slow approach is better for maintainability. Fancy tricks relying on subtleties of FileMaker just make it likely that someone later can make a little change that ruins the whole validation, without understanding its ramifications.

> **Tip from**
> *Rich*
>
> When doing any work in the Calculation Specify dialog, you should take advantage of the fact that FileMaker lets you put carriage returns into the calculation. That allows you to replace an extremely long, wrapping calculation with different lines and blank lines between sections of the calculation, so you can read the whole thing more easily. For instance, compare the rambling version in Figure 7.25 with the cleaned-up version in Figure 7.26.

Figure 7.25
Without returns, the calculation is an ugly clump.

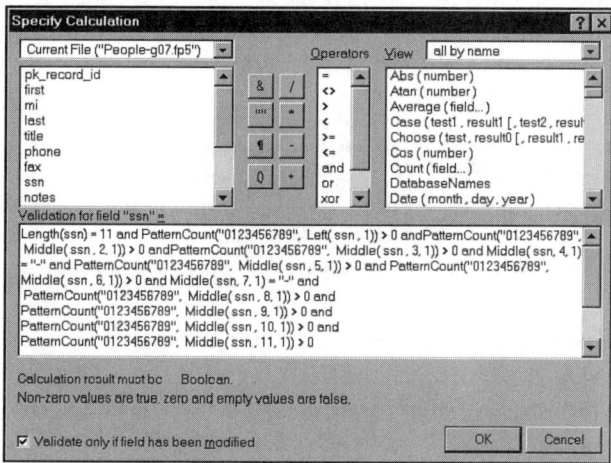

Figure 7.26
With returns, the calculation is easier to read.

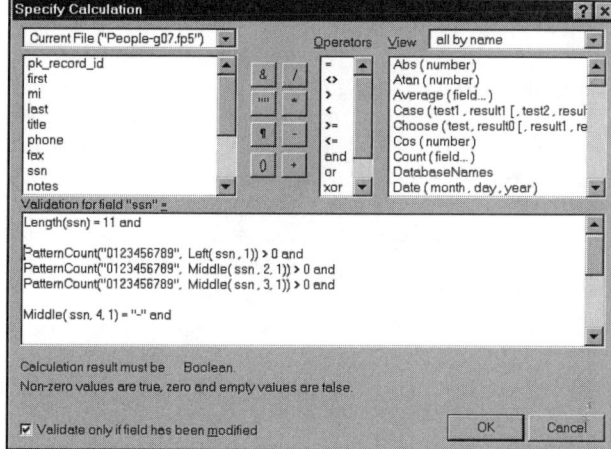

Tip from Rich

Beware the difference between AND and OR in any calculation. When you have a bunch of Boolean tests, they are usually separated by AND or OR. The AND is like glue; it binds the two tests together. Each test must pass. The OR is just a way to offer alternate ways to pass the test: either this way, or that way. OR gives you MORE chances to pass. (It is non-exclusive).

Not Allowing Users to Override the Validation

Being strict about validation means you don't allow the user to override your warnings. Soft validation just means giving the user a warning: "Um, er, this is not what we expect, why don't you, uh, re-check." Strict validation says this is not what we expect, and you can go no further until you correct this entry. You set the degree of strictness at the bottom of the Validation dialog, using the check box that says "Strict: Do not allow users to override validation."

Use this option sparingly. If there is one thing users hate more than the computer telling them they have done something wrong, it is a computer insisting that they correct the error. In general we advise using a polite warning. Users are cagey. If they cannot insert the value they want, they will enter any old value that works, and say, "The hell with accuracy."

Tip from Rich

You can tell if you are a controlling personality by the frequency with which you use strict validation. Try to pick your fights. Don't overdo this. Use strict validation only where the business absolutely requires it, because only business necessity will convince users that you are being reasonable. For instance, a good time to use strict validation would be when you are creating a database for nuclear bomb codes.

Tip from Rich

Every time you think you have validation working perfectly, another exception pops up. As circumstances change, the system turns out to get in the way of users who want to adapt the data, if you have strict validation on. Example: With a home banking service, you can enter payees and payments, and the service delivers the funds electronically or on paper checks. You have to enter your account number for each payee. For instance, if you are paying your electric bill, you have to enter the account number the utility company has assigned you (so you get credit from them).

Once, when we set up a cable TV company as a payee, the account number on the bill did not correspond to the format expected by the database. The cable company had not told the bank about the new kind of account numbers, so we could not pay the cable through the service. Workaround: we deliberately misspelled the name of the payee, so the bank said, this is not a standard payee, so they allowed us to send a check as if we were describing a new payee, and of course, the check bore the correct account number, just as it appeared on the bill. This kind of trick is what you hope your users don't resort to to bypass your validation.

Displaying a Message if Validation Fails

If validation fails, FileMaker will do its best to present a message explaining what went wrong. Sometimes that message is accurate. For instance, it might say, "This field is defined to contain a value in the range from 10,000 through 20,000. Allow this value, which isn't in this range? Yes, No, Revert Field." When you have the validation set for the numerical range, this message communicates the problem and suggests what the user has to do. But other messages are more cryptic, leaving users wondering what they should do to fix the entry. When you are doing a validation by calculation, for instance, FileMaker doesn't know what business rule you are trying to enforce, so it just issues a generic message: "This field is defined to contain only specific values. Allow this value?"

In general, create your own message, explaining the business rule and suggesting how to enter acceptable data. Think positively.

> **Tip from Rich**
>
> Don't insult your user (a true story). The validation by calculation tested for a particular user name, and if the boss was using the system, the message came up, "You ugly ..., you got it wrong again." Not a good idea, at least if you want to keep your job.

> **Tip from Rich**
>
> When creating custom messages for validation, make an effort to be really, really nice. Users get frustrated enough when a computer tells them they are not doing something right, so snotty error messages just drive them nuts. Remember that angry users soon become guerillas stalking your system, resistance fighters seeking to prove your database is oppressing them.

> **Tip from Jonathan**
>
> Give instructions or a remedy. When a user's entry fails the validation test, make up a message saying what exactly the user should do to make a correct entry. Be specific. Maybe even give an example. The user just wants to get back to work.

> **Tip from Rich**
>
> Test messages everywhere. If your application will be deployed on both Macintosh and Windows machines, test your messages on both platforms. Because of the difference in font metrics and possible font substitution, a message that fits one platform may not fit the other. It would be embarrassing if your error message was truncated because of an error on your part.

Validating Global Fields

When you are in Define Fields, and you double-click a Global field, you are taken to the Options for the Global field, not the usual validation or auto-entry screen. Thus, many folks think you cannot validate a Global field. But you can, if you know the trick. To validate a Global field, convert it to a Text, Number, Date, or Time field, depending on what type of

Global field it is. Once you have converted it, double-click the field, go into Validation options, and set the validation you want. Then convert it back to a Global field. The validation sticks with it.

In the invoicing system, when a user goes to the Set Customer screen within the Invoices tab, the user can click on a button to put a letter into a Global field called G_Selected_Cust_Letter, or the user can type into the field. If the user tries to enter more than 12 characters, a validation message appears telling the user that the field will only hold 12 characters. Thus, validation is working on a Global field.

Probably, this is unintended behavior, but lots of folks have discovered it and rely on it, so this backdoor bug has become a feature. (To see this at work, open Invoices and change the G_Selected_Cust_Letter field to Text; then double-click on the field and look at the validation. Make sure you turn it back to Global if you want the trick to continue working).

CONDITIONAL VALIDATION

In some instances, we only want to run validation on one field after the user has entered a value in another field. The validation, then, depends on what the user has entered into other fields.

EXAMPLE: VALIDATING ONE FIELD WITH VALUES IN ANOTHER

In this chapter's folder g09, the sample file called People-g09.fp5 contains two fields you should look at, one for the Social Security Number and the other for Citizenship (see Figure 7.27). The field for Citizenship has two radio buttons: U.S. and Other. The business rule says, "If a person's citizenship is U.S., then we must collect the person's Social Security Number. If the person's citizenship is Other, then we must leave the Social Security Number field empty, to avoid problems with the IRS."

In this case, we can't validate the SSN field by looking at any entry within the field. We have to look at the entry in the Citizenship field. The Citizenship field starts off with the auto-entered U.S., so by definition that field will always have a value in it. The Other is, essentially, a post-modern way of overriding the ethnocentric value saluting the United States. If the user clicks Other, then nothing much happens until the user tries to leave the record. Why? When validation depends on another field, we have a hard time deducing that the user is finished filling out the form. Therefore, we have to wait for the user to indicate that he is finished entering before we launch validation. If the user clicks Other, enters some number into the Social Security Number field, and tries to leave the record, a message appears warning "If this person is a U.S. person, please enter a valid Social Security Number. Otherwise, leave the field empty."

Figure 7.27
If the user clicks Other for Citizenship and then enters numbers into the Social Security Number field, validation will post a message insisting that the field Social Security Number be left empty.

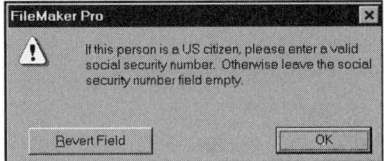

The formula for this kind of validation by calculation goes like this:

```
If (Citizenship = "US", Not (IsEmpty(SSN)), IsEmpty(SSN))
```

That means "Check the Citizenship field, and if that says U.S., make sure that the Social Security Number field is not left empty, but if the choice is something other than U.S., confirm that the Social Security Number field is empty."

In this case we are using an IF statement as part of validation, so the validation on this field can vary depending on the values entered in another field. Also, we are postponing validation until the user tries to leave the record, rather than running it immediately. Why and how do we do this? Because we do not know what order folks will be entering data into the fields on the record, we uncheck an option at the bottom of the Validation dialog, "Validate only if field has been modified." We want to run validation even if the field has not been modified. How come? If this check box is checked, then validation occurs as soon as the user leaves the field (rather than at the moment the user tries to leave the record). Hence, if the user happily types in a Social Security Number, then discovers that the person is a foreigner and clicks Other, the validation would be triggered immediately without allowing the user a chance to erase the bogus Social Security Number. We want to leave the user time to make all entries before swooping down to validate.

Tip from
Rich

> When you want validation to run when someone leaves the record, be sure to uncheck the option "Validate only if field has been modified." Now the validation will run even if the user has not made any changes to the field, and, equally important, the validation will only take place when the user tries to leave the record. This decision to check or uncheck this option is more important than you might think from its name. Perhaps this option ought to be rewritten "Validate the value in this field the moment somebody leaves the field, if she made any changes to it."

EXAMPLE: DEALING WITH THE NONSTANDARD

In the invoicing system on the CD, you'll find another example of conditional validation. When people add products to the invoice, we don't want them to be able to edit the description of the product unless they have the product identifier Misc, which stands for Miscellaneous. The business rule says, "Use this ID for any nonstandard product and write in the definition."

For standard products, we use a lookup. The description in the LineItems file is looked up over in the Products file, but the user can override it: We just want to make sure the user is not falsifying, or overriding, the standard descriptions, and is only entering an original description when the product ID indicates the product is Miscellaneous, which means it is not on the standard list.

So we need to conditionally validate the field Description to meet those business rules. Here's the validation by calculation:

```
If(fk_prod_id = "Misc", 1, description = products | prod_id::long_description)
```

This says "If the user happens to change the product description, please check to make sure that the Product ID is 'Misc.' If it is, then accept whatever the user enters."

What's the one? It represents a True condition, in Boolean terms. In other words, if the user's entry in the Product ID field does match the string "Misc," then the Boolean result is 1, or True, and whatever the user entered as a description is acceptable. On the other hand, if the test turns out False—that is, if the Product ID is something other than miscellaneous—well, then compare the description in this line item with the long description of the same product over in the Products file and make sure they are equal. If they are equal, then the user has not changed the description in the Line Items file; if they do not match, the user has illegally tried to change the description.

Note that we have also checked the option to validate only if the field has been modified, because in this case we wanted the validation run immediately if the field has been changed; if the value has not been changed, then, by definition, the value is valid.

Preventing Users from Editing a Record After It Has Been Created

You give the user a password saying the user can create new records, but not edit old ones. In this approach, the user can create—and keep editing—a new record, as long as she keeps the file open. Once the user closes the file, the record is no longer available for editing; when the user clicks in a field in the record, in a later session, FileMaker displays a standard message saying, "This field is not modifiable."

In the Password dialog, as shown in Figure 7.28, you can set these permissions password by password, so you can allow a supervisor, say, to modify a record at a later date, while preventing line workers.

Figure 7.28
The Password dialog allows you to set various permissions.

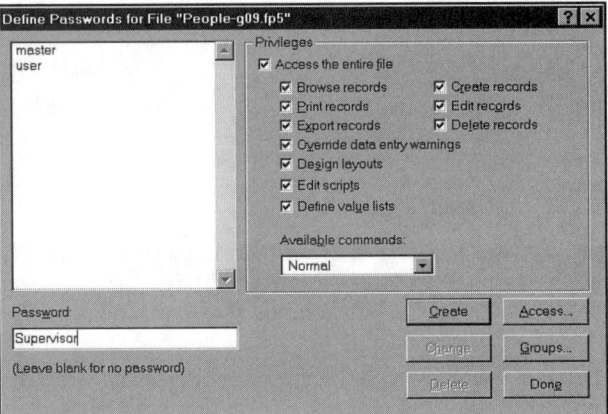

 In this chapter's folder g08, in the file named People-g08.fp5, you will see that a user with the password User can only create new records and edit during that session, but after the user puts away the file those records cannot be edited. (Of course, if you use the Master password, you can edit to your heart's content).

Adjusting the Tab Order to Suit the User's Habits

You may have built the best system in the world, but if the tab order is not the order in which the customer thinks, the system is broken. Why? People just enter data the way they think of it.

> **Tip from Jonathan**
>
> Do not assume you know what tab order people want. Check. Try your prototypes out on users. Do testing. You will be surprised how often the order in which they are used to data differs from the order you thought was "normal" or "obvious."

Also, when you are about to deliver your database, review the tab order at the last moment to make sure it corresponds to user expectations. The tab order may have gotten shuffled during your work. Also, as developers, we tend to set this up in a way we consider logical. But what if the user has spent five years using a form that delivers the information in an entirely different order?

This is critical. Too often we deliver a system and people say, "Gee, we are just having trouble with it." If you recognize this is a potential problem, take the five minutes to sit down with the users at each screen and ask them what order they like. Make it clear, too, that you can fix the order if they realize later it should be changed to match their habits.

Unless you specify to the contrary, the standard tab order is left to right, top to bottom. FileMaker considers fields as belonging to the same tab line if their tops align horizontally. So after going across all the fields whose tops are on one line, FileMaker drops down one pixel and scans for a field whose top appears in that line, and so on. This order often violates what users like or expect. You go, for instance, from first name to order number, and then back and down a line to fill in the last name. Here's how to change tab order:

1. Go to Layout mode.
2. Choose Layout, Set Tab Order. You see the Tab Order dialog.

Figure 7.29
When you ask to set the tab order FileMaker displays fields with numbers indicating the current order, and offers a dialog in which to modify the tab order.

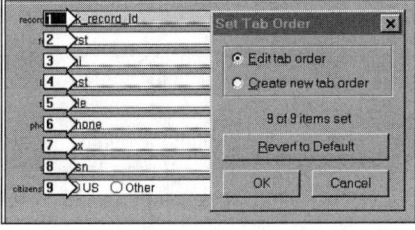

FileMaker puts an arrow next to each field, and you see a dialog box with a list of fields. A field that is part of the tab order has a number in the arrow.

3. In the dialog, create a new tab order by clicking the fields or arrows in order.

When you start a new tab order, FileMaker empties all the arrows of their numbers, so you can just click on the fields or arrows in the new tab order while FileMaker numbers the fields for you.

Tip from
Rich

> You do not have to include all fields in the tab order. There are many times when you don't want to include a field. For instance, if a field is not used very often, you may exclude it. Calculation and Summary fields cannot be entered, so they should be omitted from the tab order too.

Extra Carefulness: Keeping Carriage Returns Out of the Data

Why bother? New or casual users tend to hit the Enter key to move to the next field because they use Enter so often in word processing. Then they discover Tab, but they leave behind all the carriage returns. Later, if someone does a mail merge and there is a carriage return in the first name field, the first name appears on a line by itself. Therefore, you may find it helpful to do validation saying, "Make sure that there are no carriage returns in here, and if there are some, don't let the user out of the field until they are removed." You set a calculated validation on the field, and that calculated validation says, "Is the pattern count in the field equal to zero when the pattern of carriage return is looked for?"

```
Patterncount (First,"¶")=0
```

When the user tries to leave the field, the validation takes what was entered, counts the number of carriage returns in the field, and verifies that the count equals zero. If not, you display a message, explaining that the user needs to remove the carriage return from the data before proceeding.

EXAMPLE: AVOIDING CARRIAGE RETURNS

In the sample file People-g10.ftp, the fields for First Name, Middle Initial, and Last Name have a calculated validation to prevent carriage returns being slipped in by accident. The calculation, which is just like the one shown previously, tells FileMaker to look at what users have entered, count the number of carriage returns, and only allow the entry if the total number of carriage returns is, well, zero. If users try to insert a carriage return and move on, they see a message asking them to remove the carriage returns, as shown in Figure 7.30.

Figure 7.30
A message warns users to remove carriage returns.

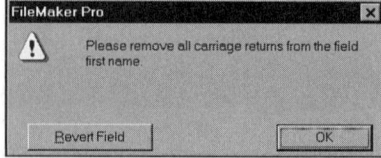

You might use this kind of validation if you intend to use the data in form letters through mail merge or in a report. (If you use fields in a layout for a report and the height is only enough to show the first line, you may not care how many carriage returns there are. But you may have a problem if you put the field into a block of text in a Merge field, because the text has multiple lines, and those carriage returns make it look mighty odd.)

Tip from
Rich

Beware the new line character when exporting. When exporting the information from a field containing carriage returns, FileMaker does not export the carriage returns as carriage returns but uses the vertical tab character instead. The reason is that the carriage return character stands as a separator between records. To avoid that confusion, FileMaker converts those to new line characters (the symbol that looks like an arrow bent back to the beginning of the next line). This still generates a new line, but does not trigger a new record. Whether this character is a problem or not depends on the receiving software.

Tip from
Rich

What if you have to restore carriage returns during export? Occasionally, people have wanted to preserve and export carriage returns, and in those cases we do the exports, and then use another application to search for the new line characters and replace those with carriage returns, or we use a FileMaker plug-in called File Toolbox from Protolight Software that allows us to do the search and replace on the exported file, cleaning it up with carriage returns. Here's the Protolight URL: `http://www.geocities.com/SiliconValley/Network/9327/index.html`

CHAPTER 8

CRAFTING THE USER INTERFACE

In this chapter

The Interface Is All There Is—for Users   214

Let Users' Tasks Shape Your Design   214

Decide Which Layouts to Focus On   215

Use Tabs for Convenience and Clarity   217

Use Menus if You Must   218

Combine the Best of Both Approaches   220

Decide on Your Default Views   220

Fit Information into a Single Record View   222

Distinguish Groups of Information by Their Functions   224

Prepare for Consistency   230

Make Data Entry Easy   237

Design Meaningful Buttons   238

Print the Reports the Users Expect   241

Test Prototypes and Get User Feedback   243

Use the Interface Prototyper   245

The Interface Is All There Is—for Users

The user interface is what people see and use. You may think of it as a cosmetic surface on the top of the real database, but for the user, the interface is all there is. In this chapter, we'll give you some tips on

- Starting with what users want to do—their tasks
- Organizing the layouts
- Deciding whether to use tabs, menus, or both as a way to move between layouts
- Squeezing information into a single record view
- Distinguishing groups of information by function
- Preparing for consistency
- Making data entry easy
- Designing meaningful buttons
- Preparing to print whatever users want
- Testing prototypes and getting feedback from users

You have now built solid data structures, which are critical. But the best data structures in the world cannot make up for a weak user interface. Users don't see data structures; they see the interface. Your interface influences the way they feel about your system, the way they use it, and the results they get from it. And over time, their interactions with your interface affect whether they choose to use your database properly, or engage in a war of resistance, dragging the data and you down with them.

So let's interface! Yes, the term is an ugly one. Originally, an interface was a plug. And the word still carries some of the overtones of fitting together a cable and a machine, or a computer and a printer. Unfortunately, users are human, and demand a lot more of an interface than two prongs and a ground.

So whenever you are building buttons, laying out fields, setting up navigation, or pondering what to put where, hark back to what the user may be thinking, feeling, and doing. Imagine the tasks the user may want to accomplish with the database, and revise it to help the person get that work done.

Let Users' Tasks Shape Your Design

As Albert Harum-Alvarez said at a recent FileMaker Developers conference, "Design that focuses on anything other than our clients' tasks is off the mark." Tasks are jobs of work that users do, not features of your database, not options in the software. Tasks are what people describe when you say, "What do you do here?" Build your interface to make it easy for people to carry out their work, and they'll be happy.

CASE STUDY: ONE SCREEN PER TASK

We have a client who has a very large Customers and Contacts database. The person we worked with was very much attuned to the work the staff needed to do, so instead of presenting one large screen full of information and forcing the user to figure out where to put things, we came up with a task list with buttons on the side. When the user had to enter particular information, the user could click a task, and be presented with a screen that contained fields relating to that task, plus a few more for context. When done with that task, the user could return to the full view of information. The users really appreciated the fact that somebody cared enough about their job to give them their own special screens, to make their lives easier. They responded by making sure that the data they entered was accurate and complete. This enthusiasm helped make the database a success.

Tip from
Jonathan

> Prepare a task list. You probably already have a good sense of the main tasks people want to do with your new database, based on all your conversations with the client and your work developing the ER diagram and other planning tools. But you should make up a list of tasks, in the user's own words, and post that over your computer as you work on laying out all those boxes, buttons, fields, forms, lists, pop-ups, and little icons the user will manipulate to get those tasks done. Users will move through what you create, taking paths you may never have imagined, backing and filling, following associations you do not anticipate. To simplify their experience, concentrate on their goals: What do they want to do, using this layout or this portal? From this point of view, your database is secondary, and their work is primary. The task list reminds you how things look from their side of the computer.

In molding the interface to your users' purposes, then, think like a visual designer, facing a blank electronic page. Often, a professional designer carves up the space into a grid, and then assigns major blocks of the space to serve different purposes: to announce content, to show what a product looks like, or to describe the product in text. Each block answers one question or a set of questions from the user; the design emerges as a response to the user's concerns.

Your user may come to your system with particular questions in mind, such as "What is the name of the contact person over at Shimer Shoes?" Or "How much do they owe us on that last order?" These questions tilt toward a particular task, such as cleaning up the overdue invoice situation, and the user has a lot of related questions, bits of advice, and worries to deal with, when approaching your interface. Think how helpful your layout will be if it responds to the user's major concerns by devoting big parts of the layout to those tasks, each in its own space, so the user can immediately see where to go to get answers to each question. That's user-centered design.

DECIDE WHICH LAYOUTS TO FOCUS ON

Your ER diagram can help you decide how to carve up the on-screen space. In task-oriented terms, your entities will become the focus for most of the work that people will be doing, so the entities deserve to get the major areas on the screen—whether those areas are individual layouts of their own or big chunks of a single layout. These are the places where people will do most of their data entry and editing. Smaller and less significant areas may show parts of the data from that file or related files, or allow data to be entered in children of those entities, through portals. In this way, your layout responds to the preoccupations of the users—reflecting the hierarchy of their concerns and the most critical tasks they have to accomplish.

In our sample Invoicing system, for instance, the major entities are invoices, customers, products, and payments. The major entities are the keys to the business, and, therefore, they form a set of frequently used layouts. As an interface designer, then, you want entities front and center, and you want to make it easy for users to move from one to another.

But there may be minor entities, too, lesser beings such as code tables with departments and department codes, or state names and their abbreviations. Users have to be able to get to those entities sometimes, but such entities are not going to be used a lot. So you may need ways for users to jump between major and minor entities without getting confused.

And there are usually some minor areas within a major entity. For example, you might have a student with information about the on-campus address, home address, and clubs. You might put each of those on a different area within your student layout, because each is a minor topic within the information about the student. Or you could have all the less important information show up in one area, with different info appearing when the user presses a different button. In Invoices, for instance, we have a special area that handles four activities: dealing with payments, making notes, identifying the customer for an invoice, and adding products to the invoice. Our goal in having those sections come and go is to make the users feel they have not gone anywhere else when switching from one to another, although we, as developers, know that we are swapping one layout for another. Each layout has the same background, and we just switch the foreground box. Users believe they are looking at the same layout, exploring it, and bringing one aspect or another to the surface. But we, as developers, have to work very hard to hold the background steady throughout, to achieve that illusion of perceptual stability, as Bruce Tognazzini, interface guru, calls it. Users prefer to stay in the same place and explore. From their point of view, they are not going anywhere, even if, in reality, you are tossing one layout after another at them.

Tip from
Rich

Decide whether to allow users to navigate from child to parent and back and forth. In some situations, you want to switch users to the child files to do data entry when they are creating a new record, so they do not overlook some fields (as they might if you allowed them to create new records in a portal that showed, say, only three of ten fields). But consider carefully whether you want to show the child records directly. In some circumstances, you may decide you only want to give users access to them through a portal. For instance, in the invoicing system on our CD, on the invoice, there is a portal for invoice line items, and although users can get to the Line Items file, it is not part of the normal interface; it is more of a hidden feature. There is no tab for Line Items. Hence, Line Items is mostly off limits unless a user happens to have an intense reason to go there. You can password protect the child files if you decide to keep them off limits. Make sure you see a firm benefit to showing the child files.

→For more on using passwords to protect your files, **see** Chapter 16, "Integrating FileMaker, Expanding Its Reach," **p. 497.**

You may start out thinking in terms of creating one layout for each major and minor entity, and then decide you want to create an interface that pulls a lot of those together in what looks like a single layout, from the user's perspective. If as a developer you were to look behind the curtain at the layouts that users are exposed to in the invoicing database, you would find that there are five layouts for Invoices, two for Customers, two for Products, and two for Payments. To break that down, in Invoices, there are four single-record views (dealing with payments, notes, setting the customer, and adding products) so two deal with data and two add functionality. Then Customers, Products, and Payments, each have one layout showing a single-record view. Plus, the four files each carry a list view. (We are not considering the many layouts that users never see, because they are part of the printing process, or for automation.)

Tip from
Rich

> Make sure that you hide layouts you don't want users to see. You may set up some layouts for your own convenience, like scratch sheets, such as code tables, bridge files, or layouts you only display by scripting, for finds on fields you otherwise prevent users from entering or editing. Remember, choose Layout, Set Layouts Order, and uncheck these in the dialog, so they will not be shown in the user's list of layouts.

USE TABS FOR CONVENIENCE AND CLARITY

Early on, you have to decide how to allow users to navigate from one major area to another. There are many methods, but the two most common are tabs and menus.

In a tabbed interface, the major areas of focus tend to get their own tabs, so these subjects are only one click away. From a user's point of view, the set of tabs all live within the same space. Clicking one tab and then another, the user explores that space without apparently going anywhere. That stability is reassuring. The tabs also offer a visual representation of the major entities, a constant reminder of what else is available in the database, and a model of the contents. The implication is that you can get to all your data from this one location (the space enclosing the entire set of tabs). Because tabs echo physical objects people know how to use, the images also communicate how to use the interface; each tab is sitting there whispering, "Click me!"

With a tabbed interface, you have to decide what data to show when users go from one tab to another. If a user was looking at a customer, and clicked Overdue Bills, would the user expect to see that customer's late bills, a list of overdue bills found the last time someone used the system, or a list of all overdue bills? To decide, you have to know what your users usually do—that is, which task they do most often. Generally, when users are working with a set of tabs, they think of the set as a unit, and therefore like to see the customer's late bills. Tabs imply that the work flows from one to another seamlessly.

> **Tip from**
> *Rich*
>
> Use one row of tabs, not two. If you give yourself two rows of tabs, your users can go to any major area or minor area with a single click. But you sacrifice a lot of screen real estate for that kind of navigation. And you face an even more complicated question of what data to show when someone clicks a tab. If you have, for example, tabs for four major areas, each with five minor areas behind it, there are 20 areas someone can go to in a click or two. How can you decide what kind of data to show when a user may be coming from 19 different take-off spots? Keeping everything visible is a commendable goal, but in many cases, the user's workflow is much simpler, and he does not need to make so many jumps. The actual work the users do should help you decide whether you really need two rows of tabs. Usually, you don't.

> **Tip from**
> *Rich*
>
> If you insist on two rows of tabs, make one for lists and the other for single records. The plus is that the user can now get to any list in a single click rather than two clicks. But the downside is the tangle of multiple rows of tabs, and the potential confusion if you move the current tab forward to indicate it is the one someone is working on. Of course, you could follow Web conventions, and leave all the tabs in the same location, and just highlight the one selected. This is not perfect because people expect the tab to extend right down into the layout, as it would on paper, but the highlighting at least indicates where the user has landed.
>
> Clicking a tab that was in the back row rearranges everything to bring that tab forward, leaving the user with a queasy feeling that all is not stable in tabland.

USE MENUS IF YOU MUST

Another approach would be to have a main menu, completely away from the data, and then allow people to go from the menu to each major entity. For instance, the Invoices database could have displayed just the options for Invoices, Customers, Products, and Payments on the first page. In that situation, if a user clicked Invoices, the Invoice information would show up, with one of the minor areas visible, but the user could not see the other aspects of the transaction, such as customers, products, and payments. Those other aspects come to seem divorced from the layout the user is on—different departments, rather than different perspectives on the problem the user is currently working on. To switch, the user returns to the menu, leaving the work in progress, makes a choice, goes somewhere else, finds a fact, goes back to the menu, and picks the original layout again. This kind of click-click-click movement may cause the user to lose focus.

With a menu system, you face the question of relevance from a different point of view: The menu suggests that these areas are distinct, so now if the user looks at a customer, and then switches to an invoice, should that invoice reflect that customer, the last invoice examined, or a list of all invoices? (In a menu environment, the user often encounters a list, and must choose the relevant invoice to get on with the work). By contrast, with a tabbed interface, the main menu approach means that after a user chooses a topic, the other options disappear from view, and the person has to go back to the main menu (or a pop-up or dropdown version of the menu) to switch to another major area, such as Customers; hence there is no visual mnemonic, no reminder of the basic organization of the database.

> **Caution**
>
> Remember that a main menu means users are two clicks away from their data, rather than one.

The main menu should contain a list of all the layouts you want people to see and use. Each layout is a button with a name the user can understand. Behind the button lies a script, which you can use to adjust the Print Setup, do any necessary sorts and searches, and run any calculations and verifications you want, before displaying the layout.

If you have a few dozen layouts, consider displaying a menu with two levels (see Figure 8.1). In this way you unveil the full structure of your database in one place, allowing the user to make quick comparisons and pick the right layout. In this situation, users make fewer mistakes, in part because they come to understand what all their options are, and don't have to make psychic guesses as to what may lie below a particular top-level button.

Figure 8.1
Multiple levels of menus let users choose correctly, and go where they want to go faster.

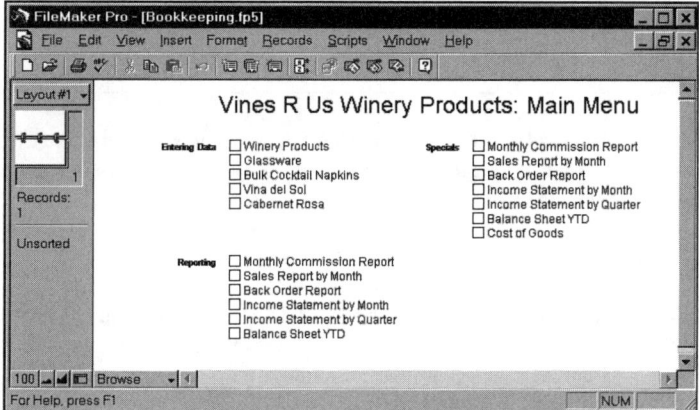

CASE STUDY: MAKING A LAYOUT TO MATCH A USER'S PAPER FORM

We were at a new customer's office the other day, a private school with a rigorous admission policy, which means they ask parents to provide a lot of information up front. Years ago, the school had bought an off-the-shelf program described as an admissions package, but it was not built from scratch for them. Basically, someone had written this program for a client, and re-marketed it. Our customer's major complaint was that their school wanted to enter information the way they had collected it, all in one screen, but instead, they had to go to 17 different screens. When we said we could build a form that looked just like their paper form, and they could enter all the data in one place, that was worth the whole cost of the database right there. That's what we mean when we say that workflow should determine the number and the content of your layouts.

Combine the Best of Both Approaches

If you feel torn between the tabbed interface and menus, consider a compromise. In a mixed approach, you might use a group of buttons to act as a menu along the left or bottom, taking people to the major areas. Once there, the user could click on tabs to move through the minor areas within each section.

The more areas you have to offer, the more you ought to consider a mixed approach. With a tabbed interface, there are limits on the number of tabs you can put into a single row, particularly if some of the names are long. So what about a second row of tabs? If you look at some Web sites, or some dialog boxes in Microsoft, options appear in multiple rows of tabs, which can get confusing. When you click on a back tab, that whole row jumps to the front, changing the stable arrangement, shuffling tabs. So if you have a dozen or more areas of focus, you may need to think about going to a mixed metaphor, where you have those dozen buttons on the left, and then when you click on those, you get its set of tabs.

Of course, if your system is even more complicated, and you generate more than a hundred files, you may want to go to a main menu with submenus. If so, try to offer the submenus on the same layout as the main menu, so that someone can explore the entire main menu without leaving. This reassures people, gives them a firmer model of the structure of your database, and increases the likelihood they will click their way to the layout they really want to see.

Tip from Rich	You can have more than 50 files. Yes, we know a FileMaker Pro client can only have 50 files open at a time, but if you are careful to close some files when not needed, you can use more than 50 files.
Tip from Rich	Avoid welcome screens. These just delay users who want to get to work. A database is not a book, so you don't need to list trademarks, put up the company logo, post a disclaimer from the legal department, or ramble on with a phony greeting.
Tip from Rich	If your client insists on a splash screen at the beginning, make it go away fast. Don't leave the darn thing staring at the user. Time it out, or include a very visible button to get rid of it, so that impatient users can get past that beautiful colored logo (and confidentiality agreement) the boss likes so much.

Decide on Your Default Views

After you decide on an interface taking people to various layouts, you must decide exactly what data will appear in those layouts when folks arrive. For instance, should you offer a list of all records, or a single record? And if you decide on a single record, should that be the first record, a random record, the last record viewed, or a record that relates to the data the user was just working on over on some other layout?

To give you an idea how tangled this issue can get, imagine starting off with the idea that whenever someone arrives at a layout in a tabbed interface, you will give them a list of all records in that database. And to be consistent, you decide that anytime anyone goes to a new layout, you will display a list. Okay, so far. But now think about the person working on a particular invoice, in single record view, who wants to know more about a particular product. Clicking on the Products tab provides a list. So the user scrolls down, finds the product, and opens it to a single record view. Having read about the product, the user decides to go back to the invoice. Clicking the Invoices tab, though, displays a list. The user loses focus, and must scroll down, recall the right invoice, and click it to get back to the work at hand. Tedious and annoying.

Three key rules of database interfacing are the following:

- **Key Rule #1:** When a user presses a button, it should always take the user to the same place. So if Stella has been working in a particular record under the Customers tab, and goes to Invoices to look at something, and then clicks Customers, the record she was looking at should come up again. No surprises, even if they seem like a convenience in the abstract.

- **Key Rule #2**: Follow the user's natural chain of association or thought. When Uma is working on a particular invoice, she probably wants to explore that customer, those products, and those payments. She should be able to switch to that individual's customer record, not a list of every customer. With the kind of investigation Uma may have in mind, picking from a list takes more time.

- **Key Rule #3:** If users set something up in one tab, they are entitled to go back to it, without our interfering, even if we think we know best.

CASE STUDY: CLICKING AN INVOICE

In our sample invoicing file, if a user clicks on Invoices, where should we take the person? Our first thought was that we should take them to an invoice. Then we got clever. Well, we said, we think we know what the user would really want to do here. If the user is coming from the Payments file and clicks the Invoices tab, then we will go to the invoice referring to that payment. But what if a user just wanted to go back to the invoice she was looking at before? Or let's say the user is in the Customers file and looking at a customer, and clicks invoice—some might think we ought to take the user to the invoices for that customer. But which one? Of course, the user might just want to go back to an invoice he was looking at before. In that case, we might bring him to the invoice list. If the customer has only one record, we could go to the single record view, showing that invoice. And if the customer has no invoices, we could go to the list and find all. But are the users going to recognize what we are doing, and why, when we react differently in different circumstances? Or are users just going to fear that if they click this button, they could end up in three different places? Probably. Best rule of thumb: If a user has done some work in one layout or tab, leave that work untouched, and if the user returns to that tab, show the work as the user left it.

Tip from
Rich

Be careful of confusing the user by swapping found sets. When you automate reporting through scripts, taking information from both parent and child files, you may want to produce the report from the child because that gives you more flexibility. But when the user presses a report button in the parent file, the user may believe the report is coming from the parent file, but in fact, very often, the magic of scripting produces the report by going over to the child file and finding a set of records within the child file without telling the user. Now if the user asks for a report based on the found set of records in front of him in the parent file, you may have to change the found set of records over in the child file to turn out the report. But when you change the found set of records, the user may well get confused. If your reporting script is going to disturb a found set, then devote part of the script to capturing the IDs of all the current found records in the child file before you change the found set of records in the child file; then, after the report has been produced, go back to that found set.

→ For more details on printing a report from the child file, **see** "Printing from the Child," **p. 363**.

Tip from
Rich

Beware of throwing away the current record during a sort. In our data entry and list views in the Invoicing system, users can sort records. When a user requests a sort, though, FileMaker loses track of whatever record the user was looking at. Hence, after the sort, the user is looking at whatever record ends up as the first one in the sort. Therefore, before doing the sort, capture the ID of the current record, and, after the sort, give the user a message saying the records have been sorted, but be sure you return to the original record.

Fit Information into a Single Record View

Although lists present some problems of sizing, the single record is where folks do most of their work, and that demands a lot of information. In the single record view, you face the question: Is there room to fit all the information on a single screen or not? On the Invoices tab in our sample invoicing system, the answer was no; with the other tabs, yes.

On screens that won't quite encompass all the data, you have to decide what data is important to have around all the time, and what data can be phased in and out, displayed, and then hidden.

In confronting the issue of what will fit, you also face the issue of scrolling. FileMaker allows a 110" × 110" layout. So you might say, what do you mean you don't have room? Well, our experience indicates that users don't like to scroll, and if you force them to scroll, they often get confused. Imagine scrolling down ten feet and then discovering you still have to scroll almost ten feet to the right to find what you want!

Tip from
Rich

Restrain the dimensions of your layout. Although FileMaker allows you to create a layout that is 110"×110", there are limits on how much of that layout you can print. The number and size of the pages depend on interacting options like those in Page Setup (orientation, margins), but when you print, only the leftmost set of pages will emerge. You can print 110" vertically, but not more than a landscape version of your page horizontally (a little less than 11" wide depending on your printer and setup).

CASE STUDY: WHAT YOU DON'T SEE...

We were taking a test that was delivered through a FileMaker database designed on a Macintosh, but displayed on both Mac and Windows machines. We were presented with one question at a time, with multiple choices—that is, four to six possible answers. We had to get the right answer before moving on to the next question. On the Windows machines, the FileMaker option to show the status bar was enabled, taking up about $\frac{3}{8}$ of an inch at the bottom of the screen. On a couple of questions where there were lots of possible answers, the status bar covered up the right answer. One person taking the test tried each of the answers he could see, but because they were all incorrect, he couldn't move on, because he still had not clicked the right answer. He finally noticed the scroll bar, and scrolled down to find the right answer, at which point he yelled in fury. Like people who rarely go below the fold in Web pages, he had assumed that he could see everything available, and did not think of looking over at the scroll bar. Out of sight is often out of mind. So we recommend designing for the real estate available within the screens of regular users. If you can't fit the information comfortably, then you may need to split it up.

Tip from
Rich

Start with a firm idea of the screen sizes you are building for. If there are several sizes, you need to build for the most common because then no one will have to scroll.

CASE STUDY: EQUIPMENT COUNTS

Make sure how much real estate you have to work with. We had a manager who was sure everyone had an 800×600 screen, and we built the system to that spec. But the president had an old portable computer that had a 640×480 display, and he kept wondering why he had to keep scrolling up and down. It was cheaper for them to buy him a new portable computer than to have us redesign the system. Don't forget antiques, handhelds, and laptops when you survey.

CASE STUDY: LETTING ACTUAL USE DETERMINE SIZE

You may need to consider actual tasks to decide on layout sizes. When we ran use studies in one company, we discovered that people in the sales group just looked up a name or address, using an old 640×480 screen, but the managers and administrators had 19" screens set to 1024×768 pixels. Because administrators had to see lots of aspects of the information at the same time, we decided to create two sets of screens, one for sales folks and another for administrators. When people logged in, we figured out from their passwords whether they were in sales or administration, and then we asked which tasks they wanted to perform, and when they chose one, took them straight to that screen, big or small.

Unfold Minor Information Gradually

You may not have enough room on the screen to show every little detail about an entity. Within a single box in the Invoices database, we offer buttons to let users switch between different kinds of information and functionality. Why not show all this right away? In our sample file, the Invoices screen is already very busy. And given the way that people are accustomed to entering information into an invoice, we decided not to segment the data entry into a series of different layouts, with one for the customer, say, and another for the products, and another for payments. We did see some priorities. Certain information has to be always visible, such as the name and contact information about the customer, line items, subtotals, shipping, taxes, and the grand total. But trailing behind the invoice come other items people might like to look up, but probably do not need to look at during data entry. So we made those subsets of the major invoice entity, in part because of limitations on real estate. If every user had 1600×1200 pixel 21" screens, we could have displayed it all. But here we limited ourselves to what would fit in an average user's 800×600 pixel screen.

To reveal additional information, you can insert a box that changes, as in the Invoices database, or you can go to other screens or forms. The first question is How do you split up the info? In a tabbed interface, you could think of this as creating tabs within tabs. What info do I want users to see all the time, and what information can I switch in and out when a user clicks a button? This decision turns out to be relatively easy to make because the information tends to fall into several groupings, and as soon as you identify what those groups are, you can decide which one to keep visible all the time, and which to toggle in and out.

Distinguish Groups of Information by Their Functions

Each group of information has its own purpose, such as preserving contact information about a customer or providing details about each product ordered in an invoice. From the user's point of view, all the parts of an information group hang together, so users like to see all of these fields in one location, apart from others. Visual isolation reinforces that this information belongs together, and doesn't overlap the content of other fields.

The Main Idea

Give each group of information its own area. If you are building a box to contain a series of less important entities, then one replaces another, in that frame; for instance, notes replace payments information, and then something else replaces notes. For information that will always be visible, separate one group from the others by white space (best), colored backgrounds (OK), patterns (distracting), or lines (dangerous, because too many lines form a grid that seems to stand between the user and the information, like bars on a window). The key is that you use some low-key way to differentiate each information group, so a user can skip from one to the other intelligently.

The interface of the Invoices tab in our sample file is busier than we would like, because we felt we had to put all these groups of information onto the same layout. The overwhelming bulk of the space is taken up by line items. If we had put those on the left side of the layout, they would overwhelm everything else. When the user clicks the New button on the Invoices tab, she is asked to set a customer, so we put that information in the upper left corner, where Westerners habitually start reading. Once she clicks a customer, she is asked to pick a product, and that is the information in the upper right corner, or secondary position. Hence, our layout follows the way Westerners read—that is, from the top left to the top right, and down. And we have organized the actions in that sequence. (By contrast, many Japanese manuals organize tables according to their natural reading sequence, so category titles often show up on the right, with facts spreading off to the left.) Again, invoice totals "naturally" drop to the bottom, where most of our users expect summaries from tables, like addition problems in school. We also segregated the buttons on the screen. The buttons along the top are for navigation. The buttons at the bottom perform actions. It's confusing enough to have a lot of buttons, but even more crazy if you mix functionality with movement.

Tip from
Rich

For some good advice on user interface, visit the Microsoft site at http://msdn.microsoft.com/ui/.

Once we had decided where customers and line items would fit, with customers taking the primary position, and line items taking up the bulk of the screen, we saw that everything else had to fit around those areas. Now, all the space we had left was in the lower left-hand corner. We wanted to add a space for notes and information on payments, but there was not room for both of those at the same time. We decided we could switch those back and forth, swapping them in and out of a box, because they were less important and less frequently consulted than the major data groups on the layout.

Plus, there were two kinds of functionality we wanted to add to the layout—setting a customer and adding a product. A lot of our automation can be performed with a click of a button or a selection from a single menu. But in other cases, automation tends to take up a lot of screen real estate. If you don't perform these automated tasks very often, you should switch them in and out, rather than leaving them gathering dust on the layout. Switching in and out is appealing because it does not force the user to leave the focus of his work, and, if it is performed only occasionally, why dedicate part of the screen to it for all eternity? So we added two more buttons bringing up information within the box at the lower left corner of the Invoices tab.

SETTING A CUSTOMER

The company might have hundreds or thousands of customers. Originally, we put customers into a pop-up list that showed the name and ID of each customer, but that kind of list loses value when you get beyond a few dozen, because as the names zip past, a user can easily miss the customer in the blur. So we sought another way to help the user find a customer. We chose to let the user see through a portal all the customers, or a subset of the customers. The user can click a button from A to Z to show all customers whose personal or company names have a word that begins with that letter, or, going a step farther, a user can type in several letters, to further filter the list. In this case, we chose to consider "customer" as a combination of Contact Name and Company Name. With this device, we have a way for a user to select a customer from an enormous list without having to remember or key in complex customer codes, last names, or critical data, and without having to scroll through all the other customers.

Adding a product to the invoice raises the same challenge. We could have had Product IDs as a pop-up list, but once you have more than a few dozen products, you may overwhelm your users. So we chose a different method, in the Add Products portion of the page. There, the user chooses a product category from a set of radio buttons, and then is presented with a smaller list of products from that category. Once again, when the user clicks on the product, the item is added automatically to the invoice, and the cursor is moved to the Quantity field, because that is the next piece of information most users want to enter.

ADD TEXT TO CLARIFY THE PURPOSE OF LAYOUTS AND AREAS

Titles, headings, and labels help users figure out where they are and what they are looking at. You can't assume that someone will know. Even if you train the team when you turn over the database, some people forget, others only use the database occasionally, and new hires come into the database without any training. So, design for these users, and even those who use your database for hours every day will appreciate the signposts you place on your layouts and over each major area.

The text doesn't have to be gigantic, but it should probably rise to the top of the layout. Consider identifying the contents of each work area within the layout, too, particularly if some areas start off empty. For instance, if you have an area for finding a customer to insert into an invoice, the fields will not start out with any values because the customer needs to pick a letter, so you can offer names beginning with that letter, or All, for all of them. A simple label such as "show" will clarify what the blank area is for, as seen in Figure 8.2.

CONSISTENCY ONLY GOES SO FAR

As a general rule, make navigation elements such as buttons, tabs, and menu items work the same way every time. If a button takes your user to Location A the first time, make sure that button always takes the user to Location A from then on. In this way, you reassure the users; they gain confidence moving around your system. But recognize that there may be times when the actual content of the target location must change.

DISTINGUISH GROUPS OF INFORMATION BY THEIR FUNCTIONS 227

Figure 8.2
Labels such as "show" tell people what will happen if they click and go.

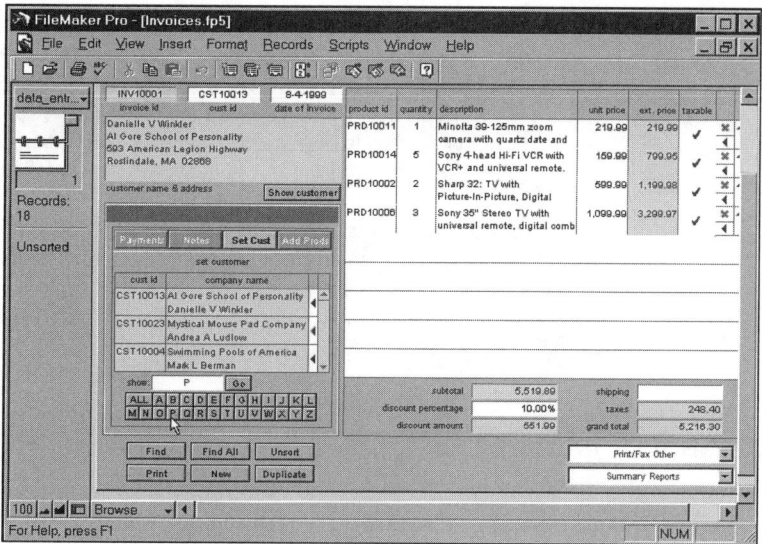

CASE STUDY: BE WILLING TO COMPROMISE

In creating the sample Invoices database, we started out with the four tabs you see now—invoices, customers, products, and payments—and each of those takes the user to a single record view, every time. But we were also looking for a way to give users access to lists of these same entities. We tried putting a list button inside the tab layout. But every other button inside the layout led to actions (such as searches), not navigation. So we created a last tab, offering a list of whatever item the person was viewing at the time, so if a user were looking at a single record of a customer, the list tab would offer a list of customers. The tab limits the user to whatever she was working on, but it is a way to dig deeper within that area. Problem: This context-sensitive tab always brings you to a list, but which list depends on the tab you have been looking at. Having a tab that changes its contents is inconsistent and impure, but we think it will probably be understandable for users after a while. The novelist Salmon Rushdie says that the biggest danger in the 20th century is movements demanding that we all should be pure, and we agree. A little dirt and grease makes the interface run smoothly.

Tip from
Rich

Don't expect a perfect solution. Any interface that works is a compromise. There isn't a right answer; instead, you make a series of choices, reflecting priorities, habits, and taste. You keep revising your design as you go as you learn more about your users and the subtle conflicts that lie below the surface of your data structures.

Tip from
Rich

Sometimes, the fewer choices you offer the user, the simpler it is to use. We considered a second row of tabs offering lists of each entity, behind the row of tabs offering single-record views of the same entities. Speedy access, yes, but also possibly confusing. Some users would, we think, be unsure whether they were going to a list of invoices or a particular invoice. Also, we have observed that users rarely jump from one task area to a list of other task objects; instead, they tend to pursue the specific ones mentioned in the current layout. The list, then, is always subordinate to data entry and editing.

> **Tip from**
> *Rich*
>
> The best peer review takes place in person, but after you get advice, you have to make your own decisions. In building the Invoicing files, we asked for and got feedback from a number of people, all of whom are topnotch professional developers. But the advice we got often differed from person to person. Person A liked what Person B disliked, so we got conflicting advice. There are certainly some fundamental rules to follow in interface, but subjectivity and taste enter in. You have to make up your own mind, finally. The most interesting and valuable sessions reviewing the files were with the Support Group team, because we could sit around and hear each other's feedback, so that a negotiation went on, and we could try things live, saying, "Will this approach resolve this issue, or not?" In this kind of discussion, we often ended up with a better result, because at the end everyone could look at the result, and nod, "Yes, that will do it!"

YES, YOU SHOULD INCLUDE LISTS

A benefit of the list layout is that the list shows multiple records in the spreadsheet grid of rows and columns. If you put the most important fields on that list (the ones they think are important), it becomes a convenient mechanism for their doing some quick scans, searches, and sorts (in ways that you can't predict, too). For example, the invoice list lets users slice and dice the data, playing what if and exploring the data in ways that go beyond the greenbar reports based on what some VP wanted to know five years ago.

> **Tip from**
> *Rich*
>
> Don't let users edit the fields in a list. When you let users edit data in multi-records view, they are likely to get off by one record and enter the wrong data. The list is not for entry. It is for querying, sorting, and reviewing. Another reason to block data entry: Often, the list does not show every field that appears in a single record view, so users may tend to leave out key information.

> **Tip from**
> *Rich*
>
> If the data comes in as a list, allow users to enter data the same way. Sometimes we do build list layouts for data entry, when users found it awkward or disorienting to enter it in a form (a single record view). So there are situations where you might do a list layout for data entry, but only when driven by a use case.

MAKE YOUR OWN SORT BUTTONS

In most databases, you will want to lock users out of the menus via passwords, so they do not change field definitions or layouts. If users get access to regular menus, they can easily violate referential integrity. But when you keep users out of the menus, the users cannot get to the Sort command under Mode. So you have to give the user buttons to let them handle sorting. Generally, you may want to include buttons in the heading portion of any list, so users can sort the records by the values in that column. In the sample file Invoices, we have included an icon of blue bars as a Sort button.

> **Tip from**
> *Rich*
>
> **Offer alternatives.** If your use cases indicate that the users sometimes want to sort in reverse order, set the button up so that if a user presses Alt on a PC or Option on a Mac, you sort in descending order rather than ascending order.

USE COLOR AND GRAPHICS TO INDICATE FUNCTIONALITY

In New Mexico and Massachusetts, the states where we live, a red light indicates that all drivers should accelerate through the intersection. But in other parts of the country, red means stop, or at least, watch out! We mention this because you should use color when offering cautionary feedback if the user could destroy data by mistake. For instance, in the invoices and payments lists, we offer red x's to allow users to delete records. Click an x, and we highlight the whole record, indicating this is what you are about to delete. We want to warn people they are about to eliminate this highlighted record, so they can make sure they are deleting the right one. And we display a message to warn that the deletion will be permanent, and that the record of the payment actually is a related record. The red x indicates danger, here.

Use graphics but do so lightly. Originally, we had the terms "Taxable" and "Not taxable" next to line items. Then we thought, why not use a graphic instead? First, we created a check box (a text field) to show whether an item was taxable, but that was not very dramatic; the x inside looked somewhat pale, as if it had faded. So we switched to a blue check mark, which is much more visible. Actually, the check mark was a Calculation field with a container result (the image of the check mark). The calculation says if the value in the field Taxable equals "taxable," then this Calculation field should equal a global container field that has a little blue check mark in it. The check mark is just a bitmap.

Colors can help make items stand out, and they can define functional areas and layers, but for larger areas, we find a set of grays can do the job without getting so interesting that the user shifts attention from the actual values to the colors. With the gray background, small blue and red icons stand out. In the Invoices sample file, six layers are suggested, modestly, with the grays from the background to the white in front, with blues and reds in the foreground.

> **Tip from**
> *Rich*
>
> **Use colors with restraint.** Colors attract the eye, particularly when the colored button is mixed in with other elements, so you can use color in little buttons you want the user to notice (like the blue triangles in the Invoicing system) or to signal negative numbers (in the red), but avoid whole swatches of color and, even though it is tempting to give every single item a different color, don't make a Times Square of bright lights. Too many colors become interesting in themselves, distracting people from the content of their work. Another valid use of color: colored backgrounds can help you distinguish one area from another without lines. Just make sure that your colored backgrounds do not overwhelm the foreground text or put someone's eye out.

Prepare for Consistency

Consistency is reassuring to users. When a set of labels look alike, from one layout to the next, the user feels relief; when the same field looks the same, it must be the same. Remember that although you know exactly what the object is, users have some doubt when they move from one layout to another, or dip into the database after several weeks away.

The poet John Keats argued that a foolish consistency is the hobgoblin of little minds. Yes, indeed, when it's arbitrary. But here consistency has a real purpose: making work a little simpler for users, moment to moment. Consistency in arrangement, font, size, color, line weight, and so on, means fewer stray thoughts raised in the user's mind, less confusion, and less likelihood of error.

Make Your Layouts Look Stable

Users prefer staying in one place and exploring. They do not like going from one place to another to another. So even when you are displaying a series of layouts, make them appear to be the same one staying put, while a little thing changes within. For instance, in the Invoices tab, when a user clicks a button for payments, notes, setting the customer, or adding products, the user sees the little box on the left change, but everything else remains the same. The user feels, "I have not gone anywhere." But, in fact, the whole invoice has been redrawn, and the user is actually looking at a different layout (one that looks exactly like the last one, with the exception of the little box area). To maintain this illusion, we have to make absolutely sure that each layout in a set of layouts looks the same, and that there is no little pixel-jiggle as we move from one layout to the next.

> **Tip from**
> *Rich*
>
> Use the Size palette for exact positioning, pixel by pixel. When you are trying to position layout objects precisely, right down to the pixel, choose Object Size on the View menu, and watch the palette because it shows the size and position of the object you are moving. Often, we click an object to see its position, and then go to a different object, perhaps even on another layout, to make sure it is in exactly the same position. Use pixels as the unit of measurement, to be precise. To change the unit of measurement, go to the Size palette, where, to the right of the number, you see the choices (inches, centimeters, or pixels). Just click one.

Set the Default Formatting for Text and Graphics

When you hunker down to turning out a bunch of layouts, set the defaults before you work, so that you end up with a consistent look to all your fields, labels, and graphics. You may have noticed how the text tool changed from plain text to bold, without your quite knowing why. Here are four ways that you can set the default attributes:

- Make sure that no object is selected and then modify a text, number, date, time, or graphic format. Those changes become the defaults.
- Create a new object on the layout and make formatting changes to it immediately (before deselecting the object). Those formats become the defaults. Evidently,

FileMaker imagines that the object is the first of a series of objects you'll want to look alike. (This doesn't work if you paste an object into the layout.)

- If you already have an object such as a field with the formatting you want as a standard, press Control in Windows or Command on the Mac at the same time as you click the object. FileMaker takes the object as an example of what you want.

COMMON MISTAKE: CHANGING THE DEFAULTS BY ACCIDENT

If you happen to change a format while no object is selected, because you intend to format the next object that way, you have inadvertently also reset the defaults. Ditto for formatting a new object the moment you create it. If you are not sure what has happened, reset the defaults, just to be sure.

Limit the number of fonts and sizes to avoid jazzy and jumpy layouts like those shown in Figure 8.3. Two fonts in a few sizes should be enough. For instance, you might use a sans-serif font such as Arial or Helvetica in 9 points for data, 10 points for button names, and 12 points for column headings. Avoid any fonts that your users might not have.

Figure 8.3
Too many fonts spoil the layout. Two fonts, or one font in several sizes, will usually be enough.

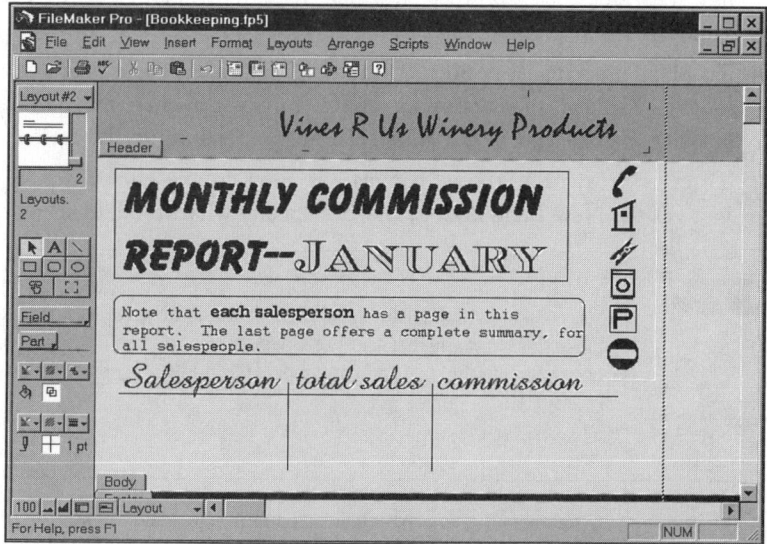

Tip from
Jonathan

Limit your emphasis to key terms. Leave your data in plain text and use boldfacing for column headings and labels only. Do not use italics on-screen, because the screen makes these tilted letters fuzzy and hard to read. In general, avoid putting anything in all-capital letters because caps make all words the same general shape, forcing folks to read letter by letter rather than "grokking" the word from the outline of its shape.

| Tip from Jonathan | Never, never use white letters on a black background. The screen renders these fuzzy and difficult to make out. |

| Tip from Rich | For a readable cross-platform font, try Verdana font. |

LET FILEMAKER HELP YOU KEEP FORMATS CONSISTENT

When you have a series of layouts that include the same block of fields, images, or text, you should copy and paste rather than creating each layout from scratch. Similarly, if you are placing the same field, text, button, or graphic in several layouts, you should rely on cloning, copy, or duplicating to ensure that the second, third, and fourth version look just like the first.

- **To clone a field's size and formatting**, hold down the Control key in Windows or the Option key on the Mac at the same time as you click the field; then drag the field to a new location. You're now asked which field you want, and when you choose, it gets the same size and format as the original. (Hold down Shift to constrain placement.)
- **To place a series of copies of one original**, select the object and choose Duplicate. Get the duplicate object exactly where you want it; then choose Duplicate again to have another copy placed in the same relationship, extending the series.
- **To copy most of a layout**, duplicate it; then double-click any field you need to change; you get the New Field dialog, and can specify what the field should be.

| Caution | You can't copy and paste layout parts. It would be great, at times, to be able to just say "Take this whole header and put it over here." You can't. Instead, you have to select all the objects within the part and copy those. (Or duplicate the whole layout, and then make changes.) |

| Tip from Rich | If you need a graphically challenging form, create it in a drawing program, copy and paste it into your layout, and lay fields on top. In this way you get the look of the original, using the rich palette of tools in a real graphics program, and the fields just fit into it. Also, ask the customer staff if they already have the form in electronic format, to avoid wasting your time reconstructing it. |

| Tip from Rich | To keep using any tool over and over, start by double-clicking. The icon turns black, and you can keep using the tool until you want to stop. To go back to the regular pointer, click it, or press Enter. By the way, there is also a preference called Always Lock Layout Tools, which you can set under Edit, Preferences, Application Preferences, on the Layout tab. |

Make Objects Line Up Consistently

Your users notice when an object gets out of alignment. Even a one-pixel shift is enough to make the object stick out oddly. Why does this make a difference? The object draws attention to itself, like a sore tooth. People get distracted; some get downright annoyed. If you haven't listened to people rant and rave about a label that doesn't end up flush left like the others, or complain about a field that begins just a few pixels to the right of the others in the stack, then you will ignore this as you create. But if you have experienced the way users obsess about issues like this, you will take the time to line objects up neatly in the first place. (Coming back later and re-jiggering them all is a pain.)

CASE STUDY: WHAT CLIENTS PERCEIVE

We developed a rough prototype for our clients at an architectural firm. We wanted to know whether the general layout was working. The clients never got to that point. They noticed that the First Name field was six pixels away from the Last Name field, whereas the State field was only four pixels from the ZIP code field. Yeah, yeah, we said, we'll fix that, but what do you think of the layout in general? We couldn't get past the misalignments. We had to go back, straighten everything out, and use a grid to pass their initial review. Of course, in a visual profession, they could spot a misaligned brick at a hundred yards, so our casual approach was particularly offensive to this team.

The ideal alignment goes something like this:

- All text labels in a stack start or end at the same place horizontally.
- The label text itself has the same baseline as the text within the fields.
- Related horizontal or vertical lines run parallel, the same distance.
- Numbers line upon their decimal points.
- The distance remains constant between objects in a series.
- The whitespace between groupings is about the same width throughout, so that the groups themselves seem to line up.

In reality, you cannot always line objects up so neatly. But to get closer to the ideal, use the T-Square and grid, the Align command, arrow keys, the Shift key, text baselines, and the Size window for guidance.

The T-Square and Grid

Like the string on an architect's drafting board, the horizontal and vertical lines of the T-Square help you see whether a series of objects are lined up correctly (see Figure 8.4). Unlike the string, the T-Square lines are normally magnetized, so any nearby object will snap to them. As you drag an object past a vertical line, one side will jump to the line, then the center will, and finally the other side will adhere to the line. On the horizontal line, an object stops at the top, center, and bottom. To release the magnetism, hold down Control on the PC or Option on the Mac while moving the object.

Figure 8.4
The lines of the T-Square help you align objects such as these fields.

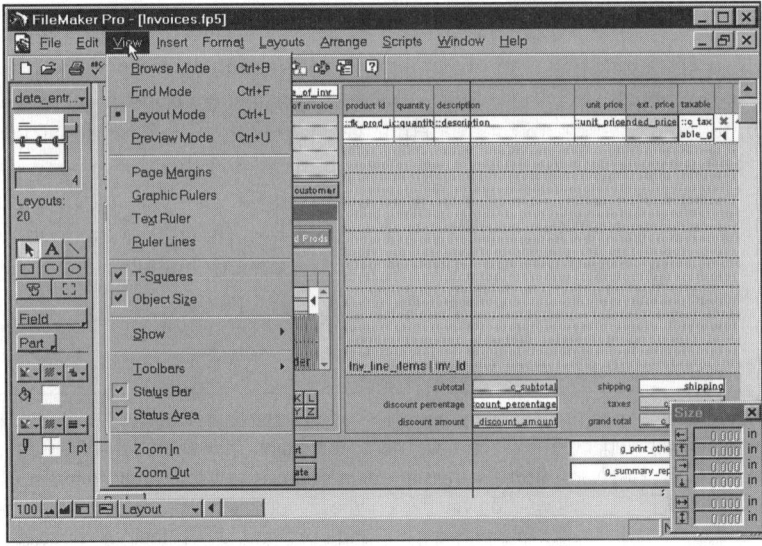

> **Tip from**
> *Rich*
>
> For extra precision in moving objects, watch the Size window to check the object's coordinates. In this way you can confirm that the object is landing in exactly the same location as the last object.

> **Tip from**
> *Rich*
>
> Keep the grid on or off most of the time. If you turn the grid off or override it by holding down Alt on Windows or Command on the Mac as you move an object so an object doesn't automatically line itself up on one of the gridlines, you can place the thing exactly where you want, but from that point on, if you turn the grid back on, the object moves the same distances as objects on the grid, maintaining its misalignment. In effect, it is following its own version of the grid, starting where it was. Better to keep the grid on permanently or off permanently, but not switch back and forth casually. Basically, when you turn the grid on, you are telling FileMaker that when you move an object, you want it to move the object in increments of a prespecified number of pixels.

THE ALIGN COMMAND

Haphazard alignment of fields can make the user feel as if an earthquake is going on, as she staggers from left to right and back again, just to enter standard information. Better to use the Set Alignment dialog, shown in Figure 8.5, to get the whole group shipshape.

Prepare for Consistency 235

Figure 8.5
In the Set Alignment dialog, the shapes in the sample change to show you what the result of each option will be, on whatever objects you have selected in the layout.

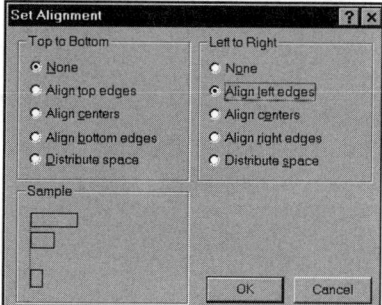

> **Tip from Rich**
>
> All the objects you have selected are aligned to the farthest object. For instance, if you select a group of objects and say you want to align their left edges, they will end up aligned with the left edge of the object that was the farthest to the left. If you choose to align to the center, FileMaker figures out where the center of the group is and centers everything around that.

ARROW KEYS

If you find using the mouse a crude way to move an object, select the object and press arrow keys to move it one pixel at a time to the left, right, up, or down. Of course, moving an item one pixel at a time is only worthwhile when you have your layout near perfection, ready for fine-tuning.

THE SHIFT KEY

If you find objects slipping a little up or down as you move them, remember that holding down Shift constrains the move to a vertical or horizontal path.

TEXT BASELINES

To avoid a bumpy ride, match the dotted line that extends to the left and right of a text label or field, as shown in Figure 8.6. When the baseline of the object you are moving is exactly aligned with the baseline of another object, it disappears. Time to release the object.

THE OBJECT SIZE WINDOW

If you have one object where you want it, check the Object Size window for one or more of the distances, as seen in Figure 8.7. (Best to measure these distances in pixels, for precision). Memorize that number. Then drag other objects watching the Size palette, and when the number matches, let go. Or just type in the right number to make the object jump to the spot.

Figure 8.6
The baseline extends to either side of a text label or a field, so you can align that text with the baseline of another label or field.

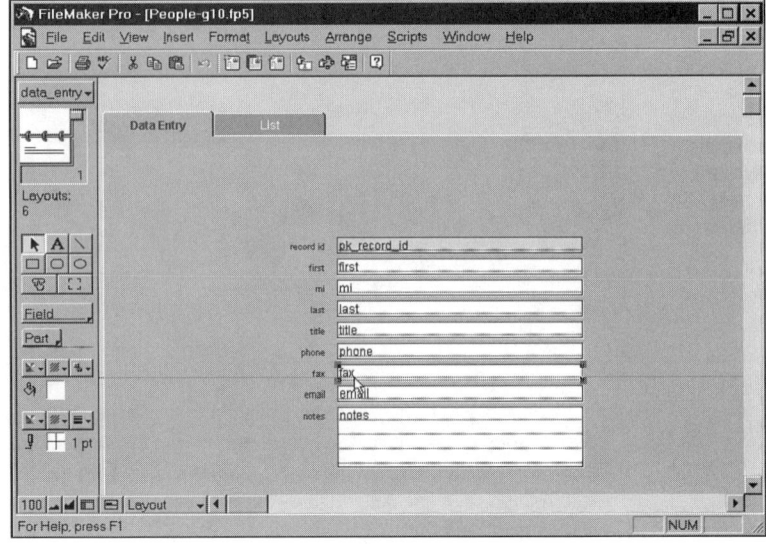

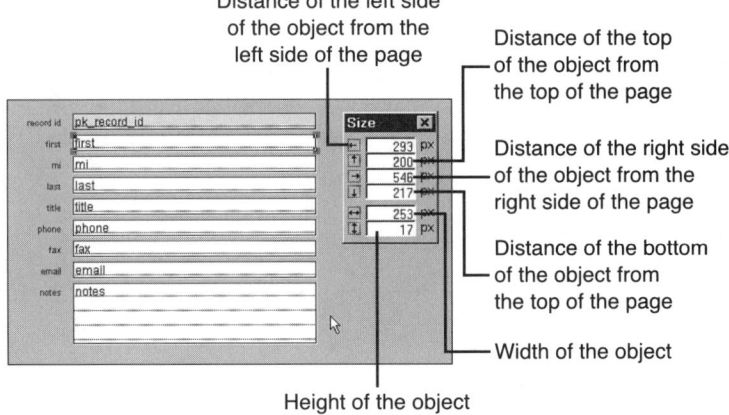

Figure 8.7
The Object Size window tracks your object's location as you move the object around.

Distance of the left side of the object from the left side of the page

Distance of the top of the object from the top of the page

Distance of the right side of the object from the right side of the page

Distance of the bottom of the object from the top of the page

Width of the object

Height of the object

Tip from
Rich

Don't zoom to move. In most drawing programs, you can zoom in to make precision movements, but this does not work in FileMaker. At the regular zoom level, you can move an object one pixel at a time if you are patient or use arrow keys. But if you zoom in 400%, objects just move four pixels at a time. You do not get greater control, just magnification.

Caution

When you are changing the size of a group of objects, changing the numbers in the Size window adjusts the size of the group as a whole, not individual members.

Tip from
Rich

Instead of deleting, archive. If you have spent a lot of work creating and formatting an element and then decide to get rid of it, consider cutting and pasting to save it in another layout for possible reuse. You might want to create a catch-all layout to collect these items, just in case you change your mind later and want to salvage a few elements.

Make Data Entry Easy

The less typing, the better. Users can enter typos faster than you can verify the entries, so you need to design your interface in ways that do some of the data entry for the users, and make it clear where to enter what, following the users' habits rather than your own idea of logic.

Never Have the Users Do What the Computer Can Do for Them

Bruce Tognazzini, former User Interface Czar at Apple and later at Sun, used to chant this mantra in meetings. You've set up a relational database, so use it to make life easier for the user.

At the top-left corner of any layout or area within a layout, try to capture information such as a person's name or the product ID, so that you can use that as a key to go and grab a lot of related information to pour into other fields in a nearby portal. And, to make sure you get the right person or product, offer a value list in some form to choose from. In this way, you sidestep having the user type in info that already exists—which is convenient for the user, and a relief to you, because your sorts and searches are more likely to work consistently in this situation. Similarly, in the Invoicing system, when a user chooses to start a new invoice, we take the user to the screen for adding customers, and then the screen for adding products, as shown in Figure 8.8, so the user does not have to remember to go to these places.

Figure 8.8
The Add Products button brings up a set of categories; when the user chooses one, we display its products, so the user can click one.

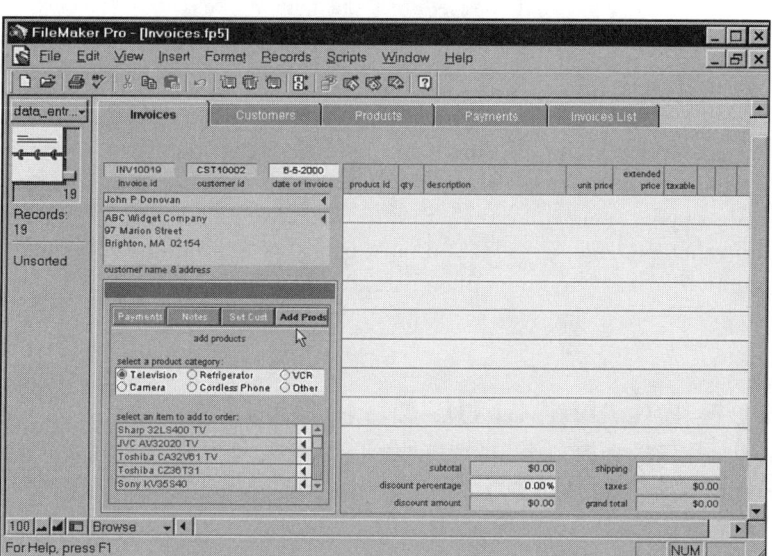

Go With the User's Flow

The reason we urge you to put the key field near the beginning of the form is that entering that value immediately triggers the filling-in process below, or to the right. The sequence seems familiar, moving from top to bottom, or left to right. On the other hand, putting the key at the bottom and having data appear mysteriously above it, seems to be disconcerting for many people. Hey, blame it on the culture.

→ To set up your tab order to match the habits of the user, **see** "Adjusting the Tab Order to Suit the User's Habits," **p. 209.**

As you look at the major areas on a layout, make sure that your arrangement follows the sequence of tasks that most users perform. For instance, if a user needs to get a customer's name before taking an order, then the customer block should move toward the top of your layout. If shipping instructions usually come up toward the end of the order-taker's conversation, put the shipping block toward the bottom. Seems simple enough, but remember that what makes perfect sense to you may be alien and weird to the actual users. Use-cases, task analysis, and testing can help you get your blocks in 1-2-3 order.

Signal Exactly Where to Enter Information

To help users spot the places where they can enter information, distinguish those visually from fields that are read-only, labels, or any other debris you put in the layout. Generally, a whitespace inside a definite border invites entry. Graying out the space slightly indicates that the field is closed to entry. Text floating in space, without a box around it or a pattern behind it, tends to be picked up as a label, so most visitors do not double-click it, imagining they can replace the label with a value.

> **Tip from**
> *Rich*
>
> Whatever convention you choose, make sure you apply it consistently. Users get quite imaginative when they detect an inconsistent use of the convention, with different shapes, colors, or patterns, and their interpretations will surprise you. They read meaning into variations you consider trivial, and those warped conceptual models of the system can get them seriously confused.

If you have some trouble convincing users that they should enter information into certain fields, consider adding tiny arrows in red pointing to the fields, or red labels saying "Required," to encourage attention. (Catching people while they enter information is better than stopping them when they want to exit, saying, "No, you can't go because you forgot to fill in the ZIP code.") And if you must insist on their entering a value, make the message specify what field has to be filled in, and if possible, put the cursor into that field, so the user can just go ahead and type the value.

Design Meaningful Buttons

From the user's point of view, a button issues a command. But what exactly will happen? You might use a graphic as a button, suggesting its purpose in the picture. Remember, though, that real icons are universally recognized, like the Madonna, but many images that mean a lot to you may be as obscure as Egyptian hieroglyphics to the user. There aren't many real icons. Most of the images that you might use as a button are, well, locally defined; so if you have room, add a label.

The text of a button label should echo the command. Use a verb in the imperative: Print, Find All, Sort. If the button takes people to a report, reduce the name of the report to a short phrase, and assume the verb phrase "Go to" in front of it. Wherever you use a label on a button, step back from the layout for a moment and make sure that a user can tell the difference between one button and another, based solely on their labels.

In some tight places, a small graphic is all you can squeeze in, as in our list of invoices; making that graphic blue or red against a gray background is enough to make it stand out from the background. In these cases, you hope that you have made the button attract attention and invite clicking, so that people can see what it does just by trying it out. If you can add pop-up text that labels such a button when someone hovers over it, great.

> **Tip from Rich**
>
> Resist putting everything in capital letters. Capitalize the first letter of each word in the label, but not every letter. Text in all capitals is hard to read and loud. Exception: OK is OK. Odd twist: In the Invoicing system, we use all-lower-case labels to indicate that the labels are subordinate to the data, but some users may find it odd, but acceptable if we are consistent throughout.

> **Caution**
>
> Don't get too creative with labels. If you use the same field in several layouts, take a pass through all the layouts, confirming that you have used the same label each time. Minor variations in the label sometimes lead users to believe there is some heavy significance to the difference, and they compound their confusion with elaborate theories to explain why you put ZIP here, ZIP code there, and Code over there.

COMMON MISTAKE: MAKING SEVERAL BUTTONS LOOK LIKE THE DEFAULT

Yes, you may want to emphasize several buttons, but resist the impulse to put double lines around them all. In most cases, there really is a single default value, and that is the one you should highlight.

> **Tip from Rich**
>
> Use Show to spot your buttons. Sometimes as you work on a layout, you forget which items are buttons. Or at least, we do. To display all the buttons with a gray border, choose View, Show, Buttons, while in the Layout mode.

Tip from
Rich

> Don't print most buttons. Buttons issue orders and take people elsewhere, but on a printout, they look like a photo of a doorknob: you can't use it, and it clutters up the printout. In Layout, select the button you don't want to print, choose Sliding/Printing from the Format menu, and in the dialog, click the check box that says "Do not print the selected objects." If you want other objects to slide into the space, you can turn sliding on.

CASE STUDY: BAN THOSE INVISIBLE BUTTONS

We were recently hired to modify a database that is sold as a complete package for a niche market. The users were saying they did not understand why they were brought to a completely different place than they expected. In observing the users, we found that sometimes, out of nervous habits, the users clicked on what they assumed was an area of the screen that had no buttons, apparently, but the developer had left invisible buttons all over the place, so the users were inadvertently jumping all over the database. The moral: Clean up all your loose buttons before turning the database over to users.

ARRANGE BUTTONS IN FUNCTIONAL AREAS

Just as you carved up the layout into functional areas, you need to make group buttons by function. Users learn what they can do in a particular area, and understand that all the buttons there relate to that task. For instance, in the invoicing system, the Customers screen shows the major tabs at the top, customer information on the left, information about individual invoices to that customer on the top right, and summaries of the data on all the invoices on the lower right (see Figure 8.9). Common areas for buttons include the following:

- **Navigation spaces**—Buttons that help people move around, going to other tabs, the main menu if you have one, and reports.
- **Actions**—Buttons that act on the data within the current layout, such as Send Reminder and Print Report.
- **Operations on lists**—Buttons that let users sort items in different ways and rearrange the sequence of items. manually.
- **Search specialties**—Buttons that offer preset searches, such as Overdue Invoices and All Invoices for Current Customer.

Figure 8.9
The functions of the Customers screen are divided up into distinct areas.

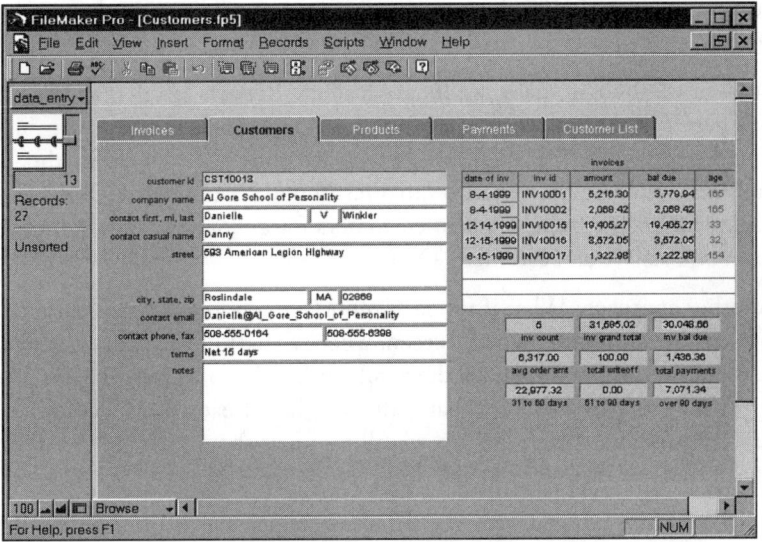

Print the Reports the Users Expect

Printing a report seems simple until you start thinking, concretely, about what data should go into that report. What would users want to print? We thought of this as "reporting," but we also realized that for many users, *reports* are only those documents you have to issue on a regular basis, like a quarterly report. Printing records does not seem like "reporting" to them.

At first we thought to have a gigantic layout with all possible reports visible. But the question came up: Which records, which found set do we print, or do we ask the user to perform a find before they print whatever records? If so, they would have to go back to data entry.

In a relational environment, the same report can be based upon a found set in any file. If you want to know sales by month, if you are in the customer file, and have a found set of customers, you might want sales by month for those customers. Or if you were in the Products file with a found set of products, you might want a report on sales by month for those products. Similarly, you might want the same report on a found set of invoices.

Our first thought was to add a Reports tab, but the question arose: Do we have a different Reports layout for each entity, so that the contents change as the user moves from Customers, say, to Invoices? Or should there be one generic Reports tab?

Displaying a separate Reports tab for each entity would be cumbersome, because if the user wanted to run a particular report, the user has to figure out which Report screen it appears on. Also, if you go to a separate Reports screen, you take the user's focus away from the data. And when leaving the data, does the user, then, really understand what the report will deal with? Do we? Do we report on something new, from scratch, or do we work on the current found set? Will this report just reflect the most recently found records, or will it contain all the records? And does the user risk losing his found set by going to Reports?

So then we thought, okay, we'll have a single Reports tab that all the files go to. But even this generic solution presents a problem: Which file is the basis for this report—that is, the found set in which file? Well, we can always remember which file the user just came from, and we could base the report on that last found set of records. But a user might want a report on invoices, click over to customers for a moment, and then choose the Reports tab, and see a report on customers. Oops!

Another approach: What if for each report we ignore whatever is found (anywhere), and just present the user with a query screen, where as part of the process, the user can enter the search criteria, and then have the results printed as a report? This is a very mainframe approach—that is, clunky. What if the user has already done a complicated search, omitted a few records, and gotten the records all set up as she wants, only to have the reporting mechanism blow all that work away?

Final decision: We make the reporting mechanism available right on the data entry screen. Therefore it relates directly to the data the user has been manipulating. The user is choosing the report from within the tab space, so the message is that the report is based on what you are seeing. This gives the user more of a feeling of being able to directly manipulate the data.

Typically, there are three ways reports are generated:

1. The report is generated on a set of records the user has found.
2. The user's found set is ignored, and a query process is built into the reporting mechanism, so prior to producing the report, the user must fill in a query with report criteria, and the report is based on the found set produced by the query.
3. A report has a hard coded query, such as "Print me a list of unpaid invoices," in which the query is always the same, and ignores the user's found set.

There may be variations, but these are the main methods of creating reports. In this case, we felt that the users of this system would be best served by reporting on their own found sets. We figured users might be playing "What if" scenarios, saying, "Find me this, and find me that, and, Oh, this is interesting, print me this, or that." This approach lets the user get closer to the data, and stay closer, without leaving to go to some Reports or Query toolshed.

> **Caution**
>
> None of these methods is really superior to another; your choice depends on the user and use-cases.

Describe Printing the Way Users Do

Users don't necessarily consider mailing labels, a list, or the invoice to be a report. They just want to print. So we separated the standard or summary reports from what FileMaker would call a detail report, that is, one showing the details of a record, for a series of specific invoices or products. Summary reports may not show the details, but they pull together a summary of all those details. Summaries are what most people think of as reports, and we list those separately as reports. The Other list shows current, found, lists, and labels: to a user, these are things you print, but not really "reports."

Tip from
Rich

> Get an expert to give you some perspective. Even if you have a brilliant eye, your idea of layout and navigation tends to be personal. If you've been going back and forth on some of your decisions, ask an outside designer to give you a critique. You don't have to follow all the suggestions, but you may be alerted to problems you would otherwise have overlooked.
>
> By the way: Thank you to Chad Novotny, who works in the Support Group, Inc. office, and built the tabbed interface we use in the invoicing system.

Test Prototypes and Get User Feedback

Create prototypes of every important layout and use those samples to elicit reactions from users. The idea here is that you can work out the worst kinks in your interface before you take the time to create an entire system (and then revise it, one layout at a time!) You might consider testing half a dozen rounds of prototypes, making changes overnight, and testing the next day. Remember that testing is a continuous process, not just some kind of pass/no pass exam. Keep asking for feedback from typical users (not your friends, or other developers).

You are looking for areas of difficulty. Often, people will point out something that confused them or disappointed them, and make suggestions about how to fix it. Listen to the problem, but not necessarily the solution. For instance, several users were disappointed in the up and down blue arrows next to line items in the Invoices tab within the Invoices database; these arrows were intended to allow users to move a portal row up or down, to reorder the list of line items. But some users complained, "When I click one, all it does is select the row." We discovered that the buttons were working correctly, but the shapes were tiny, and if a user missed by a pixel or two, the whole portal row would be selected instead.

Solution: We first measured the arrow, and the width and height of the arrow was ten by eleven pixels, so we drew a box adding two pixels both ways, so we had a box that was twelve pixels wide and thirteen pixels tall. We made the borders invisible, and chose no fill. Then we grouped this invisible box with the arrow, so that if someone tried to click the arrow, but missed by a pixel or two, the click was more likely to catch part of the hot box. (We had to do the same thing on the blue bars that acted as sort buttons in the list view, because in initial tests, if the user happened to click between one bar and the next, nothing happened, because the graphics had not been touched. So we grouped them within an invisible box.)

Sometimes, you just bump into mistakes and omissions, which at first seem easy to fix, but lead to unexpected complexity. For instance, in an early version of the Invoices database, we included an Unsort button, in the single record view, but, alas, no Sort button. We earned a

Homer Simpson "Dohhh!" Of course, when we went to insert the Sort button, we encountered a confusing situation. In the list view, the person's full name is shown as a single field, but in the single record view the name appears as part of the full address, so where do we put the Sort button? If we put it next to the whole address, would someone realize we were offering to sort by company name, as opposed to contact last name?

Also, in a lot of windows, users are accustomed to clicking a button at the top of a column to get the records sorted according to the entries in that particular field, but we weren't sure they would understand that in our interface they could get the same effect by clicking a button on the side. We disabled the Sort dialog by password protection. We did not want people to try sorting using field names that are somewhat abbreviated, and not really intended for users, such as C_age_of_unpaid_invoice. It might be traumatic for a novice user to encounter these field names, or to try to sort by contact last name, which does not exist in this file, because it is elsewhere. Solution: We added a pop-up menu like those for summary reports, to let the user sort in single record view, offering various ways to sort. This way, the users cannot sort in every way, but can sort in ways that users have indicated were important.

Sometimes, users are flummoxed by ordinary behavior of FileMaker, and you realize you need to work around the routine. For instance, you can use the up and down arrows we provide to move a line item up or down one line at a time, but when you leave the portal and return, the row you were in seems at first to have disappeared, because FileMaker has moved it to the bottom of the portal. Users express dismay. "Where did my line item go?" Also, to move intelligently, the user needs to see the rows above and below the line being moved, so the line item needs to end up in the middle of the portal, with lines above and below it.

Here, we make a Global field G_Portal_Row set equal to the status of CurrentPortalRow, which is actually the row number. To move the row up one, we have to subtract one from the row number; to move the row down one, we have to add one to the row number. When we go off to the line item file, swap values to control the sort order of the portal, and come back, the portal shows row one. So we have to tell FileMaker to go to the portal row indicated by the value in the G_Portal_Row field. That makes that row the last row visible in the portal. But to move an item up or down, you need to see items above and below, so the current row should probably be in the middle. In a nine-row portal, that would mean the fifth position. To do this, we go to the "next" portal row four times, which moves our "moved" item to the middle, although it is no longer selected. So we go to the previous portal row four times, which does not force any scrolling, but moves the selection back to the row we are interested in. Uf-dah, what a lot of work!

Unfortunately, there is still one other issue we have to deal with: If we try moving a record up and the record happens to be one of the last four records in the portal, then we may not be able to move the record to the middle of the portal using this method. So we have to add logic saying that if this record is one of the last four, FileMaker should just go to the last row and select the item, which scrolls us to the bottom of the portal. Then we use a "Go to portal row" command to select the row we just moved.

Ideally, we would bring the user back to the same scroll position within the portal because we do not like to change the user's view. But there is no good way to tell where that row is within the portal. We know which row is selected, but we do not know in advance if that will turn out to be the top, middle, or bottom row.

Tip from
Rich

> Put together a series of samples to show the customer, like examples of the latest wallpaper. Which seems most congenial? Talk about the pluses and minuses of the different options.

USE THE INTERFACE PROTOTYPER

We have created a tool to help you design an interface that relies on tabs. As a developer, you can play "What if" with the interface, come up with some concepts, and then show those to users, so they can play with the interface, giving you their reactions. Yes, you can show people interfaces like the one you plan for them, but they do not understand until they see a real interface designed just for them, and play with it themselves. You can watch them interact, listen to their comments, and make modifications quickly, so they can try out an improved version. We hope that this tool will save you many hours of experimentation, and help you carve out an effective interface in conversation with your client.

To flesh out one or more of these structure, use the Setup screen. Enter major and minor categories as shown in Figure 8.10; then see how they appear in the various looks.

Figure 8.10
Fill out the form with major and minor categories, and the prototyper goes to work.

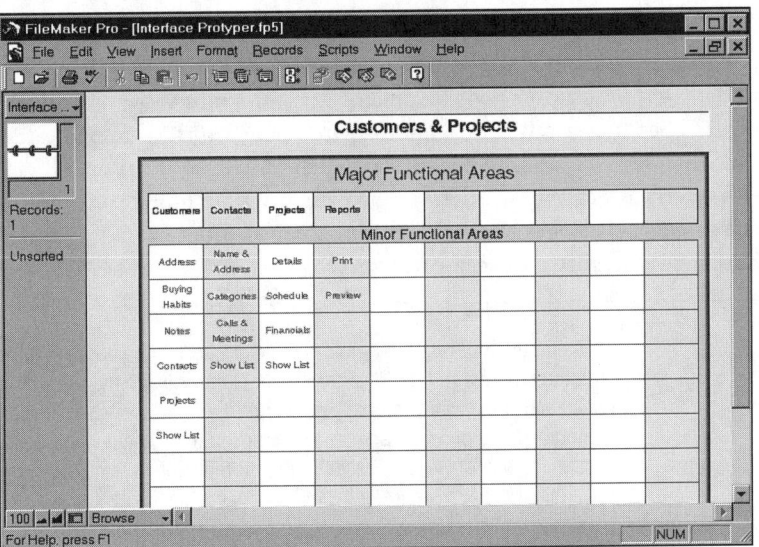

In most relational systems, you have major categories of data, and within each, you have some minor categories. The Tab Interface tool lets you enter the major categories at the top of the screen as a series of tabs, and then, under each major category, you can enter the minor categories. You can experiment with those categories in three different looks—buttons and tabs (see Figure 8.11), tabs within tabs, and main menu.

Figure 8.11
Click Interface 1 and Show at the bottom of the Setup screen, and you see this buttons-and-tabs interface with the categories you entered.

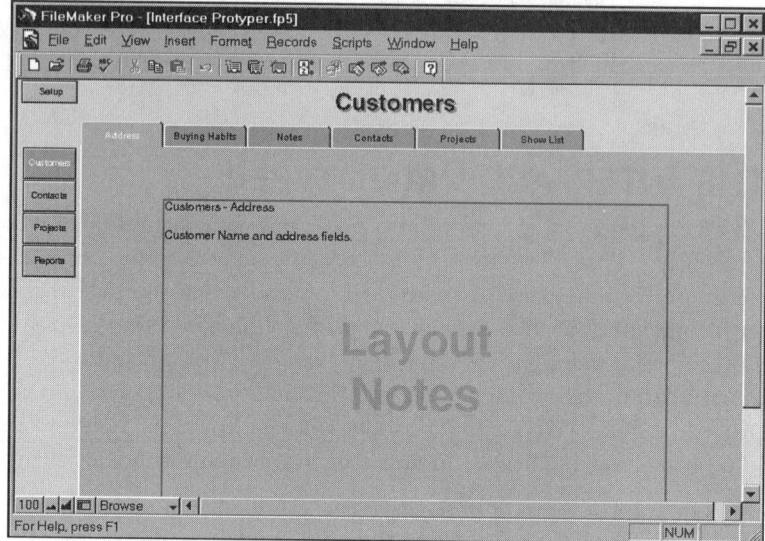

BUTTONS AND TABS

Along the left side of the screen, we have buttons that switch the user between major categories. Each time a user goes to a major category, tabs show up with the related minor categories. Then a user can click a tab to switch between these minor categories. You can type notes that describe what will appear on each screen, so the user can envision the details. This interface works best when the subcategories are going to contain a lot of data, because each tabbed subcategory gets the whole screen without having to share any space with another subcategory or a major category.

Tip from
Rich

> When building this type of interface, make sure that you include some real information on all the screens, so the client can see how the subcategory is tied to its major category. For instance, if the main category is a contact, you may want to include the contact ID and contact name on every screen, so that even if the client is looking at a subcategory, such as address information or meetings with the contact, the client can see that it is related to the contact. For instance, a list of meetings means little if you do not see what contact they were with. You do want to carry over some information from one tab to the others within the same category, so the user recognizes they are all related to the same subject.

Tabs Within Tabs

The tabs along the top of the screen represent major categories here, which stay constant, and at the bottom of the screen for each major category there is an area of subtabs, for subcategories. When a user clicks a major tab at the top, the tabs down at the bottom change to reflect that major category. For the tabs-within-tabs interface, see Figure 8.12.

Tip from
Rich

Play with top and bottom, left and right. We chose to use top and bottom, but you might prefer left and right, or you might use three-quarters of the tab area for major tabs, while in the lower left corner of the screen, taking up a quarter of the screen, you could put the minor categories.

Figure 8.12
Here is the tabs-within-tabs approach.

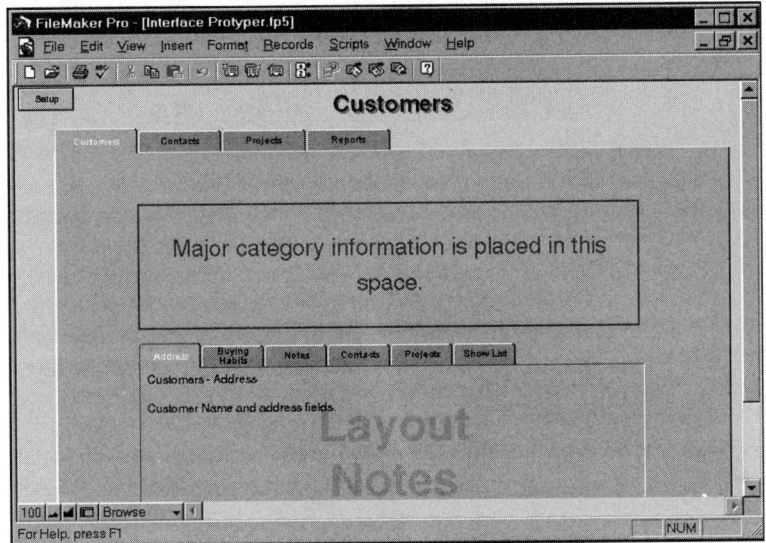

Main Menu

If you have so many major categories that you run out of space for tabs, you may have to turn to a main menu (see Figure 8.13). The problem with this approach is that users lose sight of the data. An alternative, a double row of tabs, has a different problem: When you select a tab in the top row, you expect that it will be connected visually with the information that appears below, but that means shuffling the position of tabs, as in many Microsoft dialog boxes; these changes tend to confuse users.

Figure 8.13
The Main Menu acts as the starting point for everything in this approach.

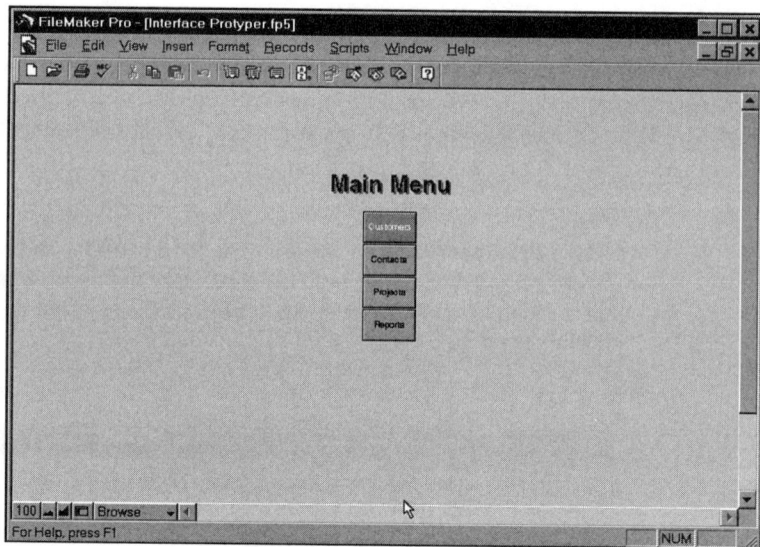

Bonus: In each interface approach, there are fields you can type into, to create a text button below, so users can envision those (even though the buttons are inactive). This is a wonderful parlor trick because you can create a button as soon as the client asks for it. "You want a Print button? Sure. Type, Here it is!"

When you are building the interface, you may want a printout to mark up or fax to a client. To print the interface, look under the Scripts menu, to print a single tab, or the tabs that are shown, or all tabs (essentially, every screen in the system).

> **Caution**
>
> If you choose to look behind the scenes to see how this little utility works, avert your eyes or, when you notice some irregularities, promise not to tell. We got this working, and we are glad it works, but some of the techniques are not ones we would recommend for a system designed for users. In fact, if you develop any enhancements for the Interface Prototyper, let us know.

> **Tip from**
> *Rich*
>
> Consider a minimal interface. Perhaps your audience does not need the handholding offered by a thoroughly developed interface. We once had to develop a system for reporting commissions, which are mathematically complex and involve complicated business rules, but this system was only going to be used by one person who was already pretty savvy, and he did not want to pay us to put in a lot of time on user interface. He just needed some fields and accurate results. He understood the data and the business rules, so he did not need a design that articulated those. He was paying, and he knew that user interface design takes a lot of time. So he chose a Spartan look, which did what he needed. The interface was sufficient for his work.

CHAPTER 9

"Webifying" Your Database

In this chapter

Letting People Interact with Your Data   250

How FileMaker Came to the Web   251

Choosing Between Instant and Custom Web Publishing   254

Instant Web Publishing   255

Custom Web Publishing   260

Understanding Security   264

How to Plan for Web Delivery   264

Putting Your Database Directly on the Internet   266

Exporting Data as HTML Pages with the Results of Calculations   267

Creating Detail Records   269

Using Lasso to Go Beyond the Web Companion   271

Letting People Interact with Your Data

In the few years during which the World Wide Web has been growing like tumbleweed in a wet season, the Web has spawned whole industries that never existed before, transformed most other businesses in the Western world, and made a lot of folks rich. In the early days of the Web, people created static HTML pages just to present information. As long as your information rarely changed, that approach worked fine, and still does even today. But if your information changed a lot, those changes probably took place within a database, so designers started asking, why not just let the data pour directly from the database onto the Web whenever someone needs the information? The database, then, would continue to enforce security and business rules, but the actual data could be available instantly for users to read on the Web, and if allowed, to edit as well.

CASE STUDY: SWEEPING AWAY CONFUSION

We have a client whose organization has both Macs and PCs, with databases of all shapes, sizes, and products. Some databases exist in FileMaker, some in Omnis 7, and some in 4th Dimension. The problem they faced was complex deployment, making sure that users who needed particular data had the right client software installed and updated. If a user needed access to one system, the IT group had to make sure that the right application was loaded on the user's PC, so the IT folks were running all over the place installing various database applications, upgrading those applications, tracking who owned what and who had been updated, and accounting for all the copies. The organization decided they had to sweep away all of this confusion by mandating that all database access would be done through a browser interface. The appeal: browsers are free, and in this scenario they have a ubiquitous client that could access any corporate information from any application, right? True enough. But a browser is not a database, and although it can display information quickly, it cannot manipulate that data or print it the way a real database can. So the organization was trading off some functionality for ease of maintenance.

A browser's display just does not offer all the capability that you can put into a FileMaker layout. For instance, controlling the look and position of a FileMaker layout is easy and precise, compared to the loose and occasionally unpredictable HTML.

Reporting gets tough, too. How will you print mailing labels? It's easy to print them from FileMaker itself, but in a browser environment, HTML may be shifting items left and right, up and down, and you may end up with the person's name printing on the gap between two labels. You're working in a world of tags, not a graphic user interface, and each person's browser is allowed to interpret those tags differently.

To bring data and some functionality to the Web pages, FileMaker provides the Web Companion. But even with the Web Companion, you can probably not recreate all the functionality of your original database on the Web, and you certainly cannot replay all the reports through the browser.

This connection takes place through a series of transactions. FileMaker users are accustomed to a persistent connection when exchanging information between the client and the host, so that if one user is looking at a record, and another user edits the record at the same time, that user's changes are shown on the other person's screen immediately, on the fly. But in the Web environment, when a user presses a button, a message is sent to the Web Companion, and the Web Companion talks to FileMaker, gets some data back, merges the data with a format page, and sends that Web page back to the browser for display. That's the end of the relationship unless the user happens to start the whole thing over again. The user, then, gets no immediate updates because the browser is not actually connected to the Web Companion, and the Web Companion itself is no longer connected to FileMaker, and FileMaker just sits there quite contentedly, because it was just asked to perform a simple task once, which it did. Web users are not really in the database. They dispatched a message, got the data back, and they are now reading the data. But any news coming into the database does not reach the users unless they decide go back and ask for an update. The Web really is a transactional environment.

This is a completely different way of thinking about the data for the user. The FileMaker user expects to be always connected to the data, live. But with the Web view, users are not really in the data; they are just seeing one snapshot, then another, then another. The data is taken out of the database and sent to the browser, but the browser doesn't have a live connection to the database. So if your data does change quite often, and if those changes are critical to the business, the browser approach risks providing users with information that is out-of-date. To draw an analogy to the stock market, using FileMaker in a client/server situation, someone else's changes to a record appear instantaneously on your screen, like a real-time stock ticker. But using the Web browser is more like watching the 20-minute delayed quotes: You have a good picture of what the data *was*.

We've had to explain to our customers that although there are major benefits to this form of deployment, you won't get the same level of capability in a browser interface that you usually have in an ordinary FileMaker layout. For example, in a FileMaker layout we can put a button that runs a script, causing lots of things to happen as the user watches. On a Web page, you can have a button that perhaps runs a JavaScript routine, but that's very different from a FileMaker button that says, "Go to this field and copy the data, and go to this other field and paste it there; then create a new record and stop." The JavaScript code controls the behavior of the browser, but it does not interact with the database, whereas a FileMaker script is actually acting directly on data in the database.

How FileMaker Came to the Web

In general, people started doing FileMaker database publishing on the Web with FileMaker 3. If you looked at both ends of the communication, you had FileMaker 3 at one end and a browser at the other end, and neither knew how to talk to the other. The browser knew how to talk to a Web server (an HTTP server), as shown in Figure 9.1. But the Web server itself did not know how to talk to FileMaker. So CGI's (common gateway interfaces) were born to act as intermediaries. Products such as Lasso, Tango, and WebFM were a few of the common gateway interfaces created to let FileMaker data appear on the Web.

Figure 9.1
At first, the browser talked to the server, but the server didn't talk to FileMaker.

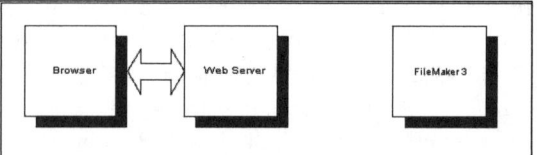

The CGI sat between the browser and FileMaker and acted as an agent to facilitate communication between them, as shown in Figure 9.2.

Figure 9.2
The CGI script helped the browser and FileMaker exchange information.

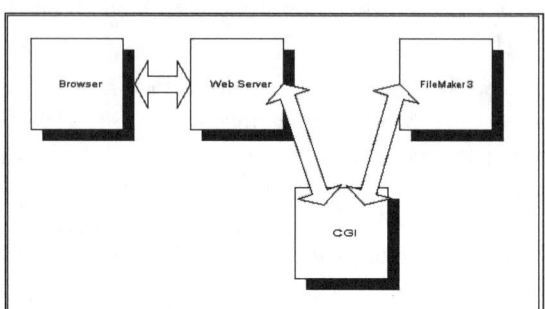

In the early days, the user would click on a hypertext link. Buried inside the link was a long string of text coded in such a way that when the Web server received it, the server would recognize the special codes that should be passed to the CGI, named something like Lasso. So the server would pass the text string to the CGI through Apple Events (yes, this was a Mac-only solution back then), and then Lasso would analyze the string and pick out instructions, such as which FileMaker file should be used, which layout should be used, and which format page should be used to send the results back. (A format page is an HTML page with tags using the proprietary Lasso Dynamic Markup Language). The instructions might also include certain field values. Finally, an action tag specified the ultimate action to perform, such as a Find, Create New Record, Delete Record, allowing the user to actually make changes to the database. Lasso took all these instructions, and using Apple Events, Lasso would make a series of requests of FileMaker. Eventually, Lasso would get data back from FileMaker.

Lasso, then, would take this data and merge it with the format page, producing a properly formatted HTML document. The HTML document would be passed back to the server software, known as Web Star, which would dispatch it to the browser (see Figure 9.3).

As you can imagine, this scenario had some limitations:

- It was a Mac-only solution.
- It required that a user buy three pieces of software: Lasso (or another CGI), Web Star (or another server), and FileMaker.
- It relied on Apple Events, which has a relatively slow messaging mechanism.

Figure 9.3
When Lasso gets the data from FileMaker, it puts that into an HTML document which is passed to the server software, which in turn sends it to the user's browser.

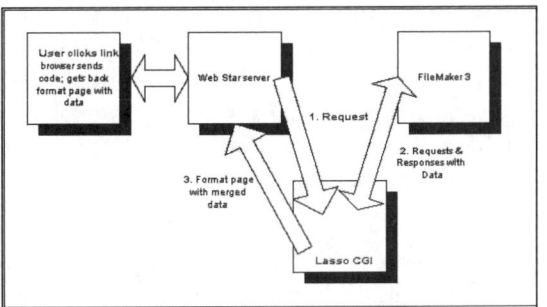

To solve these problems when they created FileMaker Pro 4, FileMaker, Inc. entered into a business agreement with Blue World Communications (the makers of Lasso) to use their technology as part of something called the Web Companion, shown in Figure 9.4. Web Companion allowed FileMaker to act as a database, CGI, and HTTP server all at once. The Web Companion software supported HTTP protocols, so it could work as a Web server; it could speak to FileMaker to get commands and data in and out; and it resided inside FileMaker.

Figure 9.4
The plug-in called Web Companion took over the job that had been performed by the external CGI.

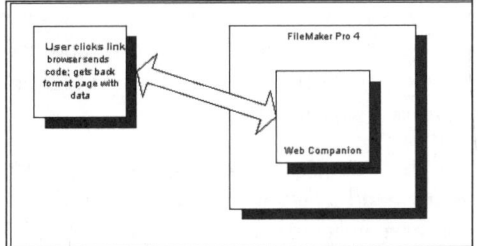

Another plus: Web Companion worked on both Mac and PC platforms, through a cross-platform Application Programming Interface (API), a specification that shows how other programs can exchange data and commands with FileMaker. Now FileMaker no longer needed Apple Events to communicate with other programs. The API meant that FileMaker, Inc. could write code to trigger actions in FileMaker and bring back the results.

So now the browser sends an ugly text string to the Web Companion, which checks to make sure the string is meant for it, then dissects the string, starts sending data or commands through the API to FileMaker, and receives information back from FileMaker. At that time, the Web Companion grabs the format page that was specified in the text string and fills it with the data it receives from FileMaker.

The format page is an HTML page with additional tags that tell FileMaker where to put information coming from the database and how to handle that information. These tags are in a markup language called the Claris Dynamic Markup Language. HTML tags are surrounded by angle brackets, whereas in CDML, the tags are surrounded by square brackets [like this]. CDML offers action tags, variable tags, replacement tags, and HTML Input tags. An ordinary browser will not recognize these tags because they begin and end with unrecognized brackets. The Web Companion strips out the CDML tag, which causes it to perform an action of some kind or to replace the tag itself with actual data from the database. If you have ever done a mail merge using a word processor, you have seen a comparable situation. In mail merge you have placeholders for data from the data document, and you might have an if/then/else statement to put different information on the page, depending on the situation.

In FileMaker Pro 5, you have a more powerful markup language, and Web Companion's functionality has been improved, but the basic process works the same way it did in FileMaker Pro 4.

Choosing Between Instant and Custom Web Publishing

You have two ways to publish FileMaker information on the Web. One method is called Instant, and it is pretty fast. The other is called Custom Web Publishing, and like so many customization routines, it gives you more control but takes more time.

FileMaker Pro 5 acts as its own Web server on any machine connected to the Internet, even without an ISP or domain name (your computer has its own IP address). Basically, with Instant Web Publishing, you just enable Web publishing. Yes, it takes a few more seconds than an instant, but the process is pretty straightforward.

The sweetness of Instant Web Publishing is its simplicity. You don't need to know a lot about HTML or CDML; you just build a layout in FileMaker, and that work is transformed for display on the Web. But you have very little control beyond that. You live with decisions made by the FileMaker design team. For many clients, those design choices are just fine.

But if you need something more sophisticated or pages that look like other parts of your company site, you may have to take the giant step into Custom Web Publishing. That's a very big giant step. To succeed, you have to be familiar with FileMaker Pro, HTML, and CDML. (That's *AND*, not *or*.) You build the presentation of the information using HTML, and you interleave groups of CDML commands into that HTML, so the Web Companion will know what data to merge into the document or what other actions to perform. The plus is that you have far more control and additional capability. The minus is the difficulty.

Tip from
Rich

You should be careful about which HTML editor you use when doing custom Web publishing. If your editor sees a command it does not recognize and removes that command, you lose your CDML. Avoid editors with Puritan parsers.

INSTANT WEB PUBLISHING

Instant Web publishing is an excellent solution. If you can live with the limitations, Instant Web publishing offers a fairly fast way to publish your data on the Web, using the Web Companion. The Web Companion is a FileMaker plug-in. So you have to start by turning it on and configuring it. The configuration is an application preference, so it impacts the way all the files are shared.

1. To turn on Web sharing, choose Edit, Preferences, Application.

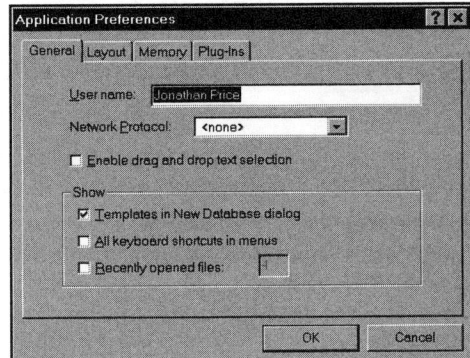

Figure 9.5
You can see the Application Preferences dialog.

2. In the dialog, choose the Plug-Ins tab.

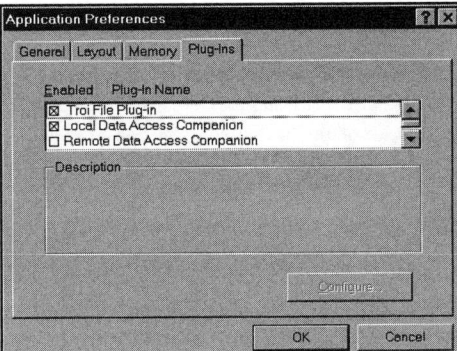

Figure 9.6
The Plug-Ins tab brings you to the Web Companion.

3. On that tab, turn on the Web Companion. (Place a check mark next to it.) The whole row is selected.

4. Click the Configure button at the bottom. You get the Web Companion Configuration dialog box.

Figure 9.7
The Web Companion Configuration dialog box lets you do instant Web publishing

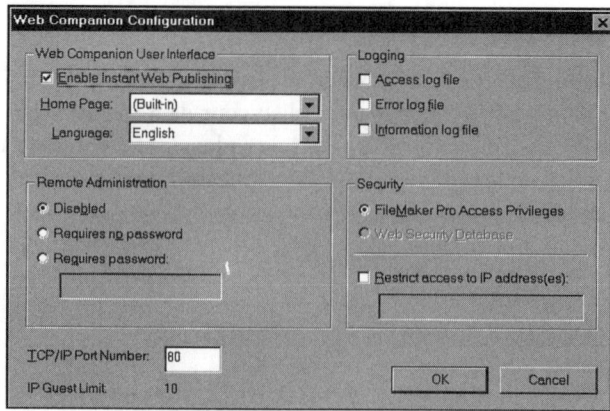

5. In the Web Companion Configuration dialog box, choose Enable Instant Web Publishing, pick what kind of home page the user will see (a built-in one or an HTML file you have placed in the Web folder inside the FileMaker Pro folder), and pick a language (to control the FileMaker Pro controlled text, such as a Delete Record button).

6. Choose options for logging, if you want.

   You are picking what kind of activities you want FileMaker to track, such as access, errors, and information logs.

7. If you want to administer the database remotely, choose whether you want that enabled, enabled without a password, enabled with a password required (enter that now), or disabled.

> **Note**
> Now you have to pick some security options. You could handle security through the regular FileMaker Pro access privileges via passwords, in which case the user will be asked to log in on arrival, to get the same functionality that was available offline. For instance, if the password prevents users from deleting records, the login assures there is no Delete Records button on the screen.
>
> The other way to handle security is through the Web Security Database, a special database located in the Databases folder inside the Web Security folder in the FileMaker Pro 5 folder. There are actually three databases that control the user's level of access over the Web, so this approach gets more complicated than using password privileges, but gives you more refined functionality.

> **Caution**
> Some of the capabilities in the Web Security Database do not work with Instant Web Publishing. These include ExactSearch, ExactUpdate, and ExactDelete.

8. Choose whether to restrict access to one or several IP addresses, if you only want people logging in from those locations.

   You can use wildcards to specify a range of IP addresses.

9. At the bottom of the dialog box, consider the remaining options and click OK.

One of the final options is the TCP IP Port Number. The default Port is 80. When information comes in via the TCP/IP protocol without another port number being specified, the information comes through Port 80. Sometimes, users run multiple applications over TCP/IP, though, and when a message comes in, the computer wonders which application to route it to. You might have personal Web sharing turned on and at the same time offer a FileMaker database. If you think Port 80 may be being used, we recommend Port 591, which is registered to FileMaker.

If you know no other software will use the port, create a link on the page that goes to the machine's IP address, something like http://260.254.254.254 and, because a port number is not specified, that message will be routed through Port 80 to any application listening on that port. If you want to specify that the message goes to a particular port, specify the whole IP address, then a colon, and then the number, for example, http://260.254.254.245:591. That identifies the hardware and the software (FileMaker) that should receive the message. In this way, you can be safe even if you have multiple TCP/IP applications running on the same machine at the same time.

Down near the port number is another section specifying the IP guest limit. This field is for your information only. It tells you how many guests can visit at the same time in the version you have. In the client version, only 10 unique IP addresses can connect to the software within a 12-hour period. If you expect that there will be more visitors than that, you must purchase the FileMaker Pro 5 Unlimited version, which is built without any limits on the number of IP addresses coming in.

> **Tip from**
> *Rich*
>
> Configuring the Web Companion, you have actually set preferences for the ways in which FileMaker will share *all* files.

Now that you have turned on the Web Companion plug-in and configured it, you can turn on sharing and set preferences for the ways in which the *current* file will be shared.

1. Go to a file you want to share.
2. Choose Edit, Preferences, Application, Plug-ins, and check Web Companion, to enable it.
3. Choose File, Sharing, to bring up the File Sharing dialog (see Figure 9.8).
4. In the File-Sharing dialog box, check Web Companion, and then click Set Up Views.

   You are presented with the Web Companion View Setup dialog box, shown in Figure 9.9, which features five tabs (count em!).

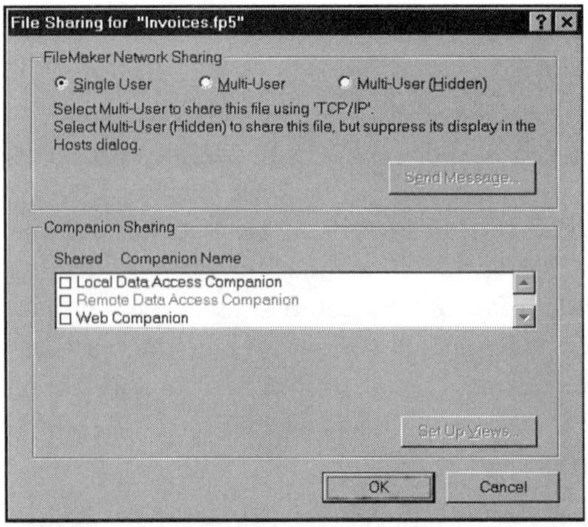

Figure 9.8
The File Sharing dialog box appears.

Figure 9.9
The Web Companion View Setup dialog offers five tabs' worth of features.

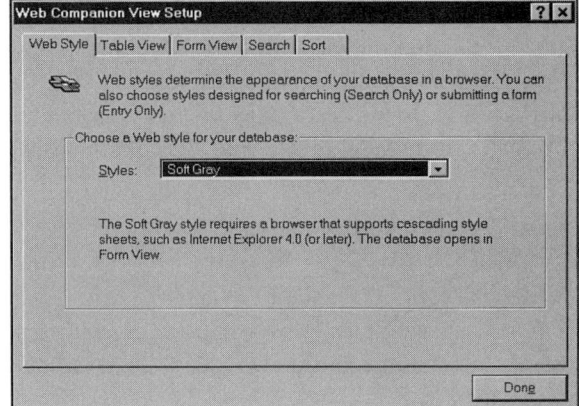

5. On the Web Style tab, pick a color scheme.

   You see a pop-up menu of styles from which you can pick a predefined color scheme and appearance for your Web presentation. Be careful. You can't just pick the pretty one. As advertised under the scheme (after you select one), some of these styles require Netscape or Internet Explorer 3.0 or later, and some require a browser such as Internet Explorer 4 or later with support for cascading style sheets (CSS). Cascading style sheets let you position objects more precisely on the screen and apply your own taste in formatting, overriding the browser's standard setup.

Tip from
Rich

The user's capability to publish a database on the Web depends on her password. If a user's password allows exporting records, she can publish on the Web.

Tip from Rich

The server is not enough. FileMaker Pro 5 and FileMaker Pro 5 Unlimited both have the capability to publish databases to the Web. But FileMaker Pro Server cannot publish a database to the Web. If you have your database open on a server machine running FileMaker Pro Server and then install FileMaker Pro 5 Unlimited on a client machine, it can open files from the server and then publish them to the Web. (The client becomes a server in its own right.) Also, browsers cannot talk directly to the server. They can only talk directly to a client because the client has HTTP capabilities. You would do this if you have a large database with a lot of users. In that environment, a server is a better way to host the file for regular FileMaker Pro guests, including the person who has just transformed her personal computer into a machine for publishing those files on the Web.

Tip from Rich

Consider publishing only copies. If you have files open on the FileMaker Pro server, any password-enabled client who acts as a guest of the server and opens the file can then publish those files to the Web. But some clients get antsy about giving the outside world direct access to their main business files. In that case, create an environment where the day-to-day business files are not actually published to the Web. Instead, a set of copies is published to the Web. In essence, you run automation on a regular basis, clearing out the data in the Web files and importing all the data from the current day-to-day files. Our customers prefer this solution. If you do that migration of data every day, then, worst case, the data seen on the Web will be no more than 24 hours old.

6. In the dialog box, click the Table View tab and pick a layout that contains the fields you want displayed in a single table in a Web page, or choose to display all fields.

   Choose the layout from the pop-up list, or click All Fields. The layout will not be recreated on the Web page. Instead, the data pours into an HTML table consistent with the theme you picked earlier. (The theme is a design look.) You are limited to a single table view, with rows and columns showing multiple records at the same time. (In Custom you can have as many tables as you like.)

7. Click the Form View tab, and for this view, pick a layout that contains the fields you want to present in a form, and the appearance.

   In this situation, the actual layout will, more or less, be recreated on the Web page. Now you have to create a search mechanism.

8. Click the Search tab and pick a layout you want users to be presented with on their Search page.

   Picking this layout does not determine the appearance of the Search page; you are actually just specifying which fields to present. On the Search page, these fields will be presented with a pop-up menu that offers several methods for searching those fields (equals, contains, begins with, and so on) and boxes into which a user types the values to be searched for. A user can choose to search multiple fields at once.

9. Click the Sort tab and decide whether to have the records left unsorted, sort them in whatever way the user specifies in the browser, or sort them in a way you specify, using the button called Specify to spell out the order you like.

> **Tip from**
> *Rich*
>
> If you want to give users access to other layouts from Form view, use buttons with Go to Layout commands. So the Form layout could, if you want, act as a menu leading to all your other layouts. Web Companion creates the HTML version of those layouts on the fly.

10. Click OK to put away the dialog box.

Custom Web Publishing

Custom Web publishing allows greater control and flexibility, but requires a deeper understanding of the way FileMaker Pro's Web Companion works.

The Web Companion lives on a computer that has FileMaker Pro 5 running and one or more databases open for your visitors from out on the Web. When the user clicks a link on one of your HTML pages, the Web Companion receives a message from the user's browser. Interpreting the message, the Web Companion then passes along commands, parameters, and data to FileMaker, which acts on these instructions and responds. Web Companion then takes the response, embeds that in an HTML page, and sends that page back across the Web to the user, who has been drumming her fingers on the desk.

With Custom publishing, there are two ways of activating Web Companion to communicate messages from a Web user to FileMaker: links and forms.

How Links Work

Links are a very controlled way of activating the Web Companion, which lives with FileMaker on a server. In the special FileMaker sense, a link is a hard-coded hypertext link containing your message for the Web Companion. When the user clicks the link, that string is sent back to the Web Companion via the TCP/IP protocol. The link contains information about the machine that the message is supposed to go to (an IP address or a domain on the Web), the port number on that machine (not needed if you expect the default port, which is Port 80), plus a long text string submitted to the Web Companion. That text contains commands, parameters, and data that tell the Web Companion what to do.

A link sends a message to the Web Companion, which passes along its interpretation of that message to FileMaker and returns FileMaker's response.

Here is an example of a text string sent to the Web Companion. It tells the Web Companion to look for the database Contacts (the database must already be open on the server), then go to the layout called Websearch, which contains the field you want to search, and any other fields that you want be presented on the Results page. Then you specify the HTML-cum-CDML page on which you want the results displayed, in this case, Searchresults.htm. Then you order an action to be performed in FileMaker—in this case, to find records that contain Coulombre in the last name field:

```
/fmpro?-db=contacts.fp3&-lay=websearch&-
format=searchresults.htm&lastname=coulombre&-find
```

The ampersand-plus-hyphen introduces any command that the Web Companion will recognize. Field names, which are not commands, do not need the hyphen (just the ampersand as a separator). The last item, beginning with a hyphen and including the command Find, is the action tag. Every link must have an action.

> **Tip from**
> *Rich*
>
> Limit the number of fields. People who are new to Web publishing tend to create a layout with all the fields on it, thinking, "What the heck, I might use them sometime." But if your database has 50 or 100 fields and you are only going to use a few of those, think how much unnecessary information must be transferred from FileMaker to Web Companion if you get, say, 40 records that match a search criterion. Under the burden of all this information, speed declines. Better to create separate layouts for results of different searches, each with a few fields, rather than trying to use one gigantic layout containing every field for the results of every search. One size may fit all of the fields, but the slow delivery may drive your users nuts.

How Links Differ from Forms

A link contains a hardcoded instruction for the Web Companion; the link is not affected by any kind of user input other than a click. An example link is a specific Find request. In this case, the user can't use the link to look up anything else.

By contrast, a form enables the user to specify data for an action, such as a Find, and to enter data. A form area contains real fields, so users can enter or edit data and define their own search requests.

How Forms Work

When you create a form in an HTML page, you still have to specify everything that you would set up when defining a link. You still have to specify a form action. To create the tag starting the form you would write

```
<form action=" fmpro" method=" post" >
```

That starts the form area on the HTML page. This says, "We are starting a form area, and it is for a process called FileMaker Pro running back on the server." So when the message comes to Web Companion on the server, it will be routed to FileMaker Pro.

There are two methods: `Get` and `Post`. One shows your hand; the other conceals your secret message. The `Get` method takes the whole ugly text string sent by the browser to Web Companion and inserts that in the address box; when that text appears, with its combination of commands, data, and an address, then you have a security problem because users can fiddle around with the combined string. (In general, with FileMaker Pro, you should use `Post` to keep from revealing your database secrets to the user).

Now you need to send some parameters that tell FileMaker Pro the following information:

- The name of the database you want to work with.
- The name of the layout you want to use.

- The name of the format page you want to use; that is, the HTML page that will return the results laid out as they are on the layout (see below).
- The name of the error page, if you are going to provide one with an apology or explanation when things go wrong.
- What actions to perform.

FileMaker uses the HTML Input tag with a name-value pair—information we want to pass back to the Web Companion. A name-value pair is the name of an operation, and the value to be used in the operation. For instance, to specify a database, you use the `-db` command, and then give the filename as a value. We don't want this gosh-awful text to show up for the user on the Web page, so we make this text hidden:

```
<input type=" hidden" name=" -db" value=" contacts.fp5" >
```

A browser handles information in the form area by converting the name-value pair to match the format of the hardcoded link. For instance, in the name-value pair, we might say to use a layout called Weblayout, but keep it hidden, by writing

```
<input type=" hidden" name=" -lay" value=" weblayout" >
```

That would be distilled to the following:

```
-lay=weblayout
```

That compressed message is what would be sent to the Web Companion.

In these verbose codes, we express the name of the layout, the format page, and error page. But the browser is smart enough to convert the long version into a single link message to the Web Companion; that message, if you could peek at it, would look just like one of the hardcoded links. But here the values may be entered by the user, through the form.

All databases get messages in this odd format; the browser itself has no idea who it is talking to; the browser is just set up to send and respond to messages in this format. Web Companion was set up to receive, understand, and act on this standard output from the browser.

Within the form area, you need to place fields so users can enter data, edit it, or search on data they themselves have put into the database. You can place fields into a form area by using any graphic Web editor, or you can write the HTML to tell the browser that the field contains text with a particular default value and width measured in maximum number of characters. (Remember that using proportional fonts may make the length vary from font to font).

```
<input type=" text" name=" fieldname" value=" defaultvalue" size=" widthofthefieldmeasuredinmaximumnumberofcharacters" >
```

You also need to add some buttons. At the least, include a Reset button to restore the values in the field to their initial states, and a Submit button to tell the browser to go ahead and collect all of the information from the form, including the tags specifying the layout and format page, combining that material with any values the user has input, to compose the ugly text string and send it off to the Web Companion for processing. The Submit button, then, is a name-value pair like this:

```
<input type=" submit" name=" -new" value=" SUBMIT" >
```

This says that there should be a button, and the name of the button will be SUBMIT (or whatever you would like it to say), and its function will be to carry out the HTML command, <submit>.

Whenever you submit a message to the Web Companion, you must specify a format page—the place where the response will appear. You are asking for some data to be returned from FileMaker to the Web Companion, but you need a Web page on which to display that—a format page. A format page is an HTML page that happens to contain some CDML code. The Claris Dynamic Markup Language offers three kinds of tags. Variable and action tags, which tell the Web Companion to do something, begin with a hyphen; replacement tags, which tell the Web Companion to replace something, like the current value in a field, with new information from a database, appear inside square brackets.

To identify the format page, you include a phrase like this:

```
-format= webresultspage.htm
```

A format page resembles the word processing document used in a mail merge because it contains fields that are populated from a database or a data document (a text file where the first paragraph names each data element, and each subsequent paragraph represents a record, with fields separated by commas). The form letters contain boilerplate text for every form letter and fields such as Name and Address, with data that comes from the database; each new record in the database triggers a new document. The word processor document might also contain an IF statement, so we can vary the content of the form letter based on values coming over from the database.

Similarly, the format page contains standard HTML, content, and, typically, references to fields in the database, and, possibly, an IF statement that allows you to vary the HTML format, the standard content, or the fields displayed.

As part of a form area, a simple reference to the format page would be

```
<input type=" hidden" name=" -format" value=" Results" >
```

Creating an Error Page

If you ask FileMaker to perform an action, but FileMaker can't carry out that task, you can specify an error page to be used instead of the format page. For example, if you ask FileMaker to find a person's name, and there are no records containing that value, you can specify an error page to be displayed to the user saying that nothing was found. If you don't specify an error page, the format page appears.

As part of a form, the reference to the error page is

```
<input type="hidden" name="-error" value=" searcherror.htm" >
```

For security reasons, the Web Companion can only serve format pages or error pages from within the Web folder (or a subdirectory within that folder). The Web folder itself lives within the FileMaker Pro 5 folder. Security is involved because, in general, you do not want to offer access to other information on the user's hard drive, such as their love letters, resumé, and proprietary reports. When you are publishing on the Web from a user's computer, you want to make sure that strangers cannot just stroll around the user's hard disk. To insure that people from the Web cannot use FileMaker as a back door to get at other stuff on a user's hard drive, FileMaker only allows access to files that appear within its Web folder.

Understanding Security

FileMaker will recognize and use passwords and group privileges, but only if these have been set up within FileMaker. (It doesn't care about AppleShare passwords, for example). If you go into Passwords, you can allow a user to do some things, but remember, not every activity is possible over the Web. You can offer Web users the following privileges:

- To create new records
- To edit records
- To delete records
- To override data entry warnings

A user can always print from the Web browser, and could, if you wanted, run a button to print records back on the server side, and this button would be controlled by the FileMaker passwords. The Web security database allows you to do more than you can do with passwords, offering or refusing other functions. It gives a little more control over user interactions. Specifically, in custom Web publishing, it gives record-level security for your database on the Web. You can limit Web user access to particular records by creating a special field value for those records that only authorized users know and enter. Then, using the ExactSearch, ExactUpdate, or ExactDelete restrictions, you can control which record a user can get at.

How to Plan for Web Delivery

Web users won't be able to do as much as regular FileMaker users, and neither will you. For instance, FileMaker layouts give you greater control over the position, size, and format of objects than HTML allows.

Also, a local FileMaker guest always has a persistent connection to the server, so data gets updated on the fly, whereas the Web guest has to rely on HTML, which establishes connections and drops them in a series of transactions. The Web user comes in, gets information, and leaves; after that, the user loses any connection with live data. Users get a snapshot of the data at the time they visited, but do not receive updates.

In the browser you do have the ability to run JavaScript code, but that language was not built to talk with FileMaker directly. ScriptMaker was. Putting the -script CDML tag into a hard link or form area lets you specify a script to be run at that moment. For instance, to run the script MyScript, you would write

```
<input type=" hidden" name=" -script" value=" MyScript" >
```

But you may run into problems. Running a script often takes time, but after that time, the user gets the information more quickly over a local area network than over the Web, so the Web user may complain about delays in getting information back from the script.

Also, what do you do about reports? Record-level data is not a big problem to display, and even tables generally appear well. But other reports offer tougher challenges. For instance, with a local printer, FileMaker does a great job of printing mailing labels. But how do you move the labels into a browser page and preserve print measurements precise enough that the text stays right within the labels? Or consider subsummary reports. How do you get those to work in a browser? If you really, really had to hack this, it would not be easy or pretty. You are moving to a different piece of software (the browser), and that software was never built with database connectivity in mind. HTML does not offer ScriptMaker controls.

There's plenty of pressure to put the data up on the Web and pretend that the browser can do the same job as FileMaker in presenting, reporting, and printing. Over the years, Information Technology (IT) departments ended up supporting a lot of database software on different users' computers, and support and maintenance became a headache. The Web browser looked like it might be a universal client for everyone's databases. The browser does solve some problems: the clients are free, and no matter where the backend data, IT only has to worry about installing one client. They don't have to have a FileMaker client, an Omnis client, or an Access client. Everything comes through the browser.

Unfortunately, each database client brings out the best in its data. With a Web browser, you have a client that is capable of displaying the results of searches, but cannot do as much as the original database software could, particularly in areas of automation, reporting, and formatting. The Web capabilities of FileMaker are best for giving users access to certain slices of data, but so far the various tools available as part of the FileMaker Pro 5 suite do not offer a fully integrated environment, such as an entire invoicing system. Many functions you take for granted are many times harder on the Web, if it is possible. For instance, if you were to move our invoicing system to the Web, you would have to change the whole user interface, reinvent the reporting mechanism, and redo the automation. Any button that performs an action in our database would not work by itself; you would have to write a hard link to substitute for it. Getting automation to work the way it does in FileMaker would be a massive challenge. A script in FileMaker can take you from file to file, collecting data from other places, but a hard link has trouble doing that; also, a script can examine conditions within FileMaker and perform actions accordingly, but doing that from the Web becomes difficult.

From the Web, you can expect to do these operations fairly easily:

- Do searches
- Show search results
- Tunnel into record detail after a search
- Create new records
- Edit records
- Delete records

But you can expect difficulty if you store data in multiple files and print complicated reports that require precision. These are possible, but compared to doing them in native FileMaker, performing these tasks on the Web will take three times as much work. If we were asked to put the invoicing system on the Web, we would decline. The Web is really a different paradigm, which requires a different approach to the database. Also, this supposedly ubiquitous client varies from vendor to vendor and version to version.

By the way, these are not just FileMaker constraints. Every database faces the same kind of problems when integrating with the Web.

Putting Your Database Directly on the Internet

Browser access is not the only way to access a FileMaker database over the Internet. FileMaker itself supports the TCP/IP protocol, the basis for the Internet, so if the user has the IP address of the FileMaker server, the user can open the database in FileMaker across the Internet by choosing TCP/IP as an application preference, then choosing File, Open, clicking the Hosts button, choosing to specify the host, and typing in the IP address. This is a good idea. The user is now using FileMaker on his desktop, and FileMaker is talking directly to the FileMaker server, not the browser, so the user can take full advantage of FileMaker's layouts, reporting, and scripts.

You have to explain to users that the performance they get will depend mostly on the nature of their Internet connection. If they are dialing in from home on a 56k modem, they will not get results back as quickly as they will by using a T1 line in the office. Or if there's heavy traffic when they dial in, or a lot of people using the server at the time, the response speed will be pokey.

For best speeds, we recommend that the FileMaker server be connected to the Internet with a T1 line, or, more inexpensively (and less robustly), frame relay, ISDN, DSL, or cable modem. The decision depends on how many concurrent users you have, and how much data will be moving back and forth.

Each user must have a copy of FileMaker. In some circumstances, to keep costs down, you might consider a mix: a few folks have this kind of direct FileMaker access, to do labels, scripts, and so on, but people who just need quick access to a fact or record can have browser access.

Exporting Data as HTML Pages with the Results of Calculations

With careful calculations, you can export your FileMaker data as HTML-tagged documents and post those on the Web for others to explore. Essentially, the calculation merges data into tags and pushes out HTML pages.

> **CASE STUDY: POSTING IN UNIX**
>
> A client had a FileMaker system that tracked some information the team wanted to display on the Web. But by policy all Web postings had to be done in a UNIX environment. So we had to figure a way to get this FileMaker database into UNIX. We calculated all the HTML pages needed—this was difficult—then we exported the raw text in files with the extension html. After we exported this whole directory and renamed the pages based on a data element and the TROI plug-in, FileMaker initiated an FTP to send the directory over to the UNIX server, and that is how we updated the Web site on a daily basis. The users could continue using FileMaker for data entry and editing, and, without violating the organization policy, display them as HTML files on UNIX.

With exporting each record as an HTML page, you can't anticipate how many pages you will have, and you probably don't want to sit there and bless each file with its own name manually. The TROI plug-in (available in demo form on our CD) lets you set up a field containing a name for the document that will be made out of the record. The TROI plug-in lets you set up directories, move files, and rename files; the TROI commands are available through the calculation engine. We can create a looping script that exports a record, doing some calculated HTML tagging, to a fixed name such as temp.htm, and then we use the TROI plug-in to rename that file by using a value in the record itself.

You can generate an entire Web site from one or more databases. You make the links between the old records (now HTML pages) by running a calculation with a text result that is a link in HTML.

> **Tip from**
> *Rich*
>
> Make sure that the value in that field is unique. This value is used to assign filenames, and you don't want to overwrite file after file by assigning the same name to each one.

For an example of creating Web pages from within FileMaker Pro 5, look in the Chapter 9 folder and launch the Companies-i01.fp5; then click the button Create Web Site. This generates HTML pages with the summary of companies, individual company details, and contact details. The names of these company files are named after the Primary key of the company because we know each of those is unique. Similarly, each contacts file is named after the Primary key plus the .htm extension. The Company summary name is hardcoded because we have only one of those and do not have to worry about varying its name. Double-click the file compsummary.htm to start using the Web site.

Before we could get FileMaker to calculate these pages, we had to map out how the Web site itself would work. We decided to start with a main page summarizing all the companies in an HTML table, with each company's name offering a hypertext link to that company's detail page. On the company detail page we would provide information about the company along with a list of contacts, and each contact's name would link to a page offering detail on that contact. In the contact detail page, we would give info about the contact in a table plus links back to the Company Detail or Company Summary.

The beauty of HTML is that you can describe quite complex formats in a file that holds nothing but ASCII text. Using FileMaker's calculations, you can therefore impose a format on the page and provide the data.

The Company Summary page, for instance, starts off with generic information that never changes (the title of the report and the column headings for the table). Then, within the table, we have a separate row for each record in the database. Then, after the final row, we need closing information to tell the Web browser that the table is complete and the body of the HTML page is over too. The first part of the body is the title of the report (Company Summary):

```
<HTML> <HEAD>   <TITLE>Companies List</TITLE> </HEAD> <BODY> <P> </P>
<H2><CENTER>Companies List</CENTER></H2> <CENTER>   <P>
```

This material was generated by the calculation in field C_Comp_Summary_ HTML_Begin, which runs like this:

```
"<HTML>¶
<HEAD>¶
  <TITLE>Companies List</TITLE>¶
</HEAD>¶
<BODY>¶
<P> </P>¶
<H2><CENTER>Companies List</CENTER></H2>¶" & "
<CENTER> ¶
<P><TABLE BORDER=1>¶
  <TR>¶
    <TD WIDTH=159>¶
      <P><B>Company Name</B></P>¶
    </TD>¶
    <TD>¶
      <P><B>Location</B></P>¶
    </TD>¶
  </TR>"
```

That generates the title for the Company Summary window, the heading at the top of the page, and the column headings at the top of the table, as the first row.

Why not put this in a Global field? When users clone a file in FileMaker, values in global fields are lost. Being cautious, we chose instead to put this information into a Calculation field with results that are saved in the file, so that if the user clones the file, the calculation is still there. Concerned that we are redundantly storing this calculation, which has the same result for every record? Yes, we are, but the amount we are storing is really negligible.

Now we needed to get record data onto that Web page. The next field we made, we calculated the HTML for each record's row in the table. (The field is called c_company_summary_record_html).

```
"<TR>" & "¶" &
"<TD Width=150>" & "¶" &
"<P><A HREF=" & g_quote & pk_company_id & ".htm" & g_quote & ">" & company_name &
"</A></P>" & "¶" &
"</TD>" & "¶" &
"<TD Width=150>" & "¶" &
"<P>" & c_csz & "</P>" & "¶" &
"</TD>" & "¶" &
"</TR>"
```

We begin a table row, and within the row we create a cell for company name and a cell for location, and then end the row. HTML expects the filename for the hypertext reference to appear within quotes, so we build up a string that starts with a quote (from the global field for quotes, described below), adds the Primary key for the company, adds the company ID, adds the extension .htm, and closes the quote. That phrase, then, will generate the filename of the Web page containing the detail about the company. The company name itself comes from the Company Name field. All of these bits and pieces are concatenated with ampersands.

When we create a calculation, of course, we use quotes to show the beginning and ending of chunks of literal text, so the quotes will not be part of the text results. Of course, if you want a quote character as part of the results, you have to use four quotes in a row to get FileMaker to put a single quote character in the result. Ugly. But here is an alternate: g_quote is a global text field, and whenever someone creates the Create Web Site button, we set g_quote equal to those four quotes.

The next cell takes data from the calculated field csz that puts together City, State, and Zip. At the end, the HTML tags close out the body and the page.

We place the Web site files at the root directory because we wanted this process to work on Windows 95/98, Windows NT, and Mac. The Web site appears in a directory called HTML Export Examples. We used the TROI plug-in to generate filenames. FileMaker can export to text files, to a fixed directory, with a fixed filename. But we were trying to write these files to a directory whose path would differ from one operating system to another. The TROI plug-in can tell us the path to the root directory of each system, and create files there. TROI allows us to calculate the path to the storage location, to create the directory there, and to grab filenames from data in the primary-key field for company and contact within each record, to make sure that each filename would be unique. (A contact name, for instance, might not be unique).

➔For more information on how plug-ins can extend your reach, **see** "How FileMaker Connects," **p. 500.**

CREATING DETAIL RECORDS

We have now created the page summarizing all the companies. In addition, we created pages giving detail on each company and on each contact within that company. The company detail shows specific information about the company and lists the contacts who work for that company. The contact detail describes each person. Basically, we use the same method to develop both sets of Web pages, with one variation: For Company details, we have to visit the Contacts file briefly, whereas for contact details, we can stay within that file the whole time.

Exporting the company detail pages, for instance, we use two scripts. One is export_single_somp_detail_HTML_page, and the other exports all of those details: export_all_comp_detail_HTML_page. The All script runs the whole process of exporting by showing all records, going to the first record, then looping through the records one at a time, performing the script that generates the HTML that will go in the middle of each Web page, and then exports a single record each time.

In creating the HTML page showing a company's details, we again have sections for the beginning of the page, the middle, and the end. To start off, we use a calculation within each record, c_comp_detail_HTML_begin. That field puts together some HTML tags, along with the name of the company and city-state-ZIP to start off the Web page. The material in the middle of the page is a list of contacts, so the Single script checks to see whether the company has any contacts (and if not, generates HTML saying "This company has no contacts"), and if the company does have contacts, goes to the Contacts file, and using the Go to Related Records, with the Show Only Related Records option, creates a found set over in the Contacts file that represents the children of the current company. Then we run a script in the Contacts file that switches to a layout that contains a calculation field that contains the raw HTML we need for the middle of the file. We copy that to the clipboard, switch to the Companies file, go to a layout containing the g_comp_detail_HTML_middle, and paste that contact HTML into the field. That field now holds valid HTML code with data about this company's contacts.

Another field, c_comp_detail_HTML_export, takes the beginning HTML, adds a carriage return, grabs the middle HTML, and adds the HTML for the closing from the field called c_comp_detail_HTML_end. In effect, it assembles the entire HTML for the page.

The Single script calls the TROI plug-in, which, with a little voodoo, lets us create an empty text file (named for the company's ID, with the .htm extension) out in the HTML Export Example folder at the root level of the computer's directory, and we append the HTML from c_compu_HTML_export, essentially filling that text file with good code. More on TROI voodoo in Chapter 15.

The trickiest part here is getting the actual HTML tags exactly right. We have done this trick for many clients, and each time the gnarliest aspect is ensuring that the calculations really spit out the right tags along with the data.

By the way, we've relied heavily on the developer log here, which we'll discuss more in Chapter 14. As we created the scripts and did troubleshooting, the scripts do so much so fast that we needed to lard the script with messages to be embedded in the log file, telling us what file is involved when and when a particular action began or ended; also, because some actions are nested within each other, we added indentations. The TROI plug-in also returns an error code if something does not work as expected, so for each action we capture the error code, if any. An error code does not necessarily mean that something went wrong; it just means that TROI was not able to complete the requested action, which may be just what we want. For example, we may ask TROI to create the HTML export example directory at the root level, but if the user has run this script before, that directory already exists, and so TROI will tell us it was unable to create the directory because it already exists. That doesn't bother us, but TROI is alerting us that it could not do what we requested.

Using Lasso to Go Beyond the Web Companion

For more features than the Web Companion offers, consider Lasso, a product that comes in three flavors—a CGI, a Web server plug-in, and a Web server with built-in CGI capabilities. A few years back, Lasso technology was incorporated into FileMaker beginning with version 4.0 as an essential part of the Web Companion. But Blue World Communications has continued to add features to Lasso, and developers turn to this product for more complex webification. A few reasons you might want to turn to Lasso are the following:

- It operates independently of FileMaker, so it can continue to serve and process pages even while FileMaker is busy processing finds, scripts, calculations, sorts, and other actions.
- It can handle multiple actions at the same time, independent of any concurrent processing going on in FileMaker.
- It can defeat hackers who want to copy your CDML code.
- It works with an SSL Web server to provide secure online transactions.
- It can protect files individually or by folder.
- It offers more complex If/Else conditional comparisons of data.
- It supports ODBC.
- It allows you to use Java for dynamic front ends, as well as applets that interact with the FileMaker data.
- The Form Builder in Lasso walks you through the process, as shown in Figure 9.10.

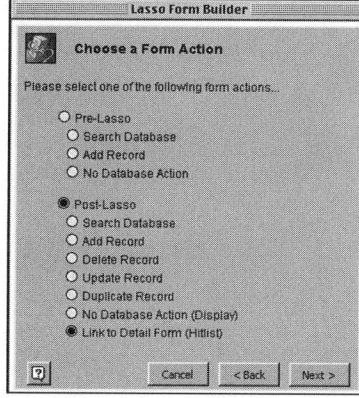

Figure 9.10
The Form Builder lets you specify the actions for a form. (Courtesy of Blue World)

- The Inline Tag Editor helps you build complex tags step-by-step (see Figure 9.11).

Figure 9.11
The Inline Tag Editor helps you put together complex tags accurately. (Courtesy of Blue World)

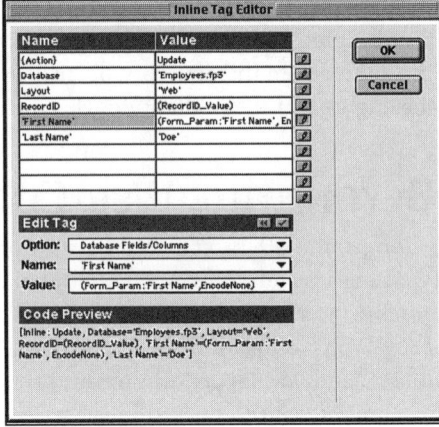

- It has built-in support for ODBC datasources, while FileMaker's Web Companion does not (although FileMaker 5 itself does have some support for this).
- Lasso also acts as a plug-in for Dreamweaver.
- Its command language has more features than CDML

If you find you are struggling with the limitations of CDML, take a look at Lasso, which may have some simple commands in its Lasso Dynamic Markup Language to solve the problem.

→Just as HTML lets you format your Web page by inserting tags that tell the user's browser what format to apply to the material they precede or surround, XML lets you create tags and use them to identify elements of meaningful content, such as a field. **See** "Going from HTML to XML and WML," **p. 517.**

CHAPTER 10

HOT CALCULATIONS

In this chapter

Why Calculations Can Get Hot   274

Welcome to the Formula   274

Mathematical and Financial Calculations   275

Text Calculations   279

Date Calculations   294

Time Calculations   305

Conditional Calculations   307

Calculations with Container Results   312

Creating a Fully Formatted Document for Database Publishing   313

Calculating with Check Boxes   316

Generating Random Numbers   326

Creating a Bar Graph   329

Exporting or Importing Fixed-Length Records   331

Handling Aggregate Functions   338

Why Calculations Can Get Hot

In their simplest form, calculations let you carry out analysis and operations on one or more fields within a record. FileMaker Pro 5 offers a rich set of operators and functions, allowing you to perform acrobatic feats of calculation for which you might otherwise need a macro or programming language. Generally, you'll define a field as a Calculation, using the Options window in which you put together the formula as shown in Figure 10.1, but you can also create calculations as part of an auto-enter or validation routine, or a script.

Figure 10.1
The Options dialog offers a list of fields, punctuation buttons, numbers, logical operators, and pre-designed functions for you to plug into a formula.

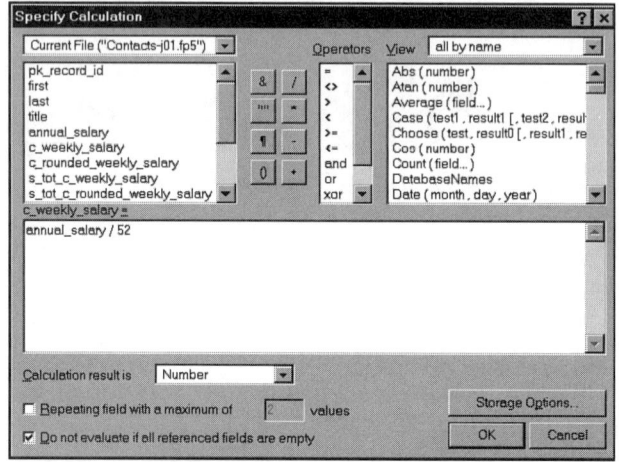

COMMON MISTAKE: TYPOS WHEN ENTERING A FIELD, FUNCTION, OR OPERATOR NAME INTO A FORMULA

Don't type these names yourself. Grab them from one of the lists in the Options dialog, so you don't get those annoying messages telling you that there is an error in your formula.

Welcome to the Formula

The most familiar operators and functions build mathematical, logical, and financial calculations. But in a calculation, you can also take apart and assemble text, run the numbers involving dates or time, and, most logically, use IF, Case, and Choose functions to test for conditions, branching to different results.

Functions put together basic math operators to perform more sophisticated tasks, such as figuring the future value of an investment, given a fixed payment, constant interest rate, and a fixed number of payment periods. The proliferation of functions offered means you don't have to spend the time working out these algorithms and formulas. The challenge you face is assembling the right combination of operators and functions for the job.

In this chapter, we explore some of the calculations we have found most useful in creating databases that really work for business.

Mathematical and Financial Calculations

In this section, we'll take a look at a few formulas that you may find useful in handling money:

- Using rounding to avoid errors in summaries
- Using the Int and Mod functions to get whole numbers
- Calculating payments

➔ For an overview of what you can put in a Calculation field, **see** "What to Put in a Calculation Field," p. **74**.

Using Rounding to Avoid Errors in Summaries

You've probably been warned a hundred times about rounding errors. To hear math teachers talk, you might think that you must keep the results of every calculation accurate to many places, and only round off at the end. But when you are talking real money, that's not true.

If you intend to summarize a series of calculations, round off the results of each calculation as you go, on each record. That way, each record's figures represent real money, in dollars and cents, or pounds and pence, not hypothetical slivers of a coin. (And never count on formatting alone to round anything off, because formatting just makes the data look better, while leaving the original figures untouched.)

Imagine you have a small departmental database tracking annual salaries and weekly pay for two dozen people, and on each person's weekly record, you figure out the weekly salary, as in the Chapter 10 file called Contacts-j01.fp5. Nobody makes more than a thousand bucks a week, so each person's salary appears in 3 digits to the left of the decimal place and 12 digits to the right, as shown in the Data Entry screen in Figure 10.2. Of course, you don't want all those digits on the person's paycheck. So you might be tempted to just format the field to show only two digits, because on any one record, that looks exactly like the result of rounding to two decimal places. But, although that looks like a solution, it leaves the other figures to the right of the decimal place, and when you add all those up, you begin to get a discrepancy. The numbers that were only rounded by formatting can easily add up to a few cents more (or less) than the total of the checks, as you can see in Figure 10.3. Hey, what's a few cents every week? Well, enough to raise an accountant's eyebrows at the end of the year.

Figure 10.2
In the individual record, rounding changes the number, whereas formatting would leave the original number, changing only its presentation.

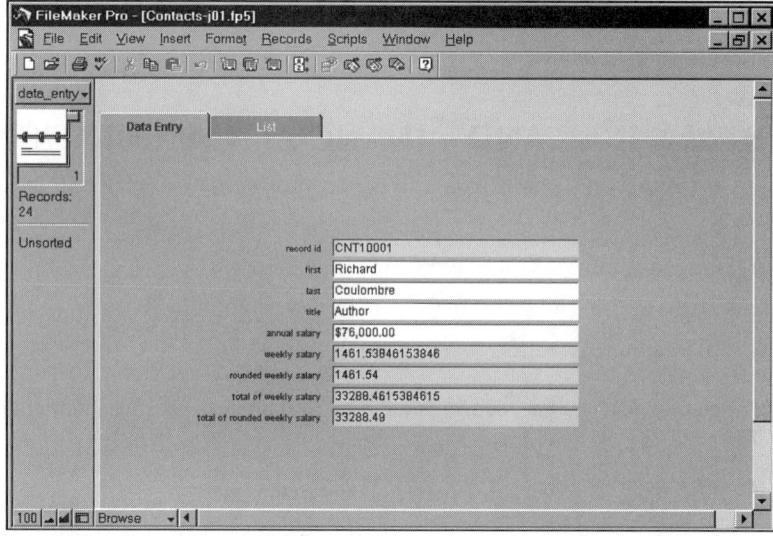

Figure 10.3
Unchanged by formatting, the extra digits in the original numbers add up, resulting in a discrepancy between the apparent total and the real total.

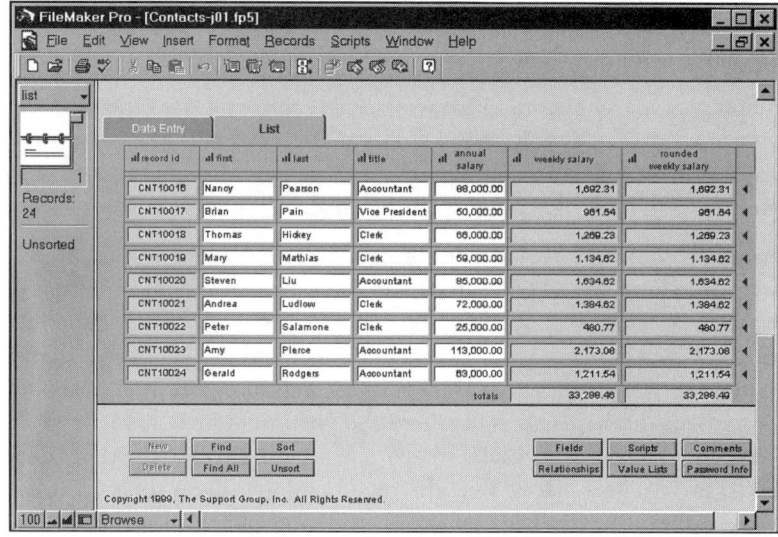

The more calculations you are handling, the bigger the difference. To avoid embarrassing audits, round off each person's weekly salary to a precision of 2 (2 digits to the right of the decimal place). FileMaker looks at the additional digits, and rounds up or down—and then discards all the other numbers to the right, forever. That's key. Rounding changes the number, whereas formatting just puts cosmetic on top.

Using the Int and Mod Functions to Get Whole Numbers

Here's the mantra: Integer grabs the whole number only, and Modulo gives you just the remainder. For instance, Int (25.67889) lops off everything to the right of the decimal point, resulting in 25. On the other hand, if you write Mod (25, 7), FileMaker divides 25 by 7, getting a result of 3 with the remainder of 4. Dismissing the integer, and focusing on the remainder, FileMaker emerges with a value of 4.

Example: Identifying What Page Each Record Appears On

Sometimes it is helpful to know what page a particular record will appear on in the report, and on that page, which slot the record will be dropped into. For instance, a catalog publisher wanted to generate a table of contents or index of all topics, showing which page each record appeared on. We then made up a separate report, printing out a list with the identifying name of the record with its page and position (third on the page, for instance), and that report acted as a table of contents for the other report.

Our example file Contacts-j02.fp5 presumes that there will be an equal number of records on every page—in this case, 5 per page. We are calculating what page each record will land on in the printed report. We are also figuring out which of the 5 records this will be—first, second, third, fourth, or fifth.

In the Calculation field named c_page_numb, we set up this calculation:

```
Int((Status( CurrentRecordNumber) - 1) / 5) + 1
```

This calculation tells us where the current record falls on the page. If we're on the sixth record, the CurrentRecordNumber is 6, so running Status on the CurrentRecordNumber returns the value of 6. We subtract 1 from that and then divide by 5, which yields a whole number 1. Taking the Integer of that, which is still 1, we add 1 to that, getting the right page number: 2.

If we just divided by 5 and got the Integer, we might get some strange results. For instance, the first 4 records would be on page 0. The fifth record would seem to be the first one on page 1.

By subtracting 1 from the page number, we squeeze the first 5 records onto page 0. But, alas, our report does not begin on page 0. So we add 1 to the result.

Now, if we are on record 23, say, we still get the right answer, despite this razzle-dazzle with adding and subtracting 1. (23-1)/5 = 4 with a remainder of 2, which we discard. Then we add 1 to the 4 to get page 5. Correct! Page 5 handles records 21 through 25. To see the results of the page assignment process, look in the List layout of Contacts-j02, as shown in Figure 10.4.

But we have set ourselves an additional challenge—to determine which position each record holds within the page, we run this calculation:

```
Mod((Status( CurrentRecordNumber) - 1), 5) + 1
```

Figure 10.4
The calculation in c_page_numb figures out which page each record belongs on (in Contacts-j02.fp5).

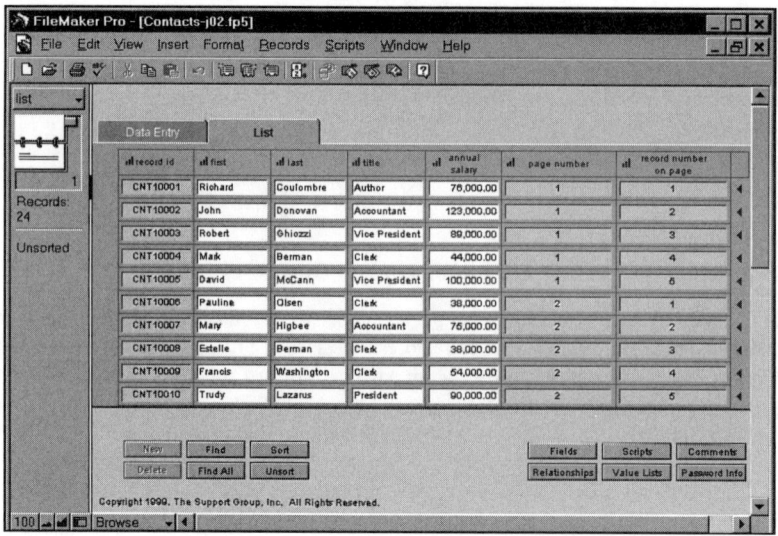

This is the same calculation (the second argument, 5, is the divisor), except that we look at the remainder, rather than the integer. Thus, if we are looking at the sixth record, we would go through this calculation: ((6-1)/5) = 1 with no remainder. Then we add 1 to the remainder of 0, so that the Modulo result is 1. Therefore, the sixth record appears as the first record on the second page.

> **Tip from**
> *Rich*
>
> Use the DayOfWeek function to sort the days of the week properly. If you want subtotals by day, using DayName, you get an odd sort: Friday starts off the week, followed by Monday, after which we get Saturday and Sunday, then Thursday, Tuesday, and, to complete the week, Wednesday. To avoid this silly calendar, you need to assign a number to each day of the week, such as 1 for Sunday, 2 for Monday, and so on, and sort by that number. To calculate that number, use this formula:
>
> ```
> DayOfWeek (Date of Transaction)
> ```

CALCULATING PAYMENTS

Now you can figure out your mortgage! In CalcPayments-j03.fp5, type in the amount of the loan, the interest rate, and the term in months, to get the monthly payment, rounded off to two figures, as shown in Figure 10.5. Here the rounding helps us maintain accuracy, after PMT figures out the payment in 18 digits.

```
Round( PMT( loan_amount, interest_rate/12, number_of_months), 2 )
```

Figure 10.5
Type a new interest rate, or term, to see the new monthly payment.

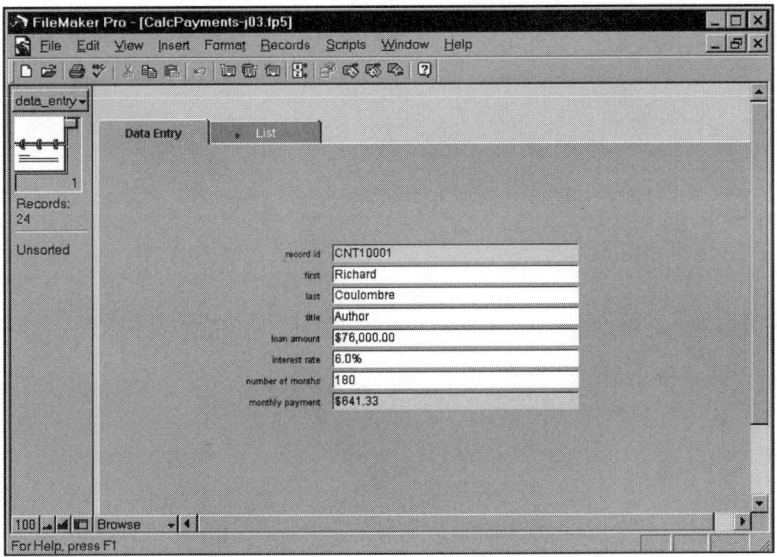

TEXT CALCULATIONS

FileMaker Pro 5 offers a surprising number of operators and functions that help you pull apart, analyze, and reassemble almost any text. You might think of these when you have a question that involves text.

Question	Operator or Function	Example
How can I glue together two passages of text?	Ampersand	"text" & "text"
Are the letters and case of the text in Text A an exact match of Text B?	Exact (text, text)	Exact (TextA, TextB)
Can I grab a certain number of characters from the left side of a text?	Left (text, number)	Left (Last_Name, 20)
How many characters are there in a certain text?	Length (text)	Length (Last_Name)
What characters appear starting at a particular position, and extending for a certain number of characters, all told?	Middle (text, starting position, size)	Middle (Social_ Security, 5, 2)

Question	Function	Example
At what position does a particular string of characters begin, if we start looking at a particular position?	`Position (text, search string, start, occurrence)`	`Position (Phone_Number, 505, 1, 1)`
How can I replace the characters in a particular text, starting at a certain position, and continuing for a certain length (or size), with a specific alternative text?	`Replace (text, start, size, replacement text)`	`Replace ("Fred is the janitor at our school", 13, 7, "custodian")`
Can I grab a certain number of characters that appear at the end of a particular text?	`Right (text, number)`	`Right (Phone_Number,7)`
How do I get rid of leading or trailing space characters (blanks)?	`Trim (text)`	`Trim (Mainframe_Data)`
How do I make sure everything in the text appears in lowercase?	`Lower (text)`	`Lower (generic_name)`
How do I capitalize a particular text so it looks like a book title, with the first letter of each word in uppercase, and all the others lowercase?	`Proper (text)`	`Proper (product_name)`
How do I turn a whole text into uppercase letters?	`Upper (text)`	`Upper (legal_warning)`
How do I convert a date into regular text?	`DateToText (date)`	`DateToText (invoice_date)`
How do I take a number and convert its type from Number to Text?	`NumToText (number)`	`NumToText (grade_level)`
How do I turn a particular time into text?	`TimeToText (time)`	`TimeToText (checkin_time)`

➔For an overview of what you can put in a Text field, for later manipulation by the following calculations, **see** "What to Put in a Text Field," p. **170**.

In this section, we apply our magnifying glass to several useful text calculations:

- Taking apart a text string to reformat it
- Putting together a full address
- Using overlapping fields to simulate typing in a Calculation field
- Using the `PatternCount` function to spot values
- Extracting the prefix to the name, first, middle initial, last name, and suffix to the last name

Taking Apart a Text String to Reformat It

Some data looks like numbers at first glance, but includes hyphens, parentheses, and multiple points, dots, or whatnots. If you put the data into a Number field, FileMaker will ignore non-numeric characters when indexing or searching. Also, if you are collecting Social Security numbers, you may be able to persuade your clerks to leave out the hyphens when entering the data, but the results are hard to read. To reformat the number as a text string with three digits, a hyphen, two digits, another hyphen, and four digits, we turn to `Left`, `Middle`, and `Right` functions, in a calculation like this:

```
Left (Social Security Number, 3) & "-" & Middle (Social Security Number, 5, 2) &
"-" & Right (Social Security Number, 4)
```

That tells FileMaker to go to the Social Security Number entry, take the first 3 characters, add a dash, take the middle 2 digits, starting at the fourth character, add another dash, and then end with the rightmost 4 characters. (This works because the Social Security Number always has the same length and format.

Tip from
Rich

The `Left`, `Middle`, and `Right` functions work best when you have text strings all of which start off with the same length, structure, and format.

This approach also works for phone numbers, as in Contacts-j04.fp5, as shown in Figure 10.6. If you have users who have to enter a lot of phone numbers, they will say, "Why can't I just type in all the numbers in a row, really fast, and let the computer put the phone number together in the right way?" Some database programs have a feature called data masking, which performs that magic, but FileMaker does not do that. So, instead, we calculate what the phone number should look like. Of course, we face three possible situations in the United States: a string of 7 digits, a string of 10 digits, and something else, which we cannot handle as a phone number (a mistake, probably).

Figure 10.6
The clerk can type only the numbers, lickety-split, and we transform those into a conventionally formatted phone number.

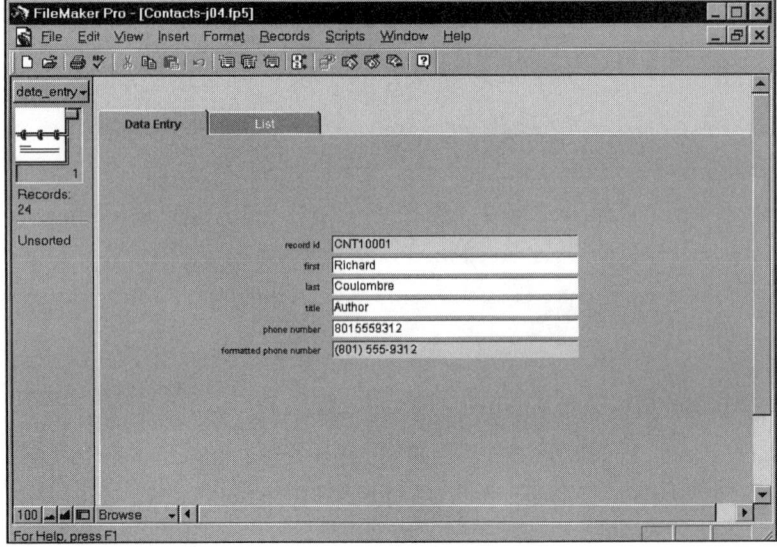

First, we examine the value in the phone_number field and use the Length function to figure out the number of characters.

- If the length is 7, then we take the leftmost 3 characters, add a hyphen, and drop in the rightmost 4 characters. (This is the easiest formatting).
- If there are 10 characters, we start with an open parenthesis, drop in the leftmost 3 characters, a closing parens, a space, and then the local number, as before.
- If the string has a length other than 7 and 10, we enter "Unrecognized Phone Number," alerting or user to the possibility of an error, or a non-U.S. number.

Here is that calculation:

```
If( Length(phone_number) = 7,
   Left(phone_number, 3) & "-" & Right(phone_number, 4),

If( Length(phone_number) = 10,
   "(" & Left(phone_number, 3) & ") " & Middle(phone_number, 4, 3)   & "-" &
       Right(phone_number, 4),

"Unrecognized phone number"))
```
The result goes into the c_formatted_phone_number field.

Tip from
Rich

Think about trapping errors when you build a calculation. Here, for instance, we recognize that there may be lengths other than 7 or 10. Think about what you assume users are entering, and develop a way to deal with mistakes (anything that violates your assumptions). You can do the error checking within the formula, or, after you get a result, you can use validation.

Text Calculations

> **Tip from Rich**
>
> Cut, copy, and paste when creating a calculation. When copying the whole calculation, make sure that you select all, so you do not lose part of the calculation. By the way, all the keyboard shortcuts for Cut, Copy, Paste, and Select All work in the Calculation dialog.

Putting Together a Full Address

If you've been careful and created individual fields for first name, last name, street, city, state, and ZIP, you may be annoyed to discover that a mainframe application expects the whole address to be wrapped up in a single value, for a single field. Or you need to provide users with a complete address they can copy and paste as a unit when moving to another application.

In creating a full address, you may also want to avoid blank lines (where there was no mail stop, say) and gaps (where a middle initial does not fill up the space you have made for it, for example).

When you are using separate fields, you can slide the entries left and up, to cover up these holes, but now we are contemplating putting the entire address into a single field, without pockmarks.

In our sample file Contacts-j05.fp5, shown in Figure 10.7, we build the address with this calculation:

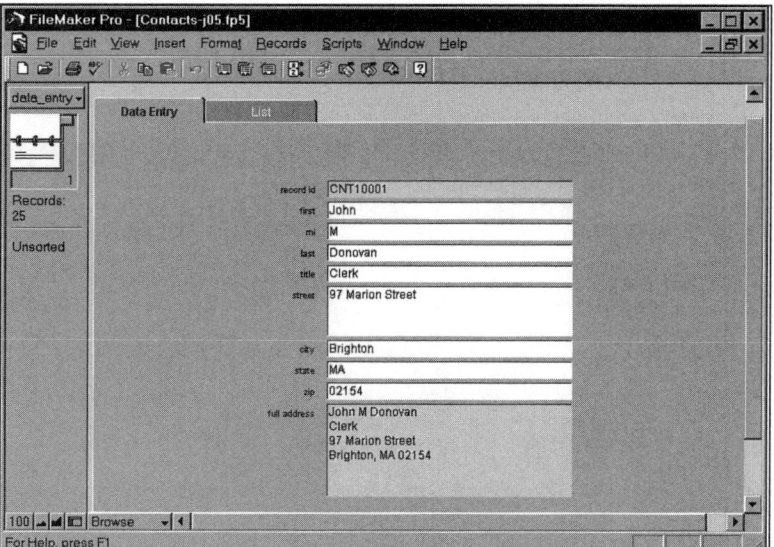

Figure 10.7
The full address appears in its own field.

```
first & " " &  If(IsEmpty(mi), "", mi & " ") & last & "¶" &
If(IsEmpty(title), "", title & "¶") &
If(IsEmpty(street), "", street & "¶") &
        city & ", " & state & " " & zip
```

The function called `IsEmpty` tests to see if a field is empty or not. If it is empty, the function returns the value of `True`, or `1`, and we are saying, if it is true that the field is empty, place absolutely nothing here; otherwise, put in the contents of the field.

Tip from
Rich

Use returns and spaces inside quotes to make your calculation easier to read. As long as returns and spaces are not inside quotes, FileMaker ignores them. We put hard returns into the calculation just to break it up for readability. In this way, the calculation matches the output, line by line. In the J04 example, we used spaces to indent subordinate parts of the calculation, so the relationships would be easier to spot during maintenance.

Tip from
Rich

Use this technique for letters. If you have to copy an entire address from a single field, to paste into a word-processing document, create the full address in a single field, instead of placing field after field into the letter as you would do when creating a form letter.

Using Overlapping Fields to Simulate Typing in a Calculation Field

Back in the j04 example file, we calculated the phone number so that when someone enters the raw numbers, we can mask the original data, reformatting it so the phone number appears in a consistent format. Now, in Contacts-j06.fp5, we want to view the formatted number in a Calculation field (which, of course, prevents data entry), but we need to allow a user to enter the field and view the raw data to edit it. Figure 10.8 shows the data entry record for Contacts.

Figure 10.8
We format the number through a Calculation, but allow the user to edit it through overlapping fields.

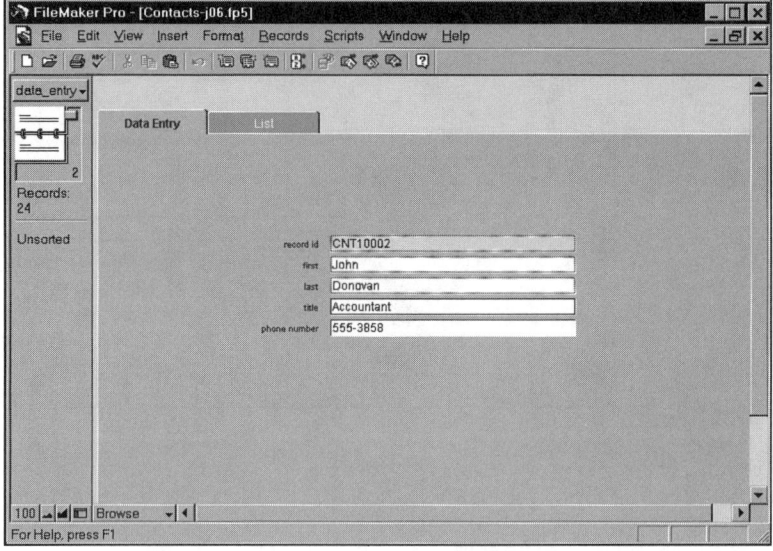

We have a field called phone_number, and that is the one the user types into. And we have another field, c_formatted_phone_number, which calculates the formatted version of the phone number; this is what the user sees.

We want the user to be able to tab into the field and see the originally entered data. So we put the field phone_number (with raw data) on the bottom. Right over that we put the Calculation field, c_formatted_phone_number. And we tweak the formatted field in two ways. First, we fill it with white, so that it normally masks out the field underneath. But we also use the Field Format dialog to choose not to allow clicking into (or entering) the formatted field. (You can normally click into a Calculation field to select the value and copy it, if you want; but you cannot type in new data, or revise what is there. Deselecting the "Allow entry into field" option, shown in Figure 10.9, blocks users from even tabbing into the field.)

Figure 10.9
We recommend deselecting the "Allow entry into field" option.

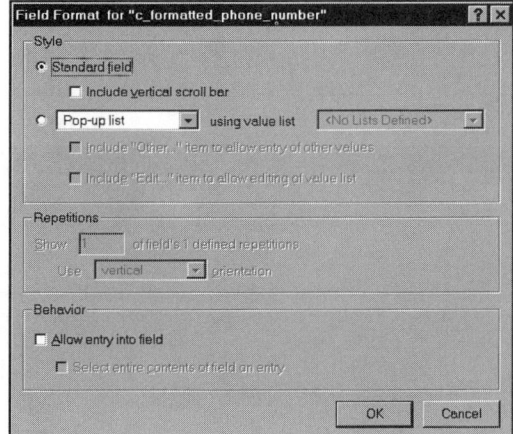

When the user clicks the area, FileMaker passes the click through the nonenterable field, brings the enterable field to the top level, and masks out the other field (as in Figure 10.10). After the user revises or types in a phone number and tabs out, the Calculation field comes back to life, displaying a formatted version of the phone number (see Figure 10.11).

286 | Chapter 10 Hot Calculations

Figure 10.10
A user types the raw data.

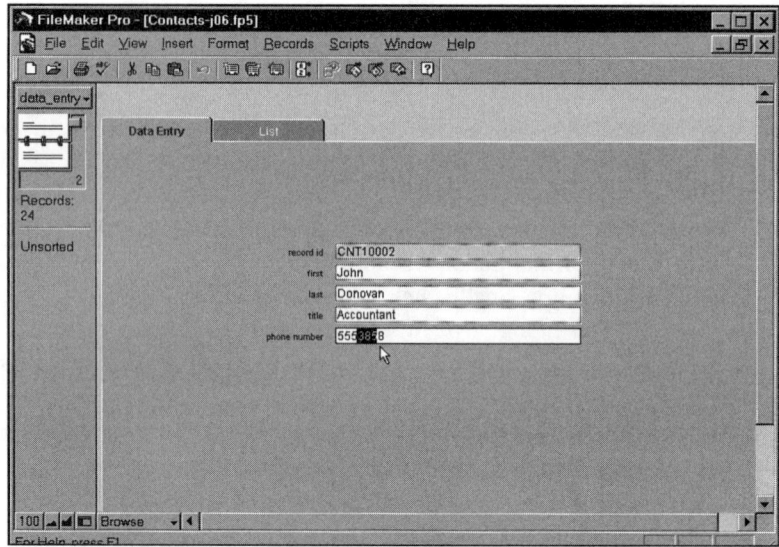

Figure 10.11
We take the raw data and display the formatted phone number.

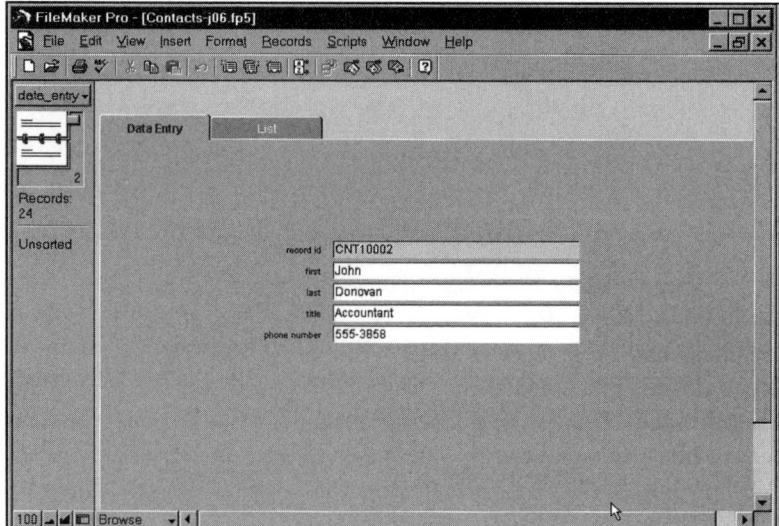

Tip from
Rich

Use a script to put a cursor in. Even when you disable the option to Allow Entry into Field, a script using a Go to Field command can still put the cursor into the field. The user, though, has no other way to click or tab into the field. You might want to use a script in this case, if you normally don't want users in there, but need to allow a superuser in, say, for adjusting a journal entry, or to let a regular user in when extraordinary circumstances arise (managed by your scripting).

If the user types in something other than 7 or 10 digits, we could send up a message saying, "Invalid phone number." But the user would have to know to click in the field to fix it. So we put the wrong number into the Calculation field, followed by the text "Invalid phone number." Then if the user clicks in the field, FileMaker puts the cursor in the underlying field. The insertion point is the same; for instance, if the user clicked after the fourth character in the formatted phone number, the insertion point would appear after the fourth character in the data-entry field. Here's the calculation:

```
If( Length(phone_number) = 7,
    Left(phone_number, 3) & "-" & Right(phone_number, 4),
If( Length(phone_number) = 10,
    "(" & Left(phone_number, 3) & ") " & Middle(phone_number, 4, 3)  & "-" &
        Right(phone_number, 4),
    phone_number & " - Invalid Phone Number"))
```

OVERLAPPING FIELDS TO MIMIC CONDITIONAL TEXT

True conditional text would be able to change, depending on circumstances. We use calculations to imitate that kind of smart text.

In our Invoicing system, if you go to the Invoice List, the Age column shows the age of the invoice in red if it remains unpaid, or black if the invoice has been paid (see Figure 10.12). To get this effect, we use two fields, one on top of the other.

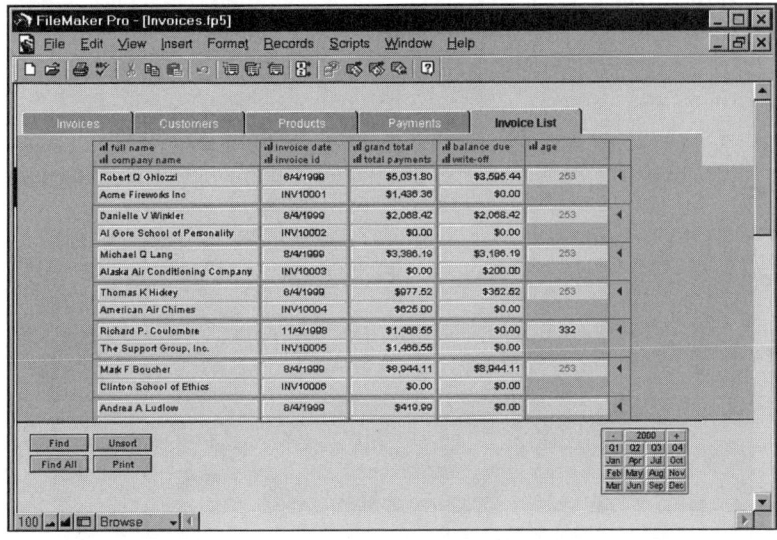

Figure 10.12
Paid invoices are distinguished from unpaid ones by color-coding the age. (Please use your imagination!)

The field on the bottom is called c_age_of_invoice, and the field on top is called c_age_of_unpaid_invoice, which contains an age *only* if the invoice has not yet been paid. Hence, if an invoice has been paid, the top field will be empty, and we will see through to the field underneath, which is in black. The field underneath always has a value, but sometimes the field on top also has a value in red, which covers up the black type, exactly.

The unpaid field has no visible fill because, using the Paint Bucket tool, we picked the transparent fill, so that if the invoice has been paid, the top field will be transparent, so we can see the age below. The calculation behind c_age_of_unpaid_invoice says, "If the invoice has not been paid, display the age of the invoice in this field, which is formatted to have red text; if the invoice has been paid, do not display anything, so users can see the other field underneath."

If a customer refuses to pay the full invoice amount, we might have to write some amount off. So if the write-off is the grand total of the invoice, or if the date of the invoice is empty so that we cannot tell how old the invoice is, then we'll make this field, Age of Unpaid Invoice, empty. In this way, if we have to deal with an invoice that will never be paid, and the user has written it off, there is no age associated with it, because it has not been paid, and we do not expect to be paid. Here's the formula:

```
If(write_off = c_grand_total or  IsEmpty(date_of_inv), "",
    If(c_balance_due > 0,
        Today- date_of_inv, ""))
```

Then we look at the age of the invoice:

- In the field for the age of an invoice, we run the same test, saying if the write-off equals the grand total, or if the date of the invoice is empty, then we have no way to figure the age, so we have no value to put in the field.

- If the balance due is less than or equal to 0, then the invoice has been paid in full, and so we take the date of the final payment from the Payments file, subtract the date of invoice from that, and show the resulting age (the number of days it took the customer to pay the invoice).

- If the balance due is more than 0, then we want the field to display how old that invoice is as of today (so we subtract the date of the invoice from today's date).

Here is the formula:

```
If(c_write_off = c_grand_total or  IsEmpty(date_of_inv), "",
    If(c_balance_due <= 0,
        Max( Payments | inv_id::date_of_pmt) - date_of_inv,
        Today- date_of_inv ))
```

Tip from
Rich

Take into account the weird things that could happen, such as a customer overpaying. We need to flag such an invoice as being paid even if the balance due is less than 0 (essentially, the customer has a credit).

Tip from
Rich

Watch out for unstored calculations because they take time to process, and in a list view, remember that FileMaker has to do that processing for every record, slowing the time to display. In this case, the fields showing the age of the invoice and the age of unpaid invoices are unstored calculations, because they each refer to another unstored calculation. And beware of creeping elegance. When we first built the Invoicing file, we got fancy, with black text for Paid, green text for Not Paid Under 30 Days, yellow text for Not Paid Between 30 and 60 days, and red text for Not Paid Over 60 days. That added a lot of value, but it visibly slowed down the presentation of the list, so even on a fast machine you could see the redraw. So, we abandoned the sophisticated color coordination.

USING THE PatternCount FUNCTION TO SPOT VALUES

When people use check boxes, the items are entered in the order they were checked as text separated by carriage returns. Sometimes, after years of entering data with check boxes, a client decides to look in a check box field to discover whether or how often a particular item was checked. In that situation, we need a way to find that text string without relying on the sequence of items, and without worrying about whether the string we are looking for happens to occur inside any other items that could be checked (as when there are check boxes for President, Vice President, and Assistant to the President, where a simple search for President would spot any record that contained any of those job titles). To see if any particular item has been checked, we use the PatternCount function, with some razzle-dazzle.

The PatternCount function looks in a given field for a specified string, and tells you how many times it finds that string. For a field offering a variety of pizza toppings, we could say:

```
If (PatternCount (pizza_toppings, "pepper")>0, "Yes, we have peppers!","No peppers here!")
```

This works as long as there is only one instance of the string "Pepper" in the field of pizza toppings. Of course, that string may show up in "Pepperoni," as well as "Hot Pepper." If either of those is selected, this calculation will say, "Yes, we have Peppers!" even if Pepper itself is not checked.

So our little IF statement won't always work, if our client offers pepperoni *and* hot pepper toppings. So what are we really looking for?

We want an entire check box entry that just says "Pepper," and nothing more.

How about carriage returns? The check box entry is, of course, the item plus a carriage return—if more than one item is checked. But "Hot Pepper" would have a return after that. Plus, if Pepper is the last item picked, it isn't followed by a carriage return.

So, maybe we are really looking for a carriage return, the word "Pepper," and another carriage return. This pattern would describe all the items in the middle, but not the first or last item.

Hence, we have to create the following formula, which adds those beginning and ending carriage returns:

```
If(PatternCount( "¶" & pizza_toppings & "¶", "¶pepper¶") > 0, "Yes", "No")
```

This tells the PatternCount function to look through the following text: a carriage return, all the values in pizza_topping, and a closing carriage return. So the PatternCount is always going to find an opening carriage return and a closing one, even though those are not actually values in the field. Now, we can have PatternCount look for the pattern of a carriage return, the word "Pepper," and another carriage return, and it will find Pepper even if it is the first or last item. And Pepperoni and Hot Pepper will no longer be spotted as patterns.

And if PatternCount does find the string of a carriage return, Pepper, and a carriage return, it shouts "Yes!" If not, "No."

If you create a field to contain these results, you can now do a count of all records containing that topping, for a report, as shown in Figure 10.13.

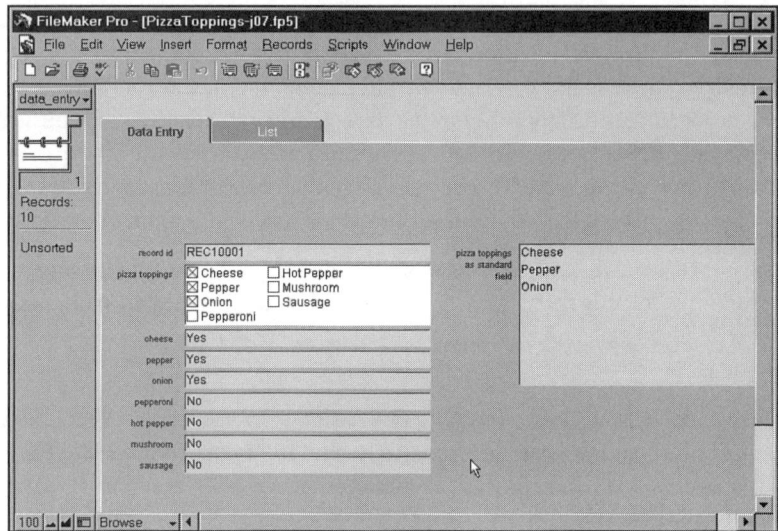

Figure 10.13
On the right, you can see the original data entry with items sequenced in whatever order they were selected. Below the check boxes, you can see the results of the PatternCount analysis for each topping. (We wouldn't display these for regular users).

EXTRACTING THE PREFIX TO THE NAME, FIRST, MIDDLE INITIAL, LAST NAME, AND SUFFIX TO THE LAST NAME

When you track people's names, you should have separate fields for anything you want to search or sort on: prefix (such as Monsignor), salutation, first name, middle name, last name, suffix (such as J.D.), and casual name (such as "Hoot"). But, sometimes we get data from other folks, who just lumped the whole name into a single field. In that situation, we may need to parse a name into its separate components.

In Contacts-j08 we have two fields, one called "Look for these name prefixes" and another called "Look for these name suffixes," as shown in Figure 10.14. We tell FileMaker, "If the first word in the full_name field is one of these prefixes, then put that word in the Prefix field." We are creating calculated fields for each part of the name, as we break it apart: c_name_prefix, c_first, c_mi, C_last, c_name_suffix.

Figure 10.14
Users enter the prefixes and suffixes to look for.

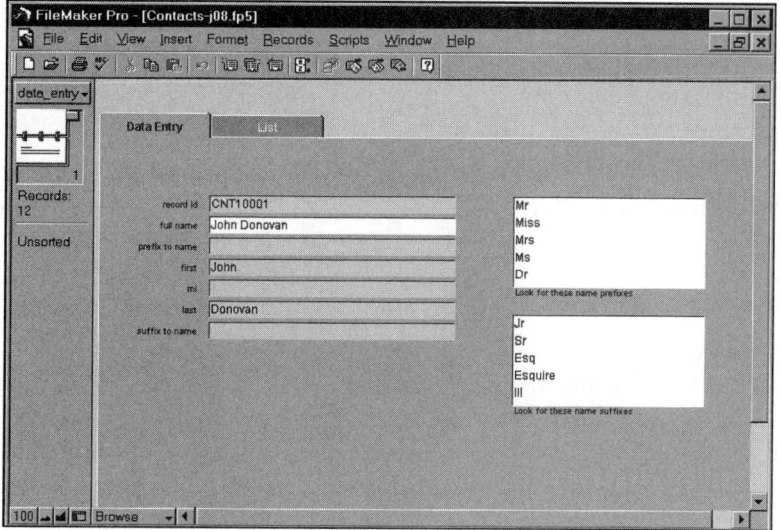

Whenever you are building an algorithm for this kind of processing, you have to make some assumptions. We presume that there will always be a first name and a last name.

> **Tip from**
> *Rich*
>
> In real life, don't count on regular names. Some cultures don't bother with last names, and users don't always catch a client's first name over the phone. We have a client at a major university, and one of the professors uses a single word as his name. It is neither a first name nor a last name; it is his entire name. And what do you do with the singer formerly known as Prince?

The second assumption we are making is that the first name comes before the last.

> **Tip from**
> *Rich*
>
> Remember that in many Asian cultures, you cannot assume that the surname will follow the given name. And even in America, we have folks like Rich's friend Paul Thomas. We call him "Bud."

In c_name_prefix, the field that will hold a prefix if we find one in the field full_name, we set up a calculation to test for prefixes using the same technique we used in the pizza parlor. First, we look through a text string made up of a carriage return, all the values in the global field in which we ask users to enter valid prefixes, and another carriage return. We compare that string to the first word in the full_name field. If we discover a match, we put the term into the field devoted to prefixes.

```
If(
PatternCount( "¶" & g_name_prefix & "¶", "¶" & LeftWords( full_name, 1) & "¶") > 0,
LeftWords( full_name, 1), "")
```

Thus, if the first word is a prefix, we grab it and put it into this field devoted to prefixes. If there is no match, we put a whole bunch of nothing into the prefix field.

The beauty of this technique is that users can add new prefixes as they come along. This openness to new prefixes (or suffixes) helps avoid accidents, like treating *Herr* or *Monsieur* as a first name, or mistaking *Emeritus* for the last name.

The calculation looking for a suffix is similar, but starts on the rightmost word:

```
If(
PatternCount( "¶" & g_name_suffix & "¶", "¶" &RightWords( full_name, 1) & "¶") > 0,
RightWords( full_name, 1), "")
```

Now we need to find words in the middle, such as the first name, middle initial, and last name. We figure that the first name must either be the very first word in the full_name field or the second word. If there is no prefix (in which case the c_name_prefix field is empty), the first name will be the first word on the left. If there is a prefix (and therefore the c_name_prefix field is not empty), then the first name is going to be the second word, so we will want to grab a single word, starting with the second word, from the middle of the mess.

```
If(IsEmpty(c_name_prefix), LeftWords( full_name, 1), MiddleWords( full_name, 2, 1))
```

> **Tip from** *Rich*
>
> Leave the order of calculation to FileMaker. Deep in FileMaker, a dependency table works out the order of calculations, so that the prefix is figured beforehand, and you can assume it has been done, so that you can proceed with this calculation. FileMaker knows that the calculation for the first name depends on the prefix calculation having been done.

Last Name is a little more gnarly. Logically, at least in our culture, the last name should be the last word in the full_name field (the rightmost word), if there is no suffix. If there is a suffix, then we can assume that the word just before the suffix will be the last name. But how do we spot that word?

To pull a word out of a field, when the word is not the first or last word, we use the `MiddleWords` function. We have to tell `MiddleWords` what the source of the words will be, what the starting word is, and how many words you want plucked out. The source is full_name. The number of words is 1. But how do we specify the second word from the end? The full name may have as few as 2 words (first and last), or may have as many as 5 words (prefix, first, middle initial, last, and suffix). To specify the second word from the end, we say, count up the number of words in the field full_name, subtract 1 from it, and that will be your starting word. Thus, if we have a full_name with just a first and last name—and a suffix—then there are 3 words, and we take away one to end up with the second word as the starting point. For example, if we were facing a full_name of Jonathan Price, III, we would have 3 words; take away 1, and start with the second word, so the last name must be Price.

```
If( IsEmpty(c_name_suffix),
RightWords( full_name, 1),
MiddleWords( full_name, WordCount(full_name) - 1, 1))
```

The full_name field can have anywhere between 2 and 5 words. We have assumed that if we exclude the prefix and the suffix, and the word count equals 3, then we must have a first name, middle initial, and last name. To get the middle initial, we take the word count of full_name, and subtract 1 from it if there is a prefix, and subtract another 1 if there is a suffix, and if the result is 3, we conclude that there must be a middle initial. (Otherwise, we presume there is no middle initial). Now, having concluded there is a middle initial, we have to figure out where it is. If the prefix name field is empty, then the middle initial will be the second word. Otherwise, it is the third word.

```
If( (WordCount(full_name) - (not IsEmpty(c_name_prefix)) - (not
IsEmpty(c_name_suffix))) = 3,
If( IsEmpty(c_name_prefix),
MiddleWords( full_name, 2, 1),
MiddleWords( full_name, 3, 1)), " ")
```

Tip from
Rich

Databases are structured, consistent animals. Names are not. We live in a global society of more than 150 countries, and almost as many conventions for creating names. This algorithm is ethnocentric, and even within our own culture, it may get tripped up. For instance, we are blithely assuming that each name will only be 1 word long. A hyphen does connect 2 parts of a single word, so Sackville-West would show up as a single word. But Sr. Jose Vargas y Vargas, III would have too many words for our simple calculations. Ditto for Sister Anne Marie H. Presley. Also, if the user enters a value in the list of prefixes or suffixes, and someone has a first name that matches one of those valid prefixes or suffixes, this simple algorithm will stumble. If you have a lot of time, you could begin to handle more of these exceptions, twists, and turns. The real problem started way back, when someone made the mistake of creating a single field for all these parts of a name. As humans, we can't always tell what's a first name or last name: therefore, we'll probably never get a perfect algorithm for sorting this out. Best to clean your data up at the start, not after the fact.

Tip from
Rich

Start with Text fields. Because this chapter deals with calculations, we made the fields Prefix, First Name, M.I., Last Name, and Suffix into Calculation fields using data from the full_name field. But if you ever need to edit a name, you can't easily jump into these fields. Instead, you have to work on the full_name value, and let the edits flow into the other fields through the calculations. In real life, we would probably handle this problem differently, by making each of these fields a Text field, using a script with SetField or a calculated Replace to physically move those calculation results into Text fields that the users could then edit in the future.

Tip from
Rich

You may want to use these calculations inside a `SetField` or a `Replace` operation within a script. `SetField` works on whatever the current record is, while a `Replace` works on all the found records. Replacing, of course, can be dicey, because a single mistake can ruin every record in the database. In fact, the `Replace` command is the second most dangerous command in FileMaker, falling just below the `Delete Found Records` command (which toggles to `Delete All Records`).

DATE CALCULATIONS

In this section we explore a few calculations you may find helpful when wrestling with dates:

- Calculating how long it's been since the last contact
- Calculating the next appointment date
- Breaking apart a date for subtotals

➔For an overview of what you can put in a Date field, on which you can run the following calculations, **see** "What to Put in a Date Field," **p. 71.**

CALCULATING HOW LONG IT'S BEEN SINCE THE LAST CONTACT

Occasionally, you need to know how many days have elapsed since a particular date, such as the day of the last contact. To find out we use the Status function, which appears more often in a script than in calculations. Status can bring back information about the file you are in, the computer you are using (Mac or Windows), what version of the operating system you are using, what version of FileMaker you are using, or what the current date or time is.

 At first, you may wonder why you might ever use a Status function, but once you try it, you begin to see its power. In our file DaysSinceLastContact-j09.fp5 (see Figure 10.15), we are looking for the status of the current date, using the argument CurrentDate, which fetches the day's date from the computer. The formula just says, "Take today's date, and subtract the date of the last contact, to yield the number of days in between." At the bottom of the Calculation dialog, we checked the box to make sure the result would be a number. Here's the formula:

```
Status( CurrentDate) - date_of_last_contact
```

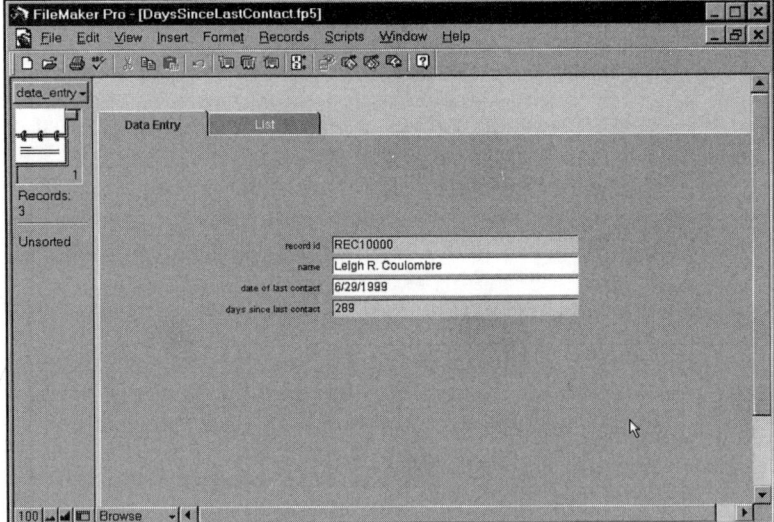

Figure 10.15
We calculate the days since the last contact.

COMMON MISTAKE: CALCULATING WHEN NOT NEEDED

In FileMaker, calculations can be stored or unstored. We'll talk more about the implications of this later in this chapter, but if you use a status function in a Calculation field and leave the result as a stored calculation, then the calculation is evaluated when the record is created, or any time a value changes in one of the referenced fields. In our current example, if we change the date of last contact, the calculation restarts and figures out the elapsed time again. Unfortunately, even though days go by, the calculation is not updated. So, we have to make sure this calculation is unstored, forcing it to be recalculated every time the value is needed, as during a search, sort, report, or display of the record. Inside the Specify Calculation dialog, down at the bottom right, is a button called Storage Options. Click that, and in the Storage Options dialog (see Figure 10.16) check the option "Do Not Store Calculation Results—Calculate Only When Needed."

Figure 10.16
The Storage Options dialog lets you choose to run a calculation only when needed.

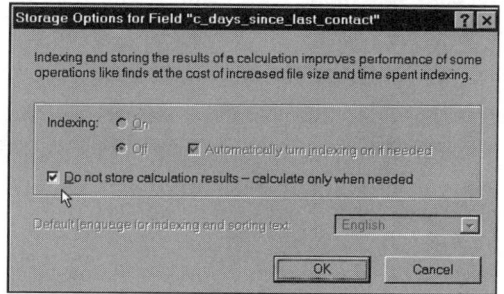

Tip from
Rich

Whenever you use the Status function, consider leaving the results Unstored because you probably want the value to be dynamic—that is, calculated every time you reach for the value. What you want to avoid is old data, rotting in the record. Status function data is generally dynamic; keeping it stored would probably defeat its purpose.

CALCULATING THE NEXT APPOINTMENT DATE

Sometimes, clients want to set up ticklers, reminding them of the next appointment date. They like to be able to pick the number of days, weeks, months, or years, and have that applied, so the record pops up with the next appointment date.

We start with the Case statement, in the file NextApptDate-j10.fp5 in folder j10, shown in Figure 10.17. In FileMaker we have long had an IF statement we could use in calculations, allowing us to put in a test, then have two different results (one if the test proves true, another if it turns out false). That works well when we have a single test with two results. But unfortunately, not all the data in the world allows us to apply such a simple test. So we created nested IFs, which were hard to read and easy to foul up if we lost track of the number of parentheses or commas.

As a substitute for a set of nested IFs, the Case statement works very well. The Case statement builds up this way: Test One, the result if the test turns out to be true; Test Two, result if the second test turns out to be true; Test Three, result if the third test turns out to be true; and so on. We *may* then have a default result at the end if none of these tests turns out to be true. As soon as any test turns out to be true, its result is returned, and no other tests are performed. Here's an example of a Case statement testing for the grade number and inserting the text name for that grade into the field.

```
Case(
IsEmpty(grade), "",
grade = 9, "Freshman",
grade = 10, "Sophomore",
grade = 11, "Junior",
grade = 12, "Senior")
```

An IF statement must always have two results—one if the test turns out true, and another if the test turns out false. In the Case statement, the default result (if all the tests fail) is optional.

> **Tip from**
> *Rich*
>
> The Case statement performs faster than the IF statement. You won't see much difference if you are only evaluating a few records, but you will if you are handling thousands of records.
>
> *Suggested by* John Mark Osborne, author of *Scriptology*.

Figure 10.17
In NextApptDate-j10.fp5 we use the Case statement to figure the date of the next appointment.

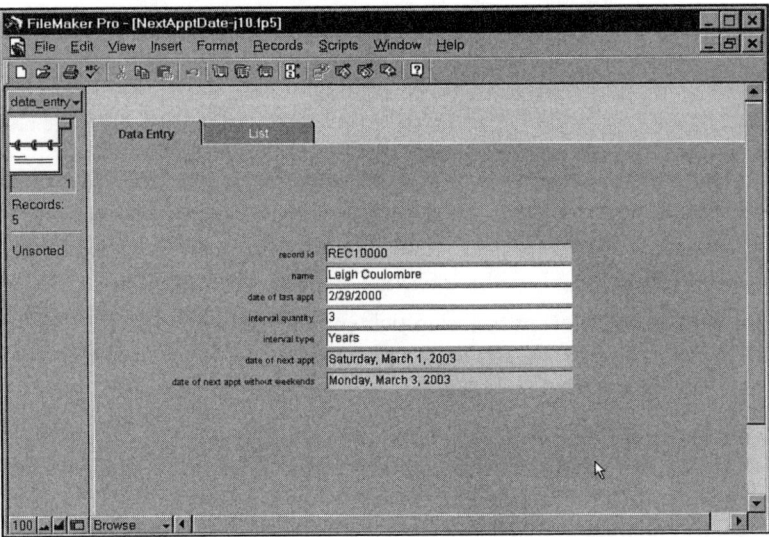

We can't do anything without the date of the last appointment, and the type of interval (day, week, month, year), and the number of intervals. So our first test examines the fields date_of_last_appt, interval_quantity, and interval_type to make sure they are not empty. If any of those is empty, we set the current field, which is the date_of_next_appt, to empty.

If all of those fields have values, we go to the next test. We say, "If the interval type equals days, then take the date of last appointment, and add the interval quantity." FileMaker understands that it should add that many days to the date, and spits out a date. For instance, if the user's last appointment was on January 15, and the user sets the interval type as days, and the quantity as 9, FileMaker figures out that January 24 will be the next appointment date.

The weeks are similar—just the quantity of weeks times 7, to get the right number of days in between appointments.

Now we face months, which challenge us because they come in different lengths. For these we take advantage of a little-known but cool feature offered by FileMaker's Date function, which takes 3 arguments (numeric values for the month, day, and year, separated by commas). We are saying, "Take the month of date_of_last_appt and add to it the interval quantity, to get the month value; then take the day component of the date of last appointment and use that as the day of the next appointment; and take the year of the last appointment, and use that again as the year for the next appointment."

Neat feature: If the interval quantity is in months and you add that number to the last month (from 1 to 12), FileMaker is bright enough to recalculate the year, when the total number of months exceeds 12. For instance, if the last appointment was in October (the tenth month), and the user sets an interval of 10 months, FileMaker adds 10+10 to get 20, and recognizes that the year must be increased, and the month must be August in that next year. The Date function also handles leap years for you. In fact, if you add years, FileMaker realizes that the day and month may also change because of leap years. For example, if you start on February 29, and end up in a non-leap year, FileMaker rolls the date forward to March 1. (Isn't it great that someone else has taken care of all this programming for you?)

To take the formula a step further, we handle years the same way as months, adding the interval quantity to the Years.

Here's the calculation:

```
Case(
IsEmpty(date_of_last_appt) or IsEmpty(interval_quantity) or
IsEmpty(interval_type), "",
interval_type = "Days",
date_of_last_appt + interval_quantity,
interval_type = "Weeks",
date_of_last_appt + (interval_quantity * 7),
interval_type = "Months",
Date( Month(date_of_last_appt) + interval_quantity, Day(date_of_last_appt),
Year(date_of_last_appt)),
interval_type = "Years",
Date( Month(date_of_last_appt), Day(date_of_last_appt), Year(date_of_last_appt) +
interval_quantity), "")
```

But what if we want to avoid setting up an appointment on a weekend? In the field c_date_of_next_appt_without_weekends, we use two tests. We say, "If the name of the day in c_date_of_next_appt is 'Saturday', then add 2 days to the date of in c_date_of_next_appt. And if that day is Sunday, add 1. If the day is neither Saturday nor Sunday, return the date as it is, unaltered."

```
Case(
DayName(c_date_of_next_appt) = "Saturday",
c_date_of_next_appt + 2,
DayName(c_date_of_next_appt) = "Sunday",
c_date_of_next_appt + 1,
c_date_of_next_appt)
```

Another file in the same j10 folder, CalcTaskBeginDate, responds to a common request. The client comes to us with a task end date, and knowing that the task will take n workdays to complete, without spending any weekends in the office, the client wants to know the day on which work should start.

We've broken this complicated calculation down into its components, so you can look at each individually, and finally we have assembled those into a single calculation, called c_task_begin_date_single_calc. The biggest challenge here is getting to the essence of the problem: We are trying to start with a date, and work backwards to another date, but we only want to use Mondays through Fridays, ignoring Saturdays and Sundays.

The first component, a calculation called c_task_duration_whole_weeks, starts with the end date entered by the user, and the user's input for task_duration_workdays. We know that an American work week has five days. So if the user says the task will take 14 days, we can figure that will take 2 workweeks, plus 4 days. Just as we used the Int and Mod functions earlier, we want to use them again to determine the number of *whole* weeks. We take the task_duration_workdays, divide by 5, and take the integer of that result as the number of whole weeks. For instance, 14 divided by 5 yields a result of 2 with a remainder of 4, and, applying the Int function to it, we conclude that we are going to need 2 complete weeks.

```
Int(task_duration_workdays / 5)
```

To find the number of days left over (the remainder_) we use the calculation called c_task_duration_remainder_days. Here we use the Mod function, which takes the value of the remainder when we divide the task_duration_workdays by 5.

```
Mod(task_duration_workdays,5)
```

If the task takes 14 days, then the remainder is 4. So now we know that we have to account for 4 days beyond the 2 solid weeks of work.

Now you might assume that we could simply take the end date, subtract from that the whole weeks times 7, and from that subtract the number of remainder days to back up to the right starting date. But the problem is that sometimes in subtracting the remainder days, we bump into a weekend. For instance, if the task ends on a Tuesday, and we have to go back 2 weeks to an earlier Tuesday and then subtract 4 more days, we end up including weekend days, so we really have to go back 2 more days. Therefore, we must determine if those remainder days take us into a weekend, forcing us to back off 2 more days, to reach the correct Begin date.

To solve this, we turn to the calculation called c_work_days_until_prior_weekend. We say, "If today is a Monday, assign it a value of 1, and if Tuesday, 2, and so on." Then we check to see if the number of remainder days is greater than or equal to some number that would take us back to Saturday or Sunday. For example, if the day of the week is Tuesday, and we have only 1 remainder day, we go back to Monday. OK! But, if the day is Tuesday, and the number of remainder days is 2 or more, we have to recognize that we are running into the prior weekend, which we will then have to skip to allow folks to go home on those days.

```
Choose(c_task_end_date_day_of_week, "", 7, 1, 2, 3, 4, 5, 6)
```

Next, in the field c_task_duration_adj_for_days_over_extra_weekend (you can see why we should never indulge in long field names!), we take the results and work on them. We now know how many days earlier the prior weekend is. If the number of remainder days is greater than that, or equal to that, then we know we have to subtract 2 more days to skip the whole weekend.

```
If( c_task_duration_remainder_days >= c_work_days_until_prior_weekend, 2, 0)
```

The result, showing the remainder days plus 2 more to give the staff a weekend off, will be used in the next calculation to figure the exact date that work should start.

Finally, in the c_task_begin_date field, we develop a calculation that lets us come up with an actual date. We start with the task-ending date and subtract 3 items from that:

1. The number of whole weeks times 7 days per week
2. The number of remainder days
3. Any adjustment needed for crossing over an extra weekend

Here is the calculation:

```
task_end_date
  - c_task_duration_whole_weeks * 7
  - c_task_duration_remainder_days
  -   c_task_duration_adj_for_days_over_extra_weekend
```

EXAMPLE: THE TASK THAT LASTED 18 DAYS

The user has a task due for completion on May 30, 2000. The boss has given the user 18 workdays to do the job. When does the user have to start, assuming the user will be devoted all day every day, except weekends, to this task? (We could have subtracted days for other tasks, but for simplicity we are omitting that here.) The task duration of 18 days reduces to 3 whole weeks (of 5 workdays each), with 3 days left over. May 30, 2000 turns out to be a Tuesday. Therefore, we have 2 workdays until the prior weekend. Our 3 remainder days are greater than those 2, so we are going to need to include the adjustment of 2 days to account for the weekend. Starting on May 30, we back up by 3 work weeks, or 21 days, and then we have 3 more days of work, and backing up we bump into the weekend, so we have to back off Monday, Friday, and Thursday, for a total of 26 days ahead of the due date. The result is May 4, 2000.

Looked at calculation by calculation, this makes sense, but when we try to grab the whole shebang at once, the mind reels, because we usually do not think backward in time.

In the same folder, the file CalcTaskEndDate-j10.fp5 addresses the reverse: starting with a beginning date, adding the workdays, and calculating the end day, avoiding weekends. (Caution: Because this calculation assumes that workers get the whole weekend off, the formula does not apply to startups or Internet companies.) This calculation differs in 2 ways from the Begin Date calculation.

1. Because we are trying to calculate a future date, we add days to the start date to get to the end date (as opposed to the eerie experience of subtracting days to move backward in time).
2. The calculation for the adjustment for the extra weekend has to move forward, not backward, so we are watching out for the next weekend, not the prior weekend. We take the workdays until the prior weekend, add the remainder days, and if the result is greater than 5 (the number of workdays in a week), we know we have bumped into a weekend, so we have to add 2 more days to get over the weekend hump.

In both files dealing with beginning and ending dates we rely on another calculation, c_task_date_day_of_week, to determine how many days away from the prior weekend we start with.

```
DayOfWeek(task_end_date)
```

We use the built-in DayOfWeek function, which returns a 1 for a Sunday, a 2 for a Monday, through 6 for Saturday. This, then, tells us what day of the week the task will end on, but not as a date, just as a numeric representation (3, not Tuesday, May 25).

We take that numeric representation of the day of the week, and convert that to a list that gives us a 1 on a Monday and a 7 on a Sunday, because Monday is 1 day away from the prior weekend, and Tuesday is 2 days away, and so on. The calculation that does this depends on the Choose function, which takes an index value as its first argument (from 0 to n), and then, a series of possible results depending on those values. We use the index values from the field we just built, c_task_date_day_of_week (from 1 to 7). So we can take a 1 and spit out another number as a result. The first result of the Choose function is for the situation in which the index starts with a value of 0. We aren't going to have one of these in our index. Hence, our first result is "" (or empty). The second result is for the situation in which the index value is 1, and the third result is for the situation when the index value is 2, and so on. So we are taking our list of days, starting with Sunday as a 1, and using the Choose function so that Monday ends up as a 1 and Sunday ends up as a 7.

COMMON MISTAKE: FORGETTING THAT 0 IS A VALID INDEX VALUE

Developers often overlook the fact that the first argument in the Choose statement is the index values, but the first result argument in the Choose statement is for situations when the index value is 0. Many folks just assume the first argument describes what to do when the first index value is 1. But all indexes potentially start with 0, and so the Choose function first looks for a 0 as an index value.

In both of the files dealing with beginning and ending dates, we include a single gigantic calculation that takes us up to the moment when we adjust for the extra days around a weekend. In the file CalcBeginTaskDate, the calculation is called calc_task_begin_date_single _calc. In the file called CalcTaskEndDate, the calculation is called calc_task_end_date_ single_calc. Previously, we built a series of 6 calculations, so you could see how the logic moves forward, moment to moment, and so we could troubleshoot it as we went. But now we put the whole set of calculations together. This final calculation grabs all the others and puts them into a single gigantic calculation. The when-do-we-begin version goes like this:

```
task_end_date
  (Int(task_duration_workdays / 5)*7)
Mod(task_duration_workdays, 5)
If(Mod(task_duration_workdays, 5)
        >= Choose(DayOfWeek(task_end_date), "", 7, 1, 2, 3, 4, 5, 6), 2, 0)
```

> **Tip from**
> *Rich*
>
> Break up complex calculations into little bits as you build, and then reassemble them into a giant one later after all the pieces prove out. Yes, this process looks wasteful because you are storing a lot of data unnecessarily, but if someone else needs to maintain the files later, your sequence will make more sense than the gigantic omnium-gatherum approach. Imagine seeing the full calculation for the first time, and trying to figure out the reasoning behind it, if you had never seen the individual calculations.

BREAKING APART A DATE FOR SUBTOTALS

In the file DateCalcs-j11, you'll see how we take apart a date many different ways, as shown in Figure 10.18, performing various calculations you might find useful when dealing with dates. We are manipulating the original date into several forms we've found we must use, from time to time, answering questions such as

- What was the first day of this month?
- Last day?
- How many days exist in this month?
- What's the first day of this quarter? Last? Days in the quarter? Which quarter is it, anyway?
- What number month is this? What day? Which month? Which day of the week? Which year?

We'll walk through these in the order they appear in the Define Fields dialog because one calculation builds on another.

FIRST OF THE MONTH

Occasionally, you have to track sales or other information month by month, or from one year to the next. The first time we used the calculation in the field First_of_Month was in a database where a customer wanted to know sales subtotaled by month. The customer had a field for each sale called Date of Sale, but the day on which the sale was made might be any day of the month, so we needed some way to group all the records from a particular month, by having a common value in one field. The first time we used the MonthName function, it worked OK, except that when we sorted by month name, we got the months in alphabetical, not chronological, order. Ugh.

Figure 10.18
We run various calculations on the date.

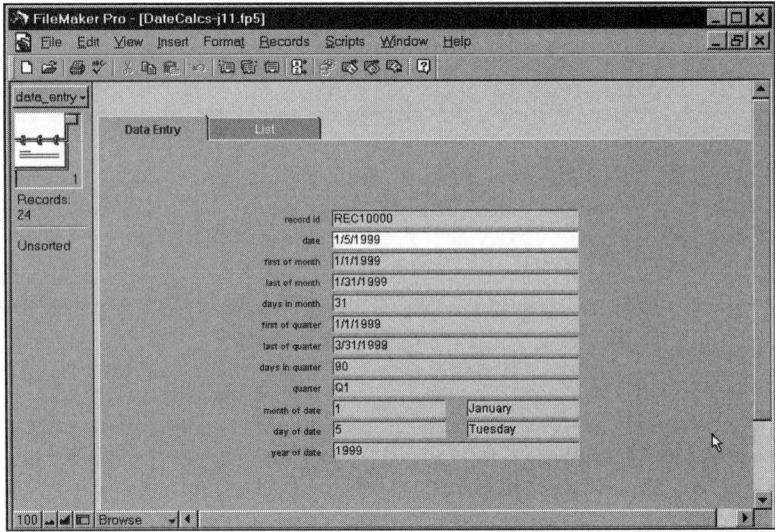

So what about summarizing by the number of the month? That was fine until the customer tried to run sales over several years, because the sales for March of 00, 01, and 02 all dropped into the same pot. Then we thought, how about the month number and the year? March 1999 would come out 3-99. But that did not work too well, either, because, this being a text field, the month 12-99 came before the month 3-99, when sorted. Therefore, we realized we needed a true date field to sort on. For every sale that occurs on any day within March, 1999, we said, this new field will have the value of 3/1/99, a real date, so we can sort on that field and get a true chronological order.

The calculation, then, turns out to be fairly simple because we use the `Date` function, which takes three arguments—a month, a day, and a year. So we build a new date for each sales record by taking the month number out of our actual date (which appears in a field called date), arbitrarily inserting a 1 for the first day of that month, and then putting in the year found in our actual date.

```
Date( Month( date ), 1, Year(date))
```

Remember: You have to make sure that the calculation result is Date because you are going to want to sort by date.

LAST DAY OF THE MONTH

We had a customer who wanted a report with a heading that would say "March 1, 2000 through March 31, 2000." So we had to look at the dates, figure out which month they were in, and put the last day of that month into the heading. Eventually, we created the field last_of_month.

But on the first go-round, we thought, "Well, 11 of the 12 months have the same number of days every year, and only February is a problem, because you have to figure out whether the year is a leap year or not." Leap years come every fourth year, but any year that ends in 00 is not a leap year, except for those evenly divisible by 400. That is why 2000 turns out to be a leap year, but 1900 was not, and 2100 will not be. But the complexity of figuring out the leap years drove us to realize that FileMaker knows all these calculations because they are built into its date engine.

So we turned to a technique using the Date function much as we did before, but adding 1 to the month, so instead of the first of this month, we get the first of next month—and then we subtract 1 day from that to get, voilá, the last day of the current month. In this way, we leave worries about leap years to FileMaker, whose programmers sweated to build all those calculations into the Date engine.

```
Date( Month( date ) + 1, 1, Year(date)) - 1
```

Again, make sure that the calculation result is Date because you are going to want to sort by date.

Days in the Month

We already have a calculation that tells us the date of the last day of the month, so now all we have to do to get the days in the month is yank the day component out of that Date field.

```
Day( last_of_month )
```

If the last_of_month field contains 3/31/2000, then this Day function returns the 31. The calculation result here is a number.

First of the Quarter

Figuring out the first day of the quarter takes a little more work than figuring out the first of the month, because there we only had to grab the month, but here we have to grab the month component of the date, and then we have to figure out what the first month of that quarter might be. The Month function analyzes the date and comes up with the number of the month. The Choose function then looks at that number and if it is 0, says, "You have no quarter" (this field will be empty), but if you have a month that is number 1, 2, or 3, you should identify the first month of that month's quarter is 1 (or January), and so on. Then we tack on the first day of the month and the year.

```
Date( Choose(Month( date ), "", 1,1,1,4,4,4,7,7,7,10,10,10), 1, Year( date ))
```

In this way we convert the month to the first month of the quarter (January, April, July, or October), slip in the first as the day of the month, and add the year.

Last of the Quarter

Here we use a technique like what we used for the last day of the month. We figure out the first day of the *following* quarter and then subtract one.

```
Date( Choose(Month( date ), "", 4, 4, 4, 7, 7, 7, 10, 10, 10, 13, 13, 13), 1,
Year( date )) - 1
```

You may complain that you cannot have a month 13. But FileMaker figures that if December of this year is 12, then January of next year can be regarded as 13. Also, the Choose function does not really care what the numbers represent; it is just figuring out a Number result at this point.

Let's imagine the date is November 22, 2000. This calculation starts off with 11 as the number for November, so the Choose statement returns a value of 13. The result so far is 13/1/2000. But FileMaker is smarter than that, and rounds the result up to 1/1/2001. Now all we have to do is to subtract 1 day from that, yielding 12/31/2000.

DAYS IN THE QUARTER

Here we are going to build on prior work again. We've already figured out the last day of the quarter and the first day of the quarter. In between are almost all of the days of the quarter. If we subtract the first from the last, we get the number of days *between* the two dates. But that is one day less than the actual *total* days of the quarter, so we add 1 at the end.

```
last_of_quarter - first_of_quarter + 1
```

QUARTER

Now the inquisitive client wants to know What quarter are we in? Intuition suggests this calculation:

```
Choose( Month( date ), "", "Q1", "Q1", "Q1", "Q2", "Q2", "Q2", "Q3", "Q3", "Q3", "Q4", "Q4", "Q4" )
```

Here we pull out the number of the month. If that's 0, well, we have no quarter at all. But if it is 1, 2, or 3, we are in Q1, and so on.

> **Tip from Rich**
>
> Use formatting to display the quarter (without changing the actual date). If all you want to do is display Q1, you can do this through a custom date format. Go into the box showing Thursday and scroll down to the items for Q4. In all the other boxes, choose None.

> **Tip from Rich**
>
> Invent your separators, if you want. In the Date Format dialog in the four pop-up menus on the right, you can ignore the choices offered for separator characters and type in your own. You can even insert multiple characters.

COMPONENTS OF THE DATE DISPLAYED AS NUMBERS OR NAME

In the fields devoted to the month, day, or year shown in the Date field, we tear apart the actual date to get at its components. You might want to do this by using your Date field to create an extract sent up to a mainframe, which expects the month component as a separate field. Instead of retyping the information, you can have FileMaker pull the date apart and place its pieces into fields for day, month (expressed as numbers or names), and year.

Expressing the day can be helpful if a client wants to summarize sales, calls, or Web hits by day of the week.

TIME CALCULATIONS

Do you keep track of your billable hours? Or do you have a client who wants to have staffers punch in and punch out to generate data for the payroll program? If so, you need to play with Time.

→For an overview of what you can put in a Time field, on which you can run the following calculations, **see** "What to Put in a Time Field," **p. 72.**

CALCULATING THE TOTAL AMOUNT OF TIME

Sometimes, you need to figure out the total length of time that something takes place, given the start and end times. For instance, you might need to set up a time-card application to track workers coming into work and leaving, to figure out the length of time each spent on the job each day. In TotalTime-j12.fp5 we show how to calculate the total time in seconds or stopwatch time (hours, minutes, seconds elapsed), and then dissect that stopwatch time into its component hours, minutes, and seconds (see Figure 10.19).

Figure 10.19
We explode time into its components.

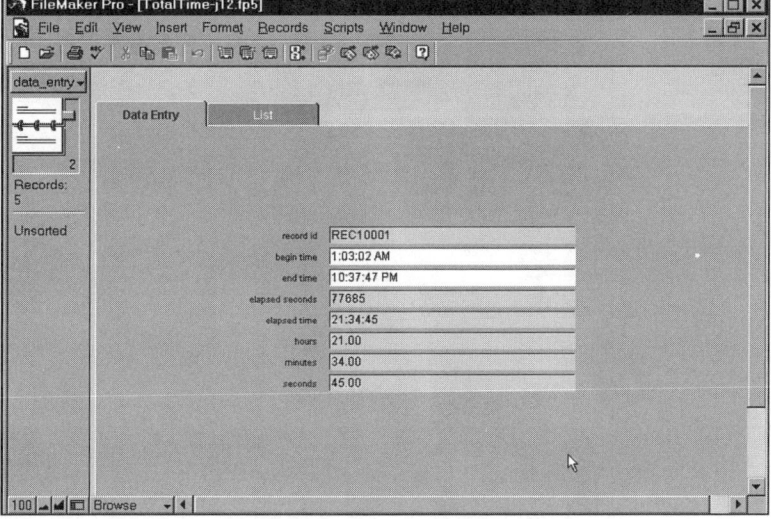

We set up two fields for users to enter start and end times. Then we create a calculation in the elapsed_seconds field, subtracting the end time from the start time to get the total time:

```
end_time - begin_time
```

Because the Calculation result is a Number (not a Time) we get the total number of seconds (see Figure 10.20).

Figure 10.20
Here is the formula, specifying a Number result.

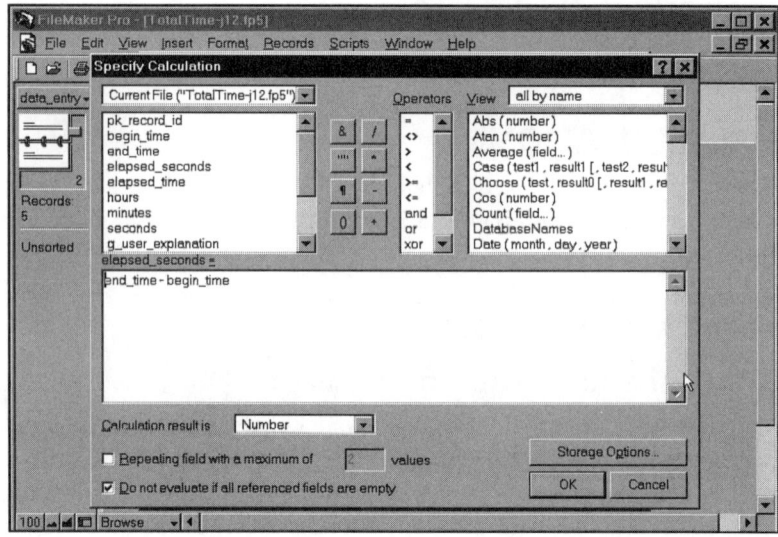

When we run the same calculation but ask for the result to be expressed as a time, we get hours, minutes, and seconds of total time in the elapsed_time field (see Figure 10.21).

Figure 10.21
This is the Time result.

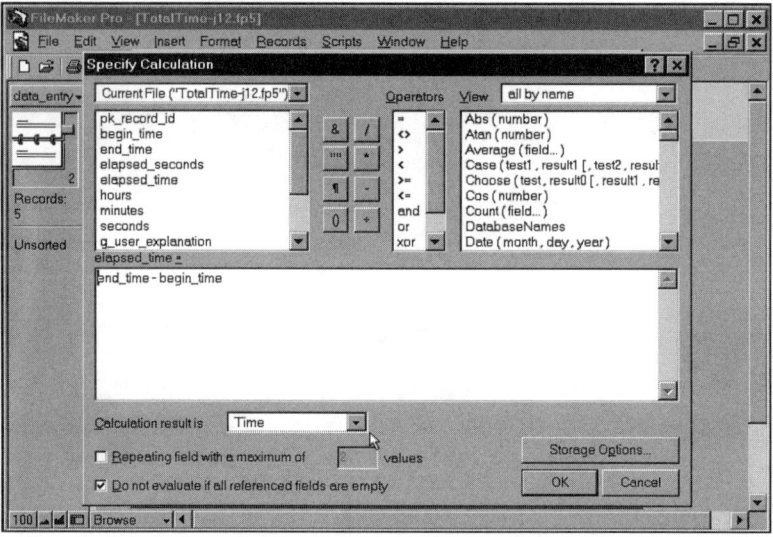

If we need to get the components of that total time (just the hours, or minutes above that, or seconds left over), as might be needed when providing separate values for a mainframe application, we use the Hour, Minute, and Seconds functions, and apply them to the time shown in our elapsed_time field.

```
Hour(elapsed_time)
```

This simply pulls out the hour component. It does not calculate the total hours.

CONDITIONAL CALCULATIONS

FileMaker Pro 5 offers 3 main ways to test for certain conditions and then take action based on the situation we discover. In this section, we'll explore

- Comparing IF, Case, and Choose statements
- Using IF statements for a multi-column report
- Using IF statements to extract the choices of radio buttons

COMPARING IF, Case, AND Choose STATEMENTS

In several of our example files, we have used the IF, Case, and Choose functions. Now you can compare the way they work, looking at our file IfCaseChoose-j13.fp5, which takes a number (such as the number of a elementary school grade) and transforms that into text in various ways.

An IF statement has these components: a test with a Boolean result of true or false, a comma; a result if the test turns out to be True, a comma; and a result if the test turns out to be False. A single IF statement works well if we have one test with two possible results. But, alas, data does not always offer such a simple form of testing. So we can create a nested set of IFs, in which we have something like this:

```
IF (test1, result1, IF(test2, result2, IF (test3, result3, result4)))
```

The first IF runs test1, and if that turns out True, returns result1. If test1 turns out to be false, we turn to another IF statement. Similarly, if test2 turns out true, we turn to result2, but if false, we go to the third IF. The third IF runs its test, which returns result3 if true, or result4 if false.

Note that result4 is only used if all of the tests fail. Also, when putting together nested IFs, you have to be very careful about inserting the right number of commas in the right places, and matching closing parentheses with their opening parentheses. If, like us, you are among the punctuation-challenged, the nested IF statement can be a bit more gnarly than the Case statement. Here, for instance, is the calculation using nested IFs:

```
If(grade = 0, "Kindergarten",
If(grade = 1, "First",
If(grade = 2, "Second",
If(grade = 3, "Third",
If(grade = 4, "Fourth",
If(grade = 5, "Fifth",
If(grade = 6, "Sixth",
If(grade = 7, "Seventh",
If(grade = 8, "Eighth",
If(grade = 9, "Freshman",
If(grade = 10, "Sophomore",
If(grade = 11, "Junior",
If(grade =12, "Senior", "Invalid Grade")))))))))))))
```

> **COMMON MISTAKE: FORGETTING THE RESULT IF FALSE**
>
> When putting together nested IFs, people tend to forget that the last IF must not only have a result if true, but a result if false. That last result is a requirement. FileMaker will reject the calculation if you fail to provide results for both true and false results of each test.

Using the Case statement, you have somewhat less punctuation, and no need to keep repeating yourself. You only have to say Case once. You have, after the opening parentheses, a test, and a result if that test is true. If it isn't true, FileMaker will just go on to try the next test, until it either finds a test that comes out true (in which case it returns that value), it hits a value you provide if all the tests fail, or, well, it just runs out of tests. Unlike IF, a Case statement can either have a default value if all the tests fail or not.

Another difference from the IF: IF does not interpret an empty field as a 0, and reacts to an empty field by ignoring the rest of the calculation. But Case and Choose interpret an empty field as a 0, even if you have chosen "Do not evaluate if all referenced fields are empty." For this reason, our Case statement starts out by testing whether the Grade field is empty; if that field does turn out to be empty, then Case returns an empty result. If we did not test for emptiness, and the Case statement encountered an empty field, Case would interpret the empty value as a 0, which would return the value of Kindergarten.

```
Case(
IsEmpty(grade), "",
grade = 0, "Kindergarten",
grade = 1, "First",
grade = 2, "Second",
grade = 3, "Third",
grade = 4, "Fourth",
grade = 5, "Fifth",
grade = 6, "Sixth",
grade = 7, "Seventh",
grade = 8, "Eighth",
grade = 9, "Freshman",
grade = 10, "Sophomore",
grade = 11, "Junior",
grade = 12, "Senior")
```

The Choose statement is less frequently used because it expects that the field we mention at the beginning has values falling into a sequence of numbers starting at 0 and going up one digit at a time. The beauty of the Choose is that you do not have to specify each test separately because the sequence of tests is implied in the statement itself, and all you have to provide, after naming the field to be analyzed, is the return values for 0, 1, 2, 3, and so on. In our example, then, the first argument is the value in the Grade field, and the Choose function can analyze this field successfully because it contains a number from 0-12. The Choose function also expects that you will provide a return value for each value from 0 on up, and, when it finds one, picks the right return value.

```
If( IsEmpty(grade), "",
Choose(grade, "Kindergarten", "First", "Second", "Third", "Fourth", "Fifth",
"Sixth", "Seventh", "Eighth", "Freshman", "Sophomore", "Junior", "Senior"))
```

CONDITIONAL CALCULATIONS | 309

Tip from	Choose does integers, only. If the value in the field in a Choose statement is not an integer (if the value is a number such as 3.8, or 4.6) the Choose statement ignores the fractional piece and uses the whole number.
Rich	

USING IF STATEMENTS FOR A MULTI-COLUMN REPORT

In the file DatainColumns-j14.fp5, shown in Figure 10.22, a manager gets one perspective on an individual invoice by looking at its age, or a standard list view by sorting all the invoices by age, to see where this one falls. But managers sometimes need to group the invoices based on the length of time it took the customers to pay. For instance, the manager might want to see how much the company collected in 1-30 days, in 31-60 days, and so on. In the List view, we present a panorama across the page, pigeonholing the data so that we see which column (1-30 days, 31-60 days, and so on) each invoice value falls into.

Figure 10.22
Here we group invoices by age.

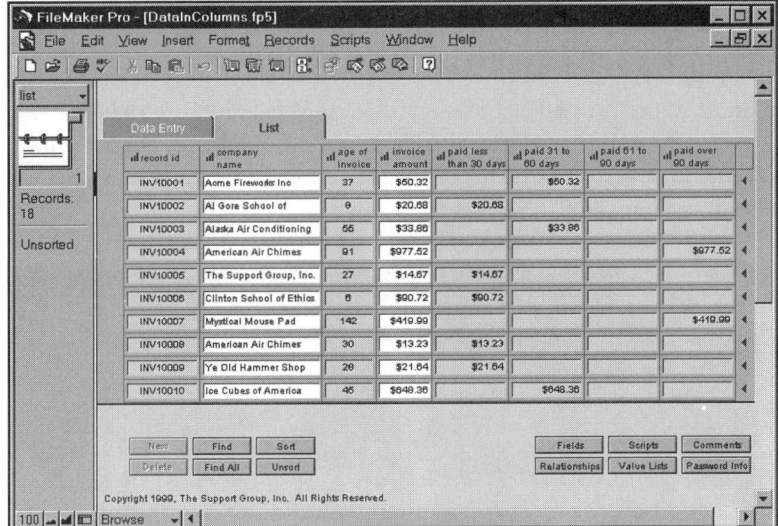

Each column shows the value in a field specially calculated to analyze the age of the invoice, and, if the invoice belongs in that column, to drop the invoice amount into that field. If the age does not belong in that column, no value goes into the field. The first calculation, for the column devoted to invoices that have an age of 1-30 days, goes like this:

```
If(age_of_invoice <= 30, invoice_amount, "")
```

There is a calculation like this for each column, but the figuring gets a little more complicated from here on. The next calculation looks to see if the age fits within a range of numbers starting with 31 and going to 60.

```
If( age_of_invoice >= 31 and age_of_invoice <= 60, invoice_amount, "")
```

Here we use an AND to require that the value undergo 2 tests. The AND operator means that for the whole expression to be true, both tests must be true.

Tip from
Rich

> Use IF and AND to test whether a value falls into a range. In this most recent case, we have created a test for a range, with upper and lower limits. In the previous example, we just asked if the invoice was paid in less than or equal to 30 days. Thus, if an invoice was prepaid (before the date of invoice), that would cause a negative number for the age of invoice, and FileMaker would drop its invoice amount into the column for Less Than 30 Days.

USING IF STATEMENTS TO EXTRACT THE CHOICES OF RADIO BUTTONS

Radio buttons may pose a problem when we want to find out whether users chose a particular selection. In this case, we just want to see if the value in the radio button field equals one particular value, rather than seeing if that particular value appears among a bunch of values, as in the check boxes for pizza toppings. But in surveying a collection of records, looking at the Radio Button field, we will likely find now this choice, now that, from record to record. In Contacts-j15.fp5, shown in Figure 10.23, we have check boxes for the field Gender, but in order to perform further summaries and calculations on the gender values, we need to extract the answer and put it into distinct fields for Male, Female, and Unknown. In this way we can easily run a count of all male records, say, or figure what percentage of all the records are female.

Figure 10.23
We use calculations to count the number of people in each gender.

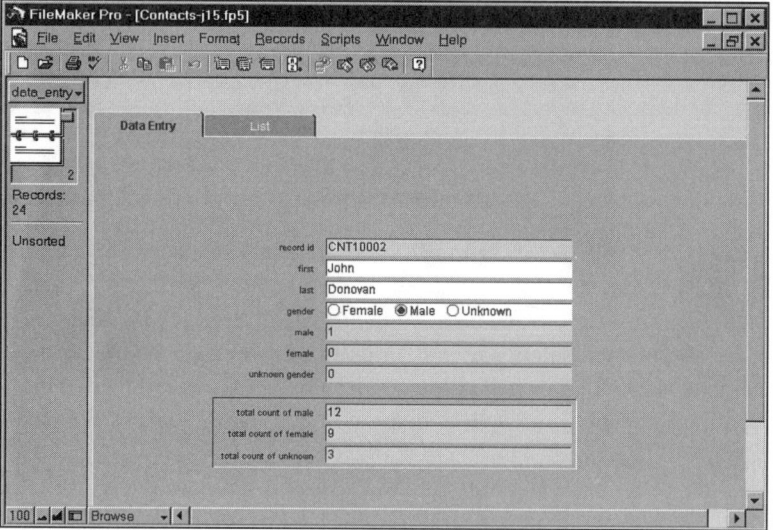

We create Calculation fields for Male, Female, and Unknown based on the user's selection of check boxes. Here is the one for the Male field:

```
If(gender = "male", 1, 0)
```

We look in the Gender field. If the text "Male" appears there, we enter a 1 in the Male field. If not, enter a 0. (The same calculation, basically, looks for the text "Female" and "Unknown" for those fields.)

> **Tip from**
> *Rich*
>
> We actually don't need to run an IF here because the results are either 1 or 0. A Boolean expression all by itself will yield a 1 or a 0. In fact, the first argument inside the IF is a Boolean expression, because it is a test with a result of True or False, and we are saying if the test turns out to be true, enter a 1, and if false, a 0. You could, then, make the expression without IF:
>
>   gender="male"
>
> This Boolean expression would be evaluated for truth or falsity, and would result in a 1 or 0.

Now that we have a 1 in one of the fields (Male, Female, or Unknown), and the other two fields contain a 0 on this record, we can run counts and percentages across the whole set of records, using a Summary field. We have one Summary field s_tot_male, which equals the total in the field c_male, which adds up all the 1s, and tells us how many people in our found set are male.

Now imagine you need a percentage for each gender choice. If we just average the values in the field, using a Summary field, s_avg_male, we get a result that is actually the percentage of male choices. For instance, if there are 10 records, and 3 have a 1 in Male, then the average is 30%.

This percentage option is often useful with check box calculations. You just need to create extra values for separate dedicated fields, such as the Cheese field and the Hot Pepper field, and then run an average on those fields. In this way, you can figure what percentage of your pizzas are going out the door with cheese.

> **Tip from**
> *Rich*
>
> You can perform a similar analysis of the values in fields for which you use check boxes, using PatternCount. Look at PizzaToppings-j15.fp5 for a delicious set of calculations going through the check box data, pulling out the choice of each topping and recording the presence or absence of that topping in its own field (with a 1 or 0), and then figuring the total number of records in which a customer ordered that topping. For instance, here's the calculation for the c_cheese field:
>
>   If(PatternCount("¶" & pizza_toppings & "¶", "¶cheese¶")
>   > 0, 1, 0)
>
> The calculations for total number of pizzas with that topping, and percentages of all pizzas with that topping then operate on the individual topping fields to get summaries, as in s_tot_cheese and s_avg_cheese.

Tip from
Steven

> We could get an identical result, in this case, by using the first argument, or the test portion of the IF statement, everything from PatternCount through the >0, and leaving everything else off. FileMaker interprets that as a Boolean expression yielding a result of 0 or 1. So we would not have to spell out the True and False results as here.

CALCULATIONS WITH CONTAINER RESULTS

Images, animations, and sound effects wake users up, help them recognize unique situations, and reward data entry. You can use calculations to determine which Container results, if any, get displayed.

- Flagging key items for management with graphics
- Creating a fully formatted document for database publishing

FLAGGING KEY ITEMS FOR MANAGEMENT WITH GRAPHICS

If you need to represent a relationship between data items in graphic form, you may want to run a calculation with a Container result, displaying an image as the result of a calculation.

In Portfolio-j16.fp5, shown in Figure 10.24, you see the client's purchase price and sales price (what the client actually sold the stock for), and the record indicates whether the client is ahead of the game, behind, or dead even.

Figure 10.24
The record uses visuals to indicate whether the client is ahead of the game, behind, or dead even.

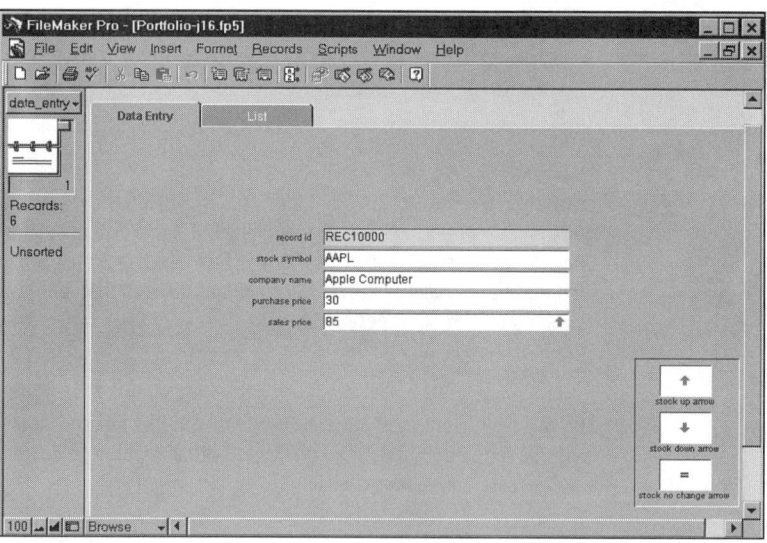

We use a calculation to provide visual icons (up and down arrows, and equal signs) to indicate the direction the stock is taking. The field is called c_up_down_no_change_graphic:

Creating a Fully Formatted Document for Database Publishing | 313

```
Case(
IsEmpty(purchase_price) or IsEmpty(sales_price), "",
purchase_price < sales_price, g_stock_up_symbol,
purchase_price = sales_price, g_stock_no_change_symbol,
purchase_price > sales_price, g_stock_down_symbol,
"")
```

Translating the calculation: In this case, we test for a variety of situations, and assign a result to each instance in which a test comes out True. (With Case, we don't have to provide a result if the test comes out False, although we can. With IF we have to.) First, we test to see if either field is empty, and if so, put nothing there, because we cannot perform a meaningful calculation. (We could have had a question mark appear as a visual cue, instead of nothing.) Assuming that the emptiness test fails, we go on to another test: Is the purchase price less than the sales price? If so, we put an up arrow into the field. That up arrow has been stored in a Global Container field called g_stock_up_symbol; the Global Container fields for up, down, and equal signs are stuck on the data entry layout, so you can see them, but normally we would hide them on a developer layout that the user would never see. We just pasted the right graphic into each Global Container field, so we could pull it out as needed.

Creating a Fully Formatted Document for Database Publishing

When you need to turn out a formatted word-processing document, such as a marketing letter or a catalog, consider using a calculation to spit out Rich Text Format (named for one of our authors), for use by a word processor or desktop publishing program. In the RTF folder for this chapter, the file Contacts-j17.fp5 contains two fields preparing Rich Text Format (RTF) and then a button for exporting the data in RTF (see Figure 10.25).

Figure 10.25
A button allows the user to export data in Rich Text Format (RTF).

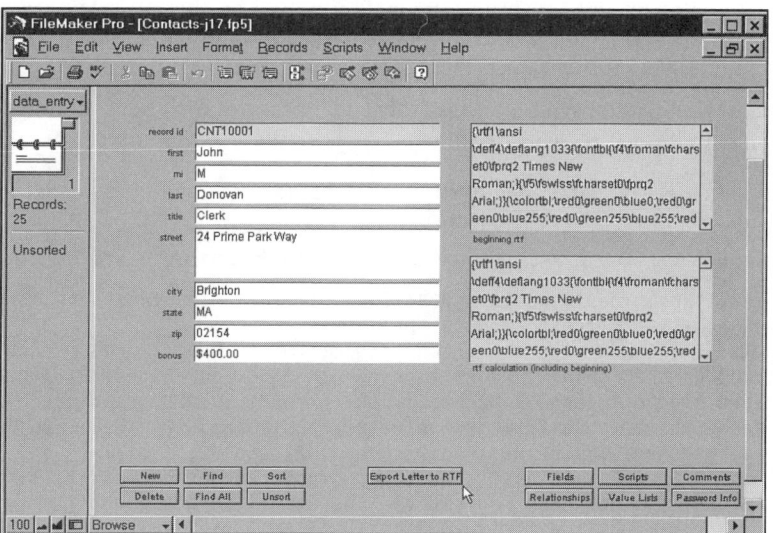

When you click the button for record one, you get a version of the following letter saved in the same directory as the file itself (if you have the file on your hard disk):

January 29, 2000

John Donovan
24 Prime Park Way
Brighton, MA 02154

Dear John,

We would like to thank you for your outstanding efforts over the past year. Our company has done extremely well, in no small part due to the efforts of you and your peers. As a token of our appreciation, shown below is a year-end bonus that will be included in your next paycheck.

Name	Job Title	Bonus Amount
John Donovan	Clerk	$400

Thank you once again for your significant contributions. We wish you continued success in the upcoming year.

Sincerely,

Dan Quayle
Management

There are two parts to this document—a standard header, setting up the document in the same way over and over, and the RTF calculation, which combines the standard header with RTF commands merged with live data from each record. The result of the second calculation is what we export to an RTF file.

You don't have to know much about RTF to pull off this trick. We created a letter in Microsoft Word, and in all-capital letters, inserted placeholders for each field, saving the document in RTF to serve as a template. We put quotes around all the literal text, and used the concatenation symbol to link those text passages with field values. Then we created a script to export the whole field.

The first RTF field, g_begin_rtf, is a Global text field with the header info. We just looked at the RTF file to spot where the actual letter began, and grabbed everything up to that point. Avert your eyes if you wish, but if you are very brave, you can look at it now:

```
{\rtf1\ansi \deff4\deflang1033{\fonttbl{\f4\froman\fcharset0\fprq2 Times New
Roman;}{\f5\fswiss\fcharset0\fprq2
Arial;}}{\colortbl;\red0\green0\blue0;\red0\green0\blue255;\red0\green255\blue255;
\red0\green255\blue0;\red255\green0\blue255;\red255\green0\blue0;\red255\green255\
blue0;\red255\green255\blue255;\red0\green0\blue128;\red0\green128\blue128;\red0\g
reen128\blue0;\red128\green0\blue128;\red128\green0\blue0;\red128\green128\blue0;\
red128\green128\blue128;\red192\green192\blue192;}{\stylesheet{\widctlpar \f4\fs20
\snext0 Normal;}{\*\cs10 \additive Default Paragraph Font;}}{\info{\title
RTFCalc}{\author Rich Coulombre}{\operator Rich Coulombre}{\creatim\yr2000\mo1\
dy14\hr10\min3}{\revtim\yr2000\mo1\dy14\hr10\min3}{\version2}{\edmins0}{\nofpages1
}{\nofwords87}{\nofchars499}{\*\company The Support Group,
```

Creating a Fully Formatted Document for Database Publishing

```
Inc}{\vern57443}}\widowctrl\ftnbj\aenddoc\formshade \fet0\sectd \linex0\endnhere
{\*\pnseclvl1\pnucrm\pnstart1\pnindent720\pnhang{\pntxta
.}}{\*\pnseclvl2\pnucltr\pnstart1\pnindent720\pnhang{\pntxta
.}}{\*\pnseclvl3\pndec\pnstart1\pnindent720\pnhang{\pntxta
.}}{\*\pnseclvl4\pnlcltr\pnstart1\pnindent720\pnhang{\pntxta
)}}{\*\pnseclvl5\pndec\pnstart1\pnindent720\pnhang{\pntxtb (}{\pntxta
)}}{\*\pnseclvl6\pnlcltr\pnstart1\pnindent720\pnhang{\pntxtb (}{\pntxta
)}}{\*\pnseclvl7\pnlcrm\pnstart1\pnindent720\pnhang{\pntxtb (}{\pntxta
)}}{\*\pnseclvl8\pnlcltr\pnstart1\pnindent720\pnhang{\pntxtb (}{\pntxta
)}}{\*\pnseclvl9\pnlcrm\pnstart1\pnindent720\pnhang{\pntxtb (}{\pntxta
)}}\pard\plain \widctlpar \f4\fs20 {\f5 \par \par \par \par \par \par \par
```

The second calculation, which is in the c_rtf_calc field, looks a lot like this gobbledygook, but includes quotes around actual text, plus concatenation symbols and field names (to grab those values).

```
g_begin_rtf & "\par " & MonthName(Status( CurrentDate)) & " " & Day(Status(
CurrentDate)) & ", " & Year(Status( CurrentDate)) & "\par \par " & first & " " &
last & "\par " & street & "\par " & city & ", " & state & "  " & zip & "\par \par
Dear " & first & "," & "\par \par }\pard \widctlpar {\f5 We would like to thank
you for your outstanding efforts over the past year.  Our company has done
extremely well, in no small part due to the efforts " &  "of you and your peers.
As a token of our appreciation, shown below is a year-end bonus that will be
included in your next paycheck." & "\par }\pard \widctlpar {\f5 \par }\trowd
\trqc\trgaph108\trleft-108 \clbrdrt\brdrs\brdrw15\brdrcf1
\clbrdrl\brdrs\brdrw30\brdrcf1 \clbrdrb\brdrs\brdrw15\brdrcf1
\clbrdrr\brdrs\brdrw15\brdrcf1 \clcfpat16\clcbpat8\clshdng3000 " &
"\cellx2193\clbrdrt\brdrs\brdrw15\brdrcf1 \clbrdrl\brdrs\brdrw15\brdrcf1
\clbrdrb\brdrs\brdrw15\brdrcf1 \clbrdrr\brdrs\brdrw15\brdrcf1
\clcfpat16\clcbpat8\clshdng3000 \cellx3504\clbrdrt\brdrs\brdrw15\brdrcf1 " &
"\clbrdrl\brdrs\brdrw15\brdrcf1 \clbrdrb\brdrs\brdrw15\brdrcf1
\clbrdrr\brdrs\brdrw30\brdrcf1 " & "\clcfpat16\clcbpat8\clshdng3000 \cellx5040
\pard \widctlpar\intbl {\f5 Name\cell }\pard \widctlpar\intbl {\f5 Job Title\cell}
\pard \widctlpar\intbl {\f5 Bonus Amount\cell }\pard \widctlpar\intbl {\f5 \row }
\trowd \trqc\trgaph108\trleft-108 \clbrdrl" &
"\brdrs\brdrw30\brdrcf1 \clbrdrb\brdrs\brdrw15\brdrcf1
\clbrdrr\brdrs\brdrw15\brdrcf1 \cellx2193\clbrdrl\brdrs\brdrw15\brdrcf1
\clbrdrb\brdrs\brdrw15\brdrcf1 \clbrdrr\brdrs\brdrw15\brdrcf1
\cellx3504\clbrdrl\brdrs\brdrw15\brdrcf1 \clbrdrb" & "\brdrs\brdrw15\brdrcf1
\clbrdrr\brdrs\brdrw30\brdrcf1 \cellx5040 \pard \widctlpar\intbl {\f5 " & first &
" " & last & "\cell }\pard \widctlpar\intbl {\f5 " & title & "\cell }\pard
\widctlpar\intbl {\f5 $" & bonus & "\cell }\pard \widctlpar\intbl {\f5 \row }\pard
\widctlpar {\f5" &  "\par }\pard \widctlpar {\f5 Thank you once again for your
significant contribuions.  We wish you continued success in the upcoming year.\par}
\pard \widctlpar {\f5 " & "\par Sincerely,\par \par \par \par Dan Quayle\par
Management\par }}"
```

> **Caution**
>
> When you are building the RTF calculation, you have a lot of literal text surrounded by quotes. Keep in mind that FileMaker allows up to 253 characters per literal text string, so if you have more continuous text than that, you have to carve it up into blocks, each of which is less than 254 characters. (Probably this odd number emerges because the two quote marks bring the total to 255, so if you had a string of 400 characters, you would need to break it up into 2 strings surrounded with their own quotes and the ampersand to concatenate them together.)

> **Caution**
>
> When you save a document as RTF from within Word, Word actually puts real hard returns into the document in addition to the \par tags indicating paragraph breaks, so if you copy the text unedited, FileMaker tends to want to export the hard returns as vertical tab characters (line breaks), which can wreak havoc with your document. So you have to go through the document and remove all those hard returns. Because RTF is just a text file, you can open it in a simple text editor, and do a search-and-replace operation to replace all return characters with nothing at all. Here, this process resulted in a single massive paragraph of RTF markup (including the tags indicating paragraph returns) and content. That's what we used to build the calculation for the body of the letter.

> **Tip from Rich**
>
> RTF is a Microsoft published standard, and if you insist on learning the ins and outs, you can pick up the standard at the Microsoft Web site. Alas, the RTF standard evolves. Systems we have built successfully with one version of Word became shaky when users moved on to the next version of Word, because Microsoft changed the specifications for RTF. We found it easier to redo the whole calculation from scratch than to figure out exactly how RTF was functioning.

> **Tip from Rich**
>
> You can perform this kind of calculation with the Sylk format to generate spreadsheets complete with calculations and formatting.

> **Tip from Rich**
>
> You can easily allow a user to export a single letter for a particular individual, but if a user wants to generate a whole set of records to a series of individual files, you should use the TROI plug-in so that you can give a unique name to each of the exported files. (The FileMaker Export command allows the user to name each file individually during an export of a single record, or assigns the same name to all the exported documents because it can only remember a single file name.)

COMMON MISTAKE: RTF

Trying to work with the nuts and grit of RTF. Enough said.

Calculating with Check Boxes

Check boxes, as we have already seen, offer a great way for users to enter values without typing, but because users can pick items in any order, we have to do some extra calculating to work with those values.

Sorting Check Box Items and Converting Values to a Comma-Separated List

Sometimes, you need to pull values out of a check box field for a summary or subsummary report, but the various sequences that people use to enter values makes it hard to spot a particular combination in the records.

Items appear in check box fields in the order in which a user selected them. Thus, if one person chooses Cheese, then Pepperoni, those toppings appear in that order; but if another person chooses Pepperoni, then Cheese, we get the toppings in that order. Later, if we tried to generate a subsummary report showing the count of pizza orders by the mix of toppings, those two records would be regarded as different, even though a hungry human would regard them as the same combination of toppings. In PizzaToppings-j18.fp5, shown in Figure 10.26, we offer a technique that takes the items in a check box field and sorts them alphabetically, to prepare them for further analysis.

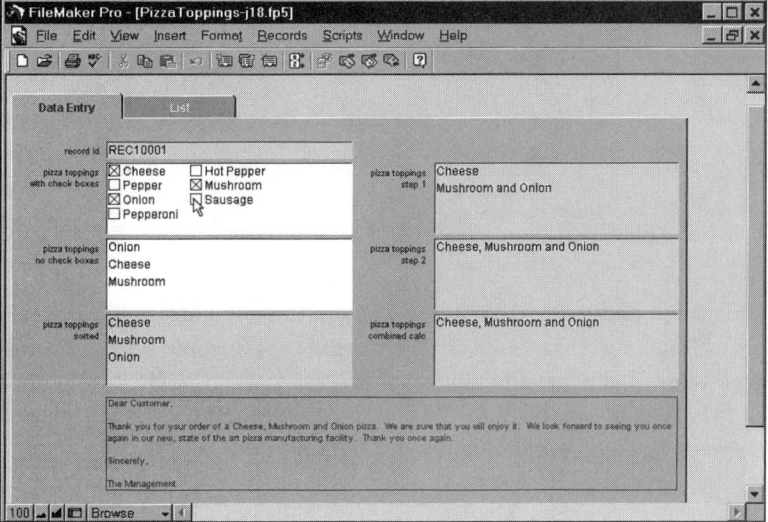

Figure 10.26
In PizzaToppings we invite entries via the check boxes.

Looking at the data entry screen in PizzaToppings-j18 (see Figure 10.26), you see our old friend the check box field for toppings. Below it, though, we show the same values entered as text (see Figure 10.27).

As a first step, we sort the values alphabetically, in the field c_pizza_toppings_sorted. This gives us a consistent ordering we can use in reports and letters. Here's the calculation.

```
Left(
Case(PatternCount( "¶" & pizza_toppings & "¶", "¶" & "Cheese" & "¶") > 0,
"Cheese¶") &
Case(PatternCount( "¶" & pizza_toppings & "¶", "¶" & "Hot Pepper" & "¶") > 0, "Hot
Pepper¶") &
Case(PatternCount( "¶" & pizza_toppings & "¶", "¶" & "Mushroom" & "¶") > 0,
"Mushroom¶") &
```

```
Case(PatternCount( "¶" & pizza_toppings & "¶", "¶" & "Onion" & "¶") > 0, "Onion¶") &
Case(PatternCount( "¶" & pizza_toppings & "¶", "¶" & "Pepper" & "¶") > 0,
"Pepper¶") &
Case(PatternCount( "¶" & pizza_toppings & "¶", "¶" & "Pepperoni" & "¶") > 0,
"Pepperoni¶") &
Case(PatternCount( "¶" & pizza_toppings & "¶", "¶" & "Sausage" & "¶") > 0,
"Sausage¶"),
Length(pizza_toppings))
```

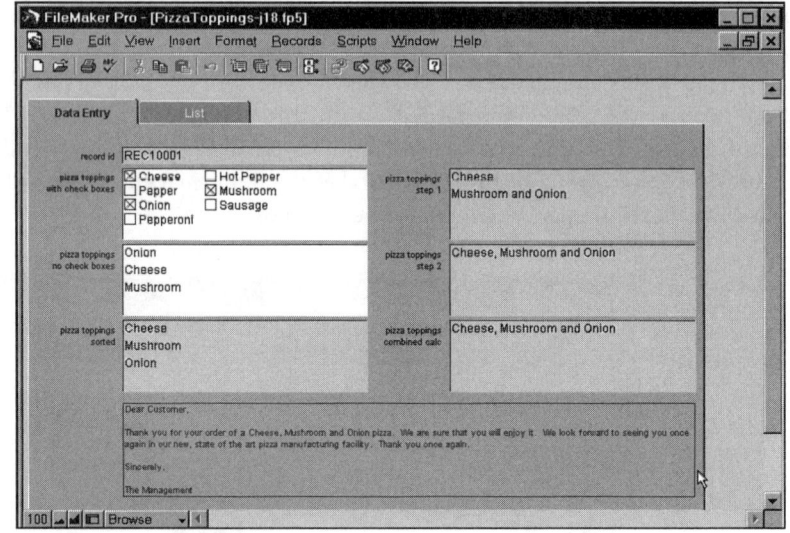

Figure 10.27
The PizzaToppings database shows the text values of the toppings chosen in the check boxes.

What we're doing here is moving values to the left with brute force. Elegant, it's not, but this technique will do the trick. We use the Case statement to test for the presence of a given value, and we test for these values in the order in which we want them to end up in the final list (alphabetically). We say, for every topping in our original value list, if you find this value in the pizza_toppings field, put that value on the list we are building, followed by a carriage return. The result: We have emerged with a list that changes the order of the items in the pizza toppings field. We have built up a new list in our preferred order.

But there is not always a next item, so we will inevitably end up with an extra carriage return—one more than we want. That's why we start off with left, so the emerging list will end up exactly as long as the original. We use the Length statement to grab only the number of characters from the *left* that existed in the pizza_toppings field. In effect, we are abandoning that extra carriage return we inadvertently created when we dropped values+returns into our evolving list.

> **Note**
>
> In the earlier example, in the Chapter 10 file called PizzaToppings-j15.fp5, we used an IF statement to accomplish this result. Here we use Case, just to show you another approach.

Another calculation shown in this file arose because a customer wanted us to take the items selected in a check box field and to merge those into a form letter. But the problem was that items in a check box field are always separated by carriage returns, which can really foul up the format of a letter. The challenge here is to get rid of carriage returns, by converting the list of values to a comma-separated list, with a comma-and-space combination following each item, and "and" between the last two items. We take the last carriage return in the check box field, and replacing it with a space, the word *and*, and another space. We think of this technique as changing check box choices into a comma-separated list.

In the field c_pizza_toppings_step1, we run this calculation:

```
If(PatternCount( pizza_toppings, "¶") = 0, pizza_toppings,
Replace(
c_pizza_toppings_sorted,
Position( c_pizza_toppings_sorted, "¶", 1, PatternCount( c_pizza_toppings_sorted,
"¶")),
1, " and "))
```

Basically, this says, "If the field c_pizza_toppings_sorted has no carriage returns, then we conclude that there is one item selected, or none. But if either of those circumstances exist, then we don't need the rest of this step, so just leave whatever is there in the field."

The rest of the step locates the last carriage return in the field, which would separate the penultimate item from the last item in the list and replaces that with a space, the word *and*, and another space character. In this part of the calculation from the beginning, we rely on the `Replace` function. It takes four arguments:

1. The text you are going to work with
2. The starting character within that text
3. The number of characters to be replaced, including the starting character
4. What you are replacing that text with (space, *and*, space)

The most difficult part of this is determining what the starting character will be. Which of several returns are we looking at? We have to locate where in the field (at what character position) the last carriage return is living. This could vary from record to record, as customers go crazy with toppings, or cut back, when dieting.

So, we use the `Position` function, which locates the character position of a given string within another string. For instance, is the last carriage return in position 53 or 66? The first argument is the text we are working on—the c_pizza_toppings_sorted field. The second argument is the string we are looking for, in this case, a carriage return. The third argument is the character position at which we want FileMaker to start looking—in this case, the first character. The fourth argument answers the question Which occurrence of this string do you want FileMaker to find? At first glance, this is a tough question to answer because each record may have a different number of toppings. But, in fact, we just want the very last item, so its number is the equal to the count of all occurrences. If the field contains 5 carriage returns, we want the fifth one. So now we have to run a little `PatternCount` of all carriage returns; the result of this calculation is the total number of carriage returns, or, looked at from the `Position` statement's point of view, the number of the last instance of the carriage return. Yes, the mind reels with wheels within wheels. But now that we have `PatternCount`, we can run the `Position` part of the calculation, and then we can carry out the full `Replace`.

> **Tip from**
> *Rich*
>
> In the `Replace` function, what you are replacing and what you are replacing it with do not have to be the same size. For instance, here, we are replacing a single character with 5.

Now, we have an alphabetical list, with the last two items separated by *and*. But there are carriage returns between all of the items, and these could disrupt the formatting of a form letter if we let them be merged with the rest of the text.

So, in the field called c_pizza_toppings_step_2, shown in the layout as Step 2, we use the Substitute function to say, "Find any carriage returns that are left after step 1, and replace those with a comma followed by a space character." This will turn the series of very short paragraphs into a list that can be dropped into a paragraph.

```
Substitute( c_pizza_toppings_step_1, "¶", ", ")
```

To put all the steps together, look at c_pizza_toppings for the total calculation:

```
Substitute(
If(PatternCount( pizza_toppings, "¶") = 0, pizza_toppings,

Replace(
pizza_toppings,
Position( pizza_toppings, "¶", 1, PatternCount( pizza_toppings, "¶")),
1, " and ")), "¶", ", ")
```

On the outside we have our substitution routine, and on the inside, the replace process:

```
Substitute(
If(PatternCount( pizza_toppings, "¶") = 0, pizza_toppings,

Replace(
pizza_toppings,
Position( pizza_toppings, "¶", 1, PatternCount( pizza_toppings, "¶")),
1, " and ")), "¶", ", ")
```

You can now go to the file and change your order for toppings, to see how the sample letter at the bottom gets modified. The payoff: The next time you order pizza, you can offer to create form letters for the pizzeria.

Allowing the User to Modify Standard Text

Sometimes, you want to allow users to put together letters inside your database, combining some boilerplate with their own comments, along with data from the records:

- Doing a mail merge on a text field
- Doing a search-and-replace within a field

Doing a Mail Merge on a Text Field

Consider Contacts-j19.fp5 (see Figure 10.28). In a FileMaker layout we can set up a mail-merge letter using the standard syntax, but sometimes our users want to be able to create their own letters. However, we don't want to give them a password to get into the Layout mode.

Figure 10.28
Contacts-j19 allows users to create their own form letters.

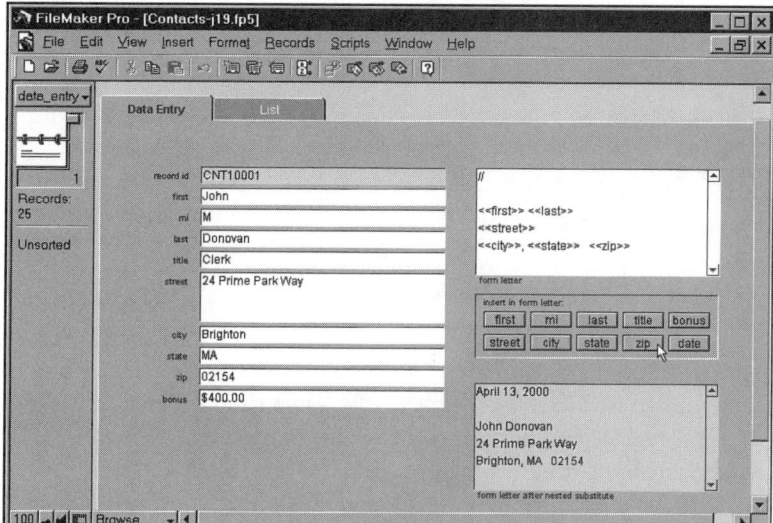

In this file, we develop a way to let users create letters within a field shown in the Browse mode, without ever letting them into the layout (see Figure 10.29).

Figure 10.29
This is the layout itself.

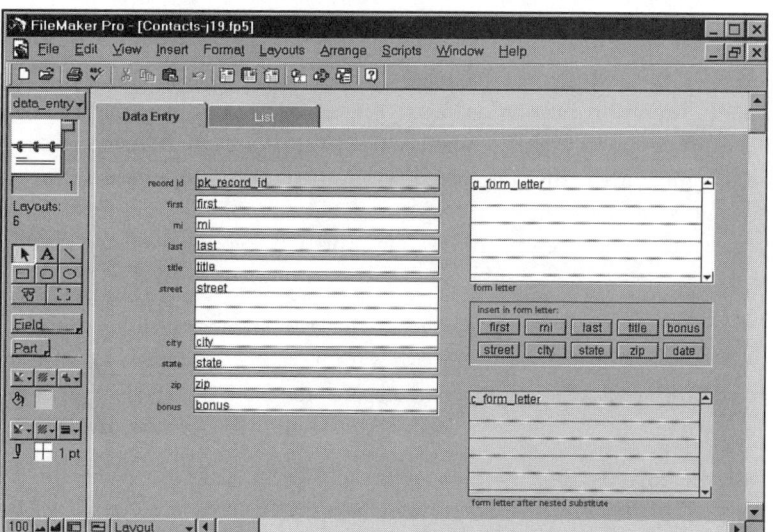

In the top right-hand portion of the screen is a Global field, g_form_letter, into which a user can put the standard text that will go in every letter, as well as the merge items (less than character, field name, greater than character).

Below that we have a calculation that replaces the merge items with actual data from the fields on this record. The calculation for c_form_letter is like the series of substitute teachers we always dreamt of in fourth grade. In fact, we are nesting `Substitute` commands.

```
Substitute( Substitute( Substitute( Substitute( Substitute( Substitute(
Substitute( Substitute( Substitute( Substitute( g_form_letter,
"<<first>>", first),
"<<mi>>", mi),
"<<last>>", last),
"<<title>>", title),
"<<street>>", street),
"<<city>>", city),
"<<state>>", state),
"<<zip>>", zip),
"<<bonus>>", bonus),
"//", MonthName(Status( CurrentDate)) & " " & Day(Status( CurrentDate)) & ", " &
Year(Status( CurrentDate)))
```

The `Substitute` command says, basically, "In this piece of text, whenever you find this string, replace it with this other string." So in a simple instance, we say, "Any time you find <<first>> replace that with the actual value in the First Name field." But we need to replace a whole bunch of strings of merge items. So, once we have taken care of the first substitution, we need to take whatever is left and do another substitution, and so on.

The alternative would be to have a separate field for each of the substitutes, saying, "Take what is in g_form_letter, and substitute just what is in the first name field." In that case, we would have a letter to Jonathan or Rich or Steven, followed by merge characters.

By nesting the substitutions, we are saying, keep working after the first name. Go on and replace the middle initial, and so on, all within the same text, so we end up with a clear text.

Consider, too, the syntax. We have a mass of `Substitute` commands, and then we list the fields in which the original values live, and a series of phrases such as "any time you find this, replace it with that." We know we have to do, say, 10 levels of substitutions, so we drop in 10 commands at the start, and then inside that, put the field we are grabbing text from, followed by a list of the 10 substitute conditions, each closed with its own parentheses and a comma. This approach simplifies our approach to parentheses, and reduces the margin of error.

If a user is accustomed to putting in two slash characters and having FileMaker replace the combination with the day's date, we want to replace that symbol with the name of the month, followed by a comma, and a space, then the day as a number, a comma, a space, and the current year. In this way, we take the // and replace it with the date of printing.

Note the buttons, too. We are giving the user an easy way to insert the merge text. If a user presses First, we insert the first name into the form letter. (Actually we put the merge characters into the g_form_letter wherever the cursor happens to be at that moment). Each button runs a script that starts by calling a subscript that makes sure that the cursor really is in that field, using the Status (CurrentFieldName) function. If not, we display a message saying, "You must be in the field form letter to insert a merge field." If the cursor is there, then we insert the double-angle brackets around the correct field name at that position. In this way a user can build up a new form letter, using the fields we offer as buttons. The calculation at the bottom would normally show up on its own layout with a Print button, so the user could approve it and send it off to be printed.

DOING A SEARCH-AND-REPLACE WITHIN A FIELD

In Contacts-j20, shown in Figure 10.30, we see a variation on this approach. In Contacts-j19, we produced a letter as the result of a calculation, which meant that once the calculation was completed, the user could not modify the letter. But now imagine that the boss wants to add individual notes at the end of some letters. Now, we can no longer use a calculated field. The question is: How do we get the results of a calculation into a field that is modifiable?

Figure 10.30
Contacts-j20 allows the boss to add notes to the form letter.

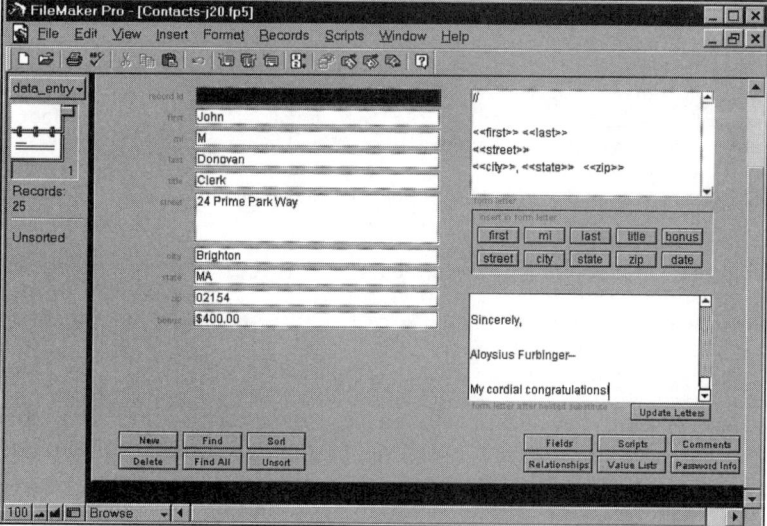

The field called results_form_letter is a Text field. Here we use script with a series of calculated Replaces to establish the initial content of the letter—the standard version. Now that this material is in a Text field, the boss can modify the text at any time.

We use a script called create_form_letters_for_found_set to perform the calculated Replaces because in this way we can avoid making the field itself a Calculation field (in which case the boss could not modify the result). Here is the script:

```
If [ Status( CurrentMode) = 1 ]
     Perform Script [ "beep_beep_not_in_find_mode_message" ]
          [ Sub-scripts ]
     Exit Script
```

```
End If
Enter Browse Mode
Replace [ result_form_letter, Replace data:Calculation: , g_form_letter ]
        [ No dialog ]
Replace [ result_form_letter, Replace data:Calculation: , Substitute(
result_form_letter, "<<first>>", first) ]
        [ No dialog ]
Replace [ result_form_letter, Replace data:Calculation: , Substitute(
result_form_letter, "<<mi>>", mi) ]
        [ No dialog ]
Replace [ result_form_letter, Replace data:Calculation: , Substitute(
result_form_letter, "<<last>>", last) ]
        [ No dialog ]
Replace [ result_form_letter, Replace data:Calculation: , Substitute(
result_form_letter, "<<title>>", title) ]
        [ No dialog ]
Replace [ result_form_letter, Replace data:Calculation: , Substitute(
result_form_letter, "<<bonus>>", bonus) ]
        [ No dialog ]
Replace [ result_form_letter, Replace data:Calculation: , Substitute(
result_form_letter, "<<street>>", street) ]
        [ No dialog ]
Replace [ result_form_letter, Replace data:Calculation: , Substitute(
result_form_letter, "<<city>>", city) ]
        [ No dialog ]
Replace [ result_form_letter, Replace data:Calculation: , Substitute(
result_form_letter, "<<state>>", state) ]
        [ No dialog ]
Replace [ result_form_letter, Replace data:Calculation: , Substitute(
result_form_letter, "<<zip>>", zip) ]
        [ No dialog ]
Replace [ result_form_letter, Replace data:Calculation: , Substitute(
result_form_letter, "//", MonthName(Status( CurrentDate)) & " " & Day(Status(
CurrentDate)) & ", " &
Year(Status( CurrentDate))) ]
        [ No dialog ]
```

We are creating a calculated Replace using the Substitute function. In this script, we check to make sure that the user is not in the Find mode because the rest of the script cannot operate in the Find mode. Next, we take whatever is in the field g_form_letter, which is where the user actually creates the letter including the merge characters, and we put that into the field result_form_letter. Replace takes only two arguments:

1. The field whose value is being replaced. (If you don't mention this, FileMaker will replace the value in whatever field the cursor is in at the moment).
2. What you want to replace that value with.

COMMON MISTAKE: RUNNING THE REPLACE COMMAND ON A FIELD THAT HAPPENS NOT TO BE ON THE CURRENT LAYOUT

The Replace command only works on a field that is on the current layout. So you have to go to its layout before using the Replace command.

> **Tip from**
> *Rich*
>
> The `Replace` command only works on the found set of records, so you need to make sure that the right records have been found before doing the replacements. (Our script here does not worry about the found set because we are assuming the user has already found the records to manipulate, but you may have to `FindAll` or perform some kind of `Find first`.)

We take the user's form letter (in the Global field g_form_letter) and move that into the text field in which the letter is created for each individual user, result_form_letter. Note that FileMaker identifies this replace script step as a calculation.

There are three different ways to use `Replace`:

1. It takes the value in the current field and uses that to replace the values in the same field throughout the current found set.
2. It enters auto-incrementing serial numbers in the field, and, optionally, when it is done, alerts FileMaker about the value to be used next, assuming FileMaker will continue to automatically enter values in the field.
3. It replaces the value in the field with a calculated result, which is a very powerful tool.

The third mode lets us create a calculated expression and, moving record by record through the found set, replace the current value with a calculated value. In this case, we are going to combine the calculated `Replace` with the `Substitute` command, which we used in the earlier example. In that way we can do a search and replace on the text within the field.

We want to locate the merge fields inserted by the users, and to replace those with actual data from the fields, record by record.

We could have used a single massive calculated `Replace`, with a bunch of replacements nested within each other. That approach would have been faster.

We chose to do the replacements one at a time because it was easier to build, and, for others who come along afterward, easier to understand and maintain.

For each field we are saying something like, "In the field result_form_letter, any time you find the string << first >>, replace that with the value in the field called first in this record." We do this for each field that a user might put into the letter. When we have replaced all the valid merge fields with real data, we stop.

The `Substitute` function spots each set of merge characters within the text, comes up with a substitute, and inserts that into the text.

Note that the `Substitute` function must be part of a calculation. It can be part of a Calculation field, but a Calculation field cannot be edited by a user. So that wouldn't allow the boss to customize the letters, record by record. But we can use `Substitute` any time the calculation engine is operating, as when we invoke `Replace` from a menu, or create a script step such as `ExitLoopIf`, `IF`, `InsertCalculatedResult`, `Replace`, or `SetField`.

In this case, we want to run the replacement across all found records, so we have turned to the `Replace` command, which operates on multiple records, and invoked its third mode, which involves calculation.

> **Tip from**
> *Rich*
>
> Contrast a calculated `Replace` with a Calculation field. The Calculation field pays no attention to found sets because it applies to all records in the database. The calculated `Replace` only applies the calculation to the found set, a nice wrinkle. Also, if you change any of the fields that a calculation depends on, a calculation is automatically updated, whereas the calculated `Replace` just takes a one-time snapshot of the calculated result, but does not stay on the alert to watch out for changes in the underlying values. Calculations, then, are live, but the results of a calculated `Replace` remain unchanged (not quite dead, but at least stable), even if the fields used in the calculation are changed, because the calculated `Replace` only occurs when the script is run. Here, after the script ran, any changes to g_form_letter would have no effect on the field results_form_letter.

> **Tip from**
> *Rich*
>
> Think carefully before using a calculated `Replace` in a multi-user environment. FileMaker does record locking to protect data from chaos, so the first user of a record has exclusive ownership of that record. If another user strolls along and clicks in that record, FileMaker tells that user to wait because someone else is already busy modifying the record. If one user is trying to do a calculated `Replace`, while other users are actively editing some of the records in the found set, FileMaker will skip those "locked" records.

GENERATING RANDOM NUMBERS

When you are writing files for a book like this, the biggest challenge is coming up with dummy data. Wouldn't it be nice to have the computer generate random data? You might need some random data to test the system, when you can't get real data from the boss, or you get a printout and say, "Ugh, I don't want to type all this." Here's how.

Looking in the folder, J20-CalcReplace, you'll find a file called RandomNumbers.fp5 (see Figure 10.31). The process is done in steps, to show you each step on the path.

We start with a field called true_random_number, which is a Number field with values between 0 and 1. On the Data Entry and List layouts, we have a button called New Random Numbers, which invokes a script called set_random_numbers. In this script, we use a calculated `Replace` to replace the last random number we put in this field with a new random number between 0 and 1, one per record through the found set of records. We use a script to generate this, because we use this technique a lot and want to be able to recycle the calculation easily. Here's the way FileMaker prints out the set_random_numbers script:

```
Enter Browse Mode
If [ IsEmpty(g_min_random_number) or IsEmpty(g_max_random_number) ]
        Beep
        Beep
        Show Message [ Buttons: "OK", "", ""; Data: "Please enter values in both
```

```
        the minimum and maximum fields before pressing this button." ]
            Exit Script
    End If
    If [ g_min_random_number >= g_max_random_number ]
            Beep
            Beep
            Show Message [ Buttons: "OK", "", ""; Data: "The minimum value must be
    lower than the maximum value." ]
            Exit Script
    End If
    Replace [ true_random_number, Replace data:Calculation: , Random ]
            [ No dialog ]
    Replace [ adj_random_number, Replace data:Calculation: , true_random_number *
    (g_max_random_number - g_min_random_number) + g_min_random_number ]
            [ No dialog ]
    Replace [ random_number_rounded_2_dec_places, Replace data:Calculation: ,
    Round(adj_random_number,2) ]
            [ No dialog ]
    Replace [ random_number_rounded_0_dec_places, Replace data:Calculation: ,
    Round(adj_random_number,0) ]
            [ No dialog ]
    Replace [ random_number_rounded_nearest_100, Replace data:Calculation: ,
    Round(adj_random_number,-2) ]
            [ No dialog ]
```

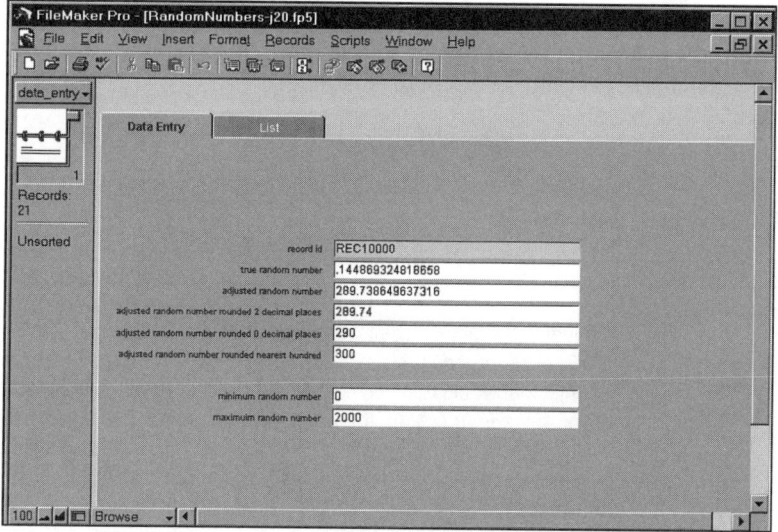

Figure 10.31
In RandomNumbers .fp5, you can generate random numbers for testing.

In this script, we tell FileMaker the range of numbers we want generated. We need minimum and maximum values before going ahead, so the first steps look in the 2 data-entry fields dealing with those, and if those are empty, prompt the user to enter values there before proceeding. Ditto, if the minimum value turns out to be greater than the supposed maximum. Once these little data entry chores have been cleared up, we can go ahead to run the calculations. We replace the true_random_number value with, well, another random number between 0 and 1, generated by the Random function.

But we may need random numbers that are larger than the ones between 0 and 1. How do we convert one of these fractional random numbers to a larger one? The smallest number we want is the one the user entered in the minimum field, and the largest is the one in the maximum field. If our goal is a number between 100 and 400, one way of thinking about that is to say, "We have to generate a random number between 0 and 300, then add 100 to it." To do so, we multiply 300 times the random number to get a number between 0 and 300, and then add the 100, to get a number that, for sure, is between 100 and 400. To get the value in the adj_random_number field, we subtract the minimum from the maximum, multiply the difference times the original random number, and then add the original minimum to make sure we beat it.

Of course, now we have a whole bunch of figures to the right of the decimal place. Normally, we don't want all those figures. So we used the Round function to create values in additional fields, rounding the result to two decimal places (hundredths), no decimal place (integers), and the nearest hundred.

The Round function takes two arguments:

1. The value that you want to round off.
2. The position on which to round, whether to the right or left of the decimal point. The first position after the decimal point is tenths; the first position to the left of the decimal point is the units column. (You can put in a negative number of decimal places to round to the nearest ten, hundred, or whatever to the left of the decimal point.) FileMaker calls this option the precision of rounding.

Tip from *Rich*	FileMaker rounds 5 up. If you say Round (1.5, 0), FileMaker looks at the .5 and rounds it up, to get 2.
Tip from *Rich*	Rounding is really different from using the Integer functions. The Int function drops all decimal places, and presents you with the whole number. The Round function may actually change that whole number, based on the values to the right or left of the precision location. If you say Round (1.3, 0), the result, which is rounded to 0 decimal places, is 1. If you say Round (1.7, 0), the result would be 2. If you say Int (1.3), you get a 1, and when you say Int (1.7), you also get 1. Rounding to zero decimal places, then, is not the same as getting the Integer value.

COMMON MISTAKE: MISTAKING A FORMAT FOR ACTUAL ROUNDING

Developers have sometimes formatted numbers on a layout to round them off to two decimal places, which changes the way the number is displayed but does not change the underlying value. Users may innocently assume that the value they see, such as $100.50, is the actual number—without understanding that the underlying number is really something like 100.499999999999 (eleven nines). If the user believes the value is $100.50, and goes into Find to locate a record with the value $100.50, FileMaker will not find that record because it indexes the true value, not the displayed value.

Creating a Bar Graph

Tip from Rich

> Just as you can use a negative number in the Round function to specify the precision in tens, hundreds, or whatever, you can put a negative number in the Format Number dialog to change the way the number is displayed (while leaving the actual value in the index). A negative 2 would format the number as rounded off to the nearest hundred. For instance, 534 would be displayed as 500.

The clear_random_numbers script empties the fields. Then the calculated Replace option replaces the value with a calculated result that is, well, a whole lot of nothing. In this way, we can erase the contents of a field.

```
Enter Browse Mode
Replace [ true_random_number, Replace data:Calculation: , "" ]
        [ No dialog ]
Replace [ adj_random_number, Replace data:Calculation: , "" ]
        [ No dialog ]
Replace [ random_number_rounded_2_dec_places, Replace data:Calculation: , "" ]
        [ No dialog ]
Replace [ random_number_rounded_0_dec_places, Replace data:Calculation: , "" ]
        [ No dialog ]
Replace [ random_number_rounded_nearest_100, Replace data:Calculation: , "" ]
        [ No dialog ]
```

Tip from Rich

> Before doing a calculated Replace, always do a backup. Things can go wrong if you happen to specify the wrong field, or if you make one false move in the calculation, and watch perfectly valid data turn to mush in a second. The calculated Replace is very powerful and very dangerous.

Creating a Bar Graph

The List view in Contacts-j21 shows bars indicating the size of each person's bonus (see Figure 10.32). Looking behind the blue lines, you can see how we generate these bar graphs by using two copies of the same field, one on top of another. If you peeled the bar graph fields apart, you would find each is filled with goalpost characters, formatted as bold. The text color is set to blue. We use the two levels to fill in the gaps between the goalpost characters. But, you may ask, how do we decide how many goalpost characters to put in?

We had to figure, first, what the range of numbers might be, and what amount of space we might have in which to chart them. For example, if we were charting the cost of a year of college, the numbers could range from $4,000 to $40,000, and we would probably not want to fit 40,000 goalposts into the field. So we had to decide on a scaling factor.

Here, our numbers range from $100 to $900, so we take the bonus amount and divide it by 10 to tell FileMaker how many goalposts to put in the field. So $250 will yield 25 goalposts. Someone with a $700 bonus will get 70 goalposts. Now we have a way to build up our lines for the chart.

Here's the calculation for c_bar_graph:

```
Left("||||||||||||||||||||||||||||||
||||||||||||||||||||||||||||||||||
||||||||||||||||||||||||||||||||||
||||||||||||||||||||||||||||||||||
||||||||||||||||||||||||||||||||||
||||||||||||||||||||||||||||||||||
||||||||||||||||||||||||||||||||",
Int(bonus/10))
```

We are saying to take the leftmost *n* characters out of the text containing many, many goalposts (250 all together). We figure *n* by running the Int function on the result of dividing the bonus by 10. So the text result is, well, a bunch of goalposts. This produces a row with gaps. So we boldface the goalposts to fatten them up, then we lay the same field on top of itself, a few pixels to one side. Also, we make sure that the field on top has no fill so it does not mask the field underneath.

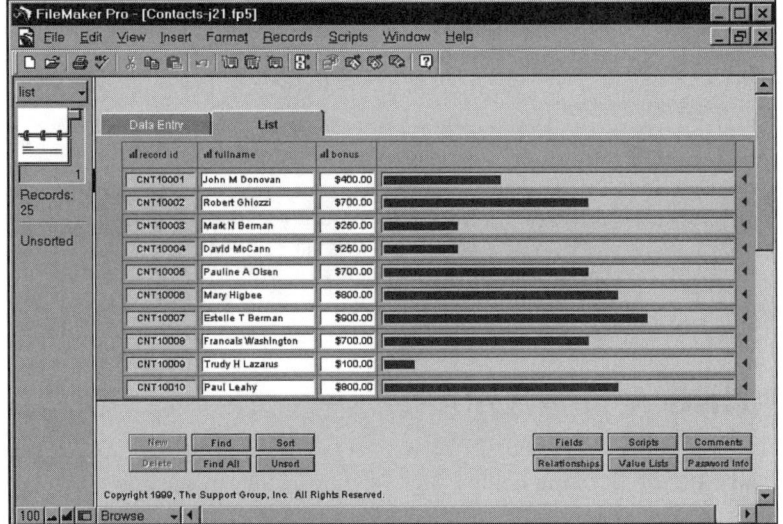

Figure 10.32
The List view in Contacts-j21 shows bars indicating the size of each person's bonus.

COMMON MISTAKE: PASTING MORE THAN 253 CHARACTERS INTO THE TEXT STRING

You get the message "This text constant does not end with a quotation mark, or is longer than 253 characters." Note that we are offering a text string of 250 goalpost characters. You face a limit of 253 characters in any single string of literal text. If you need more than that, do not despair. Create multiple chunks of no more than 253 characters and combine them with the concatenation symbol (ampersand).

Caution

The way you can edit a calculation involving text differs on Macs and PCs. In the Specify Calculation dialog on the Mac, you can use the Edit menu to copy and paste, but in Windows the Edit menu is not available. But on both systems you can use the keyboard shortcuts for Cut, Copy, Paste, and Select All, moving text into and out of the dialog.

Tip from
Rich

> To maximize the width of your charting characters, go bold.

EXPORTING OR IMPORTING FIXED-LENGTH RECORDS

The mainframe world began with fixed-length records, and many mainframe databases persist. FileMaker is unusual in that you don't have to declare, ahead of time, exactly how much room to allocate for a new field. If you have to export to a mainframe, or import from a mainframe you may have to massage your data by using special calculations to cope with fixed-length records.

EXPORTING TO FIXED-LENGTH RECORDS

In the directory j22-Custom Export, we provide two files showing you how to move your data into fixed-length fields, or export the data with customized delimiters. FileMaker offers you various flavors of exports, each an industry standard supported by many other applications. But occasionally you get a customer who needs to export the information in a fixed, record-length format (in which each field has exactly the same amount of space on each record, and each record has exactly the same amount of space as another record), or to use a custom delimiter (something other than a tab or a comma). For instance, on many mainframe systems, Last Name is assigned a fixed number of characters (perhaps 15), and if someone's last name contains fewer characters, the developer has to fill up the remaining space with something—usually some space characters.

In the file FixedRecordLength-j22, shown in Figure 10.33, we define the field c_fixed_record_length_export with this calculation:

```
Left( first & "          ", 10) &
Left( mi & " ", 1) &
Left( last & "               ", 15) &
Left( title & "                    ", 20) &
Left( street & "                              ", 30) &
Left( city & "                    ", 20) &
Left( state & "   ", 2) &
Left( zip & "          ", 10)
```

To create a 10-character entry (no more, no less) in the First Name field, we take the leftmost 10 characters of the text string made up of the field value plus 10 blank spaces. We use 10 blank spaces because there may be no entry. If someone happens to have a long first name, we are just going to truncate that name after 10 characters.

Caution

> Commonly, when people get married today, they concatenate both last names to create a new one. If this process goes on for a few generations, the length of the resulting names could blow the capabilities of many mainframes.

Figure 10.33
In the file FixedRecordLength-j22, we allow exporting to a mainframe world.

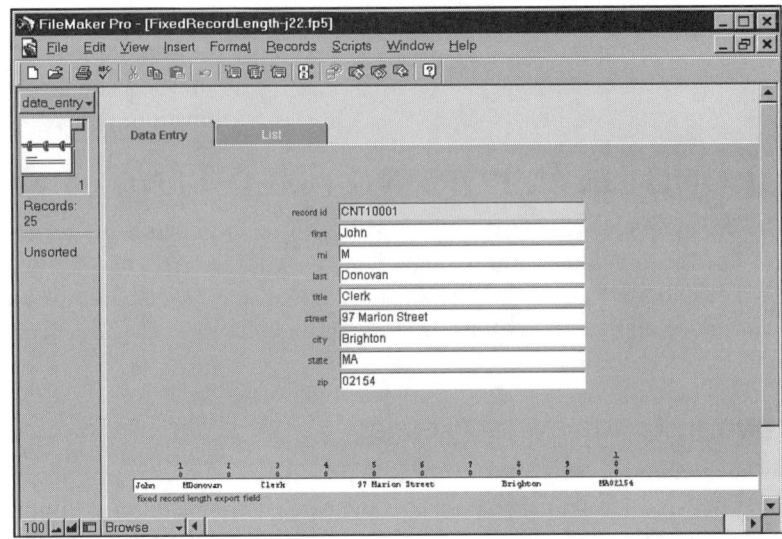

We use the same routine for all the fields, and then glue the results together. You can tell how long each field is by looking at the second argument in each Left function; for instance, the ZIP code field can only be 10 characters long.

If you look on the Data Entry screen, you see the results displayed in a long field showing how the fixed-length material emerges. To make these results display properly, we had to use a monospaced font, so that each character takes up the same amount of horizontal space. This is the field that will be exported.

 In CustomDelimiter-j22, shown in Figure 10.34, we insert a special delimiter between field values to get ready for exporting. Normally, when exporting you just specify the fields, and FileMaker itself puts in the delimiters for you. But what if you need nonstandard delimiters?

Figure 10.34
In Custom- Delimiter-j22 we insert a special delimiter between field values.

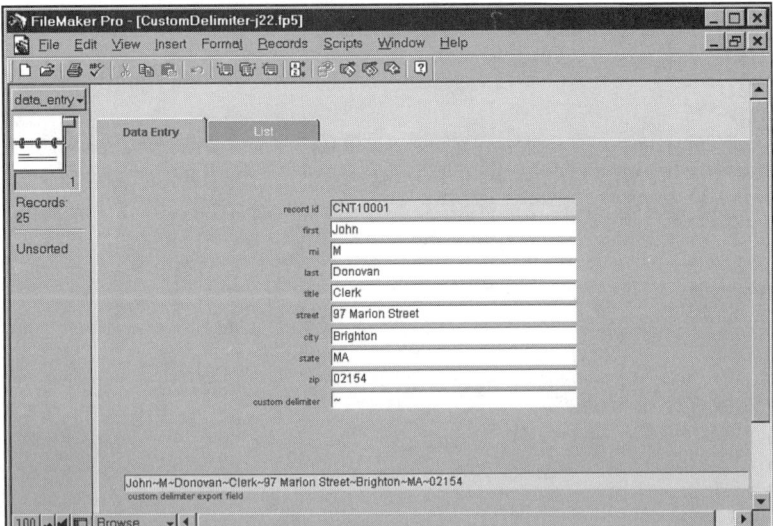

We used a calculation to put the delimiters in, and then, instead of exporting the individual fields, we export a single field—the calculated result. We put the delimiter we want to use in a Global field called g_delimiter, so you or a user can insert any delimiter needed. (In real life, you probably would need to hardwire this information, rather than offering it to an ordinary user to choose.) The field c_customer_delimiter_export contains this calculation:

```
first & g_delimiter &
mi & g_delimiter &
last & g_delimiter &
title & g_delimiter &
street & g_delimiter &
city & g_delimiter &
state & g_delimiter &
zip
```

Basically, we are just pouring field values and delimiters into a new field, and that is the field that will get exported. Because we are just exporting a single field, FileMaker does not need to add its own delimiters. It just puts in carriage returns as record delimiters.

> **Caution**
>
> In some cases, when values are separated by tabs or commas, some values get exported with quotes, following esoteric industry rules, and so you need to test the export to discover whether or not FileMaker has generated the extra quotes. If so, try a different export type. For instance, when doing a comma-separated export, if the data itself contains a comma, FileMaker encloses that in quotes so that the comma itself is not mistaken for a delimiter.

IMPORTING FIXED-LENGTH RECORDS

Importing fixed-length records can be a challenge because FileMaker doesn't have a built-in method for determining where one field stops and another field begins. (A carriage return does signal a new record.)

In folder j24, in the file FixedRecordLength-j24.fp5 (see Figure 10.35), we use a script to take apart the single gigantic field.

Here is the script, which is called import_fixed_record_length_records:

```
Enter Browse Mode
Import Records [ Filename: "FixedRecordLength.tab"; Import Order:
fixed_record_length_import(Text) ]
[ Restore import order, No dialog ]
Replace [ first, Replace data:Calculation: , Trim(
Left(fixed_record_length_import, 10)) ]
[ No dialog ]
Replace [ mi, Replace data:Calculation: , Trim( Middle(fixed_record_length_import,
11, 1)) ]
[ No dialog ]
Replace [ last, Replace data:Calculation: , Trim(
Middle(fixed_record_length_import, 12, 15)) ]
[ No dialog ]
Replace [ title, Replace data:Calculation: , Trim(
Middle(fixed_record_length_import, 27, 20)) ]
[ No dialog ]
```

```
Replace [ street, Replace data:Calculation: , Trim(
Middle(fixed_record_length_import, 47, 30)) ]
[ No dialog ]
Replace [ city, Replace data:Calculation: , Trim(
Middle(fixed_record_length_import, 77, 15)) ]
[ No dialog ]
Replace [ state, Replace data:Calculation: , Trim(
Middle(fixed_record_length_import, 97, 2)) ]
[ No dialog ]
Replace [ zip, Replace data:Calculation: , Trim(
Middle(fixed_record_length_import, 99, 10)) ]
[ No dialog ]
```

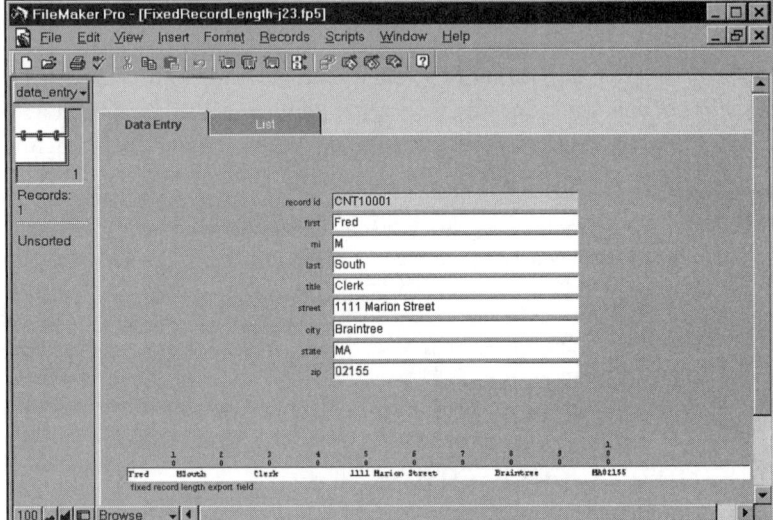

Figure 10.35
The file FixedRecordLength-j24.fp5 uses a script to take apart a single large field brought in from a mainframe.

We have created a file to import from—FixedRecordLength.tab. We start the script telling FileMaker to import that file. We then use the Import Order option to specify the order in which to import fields. Here there is only one field per record, the field called fixed_record_length_import, which is, parenthetically, a Text field.

After we have imported a bunch of records, they become a found set, and the field fixed_record_length_import contains data. Our job is now to take apart the value in that field and put the pieces into the right fields. So we need to locate, say, the position of the Last Name, grab the value, and drop that into the regular field we use for Last Name. The good news with fixed-length imports is that the data is always in the same position. Once you know the position, you can grab the data.

Because we are looking at a found set, we use a calculated Replace, which works record by record on the found set. Let's look at Last Name. We know that Last Name begins at the twelfth character position and runs for 15 characters (characters 12 through 26, inclusive), so we use the Middle function and say, "Go into the field fixed_record_length_import, and, starting at the twelfth character, pull out 15 characters for us." We use the Trim function to remove all leading and trailing spaces to get down to the meaningful data. Replace says, "Apply this calculation to determine the value for the field Last Name, for every record in the found set (the newly imported records), record by record." (Trim always works on space characters.)

> **Tip from**
> *Jonathan*
>
> The Help system for FileMaker often offers more detail than the User's Guide. For instance, the manual's index does not mention Trim, but Help does.

CUSTOM DELIMITER

When you are importing data that contains nonstandard delimiters, you may need to strip those out as part of the process of converting the data for your own database. Take a look in the folder j23-Customer Import and open the CustomDelimiters-j23 file, using the Master password. The data entry screen appears (see Figure 10.36).

Figure 10.36
The data entry screen for the file CustomDelimiters-j23.fp5.

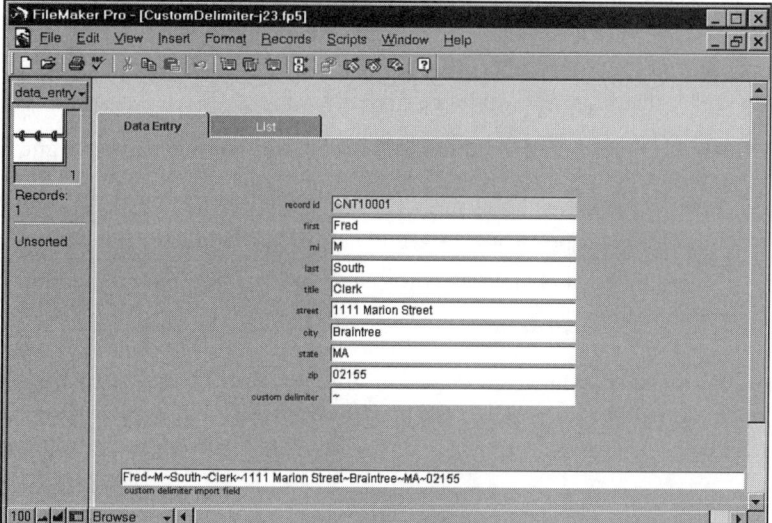

You'll discover that we run a script called import_custom_delimiter_records, which imports records from a text file we call, imaginatively, CustomDelimiter.tab. We set the Import Order option to import the data into the custom_delimiter_import field (and only that field), because that field will contain all of our data, with the custom delimiter separating the values of one field from those in the next. That gives us a found set of records, so we can use the Replace to operate on those records.

We use a series of calculated Replaces here, grabbing material from the left, middle, and right of the imported field. The first replacement is unusual: we use the Position function, which looks for a particular string, usually within a given field, starting at a certain character position (such as the first character, or the 27th), and locating the position of the nth appearance of that string. "Look in this field starting at the 27th character, and tell me the character position of the fourth occurrence of the letter L." The `Position` function therefore takes 4 arguments:

1. The field or the text you are searching in
2. What you are looking for
3. The character position at which you want FileMaker to start looking
4. Which occurrence to locate

We are saying that we want FileMaker to look in the custom_delimiter_import field, and to locate the first occurrence of the global delimiter. If the first occurrence is at character position 10, we know that the first name occupies the leftmost 9 characters. We now know we have to grab the leftmost 9 characters (the value of the first name, before we get to the delimiter between fields). The results go into the field called First. Hallelujah! We have grabbed the person's first name.

But the challenges build up. Now the text we are interested in is buried somewhere in the middle of the field. For instance, Last Name is going to be the third data element in custom_delimiter_import, and as such, it should begin 1 character after the second delimiter, and end 1 character before the third delimiter.

The `Middle` function takes a bunch of `Position` statements as its arguments.

1. The name of the field in the middle of which you want to get something.
2. The character position to start at. (Usually, the position of the nth delimiter plus 1.)
3. The number of characters you want to grab. (The assigned length of the data element, which varies.)

We use the `Middle` function to pull a chunk of text out of the middle of the field custom_delimiter_import. To tell `Middle` where to look, we are using the `Position` functions.

For middle initial, we look for the position right after the first delimiter. Then we have to figure out how many characters to grab. To get that character count, we subtract the character position of the first delimiter from the position of the second. (We are assuming that the lengths of these fields are not fixed.) The subtraction of one position from another constitutes the third argument to the `Middle` function.

At the end of the middle initial calculation, we have to subtract 1 to get the length right. How come? Assume someone has a first name of 5 characters, so the delimiter falls into position 6, and let's assume they have a middle initial of one character, which falls into position 7, so the next delimiter lands in position 8. To get the length of the middle initial, we subtract 6 from 8 and we get 2, leading us to think that the middle initial was two characters long. But it isn't. Subtracting 6 from 8, the remaining 2 actually include one of the two delimiters. That's why we have to subtract 1—to remove the delimiter from the count.

This technique also handles the circumstances in which people lack a middle initial. Presume for a moment that someone has a first name of 5 characters, so the first delimiter goes into position 6, and, lacking a middle initial, the second delimiter falls into position 7. Subtracting 6 from 7, and then subtracting 1 more, we get a length of 0, which is correct. The Middle function realizes it should go into the field, and, starting at the seventh character, grab 0 characters, which it does very well. You get just what you need: nothing.

> **Tip from**
> *Rich*
>
> Left, Right, and Middle do not object to your putting a negative number in, but the results are empty. Don't be afraid of calculating a size that dips below 0.

Here's the script called import_custom_delimiter_records:

```
Enter Browse Mode
Allow User Abort [ Off ]
Set Error Capture [ On ]
Import Records [ Filename: "CustomDelimiter.tab"; Import Order:
custom_delimiter_import(Text) ]
        [ Restore import order, No dialog ]
Replace [ first, Replace data:Calculation: , Left( custom_delimiter_import,
Position( custom_delimiter_import, g_delimiter, 1, 1) - 1) ]
        [ No dialog ]
Replace [ mi, Replace data:Calculation: , Middle( custom_delimiter_import,
Position( custom_delimiter_import, g_delimiter, 1, 1) + 1,
Position( custom_delimiter_import, g_delimiter, 1, 2) -Position(
custom_delimiter_import, g_delimiter, 1, 1) - 1) ]
        [ No dialog ]
Replace [ last, Replace data:Calculation: , Middle( custom_delimiter_import,
Position( custom_delimiter_import, g_delimiter, 1, 2) + 1,
Position( custom_delimiter_import, g_delimiter, 1, 3) -Position(
custom_delimiter_import, g_delimiter, 1, 2) - 1) ]
        [ No dialog ]
Replace [ title, Replace data:Calculation: , Middle( custom_delimiter_import,
Position( custom_delimiter_import, g_delimiter, 1, 3) + 1,
Position( custom_delimiter_import, g_delimiter, 1, 4) -Position(
custom_delimiter_import, g_delimiter, 1, 3) - 1) ]
        [ No dialog ]
Replace [ street, Replace data:Calculation: , Middle( custom_delimiter_import,
Position( custom_delimiter_import, g_delimiter, 1, 4) + 1,
Position( custom_delimiter_import, g_delimiter, 1, 5) -Position(
custom_delimiter_import, g_delimiter, 1, 4) - 1) ]
        [ No dialog ]
Replace [ city, Replace data:Calculation: , Middle( custom_delimiter_import,
Position( custom_delimiter_import, g_delimiter, 1, 5) + 1,
Position( custom_delimiter_import, g_delimiter, 1, 6) -Position(
custom_delimiter_import, g_delimiter, 1, 5) - 1) ]
        [ No dialog ]
Replace [ state, Replace data:Calculation: , Middle( custom_delimiter_import,
Position( custom_delimiter_import, g_delimiter, 1, 6) + 1,
Position( custom_delimiter_import, g_delimiter, 1, 7) -Position(
custom_delimiter_import, g_delimiter, 1, 6) - 1) ]
        [ No dialog ]
```

Handling Aggregate Functions

Prior to FileMaker Pro 3, we had to use Repeating fields to make a database look relational when it really wasn't. Certain functions were designed to work with these fields, performing different operations across the multiple rows of the Repeating field. With FileMaker Pro 3, developers started using child files and portals rather than Repeating fields; in fact, you ought not to use Repeating fields any more because they make reporting on different rows very cumbersome. But you may want to use a Repeating field as an interface trick; for instance, we use them in the Interface Prototyper. But they are a big problem when you use them to hold real data.

Tip from
Rich

> About repeating fields: Never use them for data. They look so easy to set up, but they cause problems as soon as users start asking for reports on individual line items.

The set of aggregate functions, created to handle data in Repeating fields, turn out to have some other benefits, even when we are using portals to show child records. FileMaker has extended these functions to related child records.

 The Companies-j24.fp5 file, in the j24-AggregateFunctions folder (see Figure 10.37), demonstrates how these functions can help you.

Figure 10.37
The file Companies-j24.fp5 shows the benefits of aggregate functions.

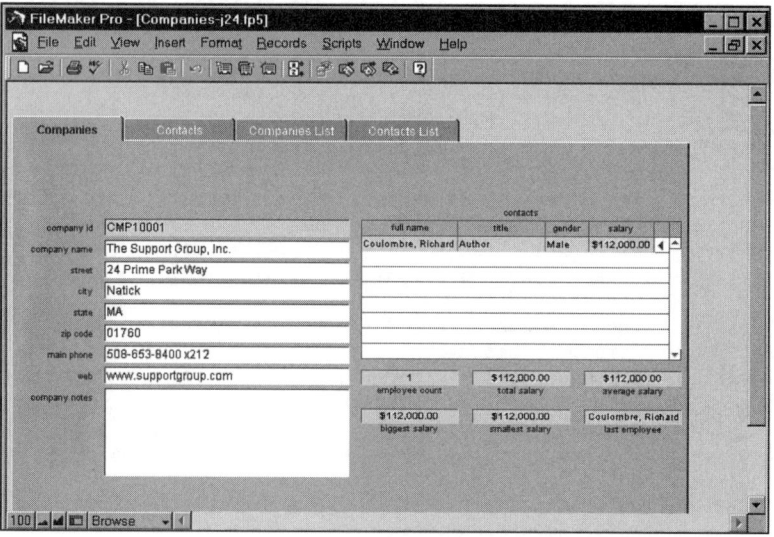

We have a Companies file, and a Contacts file; the Companies file is the parent of the Contacts file. As such, it has a portal that shows all of the contacts belonging to the company whose record a user is looking at. Looking at that portal, a user may want to derive some information from that set of children. So, we create a group of fields using aggregate functions to count for us the number of employees, to total their salaries, to average their salaries, to identify their biggest and smallest salary—and to identify the last employee entered in the portal.

> **Tip from**
> *Rich*
>
> Remember the `Last`. When you are in the Specify Calculations dialog, look above the list of functions for the choices for filtering the functions. Choose the aggregate functions. You see a list of seven functions, but you do not see the `Last` function, which works just great as an aggregate function. `Last` appears under Repeating functions, but it also works on child records. `Last` is the last record shown in the portal. If there is no sort applied to a relationship, `Last` goes to the last record entered, but if there is a sort order on the relationship, `Last` goes to the last record in sorted order.

Consider the way we figure the total of all salaries in the salary field over in the related records in the contacts file:

`sum(contacts|fk_company_id::salary)`

FileMaker goes over to the Contacts file, finds all records with a matching company ID, and then adds up all the values in the salary field across those related records. The result goes into the Calculation field c_tot_salary.

The other functions work a little differently, but operate on the same principle. You can perform a calculation in one file, based on a single or multiple values from another file, presuming you have set up a proper relationship.

COMMON MISTAKE: COUNTING ON THE RESULTS OF AGGREGATE FUNCTIONS BEING STORED

Because aggregate functions perform their magic through relationships on related fields, the results of these calculations cannot be stored.

CHAPTER 11

REPORTING

In this chapter

Layouts at the Heart   342

Using the Report Wizard   342

How Layout Parts Work   343

How FileMaker Figures Out What to Put Where   346

Creating Summary Reports   348

Putting Sub-Summaries on Every Page   355

Using Sub-Summaries without Summary Fields   357

Using the Get Summary Function in a Calculation Field   358

Where Should You Report From?   361

Interesting Reporting Techniques   366

Variations in Effect   378

Layouts at the Heart

Reports begin with layouts. We've already touched on using the FileMaker layout to create data entry screens and to display data, but now we look at the layout as a way to provide reports, whether those end up on paper, on the screen, or in that double world of Adobe Acrobat PDF files (which can be displayed on paper or onscreen). You need to understand the way different elements of a layout act (and seem to think) in reports, so you can decide

- What parts to use for different purposes
- What objects to drop into those parts
- How the different layout parts react in different circumstances
- What techniques will help you get the reports working

Using the Report Wizard

The Report Wizard, shown in Figure 11.1, is a wonderful tool for generating reports quickly, but it works best for a new user, because it walks you through dialogs prompting you to make decisions about the type of layout (detail only, detail and summary, summary only), totals (grand totals?), fields (which ones do you want?), and themes (preset designs, plus ones you build using the Cinco Group's Theme Creator, at http://www.cincogroup.com). You'll get a pretty good layout—often better than you might come up with if you are inexperienced at onscreen design. But as your client demands more from reports, you may have to get under the hood, figure out how the layouts work, and tweak them for your particular circumstances, goals, and client tastes.

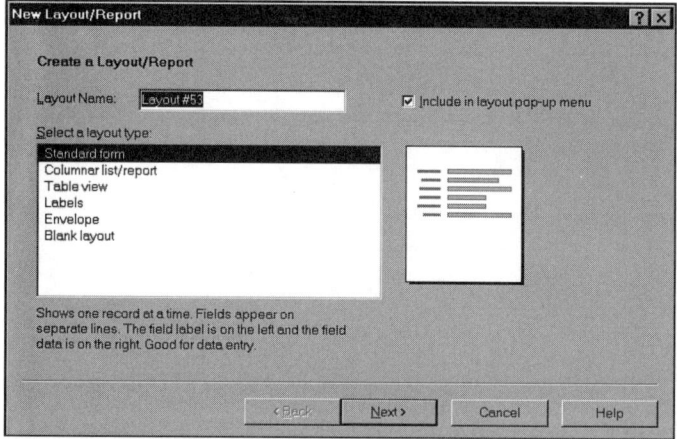

Figure 11.1
The Report Wizard walks you through creating a good-looking report in a minimum amount of time.

Tip from
Rich

If you have to cook up a report immediately, use the Report Wizard. With the Wizard you can work up fairly polished prototypes of reports, along with a script that will produce the report. Plus, the results can be modified in the usual way, for refinements.

COMMON MISTAKE: EXPECTING THE THEME TO WORK LIKE A STYLE IN WORD PROCESSING

In a word-processor, a style would apply to future paragraphs. Themes specify the initial appearance of objects on the layout, but once the wizard has created the layout, using a theme, the theme will no longer determine the appearance of any additional objects you add to the layout. If a new object looks like one of the theme objects, you're lucky, but don't count on the luck continuing. To copy the formatting from a themed object and apply it to a new object, on the Mac hold down the Apple or Command key and click the themed object, or in Windows, hold down Control and click on the original object, to soak up the formatting. From then on, any new objects that you add will follow that formatting as a default.

So the Report Wizard is a great place to start, but when you want FileMaker Pro to sing and dance, you'll probably want to explore some of the subtleties of layouts.

How Layout Parts Work

Parts offer you complex and subtle control over the report. You can drag different parts into a layout, and then place different kinds of objects into the parts to control where data prints on a page and how often those items print.

There are nine kinds of layout parts:

- Title Header
- Header
- Leading Grand Summary
- Leading Sub-summary
- Body
- Trailing Sub-summary
- Trailing Grand Summary
- Footer
- Title Footer

Except for Sub-summary parts, which can proliferate like dandelions, you can have only one part per layout—one Body, for instance, or one Title Footer.

These parts may look totally different on paper and onscreen in Browse mode. For instance, you may see a wonderful printout, but onscreen see nothing at all, or only a few pieces of the report. And even in Browse mode, the look will change when the user switches from View as List to View as Form, or back. Later, we'll discuss the ways the parts may vary in appearance, depending on the medium you use to show the report. First, though, we will talk about the ways these parts work when you are printing the report on paper.

The parts must appear in this order, but the order doesn't necessarily tell you exactly where the parts will land on the pages. For instance, all headers appear at the top of pages, and all footers appear at the bottom of pages, but the other parts may float around a bit, depending on other decisions you make.

Sub-Summaries

The Sub-summary part prints once for a group of records that hold a common value in the break field. You can have multiple instances of Sub-summaries, as you would in a multilevel subtotal report. You can have a Leading Sub-summary and a Trailing Sub-summary, both based on a single field, but you cannot get away with a third Sub-summary on the same field.

For any Text, Date, Time, Number, or Calculation field (except for a Calculation with a Container result), you can have two Sub-summaries (one leading and one trailing). But a Sub-summary part cannot be specified as depending on a Summary field, a Global field, or any kind of Container field. Why not? The Summary and Global fields do not have values that belong to any particular records, and the Container field, which does have a value that belongs to an individual record, holds graphics, which are a bit hard to summarize by.

Title Header and Header

On each page of your report, FileMaker prints or displays only one header, even though you have the option to drag both a Title Header and a regular Header onto your layout. Recall the situation in word-processing, where a header is the text that appears at the top of every page in a section or document, but you have the option to set up a special header for the first page only. In the same way, FileMaker lets you use a header to put information at the top of the first page only, or on every page. If you have information you want only at the top of the first page, use the Title header. If you want information on every page from there on, use the regular Header for that info. Key point: If you only have the regular header, it will show up on all pages, starting with the first.

COMMON MISTAKE: ADDING A TITLE HEADER AND THEREBY LOSING THE REGULAR HEADER ON THE FIRST PAGE

FileMaker prints only one header per page. You may have an existing Header on a report, and decide to add a Title Header with something like a company logo or confidentiality notice. Alas, that information only appears on the first page, and the information from the regular header no longer shows up there. If you want the information from both headers to show up on the first page, you have to duplicate the info, putting it in both headers.

Definite plus: We can be sure where headers will appear. They show up at the top of the page.

Leading Grand Summary

The Leading Grand Summary appears once at the beginning of your report, before any Leading Sub-summaries, and before any record detail. Often a report will have a Grand Summary at the end. But you may want to put a Grand Summary at the front of the report to give the big picture first. With the Leading Grand Summary, you let the reader see the key conclusions on the first page, without having to flip, flip, flip to get to the end.

Leading Sub-Summary

Where a Grand Summary offers grand totals, a Sub-summary shows subtotals. A Sub-summary part prints once for each group of records that contain the same value in a particular field. For instance, if your client wants to know total salary by department, you could insert a Sub-summary part on the layout, and as part of creating that part, you would have to define the *break field*, which is an old programming term for the field by which the records will be grouped. In this example, the break field would be department. The leading Sub-summary would appear before the first record of the group it represents, such as the salary records for the Accounting Department.

Thus, even though the Leading Sub-summary appears on the layout above the Body, the actual leading Sub-summaries could appear anywhere on the page, because they show up right in front of each group of records, if you include the detail records.

Body

The Body part offers the record details for the report, plus anything else you decide to squeeze into the part to complement the values in the individual records. If you have a database with 100 records, do a Find, discover 27 records, and decide to print a layout that includes a Body part, the Body part prints once for each of those 27 records. But even though the Body prints once for each record, the contents of the Body are not limited to the values in the records. You might, for instance, also have graphics, labels, a form (pasted in), or values in Global or Summary fields within the Body—items that are not in the actual records.

> **Tip from**
> *Rich*
>
> A layout must have one part, but you don't have to use any more parts if you don't need them. You can have a layout without a Body, if, for instance, you focus on summaries.

Trailing Sub-Summary

This part prints once for each set of records that have a common value in the break field, and the Sub-summary appears after the records it summarizes, rather than before.

Trailing Grand Summary

This part prints once, after any record detail in the Body, and after any Sub-summaries.

Title Footer and Footer

These work just the way the Title Header and Header do, except that these parts appear at the bottom of pages. To have unique information at the bottom of the first page, use the Title Footer. To have the same information at the bottom of every page, use the Footer. If you insert both, you will see the text of the Title Footer on the first page, and the contents of the Footer on all the other pages.

How FileMaker Figures Out What to Put Where

If you are printing on a regular 8.5"×11" sheet of paper, your printer probably does not put ink right up to the edge of the sheet of paper. Instead, FileMaker asks the printer driver what the nonprintable area is. Or, if you have gone into Layout Setup, shown in Figure 11.2, you may override the margins specified by the printer driver to specify fixed page margins of your own (although you cannot force the printer to put ink in the nonprintable area.) In fact, when fixed page margins have been turned off, and you shove an object to the very top or left edge of the layout, you are actually putting it at the beginning of the printable area, not at the edge of the paper. (To discover the constraints you have to work within, go to View and choose Page Margins to see a diagram showing the edge of the paper, and the boundaries of your printer's printable area.)

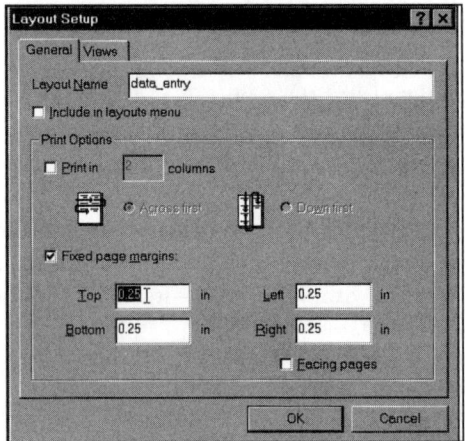

Figure 11.2
The Layout Setup dialog lets you choose fixed page margins.

So when FileMaker starts to print, it must figure out how much space it has to work with, by deducting the nonprintable area from the area of the sheet of paper. Then if the layout happens to have a header or footer, FileMaker reserves space for those, because those, too, are fixed quantities on every page. (The amount of space devoted to other parts will vary.)

Then FileMaker figures out what part it should print next, and calculates whether there is enough space left on the page to print the contents of that part. If there is enough space, FileMaker prints that part, and then calculates the amount of space left on the page. If the next part will take up more room than remains on the current page, FileMaker interrogates that part's options and attributes. For instance, in the Part Setup dialog, shown in Figure 11.3, we can allow a part to break across page boundaries. If that option is checked, then FileMaker starts pouring that part into the page, then consults the suboption (to discard the remainder of the part at the end of a page), and decides whether to pour the rest of the contents onto the next page, or throw that data away and start the next page with the next part in line. (Another option allows you to put a page break before or after a part.)

How FileMaker Figures Out What to Put Where | 347

Figure 11.3
The Part Definition dialog lets you set page-break options.

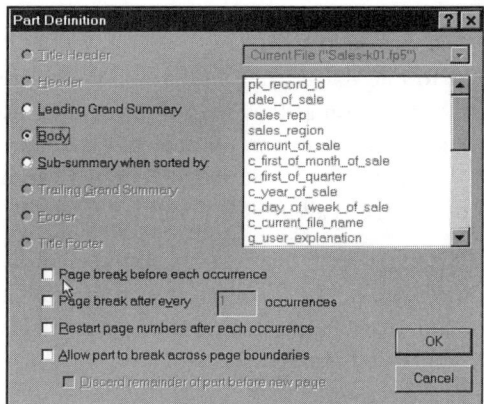

> **Tip from**
> *Rich*
>
> Think carefully about the options that allow parts to break across page boundaries. FileMaker will do its best to break the part and the page across whitespace, but that's not always possible. So if you choose to allow parts to break, you may get the top half of one line of characters at the bottom of the first page, and the bottom half of the line at the top of the next page. Yes, FileMaker really is that precise.

Examining the options for each part as it goes, FileMaker continues printing parts until it runs out of records or summaries, and prints the final footer on the last page.

If you have a large field of notes with many lines on some records, and only a few lines on other records, you probably don't want to have large blank spaces on their records. Turn to the Sliding & Printing command on the Format menu to force the data to slide up (and a sub-option lets you reduce the size of the enclosing part), to avoid unsightly gaps (see Figure 11.4).

Figure 11.4
You can slide values up and left, and reduce the size of the enclosing part, to avoid ugly blank spaces in your report.

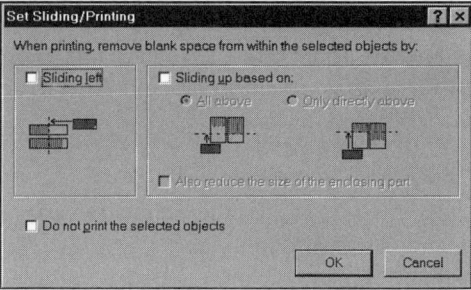

Normally, each record on a report takes up the same amount of space on the paper—exactly the size of the Body. By turning on the option for sliding items up and choosing to reduce the size of the enclosing part, you are allowing FileMaker to vary the size of records on the printed page, so a record without much text in a Notes field might take up half an inch, whereas a record with rambling notes could take up two or three inches worth of space. These decisions, then, affect the number of records that will appear on a page.

Creating Summary Reports

When ordinary users first come to FileMaker, they tend to ask you for reports showing record detail, typically in a list. But as soon as they see that long, long list of details, they ask you for an overall total, covering all the records in the report. Once they get that, they start asking for totals on different groups of records within the report. Eventually, most users long for grand totals and subtotals—they call out for Summary fields.

The role of any Summary field is to perform math across all the records in the found set (which could, of course, be the whole file), or across a subtotal group. Grand Totals offer a simple example. We create the Summary field by using the Define Fields dialog, followed by the Options for the Summary field (see Figure 11.5).

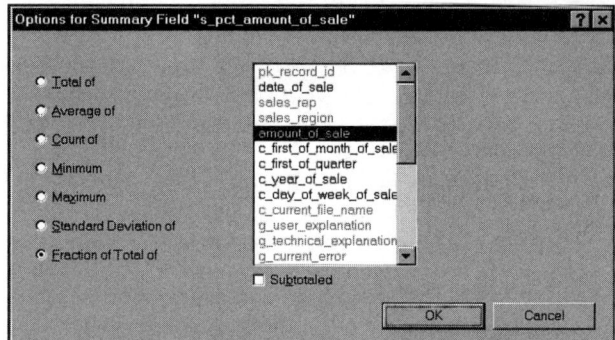

Figure 11.5
The Options for a Summary Field let you spell out options for your new field.

After we have a Summary field, we have to figure out what part of the layout to drop it into. In most cases when we put a Summary field in any part of the layout except a Sub-summary part, that Summary field will summarize all found records. If you put a Summary field in the Sub-summary part and sort by the break field, FileMaker will summarize the subtotal groups.

To produce Grand Totals, then, we can put the field anywhere *except* in a Sub-summary part, to get a total from all the records in the report. We have lots of options on placement. The question, then, becomes Where do you want the Grand Total to appear?

- If you put the Summary field in a Header or Footer, then the results will show up at the top or bottom of every page.
- If you put the Summary field in a Leading Grand Summary part, the results will show up before the first record, and before any subtotals.
- If you put the Summary field in the Trailing Grand Summary, the results show up after the last record, and after any Trailing Sub-summaries.
- If you put the Summary field in the Body, then the results appear with each record.

Subtotals can be a little more dizzying, and the Report Wizard makes them a little easier. But if you are trying to create subtotals without using the wizard, you need to take these steps:

1. Create a Summary field that carries out whatever operation you need, such as running a count or adding up a total.

COMMON MISTAKE: CREATING UNNECESSARY EXTRA SUMMARY FIELDS

If you already have a Summary field that performs the right operation, you can use it again, on different layouts, or multiple times on the same layout (in different parts). Let's say we need the value of Total of Salary in two different Sub-summary parts and a Grand Summary part. There is no need to create three different Summary fields to get these results because FileMaker easily tracks the different values calculated when the same field shows up in different parts of the layout.

2. In Layout Mode, go to the Layouts menu and choose Part Setup.
3. Click Create to create a part.

You see the Part Definition dialog shown in Figure 11.6.

Figure 11.6
Here is the Part Definition dialog.

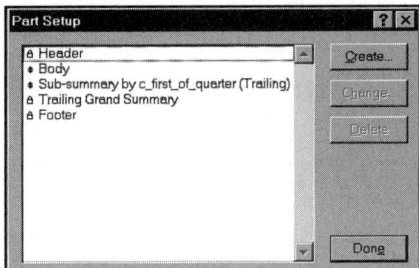

4. Choose Sub-summary, and, in the list, pick the break field.

Tip from
Rich

> To pick the break field, go past BY. In general, when someone wants a Sub-summary report, they talk about getting something like "Total salary *by* department" or "Employee count *by* city." In those circumstances, whatever follows the word *by* is the break field.

FileMaker points out (see Figure 11.7) that this part can be printed above or below the records it summarizes, which is another way to explain that the Sub-summary part can be Leading or Trailing.

Figure 11.7
FileMaker lets you make the Sub-summary part leading or trailing.

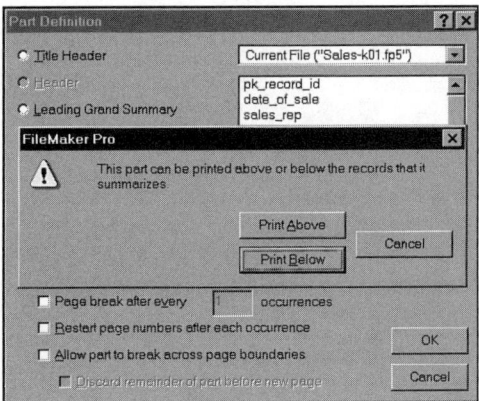

5. Choose whether to make the Sub-summary Leading or Trailing by choosing Print Above or Print Below.
6. Click OK to put away the Part Setup dialog.
7. Enter the Browse or Preview mode, and then sort the records by the break field, to put the records in each group together, so FileMaker can actually produce a subtotal on them.
8. Preview or print your report.

 In this chapter's folder on the CD, look in Sales-k1.fp5, and you'll see 46 different reports generated from fairly simple records, each of which contains very little raw material—4 fields of data. Go to Layout mode, and click the drop-down menu of layouts to pick your way through the various reports. These reports demonstrate how many ways you can slice and dice the same pile of data. We could have gone beyond these.

When you are thinking about creating a report, ponder the fact that there are 3 basic types of report you can produce:

- Pure detail reports, which require, at the minimum, the Body part
- Reports mixing details with summary information, which require the Body part for the details, and a Sub-summary or Grand Summary part
- Pure summary reports, which have no Body part, making them a bit ghostly, because they have only Sub-summary or Grand Summary parts

There's no right or wrong report, just whatever the business requires.

Looking at the Sales file, a user can pick a report from the drop-down menu, shown in Figure 11.8, and click Go. We run a script to put together the report and print it out. Note: If you want to examine the layouts, please go to Layout mode. (We have kept users from switching layouts on their own in Browse mode, by removing the layouts from the menu.)

Figure 11.8
The user can pick a report from the drop-down menu.

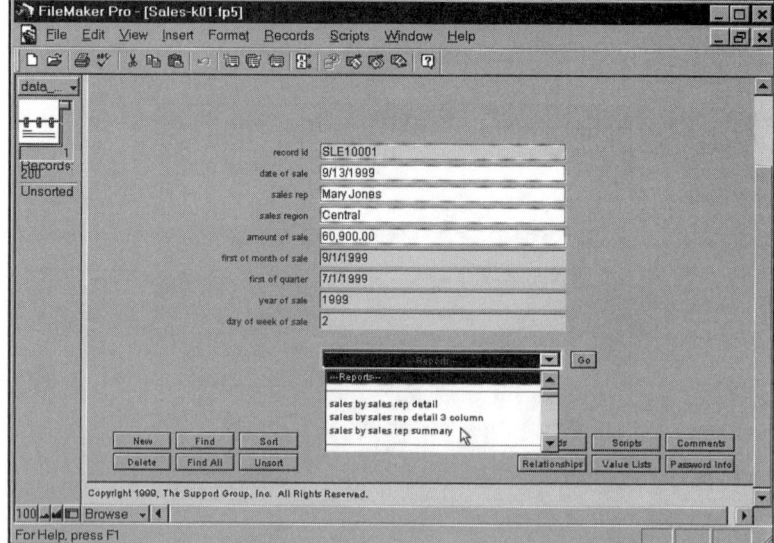

Here are a few of the scripts, with pictures of the layouts behind the reports, and the preview of the printed reports.

Sales by Sales Rep Detail offers a combination of detail and summary. We see individual sales, and then summaries at the end of the report (see Figure 11.9).

Figure 11.9
The summaries appear at the end of the report.

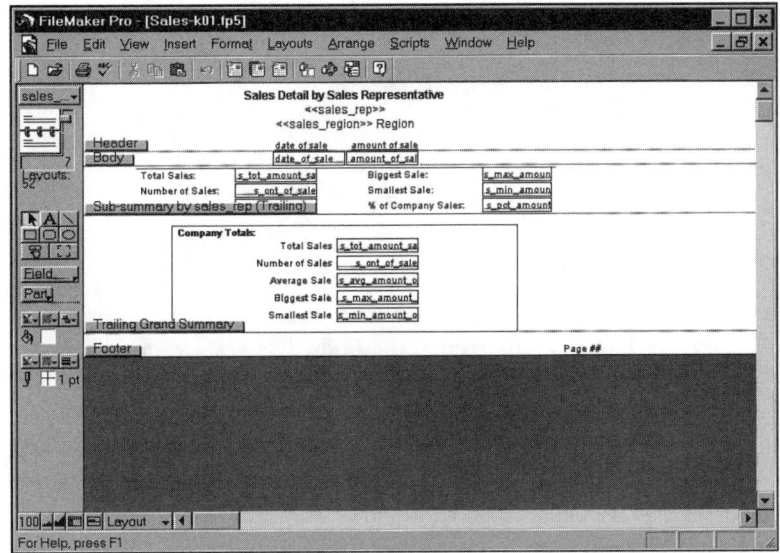

The Body part generates the detail, the Sub-summary part generates the subtotals, and the Trailing Grand Summary provides the grand totals. The Header and Footer contain items to appear at the top and bottom of every page. Because we have a Sub-summary analyzing sales by Sales Rep, we have to sort the records by Sales Rep.

Where this report shows the date of sale and amount of sale and wastes a lot of space, we asked FileMaker to put the details into 3 columns, in the eighth layout, called Sales_detail_by sales_representative_3_col because this gives us greater density of data on the page. If you sort and go to Preview, you will see the abbreviated version. To get the 3 columns, we went to Layout, then to Layout Setup, and chose to print in 3 columns (see Figure 11.10).

Tip from
Rich

Use multiple columns for detail reports to make the most economical use of your space. Most folks consider the option of multiple columns appropriate for mailing labels, but otherwise, forget it. Whenever you have a few data elements, but a lot of potential records, use columns to avoid long skinny data trails across page after page.

Figure 11.10
You can choose three columns in the Layout Setup dialog.

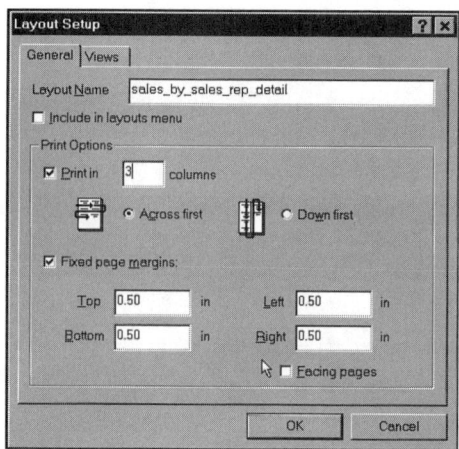

In the 3-column report, we are using the option to go across first, in the Layout Setup dialog, shown in Figure 11.10, so that the Body details show up in 3 sections across the page. You might expect that this choice would only impact the way the records get arranged. But there's a secondary impact of the decision: If we had chosen to go down first, FileMaker would split the Sub-summary and Grand Summary into 3 pieces as well. But we have a lot of info in the Sub-summary and the Grand Summary and we want it to extend across the whole page, so we chose to go across first, using the summaries as a kind of line to draw the details to a close. If you switch the Layout to go down, you'll note that the data has been cut off because the columns themselves are too narrow to show the results of the summary operations, and the summaries, oddly, show up at the bottom of each column, making it hard to tell what they summarize.

> **Tip from**
> *Rich*
>
> If you have a report with only summary information, and you only have a small amount of summary information, you can present those results in multiple columns. Just choose the Down First option, to make sure that the Sub-summary and Grand Summary fields are placed in the columns, rather than running across the whole page. With double or triple columns, you avoid wasting paper.

In sales_by_sales_rep_summary, the eighth layout in Sales-k1.fp5, we have a pure summary report. When you choose this report from the menu, we set the orientation to Landscape, because this is a wide report. You'll see that we have a Trailing Sub-summary and a Trailing Grand Summary. (If we had made the Grand Summary a Leading, not Trailing, one, the totals would print above the Sub-summary, which would be odd, because people expect the subs to add up to the grand.) As you look at this layout, you'll note that all the fields begin with the letter *s*, indicating that they are summary fields, as seen in Figure 11.11. (The rest of each field name indicates the operation, so we can tell right away what the field does.)

Creating Summary Reports 353

Figure 11.11
Note that because we have nothing but summaries here, we have no Body part.

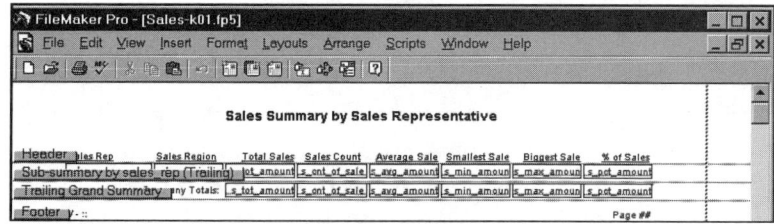

To look at multiple levels of subtotals, take a look at the layout called sales_by_sales_rep_by_quarter_summary, shown in Figure 11.12. Sort the records by sales_rep and c_first_of_quarter, and then go to Preview to see the many levels, as shown in Figure 11.13. You see summaries by sales rep, and then, within each sales rep's section, sales by quarter. Remember, you aren't limited to a single level of subtotals. You can have as many as you care to, provided you do all the right sorts before previewing.

Figure 11.12
The layout allows multiple levels of subtotals.

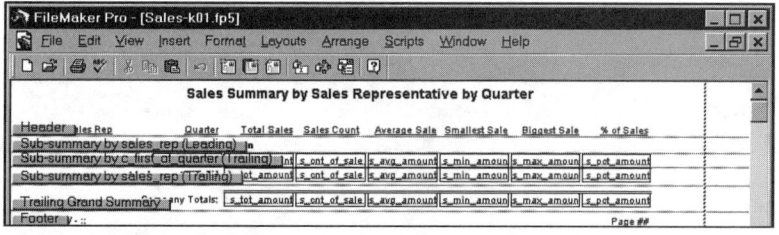

Figure 11.13
The Preview shows summaries by quarter, and then by sales rep, with a grand summary at the bottom.

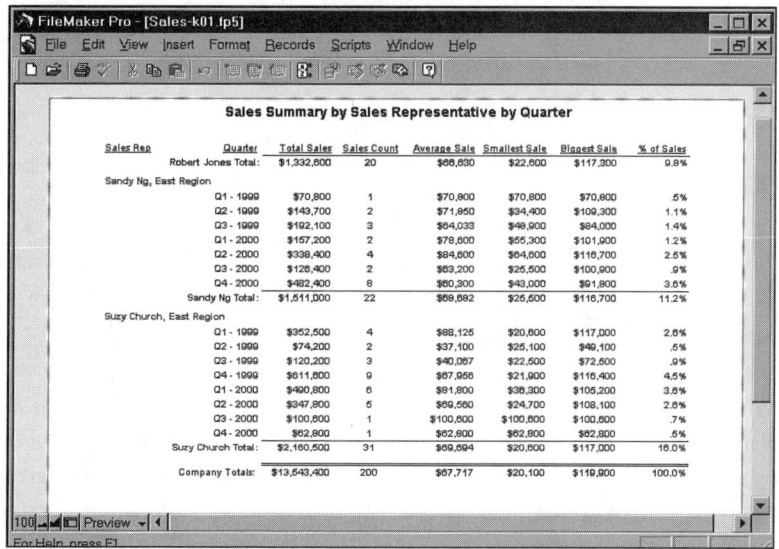

The Leading Sub-summary has the sales rep's name and region in it, but the Trailing Sub-summary has the rep's totals for all quarters, adding up the figures we see broken out by quarter, in the Sub-summary part by c_first_of_quarter field.

> **Tip from**
> *Rich*
>
> We recommend FileMaker as a very nice reporting tool because it brings the power of reporting to users. With its capability to import data from a variety of sources, including an ODBC source, FileMaker gives users a way to take data out of mainframe or legacy systems, and to generate reports any which way they need them, rather than troubling the IS folks to make up the reports.

GENERATING REPORTS WITH SUBTOTALS BY MONTH OR QUARTER

If you look at the file sales-k01.fp5, you'll see that in the data entry layout each sale has a date of sale, as shown in Figure 11.14, so you can report on sales by date, showing all the sales that took place on a particular day. But you have to do a little magic to get subtotals by month, quarter, or year.

Figure 11.14
Each sale record includes a date of sale.

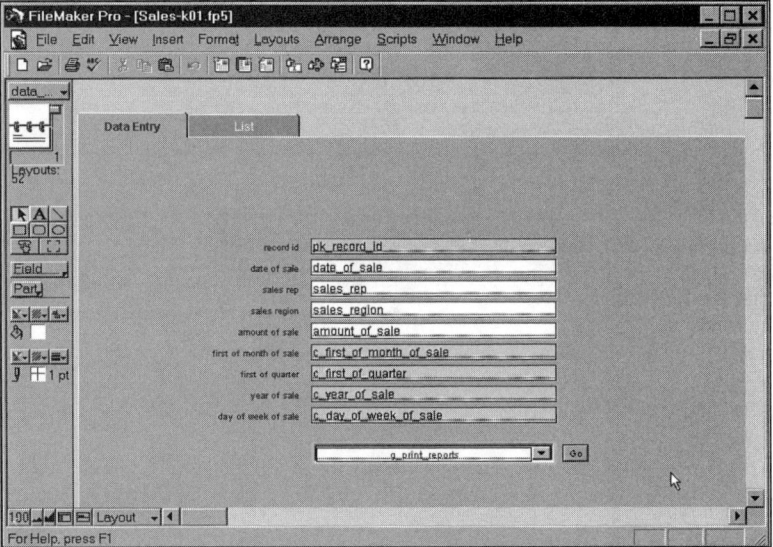

To get ready for subtotaling, we pick an arbitrary date, and we say, "If the sale is within this month, assign it this single arbitrary date. Or if it is within the quarter, assign it to this single arbitrary date within the quarter." Looking at the data entry screen, you'll see that the first record shows a sale on 2/23/99, and after that we have a field First_of_month_of_sale and that figures out the first of the month. (We talked about the way this calculation works back in Chapter 10, "Hot Calculations.") In a similar way, we figure out the first day of the quarter, and the year in which the sale took place. Now, if we break on the field showing the first of the month, we capture all of the records for that month.

➔ For more twists and turns on figuring dates, **see** "Calculating the Next Appointment Date," **p. 295** and "Breaking Apart a Date for Subtotals," **p. 301**.

All the reports that do summarization by month, quarter, or year depend upon these calculations to arrange the records in those time periods, for sub-summarization. In sales_by_month_summary, you'll see that the layout includes a Sub-summary based on the field c_first_of_month_of_sale (the calculation of the first day of the month in which the sale took place), and a Trailing Grand Summary, as shown in Figure 11.15. When sorted on the break field, you get both Sub-summaries and the Grand Summary (see Figure 11.16).

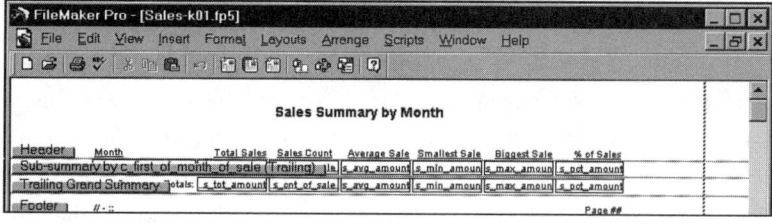

Figure 11.15
The layout includes a Sub-summary Part based on the field c_first_of_month_of_sale.

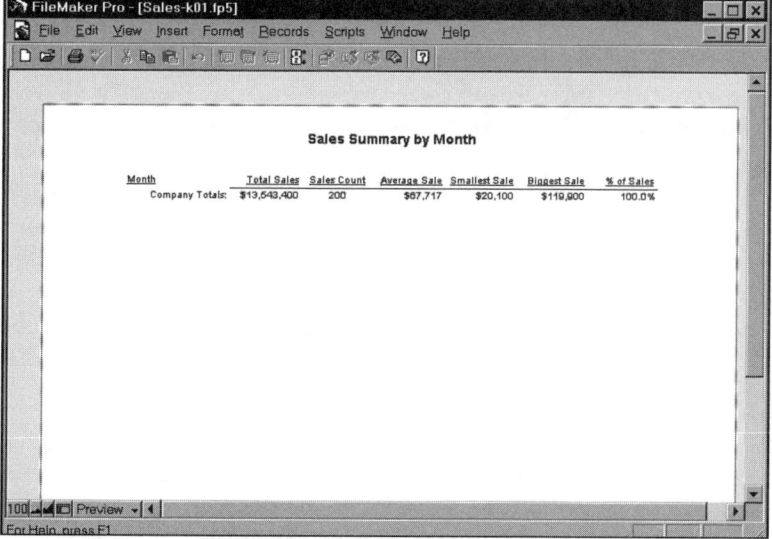

Figure 11.16
The report includes Sub-summaries and a Grand Summary.

Putting Sub-Summaries on Every Page

Occasionally, a client asks for Sub-summaries on every page. For instance, an auditor once told us that he needed totals on every page because the IRS was going to select random pages and verify that those totals were correct before accepting their grand totals.

The key is to calculate which records will end up on which page. The Sub-summary will use the page number as a break field; all the records being summarized will have the same value in the field devoted to Page Number. Here is the calculation for that field:

```
Int((Status( CurrentRecordNumber) - 1) / 35) + 1
```

We figured that 35 records would fit on a page. So for records 1 through 35, we need an arithmetic operation resulting in a value of 1 for each of those records. For records 36 through 70, we need a result of 2, and so on.

The key function is Status (CurrentRecordNumber), which returns the position of the record within the found set, so the twelfth record is, well, 12, and so on. CurrentRecordNumber is just one of the arguments you can use with Status. Using this function we can tell what number record we are looking at, within a found set of records.

Assume for a moment that we are looking at Record 35. If we subtract 1, we get 34. Then we divide that by the 35 records per page, to get a result of 0.9714. We take the integer of that (which drops the decimal, and leaves the whole number). So now we have 0, and add 1, to get a result of 1. Ergo, Record 35 is on Page One. To get the subtotals, then, all we have to do is sort by c_report_page_number. Note that this must be an unstored calculation, because if the Status function results were stored, we would be stuck with one order forever. The unstored calculation is refreshed as needed.

This method works fine as long as we accept the order in which the records appear, and don't need to get other subtotals. Of course, the sort by page number may blow away other sorts, leaving the records in the order in which they were entered.

In sales-k02a.fp5, we do a little more processing, to allow us to maintain a sort order put in place by the user. Now we offer a record sequence number, as well as the page number. The user can run a sort, leaving the records in a certain order. Then, if the user wants a report, we run a script called print_sales_detail_totals_by_page that produces the report using a Replace function. The Replace function says take the value in the field record_seq_number and replace that, starting with the first record with the number one, and incrementing that by one for each subsequent record. Now we have a field that will maintain that record's position even after the records have been sorted. The calculation of c_report_page_number is based on that record sequence number we just generated. So our Sub-summary part, based on c_report_page_number, can recognize the records as they fall into the groups by page number.

If we were just to sort the records by c_report_page_number, FileMaker would put all the records on the right pages, but they might not be sorted as they were when we originally numbered them, because, if we sorted only by this field, without specifying a secondary sort, FileMaker would place all the records within the same page in the order in which they were created. To resurrect the previous sort, our first sort must be by page number, and our second sort by record sequence number.

COMMON MISTAKE: FORGETTING THAT A FIELD MUST BE ON THE CURRENT LAYOUT FOR CERTAIN SCRIPT OPERATIONS TO WORK

Some script operations require that whatever field you're specifying be on the *current* layout. The Replace command is one of these. When using a Replace in a script, issue a Go To Layout command to bring the script to a layout where you are confident the field will *always* exist. Sometimes, we create a layout called a Developer Layout to which we add all of the fields in the current file, so we always know that one layout will have a field we need for this kind of operation.

Using Sub-Summaries Without Summary Fields

 In sales-k03.fp5, we show you how to make name tags. No, seriously, this file has 200 records in it, and if we created a normal Name Tag layout, we would get 200 tags, one for each sale, because the Body part, which prints the detail, prints once per record. And there is a record for each sale. If Al makes 31 sales, he would get 31 nametags. To avoid this terrible waste of gummed labels, we create Sub-summary parts without bothering with any fields that do summarization (see Figure 11.17). A Sub-summary part prints once for every group of records with a common value in a field. If we put the field for name and region in a Trailing Sub-summary, those detail fields present the values from the last record in that Sub-summary group, once. In essence, for each sales rep, we get one sales tag. (The break field is the sales rep).

Figure 11.17
We create Sub-summary parts without Summary fields to avoid massive duplication.

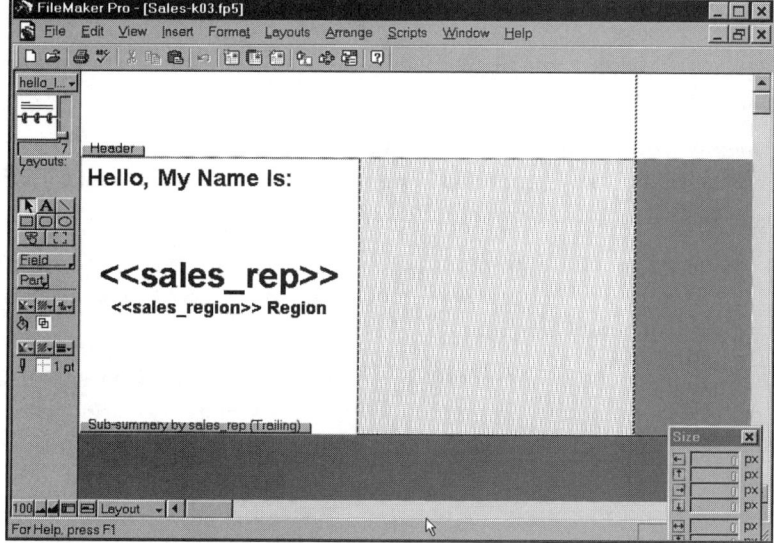

Tip from
Rich

If you find yourself using this technique (using Sub-summaries to print nametags), you may need another table. Here, for instance, we need a table for sales reps, where each sales rep has a separate ID. In real life, we would likely have a sales file and a salesperson file, so we could use the salesperson file to avoid the potential of having non-unique names to break on. What if we had two people named Peter Dimwit? We would get one tag for each salesperson ID. In that situation, we wouldn't have to worry about Sub-summaries. Of course, we aren't always given data so neatly organized.

Using the GetSummary Function in a Calculation Field

Imagine a client wants a report that will tell the sales reps how their average sales compare to the regional average and the company average. You'll need to calculate the sales rep's average sales, and then compare that to the values in two Summary fields, one that averages all sales in the region, and another that averages all sales in the company. In our file Sales-k04.fp5, we generate this report.

A Summary value appears in memory, for the purposes of generating a report, but the values in a Summary field represent a mathematical operation on one field across a found set of records at a moment in time, and so the value does not belong to any one record. A single edit on one of those records, or a change in the found set, would change the value. Hence, Summary values do not live on any one record. (If the values did live on a record, then you would face massive slowdowns every time you changed a value on one of the records being summarized, because the math operation would have to be performed again, and again, and again.)

Remember, too, that a Summary field can act differently in different parts of the layout. So, referring to one in a Calculation is not being specific enough about what you want. For precision in fetching values from Summary fields, we turn to the GetSummary function.

Sometimes, you want to perform a record-level calculation based on a summary value. To bring a summary value back to the record, we have created a couple of Calculation fields using the GetSummary function.

The GetSummary function has two forms—one for generating a subtotal, and another for generating a grand total. In the subtotal version, you use two arguments: the Summary field and the break field. A Summary part is what normally ties a Summary field to a particular break field, but here we're not in any particular part, because this is a value we are bringing back to the record irrespective of the way the data may be presented.

In the Calculation field called c_sales_rep_avg_sale, we write this formula:

```
Round( GetSummary( s_avg_amount_of_sale, sales_rep), 2)
```

We are rounding off the result of an operation by using GetSummary, which summarizes the average amount of sales by sales rep, so the result is in dollars and cents.

Tip from Rich	Whenever you have an operation using division, and the results involve money, you probably should round to two decimal places, particularly if you might be going to use the results in further calculations or in a Summary field. (Otherwise, you could just format the number as currency.) Unrounded figures may throw later totals off, because of all those digits to the right of the decimal point.

Using the GetSummary Function in a Calculation Field

The GetSummary function grabs a value from the Summary field called s_avg_amount_of_sale when using the sales_rep field as the break field. We bring the sales rep's average sale in the current found set back to the record, in a field value that can now be referenced by other calculations.

Normally, the values in Summary fields cannot be used in a record. But the GetSummary function lets us bring back the value from a Summary field to the record in a form we can use in another calculation.

Tip from
Rich

> Sort by the break field before trying GetSummary. In returning a subtotal to a record, the GetSummary will only work when the records have been sorted by the break field. In this case, when we sort by Sales Rep, then all of an individual's sales appear in a group, making it easier for FileMaker to total those records than by looking throughout the database for each of them.

Sorting makes the GetSummary function work correctly. To see this in operation in the file, go to List view and click the icon at the top of the Sales Rep column, shown in Figure 11.18 to sort by Sales Rep. Now the column showing the average of a Sales Rep's sales fills with numbers. Click the icon for the Sales Region (see Figure 11.18), and the next column appears with numbers showing the average sale for each region. Now, if you want to see both columns at once, click Show Sales Averages, which does a two-level sort, first by sales region, and then by sales rep. A sales rep only works for one region, so that double-sort is enough to trigger both calculations.

Figure 11.18
Note the icons at the top of the columns; clicking one sorts the list by that subject.

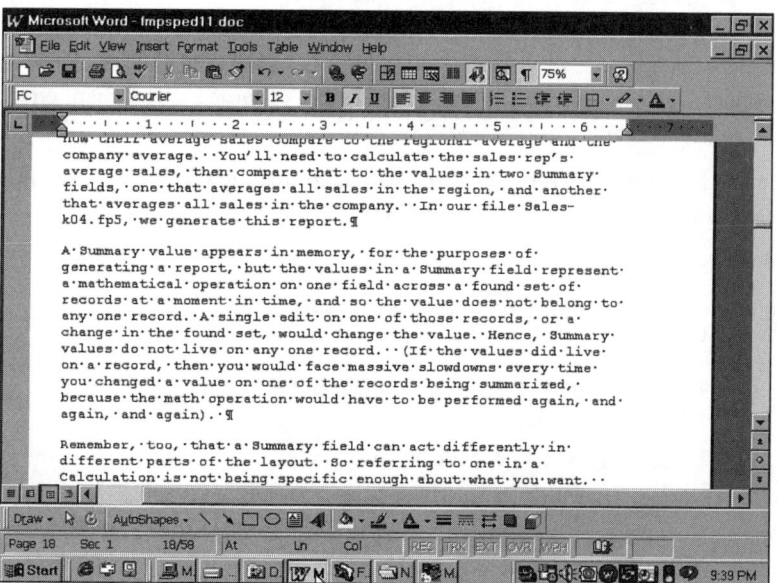

The second calculation brings the Grand Total summary back to the record. In the Calculation field, c_company_avg_sale, we write this formula:

```
Round( GetSummary( s_avg_amount_of_sale, s_avg_amount_of_sale), 2)
```

As before, the rounding puts the result into a format showing currency. Then the grand-total version of the `GetSummary` takes the value from the Summary s_avg_amount_of_sale. The second argument, showing the Break field, repeats the field used in the first argument; FileMaker understands that we want it to perform this operation on all found records, rather than bringing back subtotals on different groups of records. (Essentially, there is no break field).

By the way, this particular syntax doesn't require any sort. If you look at the List view, you'll see that this value is always present, no matter how you sort.

Now we can send a letter to each sales rep, as a report, evaluating performance. To prepare the prose, we write a standard letter with placeholders for calculations, saying "As you can see, your individual average is <<c_sales_rep_vs_region>> the regional average, and is <<c_sales_rep_vs_company>> the company average. This is <<c_good_or_bad>>." Then we do a few calculations to fill in the blanks.

In c_sales_rep_vs_region we create this formula:

```
Case(
c_sales_rep_avg_sale < c_region_avg_sale,
"less than",
c_sales_rep_avg_sale = c_region_avg_sale,
"equal to",
c_sales_rep_avg_sale > c_region_avg_sale,
"more than")
```

We are using the `Case` function to lead up to a phrase in the standard letter, "the regional average." So we want to know if the sales rep's average is less than, equal to, or more than the regional average.

To see how the sales rep compared to the company average, we run another `Case` analysis, leading up to the phrase "the company average."

```
Case(

c_sales_rep_avg_sale < c_company_avg_sale,
"less than",

c_sales_rep_avg_sale = c_company_avg_sale,
"equal to",

c_sales_rep_avg_sale > c_company_avg_sale,
"more than")
```

In this way, we prepare alternate versions. If the Sales Rep averaged less than the company, we get prose that reads "less than the company average." If the Sales Rep's average equals that of the company, the letter tells him that, and if the Sales Rep's average beats the company average, the letter says that.

Now comes the judgement on whether or not the sales rep's performance qualifies as good or bad. The field c_good_or_bad has the following formula:

```
Case(
c_sales_rep_avg_sale < c_region_avg_sale and c_sales_rep_avg_sale <
c_company_avg_sale, "an unacceptable performance",

c_sales_rep_avg_sale >=  c_region_avg_sale and c_sales_rep_avg_sale >=
c_company_avg_sale, "an exceptional performance",

"reasonable performance, with some room for improvement")
```

This is a set of Boolean tests. If the Sales Rep's average is less than the region and the company averages, we pronounce this performance "unacceptable." If it is greater than the region and the company averages, wow, this is an "exceptional" performance. Anything else is, well, reasonable, with room for improvement. The beauty of this report is that it drives every Sales Rep to try to achieve sales that are above average, thereby increasing the average, and, well, you get the idea.

The GetSummary function, then, lets you refer to a Summary field, and specify whether or not you want a subtotal (with a particular break field) or a grand total on all the found records.

WHERE SHOULD YOU REPORT FROM?

It depends. Deciding where to report from may involve you in balancing lots of trade-offs and constraints.

When you are producing reports in a relational environment, the information often comes from different files, and these are often in parent-child relationships. The question arises: Do you report from the parent or the child? If you are in a parent, you can show data from the children, and if you are in a child, you can show data from the parent. So where does it make sense to report from?

Portals were created as a mechanism to display child records in the Browse mode, not as a mechanism for printing, even though they do print. In fact, FileMaker folks advise printing from the child where possible to avoid the limitations of portals during printing. There are times when you will decide to print in a parent file by using data from the child, despite that advice, but you may want to know some of the twists and turns you need to wriggle through to do so.

PRINTING FROM THE PARENT

If you are printing a report from the parent, including data from the child, FileMaker shows that information in a portal, so you need a layout including that portal along with any fields native to the parent records. Printing from a portal tends to be easy; you create a Body part on the layout, place fields from the parent, and add the portal with fields from the child.

Of course, you have to specify the number of rows you want shown in the portal. In a report, how many will that be?

You need to show a number of rows equal to or greater than the largest number of children any parent might possibly have. So you set the portal to accommodate the maximum number of children, and then blank space appears for every parent with fewer than the max. You can slide objects up and also reduce the size of the enclosing part (options under the Format menu in Layout mode), to keep FileMaker from printing any empty rows. In this way, you remove whole rows of the portal. But the tricks do not vary the size of each row, as you might want if you had a large Notes field with anywhere from nothing to eight or ten lines. The portal row size, then, is fixed, so the field size within that portal row is also fixed; by contrast, if we were putting the field in the Body part by itself, we could vary its size by using those options of sliding and reducing the size of the enclosing part. Of course, in Browse mode you would have a scroll bar so users could move through a lot of children even though the portal only shows a few rows; but paper does not scroll very well.

So if you have varying amounts of information in a field, and you want to be able to slide that up (and reduce the enclosing space), avoid portals.

Another wrinkle: If the portal has multiple rows spanning many pages, you may end up with information broken across pages. A single row may end up split between one page and the next.

The good news is that putting a portal together is easy. You don't have to sort the records ahead of time. You can include parents without children in the report, whereas if you were reporting from the child file, those childless parents would never appear. Another benefit of printing from the parent is that you can have aggregate functions that perform math on the children, yielding the equivalent of subtotals, in a form that users can search and sort on. These functions live in a field on the parent record, and summarize data from that parent's related children.

Printing from a portal is similar to a Sub-summary report, but a portal only allows one level of subtotals. If you need a multi-level, Sub-summary report, you have to go beyond portals or switch to the child file. (Even if you have a second portal in the parent, you cannot get multi-level subtotals, such as sales by sales reps within districts within regions.)

Typically, a portal in the parent shows all the children. Yes, you can find any set of parents you want, but once you have found them, you usually get all their children, no matter what. If you don't want the report to show all the children, but just some of them (a common requirement), then you are going to have to work very, very hard, using the techniques in Chapter 12, but you probably won't want to perform these acrobatics on a regular basis.

→If you want to perform some fancy feats with portals, **see** Chapter 12, "Dumb Portal Tricks," **p. 395.**

Also, portals have limits. You can't make a portal larger than 1,000 rows. So if a parent has more than 1,000 children, only the first thousand will appear on paper through the portal. The information you can see and scroll to within the portal is limited to 32,767 pixels in height, all told. For instance, if the portal shows 10 rows and each row is 10 pixels high, the portal would be able to show 3,276 records.

The maximum length of a layout is approximately 110 inches, so if the information you need about the children exceeds that length, you might lose some data. If each child requires a full 11-inch page to print, you could print a maximum of 10 children.

One other time when you might decide to print from the parent: When you have a parent with multiple child files, and users want to print out reports that include multiple related records from those different child files, we might choose to print from the parent through a portal, rather than from the child. (Reporting from one child file was fine, but how would we get the data from the other child files?)

PRINTING FROM THE CHILD

When you print a report from a child, including data from both the child and the parent, you can get good detail quite simply. You are just combining the fields from child and parent in the Body part of the layout.

If you need subtotaling, though, you must add a Sub-summary part on the layout and specify a sort to trigger the Sub-summary process. Whereas printing from the parent does not require a sort, printing from a child does require a sort if you want to emerge with some form of Sub-summary.

Pluses: In a detail or Sub-summary report, each record is produced in the Body, and we generally do not face page breaks interrupting our data. If a Body would break, FileMaker bumps it to the next page, trying to preserve the Body as a unit on one page or another. Also, if you have a Notes field with varying amounts of information, you can use the options for sliding the object up and reducing its size, to get rid of unnecessary blank spaces on the page. And since you are dealing with individual child records, rather than a portal where they get clumped together, you can produce reports with multiple levels of subtotals. Most importantly, you can include different found sets of children in the same report, so users can print out their own found sets. (Note that the report will still not include those parents without children, unless you try the trick of self-joins, described in Chapter 13.) There are no limits on the number of rows because the information appears in the Body part, one per record, rather than in one giant Body part, as was the case when we used a portal in a parent.

➔If you want to learn more about self-joins, **see** Chapter 13, "The Joys of Self-joins and Other Interesting Relationships," **p. 421.**

 In one of our sample files on the CD, we demonstrate that the reporting glass can be half full, or half empty, depending on your perspective. In the file Companies-k05.fp5, you'll see two buttons at the bottom of the Companies tab. The button called Print Contacts from Parent File shows you that you can get a list of all the parents, including those without a child, when printing from this location. (Note that the company Swimming Pools of America appears, even though it has 0 contacts.) You'll see a whole lot of blank space underneath the Swimming Pools of America. Click to the next page, and you can see the archery company starting at the top of the page. Because all the children did not fit on the remaining space on the first page, FileMaker bumped it to the next page, because all the contacts belong to a single portal, which is in a single Body part (the one for the American Archery

Alliance). Here you see the good and the bad: the blank space left on Page One, as shown in Figure 11.19, but the grouping of all the related contacts under their parent company, shown in Figure 11.20.

Figure 11.19
Here is Page One of the report, complete with some blank space at the end.

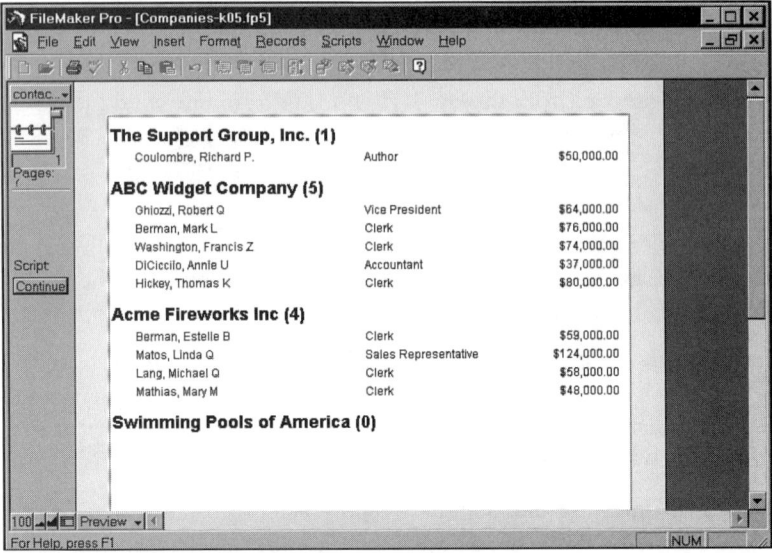

Figure 11.20
In the report, this is Page Two, with contacts grouped with their companies.

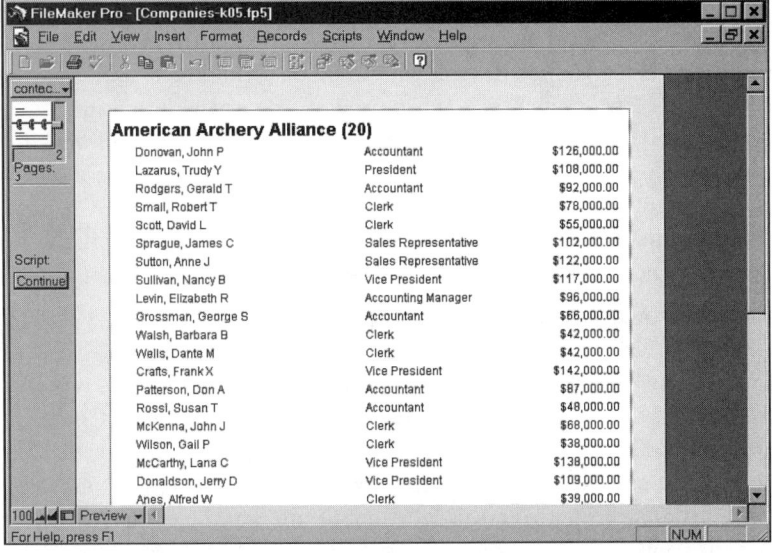

If you click the button Print Contacts from the Child file, you see a similar report, but from the Contacts file. First of all, notice that Swimming Pools of America no longer appears (having no children, it is not referenced by any record in the child file, and will not appear). Also, as shown in Figures 11.21 and 11.22, note that in this report, the American Archery

Alliance has 18 of its members on the first page, while 2 more get rolled onto the second
page, because these are individual records, not a clump inside a single humongous portal. Of
course, the way we have set up this report, nothing on the second page tells a reader where
those contacts come from.

Figure 11.21
Page One has almost all the members of the American Archery Alliance, but not quite.

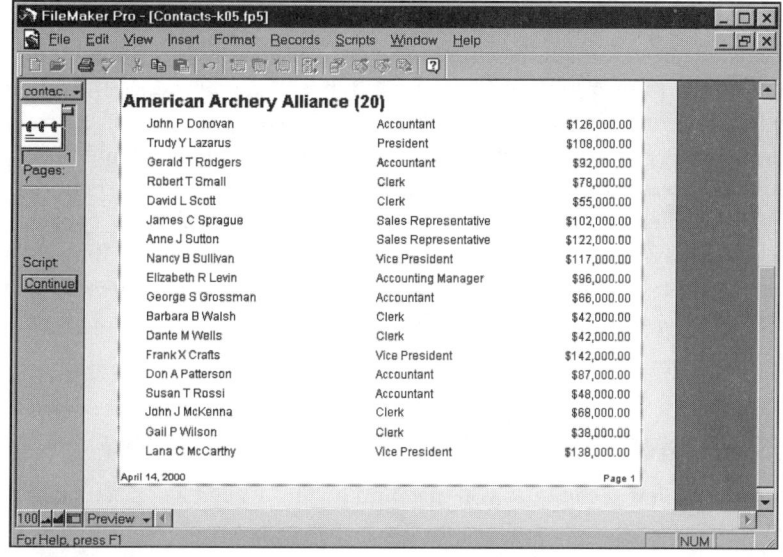

Figure 11.22
Page Two shows the 2 members who did not fit on the first page; readers may not know where these folks came from.

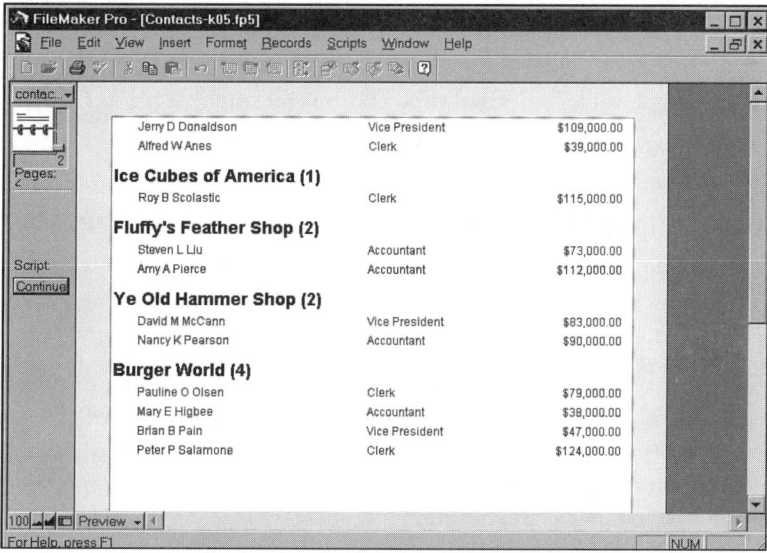

MANY TO MANY

We generally resolve a traditional many-to-many situation, such as invoices and products,
by creating a join file, such as a line items file sitting in the middle. The line items file, then,

becomes a child of both parents—invoices and products. The middle file is the ideal place from which to create reports. Not only is it a child file, but it can include data from both parents. All the data flows into the middle file, which makes it the most convenient spot to report from.

By the way, if you look at our Invoicing solution, you'll find files for customers, invoices, products, payments, and invoice line items. Most of the reports are generated from the line items file, even though that is not always visible to the user. Our scripts create the correct set of records over in the Invoice Line Items file, and produce the report from that vantage point, bringing the user back to the starting point at the end of the reporting process. (This magic takes place behind the stage curtain, and most users would never know that the Line Items file was involved.) But you may want to look at the reports in the Invoices file, and note that there are a lot of Accounts Receivable reports; those reports live in Invoices because they draw information from two different children, pulling the total amount purchased from the Line Items file, and the total amount of payment from the Payments file. In that case, the receivables reports are easiest to churn out when we are standing in the Invoices file.

Interesting Reporting Techniques

Here are a few techniques you may find helpful when clients start talking about refinements in your reports:

- Providing the user with editable report headers and footers, without letting him mess up the layout
- Creating a script to allow the user to perform a search as the basis for a report
- Taking advantage of fixed page margins for multiple printers
- Finding the median in subtotals and grand totals

Providing the User with Editable Report Headers and Footers

In Sales-k06, when a user clicks the Data Entry button called Print Sales by Sales Rep, a dialog appears, allowing the user to modify the headers and footers on the report, as seen in Figure 11.23.

Customers might want the same report for different purposes, or on a particular set of records, or for delivery to a certain person. They might want the header or footer to tip someone off to these special circumstances. The report itself may be routine, but the users seem to want to add a word or two, or change a word, so they can tell one version from another by looking at the header.

The technique is fairly simple. Normally, when you build a layout, you create the text in the Header or Footer part by using the Text tool, so the text is hardcoded to that layout, and cannot be changed programmatically. To allow users to modify the text, without giving them the ability to edit (read, mess up) our layout, we use Global text fields g_header_message and g_footer_message. A script allows the user to modify the value in the Global field. It brings the user to the layout that looks like a dialog box (with the status area hidden, to disguise the fact that the script is now in Pause mode), with the Global fields for the text in the Header and Footer, and the script puts the default text into these fields, so the user does not have to cope with her own text from the last time. Then the user can edit the values. We offer the Continue button to tell the script to continue (it says "Resume script"), after this brief pause. The script then resumes and builds the report, using the layout that goes and grabs the new values from the global fields, and proceeds with previewing and printing the report. The beauty of Global fields is that they have a single value for the whole file, so we don't have to worry what record we are looking at, or what page we are describing in the header or footer.

Figure 11.23
Users can modify the headers and footers.

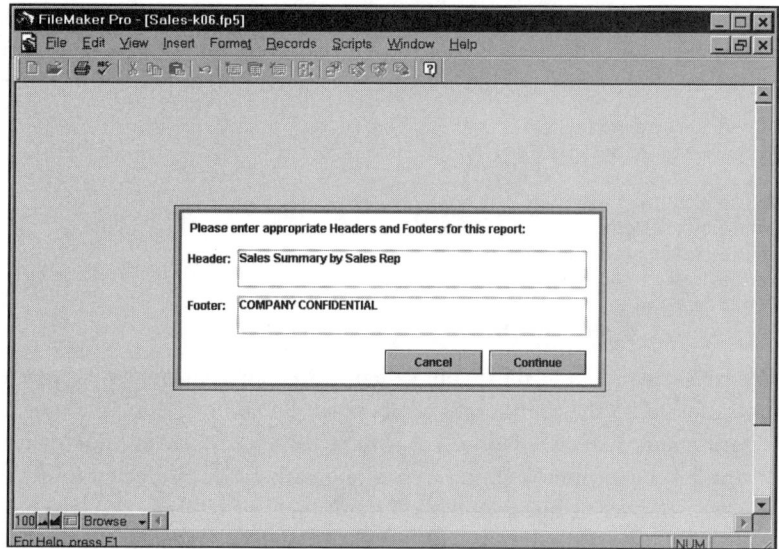

CREATING A SCRIPT TO ALLOW THE USER TO PERFORM A SEARCH AS THE BASIS FOR A REPORT

Sometimes when we produce a report, we use whatever found set of records the user has come up with. Some users want to scan through the found records, omitting this one and keeping that one. But at other times, we need to build a search into the process, which eliminates the opportunity for the user to pick and choose among the found records, but clarifies exactly what will appear in the report. For instance, some clients say they prefer having the database ask the user which records to use because this ensures the user knows exactly what will be in the report, and regularizes the found set (overruling the chance to pick and choose within that set). In our sample file Sales-k08.fp5, the script process_sales_summary_by_sales_rep_report stops to ask the users what they want to find, does some error checking to make sure the user entered a reasonable search criterion, then does the find, and, if at least one record is found, runs the report.

```
Enter Browse Mode
Allow User Abort [ Off ]
Set Error Capture [ On ]
Set Field [ g_last_layout, Status( CurrentLayoutNumber) ]
Perform Script [ "find_records_for_reports" ]
        [ Sub-scripts ]
Perform Script [ "test_for_error_in_search" ]
        [ Sub-scripts ]
Perform Script [ "print_preview_sales_summary_by_sales_rep" ]
        [ Sub-scripts ]
```

Assuming the user is starting on a particular layout, we want to bring that person back to the same layout later. We capture the number of the layout the user is on before we leave it, so we can go back to it after generating the report. We put the layout number into a Global field, g_last_layout. SetField is a way to do a calculation within a script, and here we use the Status function to fetch the CurrentLayoutNumber and place it in the Global field. Now we run a script called find_records_for_reports. (We could make a single giant script, but here we are working with modules.) The script called find_records_for_reports looks like this:

```
Enter Browse Mode
Allow User Abort [ Off ]
Set Error Capture [ On ]
Go to Layout [ search ]
Enter Find Mode
Go to Field [ date_of_sale ]
Pause/Resume Script [ ]
Perform Find
Set Field [ g_current_error, Status( CurrentError) ]
```

We are saying, "Go to the layout called Search and put the cursor in the first field, which is date_of_sale, so the user knows where to type." We pause for the user to enter the search criterion and then click Continue. Whenever a script pauses, FileMaker puts a Continue button on the left in the status area, along with a Cancel button (unless we say not to). In this case, our script turns off the ability of the user to abort the script; in essence, we have told FileMaker not to let the user cancel. Hence, we only offer a Continue button. We have created a similar button, which issues a Resume Script command to FileMaker, which starts rolling the script again. Then we run the Find.

We set the error capture on, to prevent FileMaker from stopping in the middle of the script and generating some obscure error message. Still, we have to deal with errors if they do occur. The Status (CurrentError) function lets us grab the current error code number, which we put in the Global field g_current_error, and use to tell the user about the problem. Remember that FileMaker generates a different error code after each step, to tell us whether each step was a success or failure. (Odd to think of success being represented in an error code!) If we didn't stash the error code in a Global field right after the search, the message would disappear as soon as any script took another step. (A new error code would be generated after this Set Field step, for instance.) A Status (CurrentError) of 0 indicates, "It worked!" Any number other than 0 indicates the step got derailed.

You can look up the meaning of error messages in the Help system, using Find to look up CurrentError (all one word) and then looking at Status (CurrentError) function. Relying on that list of errors with explanations, we create another script, test_for_error_in_search, to explain what went wrong to the user.

```
Enter Browse Mode
Allow User Abort [ Off ]
Set Error Capture [ On ]
If [ g_current_error = 400 ]
        Enter Find Mode
        Beep
        Beep
        Show Message [ Buttons: "OK", "", ""; Data: "The Find request is empty." ]
        Enter Browse Mode
        Go to Layout [ g_last_layout ]
            [ By Field Value... ]
        Halt Script
End If
If [ g_current_error >= 500 and g_current_error <= 510 ]
        Modify Last Find
        Beep
        Beep
        Show Message [ Buttons: "OK", "", ""; Data: "FileMaker has tried to
perform the search, but could not make sense of one or more of the items you
entered in the form."]
        Perform Script [ "clear_out_find_request" ]
            [ Sub-scripts ]
        Enter Browse Mode
        Go to Layout [ g_last_layout ]
            [ By Field Value... ]
        Halt Script
End If
If [ g_current_error = 401 ]
        Modify Last Find
        Beep
        Beep
        Show Message [ Buttons: "OK", "", ""; Data: "No matching records were
        found." ]
        Enter Browse Mode
        Show All Records
        Go to Layout [ g_last_layout ]
            [ By Field Value... ]
        Halt Script
End If
```

In this script we translate numeric error codes into messages that the user might understand, and we change the situation to avoid any further confusion. For instance, when an error 400 occurs during a scripted find, with SetErrorCapture on, meaning that the user forgot to enter any search criteria, FileMaker normally puts the user into Browse mode and finds all the records. We take the user to a layout with a fake dialog box, with our own message to the user, saying, essentially, "You left the Find form blank." Behind that dialog a record appears, and users often think, "Gosh, my Find was successful because I see a record came up." Therefore, just before showing the message, we put the user back into the Find mode, so that the user sees an empty Find request, which is what the message refers to. The user, then, doesn't wonder whether or not the original search turned out OK after all, despite our message.

The `ShowMessage` function takes four arguments, beginning with up to three buttons, and the data for the message. A script can run `Status(CurrentMessageChoice)` to find out which button the user pressed. In this case, we are not offering any choices beyond an OK, to get rid of the message. When you show a message, FileMaker pauses the script. When a user clicks OK, that has the effect of dismissing the dialog and resuming the script. (In fact, if the user clicks any button, or a Windows close box, the script will resume). In this case, we don't have to worry about which button someone clicks. We just need to know that the user has clicked. We go back to the Browse mode, and halt the processing of all scripts. (We could go back to the Find mode, if we thought the user would want that, but we figured we would offer the user a way out of Find, in case the failure to enter anything indicated that the user did not want to find anything after all.)

> **Tip from**
> *Steven*
>
> Clicking the close box in Windows has the same effect as clicking the default button. It does not automatically abort the script if the default button's choice is supposed to trigger an action.

We return to the last layout, using the number we stored in the Global field g_last_layout. (In the script process_sales_summary_by_sales_rep_report, we captured the sequence number of the layout before jumping into the actual report process.) We may need this general reporting script to run from any number of layouts, and in general we want to return to the layout the user started with. We captured the sequence number of the layout the user was on when requesting a report, and now we go back there, so that the user doesn't develop an unnatural fear of asking for a report, as happens when the user is brought back to a different layout after the reporting process.

Errors 500 to 510: Instead of searching for a particular message, we are looking for a range. All the error messages in the low 500s refer to validation errors, such as the user putting an incorrectly formatted date into a Date field. There are many different mistakes the user might have made, and we don't want to bother identifying each one. Instead of trying to pick off individual problems, we are catching a whole bunch at once by saying, "If the error number is greater than or equal to 500 and less than 510, tell the user that the Find request was invalid." The Find has already been performed, so we no longer know what field the user was in when entering the invalid criteria, and therefore we cannot specify exactly what the problem was, or put the cursor back into the problematic field. Our message, then, must also be fairly generic. "FileMaker has tried to perform the search, but could not make sense of one or more of the items you entered in the form." Now we clear out the invalid Find request, because if we left it there, FileMaker would again try to validate it before letting you go back to the Browse mode, trapping the user in Find hell. Then we put the user back in the Browse mode. We use the script clear_out_find_request to tell FileMaker to empty every field on the Find form. (There are four fields, so we use `SetField` four times, setting the value to nothing at all.)

> **Tip from Rich**
>
> Another way to clear the form is `EnterFindMode`. We cleared the form by issuing a series of `SetField` commands, setting each of the fields equal to nothing. If you include the `EnterFindMode` command with the Restore and Pause options turned off, you get the same effect.

The next error message is 401, which says, essentially, "We didn't find any records that matched the criteria you entered." Normally, when doing a find in a script with error capture turned on, FileMaker would just present the user with a found set of records containing, well, zero records. What do 0 records look like? Not much. So the user is normally returned to a blank form with an error message saying how many records there are and pointing out that no records match this request. But in this case, we have intervened to trap for other errors. We turned on error trapping earlier, using Set Error Capture on, to grab the actual error codes behind the scenes (they are never visible to the user). So now FileMaker won't automatically display any messages except the really terrible ones: ("Your file is completely corrupted; please shut down and take a walk.") Therefore, we have to come up with messages for any other common errors, such as 401. In this case, FileMaker has actually performed the Find, so we tell the user the bad news, using text rather than the numeric code.

Now the script called clear_out_find_request sets each of the fields to contain absolutely nothing.

```
clear_out_find_request
Set Field [ date_of_sale, "" ]
Set Field [ sales_rep, "" ]
Set Field [ sales_region, "" ]
Set Field [ amount_of_sale, "" ]
```

Having passed the testing for error, we know we have a valid found set, so we can preview and print that. The script that pulls everything together is print_preview_sales_summary_by_sales_rep. This script generates the report. It contains the components we generally include whenever we are creating a script to run a report.

1. We enter Browse Mode because we like to know where we are when we start. We start almost all scripts this way. In some cases, the mode makes no difference, but every once in awhile this move saves our butt. We've seen scripts that assume Browse Mode, but go haywire when the user is actually in Preview, where the menu commands are different. If the current mode does not support a particular command, FileMaker skips the step.

2. We prevent the user from canceling because that would stop the script in midstream. We wouldn't know what layout and what data would be presented to the user at that moment.

> **Tip from Rich**
>
> Only enable Allow User Abort (Off) when you are convinced that the script is working properly—particularly if the script is designed to loop. You need a way to stop the looping, or else it will go forever. If your looping script is not working right and you have turned off this flag, you have no easy way to kill the script without turning off the computer.

> **Tip from**
> *Steven*
>
> On the MAC OS you can often stop a loop that's hung by running a simple AppleScript or applet telling FileMaker Pro to quit. This does not work in every instance, but more often than not, it will. Use the Application Switcher to go out to the Finder to run the script or applet.

3. We set ErrorCapture on, because if the script does generate an error, the message will probably not make a lot of sense to the user. The cause of the error may have nothing to do with what he or she did, and the messages themselves are so general as to be cryptic. We are making it possible, too, to use a subscript to test for certain error codes and present them as messages.

4. We tell FileMaker to go to the layout we set up for the report, which in this case is sales_total_by_sales_rep.

5. We tell FileMaker to perform the script print_setup_portrait_found_records, which makes sure that the page setup and print setup are in portrait orientation, and set to print "records being browsed." (We need to make sure of these settings because some of our other reports may be in landscape orientation, or may offer to print only the current record.)

6. In order to get Sub-summaries, we sort by the break field, which in this case is the sales_rep. We choose to restore because we want to use a specific sort order. If we had the Sort command in there without the Restore option, the records would be sorted the same way they were the last time this file was sorted. The Restore says, "Do the sort based on the settings in this script, which says to sort by sales_rep." Before we created the script, we had sorted by sales rep, and when we wrote the script we were saying, "Please restore the sort order that now exists." (These are options in the Sort dialog.)

7. We enter Preview mode to show the user what the report looks like. Seeing the report onscreen may be enough for the user. If that would not be enough, we would offer a Print button. At the moment, because we turned off the option for allowing the user to abort, the user is presented with a Continue button. After a pause, when the user clicks Continue, the script starts up again.

8. We return the user to Browse Mode.

9. We tell FileMaker to print the report.

10. We return to the last layout, whose number is stored in the Global field g_last_layout. (To store that number, we used the script called process_sales_summary_by_sales_rep_report earlier). We set the option By Field Value, meaning, Take the sequence number in the Global field as the number of the layout.

11. At the very end, we undo the sort because the user might not recognize the sorted order (not having personally ordered it). We are returning to the default order.

Here is the script called print_preview_sales_summary_by_sales_rep:

```
Enter Browse Mode
Allow User Abort [ Off ]
Set Error Capture [ On ]
Go to Layout [ sales_total_by_sales_rep ]
Perform Script [ "print_setup_portrait___found_records" ]
        [ Sub-scripts ]
Sort [ Sort Order: sales_rep (Ascending) ]
        [ Restore sort order, No dialog ]
Enter Preview Mode
        [ Pause ]
Enter Browse Mode
Print
Go to Layout [ g_last_layout ]
        [ By Field Value... ]
Unsort
```

This is a time-tested report script. We have used variations on this script in many different situations, and found the basic approach reliable and steady.

> **Tip from**
> *Rich*
>
> Use scripts to remember. Scripts are perfect ways to store information about what layout to go to, what sort to perform, and what page setup and print setup to choose, because users won't recall these details. Just offer the users a button and put the script behind it.

Taking Advantage of Fixed Page Margins for Multiple Printers

Only high-end printers print to the edge of the paper, and different printers have different printing areas. As a result, the nonprintable areas range from an eighth of an inch to half an inch. FileMaker looks at the printer driver to find out what the nonprintable area will be, and then works within the remaining space in laying out pages.

If you are designing reports for a particular printer, you can confidently use its specific printable area. But often you don't know what printers the users will be using. In that situation, you would like to be able to specify a nonprintable band ahead of time, rather than relying on the various printer specs in the drivers of the different printers.

You need to set this up layout by layout:

1. Enter Layout Mode.
2. Use one of the following techniques to pick one of the three units of measurement—pixels, centimeters, or inches (so you are using the units you like, and don't have to translate on the fly).
   - Choose Layout, Set Rulers, and pick the unit.
   - Choose View, Text Rulers, and right-click the ruler (or Control-click on a Mac) to bring up a menu that allows you to pick the unit of measurement.
   - Choose View, Graphic Rulers, right-click the ruler (or Control-click on a Mac).
   - Choose View, Object Size, and in the floating Size palette, look on the right side, which shows the current units of measures; then click to cycle through the units.

- Where the horizontal ruler meets the vertical ruler, click the little marker saying what unit of measurement you are currently using (Px means pixels, IN means inches, and CM means centimeters). The button lets you change units of measure.
3. Choose Layout, Layout Setup.
4. At the bottom of the Layout Setup dialog, check the option for Fixed Page Margins.
5. Specify bottom, top, left, and right page margins for that layout.
6. Click OK.

Remember that this "page margin" is measuring from the edge of the paper. Unlike regular margins, these page margins override the printer defaults. A good compromise is to set the page margin to half an inch.

Now you don't have to worry that a particular printer might force information to shift left or right on a page, and we can be specific about exactly where that information will fall.

Finding the Median in Subtotals and Grand Totals

Mean and *average* are the same, but *median* is the item in the middle. FileMaker has built-in functions to calculate standard deviation, average, and count, but it does not have a median function, so you may need to build one yourself. Typical situations in which you might want to find the median in a subtotal or grand total field: a company wants to know the average salary, which you calculate by adding up all the salaries and dividing by the number of people, but if the company has some very well-compensated folks, and a mass of poorly paid staff, the top salaries tend to skew the average, so the boss might want to know "What's the median salary?" The median salary is the one dead center, so there are an equal number of salaries above and below.

For example, if a company has seven people, with one getting an outrageous salary and the rest making bucks in the normal range, the average would look very good, but the median would show that most folks are not getting anywhere near the average. Sorting the records by salary, we seize on the fourth record as the median.

Calculating the median is easiest when you have an odd number of instances. But what if you have an even number of instances? There is no record sitting exactly at the mid point. So we look at the middle two items and average those to get the true median point. If there were 6 records, we would average the values of records 3 and 4 to get a mathematical median.

When you work in a Sub-summary part, you are trying to calculate the median for different groups of records. If there were 7 sales reps, then the median of their salaries would be the fourth item, when sorted by salary. Similarly, if there were 11 accountants, the median salary would be the sixth. And if there were 15 clerks, then the eighth record would be the median. Looking at the whole company, then, we have 33 salaries, and the median for the whole company would be the seventeenth record.

The sample file Sales-k09.fp5, on the CD, shows one way to calculate medians on a group of records when you aren't sure, in advance, whether the total number of records for that group will be odd or even.

We start with a script called calculate_median_for_company.

```
Enter Browse Mode
Allow User Abort [ Off ]
Set Error Capture [ On ]
#
# "Determine the median amount of sale for the company."
#
# "Sort by amount of sale."
Perform Script [ "sort_ascend_by_amount_of_sale" ]
        [ Sub-scripts ]
# "Calculating the median works a little differently, depending upon whether there
is an even number of records, or an odd number of records."
If [ Right(Status( CurrentFoundCount),1) = 0 or
Right(Status( CurrentFoundCount),1) = 2 or
Right(Status( CurrentFoundCount),1) = 4 or
Right(Status( CurrentFoundCount),1) = 6 or
Right(Status( CurrentFoundCount),1) = 8 ]

            # "If there are an even number of records, take the values from the middle
            two records and average them to determine the median."
            Set Field [ g_record_number, Status( CurrentFoundCount) / 2 ]
            Go to Record/Request/Page [ g_record_number ]
                        [ By Field Value... ]
            Set Field [ g_company_median, amount_of_sale ]
            Go to Record/Request/Page
                        [ Next ]
            Set Field [ g_company_median, Round((g_company_median + amount_of_sale)/2,2) ]
Else
            # "If there is an odd number of records, take the value from the middle record."
            Set Field [ g_record_number, Int(Status( CurrentFoundCount) / 2)+1 ]
            Go to Record/Request/Page [ g_record_number ]
                        [ By Field Value... ]
            Set Field [ g_company_median, amount_of_sale ]
End If
```

First, we sort all the records in the found set by salary. Then we wonder how many records are in the found set. Starting with the rightmost digit, if the digit is 0, 2, 4, 6, or 8, we know we have spotted an even number. If the number of records turns out even, we need to average the middle two records. We take the current count and divide that by 2. If we had 10 records, we would go to the fifth record. And, while on the fifth record, we capture the amount of sales, and put it in a Global field called g_company_median. Now we go to the next record (the sixth), and take that value and add it to the g_company_medium value, divide that total by 2, and round it off to 2 decimal places. Essentially, we are setting the value for the Global field by averaging the middle 2 records. That field now holds the company medium for the found set of records when their count is even.

> **Tip from Rich**
>
> Put the median in a Global field. Since the company median will be the same for all records in the found set, we capture that value in a Global field. There is no point to storing this value on each record when we can store it once.

Turning to the odd number in the Else portion of the script, we take an integer of the count of records, divided by 2, to which we add one. If we have 7 records, we get 3.5, take the integer, which is 3, and add 1, to determine that our median is the fourth record. We say, "Go to that fourth record, and set the value of the field g_company_median equal to the value in the field amount_of_sale in the fourth record."

> **Caution**
>
> If the user finds a different set of records, adds, edits, or deletes some records, the true median would change, so the median values would need to be recalculated. Right now, that only happens if the user runs this script by pressing the button Calculate Medians.

That was the easy set of calculations. In the next script we deal with a subgroup within the company, looking only at the sales reps. We want to know what the median sales are for the sales reps. For this, we use the script called calculate_medians_for_sales_reps.

```
Enter Browse Mode
#
# "Calculate Median for Sales Reps"
#
# "Clear out old Sales Rep sequence numbers."
Replace [ sales_rep_sequence_number, Replace data:Calculation: , "" ]
[ No dialog ]
If [ Status( CurrentFoundCount) <> Status( CurrentRecordCount) ]
        # "Clear out old Sales Rep sequence numbers in records in not found set."
        Show Omitted
        Replace [ sales_rep_sequence_number, Replace data:Calculation: , "" ]
             [ No dialog ]
        Show Omitted
End If
# "Sort by Sales Rep and Amount of Sale"
Sort [ Sort Order: sales_rep (Ascending)amount_of_sale (Ascending) ]
[ Restore sort order, No dialog ]
# "Set new Sales Rep sequence numbers. These new sequence numbers will allow the
median calculations to work properly."
Replace [ sales_rep_sequence_number, Replace data:Calculation: , Count(sales |
sales_rep::sales_rep_sequence_number) + 1 ]
[ No dialog ]
```

First, we clear any lingering sequence numbers out of the records that are not found. (We intend to rely on a self relationship later, and relationships just find related records, in or out of the found set, and we don't want to find any other values in the sequence number field). Our aim is to have that field empty in every record, found or not.

In this situation, we sort primarily by sales rep, secondarily by amount of sale, to produce groupings by sales rep, ordering all the sales rep's records by the amount of sale. We now number the records within these groups. Using a field called sales_rep_sequence_number, we identify each rep's lowest sale (#1), next lowest (#2), and so on, so that we end up with a number line of all the sales, and can then pick out the middle item of each group, or average the middle two items. The first `Replace` removes all existing data from that field. The `IF` statement removes any leftover values in the not-found set.

Now, how do we put the right numbers in? Each record has a sales_rep_sequence_number field and a sales_rep field. Now that the records are in the right order, we use a calculated `Replace` which starts with the first record and uses the self-relationship that says, "Count the number of records belonging to the sales_rep, count the number of times you find that the sales_rep_sequence_number has a value in it." Since we just emptied the field, the result is 0. Now we add 1 to that value. In this way, we identify this as the first record. When we do the calculated replace on the second record, if it is the same sales rep, and it should be because we sorted the records by sales rep, FileMaker will count the number of times the sales_rep_sequence_number has a value in it. Answer: 1. Add 1 to that, to get 2. Now we have two records, identified as 1, and 2. The self-relationship prevents this replacement from spilling over to a record belonging to the next sales rep. When the processing hits a record by another sales rep, the process begins again, and so on, through all the sales reps. So each sales rep emerges with a numbered set of records. (The trick depends on starting with the field being empty.) By the way, the filename is Sales, and in the second `Replace`, the word Sales just refers to the file we are working in.

The field c_sales_rep_median_sale uses these sequence numbers to identify or figure out the median.

```
Round(
(sales | bottom_median_sales_rep_id::amount_of_sale +
sales| top_median_sales_rep_id::amount_of_sale)/2,2)
```

Here, rather than calculating differently depending on whether we have an even or odd number of records, we calculate the same way. If there are an even number of records, we average the top of the middle two values and the bottom one of the two middle values. If we have 10 records, then, we average records 5 and 6. If there were 7 records, the bottom record would be 4 and the top would be 4, and we average those. Then we round the results off to 2 decimal points. The c_bottom_median_sales_rep calculation goes like this:

```
sales | sales_rep::sales_rep & "-" &
Int(((Count(sales | sales_rep::sales_rep_sequence_number)-1)/2)+1)
```

Essentially, we are figuring out which record is the lowest of the 2 records in the middle. For instance, if we have 10 records, the bottom record in the middle would be 5, and the top would be 6. So the bottom calculation says count the number of records and divide by 2.

We apply the same logic to dealing with the top of the two middle values in the calculation c_top_median_sales_rep:

```
sales_rep & "-" &
Int((Count(sales | sales_rep::sales_rep_sequence_number)/2)+1)
```

Another script, calculate_medians, puts it all together:

```
Enter Browse Mode
Allow User Abort [ Off ]
Set Error Capture [ On ]
GotoLayout ["list"]
Perform Script [ "calculate_median_for_company" ]
        [ Sub-scripts ]
Perform Script [ "calculate_medians_for_sales_reps" ]
        [ Sub-scripts ]
GotoLayout [original layout]
```

Here we switch to the List layout because that has a field we want to use in a Replace command. We now run the two calculations we have already prepared, calculating the median for the company and for sales reps. (At the end we will switch back to the user's original layout, whatever that was.)

> **Tip from**
> *Rich*
>
> Revising names goes easy inside FileMaker, but not outside FileMaker. FileMaker uses an internal database to keep track of your relationship names, field names, script names, and value lists, assigning each a persistent ID. (The name is just an attribute of the ID). Then, when you change a name, FileMaker very generously updates the name everywhere you have used it—within FileMaker. Alas, FileMaker does not have the power to extend updates into files outside, such as Web pages, XML connections, and ODBC connections, all of which refer to items inside your FileMaker database by the name, not the persistent ID.

> **Tip from**
> *Rich*
>
> The developer edition of FileMaker Pro lets you update references to files throughout your database. Thus, references to filenames are updated across the entire system (but not outside of FileMaker).

> **Tip from**
> *Steven*
>
> But FileMaker Pro cannot update a file's name if that file is referred to literally, as in a Design Function or an embedded AppleScript.

Variations in Effect

You'll see varying effects when you put a particular field type into different parts of the layout under different conditions. Alas, there are no general rules to predict exactly how behaviors will change. Instead, there are many small surprises. For example, when you are in the Browse mode, the same layout you developed viewing it as a form (with a single record) may look dramatically different when viewed as multiple records in a list, as you will see in our sample file Parts-k10.fp5.

To control the way information is presented in Browse or Preview modes and in Print, you need to understand the many possible combinations and permutations of interactions between field type, part, and situation. (By situation, we mean the nitty gritty circumstances such as the exact way you have sorted, or not sorted, the records.) We'll start our analysis of the possibilities by looking at the Print or Preview mode, and then turn our attention to the way the same reports may show up in Browse Mode when you choose to View as List or as Form.

Print or Preview

When you are printing or previewing, all parts on the layout are *potentially* viewable. Even when parts are on the layout, though, circumstances may intervene to dictate that a particular part is not used when you actually go to print or preview. For instance, a Title Header on a one-page report will show up, but because the report itself is only one page, the regular header will never appear, because that normally starts on the page after the Title Header, but in this circumstance there is no such page. Another part that may appear on the layout but not show up on a report is a Sub-summary, because this part requires that there be a sort by the field that the Sub-summary part is built around, and if you haven't sorted by that field, well, you don't get the Sub-summary.

> **COMMON MISTAKE: FORGETTING TO SORT FOR SUB-SUMMARIES**
>
> The field specified in the Sub-summary part must be the field by which you have sorted records, or else the Sub-summary will not appear.

When we look at the way different field types react during Preview or Print, we discover that there are seven categories of field types:

- **Text, Number, Date, Time, Container, and Calculation Fields** have a value for each record. When you have one of these fields in a Title Header, which prints only once (on the first page), you see the value from the first record in the found set. A regular Header prints the value from the first record on the page. And if you have one of these fields in a Title Footer or regular Footer, you see the value from the last record on the page. The Leading Grand Summary takes the value from the first record in the found set, and the Trailing Grand Summary shows you the value in the last record in the found set. The Leading Sub-summary part gives you the value from the first record in the current subtotal group, while the Trailing Sub-summary gives you the value from the last record in the subtotal group—assuming that you have sorted the records on the field the Sub-summary part was created around. The Body part appears once for each record in the found set, showing the value in the record.

- **Global Field Types** offer a constant value for the entire field, or one value throughout the file. No matter what part you put a Global field in, you see that value. Of course, you have to sort the records correctly to get the value to show up in a Sub-summary part.

- **Summary Fields** have no value for a particular record, and no value for the file as a whole, but generate a value depending on circumstances. These values are a bit amorphous because they do not belong to any one record, and may not summarize every record in the file, either. They summarize those records that have just been found, or the records that belong to different groups. The way Summary fields act in different parts depends on the actual operations they perform.

- **Summary Fields That Offer Total, Average, Count, Minimum, Maximum, Standard Deviation, and a Weighted Average.** If one of these fields appears in a Title Header, Header, Leading Grand Summary, Body, Trailing Grand Summary, Footer, or Title Footer (anywhere but in a Sub-summary part), then that Summary field operation is performed on the found set of records. In a Sub-summary part, the operation is performed on the current subtotal group, presuming the records have been sorted by the values in the field you are sub-summarizing.

- **Summary Fields That Offer a Fraction of a Total**, when placed in the Title Header, Header, Leading Grand Summary, Trailing Grand Summary, Footer, or Title Footer, give a result of 100% because they are totaling up all the records, and all the records add up to 100% of the records. But put one of these fields into a Body, and you get that record's percentage of the grand total of the found set of records' values in the field you are summarizing. Place one of these fields into a Leading or Trailing Sub-summary, and you get that subtotal group's percentage of the grand total.

- **Summary Fields for Running Total and Running Count.** If you are showing a report on Count of Sales and Total of Sales, you get a count of all records, and a total of the value of all the sales in those records. And in a Sub-summary section, you get a count or total of that subtotal group. But that count or total will be reset to zero for each new group. These field types accumulate as you go through the records, rather than resetting to zero. Therefore, these two field types behave similarly in a Header, Title Header, Leading Grand Summary, Trailing Grand Summary, Footer, or Title Footer: You get a total or count of all records in the found set. When you place these fields in the Body, though, you get a total or count up to and including the current record. If you place these fields in a Leading or Trailing Sub-summary part, you get a total or count up to and including *all* of the records in the current subtotal group.

- **A Summary Field for a Fraction of the Total When Subtotaled by Another Field.** Normally, the Fraction of a Total gives you a percentage of a grand total. In this situation you are taking a percentage of a subtotal. For instance, if you have a field with the fraction of the total of the amount of sale, and you put the field into a Sub-summary part showing sales by sales rep, you get that sales person's percentage of the company sales. But if that sales person belongs to a sales region, and you want to know the sales person's percentage of the region's sales, then you have to create a Summary field that figures the Fraction of the Total of Amount of Sales, and check the box "Subtotaled by" and choose region, as shown in Figure 11.24. The operation, then, takes the subtotal and figures out what fraction of that total the person's salary represents. Hence, this field has the most value when put into the Body part because it gives you that record's percentage of the subtotal for a group. If you put the field into a Sub-summary, such as a Sub-summary by region, you get a value of 100%, because the total sales in the Sub-summary are 100% of the sales in the Sub-summary, assuming the Sub-summary matches the field. One other wrinkle: If within region you have subtotals by sales districts within the region and you put this field into a Sub-summary by district, you get the district's percentage of the region total. If you put it into any other part, the field is empty, because, like the famous Chewbaca defense in South Park, it just doesn't make any sense.

Figure 11.24
Here we choose to subtotal by region.

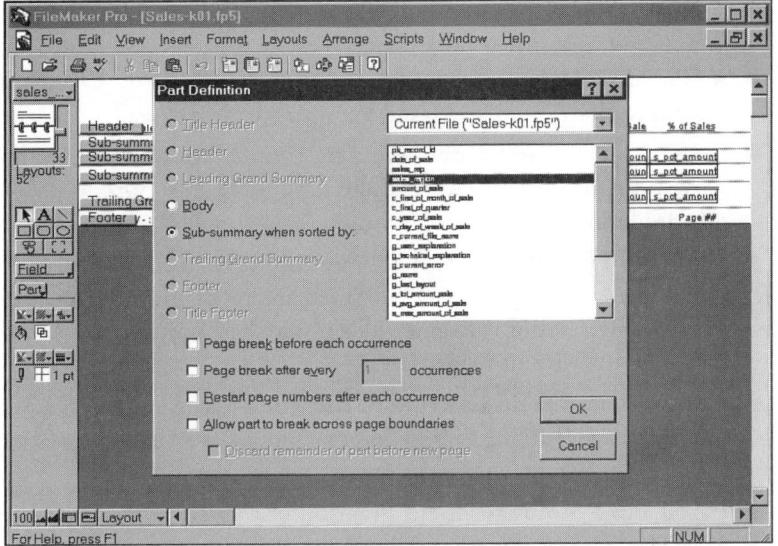

BROWSE MODE–VIEW AS FORM

Reports in Browse mode viewed as Forms display the same behavior we have seen in Print and Preview, in Global and Summary fields, which do not belong to any one form anyway. But values that belong to individual records will act differently because you are displaying one record at a time as individual forms.

So if you have a Text, Number, Date, Time, Container, or Calculation field in *any* part of the layout, you see the value from the current record in this mode. If you have sorted the records for a Sub-summary, it will be visible but the Sub-summary you see onscreen will refer only to the current record, so the value will be the value in that field in the current record. Also, remember that in Browsing a Form, the Text, Number, Date, Time, Container, or Global fields are editable without restrictions.

BROWSE MODE–VIEW AS LIST

When a report is displayed in Browse Mode, viewed as a List, then some parts go away. Say goodbye to the Title Header, Leading Sub-summary, Trailing Sub-summary, and Title Footer—they are never visible.

- If you take a field that has values on each record (Text, Number, Date, Time, Container, and Calculation fields), and put that field into a Header or Footer, then you see the field's value in whatever record is currently selected. (In viewing as a list, the selected record is marked with a vertical black bar to the left.) If you put any of these fields in a Leading Grand Summary, you get the value from that field on the first record in the found set; in the Trailing Grand Summary, you get the value from that field in the last record in the found set. If you put one of the fields into the Body, you see values of one record after another in one long scrolling list. By the way, Text, Number, Date, Time, Container, and Global fields are only editable in the Body part when viewed as a List.

- **A Global Field** has only one value, so that appears in the Header, Leading Grand Summary, Body, Trailing Grand Summary, or Footer.
- **Summary Fields for Total, Average, Count, Minimum, Maximum, Standard Deviation, and Weighted Average** summarize the entire found set when displayed in the Header, Leading Grand Summary, Body, Trailing Grand Summary, or Footer parts.
- **Summary Fields for Running Count or Running Total** in the Header, Leading Grand Summary, Trailing Grand Summary, or Footer give you a total or count of the entire found set. But the same fields inside the Body, give a count or total up to and including the current record.
- **The Summary Field Fraction of the Total** inside a Header, Leading Grand Summary, and Trailing Grand Summary gives you 100%. Inside the Body, it gives you that record's percentage of the grand total for the found set.
- **If You Put a Summary Field Fraction of the Total When Subtotaled** in a Header, Title Header, Leading Grand Summary, Trailing Grand Summary, Title Footer, or Footer, it is empty. In these parts, there is no subtotal to work with, because these parts are not related to any particular subtotal. Hence, the operation cannot take place, and the results are, well, nothing. In the Body, the field gives the current record as a percentage of the subtotal when the records have been sorted. When you create the field, you define the subtotals by a field, so you have to sort the fields by that second field to make this work.

Looking over all of these variations, we have summed up the ideas in Table 11-1, included as a file on the CD. In the sample file Parts.fp5, you can experiment with all of these variations, too.

In our Chapter 11 folder on the CD, the file called Parts.fp5 has fields of the types Text, Number, Date, Time, Container, Calculation, Global, so you can watch how different types behave in different parts of a layout. Important: In the Scripts menu, you'll find the commands you can use to navigate to these other layouts.

- **Data Entry and List:** These are the ordinary layouts, visible when the file opens, as seen in Figure 11.25.

Figure 11.25
The Data Entry and List layouts are visible on opening.

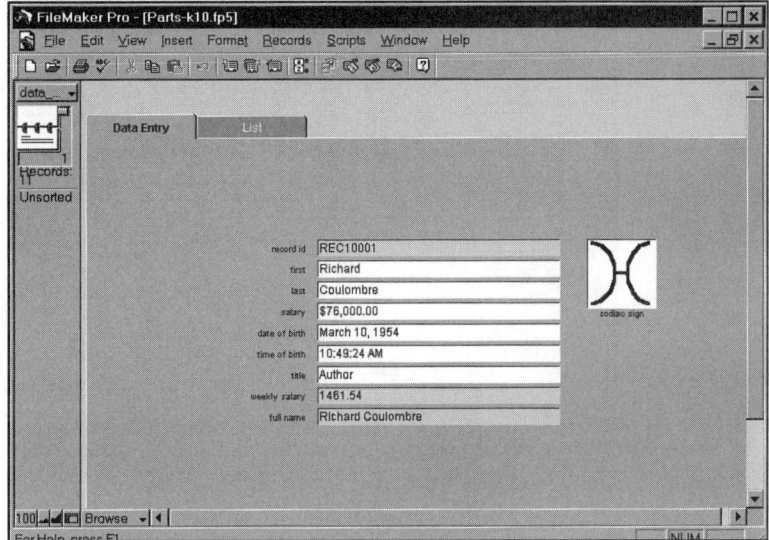

- **Show Fields** displays a layout with samples of each of these field types in every possible part (see Figures 11.26 and 11.26b). Note that in this mode, the Title Header, Leading Sub-summary, Trailing Sub-summary, and Title Footer are visible. Notice that you can click in any field in any part and edit the values.

Figure 11.26
The Show Fields layout is visible in Layout Mode.

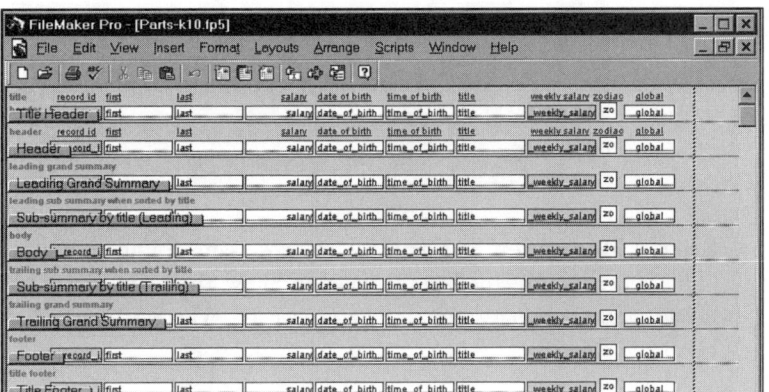

Figure 11.26b
You can see the Show Fields layout in Browse Mode.

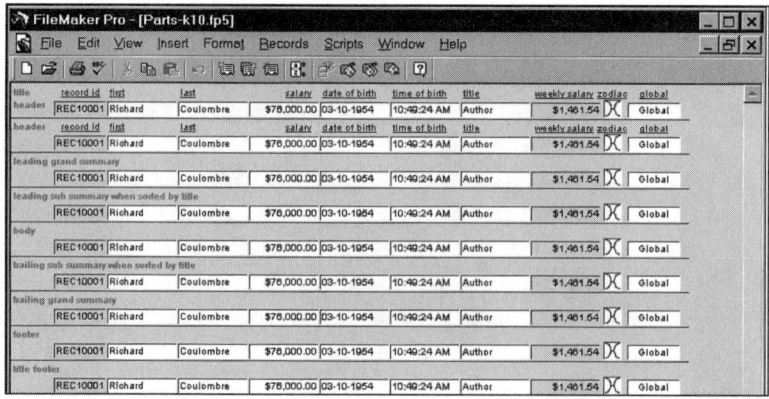

- **Show Summary Fields** offers a layout that has an identical structure, but includes only Summary fields, such as Total Salary (see Figure 11.27).

Figure 11.27
Show Summary fields shows a layout with only Summary fields.

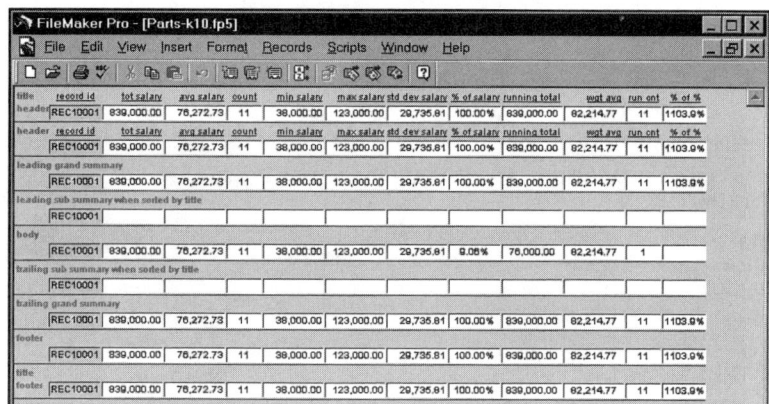

- **Browse Mode-View as Form** shows us the same Summary fields in a single record. (This is the same as the layout shown in Show Summary Fields.) You see the Title Header, Sub-summary, and Title Footer parts, whereas View as List does not (see Figure 11.28).

Figure 11.28
Browse Mode–View as Form shows Summary fields in a single record.

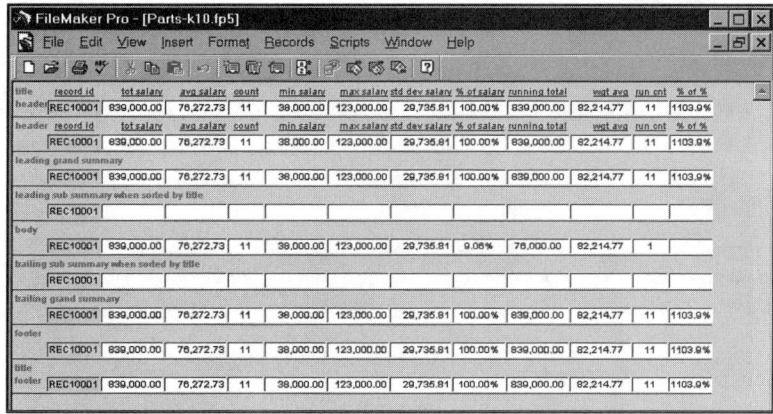

- **Browse Mode-View as List** shows the same Summary fields, but in a list arrangement, shown in Figure 11.29, so there are many bodies (records) in the middle. Note that the Title Header, Sub-summary, and Title Footer parts are no longer visible, although they are on the layout. (If you switch to Layout view, you will see these parts do exist in the actual layout; they just do not appear when viewed as a list.)

Figure 11.29
The List View hides some parts that are actually on the layout, such as Title Header and Sub-summary parts.

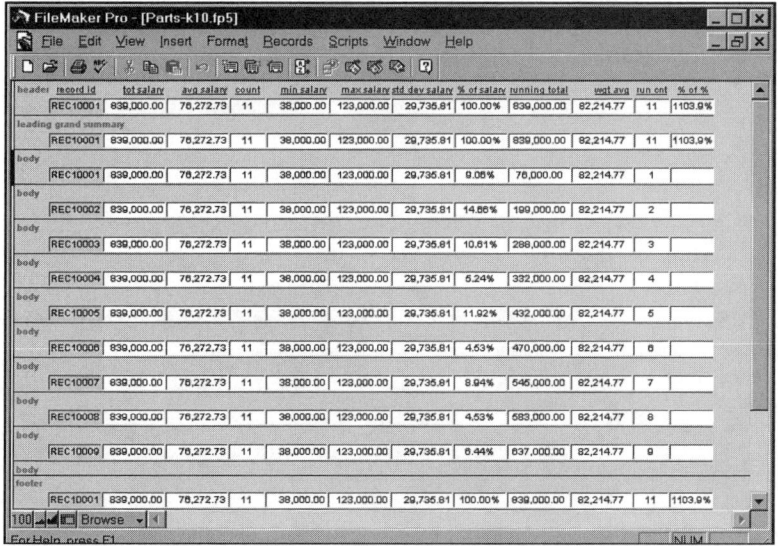

- **Preview Mode** shows what the same layout will look like when it prints, as shown in Figure 11.30. Note that we get the Title Header on the first page only, but the Header shows up on subsequent pages. The Leading Grand Summary appears before any Sub-summaries or record detail, and the Trailing Grand Summary comes afterward. We get different clusters of records for each subtotal group, sorted by title (a group of records with the same value in the field Title, such as Accountant or Clerk). For each subtotal group, we have a Leading Sub-summary, put just ahead of the first record of the group, then the record detail printed as part of the Body, and finally the Trailing Sub-summary, which prints after the last record in the subtotal group. And, after the final Trailing Sub-summary, we get the Trailing Grand Summary. On the first page, we get the Title Header and Title Footer, and on the subsequent pages we get the regular Header and Footer. (Now, if you choose Unsort, you lose your Sub-summaries, but when you choose Sort Titles, you get them back.)

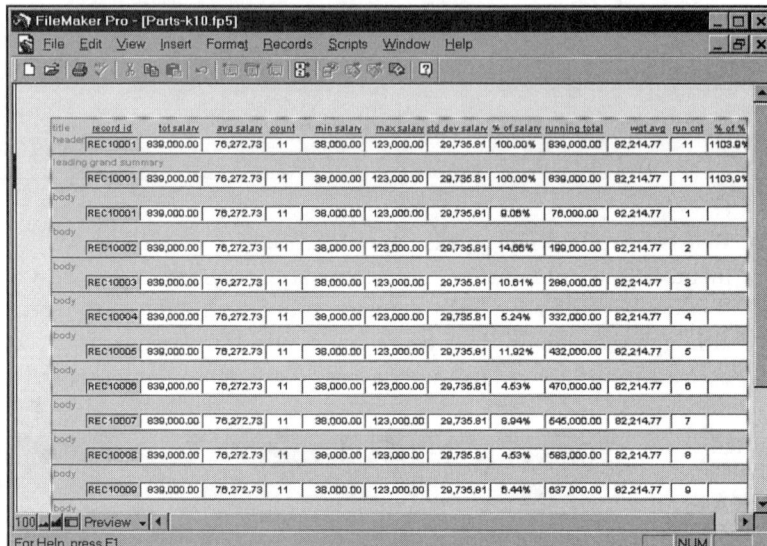

Figure 11.30
Here is an example of Preview Mode.

- **Unsort** removes the Sub-summaries from the Preview and Browse Mode View as List.
- **Sort Title**s brings the Sub-summaries back into the Preview and Browse Mode View as List (see Figure 11.31).

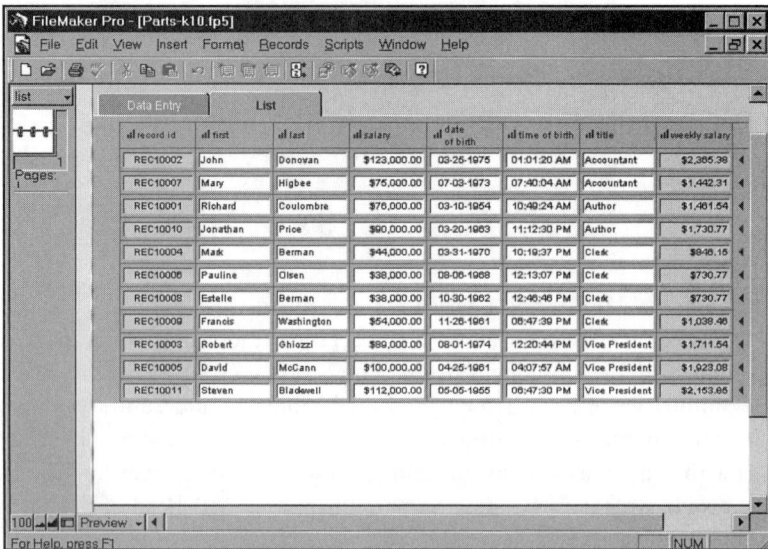

Figure 11.31
Sort Titles brings the Sub-summaries back in Preview and Browse Mode View as List.

TABLE 11.1 How Different Field Types Behave in Different Parts of the Layout

Browse Mode - View as List

Field Types	Title Header	Header	Leading Grand Summary	Leading Sub-summary	Body	Trailing Sub-summary	Trailing Grand Summary	Footer	Title Footer
Text	Part Not Visible	Value from Selected Record	Value from First Record in Found Set	Part Not Visible	Value from Multiple Records***	Part Not Visible	Value from Last Record in Found Set	Value from Selected Record	Part Not Visible
Number	Part Not Visible	Value from Selected Record	Value from First Record in Found Set	Part Not Visible	Value from Multiple Records***	Part Not Visible	Value from Last Record in Found Set	Value from Selected Record	Part Not Visible
Date	Part Not Visible	Value from Selected Record	Value from First Record in Found Set	Part Not Visible	Value from Multiple Records***	Part Not Visible	Value from Last Record in Found Set	Value from Selected Record	Part Not Visible
Time	Part Not Visible	Value from Selected Record	Value from First Record in Found Set	Part Not Visible	Value from Multiple Records***	Part Not Visible	Value from Last Record in Found Set	Value from Selected Record	Part Not Visible
Container	Part Not Visible	Value from Selected Record	Value from First Record in Found Set	Part Not Visible	Value from Multiple Records***	Part Not Visible	Value from Last Record in Found Set	Value from Selected Record	Part Not Visible
Calculation	Part Not Visible	Value from Selected Record	Value from First Record in Found Set	Part Not Visible	Value from Multiple Records	Part Not Visible	Value from Last Record in Found Set	Value from Selected Record	Part Not Visible
Global	Part Not Visible	Global Field Value	Global Field Value	Part Not Visible	Global Field Value***	Part Not Visible	Global Field Value	Global Field Value	Part Not Visible
Summary - Total	Part Not Visible	Total of Found Set	Total of Found Set	Part Not Visible	Total of Found Set	Part Not Visible	Total of Found Set	Total of Found Set	Part Not Visible
Summary - Average	Part Not Visible	Average of Found Set	Average of Found Set	Part Not Visible	Average of Found Set	Part Not Visible	Average of Found Set	Average of Found Set	Part Not Visible
Summary - Count	Part Not Visible	Count of Found Set	Count of Found Set	Part Not Visible	Count of Found Set	Part Not Visible	Count of Found Set	Count of Found Set	Part Not Visible

TABLE 11.1 CONTINUED

Browse Mode - View as List

Summary - Minimum	Part Not Visible	Smallest in Found Set	Smallest in Found Set	Part Not Visible	Smallest in Found Set	Part Not Visible	Smallest in Found Set	Smallest in Found Set	Part Not Visible
Summary - Maximum	Part Not Visible	Biggest in Found Set	Biggest in Found Set	Part Not Visible	Biggest in Found Set	Part Not Visible	Biggest in Found Set	Biggest in Found Set	Part Not Visible
Summary - Standard Dev	Part Not Visible	Standard Deviation of Found Set	Standard Deviation of Found Set	Part Not Visible	Standard Deviation of Found Set	Part Not Visible	Standard Deviation of Found Set	Standard Deviation of Found Set	Part Not Visible
Summary - Fraction of Total	Part Not Visible	100%	100%	Part Not Visible	Single Record Percentage of Found Set	Part Not Visible	100%	100%	Part Not Visible
Summary - Running Total	Part Not Visible	Total of Found Set	Total of Found Set	Part Not Visible	Total of Records up to and Including Current Record	Part Not Visible	Total of Found Set	Total of Found Set	Part Not Visible
Summary - Weighted Average	Part Not Visible	Weighted Average of Found Set	Weighted Average of Found Set	Part Not Visible	Weighted Average of Found Set	Part Not Visible	Weighted Average of Found Set	Weighted Average of Found Set	Part Not Visible
Summary - Running Count	Part Not Visible	Count of Found Set	Count of Found Set	Part Not Visible	Count of Records up to and Including Current Record	Part Not Visible	Count of Found Set	Count of Found Set	Part Not Visible
Summary - Fraction of Total when Subtotaled	Part Not Visible	Empty (when sorted)	Empty (when sorted)	Part Not Visible	Current Record Percentage of Subtotal Group (when sorted)	Part Not Visible	Empty (when sorted)	Empty (when sorted)	Part Not Visible

Variations in Effect

Field Types	Title Header	Header	Leading Grand Summary	Leading Sub-summary	Body	Trailing Sub-summary	Trailing Grand Summary	Footer	Title Footer
Text	Value from Current Record***	Value from Current Record***	Value from Current Record***	Value from Current Record*** (when sorted)	Value from Current Record***	Value from Current Record*** (when sorted)	Value from Current Record***	Value from Current Record***	Value from Current Record***
Number	Value from Current Record***	Value from Current Record***	Value from Current Record***	Value from Current Record*** (when sorted)	Value from Current Record***	Value from Current Record*** (when sorted)	Value from Current Record***	Value from Current Record***	Value from Current Record***
Date	Value from Current Record***	Value from Current Record***	Value from Current Record***	Value from Current Record*** (when sorted)	Value from Current Record***	Value from Current Record*** (when sorted)	Value from Current Record***	Value from Current Record***	Value from Current Record***
Time	Value from Current Record***	Value from Current Record***	Value from Current Record***	Value from Current Record*** (when sorted)	Value from Current Record***	Value from Current Record*** (when sorted)	Value from Current Record***	Value from Current Record***	Value from Current Record***
Container	Value from Current Record***	Value from Current Record***	Value from Current Record***	Value from Current Record*** (when sorted)	Value from Current Record***	Value from Current Record*** (when sorted)	Value from Current Record***	Value from Current Record***	Value from Current Record***
Calculation	Value from Current Record	Value from Current Record	Value from Current Record	Value from Current Record (when sorted)	Value from Current Record	Value from Current Record (when sorted)	Value from Current Record	Value from Current Record	Value from Current Record
Global	Global Field Value***	Global Field Value***	Global Field Value***	Global Field Value*** (when sorted)	Global Field Value***	Global Field Value*** (when sorted)	Global Field Value***	Global Field Value***	Global Field Value***
Summary - Total	Total of Found Set	Total of Found Set	Total of Found Set	Total of Current Subtotal Group (when sorted)	Total of Found Set	Total of Current Subtotal Group (when sorted)	Total of Found Set	Total of Found Set	Total of Found Set

TABLE 11.1 CONTINUED

	Browse Mode - View as List								
Summary - Average	Average of Found Set	Average of Found Set	Average of Found Set	Average of Current Subtotal Group (when sorted)	Average of Found Set	Average of Current Subtotal Group (when sorted)	Average of Found Set	Average of Found Set	Average of Found Set
Summary - Count	Count of Found Set	Count of Found Set	Count of Found Set	Count of Current Subtotal Group (when sorted)	Count of Found Set	Count of Current Subtotal Group (when sorted)	Count of Found Set	Count of Found Set	Count of Found Set
Summary - Minimum	Smallest in Found Set	Smallest in Found Set	Smallest in Found Set	Smallest in Current Subtotal Group (when sorted)	Smallest in Found Set	Smallest in Current Subtotal Group (when sorted)	Smallest in Found Set	Smallest in Found Set	Smallest in Found Set
Summary - Maximum	Biggest in Found Set	Biggest in Found Set	Biggest in Found Set	Biggest in Current Subtotal Group (when sorted)	Biggest in Found Set	Biggest in Current Subtotal Group (when sorted)	Biggest in Found Set	Biggest in Found Set	Biggest in Found Set
Summary - Standard Dev	Standard Deviation of Found Set	Standard Deviation of Found Set	Standard Deviation of Found Set	Standard Deviation of Current Subtotal Group (when sorted)	Standard Deviation of Found Set	Standard Deviation of Current Subtotal Group (when sorted)	Standard Deviation of Found Set	Standard Deviation of Found Set	Standard Deviation of Found Set
Summary - Fraction of Total	100%	100%	100%	Current Subtotal Group Percentage of Found Set (when sorted)	Single Record Percentage of Found Set	Current Subtotal Group Percentage of Found Set (when sorted)	100%	100%	100%

Field Types	Title Header	Header	Leading Grand Summary	Leading Sub-summary	Body	Trailing Sub-summary	Trailing Grand Summary	Footer	Title Footer
Summary - Running Total	Total of Found Set	Total of Found Set	Total of Found Set	Total of Records up to and Including this Subtotal Group (when sorted)	Total of Records up to and Including this Record	Total of Records up to and Including this Subtotal Group (when sorted)	Total of Found Set	Total of Found Set	Total of Found Set
Summary - Weighted Average	Weighted Average of Found Set	Weighted Average of Found Set	Weighted Average of Found Set	Weighted Average of Current Subtotal Group (when sorted)	Weighted Average of Found Set	Weighted Average of Current Subtotal Group (when sorted)	Weighted Average of Found Set	Weighted Average of Found Set	Weighted Average of Found Set
Summary - Running Count	Count of Found Set	Count of Found Set	Count of Found Set	Count of Records up to and Including this Subtotal Group (when sorted)	Count of Records up to and Including this Record	Count of Records up to and Including this Subtotal Group (when sorted)	Count of Found Set	Count of Found Set	Count of Found Set
Summary - Fraction of Total when Subtotaled	Empty (when sorted)	Empty (when sorted)	Empty (when sorted)	100%	Single Record Percentage of Subtotal Group (when sorted)	100%	Empty (when sorted)	Empty (when sorted)	Empty (when sorted)
Text	Value from First Record in Found Set	Value from First Record on Page	Value from First Record in Found Set	Value from First Record in Current SubTotal Group (when sorted)	Value from Each Record in Found Set	Value from Last Record in Current SubTotal Group (when sorted)	Value from Last Record in Found Set	Value from Last Record on Page	Value from Last Record on Page
Number	Value from First Record in Found Set	Value from First Record on Page	Value from First Record in Found Set	Value from First Record in Current SubTotal Group (when sorted)	Value from Each Record in Found Set	Value from Last Record in Current SubTotal Group (when sorted)	Value from Last Record in Found Set	Value from Last Record on Page	Value from Last Record on Page

TABLE 11.1   CONTINUED

Browse Mode - View as List

Date	Value from First Record in Found Set	Value from First Record on Page	Value from First Record in Found Set	Value from First Record in Current SubTotal Group (when sorted)	Value from Each Record in Found Set	Value from Last Record in Current SubTotal Group (when sorted)	Value from Last Record in Found Set	Value from Last Record on Page	Value from Last Record on Page
Time	Value from First Record in Found Set	Value from First Record on Page	Value from First Record in Found Set	Value from First Record in Current SubTotal Group (when sorted)	Value from Each Record in Found Set	Value from Last Record in Current SubTotal Group (when sorted)	Value from Last Record in Found Set	Value from Last Record on Page	Value from Last Record on Page
Container	Value from First Record in Found Set	Value from First Record on Page	Value from First Record in Found Set	Value from First Record in Current SubTotal Group (when sorted)	Value from Each Record in Found Set	Value from Last Record in Current SubTotal Group (when sorted)	Value from Last Record in Found Set	Value from Last Record on Page	Value from Last Record on Page
Calculation	Value from First Record in Found Set	Value from First Record on Page	Value from First Record in Found Set	Value from First Record in Current SubTotal Group (when sorted)	Value from Each Record in Found Set	Value from Last Record in Current SubTotal Group (when sorted)	Value from Last Record in Found Set	Value from Last Record on Page	Value from Last Record on Page
Global	Global Field Value	Global Field Value	Global Field Value	Global Field Value (when sorted)	Global Field Value	Global Field Value (when sorted)	Global Field Value	Global Field Value	Global Field Value
Summary - Total	Total of Found Set	Total of Found Set	Total of Found Set	Total of Current Subtotal Group (when sorted)	Total of Found Set	Total of Current Subtotal Group (when sorted)	Total of Found Set	Total of Found Set	Total of Found Set

Variations in Effect

Summary - Average	Average of Found Set	Average of Found Set	Average of Found Set	Average of Current Subtotal Group (when sorted)	Average of Found Set	Average of Current Subtotal Group (when sorted)	Average of Found Set	Average of Found Set
Summary - Count	Count of Found Set	Count of Found Set	Count of Found Set	Count of Current Subtotal Group (when sorted)	Count of Found Set	Count of Current Subtotal Group (when sorted)	Count of Found Set	Count of Found Set
Summary - Minimum	Smallest in Found Set	Smallest in Found Set	Smallest in Found Set	Smallest in Current Subtotal Group (when sorted)	Smallest in Found Set	Smallest in Current Subtotal Group (when sorted)	Smallest in Found Set	Smallest in Found Set
Summary - Maximum	Biggest in Found Set	Biggest in Found Set	Biggest in Found Set	Biggest in Current Subtotal Group (when sorted)	Biggest in Found Set	Biggest in Current Subtotal Group (when sorted)	Biggest in Found Set	Biggest in Found Set
Summary - Standard Deviation	Standard Deviation of Found Set	Standard Deviation of Found Set	Standard Deviation of Found Set	Standard Deviation of Current Subtotal Group (when sorted)	Standard Deviation of Found Set	Standard Deviation of Current Subtotal Group (when sorted)	Standard Deviation of Found Set	Standard Deviation of Found Set
Summary - Fraction of Total	100%	100%	100%	Current Subtotal Group Percentage of Found Set (when sorted)	Single Record Percentage of Found Set	Current Subtotal Group Percentage of Found Set (when sorted)	100%	100%

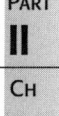

TABLE 11.1 CONTINUED

Browse Mode - View as List

Summary - Running Total	Total of Found Set	Total of Found Set	Total of Records up to and Including this Subtotal Group (when sorted)	Total of Records up to and Including this Record	Total of Records up to and Including this Subtotal Group (when sorted)	Total of Found Set	Total of Found Set
Summary - Weighted Average	Weighted Average of Found Set	Weighted Average of Found Set	Weighted Average of Current Subtotal Group (when sorted)	Weighted Average of Found Set	Weighted Average of Current Subtotal Group (when sorted)	Weighted Average of Found Set	Weighted Average of Found Set
Summary - Running Count	Count of Found Set	Count of Found Set	Count of Records up to and Including this Subtotal Group (when sorted)	Count of Records up to and Including this Record	Count of Records up to and Including this Subtotal Group (when sorted)	Count of Found Set	Count of Found Set
Summary - Fraction of Total when Subtotaled	Empty (when sorted)	Empty (when sorted)	100%	Single Record Percentage of Subtotal Group (when sorted)	100%	Empty (when sorted)	Empty (when sorted)

CHAPTER 12

DUMB PORTAL TRICKS

In this chapter

What Shows Up in a Portal—and How   396

Dumb Portal Trick #1: Lets You See in a Portal All Records from Another File   396

Dumb Portal Trick #2: Lets You Use Conditional Value Lists with Portals   398

Dumb Portal Trick #3: Highlights Selected Items in Portals   401

Dumb Portal Trick #4: Moves Records from One Portal to Another   403

Dumb Portal Trick #5: Uses Calculated Multivalued Keys to Filter Which Child Records Show Up in the Parent Record   405

Dumb Portal Trick #6: Moves Portal Rows and Inserts a Portal Row   406

Dumb Portal Trick #7: Allows the User to Choose the Sort Order in a Portal   412

Dumb Portal Trick #8: Makes the Portal Disappear!   414

Dumb Portal Trick #9: Uses a Portal to Control Access to Records in Another File   417

WHAT SHOWS UP IN A PORTAL—AND HOW

In this chapter, we help you think outside the portal, or at least outside the standard model of a portal. Traditionally, the portal simply served to show child records within a parent. But you can use portals in other ways, to satisfy special requests from your client and provide a livelier and more responsive interface. Because these techniques go against convention, we call them *dumb portal tricks*.

Imagine that you have a Customers file and an Invoices file. The Customers file is the parent, and the Invoices file is the child. In the traditional sense, a portal goes into the parent, showing the children who are related to the current parent. In the Customers file, then, each customer would have a unique ID (the customer ID, also known as the Primary key). Each invoice also has a Primary key (the Invoice ID) and a Foreign key identifying its particular parent (the Customer ID). When you are looking at a particular customer, the portal gets filled with all of that customer's invoices. FileMaker figures out which records to load into the portal by getting the primary-key value from the parent, and searching through the child file to locate all records containing that value in the Foreign key field. In essence, what FileMaker is doing behind the scenes is a super-fast Find. (Relational computer scientists don't like to think this way, of course, but loosely, what shows up in the portal can be thought of as a found set of records).

Through script control or calculations, we can manipulate the two match fields in the parent and the child to expand what shows up in the portal. The portal can go beyond the parent/child model to become an element of our user interface, giving access to a wide range of information. In this chapter, then, we will show you several techniques you can use to take advantage of the portal's ability to show multiple matching records.

> **Caution**
>
> When you start using portals in a nontraditional way, even though the portal may be within a parent file, you need to distinguish between the keys used to hold our data model together and those other keys we will be suggesting for a variety of user interfaces. The relationships we create in this chapter never showed up on your Entity Relationship diagram; they are not part of the original data model. They are created just to get the job done.

DUMB PORTAL TRICK #1: LETS YOU SEE IN A PORTAL ALL RECORDS FROM ANOTHER FILE

Problem to be solved: You want to show all the records from the parent file when you are within a child—every parent irrespective of relationship.

 To help users pick a company to assign to a new contact, when the individual contact is set up as a child of the file Companies-l01, we offer a portal in the file Contacts-l01, showing a list of *all* the companies living in Companies-l01. This portal shows all parents, not just the records related to this particular contact. How did we pull that off?

We started by asking ourselves, "How do we set up a pair of match fields in the child and the parent so that when we look at any child, that child automatically has a field value matching all the parents?" We create a Constant field equal to the value 1. The field is defined the same way in both the parent and child files as a Calculation with a Number result of 1 (see Figure 12.1).

Figure 12.1
This is a really simple calculation.

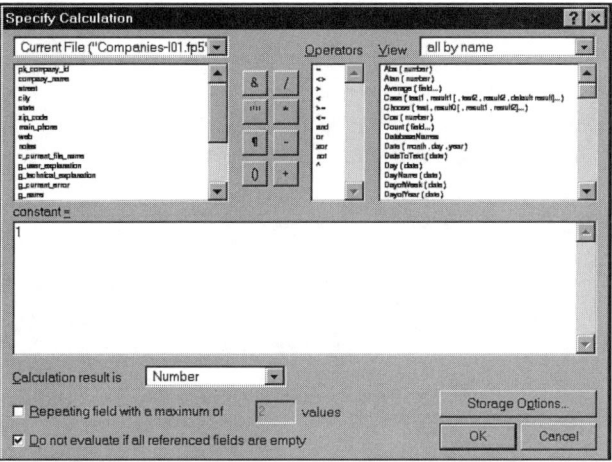

Now that we have the Constant field in both files, we create a relationship from the child to the parent (see Figure 12.2). This relationship is based upon the Constant value, which is always and everywhere 1. Now every child is related to every parent through this special relationship. So looking at any child, we find its Constant value is 1. And when we ask FileMaker to load all records from the parent containing a Constant value of 1, FileMaker loads every parent record into the portal in Contacts (see Figure 12.3) because every parent has that value in the field.

> **Caution**
> When creating the Constant relationship, do not under any circumstances check the option that says, "When deleting a record in this file, also delete related records." Your user could accidentally wipe out your whole parent file just by deleting one child.

> **Caution**
> In a relationship where the field on the right-hand side of the relationship is a calculation, you should not check the option to allow creation of related records. When you allow that, FileMaker attempts to set the key values behind your back to keep the records properly related, but if the field it is trying to set is a Calculation, well, it can't modify the value, so you will get an error message such as, "The relationship "Companies | Constant" is not valid and must be corrected before this field can be modified."

Figure 12.2
The dialog for Define Relationships for
`Companies | constant`.

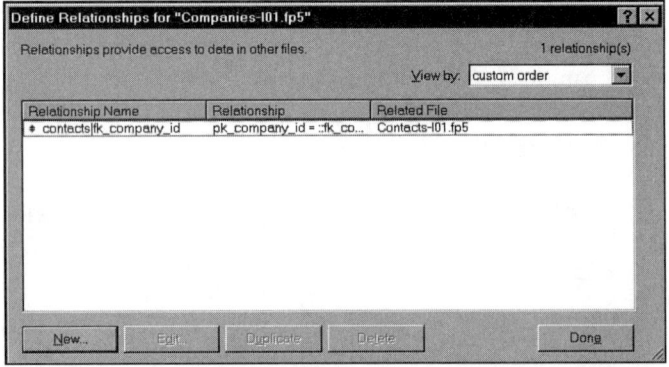

Figure 12.3
Here is the data-entry screen in Contacts-l01.

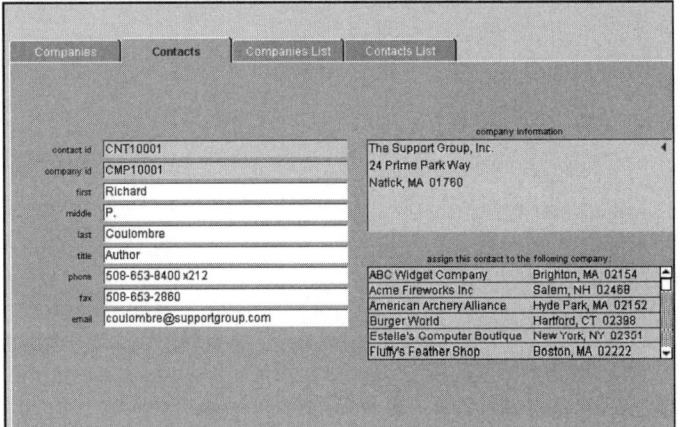

Dumb Portal Trick #2: Lets You Use Conditional Value Lists with Portals

Rich recently went car shopping on the Web, looking at exchange sites that asked him for information about the car he wanted, and then pointed him to dealers. One site had a single pop-up list of every manufacturer, make, and model. It was a very long list. Rich felt tired just looking at it. Other sites let him drill in by choosing a manufacturer, then picking a make, and finally identifying a model. He found that process a lot easier, making three simple choices from short lists.

Users often prefer to drill down to find an item, particularly if they arrive not knowing exactly what they want. In this trick, we show you how to do that.

> **Note**
> This trick resembles the tips we gave on conditional value lists back in Chapter 5. But you might prefer to do the trick through a portal, because
>
> ■ You may prefer the look of a portal.

- With a value list, you can only show two fields, max, whereas a portal can show as many as you want, and you have more control over their arrangement and appearance.

  When a user selects an item from a portal, you can have a button action trigger a script, automating some process at that moment. (You can't do this as easily with an ordinary value list.)

 So, in the file CustomerInterests in the second folder for this chapter, we have records of customers being interested in a particular product. (The user would be a sales person). So, instead of presenting a massive list of products, we offer a way for the salesperson to identify a product category by clicking the category on the left. Then a list of those products appears on the right (see Figure 12.4). And when the user picks one of those, the product information flows into the fields at the top, as shown in Figure 12.5

Figure 12.4
The user picks a category on the left, and products appear on the right.

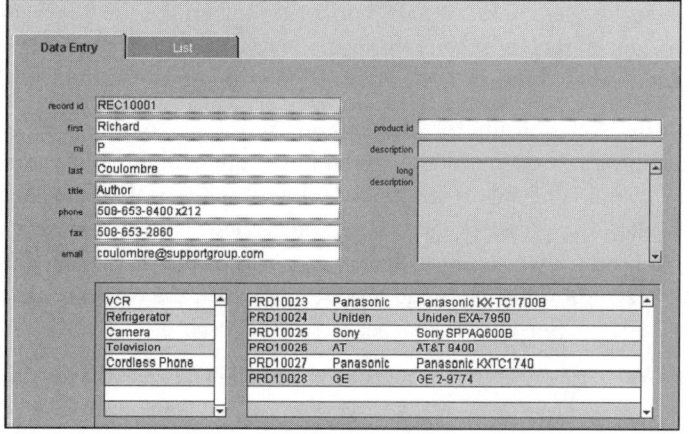

Figure 12.5
The user picks a product, and the information about that pours into the fields at the top.

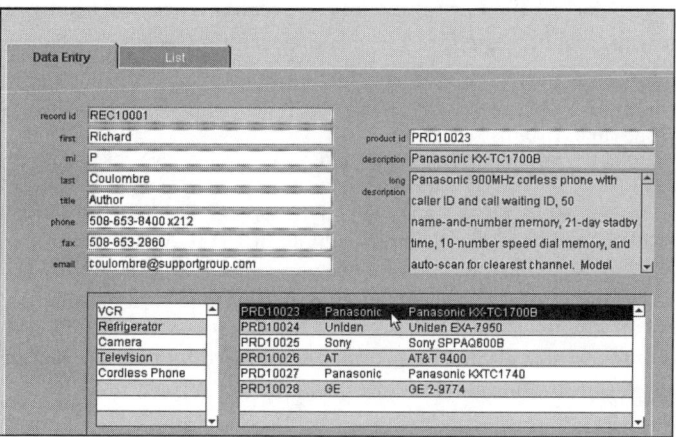

The first portal offers product categories, such as VCR, camera, and TV. We are using the technique we looked at in the first dumb portal trick—a constant portal. The portal goes to a file called Product Categories, and brings back all the records from that file. Simple enough.

Our first challenge: When a user clicks one of those categories, we want to show the products that belong to that category. To do that, we fit together several pieces. First, in the first portal, we make the field called `category_name` into a button, running a script called `select_a_category`. When a user clicks a particular portal row, which has one field, which is itself a button, that action triggers the script:

```
Enter Browse Mode
Allow User Abort [ Off ]
Set Error Capture [ On ]
Set Field [ g_selected_category, ProductCategories | constant::category_name ]
```

We use a global field, `g_selected_category`, to store the name of the category the user selects. When the user clicks, we take information from the field `category_name` in the file ProductCategories, through the relationship `ProductCategories | constant`, (the relationship the portal is based on) and pour that name into our global field.

Now we create a relationship for a second portal (the one on the right), that is based on the category name we just captured and stored in the global field. The moment we capture that value in the global field, FileMaker reloads the second portal because that field is defined as part of the relationship that portal is based on. When that value matches the category associated with a product, we want the product records displayed. When a user clicks VCR, then, we are saying, "Only show the products in which the category field equals VCR." So FileMaker loads the portal with that set of product records.

Then, when the user clicks a particular product, FileMaker soaks up all the values from that record, and we run another script, `select_a_product`, which says, "Go ahead and set the field `selected_product_ID` equal to the Primary key value of that product," which is the Product ID. As part of the Customer Interest record, then, we are capturing the Product ID that the customer is interested in. Here is the script `select_a_product`:

```
Enter Browse Mode
Allow User Abort [ Off ]
Set Error Capture [ On ]
Set Field [ selected_product_id, Products | category::pk_record_id ]
```

Hence, we set the value for the `selected_product_id` field by looking in the Primary key field called `pk_record_id` over in the Products file. (FileMaker knows which record to look at because of the relationship).

Now we set up another relationship between the CustomerInterest and the Products files, to fetch other information about the product whose Product ID we just discovered. We don't bother with portals because we are just going to use related fields to display the description and long description as recorded over in the Products file. Here a child record is showing data from the parent.

Dumb Portal Trick #3: Highlights Selected Items in Portals

Following this drill-down scenario, what if you want to give the users feedback when they select a particular category? The third set of files for this chapter show how you might highlight the item selected. Here we are providing blue highlighting on the category selected, to make clear what was chosen, and we leave that item highlighted as the user picks a product within the category. (We allow standard highlighting for the product—that is, a flash of inverted white-on-black background during the click—and additional feedback comes when all the data about that product pops into the fields above).

When the user clicks a category, we capture the name of that category (in part to trigger the product list in the neighboring portal) and then set that value in a global field over in the ProductCategories file. The category_name field is a button that launches a script called select_a_category:

```
Enter Browse Mode
Allow User Abort [ Off ]
Set Error Capture [ On ]
Set Field [ g_selected_category, ProductCategories | constant::category_name ]
Set Field [ ProductCategories | constant::g_selected_product_category,
ProductCategories | constant::category_name ]
```

In the first SetField, we put a value into the g_selected_category field in the CustomerInterest file, by performing some magic via the portal in which we show all the records from the ProductCategories file, through a constant relationship ProductCategories | constant. We take the value out of the field category_name over in ProductCategories. Which name? Well, whichever one the user clicked in the portal.

In the second Set Field we define the field we will set, which lives over in the ProductCategories file, and can be reached via the relationship ProductCategories | constant. We are pushing the value from g_selected_product_category into g_selected_category. (Both fields live in the ProductCategories file). We perform this complex round trip so that over in Product Categories, each record has its own category name, and through the global field, has access to the value that the user just selected—the category of the moment.

> **Tip from**
> *Rich*
>
> When setting or retrieving global values in a related file, you can use any relationship to that file, and you don't even have to be standing on a record that matches. Any old relationship will give you access to all the globals in the other file, irrespective of data matches.

Over in ProductCategories we create another global field, g_box, which is a Container field into which we paste a blue box. This is not a layout element. That blue box is a piece of data stored in the Global Container field.

> **Tip from**
> *Rich*
>
> Use graphic formatting to fill a field, by reducing or enlarging as much as needed, and then aligning to the top and left.

If you go over to ProductCategories and flip through the records, you'll see that the g_box field is completely filled with the box. We weren't that careful in creating the box to the exact dimensions. Instead, in the Graphic Format dialog shown in Figure 12.6, we set the graphic format for that field with the options to Reduce or Enlarge, unchecked the option to Maintain Original Proportions, and chose Left and Top alignment. These settings work all the time. (Other settings work sometimes).

Figure 12.6
You can use the Graphic Format dialog to reduce or enlarge, maintaining the original proportions, and to adjust the alignment

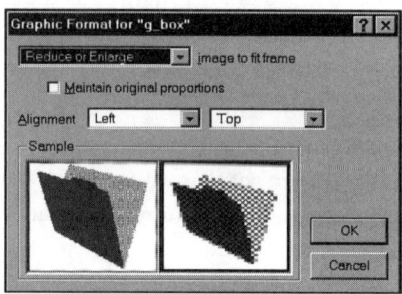

Now we have a field with a blue box. We create a Calculation field called c_selected_highlight, with a Container result. This calculation compares the category_name to the g_selected_product_category, and if they are the same, inserts the blue box grabbed from the Global field g_box. Otherwise, the field is empty. (Flip through the records in ProductCategories to see the effect).

Over in CustomerInterests, we now put the field c_selected_highlight (the calculated blue box) into the lower level of the category-list portal. The top level is the field category_name. We stack them one on top of the other in that order because if the highlighting went on top, it would block out the text. We also make sure that the category_name field on top is transparent, so the blue box will show through from underneath.

So this technique goes round robin. We start with category names from ProductCategories showing in the portal in CustomerInterests. A user clicks a row there, which resets the Global field in the ProductCategories file, and that in turn adjusts the Calculation called c_selected_highlight, which then is shown back in the same portal, at the bottom of the stack, in CustomerInterests.

> **Caution**
>
> This technique only works if the highlighted record will be visible in the portal. Whenever a user clicks out of a portal, FileMaker scrolls back to the top. If there are a lot of records in the portal, the selection will be highlighted briefly, but alas, the user will not see the special effect after clicking a product.

Dumb Portal Trick #4: Moves Records from One Portal to Another

Imagine a client who wants to rank all of a company's contacts by the amount of business each person generates. The user gets to flag a contact as Low, Medium, or High Volume. The client wants to see all the contacts in one area on the company record, and then have them sorted into three other areas, one for Low Volume, another for Medium, and a third for High.

In the Companies-l04.fp5 file, we define three fields (that do not live on any layout) to calculate three composite keys, combining the company ID, a space, and the text *Low*, *Medium*, or *High*. We are not identifying any particular person as low, medium, or high; we are just generating three keys we can use later to identify the company-cum-volume-level over in the portal. We control the key in order to control what shows up where.

The Calculation field c_low_calc_key is designed to put records into the first portal; the c_med_calc_key calculation puts records in the middle; and the c_high_calc_key calculation puts records in the right-hand portal. In each portal, we want to see only someone who has a particular volume and works within this particular company. These Calculation fields live in the Companies file, but we need something in the Contacts file to match, so we can fetch the right records for our portals.

In Contacts we create c_calc_key, a single calculation that combines the company ID, a space, and the volume attribute assigned to the contact. Now if you have a company CMP10010 and a contact who has Low volume, you get a composite key CMP10010 Low. Remarkably, that just happens to match the calculation that we already ran over in the Companies file, and therefore we can use that calculation to determine which records will show up in the first portal.

Tip from
Rich
> Fields that you create for strange relationships do not have to appear on any layout. (Or, if you have a developer layout, you could drop them there.)

As business develops with a particular contact, we need a way to be able to move a person back and forth among the categories, so we add an arrow that lets a user push a contact to an adjoining list. If you look at the arrows (see Figure 12.7), you will see that low-volume contacts can be moved up; medium-volume folks can go up or down; and high-volume people can only go downhill.

Of course, a user could go to the Contacts file, change the rating, and come back. But offering the opportunity to make the change right here adds convenience, particularly with the graphic components. The arrow interface feels more like something you can directly manipulate without going anywhere.

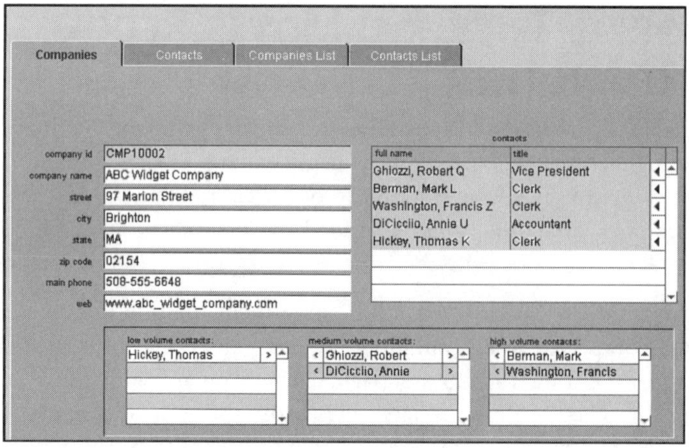

Figure 12.7
The arrows show where a user can move a contact.

The arrows act to change the value in the Volume field, and as soon as that happens, the record switches to the other portal. Then the relationship and the calculated keys take care of the rest. Hiding behind the little blue arrows are scripts such as move_contact_low_to_medium:

```
Enter Browse Mode
Allow User Abort [ Off ]
Set Error Capture [ On ]
Set Field [ contacts_low | c_calc_key::volume, "Medium" ]
Go to Field [ ]
```

The arrow is in a portal based on the relationship contacts_low |c_calc_key, so we are saying, "Through this portal's relationship, set the field volume to Medium, in the record the user just selected." FileMaker knows that is the record to modify, because it just saw the click.

Tip from
Rich

When you have a relationship, remember that can be used to push data into related records as well as to pull data out of related records. The relationship allows data to flow in both directions.

When we are in the Companies file looking at a portal showing records from the Contacts file and the user clicks an arrow, we push data from the Companies file into the Contacts file. But sometimes when you send data from one file to another, FileMaker forgets that it must update the portal itself, so Go to Field has the effect of a click, which is just enough to bring about the refresh. (We could have used Exit Record, which is like clicking a blank spot on the layout, but we wanted to show that Go to Field has a similar effect as long as you refuse to specify any particular field. Also, sometimes Go to Field works when Exit Record fails to get the refresh).

Dumb Portal Trick #5: Uses Calculated Multivalued Keys to Filter Which Child Records Show Up in the Parent Record

 Sometimes, you want to allow the user to show a subset of the related records through the portal as an alternative to the entire set. Here's how to make that happen.

In Contacts-l05.fp5, looking at a company record, we see all that company's contact folks through a portal. Sometimes, though, we don't want to see all the records. Instead, we want a subset. So here we add buttons that let us filter out a subset of the child records, showing, say, only male or female records, only sales people with low, medium, or high volumes, or only certain job titles.

On the company side, we need a relationship to show the records that we want to see in the portal. Logically, the records we want to show are based on two criteria: 1) the company ID, because we only want to see records from that company, and 2) the choice of subset, made by the user. We make a calculated key on the company side combining the company ID and a blank space and then whatever is in the global field g_show, the field in which the user picks an item from the value list.

If we look at an ordinary contact record, that person may have to show up in the portal under four different circumstances—gender, sales volume, job title, or the you-name-it-collection, "all." If on the second record the user chooses All, Male, Medium, or Vice President on the Show field, those are four separate conditions under which Robert Ghiozzi's record must be displayed in the portal (see Figure 12.8). We ask ourselves, "How do we create a match field in the Contacts file that will match four different values in the calculated key field, c_calc_key?"

Let's go over to Contacts. There we create a single calculated field with four paragraphs, c_calc_key. When FileMaker indexes a field, the index that is used for relationship purposes identifies each paragraph separately. Therefore, each paragraph inside a match field represents a separate possible match. Hence, in c_calc_key, we calculate all possible calculated keys for this record. Here is the calculation.

```
fk_company_id & " All¶" &
fk_company_id & " " & gender & "¶" &
fk_company_id & " " & volume & "¶" &
fk_company_id & " " & title
```

Tip from
Rich

> To get separate matches, include carriage returns between the potential match values. FileMaker keeps two indexes. One stores values that have been entered in Text, Number, Date, and Time fields, and Calculation with results of these types; this is the index FileMaker uses to perform finds. When indexing a Text field, each word is indexed separately. The other index includes paragraphs, to be used in relational joins. Here, FileMaker will match any sequence of words (to a maximum of 60 characters), each word having a maximum of 20 characters; it considers that sequence to be a paragraph, and stores each one as a separate index item. In the calculated key field, all we have to do is let FileMaker know that we are generating different paragraphs, and thus potentially different matches, by inserting carriage return symbols within the calculation.

Tip from
Rich

> Use a space character to separate the composite key into individual words, to fit within the 20-character-per-word limit. In calculating this multiple key, we put a blank space between the Company ID and the value from the field Show. How come? The Company ID itself takes up 8 characters. If we concatenate another word greater than 12 characters, then the total would exceed the limit of characters allowed for a word, and the index would have cut off any characters beyond the limit, resulting in an index term that would not match correctly, or worse, several keys that were the same for the first 20 characters, and lost the final characters by which they could be distinguished.

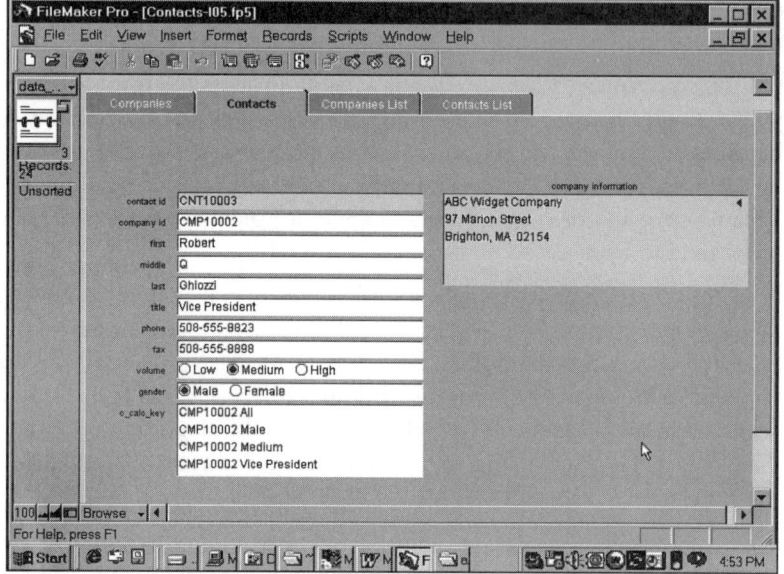

Figure 12.8
All, Male, Medium, or Vice President on the Show field, are four separate conditions under which Robert Ghiozzi's record must appear.

Dumb Portal Trick #6: Moves Portal Rows and Inserts a Portal Row

Normally, records appear in a portal in the order in which they were created, or in a sort order you specify as part of the relationship used by the portal. For instance, you may normally want to see people listed alphabetically or sales listed chronologically by date, but sometimes you want to allow items in the portal to be ordered in a way the user can choose on the fly.

EXAMPLE: WHEN A LOGIC TREE JUST WON'T GROW

We have a neighbor who sells office furniture. When he puts together a quotation, he likes to arrange the items in a particular sequence for a particular customer. He has learned that by customizing the order of items, he has a better chance of getting the order. But there is no all-purpose order, and because this decision grows out of his experience, we cannot really build a logic tree representing the choices, which depend on the personality of the customer, the type of items on the order, and the overall situation. So he needs manual control over the order in which items appear in the portal. Our sample file Companies l06.fp5 shows how you can provide that kind of user control in different circumstances.

To give the user the freedom to change the sequence, we need to have a firm grasp on the way we are ordering the records. The underlying principle is that every time we create a new record in the Contacts database, we auto-enter a value in a field called portal_row_seq_no. Each new record, then, gets an incremented serial number, so the newest record has the highest value in that field, and because the portal is sorted by that field, that record will drop to the bottom.

In the portal, we have (from left to right) diagonal arrows that let the user insert a new row above or below their row, up and down arrows that let the user move a record up or down in the sequence, and a left-pointed triangle that takes the user to the detailed version of the record (see Figure 12.9).

Figure 12.9
Arrows and triangles allow the user to insert new rows, move records up or down, or go to the details.

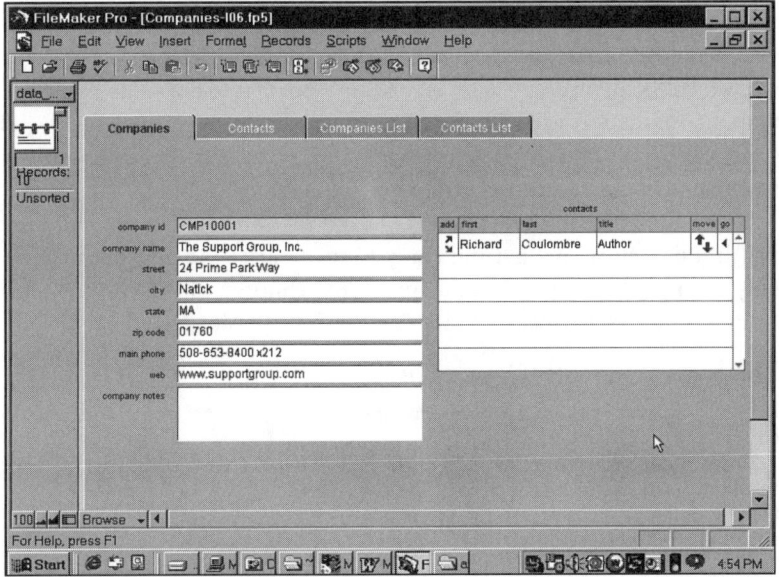

Let's look behind the up arrow first. We use a script called move_related_contact_up.

```
If [ Status( CurrentMode) = 1 ]
        Perform Script [ "beep_beep_not_in_find_mode_message" ]
                [ Sub-scripts ]
        Exit Script
End If
Enter Browse Mode
Freeze Window
If [ Status( CurrentPortalRow) = 1 ]
        Beep
```

```
                Beep
                Show Message [ Buttons: "OK", "", ""; Data: "The first row cannot be moved
                              up any further." ]
                Exit Script
End If
# "Capture the number of the current portal row minus one so that the user can be
brought back to the row that they are moving."
Set Field [ g_target_portal_row_new_position, Status( CurrentPortalRow) - 1 ]
Set Field [ contacts | constant::g_record_number, Status( CurrentPortalRow) ]
Go to Related Record [ contacts|fk_company_id ]
        [ Show only related records ]
Perform Script [ Filename: "Contacts-106.fp5", "move_contact_record_up" ]
        [ Sub-scripts ]
Go to Portal Row [ g_target_portal_row_new_position ]
        [ By Field Value..., Select entire contents ]
```

First, we check to see whether the row is the first one in the portal by looking at the status. If the status of the current portal row is 1, then we beep a few times, and tell the users they cannot move the row any higher. If we are on row 2 or later, we have to move the row. If we are moving row n up, then we are moving it into position n-1. The record for row n has a value in portal_row_seq_no that is greater than the value in the record n-1. But by scripting, we swap those values, and then when FileMaker redraws the portal, those records will have swapped positions in the sequence. The script move_related_contact_up stores a value in the Global field g_target_portal_row_new_position; the value is the current portal row's number, minus 1. That's the position we want this row to take (up 1). Then, over in the Contacts file, in a field called g_record_number, we put the value of the number of the portal row that is being moved. Then we go to the related records, using the Show option, which creates a found set in the Contacts file and the found set of the children of the current parent. In this way, we are getting ready to manipulate the field portal_row_seq_no, but we only want to change its position among the children of the current company. Then, in the Contacts file, we perform a script move_contact_record_up.

The script move_contact_record_up runs like this:

```
# "This script moves a selected portal row up one position in the portal in the
companies file."
# "The technique that we are using is as follows:
1. Each line item record has an auto-entered serial number.
2. The portal is sorted by this auto-entered serial number
(portal_row_position_value).
3. To move a record up one position, we simply swap that record's serial number
with the serial number of the previous record in the portal."
Enter Browse Mode
# "Before this script is called from the companies file, a Go To Related Record
command with the Show option puts all of the records in a found set. Therefore, we
are only working with the records that were seen in the portal."
# "Since the portal in the companies file is sorted by portal_row_position_value,
we need to sort the records here in the same way."
Perform Script [ "sort_ascend_by_portal_row_seq_no" ]
        [ Sub-scripts ]
# "After records are sorted, the current record may change. The Go to Record
command puts the script back on the record that the user has selected to move. Now
```

```
the records are in the same order as the portal, and the current record is the
record that the user has selected to move."
Go to Record/Request/Page [ g_record_number ]
        [ By Field Value... ]
# "Memorize the serial number from the record being moved."
Set Field [ g_first_portal_row_position_value, portal_row_seq_no ]
Go to Record/Request/Page
        [ Previous ]
# "Go to the previous record and memorize its serial number in a separate global
variable. Also set the serial number of this record to that of the record being
moved."
Set Field [ g_second_portal_row_position_value, portal_row_seq_no ]
Set Field [ portal_row_seq_no, g_first_portal_row_position_value ]
Go to Record/Request/Page
        [ Next ]
# "Now go back to the original record and set its serial number equal to that of
the previous record. Voila, it's done!"
Set Field [ portal_row_seq_no, g_second_portal_row_position_value ]
# "Now just do a little cleanup on the file. Find All and Unsort."
Show All Records
Unsort
```

In this script, we want to make sure that the records here in Contacts are, in fact, arranged in the same order as in the portal. The little script with the long name, sort_ascend_by_portal_row_seq_no, takes care of that. The relationship for the portal is set up to sort by portal row sequence number, and this script does the same thing in the Contacts file. Any time you sort, FileMaker takes the user back to the first record, but that isn't the one we want to work on, so now we have to tell FileMaker to go into the Contacts file and move to the same number record that the user just clicked over in the Companies file. If the user clicked row 4 in Companies, we want to pick record number 4 in Contacts as the current record. Because the found set in Contacts matches the records in the portal and those records are sorted in the same way, we can presume that we have found the same record.

Now, we want to swap the value in the portal_row_seq_no in Contacts with the value in the same field in the previous record. To start, we memorize the value in the field portal_row_seq_no by putting it into the global field g_first_portal_row_position_value. Then we capture the value of the field portal_row_seq_no by putting it into the global field g_second_portal_row_seq_position value. Now that we have captured both values, we can set the value in the second record equal to the value we grabbed from the first record. Then we go to the next record and set its value equal to the one we grabbed from the second record. We started on record n, went to the previous record, or n-1, and then we go to the next record, or n. Now the position numbers have been swapped. As soon as FileMaker refreshes the portal, the record is "moved" up or down.

Our next job is to insert a new record. Traditionally, a new record appears at the bottom of the portal. The user would then have to move that record up, up, up to the right location. Better to offer the user a button that moves that bottom row up to the right location. So we added diagonal arrows and said, "If someone clicks the upward diagonal arrow, meaning, insert a row at the position above row n, then the desired position is n, and the current record will be shoved down a row, to become row n+1. And if a user clicks the arrow pointing diagonally down, the current record will retain its position, but the new record will land in the position n+1." So in the Companies file, we wrote a script called `insert_related_contact_above`.

```
If [ Status( CurrentMode) = 1 ]
      Perform Script [ "beep_beep_not_in_find_mode_message" ]
            [ Sub-scripts ]
      Exit Script
End If
Enter Browse Mode
Freeze Window
Set Field [ contacts | constant::g_new_record_position, Status( CurrentPortalRow) ]
Set Field [ contacts | constant::g_temp_fk_company_id, pk_company_id ]
Go to Related Record [ contacts|fk_company_id ]
      [ Show only related records ]
Perform Script [ Filename: "Contacts-106.fp5", "insert_contact_record" ]
      [ Sub-scripts ]
Enter Browse Mode
```

This operation would make no sense in Find mode, so we trap for mode right away, and if someone is in Find, we run the subscript that beeps and waves them off, telling them they can't do this operation when in Find mode. We exit the current script at that point, at the end of the IF test, on the theory that continuing would be crazy.

Tip from *Rich*	Be careful about the difference between Exit Script and Halt Script. Exit Script terminates the current script. Any other scripts that are running (calling this subscript, for instance) will continue. Halt Script, on the other hand, stops this script and every other script that is running anywhere. You might think of Halt Script as "Achtung! Stop All Scripts!"

To get ready for the work we are going to do, we go to Browse mode and freeze the screen that way. (Basically, we want to prevent a lot of screen flicker, flash, and redraw).

We go to the Contacts file, and set the global field `g_new_record_position` equal to the row position that the new record should occupy. The second Set Field tells the Contacts file, "When you create that record, you need to assign that record to this Company ID," putting the ID into the Global field `g_temp_fk_company_id`. We are therefore passing two values over to the Contacts file, one identifying the new record's row position, and the other the parent for the new record.

Having set up the new record, we go to the related records, because in the Contacts file we want to create a found set of records matching those in the *current* portal.

Now, we perform the script `insert_contact_record` in Contacts, to create the record and move it to the right location.

```
Enter Browse Mode
New Record/Request
Set Field [ fk_company_id, g_temp_fk_company_id ]
Set Field [ g_temp_pk_contact_id, pk_contact_id ]
Loop
```

```
            Perform Script [ "sort_ascend_by_portal_row_seq_no" ]
                    [ Sub-scripts ]
            Go to Related Record [ Contacts | pk_contact_id ]
Exit Loop If [ g_new_record_position = Status( CurrentRecordNumber) ]
            # "Memorize the serial number from the record being moved."
            Set Field [ g_first_portal_row_position_value, portal_row_seq_no ]
            Go to Record/Request/Page
                    [ Previous ]
            # "Go to the previous record and memorize its serial number in a separate
global variable. Also set the serial number of this record to that of the record
being moved."
            Set Field [ g_second_portal_row_position_value, portal_row_seq_no ]
            Set Field [ portal_row_seq_no, g_first_portal_row_position_value ]
            Go to Record/Request/Page
                    [ Next ]
            # "Now go back to the original record and set its serial number equal to
that of the previous record. Voila, it's done!"
            Set Field [ portal_row_seq_no, g_second_portal_row_position_value ]
End Loop
# "Now just do a little cleanup on the file. Find All and Unsort."
Show All Records
Unsort
```

This script creates a new record, auto-entering the next value into the field `portal_row_seq_no`. By definition, that value will be the largest in the field anywhere in the database, so this record must end up last in the portal (where records are sorted by this field). Now that the record exists in the wrong position, we need to move it. We set the `fk_company_id` field value equal to the Company ID we captured in the global field `g_temp_fk_company_id`, so the record knows who its parent is. We then capture the `pk_contact_id`, the Primary key value, in a global field called `g_temp_pk_contact_id` because, in a moment, we are going to perform looping, and we will need a way to get back to the record we are moving, and the Primary key value is the best way to locate that record.

Now, we enter the looping section of the script. We go through a set of steps moving our new record up one position for each loop, in somewhat the same way that we moved a contact record up or down one position. We loop through until the moment when the new record is in the position that we placed in the global field over in the companies file, `g_new_record_position`.

The loop takes the found set of records in the same order as the portal records, using the script `sort_ascend_by_portal_row_seq_no`.

Tip from
Rich

> Put sorts into a separate script, with a meaningful name. Having your sorts saved in a separate script makes the script self-documenting. Normally, when you look in ScriptMaker, you see the command Sort [Restore, No Dialog], but you see nothing else to tell you what things are being sorted by. By performing a script that has an easily understood name, you can look at the script name to recall exactly how it is going to sort your records.

After a sort, FileMaker makes the first record the current record. So we go to the related records, using a self-join (more on that in the next chapter). Essentially, this step says, "Go to the record where `pk_contact_id` matches `g_temp_pk_contact_id`." This step ensures that the new record will become the active record. We check to see whether the record number of the current record does, in fact, match the position we wanted. If so, we exit the loop. If not, the looping continues, copying the portal row sequence number from the new record and from the previous record, and then swapping those values. Then we go back through the loop again, resorting by portal row sequence number, in effect moving our new record up one position. We keep looping until our portal row number hits the target position.

> **Tip from**
> *Rich*
>
> Make sure that you bring people back, after running a subscript in another file. If you go back and look at the `insert_related_contact_above` in the Companies file, you'll see a weird Enter Browse step, at which point you may have wondered, "What the heck is this doing here?" If the last step in the Companies script were the Perform Script over in Contacts, then when that script was done, the user would be left over in the Contacts file. By putting a benign command like Enter Browse Mode after that script, we force FileMaker to come back to the Companies file.

Dumb Portal Trick #7: Allows the User to Choose the Sort Order in a Portal

Records come to a portal through a relationship, and the relationship may have its own sort order, so the records in a portal usually appear sorted in one way, and only one way. But sometimes a customer wants to sort the records in some other way or several ways, and in addition, wants to pick that sort order on the fly. Here's another way to make that flexibility possible.

In Companies-l07, the user can sort contacts by first name, last name, title, or gender, just by clicking a blue icon at the top of the column (see Figure 12.10).

In the Contacts file, we place a field called `c_sort_portal_by`, which has this calculation:

```
Case(
g_sort_by = "Unsorted", pk_contact_id,
g_sort_by = "first_name", first,
g_sort_by = "last_name", last,
g_sort_by = "title", title,
g_sort_by = "gender", gender
)
```

The Global field `g_sort_by` in the Contacts file gets information when a user clicks a column sort button in the region just above the portal in the Companies file. For instance, when a user clicks First, the script says, "Put the name `first_name` into the field `g_sort_by` over in the Contacts file." As soon as the value in `g_sort_by` is updated, FileMaker launches a recalculation of our calculation because it uses this value. Now the field c_sort_portal_by has a value that matches the value first_name in every record. The portal is sorted by the c_sort_portal_by field, so in essence, the records in the portal end up being sorted by first names.

Figure 12.10
The icon at the top of the column lets the user sort contacts by first name, last name, title, or gender.

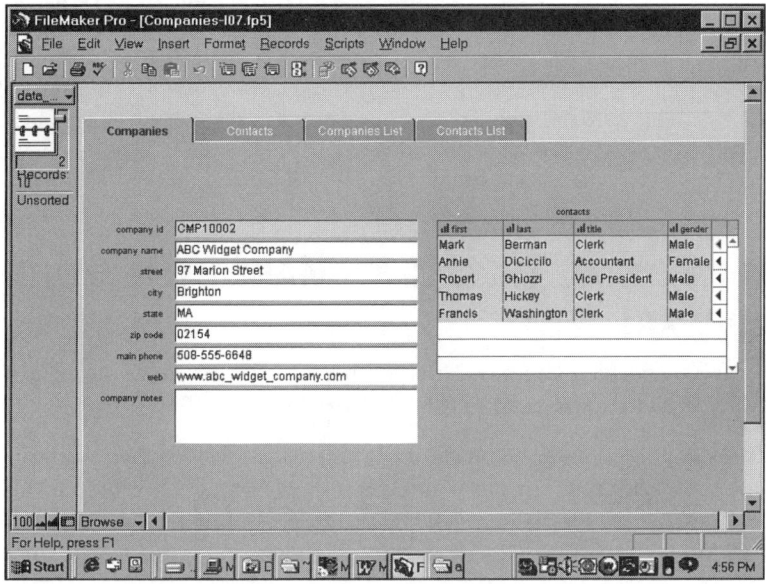

Let's look at one of the four scripts over in the Companies file that set the value for g_sort_by. (All four scripts are identical, except for their names!) You might expect to set the field g_sort_by in Contacts equal to the value in the field first_name. But we use this trick. Let's say we create the first script, sort_portal_by_first_name:

```
Enter Browse Mode
Set Field [ contacts | constant::g_sort_by, Middle(Status( CurrentScriptName) ,
16, 99 ) ]
Set Field [ pk_company_id, pk_company_id ]
```

Instead of setting the field g_sort_by equal to a hard-coded text string, we set it equal to 99 characters grabbed from the 16th character forward in the name of the script itself, using the CurrentScriptName function. (99 characters just grab plenty of characters; there is no magic to the number itself). Now all we have to do is change the name of the script to get different output. (Of course, if a client changes a script name, this automation goes to hell). This is just an easy way to use the same script in a number of different circumstances.

> **Caution**
> Automation relying on the name of a script may not be a good practice, because someone else might change that script name without realizing the impact on automation. We are just showing this trick because it is cool—if you are careful.

Tip from
Marc Norman

> You can force a portal to update by setting the primary key equal to itself. The second `SetField` command in the script seems nonsensical. In the current record, we set the Primary key equal to the Primary key. Why waste time doing this? Because this script is setting a value over in the Contacts file, in `g_sort_by`, and in turn `g_sort_by` triggers a recalculation in the field `c_sort_portal_by`. And because we have this circular process where we look at a portal with values from another file, and adjust a value referenced by fields over there, we need to make sure that FileMaker is aware that it must redraw the portal after all of our acrobatics. Setting the Primary key equal to itself causes FileMaker to redraw the portal.

DUMB PORTAL TRICK #8: MAKES THE PORTAL DISAPPEAR!

Poof! The portal goes away. Now, when you first hear about this idea, you probably think: "Why would anyone want to turn the portal invisible?"

Think conditional, as the inventor of this trick, Marc Norman suggests. Sometimes, you have information or buttons you want to show at times then hide at other times. You could use one layout with the item, and one without, and switch between those layouts using some kind of automation. But sometimes we don't have the luxury of running a script. We may want the appearance and disappearance to be based on data the user has just entered. That's when you want to be able to make the portal appear and disappear, depending on what the user does.

In this approach, the data actually goes away. It not only becomes invisible, it really dissolves. With a button, for instance, you can make it appear or disappear by using a Calculation field with a container result. But if the user happens to click in that area of the window, even when no button is visible, the user gets the feedback showing the button has been clicked. Our technique here avoids that problem.

Basically, we are using a portal to hold the information that we want to make appear and disappear. The crux of the technique lies in a reasonable approach taken by FileMaker's designers: If the relationship driving the portal does not match, then FileMaker does not create the portal (and therefore nothing shows up).

In Contacts-l08 we have a check box that allows the user to choose whether to show (or hide) related company information. When the user checks "Show related Company information," the portal appears, showing details from the parent record, and when the user unchecks that button, the portal goes away. (And afterward, if you click in the area where the portal was, you do not get the kind of highlighting indicating that an object has been selected.)

We're using a calculated key to perform this sleight of hand. The relationship is based on the company ID, and on the value in the check box field (checked or not checked, which is to say, "show related Company information" or nothing). In the field `c_calc_key` we concatenate the Company ID with the value in the field show_related_Company_information. Therefore, c_calc_key will end up with one of two possible values: the Company ID by itself, or the Company ID plus the text "show related Company information."

Over in the Companies file, we create another field called c_calc_key, which combines the Company ID and the words "show related Company information." But here we have no button.

If the box is checked in Contacts, then c_calc_key equals the company ID plus the button text, and that exactly matches the value in c_calc_key back in the Companies file, and so FileMaker enables the portal and the records appear, along with the graphics.

In Contacts, if the box is not checked, FileMaker looks at the relationship based on the c_calc_key, and sees that the field in Contacts contains only a Company ID, which does not match the field of the same name over in Companies, because that contains the Company ID plus the text (all the time). FileMaker says, "There are no matching records, so I won't show this portal at all."

Tip from
Marc Norman

You can use a disappearing portal to show or hide buttons. In this example, the technique shows related data, but you can use the technique to have a button or set of buttons appear and disappear. For instance, you might want a button to appear only when the user has typed a particular value in a field. By putting a calculated key behind the scene, you can look at the value the user just entered to determine whether or not to make the portal come to life, displaying the buttons.

Tip from
Marc Norman

You can make fields appear and disappear the same way. If the user chooses Married in the Marital Status field, you can cause a portal to come to life with fields for Spouse's Name and Spouse's Date of Birth. In essence, you are showing these fields conditionally.

If you are in Contacts, with the company information showing, and click anywhere in the portal, the whole portal area is highlighted because FileMaker figures you want to select the whole portal.

To go behind the scenes, go to Layout, select the portal (not a field inside it), and then choose Portal on the Format menu and look at status area and the dialog box (see Figure 12.11).

Figure 12.11
When a portal is selected, the Portal dialog shows that we have chosen to show one row, no vertical scroll bars, and no alternating pattern.

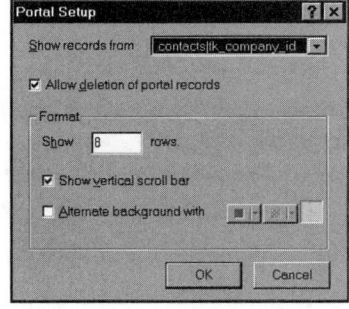

You'll notice we have chosen to show one row, no vertical scroll bars, and no alternating pattern. Over on the left in the status area, you'll see that the fill pattern is set to transparent and the border is set to none. In this way, we make the portal almost invisible. (We do draw a box inside the portal region as a way to tie the information together, but the box is part of the content of the portal and comes and goes with the portal, which itself has no border and no background—making it easier to get rid of. If you include a border with a portal, then the border shows up even when there are no related records, and you get a weird empty box on the layout with nothing inside. Similarly, if you put in a background fill, it will show up even if the portal rows do not appear. Essentially, the visual aspects of the portal always show up, whether or not the data is there (so we make those aspects, well, invisible). See Figures 12.12 and 12.13 to show the way the portal appears and disappears.

Figure 12.12
The portal appears....

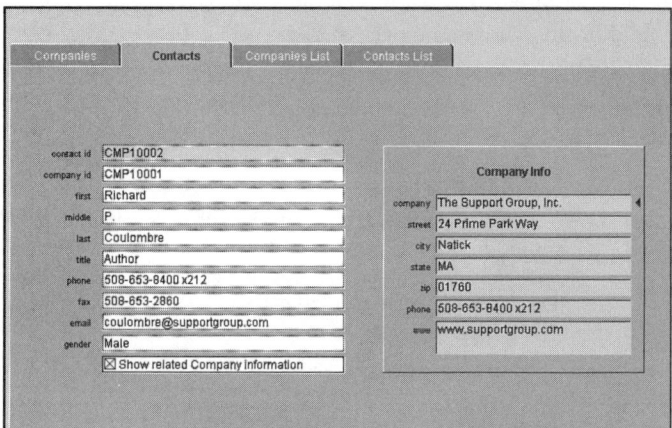

Figure 12.13
The portal disappears....

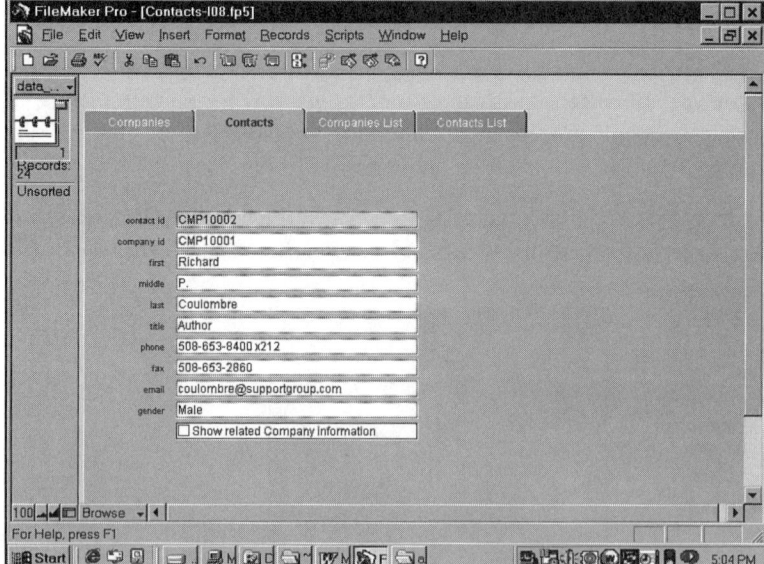

Dumb Portal Trick #9: Uses a Portal to Control Access to Records in Another File

Some customers want their staff to see but not manipulate whole swatches of data. Or the boss wants to control record-level access, allowing only certain staff members to edit particular records. Or the boss wants to control what operations a staff member can perform on some records, but not on others. For these situations, we suggest an access file, such as SalesViewer-l09.fp5, which has only one record, built to show the user the sales data that lives over in Sales-l09.fp5. In a real implementation, we would probably use passwords to define different access levels for the two files.

Another situation in which an access file might prove useful is a user trying to look at a big database over a slow connection. Imagine you have a FileMaker database with a half million records, and a user needs to access the database over a 28.8 connection. Just opening the file across that kind of Internet connection could be painful. Instead, we might want to put a small file on the user's computer and manipulate the keys to control what records have to be displayed so that we just draw down the data without a lot of scripts, formatting material, graphics, and unnecessary records. An access file might offer you a way to improve performance.

In Sales Viewer, we present a particular user with a simple viewer file (see Figure 12.14). The user can search, sort, and edit records through this file. In this example we let the user see all the records, but you could also lock out certain records if you wanted to. Hint: Here, the user chooses which sales rep to show. But you could set that value behind the scenes, so that an individual user could only view his or her own records.

Figure 12.14
The Sales Viewer lets a user search, sort, or edit records.

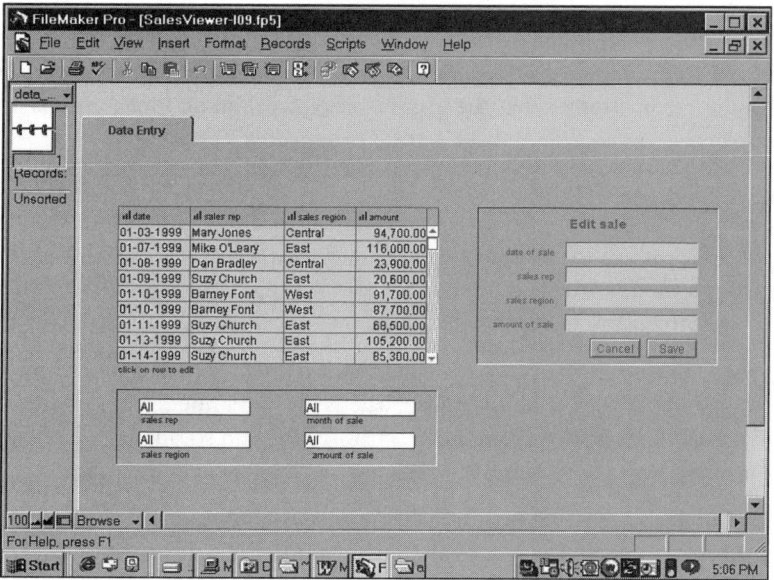

Filtering the Records

The portal in the Sales Viewer file shows a portal on the left. Below it are pop-up buttons that let the user choose whether to view all the records in a particular category or just the records in a particular subcategory. Users can make choices from several pop-up menus, filtering the records so that only records meeting all the criteria show up in the portal. For example, if a user says, "Show me all the sales from the East region in the month of February, with volumes over $100K," then the only records that appear are the ones that satisfy all three criteria. Thus, there is an implied AND between the choices.

→This technique resembles the approach in I05 –CalcMultikeys; **see** "Dumb Portal Trick #5: Uses Calculated Multivalued Keys to Filter Which Child Records Show Up in the Parent Record," **p. 405.**

In `SalesViewer`, `c_calc_key` puts together several components like this:

```
g_sales_rep & " " & g_sales_region & " " & g_sales_month & " " & g_sales_amount
```

We grab the values from four global fields and stick them together with spaces in between. The global fields are the four pop-up fields: g_sales_rep, g_sales_region, g_sale_month, and g_sale_amount.

Now we go over to Sales, and create a similar Calculation field, c_calc_key, which says

```
g_sales_rep & " " & g_sales_region & " " & g_sales_month & " " & g_sales_amount.
```

You'll see the results in Sales if you look at the data entry screen. We apply four different filters to determine whether a record should appear. For each filter, the record should show up if the user has chosen All, or if the user has chosen a value that matches the value in the record. Essentially, for each criterion, there are two possible answers. Thus, we have 16 possible combinations to account for. The calculation deals with all potential matches with the user's choices over on the other side.

The structure of the calculation, which follows, deals with these combinations one at a time. To start off: If the user has chosen All, we want the record to show up. We need four Alls to handle the possibility that the user has chosen All in all four pop-ups or left the default Alls in place.

The following sections deal with all possible combinations that include the sales_rep. We deal with the situation when a user has made a single choice plus three Alls; two choices and two Alls; three choices and one All; and finally, four choices (no Alls at all). We walk through the four fields in the same order in which we captured the values over in Sales Viewer, to ensure matching.

Wrinkles: Rather than take the full month name, we grab the first three letters of the month name, in both files. The amount of sale is just a number, but we have chosen to put those numbers in clumps, such as 0-50K, 50K-100K, and so on, using the calculation c_amount_of_sale to identify which clump the record belongs to.

Essentially, we are creating 16 different paragraphs that will match the 16 different conditions under which this record should appear in the Sales portal over in the Sales Viewer file.

```
"All All All All¶¶" &

sales_rep & " All All All¶" &
"All " & sales_region & " All All¶" &
"All All " & Left(MonthName(date_of_sale),3) & " All¶" &
"All All All " & c_amount_of_sale & "¶¶" &

sales_rep & " " & sales_region & " All All¶" &
sales_rep & " All " & Left(MonthName(date_of_sale),3) & " All¶" &
sales_rep & " All All " & c_amount_of_sale & "¶" &
"All " & sales_region & " " & Left(MonthName(date_of_sale),3) & " All¶" &
"All " & sales_region & " All " & c_amount_of_sale & "¶" &
"All All " & Left(MonthName(date_of_sale),3) & " " & c_amount_of_sale & "¶¶" &

sales_rep & " " & sales_region & " " & Left(MonthName(date_of_sale),3) & " All¶" &
sales_rep & " " & sales_region & " All " & c_amount_of_sale & "¶" &
sales_rep & " All " & Left(MonthName(date_of_sale),3) & " " & c_amount_of_sale & "¶" &
"All " & sales_region & " " & Left(MonthName(date_of_sale),3) & " " & c_amount_of_sale & "¶¶" &

sales_rep & " " & sales_region & " " & Left(MonthName(date_of_sale),3) & " " & c_amount_of_sale
```

Now the four pop-ups back in SalesViewer determine what will show up in the portal. At the top of the portal, we have sort buttons like those in the l07-PortalSort example.

→ To find out more about buttons for sorting, **see** "Dumb Portal Trick #7: Allows the User to Choose the Sort Order in a Portal," **p. 412.**

Tip from
Rich

> Protect your data. In this example, users could simply open up the Sales file and mess up the data. But in real life, the Sales file would be open to a layout that is password-protected to prevent users from changing the data.

ALLOWING USERS TO EDIT

Over on the right, there is a dimmed-out area called Edit Sales. How does a user edit a sale? The user clicks on the record in the portal, which takes the user to another layout in which the portal itself is dimmed, but the Edit Sales area comes alive. Now the user can edit the record, click Save, and return to the layout that shows the portal in its full glory.

During the moment after the first click, we use the highlight technique, described in our discussion of l03-PortalRowSelect. We dim all the rows in the portal to indicate that they are not usable right now. The Edit Sales area comes to life with its four fields. We could have let people operate directly on the original records. But some clients want to be able to Cancel changes, or Save them, rather than having FileMaker make the changes right away (as soon as a user clicks out of the field). Therefore, we made up global fields and created a script that takes the field values from the selected record for date of sale, sales region, amount of sale, and sales rep, and placed those in the global fields shown in the Edit Sales area. When a user clicks Save, we grab those values, and put them into the matching fields in the selected record, clear out the globals so they are ready to use again (a safety precaution), and return the user to the main interface. If a user clicks Cancel, we just clear out the global fields and bring the user back to the main interface.

The other benefit of forcing the user to go to a new layout is that we can control via scripts which records the user can edit and which records the user cannot touch. Users can look at any record, but we can lock a few records, using logic that says, "If this record has been locked, display a message telling the user, 'You cannot edit this record.'"

In conclusion, we hope we have expanded your idea of portals. These tricks all grew out of an effort to respond to repeated requests from our customers. In solving their problems, we discovered that we could use portals for more than showing related data. Portals can act as user interface devices, to improve the user's experience:

- Making the database more convenient for the user, requiring fewer trips from one file to another
- Letting the user move rows around to control the order
- Letting users change the way records are sorted
- Letting the user avoid extra typing or choosing from value lists, because we already offer the data in various slices on the record

Caution

Just because you can pull off a trick does not mean that your customer really needs it. Please consider these techniques as options for responding to customer requests, not for imagining what customers would want, if they only knew.

CHAPTER 13

THE JOYS OF SELF-JOINS AND OTHER INTERESTING RELATIONSHIPS

In this chapter

The Miracle of a Self-Join   422

Assembly-Subassembly, a.k.a. the Hamburger Example   426

Many to Many to Many   431

An Outer Join   435

THE MIRACLE OF A SELF-JOIN

When we first think about relationships, we generally imagine a parent-child pair as separate files, such as a company and its invoices. And, yes, usually the parent and child are different entities. But there are times when you may want the parent and the children to represent the same kind of entity. For example, in a database holding employee information, there could be a parent-child relationship from a manager to the employees reporting to that manager, even though the parent record and the child records all belong to the same file, Employees. You could make the argument that the managers ought to go into their own file, and the employees in another. But if you have exactly the same fields on these records, what's the benefit of putting them into separate files?

And what if you have multiple levels of management and employees? Do you then create a file for each level of management? And if so, when you want to look up an employee's record, which file do you look in?

The purpose of a relationship is not to link one file with another file, but to link a record with another record. If you need to link one record to another and they both have exactly the same fields, what reason would you have to create a separate file if you can manage that relationship through the miracle of a self-join? A self-join is a relationship between one set of records inside a file and another set of records in the same file.

In Employees-M01.fp5, we have a database with three enterable fields—the name of the employee, the job title, and the ID of the manager. Another field is the employee ID, which is auto-entered by FileMaker. But the data entry screen (see Figure 13.1) displays a whole lot more than those four fields, thanks to the self-relationship diagrammed in Figure 13.2. On each employee's record, you can see four portals, showing a list of "My Employees," if any, "My Management" (people who are above me in the hierarchy), "People who work for the same manager (including me)," and "People who work for the same manager (not including me)." The manager, in this scheme, is the first person immediately above me in the organization.

Figure 13.1
An employee in the middle of the organization has people above and below.

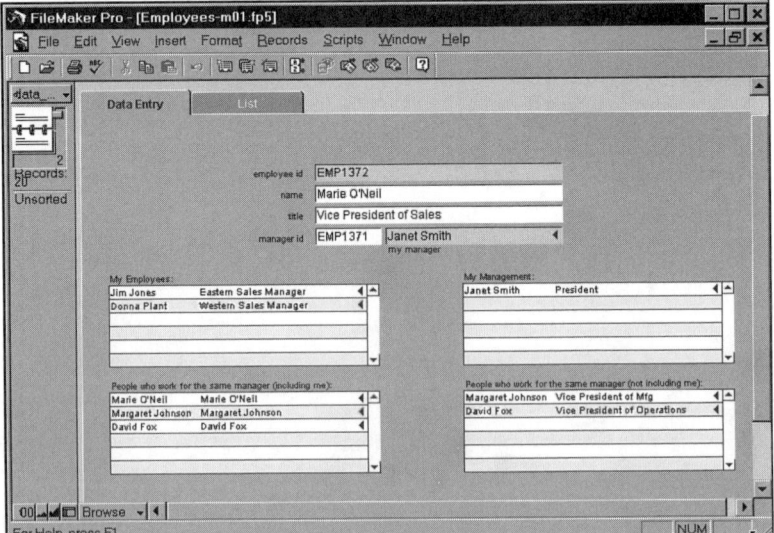

Figure 13.2
The employee file has a one-to-many relationship with itself. Can this be legal?

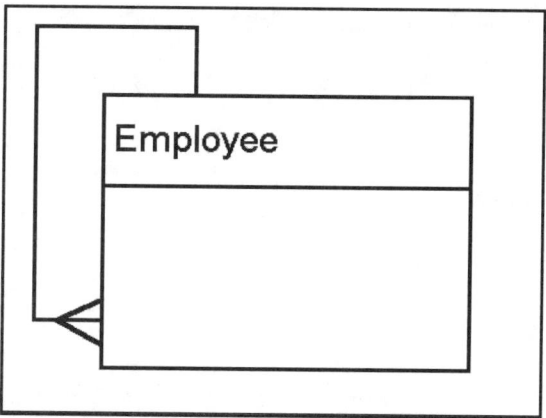

> **Caution**
>
> We are assuming a traditional organization in this example. In this old-fashioned world, an employee who is a manager may have many other employees working for him or her, but reports to only one manager. Thus, a record may have many children, but can have only one parent. A contemporary organization with multiple reporting relationships could not be handled in this way.

Let's look at the portals first. If we are looking at Jim Jones' record, we want to see all the employees who have identified him as their boss. How do we know who they are? Each of his employee's records will have his ID in the field for their manager. As shown in Figure 13.3, when an employee ID on the left matches a manager ID on the right, we display the records in the portal. (This relationship is the mirror image of the one that pulls in data above, in the field showing My Manager, as shown in Figure 13.4.)

Figure 13.3
The Edit Relationship dialog for my_direct_employees.

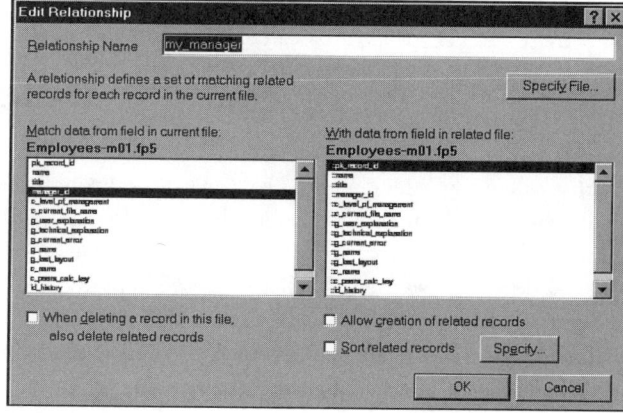

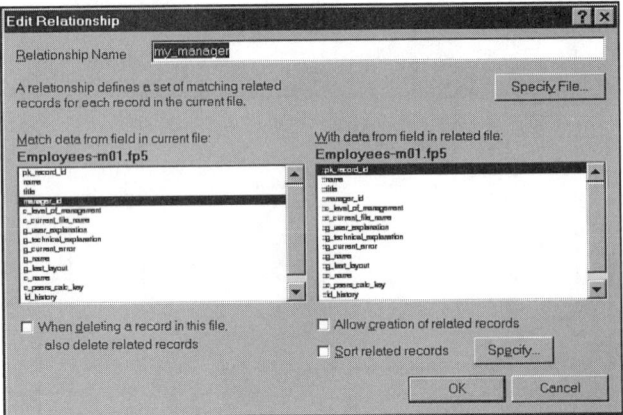

Figure 13.4
The Edit Relationship dialog for my_manager.

Essentially, we are playing with different combinations of match fields on the right and left.

The next portal shows everyone who works for the same boss as the employee whose record we are on. How do we identify those fellow employees? Well, they all have my manager's ID in their manager ID field; we are looking at all the children of the same parent, and displaying those records on the child side.

The third portal (on the bottom right) shows all the other children of the same parent, without including the record owner (everyone but me). We are not using a traditional relationship to make this work. Instead, we use a technique we looked at in the last chapter, putting multiple keys into a field to control what shows up in the portal.

→If you want to see how to use calculated multi-valued keys to filter which child records show up in the parent record, **see** "Dumb Portal Trick #5," **p. 405.**

The question we are trying to answer is "How can we get a list of all of the IDs of all of the other related children?" For that, we turn to a neat function called ValueListItems, which lets you bring back the value list for use in a calculation. In c_peers_calc_key we run this calculation:

```
Substitute(ValueListItems( "Employees-m01.fp5", "my_peers") & "¶", pk_record_id & "¶", "")
```

We create a value list called my_peers, which gives us values through the relationship that we used to populate the portal that shows people who work for the same manager (including me). In the calculation, we say, "Give us the IDs of all the employees who have the same manager ID as I do." We use the value list from the field my_peers, which shows me and my peers. To get rid of me, we use the Substitute command, which looks at the Primary key for this record, adds a carriage return at the end of the value list, and finds my ID, followed by a carriage return, and substitutes an absolute nothing for that ID. Now we have a carriage-return separated list of all of my peers, minus me.

> **Tip from**
> *Rich*
>
> Use carriage returns to clean up. When I first did this calculation, I just said "Find the Primary key and replace it with nothing," which worked just fine most of the time. But occasionally there was a hole in the middle of the items, where the nothing had landed. That offended my sense of aesthetics. By using the carriage return technique described in the chapter on calculations, I was able to get rid of the blank spots.

→ To see how adding carriage returns to the data can help you avoid accidental gaps in your results, **see** "Using the `PatternCount` Function to Spot Values," **p. 289.**

Now that we have the c_peers_calc_key calculated, we use that field on the left-hand side of the relationship, matching the Primary key for the record, to pull out the correct records for the portal (see Figure 13.5). When the list of IDs of records in c_peers_calc_key matches the Primary keys of the records in the file, we bring those records up in the portal.

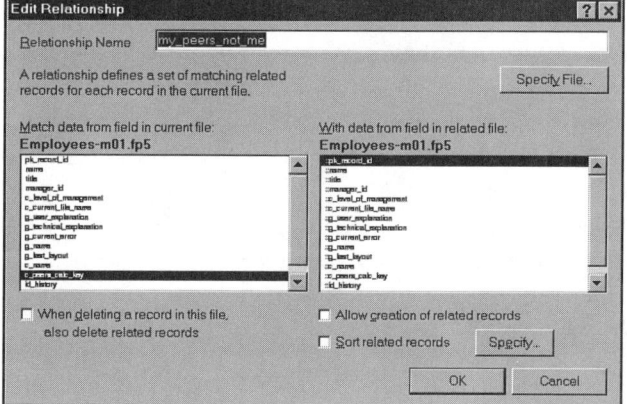

Figure 13.5
Creating the relationship my_peers_not_me.

In the My Management portal, we want to see everyone who ranks above the person the record is about, ranked in the order of importance. To achieve this, we have to do some complicated jiu-jitsu. We use the same trick we used in "People who work for the same manager (not including me)"—creating a field that will hold the IDs of all candidate records we want to appear in that portal. Imagine Noah is a 4th level employee with three levels of management above, so we need to get the IDs of all three of those managers into a single field. So we dreamt up the history of the ID, recording my manager's ID, and the ID of his or her manager, and the ID of that person's manager. There is a field in each record called id_history, which equals my manager's history, plus a carriage return, and my own ID. In turn, my manager's history equals his or her own manager's ID. In this way we pile up a vast history of managerial IDs for low-level employees.

> **Caution**
>
> At first, we tried to make the id_history directly equal to the id_history of the manager, and FileMaker refused to do so, because that would become a circular reference, setting the field ID history equal to the field id_history, even though that field was in another record. To get around that impasse, we created a field called parent_id_history that equals

> the id_history through the relationship to the parent record. Then we take the value from the field called parent_id_history, and we add a carriage return and the ID of the current record. For some reason, this gets around FileMaker's objection to circular references.

This recursive building of a calculation by building up the IDs of parents and children works well in FileMaker Pro 5 (although it would not work in earlier versions of FileMaker Pro). Now we create a relationship for the portal called My Management, from the field called parent_id_history to the field employee_id, and because the parent_id_history has the grand collection of IDs for all managers going up and up, above me, those records show up in the portal, revealing the names of my management chain.

How, now, do we determine the order in which the various bosses should show up? At first glance, the data does not say who is more important than someone else. If we count the number of words in a person's management history, though, that can give us a clue as to what level that person lives on. A low-level employee would have a lot more words than the president, because the president has only her own ID. The VP has her own ID, plus that of the President. Therefore, we can look at the id_history field and derive a number indicating what level someone is within the hierarchy. We calculated the words in c_level_of_management, which is simply WordCount (id_history). The portal for My Management is defined to sort by c_level_of_management.

You might find this last trick useful when dealing with hierarchies, where you need to show more than one level of the hierarchy on each record. This is just one area in which you can see the odd usefulness of self-joins. Sometimes, we use them for genuine data, but sometimes we use them for automation, interface, or just plain fun.

Assembly-Subassembly, a.k.a. the Hamburger Example

Imagine that you work for a burger joint. Big semis pull up with raw materials like cheese slices, hamburger patties, pickles, onions, ketchup, mustard, and sesame-seed buns. The cooks combine those ingredients to make the mega burger, the double-mega burger, and other specialties. But the mega burger is itself part of the special mega meal, which is made up of the mega burger, an order of fries, and a large drink. We have a hierarchy of fast food here. Items at the lower end of the food chain all go into other items, but items in the middle of the food chain have a double life: they are made out of other things, and in addition they drop into other, larger entities such as the mega meal. At the very top, with something like the mega meal, we have a tray full of stuff made from other identifiable items, but no one uses the mega meal to build something even grander. The top items, then, never become components of anything else, while the bottom items always end up as components, because the store doesn't sell individual slices of cheese at the drive-through.

Because the items in the middle are made out of other components, and in turn may become components in some larger product, such as the mega meal, the Components file has a many-to-many relationship with itself. This is, of course, illegal in conservative states such as Massachusetts, Virginia, and Tennessee.

Assembly-Subassembly, a.k.a. the Hamburger Example

We start with the Components file in the m02 folder having a many-to-many relationship with itself (see Figure 13.6). Unless you have dealt with this kind of situation before, you may find this self-join hard to grasp. Another way to think of this situation is to develop it as a traditional many-to-many relationship, as shown in Figure 13.7. Having defined the relationship as many-to-many, we then insert a join file as shown in Figure 13.8, imagining two versions of the Components file (just to sort things out in our head). Finally, at the end of our design process, we collapse the two imaginary versions of the Components file back into it, recognizing that it is really a single entity, as shown in Figure 13.9. The result is two distinct one-to-many relationships, each going from the Components file to the Components Roster.

Figure 13.6
Components with a many-to-many relationship to itself.

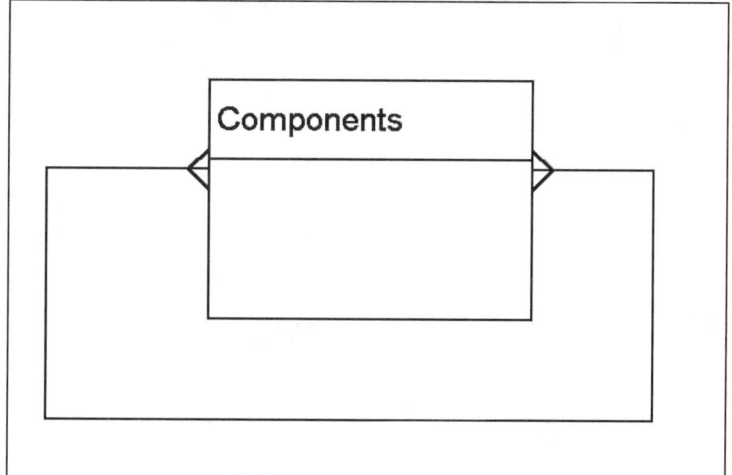

Figure 13.7
Components with multiple relationships in both directions.

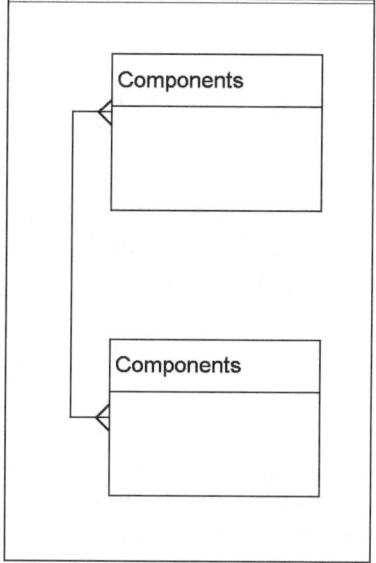

Figure 13.8
A Components Roster forms a join file in the middle.

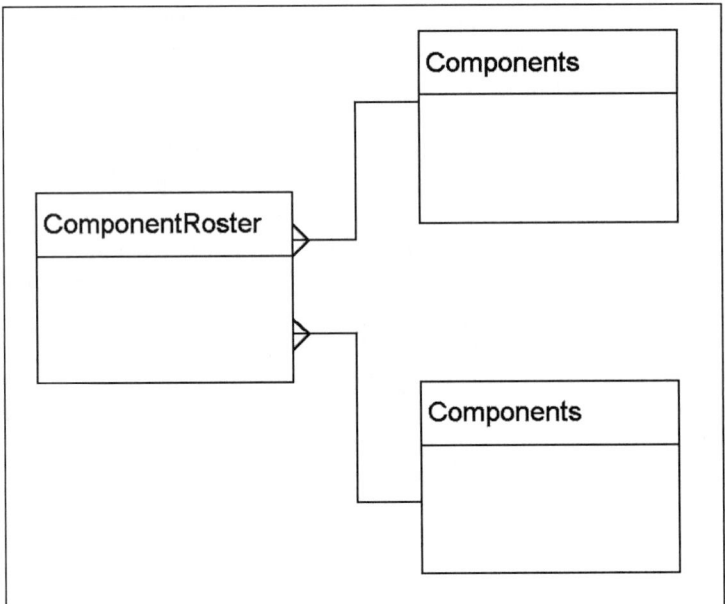

Figure 13.9
Components has two one-to-many relationships with Components Roster.

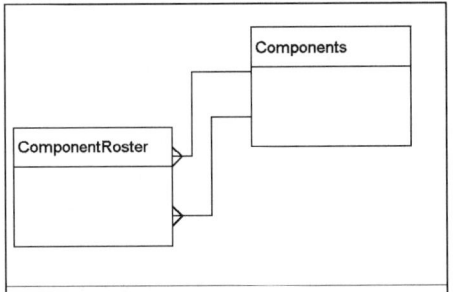

The many symbol is attached twice to the Components Roster file, meaning that there are two Foreign keys there, taken from the Components file. One is the ID of the item being made, and the other is the ID of the item used to make it.

Because the Components file has two one-to-many relationships with the Components Roster file, we can create two portals in Components. One shows all of the items that the record item is made from, and the second portal shows all the items this particular item is used to make.

The first portal, showing what the record item is made from, shows all the items from the Components Roster file where the record ID of this item matches the ID of the id_of_item_to_make over in the Components Roster file. In the Edit Relationship dialog (see Figure 13.10), we are saying, "Go to Components Roster file and find all the records describing the components used to put me together, and then show the IDs of each item, along with the name, quantity, unit price, and extended price."

Figure 13.10
Edit Relationship dialog showing the relationship I_am_made_from, which sets up a one-to-many relationship with `ComponentRoster`.

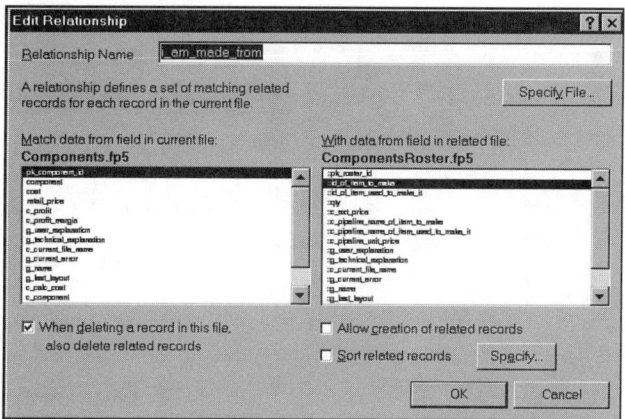

In the second portal, on each item's record, we want to see all the other items this item is used in, (see Figure 13.11). In the Edit Relationship dialog, as shown in Figure 13.12, we create the relationship that says, "Show me all the records where my record ID appears in the field id_of_item_used_to_make_it in the Components Roster file," which should bring back all the records showing the bundles, meals, or packages of which the current item is a component.

Figure 13.11
A sample data-entry record in Components.

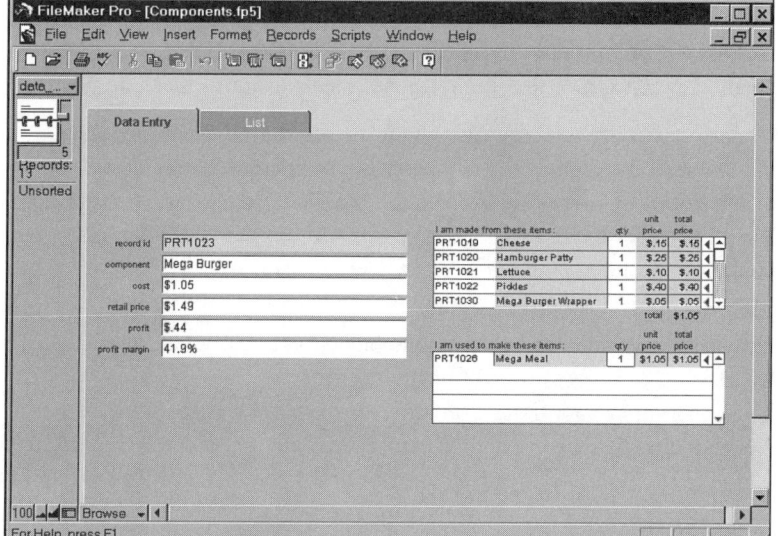

Figure 13.12
The Edit Relationship dialog for the relationship I_am_used_to_make, a one-to-many relationship of Components to ComponentRoster.

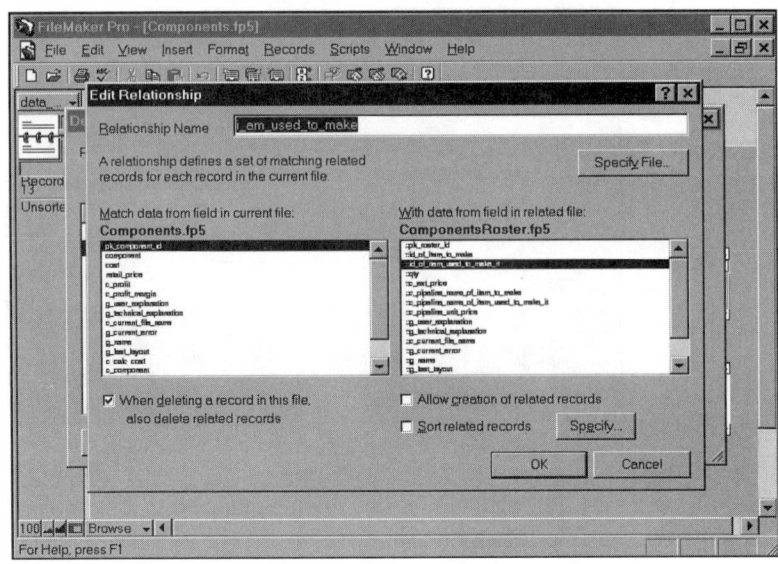

Having created relationships in this way and put two portals showing the records from the Components Roster file, we can show the IDs of the items being made and the items used to make it, as well as quantities. But what would not be available would be the names and cost of the items because those attributes live in the Components file. We are looking at two portals in Components showing data from the Components Roster file, but we now need some data from the Components file as well, in the same portal.

Therefore, we have to use the pipelining technique, grabbing the name and cost, and moving those to the Components Roster file as unstored calculations, so we can add those fields to the portal in Components. We are pipelining data from Components to Components Roster just so we can see it again within Components. This recursive relationship makes the portal more understandable for the average user, who might not know what we were referring to if we just displayed the ID numbers by themselves.

→ To learn more about the pipelining technique, **see** "Using Data That Is More than One File Away," **p. 128.**

To allow users to get details on any row in the portal, we add the little blue triangles. In the Components file, we create a Global field called g_selected_record_id. When the user clicks a blue triangle in either portal, a script grabs the record ID of the item clicked and puts that into the Global field. Then we set up a self-relationship called components | pk_component_id, in which the Global field value matches the Primary key value, (see Figure 13.13).

Now, in the script, after we put the record ID of the selected item into the Global field, we can use the Go To Related Records command without checking the Show Only Related Records option, through that self-relationship, to make that selected record the current record of the Components database. (Because the Primary key is unique, there is only one related record).

MANY TO MANY TO MANY | 431

Figure 13.13
The relationship components | pk_component_id has a Global field value matching the Primary key.

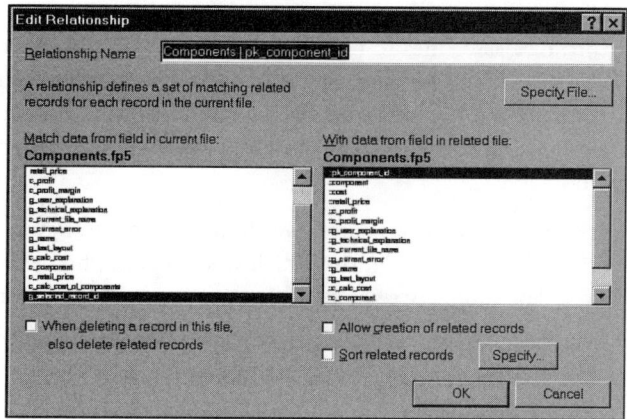

> **Caution**
>
> If you use the Go to Related Record command—with or without the Show Only Related Records option checked—you might disturb your current found set. If the record you are going to is within the current found set, and you have unchecked the Show Only Related Records option, then FileMaker brings you to that record without disturbing the current found set. But if you use the Go to Related Records command without the Show Only Related option set, and the record is not in the found set, FileMaker does a Find All, and then brings you to the records. (If you check Show Only Related Records, FileMaker virtually always changes the found set in the related file, because whatever records are related, the Show option puts them together in a new found set, and shows only those.)

MANY TO MANY TO MANY

 Sometimes you have too much of a good thing, with a many to many to many relationship, as shown in Figure 13.14.

Figure 13.14
A diagram of a many to many to many relationship. Too much!

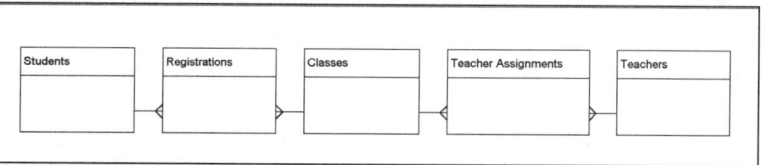

In the directory `m03-ManytoManytoMany`, we have files exhibiting a many-to-many relationship between students and classes, resolved through registrations, and we have a many-to-many relationship between classes and teachers, resolved through the teacher assignments. This model reflects the way our example school operates, allowing team teaching. But now the principal wants to know which students a particular teacher has taught, and which teachers a particular student has been taught by. The challenge is to establish these connections through this web of relationships. The student's class information lies on one side of the class relationship, and the teacher's information lies on the other side. There is nothing in teachers, students, or classes files to tie them *all* together. For instance, there is no data in Students you can tie directly to any particular teachers. The only places in which we have common information are the Registrations file and the Teacher Assignments file. Perhaps we could do some reporting through a relationship between those two, but, alas, that poses some challenges, too.

If we know what classes a student has taken, we should be able to figure out the teachers involved, and we should be able to identify which students have had which teachers, and vice versa. Examining the data model, we see that the only places holding common information allowing us to tie student information to teacher information are by relating the registrations with the teacher assignments. Both of these files are children of the Classes files, so the records in both contain a Class ID. If we create a relationship from Registrations directly to Teacher Assignments via a matching Class ID, we can put a portal in Registrations showing a list of all of the teachers associated with a particular class registration, and we can create a Sub-summary report by student ID, and use the Body of the layout to hold the portal showing the names of the teachers who taught that course. We use the Slide Up feature and reduce the size of the enclosing part to eliminate any blank space created by unused portal rows. Then we can produce the report if users press the button on the Classes screen labeled Student/Teacher Report via Portal.

But this approach leaves two problems unresolved.

- We have all the issues of reporting from a portal because portals weren't designed for reports. (We discussed this in the chapter on reporting through portals.)
- If a student has participated in more than one class with a teacher, that teacher's name shows up over and over.

So, yes, we can generate the report through a portal, but that is not such a great choice.

When we look at the existing structure of this database, we conclude that there is no good place to generate the report. What we need is a file in which a record represents a student taking a class with a particular teacher. If that class had three different team teachers, then there would need to be a separate record for each combination (student/class/individual teacher). Thus, if Rich took Freshman English, and the class was taught by the instructors Mr. Abc, Ms Def, and Mrs. Ghi, there would be three records with Rich's ID, the Freshman English class ID, and the IDs of one or another of the teachers. Therefore, we decided to create a special file just to do the reporting. In that file, there would be a record for every combination and permutation of student ID, class ID, and teacher ID. Fragmenting the data this way allows us to run Sub-summary reports showing the data in various ways, indicated in the buttons at the bottom (see Figure 13.15). (By the way, in a network set up for multiple users, this report should reside on the individual user's machine, not on the central server). The buttons are as follows:

- Show Teachers by Student
- Show Students by Teacher by Class
- Show Students by Teacher

Figure 13.15
Buttons lead to Sub-summary reports.

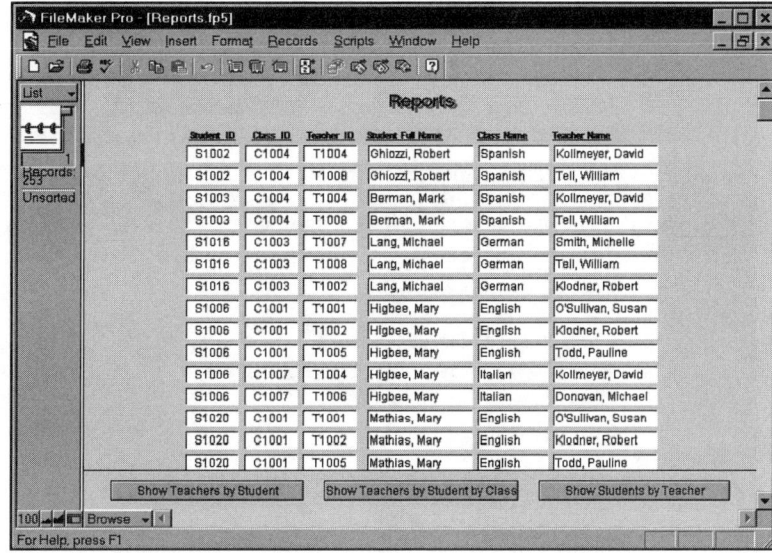

The hard part, here, was coming up with an algorithm to create all those different combinations on individual records. For every registration record, we would have to create at least one record in the reporting file. And if a class associated with that registration happened to have more than one teacher, we would have to create multiple records over in the reporting file.

To do this, we go to Registrations and create the script Generate Report in Reports file:

```
Allow User Abort [ Off ]
Set Error Capture [ On ]
Enter Browse Mode
Freeze Window
Show All Records
Go to Record/Request/Page
        [ First ]
Perform Script [ Filename: "Reports.FP5", "Delete all records in Reports file" ]
        [ Sub-scripts ]
Loop
        Go to Related Record [ Teach_Assigns | Class ID ]
           [ Show only related records ]
        Set Field [ Reports | Constant::g_temp_student_id, Student_ID ]
   Perform Script [ Filename: "Reports.FP5", "Import Teacher\Class records from
   Teacher_Assigns" ]
           [ Sub-scripts ]
        Go to Record/Request/Page
        [ Next, Exit after last ]
End Loop
Perform Script [ Filename: "Reports.FP5", "Find All in List View" ]
        [ Sub-scripts ]
```

We start with our usual `Allow User Abort [off]` to make sure that no sudden clicks or Escapes can interfere with the process, thus ruining the data. (If a user stopped the processing and then reported on the results, the report would be a mess).

> **Tip from**
> *Rich*
>
> It's a really good idea to postpone the `Allow User Abort [off]` until the moment you put the script into production. You may want to leave out this command until that moment because this is a looping script, and by definition, looping scripts need a way to end the loop, such as an exit loop statement. But we don't always build the loop properly at first, and sometimes we need to abort the script because it has gone haywire. But if you have enabled User Abort Off and you are stuck in an endless loop, you have to crash the application or pull the plug. Not a pretty ending.

> **Tip from**
> *Steven*
>
> If you are on a Mac and are stuck in an endless loop, and you have enabled `Allow User Abort[off]`, there is an AppleScript that will bring you to a soft landing rather than a crash. (See the file on the CD.)

We freeze the window, collect all the records, and go to the first one. Then we run a script over in Reports to delete all the current records there, to get a clean slate. The script Delete All Records in Report File operates in the Reports file by showing all records and deleting them all, without showing a dialog.

Now we make up a loop to create a new set of reporting records over in the Reports file. A record in Registrations represents one student participating in one class. So the first step in this loop says "Go to the related records (we assume that there will be one or more) over in the Teacher Assignment file—that is, the Teacher Assignment records that have the same Class ID as in the Registrations record." Each of these records represents a single teacher participating in the instruction in that class (remember, because of team teaching, there may be several teachers running the class together). We are, then, creating a found set of the Teacher Assignment records for this class over in the Teacher Assignment file.

Now we take the student's ID from the current registration and pass that along to the Global field g_temp_student_id over in Reports. Next, we run a script over in the Reports file, Import Teacher\Class records from Teacher_Assigns, to import two fields from those records: the Class ID and the Teacher ID. In this way, if the class in the Registration record has two teachers, we import two records, both with the same Class ID, but with different teacher IDs. The only field we haven't filled in in those new records is the student ID. But if we look back, just before we imported those records, we had taken the student ID from the Registration record, and put that into a Global field in the Reports file, so now we can pull that out and put it into the Student ID field in these newly imported records. We use the Replace command to do that on all of the found records (that is, whatever records we just imported).

> **Caution**
>
> You have to be in the right place to replace. Notice that the beginning of the Import script in the Reports file has a Go to Layout command taking us to the List layout, because the Replace command requires that the field being replaced be on the current layout. We use the Go to Layout to make sure we start off in the right place.

After we have imported records into the Reports file, we bounce back to the script in the Registrations file (the one we display above), which goes to the next record, and runs the same loop again, unless that's the last record. Hence, the loop continues to the last record, and then exits, moving us to the last steps of the script. At the end, we go to the Reports file and display the results in a list. The list shows the IDs of the student, class, and teacher—and their names. (The names themselves show up through relationships in related fields.)

We add a few Sub-summary reports showing teachers by student, teachers by students by class, and students by teacher. (You could perform additional mix-and-match reports, if you wanted to). Here the main trick was to eliminate duplicates, so that the same teacher's name does not show up over and over, if a student took several courses with that person.

The script for Preview Teachers by Student by Class Report runs like this:

```
Enter Browse Mode
Allow User Abort [ Off ]
Set Error Capture [ On ]
Go to Layout [ Teacher List by Student by Class ]
Print Setup
        [ Restore setup options, No dialog ]
Sort [ Sort Order: Student_ID (Ascending)Class_ID (Ascending)Teacher_ID
(Ascending) ]
        [ Restore sort order, No dialog ]
Enter Preview Mode
        [ Pause ]
Enter Browse Mode
Unsort
Go to Layout [ original layout ]
```

These buttons are fairly standard for Sub-summary reports. We get rid of the duplicates by using the Sub-summary part, because that prints only once for each group sharing a common value. In this way, even if a teacher or student shows up several times, we only see it once in this part.

An Outer Join

In the SQL world, a join between tables is often described as being an inner or an outer join. Roughly, an inner join is the kind we use most often in the FileMaker world. An example in FileMaker: If we have a file such as Companies, with the child file Contacts, and run a report in Contacts, all of the records found in the Contacts file would show up, but we would only see those company records that have a relationship with the records already found in Contacts. An outer join reaches out farther: The boss comes along and says she wants the same report, with just these contacts, but with all companies, even if the company has no contacts yet.

In the FileMaker Pro 5 world, we don't use that distinction between inner and outer, but we may have to include all parent records in a report being issued from the child file. We would, then, need to include parents who are not related to the current found set, and parents who have no children yet, as well as the parents who are related to the current found set.

In the directory m04-Outerjoin, we have a number of files that describe Companies and Contacts, and then in Reports we put together the records we need for particular reports. The Reports file shows two techniques, one of which stinks.

THE NOT-SO-HOT BUTTON

This button says "Show found Contacts and all Companies v1." The only way we can do this in the Contacts file would be if the found set of records in Contacts included a related contact for every company in the Companies file, and we know that isn't going to be true in every case. But if we run the report from the parent file, Companies, using a portal there to show the related contacts, the normal parent-child portal will show all the contacts, not just the ones in the found set. So we face a head-scratching challenge: Starting with a found set of children, how can we produce a report that includes even those parents who have no children in that set?

The v1 button uses a technique to get around this problem. We mark the records in the Contacts file that we want included—all of the found contacts. We make the script Show Found Contacts and All Companies:

```
Enter Browse Mode
# "Mark all found records with "X~Company ID". Go to List layout where field Mark
for report is available for the Replace command."
Go to Layout [ List ]
Replace [ Mark_for_Report, Replace data:Calculation: , "X~" & Company_ID ]
        [ No dialog ]
# "Set Mark on not found records to ""."
Show Omitted
Replace [ Mark_for_Report, Replace data:Calculation: , "" ]
        [ No dialog ]
Show Omitted
Go to Layout [ Data Entry ]
# "Now go to layout in Companies that shows only marked records in the portal."
Perform Script [ Filename: "Companies.FP5", "Show all Companies and found
Contacts" ]
        [ Sub-scripts ]
```

If we want a record to appear in the report, we are going to put an X, plus the tilde character and the company ID into the field Mark_for_Report. When the user clicks the button, we put the X combination into the Mark_for-Report field in all of the found records, and then we say, "Show Omitted," to see all of the records that weren't found. We make sure the Mark_for_Report field is empty in all of those records, so there are no X combinations left over from some earlier report. Then we go back to the original found set by running Show Omitted again, go over to Companies, and run the report. In the Companies file, the script "Show all Companies and found Contacts" is fairly simple; it says, "Show all the companies, and then go to the layout called Report–Found Contacts (Marked)." If you go to the layout, you'll see it involves a technique we don't recommend: using a portal as a reporting mechanism.

Normally, in the Companies file, with a portal showing all of the related contacts, we would see all contact records for each company. But we only want to see the contact records that belong to the current found set. So, over in the Contacts file we turn to the field Mark_for_report, which contains an `X~companyID` on every record we want to appear in the report. In the Companies file, then, we create a field called Mark, defined as `"X~"` & `Company_ID`, and we can use this field to relate to the field Mark_for_report over in the Contacts file, ensuring that only the found set of records from Contacts shows up in the portal in Companies, because the portal is defined through the relationship of Mark to Mark_for_report.

Unfortunately, as mentioned in the Reporting chapter, this approach raises questions such as how big do we make the portal? Where do page breaks fall? Portals were never created for reporting purposes. Although they print, they were designed to allow data entry and browsing on-screen.

→ If you would like to see more consideration of the tradeoffs and constraints of reporting, **see** "Where Should You Report From?" **p. 361.**

Also, if this system is being used by several users at once, then they could trample on each other. When you look at the Contacts script called Show Found Contacts and All Companies, you'll see that the script puts the x combination into the field Mark_for_report in all the found records, and then empties the same field in the omitted records. Essentially, that script changes a value in every record in the file. With multiple users, though, FileMaker locks a record when a user starts using it, to guard against the confusion that could arise if two people tried to edit the same record at the same time. But if a script starts marking records, and another user is already working on one or two of those records so they are locked, the Replace command skips whatever records are locked, so those records will retain whatever values they had before the script ran. This glitch may lead to garbled reports, in which we could no longer be confident that we had identified the entire found set (or the not-found set). We could easily end up with X's in some records that should *not* have them, and empty fields in records that ought to have X's.

A Hotter Button

To recap, the purpose of this report is to show the found contacts—that is, the names of a group of people, arranged under their companies—but we also want to show the other company names without any contact info under them. Essentially, we want a subgroup of records from one file, but all the records from another. For instance, we might want to show all customers who bought electronic gear, reported by state, but even if no one in New Mexico bought anything, we would want New Mexico, and every other state, to show up in the list.

In the V2 option, we use a separate reporting file, much as we did in the M03 example. We are importing the found contacts along with the IDs of their companies, and then we import *all* of the company records (none of which have any contact data in them). Now we want to get rid of the duplicates—those company records that were already referred to in the found contact records, because we already collected those company records once, before.

In looking for the unneeded duplicates, we want to locate all company records in which the Contact ID field will be empty, proving this record is one we just imported, and where the count of related records through the self-join is greater than 1 (because that Company ID shows up in more than 1 record since it is on the contacts). In essence, we are saying, "Find all the Companies that already have records in the Reporting file."

What we discover, then, are any company records we just imported, but don't need. Here's the script called "Create report record set."

```
Allow User Abort [ Off ]
Set Error Capture [ On ]
Enter Browse Mode
# "Delete all records in reporting file."
Show All Records
Delete All Records
        [ No dialog ]
# "Import all found records in the Contacts file."
Perform Script [ "Import found records from Contacts" ]
        [ Sub-scripts ]
# "Import all Company records."
Perform Script [ "Import all records from Companies" ]
        [ Sub-scripts ]
# "Delete Company records that are not needed."
Perform Find [ Request 1: Contact_ID =, Count of company records >1 ]
        [ Restore find requests ]
If [ Status( CurrentFoundCount) > 0 ]
        Delete All Records
            [ No dialog ]
End If
Show All Records
```

The Perform Find looks for all records where Contact_ID is empty, and where the count of related company records (through the self relationship on the Company_ID field) is greater than 1. Having done the find, we say, "If the count of the current found set is more than 0, delete those records, as unneeded." Then we show all the records that remain in the Reports file.

As with the previous button, multiple users might want to run the same report at the same time, and could trample each other's found sets, or inadvertently make the report incomplete. If this is a rarely issued report, we could probably chance making it a multi-user file. If people want to use this report often, we might make the file a single-user file that is distributed only to those people who must run the report. Under those conditions, we would want the file to be stored locally on the user's desktop, set to single user, even though we might have multiple copies out there. It is okay for the single user file on the user's desktop to have a relationship with the centrally stored multi-user file, but you should not try to establish a relationship between that central file and the many possible single-user files because that could lead to chaos. Also, if we decided to make this a distributed file, rather than one living on the central server, a real bad idea would be to have relationships from the central file to the distributed file, because by definition the distributed file is on many people's desktops, and we cannot be sure which one will be accessed.

Early in our career of creating relational environments, we learned to think of parent-and-child relationships as separate files. But in this chapter, we show that relationships really relate records, and there is no reason those records can't live in the same file, particularly if they contain the same fields.

Sometimes, we have to twist and turn our data, moving it in and out of other files, in order to provide the kind of reports a client wants. In this chapter, then, we have looked at ways you can create records in a separate file, just to be able to provide certain reports.

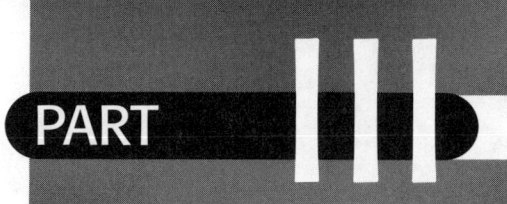

PART III

SCRIPTING

14 Scripting 443

15 Troubleshooting a Script 481

In this part we'll offer some scripts you might need over and over. Then we'll talk about ways you can troubleshoot your scripts, and finally, with the help of some generous developers, we'll provide a cautionary list of scripting "gotchas."

CHAPTER 14

SCRIPTING

In this chapter

The Benefits of Scripting   444

Creating and Editing Scripts   444

Good Scripting Practices   448

Write Once, Run Many Ways   453

Startup Scripts   453

Shutdown Scripts   458

Scripts to Help Users Navigate Among Layouts   459

Scripts for Navigating Among Parents and Children   461

Scripts That Delete   465

Scripts for Creating New Records   468

Scripts for Sorting   468

Scripts for Reporting   470

Scripts Asking Users What They Want to Print   473

Scripts for Preparing Canned Finds   474

Scripts That Duplicate Records   476

Handling Button Actions in Your Scripts   476

The Benefits of Scripting

A script in FileMaker is a way to automate a process. Sometimes you use a script only once, but most scripts automate repetitive processes. A script in FileMaker, then, acts like a macro in a spreadsheet.

If you've looked at our example scripts on the CD accompanying this book, you've seen a wide range of special-purpose scripts. In this chapter, we are going to get boring and give you advice about best practices for building the most common business scripts efficiently and successfully.

Scripts and relationships are the glue holding together the files in a FileMaker Pro 5 database system. We use scripts to keep track of a set of choices and selections so that users don't have to. If we were to ask the user to run a summary report without a script, the user would need to know which layout to use, which kind of page setup to establish, and which sort to run. But we cannot reasonably expect to teach all our users the complete configuration for every report, operation, or event. That's what scripts are for. Scripts build that intelligence into the system, so the user only needs to know how to trigger it. Scripts, then, represent a way to help users by automating actions, without forcing the users to remember the details. In effect, good scripts act the way Bruce Tognazzini, former Apple user-interface czar, recommends "The computer should remember so the user doesn't have to."

Creating and Editing Scripts

ScriptMaker is home base for scripting. When you first choose ScriptMaker from the Scripts menu and get the Define Scripts dialog, shown in Figure 14.1, you can see any existing scripts, with buttons allowing you to perform, print, edit, rename, duplicate, or delete individual scripts. You can now create or import a new script.

Figure 14.1
The Define Scripts dialog shows you existing scripts and lets you create new ones.

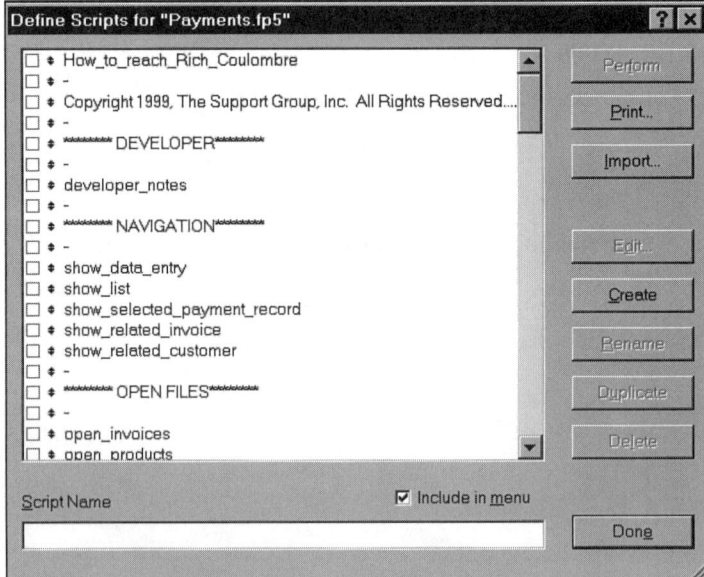

Double-clicking the name of an existing script opens the Script Definition dialog, showing most of the details for that script (see Figure 14.2).

Figure 14.2
The Script Definition dialog shows the script steps and lets you create more steps or edit the existing steps.

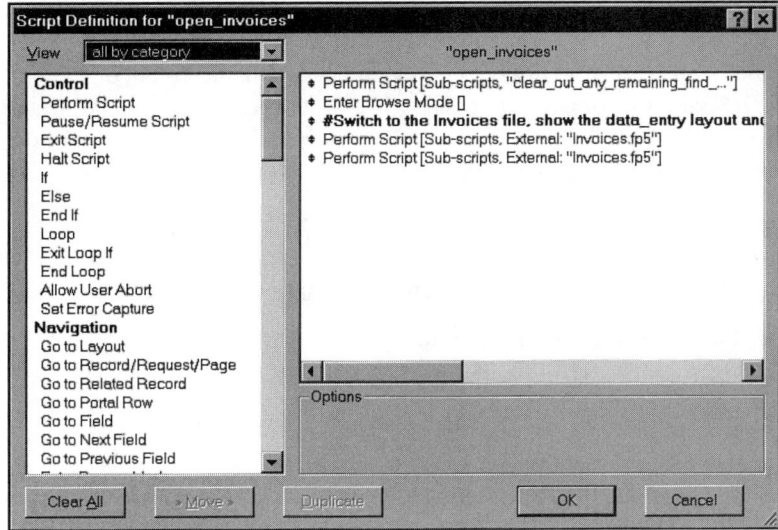

A script lives inside an individual file. To use data from another file, we use a relationship to that other file, or we call a script that will run inside that other file. FileMaker's Perform Script step lets you run a script inside your current file, or in an external file. Here is a diagram showing the components:

File				
	Script			
		Steps		
			Options	
				Specified in the Options area of the Script Definition menu
			Settings	
				Specified by example before the script is created
				Available for:
				Find
				Sort
				Import
				Export
				Page Setup
		Print Setup		

The Script Definition dialog box is carved up into several functional areas. On the left is a list of all available steps (more than 100 commands you can use inside of steps). Many of these steps resemble FileMaker's own menu commands such as Sort, Print, Cut, Copy, and Paste. But other steps resemble common programming constructs such as If, Else, End If, Loop, and End Loop. And still other steps are platform-specific, such as the Windows command Send DDE Execute or the Macintosh commands to Send Apple Event or Perform AppleScript. Of course, ScriptMaker breaks all these commands down into different categories. (The View menu lets you look at a particular category, or all categories, and you can sort by category or name).

To make a script, we assemble a sequence of these steps, configuring their options and settings so that we perform some form of automation. When you move a script step from the list over to the list of steps in the current script on the right, several things happen:

- That step is added to the script.
- That step is selected in the list of steps in this script.
- The options for that step become visible down below.
- If the step is followed by square brackets, the text inside tells us what options are selected. For example, the Print step is followed by a pair of square brackets around the text Perform without Dialog. But if we move the Unsort command over, it has no square brackets, indicating that it offers no options.
- Up and down arrows appear to the left of the step, allowing you to drag the step around within the script, creating a new order. (On arrival, the step lands just below the currently selected step; if no step is selected, the new step goes to the very end.)

Tip from
Rich
> Use keyboard controls to move the steps up and down. In Windows, for instance, if you have a particular step selected, hold down Control and press the Up and Down arrow keys on the keyboard; you can nudge the step up or down, one step at a time. On the Mac, you can use the Command key with the up or down arrows.

Now for the options! When you move a step over or click on an existing script, the step's options appear, if there are any, letting you control how the action is performed.

Tip from
Rich
> To bring up the dialog, just double-click the step. When you are in ScriptMaker, some of the steps have options that must be set in dialogs. With Set Field, for instance, there are two different dialogs that can come up. You can use buttons to bring these up, or, if your pointer is already up around the step, turn to double-clicking the step to bring up one, and Alt-double-clicking (in Windows) or Option-double-clicking in Mac, to bring up the other.

Some steps also have settings, which are set by example, because they are based on performing the step manually before you actually create the step in the script, so FileMaker can follow the way you configured the action earlier, embodying those decisions in the step, as its settings. Steps that have settings are Perform Find, Enter Find Mode, Sort, Import, Export, Page Setup (the Mac version of Print Setup), and Print Setup (the Windows equivalent of Page Setup on the Mac). The Page Setup and Print Setup settings take their settings from two dialogs: some of the settings come from your last use of the command of the same name, as well as the Print dialog, where you choose exactly what to print. These all depend on any setups you have done just before you created the step.

Tip from
Rich

When setting up a Find by example, before creating the step in a script, you don't have to actually run the Find. You just have to go into Find mode and set up the criteria. Then, while still in the Find mode, create the script.

Tip from
Rich

For a sorting script, go into Sort and set up the sort. You can now click Done, without having to do the actual sort, because FileMaker remembers the sort criteria, and you now have those settings applied in your script. Just create the script before doing another sort.

Tip from
Rich

You have to pretend to start printing to commit the Print dialog settings to FileMaker's memory. If you are changing something in the Print dialog, you have to initiate the printing; you can then abort the print job before anything gets printed. As long as you have clicked OK or Print, the settings are stored.

Tip from
Rich

If you realize you put the wrong sort in, or the business requires a different Find, you can change the settings by example, too. You set up the action again, go into ScriptMaker, double-click the script, and click OK. ScriptMaker will ask you whether you want to keep or replace the settings for these steps, as shown in Figure 14.3. Just click Replace for the step.

Figure 14.3
The Keep/Replace dialog lets you modify settings by example, but alerts you that those settings are about to change, if you happened to open the script and click OK without pondering the consequences.

Good Scripting Practices

Here are umpteen habits of successful developers. You'll find a lot of lore here, most of which we have learned through sad experiences, followed by vows such as "I don't want to go through that again!" You might think of some of these practices as preventive or defensive because they are designed to protect you against confusion, inconsistency, and late nights spent debugging.

→ If you are already in trouble with a script, **see** Chapter 15, "Troubleshooting a Script," **p. 481**.

Naming Your Script

Any name is a good script name if it tells you what the script does. But when you have dozens, hundreds, or even thousands of scripts, as you might in a standard business application, you probably need to establish a routine for creating those names. Following a standard approach to the creation of script names will help you later, when you have to tinker with the scripts. Also, if you are part of a team, and the whole team follows those conventions, you can all open and modify the right scripts faster, with less annoying false starts and wrong turns.

The conventions for script names resemble those for field names. For instance, you should probably keep spaces out of your script names, because in a Web environment, if you are sending a request to FileMaker to run a script, some browsers and operating systems may choke on the space character, truncating the name or drastically shrinking it.

The safest characters are letters of the alphabet and numbers. You can be sure that these are recognized by various operating systems, applications, and browsers.

We use the underscore character in our names because reading a wholebunchofwordsasoneword is hard. We've never run into problems with the underscore, but we should warn you that some of our colleagues caution against it.

Also, we use all lower-case characters, so that in environments that are case-sensitive, we don't risk accidentally typing a capital letter and having the system say that it can't find the script. (We recently got a letter from a UNIX designer with everything lower-case).

Write the name so you can tell, months later, what the heck the script does. Examples of pretty good names include the following:

- print_landscape_found_records
- print_setup_portrait_current_record
- print_avery_5160
- sort_by_date_invoice_ascend
- startup_script
- shutdown_script

In modular scripting, good names help you document the purpose of each subscript inside a larger script. Breaking a giant script into small chunks, then calling those with the Perform Script command, you won't have to add any comment lines if the names of the called scripts are meaningful enough. For instance, in the Invoices file, the show_selected_customer script performs show_data_entry, find_all, and maximize_window as subscripts. The names alone telegraph what each script does.

```
show_selected_customer
If [ Status( CurrentMode) = 1 ]
        Perform Script [ "beep_beep_not_in_find_mode_message" ]
                [ Sub-scripts ]
        Exit Script
End If
Enter Browse Mode
If [ IsValid(Customers | cust_id::pk_cust_ID) ]
        Go to Related Record [ Customers | cust_id ]
        Perform Script [ Filename: "Customers.fp5", "show_data_entry" ]
                [ Sub-scripts ]
        Perform Script [ Filename: "Customers.fp5", "find_all" ]
                [ Sub-scripts ]
        Perform Script [ Filename: "Customers.fp5", "maximize_window" ]
                [ Sub-scripts ]
Else
        Beep
        Beep
        Show Message [ Buttons: "OK", "", ""; Data: "There is no customer assigned to this invoice." ]
End If
```

Some people begin their script names with an identifier such as *btn* for *button* or *dev* for *developer-only*. You'll probably want to come up with your own conventions and stick to them. Consistency, here, guarantees that you will understand the meaning of the names later—and that can save you a lot of time when you return to make changes.

In ScriptMaker, you may want to group your scripts so you can find a particular script quickly and compare related scripts. For instance, in the Invoicing system, we use categories such as the following:

- Developer
- Navigation
- Open Files
- Operations
- Printing
- Searching
- Sorting
- Startup/Shutdown
- User Scripts

Add Comments

Think of comments as notes you leave for yourself or others, indicating what is going on. You should comment in detail as you go because you are fully aware of the reasons for each step right now, but may not recall the rationale in a few months, and if someone else has to work on the script, that person certainly hasn't much idea of what you were thinking. Taking the time to write a comment now will save you and others from wasting time and making mistakes later.

When you are writing a script, you are working your way through an algorithm, moving from a high-level understanding down to specific actions. In this way you are taking a business requirement that you first heard about in conversation with the client and converting it into a series of steps that direct the computer to perform a series of tasks. The problem is that someone reading the script may not be able to translate it back into the business concepts. The comments help anyone—even you—understand the business problem that is being solved.

Expressing the technical gobbledygook going on can be useful, too. When we modify a script, subtle changes may have bad effects on its performance, without our recognizing them right away. If you want to warn your future self or a colleague away from making those changes, add a comment. Talk about the implications and impact of a delicate step to make maintenance go smoothly.

For example, sometimes the order of steps makes a dramatic difference to the results, and changing that order may create a subtle, or intermittent, effect. The innocent newcomer to your script may not realize that this step must, absolutely, come last, unless you say so in the comment.

Yes, there is never enough time to insert comments, but think of comments as an absolute requirement for your future sanity, not an optional add-on. Commenting a script takes a lot less time than trying to figure it out later without the help of these hints, asides, and warnings.

> **Tip from**
> *Rich*
>
> Start every script with a comment giving a 20,000-foot view of the script's purpose.

> **Tip from**
> *Rich*
>
> Create a script called Developer's Notes, where you can leave reminders for yourself, notes about changes you are thinking of making, improvements you wonder about, and warnings. Look in our Invoicing system for an example.

Modularize Your Scripts

Carving up a large script into smaller, more manageable chunks lets you test each chunk separately, use the same chunk in many different situations, and understand the step-by-step progress of the larger scripts that call these chunks in as subscripts.

When creating a set of scripts, we focus on the main actions, not the details: "First we have to do this, then we need to do that, and in the end, we must wrap by doing this other thing." And, "If this is true, then we do x, but if it is false, we do y." Instead of building one giant script with all those details, we do better when we create a separate script for each of those high-level actions. Only at the end do we create a larger script whose flow mimics the high-level process we imagined before, and most of the actions take place within those subscripts, so the larger script is a kind of skeleton key to the overall process.

Each chunk represents a high-level activity. If we want to move mulch from one side of the yard to another, we have to get the tools out of the garage, bring the tools to the mulch pile, loop into shoveling mulch into the wheelbarrow, move the loaded wheelbarrow across the yard, perform the wheelbarrow-dump, go back, and continue until we run out of mulch, or a backache intervenes. That's the high-level process. Each activity has steps, such as opening the garage door, backing the car out, moving the snow blower out of the way, hefting the pitchfork onto the wheelbarrow, and wheeling the wheelbarrow out. Those are the steps inside the algorithm for getting the tools out of the garage.

Breaking the job down into these pieces lets you troubleshoot an individual module without worrying about the effect of other modules or the larger process. For instance, we can make sure the pitchfork is really on top of the wheelbarrow before exiting the garage and getting to the mulch pile, only to discover that the pitchfork fell off when we navigated around the tricycle and the garbage can just inside the garage door.

Another benefit of the modular approach is that the modules can be reused. You can, for instance, use the same shoveling technique for tossing hay into the wheelbarrow. In FileMaker Pro 5, if you create a reusable module that is fairly generic (that is, one that could work in another file) you can import that into another file and save yourself time and effort on your next project. For instance, in every file we create, we include scripts for

- print_setup_found_records_portrait
- print_setup_found_records_landscape
- print_setup_current_record_portrait
- print_setup_current_record_landscape

Benefits: We can import these scripts from one file to another, because they are not file-specific, and do not require any alteration. Also, if we go to a new environment and discover a strange printer, we no longer have to go to a dozen reporting scripts to change the portrait or landscape or percentage of reduction or enlargement to suit that printer; we would make the changes in these four scripts, period.

> **Tip from** *Rich*
>
> Create a library of scripts that can be imported. Devote the file to that library—and nothing else.

> **Caution**
>
> Importing scripts, a new feature in FileMaker Pro 5, can save you a lot of time, but listen carefully to the message that comes up after the import: "Script Import is completed. Verify that script references are valid before running the script." Steven Blackwell and Danny Mack, Partner-level members of the FileMaker Solutions Alliance, point out that problems may arise if the file you import the script into happens to have a field or relationship with the same name as the source file, but with a different definition (the fields are, perhaps, of different types or the relationships point to different files). Thus, the script may set a field in a related file, but when you import the script, the results may not be what you expect when running the script in the target file. Other potential discrepancies include
>
> - If the relationships with the same name sort differently (one ascending, the other descending, or with different break fields)
>
> - If the relationships differ on allowing creation of records or cascading deletes
>
> To sidestep some of these problems, adopt a rigorous naming convention, so that your relationship names embody the attributes, and you can rely on the name as an accurate expression of the relationship. Verify the results of the script.

> **Tip from Rich**
>
> FileMaker will change the name of the Page Setup command based on the platform. On a Mac, it will be called Page Setup; on the PC, Print Setup. Normally, if you have a Sort script, FileMaker can store one sort order, but Page Setup and Print Setup store two different settings, one for the Mac, and one for the PC. If you create a script on the Mac, include the Page Setup command, define that as Landscape, and then move the whole file over to Windows, the Windows version of FileMaker would not recognize that Landscape setting. Having moved the file, you would need to manually set the Print Setup to the Landscape orientation, then open the script, and just click OK. You don't have to change anything in the script, but you do have to go through this little piece of voodoo to encourage FileMaker to show the Keep/Replace dialog so you can say, "Yes, replace the existing Print Setup with the option I just set." In this way, FileMaker saves the Mac setup and adds a Windows version. (If we took the file back to the Mac, it would work just fine without further tinkering.) Here, of course, Replace really means Append.

But don't make the chunks too small. If you break things into a bunch of tiny scripts, maybe one or two steps, you have not gained any advantage from modularity. Better to identify a set of chunks, each of which performs a specific function. Also, look for a function in which you can easily identify the entry point and exit point of the script. If someone asks you what a script will do, and you say, "It will perform this function," then you have spotted a module. But if you say "It does this, and that, and the other thing," then you probably ought to carve that up into three modules, plus a parent script that calls them one after another.

> **Tip from Rich**
>
> No matter how good your scripts are, if you let users tinker with them, you can be sure that the scripts will turn to a tangled pile of spaghetti. Never give users a password that lets them modify a script.

Write Once, Run Many Ways

John Mark Osborne, co-author of *Scriptology*, points out that there are many ways you can run scripts from inside FileMaker Pro 5:

- From the Script menu or Scripts dialog
- Using keyboard shortcuts
- From a button
- On opening the file (Startup Script)
- On closing the file (Shutdown Script)
- As a subscript from another script

Several other methods involve applications outside of FileMaker Pro 5:

- Web Companion
- Plug-ins, such as Waves in Motion's Script_Scheduler.
- AppleScript
- Active X
- Java
- WinBatch
- QuickKeys

In the rest of this chapter, we walk through some of the most useful modules you might want to prepare for multiple reuse.

Startup Scripts

You may want to create a standard startup_script to help you get everything set up correctly for your database to work well as soon as the user glimpses it. You can tell FileMaker which script to run at launch by setting a Document Preference under Edit, Preferences, Document, General, as shown in Figure 14.4; you can say whether you want a startup script or shutdown script and identify which ones to use.

> **Caution**
> Sometimes, startup scripts do not run. If the file opens due to a relationship (a related field on a layout requires information from the related file, so FileMaker opens the file, and if that is how the file opens, it is not considered a startup), or if the file is opened during the performance of an external script, or if a value list in another file is drawn in, then FileMaker ignores the startup script.

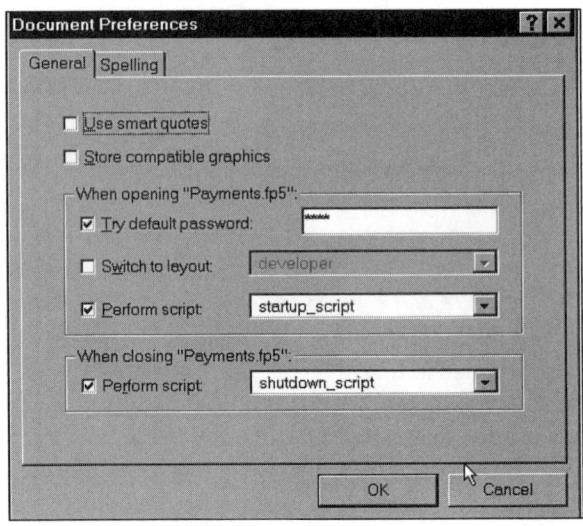

Figure 14.4
Set the Document Preferences to tell FileMaker which script to launch at startup.

Here are several components that we find useful as part of a startup script, to be performed when a user opens a file.

STARTUP PART 1: OPEN ALL THE FILES AND MAXIMIZE THE WINDOWS

You may want to do this because in FileMaker, particularly on a Windows machine, if you open File A via a script and maximize the window, and then a particular layout in File A draws on related data from File B and File C, FileMaker opens those files behind the scenes and Windows decrees that none of the windows are maximized. (Send your protests to billg@Microsoft.com.)

As developers, we design around an expected window size, so when a window is unmaximized, we have no idea how big it will be and how much info a user will see. Therefore, in your startup script, we recommend opening all the files at the beginning because each one's startup script will run, maximizing its windows. After that, you have all your files open and all your windows maximized. You have a window size you can rely on from now on. By the way, in the startup script for Invoices, we open all the files from the Invoices startup script, so we make the startup scripts in those other files say, "Go start the main file, because that file's startup script will launch everything else."

Kelvin Limm, of DataBasix at www.databasixtechnologies.com, points out that in Windows, a window can have three states: maximized, minimized, or restored (taking the window back to whatever size it was before the user minimized it). Restored is the ringer. If a file is opened and its startup script says to maximize the window, the window will stay maximized until you change its size, or until another window opens as Restore, because Windows dutifully restores all the windows in the application window, including any ones that you maximized. So if a file opens without running the startup script (through a relationship, a value list, or an external perform script), FileMaker always opens the file as

Restored because it doesn't read the startup script in those circumstances, and lacking any guidance, it just assumes the window should come up as restored. The moment one file opens as Restored, your other windows get restored too—not a pretty sight. One workaround: When a user opens any of the files, the file will include a startup script that opens a main file, which itself contains a script that opens all the other files and maximizes their windows. (By the way, Limm and his company have a tool for sale that lets you control window sizes and positions in a Windows environment.)

When using FileMaker Pro in a multi-user environment, we would have an opening file with no data or records, but just a startup script, which says, "Open all these other files on the server, in this order, maximizing their windows as you go—and when you are all done, come back to this opening file, and close it." (This way, the user doesn't have to open FileMaker, go into the Host dialog, and hunt for the proper files to open. We put the opening file right on their desktop, so it is easy to find, or we stick it into the Apple menu or Start menu. All users know is that when they choose the item, their database opens up.)

Tip from
Rich

> Put an opening file on the user's desktop or within easy reach, to make the user's life a little easier. Considerations like this go a long way toward encouraging people to accept the database and use it productively, rather than ignoring it, dragging their feet, protesting, or fouling up the data in passive aggression.

STARTUP PART 2: DECIDE WHAT TO DO WITH THE STATUS AREA

Started as an interface element to allow users to flip through records, the Status Area runs top to bottom on the left, offering the bookmark, plus the record flipper, number of records, number in the found set, info on whether or not the records are sorted, and so on. Developers often debate whether or not the status area should show; some say the area tastes good, and others prefer it to be less filling. Some users like dragging the bookmark, and we don't know a good way to offer the same functionality without the status area. Still, the status area uses up a lot of real estate that we could devote to significant data. And sometimes we want to control the way the user gets access to particular records or sets of records, so we tend to hide the status area. For example, in the folder I09-PortalView, you'll see that we do not let the user get at the records directly; in this situation, before passing the file along to users, we might lock and hide the status area.

Compromise: Emulate the functionality of the status area via objects on the layout.

(Two suggestions to FileMaker, Inc.: It would be nice if developers could add the little Rolodex and bookmark functionality to a layout as an object. Also, you might give us the ability to add our own buttons to the status area.)

STARTUP PART 3: GO TO THE RIGHT LAYOUT

When we are writing a database system, we tend to focus on a single window full of information (although some folks do position a number of windows on-screen at the same time). Narrowing our focus, we ask ourselves what window should be the first item? Should it be a main menu, a query screen, or the actual data? The answer helps us identify the layout we want to bring the user to, right off.

In FileMaker, normally, our startup script brings the user to a particular layout within a particular file. But the user often has access to the Window menu (unless we have blocked that access), so the user can switch from file to file. If a user does that, the other window comes to the front without running a script, and that window may or may not be maximized, and worse, the layout that comes up is the last one the user looked at in that file. So one of the techniques we use to discourage the user from picking another window on the Window menu is to bring the user to a layout we call, "Go Away." That layout displays a message saying, "You have gotten to a place you shouldn't ought to be, no-how. Click this button to go back where you belong." For instance, in the invoicing system, the Line Items file acts that way. If a user goes to the Window menu and chooses Inv_Line_Items, a message comes up saying, "You do not belong here: Click Continue to return to the invoicing system."

You should use Layout Setup to prevent layouts from showing up in the Layouts pop-up menu, so that route is closed off to the user. You can use a plug-in to dim out or to remove the Window menu. SecureFM, a plug-in from New Millennium (www.newmillennium.com), lets you disable individual menu items or whole menus, including the Window menu. Having put these two controls in place, you force the user to rely on your buttons and scripts for navigation, so your startup script for each file puts you in charge of what layout shows up and what size the windows will be.

STARTUP PART #4: SHOW ALL AND UNSORT

These steps are a carryover from our days of writing databases for single users. In that environment, FileMaker remembers the last sort and the last find, and if you close the file and reopen it, you get those criteria again. Of course, in a multi-user environment, each user can have a different find and sort, those criteria are thrown away when the file is closed, and the next time the user opens the file, FileMaker automatically finds all and unsorts the records. Including the steps requesting that FileMaker show all records and unsort them may not be necessary, but we put those steps in anyway just to make absolutely sure that a user is starting with a full deck.

Of course, if the business requires that the user be presented with a particular subset of the records, or a particular sort, we could do that as part of the startup script instead.

STARTUP PART #5: INITIALIZE THOSE VARIABLES

When we open a file or a system, we often want the variables to start life with a particular value, so we use the startup script to set the beginning values. Typically, these values appear in Global fields. But in a multi-user environment, the starting value in a Global field is that field's value in the host, which may not be the value we want to start off with, because an earlier user may have modified it, or one of our scripts may have changed it during its processing. If we clone a file, creating the same file without any records, FileMaker empties out values in Global fields, so we have to insert the proper values; we can do so manually or rely on the startup script to do so.

In our startup script, we use Set Fields to set the starting values of all Global fields, just to make sure they are correct. In the Invoicing system, we created a subscript called reset_value_lists to handle this initialization process here and elsewhere.

> **Tip from**
> *Rich*
>
> We often use Global fields as variables in scripts because the field has one value throughout the file, but each record can share that value. Therefore, a Global field is great for holding a single value we want to use everywhere. But each user in a multi-user environment can change the value of that Global. The change only applies to the user's own instance of the Global field value. If you are using FileMaker Pro Server, and you have ten guests, each guest's Global field values will start off being whatever is stored at the host server, but each user can change the Global field value, on his or her own instance of the field. Global fields are local to the guest. Every user, then, starts with the same value, and may diverge after that. This makes sense. For instance, if we are using the Global as a counter, and two people are using the system at the same time, we would not want one person's count to trounce the other person's count. Therefore, Globals start off as universals, but once a user gets hold of the file, the Global values can only change within the individual user's world, not throughout the whole universe.

> **Tip from**
> *Rich*
>
> Use a Constants file. Sometimes we need a field that can be changed by any user and must be shared by all users, contrary to the way a true Global field works. In those circumstances, we create a Constants file, and that file has only one record, which contains a Date, Number, Text, or Time field. Through a relationship, any user can change the value, and at that moment, all the other users see the updated value on their screens.

STARTUP PART #6: SHOW A WELCOME SCREEN, IF YOU HAVE ONE

You don't have to have a welcome screen, but if you do, launch it in the startup script. Clients sometimes insist on these Hello pages to remind users about security, confidentiality, or the company slogan. The script can point to this opening layout, pause the script for a few seconds, and then move on to a screen with data entry. Or, worst case, a script takes the user to the so-called welcome screen and sits there until the user clicks Continue or OK. Not much of a welcome.

STARTUP PART #7: SET PAGE SETUP/PRINT SETUP, IF USERS CAN SELECT PRINT FROM THE MENU

In the early days with FileMaker 2, you couldn't keep users out of the menus, so the user could go to File and choose Print at any moment. In those days, you had to make sure that the page was set up for the layout you were going to, so that if the user happened to choose Print, the printout would emerge in the proper orientation.

More recent versions of FileMaker allow us to keep users out of the menus; in fact, we *should* keep users out. So users have to use our scripts to get printing done, and our printing scripts should, by definition, ensure that the page is set up in the correct orientation. So why do we still guard against this unlikely problem? Old habits die hard. And sometimes we do need to let users into the File menu. Also, in this way, you can be sure you're ready to print.

Make sure that the orientation is right, reduction or enlargement set up the way you want, and print records being browsed.

STARTUP PART #8: CREATE A LOG OF WHO ENTERS THIS SYSTEM AND WHEN

This kind of log might be useful in secure facilities, where the confidential nature of the information requires that the system administrator be able to track exactly who logged into the system, when. Create a log file, with records for each visit, and in the startup script, open the log file and create a record for the visitor. (We have not created a sample log file on our CD).

STARTUP SCRIPT

Here is a sample startup script, taken from the Invoices file.

```
# "To be run when file opens. Customize to meet system needs."
Allow User Abort [ Off ]
Set Error Capture [ On ]
Enter Browse Mode
Open [ Filename: "Customers.fp5" ]
Open [ Filename: "Inv_line_items.fp5" ]
Open [ Filename: "Payments.fp5" ]
Open [ Filename: "Products.fp5" ]
Perform Script [ "show_data_entry_payments" ]
        [ Sub-scripts ]
Show All Records
Unsort
Toggle Status Area
        [ Show ]
Toggle Window
        [ Maximize ]
# "Initialize a couple of variables."
Perform Script [ "reset_value_lists" ]
        [ Sub-scripts ]
Set Field [ g_selected_cust_letter, "All" ]
Set Field [ g_product_category, Left( ValueListItems(Status( CurrentFileName),
"product_categories"),
Position(ValueListItems(Status( CurrentFileName), "product_categories") , "¶",1 ,
1) - 1 ) ]
```

SHUTDOWN SCRIPTS

There may be certain actions you want performed whenever the file is closed, such as closing all the files, logging the fact that the user is leaving the system at this time, or capturing data and storing that for the next session. For instance, you might want to capture the fact that the last time this file was used was today.

Close All Files in the System

You might think it should be easy to close a file, but, in a relational world, you may discover that as soon as you close one file, it gets reopened. How come? Well, imagine you have the invoicing system open, with the Customers file on top of the Invoices file. The user clicks the Close box on the Customers file. FileMaker closes the Customers file, goes to the Invoices file, and realizing it needs information from Customers, brings the Customers file back to life. Unsuspecting users end up in a frustrating click-click-click to close the file. The user must close the windows faster than FileMaker can open them—or you can have a Shutdown script. "If a user closes this file, close all these other files," so that when the user closes any window, you close all the other windows as well.

Put this kind of shutdown script into each file, so no matter what the user closes, all the windows close and the original window does not spring back to life.

Idea: If you have a system with a lot of files, you might put a shutdown script into one master file to close down all the others, and in the shutdown scripts in the other files, just say "Close down the master file."

A Shutdown Script

Here is a sample shutdown script.

```
(Removing the parts here, because this is not a part, but the whole)Enter Browse
Mode
Close [ Filename: "Customers.fp5" ]
Close [ Filename: "Inv_line_items.fp5" ]
Close [ Filename: "Payments.fp5" ]
Close [ Filename: "Products.fp5" ]
```

Scripts to Help Users Navigate Among Layouts

As developers, we create many layouts, and we allow users to switch layouts by using buttons. In the invoicing system, for instance, when the user is looking at the Invoices system, we offer buttons for Payments, Notes, Set Customer, and Add Products, and when the user clicks one of those buttons, we jump to an entirely different layout (although we hope the user doesn't realize this). In going to a new layout, you may want to make sure that the user is in the right mode, set some values, reset page setup or print setup, or run a script.

1: Make Sure You Know What Mode You Are In

All buttons come up in Find mode, so innocent users might click them, leading to unforeseen results. So as part of your button script, you probably ought to check what mode the user is in. If a user is in Find and clicks the Notes button, we take the user to the Notes layout (because the user may want to do a Find in the Notes layout), and then we abort the rest of the script.

If the user isn't in the Find mode, we choose to enter Browse Mode. We get militant about this. We recommend starting most scripts by going into Browse mode because scripts' behavior can change dramatically in different modes. For example, if FileMaker is in Preview mode, then the available menu commands are quite different from those available in Browse mode. Therefore, if you have a script using the New Record or Delete Record commands, and your user wanders into Preview mode, ScriptMaker will attempt to perform those steps, but because those commands are not available in Preview mode, ScriptMaker will just skip the steps. So to be conservative, you'll probably want to guarantee what mode the user is in right at the start of the script.

Going into Browse mode makes no difference 99% of the time, but the rest of the time, this decision can save your hide.

2: Go to the Right Layout

You don't want to leave the choice of layout up to the user. You know best, and you should build the right layout into the script.

3: Initialize Any Variables You Need

You might have some value lists presented in Global fields, as in the Invoices file. Whenever we switch to a new layout, we want to make sure that these fields have a particular starting value. So we run a subscript to reset the value lists, initializing the values in the Global fields.

The show_data_entry_notes Script

```
# "The following IF statement causes the script to switch to a different layout
only and abort the rest of the script if the user presses a button while in the
FIND mode."
If [ Status( CurrentMode) = 1 ]
        Go to Layout [ data_entry_notes ]
        Exit Script
End If
Enter Browse Mode
Go to Layout [ data_entry_notes ]
Set Field [ g_last_layout_number, Status( CurrentLayoutNumber) ]
Perform Script [ "print_setup_portrait___found_records" ]
        [ Sub-scripts ]
# "Initialize a couple of variables."
Perform Script [ "reset_value_lists" ]
        [ Sub-scripts ]
```

> **Tip from**
> *Rich*
>
> Create a script called Developer Notes, to leave notes to yourself (months from now) and to future developers. You might say, "The next time we take the server down, add these fields." This script has no functionality other than preserving comments that follow the file wherever it goes.

> **Tip from**
> *Rich*
>
> In FileMaker Pro 5.0v3 with FileMaker Server 5, if the server has a single guest, and only one, that guest can open and get at Define Fields.

Scripts for Navigating Among Parents and Children

Most of the files in your system will be related through parent-child relationships. Often, users looking at a parent that shows child records, or a child that shows related parent fields, want to move from child to parent and back. You may find it useful to build some standard scripts to handle this kind of navigation.

Child-to-Parent Navigation

If a user looks at the Invoices file, which is both a child of Customers and a parent of Line Items, the user sees two fields in the upper left-hand corner of the screen. One field shows the customer contact ID and the other shows the name and address of the company. In both of those fields we have our favorite blue triangles that, when clicked, bring the user to the parent record within the Customers file.

1: Check or Set the Mode

Just as we do in every script that can be triggered by a button, when we know that the button can be pressed in Find mode, we check the mode right away, stop if the user is in Find, and if not, continue to go into Browse mode. (In Find, there is no related record, so pressing this button makes no sense, and we are telling the user to forget about it.) By the way, the subscript that beeps at them is a distinct module, so we can modify the message once, rather than tracking down every script that might need to show that message.

2: Make Sure That the Related Record Is Valid (That Is, Check to See Whether the Parent Exists)

We don't assume that the related record is valid. We test, using the IsValid function, which returns a 1 if the related record and field do exist, and if the data in the field is of the expected type. We get back a 0 if the related record is missing, or if it lacks the field, or if the field itself is the wrong type. Here we want to make sure that Customer ID matches a valid Customer ID over in the Customers file.

The function goes like this:

```
IsValid(relationship name::related field)
```

Basically, before we even try to navigate to the record, we verify that it exists. If the customer record does exist, then we go to the related records. The current record will be that customer.

The step in which we went to the related records makes this customer's record the active record in the Customers file. If this customer record is part of the current found set, then there will be no change made to the found set. If this customer record is part of the "not found" set, then FileMaker will do a Find All, and then make this customer record the active record.

Therefore, the Go to Related Records may not disturb the found set, but it may find all in order to show the customer record. We will deal with this uncertainty in a moment.

3: Go to the Right Layout

Having determined that the record is valid, we go to that record and open the right layout (in this case, using the script called show_data_entry in the Customers file, which brings up the data entry layout in Customers).

4: Find All

We just located the related record, and may or may not have set off a Find All. Sometimes going to a related record triggers a Find All, and sometimes it does not. To be consistent, we force a Find All on the records.

5: Maximize the Window

Because users can maximize windows and shrink them, but we design for the maximized condition, we maximize the window whenever we move from one file to another, just in case.

> **Tip from** *Steven*
>
> You can prevent a user's maximizing or minimizing a screen with the use of the SecureFM 5 plug-in from New Millennium Communications (http://www.newmillennium.com).

The show_selected_customer Script

Here's the complete child-to-parent navigation script show_selected_customer in Invoices to handle navigation:

```
If [ Status( CurrentMode) = 1 ]
        Perform Script [ "beep_beep_not_in_find_mode_message" ]
                [ Sub-scripts ]
        Exit Script
End If
Enter Browse Mode
If [ IsValid(Customers | cust_id::pk_cust_ID) ]
        Go to Related Record [ Customers | cust_id ]
        Perform Script [ Filename: "Customers.fp5", "show_data_entry" ]
                [ Sub-scripts ]
        Perform Script [ Filename: "Customers.fp5", "find_all" ]
                [ Sub-scripts ]
        Perform Script [ Filename: "Customers.fp5", "maximize_window" ]
                [ Sub-scripts ]
Else
```

Scripts for Navigating Among Parents and Children | 463

```
        Beep
        Beep
        Show Message [ Buttons: "OK", "", ""; Data: "There is no customer assigned
to this invoice." ]
End If
```

Parent-to-Child Navigation

This kind of navigation is very similar to going from a child to a parent, as you will see if you go to the show_selected_payment script in Invoices.

EXAMPLE: EXPLAINING THAT A RECORD DOES NOT REALLY EXIST

In the case of the Payments portal inside Invoices, as shown in Figure 14.5, the relationship to the Payments file was set up with the option to allow creation of related records. That puts an extra blank row at the bottom of the portal, ready to receive a new payment when it arrives. That empty row does not actually represent an existing record, so its blue arrow, if clicked, needs a message saying, "This payment record does not yet exist." Metaphysical, huh!

Figure 14.5
The Payments portal (lower left) shows payments on this invoice, taking information from the Payments file.

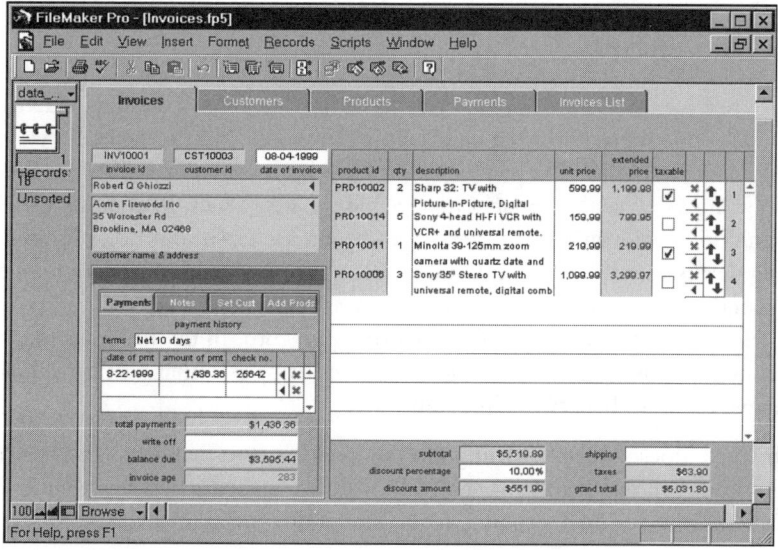

Here is the show_selected_payment Script

```
If [ Status( CurrentMode) = 1 ]
        Perform Script [ "beep_beep_not_in_find_mode_message" ]
                [ Sub-scripts ]
        Exit Script
End If
# "Go to the selected payment record. The IF statement below checks to make sure
that the payment record is valid (exists). Since the relationship that this portal
uses has the option to "Add related records", there will always be one blank
portal row at the end that enables users to add an additional payment."
```

```
Enter Browse Mode
If [ IsValid(Payments | inv_id::pk_pmt_ID) ]
        Go to Related Record [ Payments | inv_id ]
        Perform Script [ Filename: "Payments.fp5", "show_data_entry" ]
                [ Sub-scripts ]
        Perform Script [ Filename: "Payments.fp5", "find_all" ]
                [ Sub-scripts ]
        Perform Script [ Filename: "Payments.fp5", "maximize_window" ]
                [ Sub-scripts ]
Else
        Beep
        Beep
        Show Message [ Buttons: "OK", "", ""; Data: "This payment record does not yet exist!

        I feel your pain.  ☺" ]
End If
```

PARENT-TO-PARENT NAVIGATION IN A MANY-TO-MANY RELATIONSHIP

This script resembles the one for navigating from the child to the parent, but lets the user jump from one parent to another, skipping past the join file that is the child of both.

In our Invoicing system, we have a many-to-many relationship between invoices and products. One invoice can have many products, and one product can appear on many invoices. We resolve this many-to-many relationship with the middle file of InvLineItems. The invoice line items file is the child of both Invoices and Products. So we have a portal in Invoices to show all the products that have been ordered, and in Products, we have a portal showing us all of the invoices that include that product. In general, the line items file is not something we would show users. We let you look at it, but because we hide this file from regular users, we face the question: What happens when the user clicks the little blue triangle next to the product line in the portal inside Invoices? We now take the user to the Products file and show the user the product record. In the Products file, in the list of invoices, if the user clicks the blue triangle, we take the user to that particular invoice. In both situations, then, we bypass the line items file.

Invoices doesn't have anything directly relating it to Products, and Products doesn't have anything relating it to Invoices, so how do we navigate between them? We rely on a script called show_selected_product_from_line_item_portal in Invoices.

COMPONENTS OF THE SCRIPT

The script checks on the mode and bounces anyone who is in Find mode. Then we resolutely enter Browse Mode.

Because the Invoices file doesn't have a direct relationship with the Products file, we use a Global field, g_selected_prod_ID, which lives in the Invoices file. The script says, "If the user clicks the blue triangle, grab the product ID from that row and put it into our Global field." Now we invent a relationship between Invoices to Products, where g_selected_prod_id matches pk_prod_id over in the Products file. With this get-the-job-done relationship, we use the Go to Related Record command to bring up the record for that particular product.

The rest of this script resembles the other navigation scripts.

THE SHOW_SELECTED_PRODUCT_FROM_LINE_ITEM_PORTAL SCRIPT

```
If [ Status( CurrentMode) = 1 ]
        Perform Script [ "beep_beep_not_in_find_mode_message" ]
                [ Sub-scripts ]
        Exit Script
End If
Enter Browse Mode
Set Field [ g_selected_prod_id, Inv_line_items | inv_id::fk_prod_id ]
If [ IsValid(Products | g_selected_prod_id::pk_prod_id) ]
        Go to Related Record [ Products | g_selected_prod_id ]
        Perform Script [ Filename: "Products.fp5", "show_data_entry" ]
                [ Sub-scripts ]
        Perform Script [ Filename: "Products.fp5", "find_all" ]
                [ Sub-scripts ]
        Perform Script [ Filename: "Products.fp5", "maximize_window" ]
                [ Sub-scripts ]
Else
        Beep
        Beep
        Show Message [ Buttons: "OK", "", ""; Data: "This product ID is invalid." ]
End If
```

SCRIPTS THAT DELETE

If you keep users out of the menus, as we suggest, then the only way a person can delete a record is through a button you create with a script. You may, of course, decide you never want users to be able to delete records. In the invoicing system, the user might intend to delete the customer, and therefore get rid of all the children of that customer, including all the invoices, and all those invoices have children, called payments and line items; that cascading disaster can be avoided via scripts, or total refusal to allow users to delete anything.

DELETING A PARENT

If you do decide to let people delete a parent, you have to figure out what to do with the kids. Are you going to delete the children, force another parent to adopt them, or set up a restricted delete, where they have to get rid of all children before being able to delete a parent? If you have decided to allow some form of deletion, you might start by warning the user, explaining the implications of the delete, so her decision can be informed.

If the user presses ahead with the deletion, then you have to make sure that all business rules are satisfied. For instance, the business may insist that you archive all records before removing them from the active database—just in case. Or the business might say, "Don't let anyone delete a customer unless that customer's last order is more than three years old."

If those requirements are satisfied, you delete the record.

> **Note**
>
> In most of our files, you'll see that there are no buttons letting users delete records. The user cannot, for instance, delete any invoices (although an individual line item or a payment can be erased).

DELETING A CHILD

There are two places in the invoicing system where we delete a child: in Invoices, we let users delete payments and line items. These deletions take place in a portal (see Figure 14.6). The little red x invites the user to knock out the whole row.

Figure 14.6
The red x invites the user to delete a row.

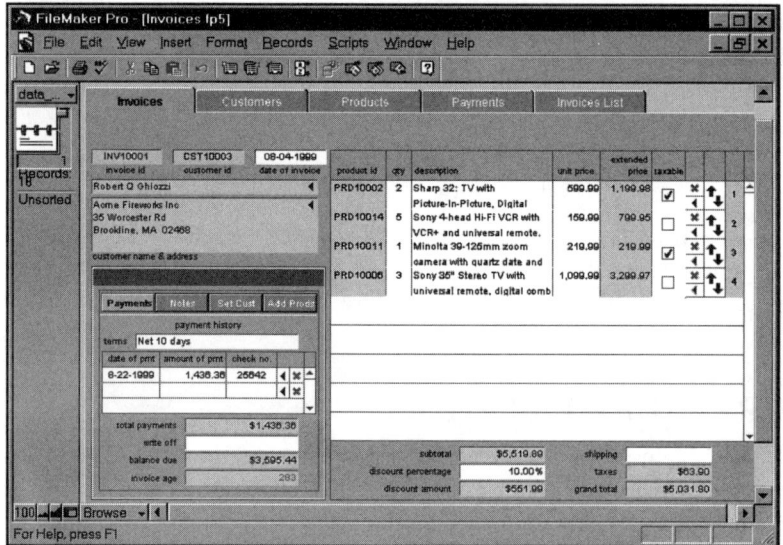

BEHIND THE RED X

The script behind the red x checks for mode, as usual, takes us into Browse Mode, checks that the record is valid as we did in the button that navigates us to the parent record, and then captures the number of the selected portal row. We go to that whole row and select it, so it shows up with black highlighting. We refresh the window, to make sure that the window is fully up-to-date. (FileMaker doesn't redraw after each step in a script because that would slow down performance. But here we want to refresh the window, to show the user that highlighting.)

Now we ask the users whether or not they really want to delete the record. "Do you wish to delete this payment record?" We offer an OK and a Cancel button on the message. Behind the message, remember, users can see the record they are thinking of deleting.

> **Tip from Rich**
>
> Make the first button the safe choice in Show Message. The first button is the default button. If the user hits the Enter key, the action that occurs is the first one, and just in case the user is not paying close attention, you ought to make your first option the least dangerous. In this case, that's Cancel. Also, clicking the close box in Windows dialog activates the same choice as button 1.

> **Tip from Rich**
>
> Buttons are numbered from right to left. Button #1 is on the far right, button #2 is second from the right, and so on. The designers clearly expect buttons to start on the far right of the dialog and move left.

> **Tip from Steven**
>
> But on the Mac, it's different. In FileMaker Pro for the Mac, in Perform Apple Script dialogs, the buttons are numbered left to right following the standard Mac OS convention. Thus button #1 is the leftmost button, button #2 the middle one, and button #3 the rightmost one, if all three buttons are selected. This difference can cause no end of confusion.

If someone chooses the second button (the OK), we just delete the record without any dialog to sidestep FileMaker's usual warning (because we already presented our own more specific warning).

Of course, if the record turns out to be invalid, we beep at the user and announce that fact. (At the end, we complete the first IF, which tested the validity of the related record.)

The delete_related_payment_record script:

```
If [ Status( CurrentMode) = 1 ]
        Perform Script [ "beep_beep_not_in_find_mode_message" ]
                [ Sub-scripts ]
        Exit Script
End If
# "This script deletes a related payment record. The IF statement makes sure that
the user has selected a valid portal row, rather than the extra row at the end of
the port used for adding new payments."
Allow User Abort [ Off ]
Set Error Capture [ On ]
Enter Browse Mode
If [ IsValid(Payments | inv_id::pk_pmt_ID) ]
        Set Field [ g_portal_row, Status( CurrentPortalRow) ]
        Go to Portal Row [ g_portal_row ]
                [ By Field Value..., Select entire contents ]
        Refresh Window
        Show Message [ Buttons: "Cancel", "OK", ""; Data: "Do you wish to delete
this payment record?" ]
        If [ Status( CurrentMessageChoice) = 2 ]
                Delete Portal Row
                        [ No dialog ]
        End If
Else
        Beep
```

```
        Beep
        Show Message [ Buttons: "OK", "", ""; Data: "This row cannot be deleted." ]
End If
Exit Record/Request
```

Scripts for Creating New Records

Building a script to create a new record can be as simple as saying just "Create the darn record." But if the business rules are complicated, this script can get as gnarly as an old cottonwood. For instance, you might have to walk the user through a wizard's sequence of screens, each with options and requests for data, followed by some validation, to make sure that all the choices are in fact consistent with the business rules.

Some folks run a check for duplicates before the user continues with data entry. If the user is entering a new contact, for example, the wizard would ask for the name and address of the contact, then go off and check those against current records to verify that there are no records for that person. If the wizard found any matches, it might show those to the user, saying, "Can you make sure this person isn't already in our database, in one of these records?" In this way, the wizard prevents unintended duplication.

Easy Example of Creating New Records

In Invoices, we have a simple scenario. We check to make sure that the user has not accidentally pressed the New button while in the Find mode, because there is no such thing as a new record when you are in Find. We insist on going to the Browse mode, creating a new record, and bringing the user to the SetCustomer screen via a subscript, hoping to encourage the user to pick a customer for the new invoice.

The new_invoice script in Invoices

```
If [ Status( CurrentMode) = 1 ]
        Perform Script [ "beep_beep_not_in_find_mode_message" ]
                [ Sub-scripts ]
        Exit Script
End If
Enter Browse Mode
New Record/Request
Perform Script [ "show_data_entry_set_customer" ]
        [ Sub-scripts ]
```

Scripts for Sorting

We recommend preparing a standard sorting script as a module, to call from various other scripts or modify as needed. By the way, the actual sorts are in subscripts we call from this one.

We start off by checking the mode to make sure we are not in the Find mode. We enter Browse mode. Now, before we do any sorting, we capture the ID of the record the user is looking at, storing that in the Global field called g_current_record_id, for future use. Here's why. Whenever we perform a sort, FileMaker puts the user in the first record in the new sort. Users find this experience confusing. They start off in a particular record, do the sort, and, wow, end up in a different record. So we want to return the user to the same record after the sort.

TO ASCEND OR DESCEND

Our standard script allows the user to sort in ascending order by default, or using the Alt key in Windows or the Option in Mac, to sort in descending order. Part of our script makes this option possible. The script looks to see which modifier keys are being held down, so we can tweak the sort for the user to ascend or descend. The script decides whether to run the subscript for descending or the subscript for ascending order.

Modifier key	Value
Shift	1
Caps Lock	2
Control (Mac) or Ctrl (Windows)	4
Option (Mac) or Alt (Windows)	8
Command (Mac)	16

We are saying, "If the modifier key value is 8, that means the Option or Alt key is being held down, but if the value is 10, the Caps Lock is also being held down." If the user is not pressing any modifier keys, we go ahead and sort ascending, using a subscript; pressing the modifier keys, we sort by descending, using another subscript.

> **Tip from**
> *Rich*
>
> Put sorts in their own subscripts so you can call them from anywhere; they are self-documenting modules. Here, for instance, we had to farm out the ascending or descending sorts because any given script can hold only one setting for a sort, find, import, export, page setup, or print setup, such as the sort order. Also, any one script can only perform a single sort; any others must be performed by subscripts. So we had to create one script for descending and another for ascending. We use the Perform Script to call them as needed.

> **Caution**
>
> Letting the user sort forward or backward adds a fair amount of hard work to your job as a developer. Take on this chore only if your users really need the capability. If so, the feature can wow them, because of the convenience and extra power it gives them.

RETURNING THE USER TO THE ORIGINAL RECORD

At the beginning of the script, we caught the ID of the record the user was on, so now we run the subscript return_user_to_current_record, ensuring that the user goes back to the original related record, based on a relationship between the field g_current_record_id and the pk_inv_id.

The sort_by_date_of_invoice Script

```
If [ Status( CurrentMode) = 1 ]
      Perform Script [ "beep_beep_not_in_find_mode_message" ]
            [ Sub-scripts ]
      Exit Script
End If
# "If the user is holding down the Alt key on Windows or the Option key on a
Macintosh, sort descending. Otherwise sort ascending. Note that we check to see
if:
Status( CurrentModifierKeys) = 8 or Status( CurrentModifierKeys) = 10
In this way, the script will work if the Caps Lock key has been pressed when the
Alt or Option key is pressed."
Enter Browse Mode
Perform Script [ "capture_id_of_current_record" ]
      [ Sub-scripts ]
If [ Status( CurrentModifierKeys) = 8 or Status( CurrentModifierKeys) = 10 ]
      Perform Script [ "sort_by_date_of_invoice_descend" ]
            [ Sub-scripts ]
Else
      Perform Script [ "sort_by_date_of_invoice_ascend" ]
            [ Sub-scripts ]
End If
Perform Script [ "return_user_to_current_record" ]
      [ Sub-scripts ]
```

Scripts for Reporting

Whenever you create a report, consider using a script to ensure that

- You have restored the page setup or print setup properly.
- You have chosen which records to print, inside the Print dialog.
- You have gone to the right layout.
- You have applied a special Find, accepted the current Find, or stopped to ask the user to enter criteria. In this way, you identify which records to include.
- You have applied the right sort.

Given these conditions, many of which may be specific to a particular report and not others, you may not want a universal reporting script, but instead a series of carefully tailored scripts handling these issues for the individual reports.

In the invoicing system, if the user is on the Customers tab (that is, inside the Customers file), finds a set of records, and clicks a button at the bottom to get a report, then any report will be based on the found set. In the Reports chapter, we recommended reporting from the child in most cases, because you can get more complete information there. This report is being run in Invoices, but the found set there probably does not match the found set in Customers, which are the ones we want to report on. So we have to alter the found set in Invoices to represent the invoices from the found set of customers. Unfortunately, that means we will be changing the found set of records in Invoices, which might confuse the users because when they return, there could be a different set of found records. Therefore, at the end of the reporting process, we need to restore the set of records we found at the start.

In the Customers file, print_ar_aging_by_customer runs another script there, capture_id_of_found_set_of_customers, to collect the right invoice records relating to those customers.

THE CAPTURE_ID_OF_FOUND_SET_OF_CUSTOMERS SCRIPT

```
Enter Browse Mode
Allow User Abort [ Off ]
Set Error Capture [ On ]
Go to Layout [ customer_id ]
Copy All Records
Go to Layout [ developer ]
Paste [ g_found_set_record_id_list ]
       [ Select entire contents, No style ]
Go to Layout [ original layout ]
```

We learned earlier that if you have multiple keys separated by carriage returns all put together in a field, each can be a potential match in a relationship. We are putting all the IDs of the found customers into one field so we can locate matches in a while. Later, we will go to the related invoice records for these customers, creating a new found set in Invoices, matching this set of customers, because we want to create the report in Invoices based on the records that have been found over in Customers. But right now, this particular subscript just finds the IDs using the Copy All Records command, which takes the values in all the fields on the current layout and puts them in the clipboard in tab-separated format, so we can paste that data into a Global field we use in a relationship to the Invoices file. We go to a layout that contains only the Customer ID, so when we copy all records that puts the found set of Customer IDs on the clipboard. Then we paste those into the Global field g_found_set_record_id_list on a different layout, replacing anything that may have been in that field earlier.

Tip from
Rich

> You can use the Copy All Records outside of a script. In Windows, make sure that you have not clicked inside any particular field; then hold down Shift and choose Copy from the Edit menu. Or if you hold down Option on a Mac and choose Copy, FileMaker will take the values in the current found set of records and put them on the clipboard. This trick lets you grab data from FileMaker and paste it into a spreadsheet or a table in a word-processing document. If you have not clicked in a field so you no longer see the flashing insertion point in a field, choose Copy without any modifier key held down to take all the values from the fields in the current record and place those on the clipboard.

At the end of this subscript, we return to the original layout in Customers to avoid confusing the user by displaying layouts the user never sees and never expected to see. We return to the main script, print_ar_aging_by_customer.

Capturing the IDs of the Current Invoices

Now, we capture the IDs of the original set of invoices so that later we can restore this set for the user. This capture takes place through the subscript capture_id_of_original_found_invoices, which acts like the script we just looked at for customer record IDs.

Printing, at Last

In the Customers script, print_ar_aging_by_customer, we then go to the invoices that relate to the found set of customers and launch the report. We use the following subscript, print_ar_aging_by_customer, which is the same name as the master script, but exists in Invoices.

The print_ar_aging_by_customer Subscript in Invoices

```
Enter Browse Mode
Allow User Abort [ Off ]
Set Error Capture [ On ]
If [ Status( CurrentFoundCount) = 0 ]
        Beep
        Beep
        Show Message [ Buttons: "OK", "", ""; Data: "There are no records in this report!" ]
        Exit Script
End If
Go to Layout [ print_ar_aging_by_customer ]
Perform Script [ "print_setup_portrait___found_records" ]
        [ Sub-scripts ]
Sort [ Sort Order: fk_cust_id (Ascending)s_tot_balance_due (Descending) ]
        [ Restore sort order, No dialog ]
Enter Preview Mode
        [ Pause ]
Enter Browse Mode
Print
Go to Layout [ original layout ]
Unsort
Perform Script [ "reset_value_lists" ]
        [ Sub-scripts ]
```

We start this subscript by checking to make sure that there are some found records. If the current count equals zero, we conclude that the current found set of customers has no related invoice records and we exit the script, alerting the user that there are no records to put in the report. Unlike a Halt, merely exiting this subscript sends us back to the script over in Customers, so we can finish that gracefully, cleaning up the debris before we turn control back to the user.

If there are some related invoices, we go to the right layout, set up the print setup, sort the records, enter Preview, and pause for the user to decide to go ahead. We've turned the User Abort option off earlier, so the Status Area will only contain a Continue button (no Cancel), because we don't want the user left in limbo through cancellation. When the user continues, we bring her back to Browse Mode, print the report, and go back to the original layout, unsorting and resetting our value lists.

The last step, resetting the value lists, restores the pop-up menus from which the user selects the report in the Invoices file. This command isn't required, because the user is running the current report from over in the Customers file, so presumably the Invoices pop-up menus do not need to be restored right now, but the user can run this script from Invoices, and in those circumstances, we need to restore the pop-ups.

Let's take a look at the master script, print_ar_aging_by_customer, in Customers, to restore the original found set of invoices and reset value lists inside Customers.

THE PRINT_AR_AGING_BY_CUSTOMER SCRIPT IN CUSTOMERS

```
Enter Browse Mode
Allow User Abort [ Off ]
Set Error Capture [ On ]
Perform Script [ "capture_id_of_found_set_of_customers" ]
        [ Sub-scripts ]
Perform Script [ Filename: "Invoices.fp5", "capture_id_of_original_found_invoices" ]
        [ Sub-scripts ]
Go to Related Record [ Invoices | g_found_set_record_list ]
        [ Show only related records ]
Perform Script [ Filename: "Invoices.fp5", "print_ar_aging_by_customer" ]
        [ Sub-scripts ]
Perform Script [ Filename: "Invoices.fp5",
"restore_original_found_set_of_invoices" ]
        [ Sub-scripts ]
Perform Script [ "reset_value_lists" ]
        [ Sub-scripts ]
```

Tip from
Rich

> Choose the subscripts option. If you are saying "Perform another script," and you choose the subscript option, then the other script will run along with any of its subscripts. Without this option chosen, the other script will run but will not call its own subscripts. We almost never deselect the subscripts option.

SCRIPTS ASKING USERS WHAT THEY WANT TO PRINT

If you have a Print button on a single record, you might want to ask the user whether you should print the current record or the found set. For instance, if a user is looking at our Invoices screen and clicks Print, we ask which records to print, offering buttons for All Found or Current (see Figure 14.7). We also offer a drop-down list called Print Other, distinguishing the Current from the Found records. We also offer a pop-up list of summary reports, all of which work on the current found set.

Figure 14.7
The modal dialog pops up when you click Print on the Invoices data entry screen.

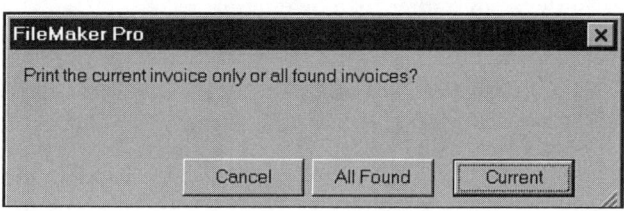

The print_invoice_button Script Behind the Print Button

```
If [ Status( CurrentMode) = 1 ]
        Perform Script [ "beep_beep_not_in_find_mode_message" ]
                [ Sub-scripts ]
        Exit Script
End If
Enter Browse Mode
Allow User Abort [ Off ]
Set Error Capture [ On ]
Show Message [ Buttons: "Current", "All Found", "Cancel"; Data: "Print the current
invoice only or all found invoices?" ]
If [ Status( CurrentMessageChoice) = 3 ]
        Exit Script
End If
If [ Status( CurrentMessageChoice) = 1 ]
        Perform Script [ "print_this_invoice" ]
                [ Sub-scripts ]
Else
        Perform Script [ "print_found_invoices" ]
                [ Sub-scripts ]
End If
```

This script posts the buttons and acts on the user's decision, using subscripts to print the current record or the found set.

Scripts for Preparing Canned Finds

If you are going to perform a find or enter the Find mode, you have the option to Restore. That means "Run the Find that I ran manually before I created this script, so those settings become part of this script." During the actual performance of the step, we will restore the Find settings that exist at the moment you are working on the script. These settings become part of the script by example. (This process works for all the commands that use settings—Enter Find Mode, Perform Find, Sort, Page Setup or Print Setup, Import Records, and Export Records).

One downside of using the Restore option in a Find is that you cannot see the settings or change them from within ScriptMaker. If you want to be fully aware of your settings, enter Find Mode without the Restore and Pause options, and then use Set Field to spell out the values that should be searched for and perform the Find (again without the option to Restore). Defining your Find this way, your script documents itself so you can see what the search criteria are rather than guessing. You can also adjust those criteria within ScriptMaker without having to back out, set up a new Find, perhaps running it to make sure it works, and go back into ScriptMaker. You can also set criteria conditionally because you are working in the script rather than by example.

Tip from *Rich*	You don't have to do the Find for ScriptMaker to pick up on the criteria. If you enter the Find mode and enter criteria, then go into ScriptMaker, and that is enough. Of course, you may want to run the Find just to make sure it works the way you expect it to.

Tip from
Rich

Use Globals to set up criteria. If you want to grab one or more values from the Browse mode and drop those into the Find, you could use Copy and Paste, but that only works for single values. If you put a value in a Global field, that value is available in the Find mode. Global fields are a good way to move values into the search criteria in a Find.

Tip from
Rich

Omit Record normally takes a record from the found set and puts it in the not-found set. But if the script is in Find mode for a moment, and the Omit Record command is performed, then FileMaker checks the Omit box visible in the status area of the Find screen, giving us more ability to create custom Finds on the fly. The Omit command, in Find, has the effect of a Boolean NOT. If you are building up a set of Find requests, you can use the Omit Records step to avoid certain records.

COMMON MISTAKE: USING A RANGE TO FIND A DATE

Perhaps you want to put variable search criteria into a Date field, such as "Find all meetings from Today through Today's date plus seven days." In Find, if Today is 4/22/2000, we would put 4/22/2000 into the Date of Meeting, followed by three dots, and 4/29/2000 to cover that range. You might be tempted to use the `SetField` command to do this. But `SetField` insists that the type of data should match the field type even in Find mode. But the date range is not a date, so FileMaker refuses to use these "invalid" search criteria. Instead, use the literal paste (Insert Calculated Result) to do that.

Tip from
Rich

Check that your found record count is more than 0 to make sure you get something other than frustration. You cannot always be sure you will get a match, so check the found count first.

```
If [ Status( CurrentFoundCount) = 0 ]
        Beep
        Beep
        Show Message [ Buttons: "OK", "", ""; Data: "There are
        no records in this report!" ]
   Exit Script
End If
```

Tip from
Rich

Consider taking users to another layout, using buttons for Find, Duplicate, and so on, if you want to make your own life easier. In doing this, duplicate the data entry layout, dimming out all the buttons and deactivating them. In the invoicing system, we decided to allow users to do searches from the data entry screen. That way, users are familiar with the screen. But getting this convenience to function properly may take a lot of work. Going to another layout is easier because then you don't have to worry about whether the user is on the data entry screen in Browse or Find, and you don't have to consider what mode they might be in, coming up with alternative ways of handling their situation. In this way, you are exerting more control over when buttons are active or inactive.

Scripts That Duplicate Records

When you are duplicating a parent record, you have to ask whether the user wants to duplicate the parent or the parent and the children. For example, does the user want to duplicate just the invoice without the line items, or the entire invoice with all its line items? You might want to ask via a message that offers the opportunity to duplicate with line items, without line items, or just cancel the whole thing. Here is the script called duplicate_invoice.

```
If [ Status( CurrentMode) = 1 ]
        Perform Script [ "beep_beep_not_in_find_mode_message" ]
                [ Sub-scripts ]
        Exit Script
End If
Allow User Abort [ Off ]
Set Error Capture [ On ]
Enter Browse Mode
Show Message [ Buttons: "With Line Items", "W/O Line Items", "Cancel"; Data:
"Duplicate Invoice with or without line items?" ]
If [ Status( CurrentMessageChoice) = 3 ]
        Exit Script
End If
# "If the user chooses to duplicate the invoice and the line items, and the count
of line items is greater than 0 (just in case the invoice being duplicated does
not yet have any line items), then go to the Line Items file and duplicate all the
line items."
If [ Status( CurrentMessageChoice) = 1 and
        Count(Inv_line_items | inv_id::pk_line_item_ID) > 0 ]
        Go to Related Record [ Inv_line_items | inv_id ]
                [ Show only related records ]
        Duplicate Record/Request
        Set Field [ Inv_line_items | constant::g_temp_inv_id, pk_inv_id ]
        Perform Script [ Filename: "Inv_line_items.fp5", "duplicate_found_
➥set_of_records" ]
                [ Sub-scripts ]
Else
        Duplicate Record/Request
End If
Perform Script [ "show_data_entry_add_products" ]
        [ Sub-scripts ]
```

Handling Button Actions in Your Scripts

If you run scripts through buttons, consider how important the button actions of Pause, Resume, Exit, and Halt can be. In the file ButtonAction, go to Layout mode, and when you double-click the button, you get the Specify Button dialog (see Figure 14.8) with a drop-down menu offering the choice of these four options, which look innocent enough, but in some circumstances, can have dramatically different effects. Each deals with the circumstance when a user has pressed another button while this script is running. In theory, the user is telling FileMaker to do something else. But what?

Handling Button Actions in Your Scripts 477

Figure 14.8
The Specify Button dialog offers options that look innocent enough, but watch out!

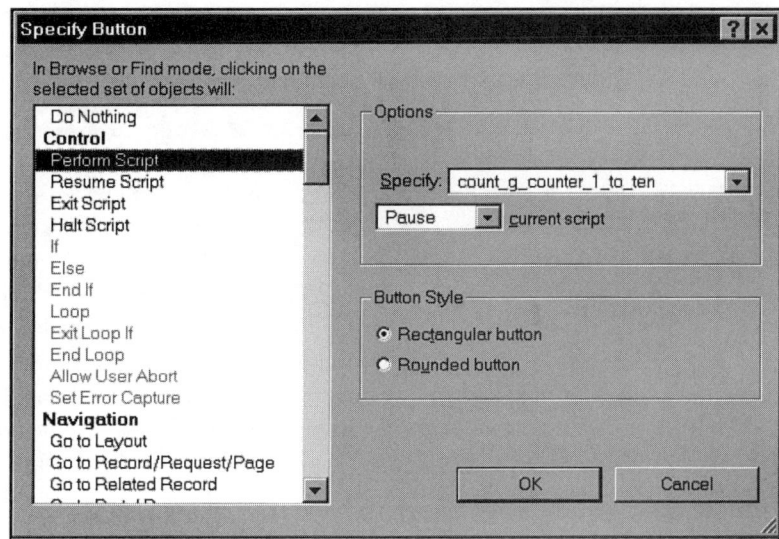

You might want to start the first counter rolling by clicking Count to Ten over on the left, which starts the numbers going as shown in Figure 14.9.

Figure 14.9
The numbers start rolling away from 1 to 10.

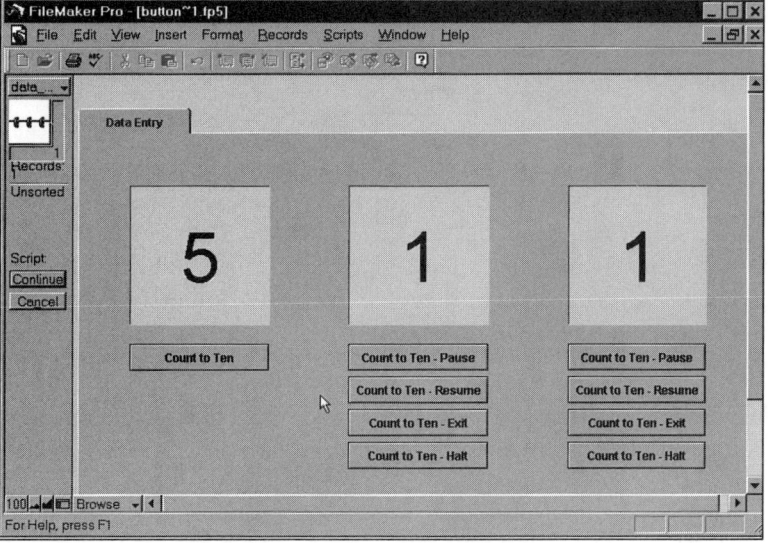

Once that script is counting away, move to the second column and click Count to Ten–Pause. The first script is paused and the Status Bar shows the Continue and Cancel buttons, and then the second display starts counting to ten. The first script stays paused until you click Continue.

To see more drama, go to the Scripts menu and choose Reset Values so we can be absolutely sure nothing is still paused. (Please do this between each trial sequence in what follows).

PART
III
CH
14

> **Note**
>
> If you try to click a button while another script is in process, you have to watch carefully for the feedback to be sure your click really got through.

Now try the Resume buttons in this way: Start the counting in the first column, then quickly click Count to Ten Resume in the second column, which temporarily pauses the first column. Then to really introduce confusion, click the Count to Ten Resume in the third column. That pauses the second column. Note that when the third column hits 10, then the second column resumes, and plays out its climb to 10, and when that finishes, then the first script finally gets to resume. The Resume function pauses whatever script is currently running, and then restarts it after doing whatever you like, such as playing Dixie with beeps, displaying a meaningful message, or running a subscript. Where Pause depends on a user clicking Continue before the script can go on, Resume just starts over, when any intervening action is completed.

Exiting: If you start the first counter running, then click Count to Ten–Exit in the second column, the script starts rolling in the second column, and the Continue and Cancel buttons go away, so that we know the first script has not actually been paused, but aborted. Exit, then, causes whatever the current script is doing to stop, but any other scripts in the cue above will finish up. So choose Scripts, Reset Value, then click the first-column button, and in the second column, click Count to Ten–Resume. When that is rolling along nicely, click the third column button called Count to Ten–Exit, and you will see that the second script stops, altogether, but once the third column reaches ten, the first column resumes its progress.

Halt stops the current script, and all others in the queue, essentially blocking all scripts in line. To see this in operation, click Scripts, Reset Values, then click the first-column button, then Count to Ten-Resume in the second column, and finally, Count to Ten–Halt. After the third column reaches ten, the Continue and Cancel buttons disappear, and the other columns remain unchanged. The scripts driving the numbers in the first two columns have been halted, altogether, even though in the second column we said it should resume after we finish the numbers in the second column. Halt, then, overrides the stack of scripts waiting to be resumed.

Another scenario, to show you how important the difference between these four approaches can be: Click Count to Ten on the left, then, once it gets going, click it again. The numbers go to 10, but then Continue and Cancel buttons show up on the left. Click Continue, and the numbers go on up above 10.

We set the field g_counter_1 to 1 as a way to initialize the variable. Then we go into a loop. We pause for one second, increase g_counter_1 by 1, and exit when that field equals 10. If someone presses the button once, the field starts off at one, and goes on up. When pressed a second time, the button action is set to pause, so it stops counting at 5, puts that first iteration of the script on hold, and begins running the same script again, starting off from 1. When it reaches 10, it goes back to the first version of the script. But going back to the first iteration of the script does not set the value back to 1, because it was paused in the middle of a loop, and the loop is beyond the step that initializes the variable. So when you click Continue, the script says to increase the counter by 1, and it goes on and on and on, past 10. How come? The user likely presses the button during the pause, which takes a full second (compared to the split second for other steps). When after reaching 10, we click Continue, the loop will never find 10 again, so the count goes on forever.

We recognize that we could have prevented this behavior (by testing for equal to or greater than 10). We included this craziness to show how the action choice can cause weird behavior. Here, the choice was pause. Exit would have done better, because that would have aborted the first iteration before going on. Halt would have gotten rid of every script.

CHAPTER 15

TROUBLESHOOTING A SCRIPT

In this chapter

Looking for Trouble 482

Scripting Gotchas 484

LOOKING FOR TROUBLE

Not that you will ever have problems with a script, but if your friend does, you might recommend these techniques.

Scripts may work well under most circumstances, but act up now and then. The intermittent problems are really hard to identify and solve.

Or a script may work for a long time and then break. You have to wonder what has changed in its surroundings.

Most frustrating of all is the problem that is, in theory, easiest to fix. You stare at the script and cannot figure out what the heck is wrong, even though it breaks consistently.

For all these moments, we recommend trying out some of these approaches.

INTERRUPTING WITH Pause

You may need to interrupt the script at some point to see whether the script has worked so far. These techniques work best when you have conditionals or loops misbehaving.

Putting pauses into the script lets you see what the script has done so far, and compares that with what you expected. You need to choose moments when the results will really show up in fields, so you can check.

Pause does let us examine the database at that moment, but if you have multiple pauses, how can you tell which one you are at? Show Message may help.

INTERRUPTING AND SHOWING MESSAGES

Show Message lets you identify which pause you are looking at. Show Message pauses the script anyway, but allows you to put up a message telling yourself where you are, and maybe what you hope is going on at this moment.

HALTING THE SCRIPT AT DIFFERENT PLACES TO SEE WHETHER IT WORKED SO FAR

If you put a Halt Script in, you abort that script and all others that were running at that point. This quick-and-dirty technique lets you examine everything in the database to see what is going on. If the script seems to be working to that point, then you can move the Halt Script down a step to see if the trouble intrudes there.

> **Tip from**
> *Rich*
>
> Don't delete. Sometimes if you suspect a particular step, don't delete the step right away, because you might have trouble recreating all its settings and options. Instead, put an Exit Script at the end of the script, and put all potential offenders below the Exit Script, where they will never be performed, but they are available to be moved back in later.

> **Tip from**
> *Steven*
>
> If you have a particularly large script, another way to accomplish the same result is to put another IF statement in, putting a condition that you know will always be false, such as a 0, or the text `"If hell freezes over."` Put the IF ahead of all the steps you want to keep but not activate and put the END IF after them. Thus, the steps will still be there, but they will not be performed because the test is always false.

Writing Script Results to a Log Field or File

Writing out the results of the script operation as it happens lets you watch the results as they go. Setting up the log operation may take a little work, but for a long and complex process, the log can help you spot the problem.

CASE STUDY: USING A LOG FILE TO SPOT TROUBLE

We were doing work for a large company, and every night they had their backend Oracle system dump an extract to a text file, and we had to grab that extract and add it to their existing FileMaker system. In the middle of the night, we would quit FileMaker server, open the files in regular FileMaker, and perform a sequence of operations. First, we ran an FTP to bring the extract down from the directory used by the Oracle database. Then we imported the material, got rid of duplicates, and closed the file, quit regular FileMaker, and reopened it in FileMaker server. The problem was that this process ran at 2 AM when no one was looking at it. When the first trials experienced problems, we did not know why. So at the beginning of every script, we wrote to the log file the date and the time, and a note that said, "Beginning the such-and-such script," and if there were significant milestones within a script, we wrote out a log file whenever we began and ended those processes. We also did some error trapping. For example, after we did the import, we tested the found count of records and wrote that count to the log file, along with any notes on success or failure. By rereading the log file, we were able to pinpoint the source of the intermittent errors.

EXAMPLE: USING THE DEVELOPERS LOG

In the example files for Chapter 9, look at Companies tab in the Companies-l01.fp5 file and locate the field Developers Log. Here, you can see what file the users were in, what action was going on, and when. We also track the TROI plug-in error codes.

Beeping at Yourself

Some may consider this technique bizarre, but when a loop seems to be going off track, we put a Beep step into the loop. We don't want to pause at every step, but the beeps give audible feedback about what is going on, and the pattern of the beeps suggests the way the script is behaving. Those little beeps have bailed us out on several occasions.

Using Analyzer—A Two Thumbs Up Product

Analyzer, from Waves in Motion (www.wmotion.com), tells you everything you wanted to know about your database but were afraid to ask. It looks at fields, layouts, value lists, scripts, and relationships. When it looks at your script, it reports potential problems.

Analyzer puts all the results into a database, so you can look at the information many different ways. If you are serious about FileMaker development, Analyzer is a must-have tool. It also lets you generate technical documentation for a customer or someone who will be maintaining the database. Alas, it runs only on the Mac because it relies on Apple Events and AppleScript. Even if you are working in a pure Windows environment, we'd recommend you buy a Mac just to run Analyzer.

PRINTING THE SCRIPTS

Printing gives you information that you don't see inside ScriptMaker, such as settings alongside the steps and their options. Sometimes, a glance is enough to spot the wrong setting.

By the way, in FileMaker Pro 5, scripts indent properly when you print them. This is a real godsend.

Tip from *Rich*	Print the scripts to PDF files, because that format is searchable. If you have hundreds of scripts and you don't remember where you put a particular item, you can find it through Acrobat Reader.

Tip from *Rich*	Ask someone else. This is often the best approach, if you are fortunate enough to be around folks who could look through the script. We do this all the time. Better to have someone point out your error in a few minutes than bang your head against the wall for a few hours.

Tip from *Rich*	Duplicate a script and play with the dupe. Don't screw up the original. If a script is particularly problematic, don't start hacking away at the original, because you can lose track of your changes. Duping and working on the copy lets you preserve the original until you discover the problem and fix it.

SCRIPTING GOTCHAS

Becoming a professional scriptwriter involves a lot of trial and error, learning, sadly, to protect yourself against little surprises by a series of good habits, conservative routines, and diligent practices. Here are some scripting "gotchas" to watch out for, with some suggestions for ways to avoid them. Many of these alerts have been generously contributed by professional developers, whose names appear next to the gotchas. We have to say, though, that we are responsible for the way these reminders are written, so if you spot a problem, please email us, not them.

GOTCHA #1 CONFUSING Exit AND Halt.

Exit only interrupts the current script, but other scripts in the queue will continue to run. Halt stops every script.

Gotcha #2: Leaving Yourself No Way Out of a Loop.

When writing the loop, remember to leave the backdoor open while testing to make sure the loop works. Do not allow `User Abort [off]` until you are sure that you, as the first user, have no need to stop the loop, because it works perfectly.

Tip from
Marc Norman

> Include an `exit loop if` statement inside the loop, saying "Exit Loop If [Status (CurrentModifierKeys) = 13 or Status (CurrentModifierKeys)=15]." This tests to see if the Shift, Alt, and Control keys are all being held down at the same time on a Windows machine, or, on the Mac, if the Shift, Command, and Option keys are all being held down at the same time. We check both 13 and 15 because we do not know in advance whether the Caps Lock key has been pressed down; 13 is without Caps Lock, and 15 is with.

Gotcha #3: Tracking Script Variables in a Field That Is Not Global.

If you try to keep track of a variable in a non-global field, alas, that value is likely to change from record to record. *Note: Rich was banging his head against the wall at some bizarre behavior. After much thinking, he realized that he had fallen into this pit. Don't let it happen to you.*

Gotcha #4: Leaving Restore on When You Don't Really Mean It.

Restore takes the settings for Find, Sort, Import, Export, Page Setup, and Print Setup, for example, and applies them in your script. But you might just not notice that Restore was on, and you might innocently apply settings that really don't work for the script, by accident. Always ponder whether or not you really want to use Restore.

Example: If You Left Restore Checked

Your script enters Find mode, and you use Set Field to specify the Find request and Perform Find to trigger the find operation. At that moment, you would not want to have Restore checked. If you did leave it checked, alas, the search criteria that were originally stored with the script, for example, would be applied, not the criteria you carefully built up during `SetField`.

Gotcha #5: Portals Don't Redraw While a Script Is Running or Afterward.

FileMaker Pro generally suspends Refresh during the running of a script, to spare users the flashing lights and changing scenery. But sometimes you want the screen redrawn during or after a script. To make sure it is refreshed, try

```
Go to Field [] (with no field specified inside the brackets)
Set Field (primary key, primary key)
Refresh Window
Enter Find Mode followed by Enter Browse Mode.
```

Gotcha #6: Going to the right row in the wrong portal.

The `Go to Portal Row` command cannot specify which portal to use. The workaround is using `Go to Field` just before you go to the portal row, because `Go to Field` lets you specify the name of a relationship, implying which portal to go to. If this does not work right, put an `Exit Record` in front and that will often fix things right up.

Gotcha #7 from Steven H. Blackwell: Scripts tripping on themselves in fast processors.

Processors run so fast today that scripts can get ahead of themselves. For instance, if you are integrating with an outside technology such as AppleScript, putting a pause of `0` seconds lets the script catch up and work correctly. But even within ScriptMaker, an occasional pause of `0` seconds can clear up a balky script.

Gotcha #8: Letting the screen vibrate during the running of a script.

If you don't freeze the window, FileMaker may flash and bleep and bop the screen around during the processing of the script. Freezing the screen just makes everything look calm and professional.

Gotcha #9 from Jeff Gagne: Scripts running slowly with `If`, `Case`, or `Choose` calculations.

Don't use large `IF`, `Case`, or `Choose` calculations within a single calculation in a script step like `SetField`. Better split that chunk up into separate script steps. For example

```
If [fieldA = 1]
        Set Field [fieldB, some_calc_1]
Else
        Set Field [fieldB, some_calc_2]
End If
```

would be faster than

```
    Set Field [fieldB, "If(fieldA = 1, some_calc_1, some_calc_2)"]
```

Gotcha #10 from Jeff Gagne: Slowdowns when using `Set Field`.

If you have a bunch of `Set Field` script steps in a row, be sure that there is a `Go To Field [x]` step before the `Set Field` steps, and an `Exit Record` step at the end. Otherwise, every single `Set Field` step will (1) open/lock the record, (2) upload the changed record, and (3) unlock the record. By doing the `Go To Field` first, the record will be locked once then, and uploaded/unlocked just once on the `Exit Record`. This modification to your script can bring a major performance improvement.

Gotcha #11 from Aileen Silver: Confusing nested IFs with a sequential series of IFs.

The result of a group of nested `IF`s can be different from the result of a group of sequential `IF`s. Nested `IF`s are mutually exclusive, while sequential `IF`s may give you more than one `True` result.

Gotcha #12 from Darren Terry: Scripts don't work because the fields needed are not on the current layout.

All the following script steps insist on having the target field on the current layout:

- Cut
- Copy
- Paste
- Clear
- Insert Calculated Result
- Insert User name
- Insert Date
- Insert Time
- Replace
- Relookup
- Go To Field

If the field isn't on the current layout, that step is skipped.

Gotcha #13 from Darren Terry: Expecting that the script will wait until AppleScript or some other external technology has completed its chores.

When you use a script step such as Perform AppleScript, Send Apple Event, Send Message, or Perform DDE, FileMaker only waits until the message has been sent off to the other technology. When the "Wait for event completion before continuing" check box is checked, the "event" in question is the message or Apple Event being sent, not the actual execution of the orders contained within the message, in AppleScript or some other outside technology. If a long AppleScript is executed, FileMaker will not wait until the AppleScript is done. FileMaker simply waits until the message has been sent out requesting that the AppleScript be executed.

Gotcha #14 from Darren Terry: Thinking that Speak will work on Windows machines.

Speak is a Mac-only script step. (Its control panel is called Speak.)

Gotcha #15 from Darren Terry: Pausing a script by mistake, by using Show Message.

If you are running a script that involves a long, complicated process, you might want to post a message to the user saying, "Sorry, we are very busy running these big ugly calculations, and could you please be patient?" The minute the message goes up, though, the script is paused until the user notices it and dismisses the message. The workaround is to go to a layout that contains the message, and when the script is done, go back to the original layout.

GOTCHA #16 FROM DARREN TERRY: RECURSIVELY CALLING THE SAME SCRIPT OVER AND OVER.

Better to use a Loop. If your script gets called over and over, then you can create a stack overflow that ultimately crashes the script.

GOTCHA #17 FROM DARREN TERRY: FORGETTING TO COMMENT.

You never know when that comment will come in handy. The right comment can save you a lot of time in a few months, when you have forgotten the 43 considerations that led you to write the script in just this way.

GOTCHA #18 FROM DARREN TERRY AND JEFF BENJAMIN: IF A SCRIPT PERFORMS A Replace COMMAND IN A MULTIUSER ENVIRONMENT, ANY RECORDS CURRENTLY IN USE BY OTHER USERS WILL BE LOCKED AND NOT UPDATED.

In a multiuser situation, if you need to do a Replace on more than one field, use a looping Set Field script that moves through the database record by record instead of a script that does multiple Replace steps. Why? First, the script will probably execute noticeably faster. (Far fewer packets are passed back and forth between the guest and the host with a looping Set Field script than with a Replace script). Second, it's safer, in that you can check whether the record is in use with Status [currenterror] in the looping script, while the Replace will simply fail if the record is in use.

GOTCHA #19: RELYING ON FEATURES THAT ONLY WORK IN CERTAIN VERSIONS OF FILEMAKER.

This "gotcha" is like counting on a bug, only to find it has been fixed—or vice versa, counting on the user having a version in which the bug has finally been fixed, only to discover the user has clung to the older version, where the bug is still rampant. Check the version number in the startup script. Use Status (CurrentAppVersion) to check the version the user is running.

GOTCHA #20 FROM ANNE VERINDER: SKIPPING A RECORD BY MISTAKE, WHEN LOOPING THROUGH AND OMITTING OR DELETING RECORDS.

If you have a script step that omits or deletes a record, FileMaker assumes it should go to the next record, so if you tell it to go to the Next record, it skips one to get there.

Workaround: Start by using Go to Record (Last), and then use Go to Record (Previous), or use a structure where you advance a record only if the Omit or Delete did not take place:

```
Go to Record/Request/Page [First]
Loop
   If [" email = "Coulombre@supportgroup.com" "]
      Omit Record
   Else
      Go to Record /Request/Page [Exit after last, Next]
   End If
End Loop
```

Gotcha #21 from Anne Verinder: Using `Set Field` to find a range of dates.

Sometimes in a script, we enter the Find mode and want to locate records within a range of dates. At first, you might assume you could use `SetField` to do this, but it doesn't work, because `SetField` recognizes the field as a Date, and a range of dates is not a valid date, so the find fails.

Workaround: Use the `Insert Calculated Result` command, using the `DatetoText` function in the calculation, to put the range into the Date field during Find. For some reason, `Insert Calculated Result` does not balk at putting a range into a Date field. Go figure.

Gotcha #22 from Patricia Schiffman: Leaving the user in another file.

Sometimes, we put a `Perform Script` step at the end of a script, sending FileMaker off to another file to run the script. But in that situation, FileMaker has no reason to come back to the original file, and the user may be surprised to discover he or she has been transported to a new location by magic. To make sure the user is brought back to the original file at the end of the script, insert a benign command at the end of the script in the original file, such as `Enter Browse Mode`, so that whenever a subscript is performed in another file, FileMaker will know to come back to the original file, rather than leaving the user in some unexpected file.

Gotcha #23 from Patricia Schiffman: Forgetting to return the user to Browse mode after a Preview.

If you have a script that previews a report for the user, don't leave the user in Preview. Go back to Browse.

Gotcha #24 from Patricia Schiffman: Forgetting to set `Print to Current Record` and printing every record by mistake.

In FileMaker the Print dialog lets you pick which records to print. If you inadvertently set that to Records Being Browsed, that setting may be stored in your script, for example, as part of the Page Setup or Print Setup step. Your user might get a printout of every record in the database, instead of the one needed.

Gotcha #25 from John Morina: Wiping out each insert with the next one in a sequence, rather than appending one after another.

Sometimes, you use a series of insert operations (`Insert from Index`, `Insert from Last Record`, `Insert Current Date`, and so on) to build up a field value or a Find request, but when you have one insert after another, you should make sure that the first one has the option to Select Entire Contents checked, so the first insert replaces the current contents, and then each subsequent `Insert Calculated Result` should not have this option checked, so the additional inserts are appended rather than wiping out the ones you just inserted.

Gotcha #26: Startup scripts that don't always run.

Startup scripts won't run if the file has been opened incidentally for the purpose of showing a related field or a value list, or if it is just opened to perform a script that lives there.

Gotcha #27: Having an operation performed on the first row of the portal, not the one you intended, because you left the portal for a moment and FileMaker lost track of which row was selected.

Sometimes, a developer has a button in a portal row, and when a user presses the button, the script leaves the portal briefly to do something, and then the script expects to operate on the row in the portal, but FileMaker is no longer there, so it comes back to the portal, and, not knowing which row to work on, operates on the first row. In leaving the portal, FileMaker loses track of which row was selected.

Workarounds: Capture the portal row by using the Status (CurrentRow) before leaving, or just don't leave the portal row before leaving, as when going to a related record.

Gotcha #28 from Jeff Benjamin: Comparing fields that aren't of the same type.

You get unexpected results, to say the least, if you try something like comparing Date and Text fields in an IF script step.

Gotcha #29 from Jeff Benjamin: Not seeing the settings in a script onscreen.

When looking at the script in ScriptMaker you see the options, but not the settings. Onscreen, the settings for steps such as Import, Export, Find, Page Setup, and Print Setup are hidden, but they show up when you print. To check the settings, print the script out.

Gotcha #30 from Melissa Kurtz: Forgetting that a user's password may make an action impossible.

A script can only run properly if the user's password lets him perform all the actions that you have put into the script. For example, a script that attempts to delete a record will fail if the user lacks password privileges allowing deletion of records.

Sometimes, a multifile system will restrict delete privileges to the db manager. But a lower level user may try to run a script that deletes records, and FileMaker just refuses to perform the deletes. Melissa Kurtz recalls: "This happened with a system that daily imported records into a child file from an accounting source file after deleting a found set of duplicate records. The file normally should have about 300 records. One day the client called saying the file had 15,000 records and was taking 45 minutes to run the script. After going over there, I found out the user (who was new) was using the wrong password so no records were being deleted, though more were being imported each day. I cleaned out the file, gave him the correct password to use, and now the script runs in 30 seconds."

Gotcha #31 from Scott Key: Testing for `Status[CurrentError]` a few steps too late.

`Status [CurrentError]` does not last forever. After completing each step in a script, FileMaker generates this status, and mostly that is 0, meaning that there was no error. But if you wonder whether or not a particular step has been performed successfully, the safest way is to store `Status [CurrentError]` in a global field right after the step, because as soon as FileMaker carries out the next step, the error number will be changed and the code you care about will have disappeared.

Gotcha #32: Expecting the Mac Page Setup to work in Windows Print Setup or vice versa.

You may set up landscape orientation on the Mac and be surprised to find that on Windows you get the report in portrait. The settings do not carry across platforms.

Workaround: You can add the settings in the other platform by going there and setting up the dialog, then opening the script again without changing any steps, then clicking OK and choosing Replace for this step (a bit of a misnomer in this case). Here, FileMaker does not actually replace the existing settings but adds the new ones, so that the step contains the settings for both the Page Setup (Macintosh) and the Print Setup (Windows) in the same step.

Gotcha #33: Going haywire because you're in the wrong mode.

Occasionally, a script can get fouled up if you are in the wrong mode. For instance, if the user goes into Preview, where the `New Record` or `Delete Record` commands are not available, and if your script references one of those, the step is skipped. The mode can make a huge difference to the success or failure of a script, so a conservative approach is to start each script with `Enter Browse Mode`, so you can be sure what mode you are in rather than just hoping the user or system has left you in the right mode.

Gotcha #34 from Steven H. Blackwell and Danny Mack: Importing a script without checking the validity of the references in the new situation.

When importing scripts, always double-check that the references to fields, relationships, value lists, and other scripts are still okay inside the new file.

Gotcha #35 from FileMaker Tech Info: Wasting a step to open a file when you need to use one of its scripts.

Referencing an external script is enough to open the script, and you do not need to open the file first. However, do use Open File first if you want the file's startup script to run.

Gotcha #36 from FileMaker Tech Info: Wasting a step to enter Browse Mode after exiting a Find or Sort.

When FileMaker completes a Find or Sort script step, it places you back in Browse Mode, showing the first record in the found set or sort order. You don't have to use the Enter Browse Mode command or go to the first record.

GOTCHA #37 FROM FILEMAKER TECH INFO: CONFUSING SetField WITH COPY AND PASTE.

Understanding the difference between `SetField` and Copy and Paste can help you avoid many small gotchas. `SetField` will work even if the source field and the field to be set are not on the current layout; both fields could be in related files. Copy and Paste only work if both fields are in the current layout.

The steps also have different effects in the field you are putting data into. `SetField`, by default, replaces the contents of the field. Paste, though, only replaces the contents if you check Select Entire Contents; otherwise, it appends the material. Text style, too, may be affected. Copy copies with text style, and Paste can paste with or without the text style. `SetField` ignores the text style. (Anything that goes through the calculation engine, like `SetField` or `Paste Calculated Results`, loses its text style). Lookups, though, preserve text styles.

If you want to work in Find, you can use either script step, but `SetField` is very sensitive to matching field types, where `Insert Calculated Result` is less sensitive. For instance, if you want to put a range of dates in a Date field (that is, material that is not strictly speaking a date), you can get away with that by using `Insert Calculated Result`, but not `SetField`.

GOTCHA #38 FROM FILEMAKER TECH INFO: WASTING A STEP GOING TO A FIELD WHEN YOU CAN SPECIFY THE FIELD IN THE STEP ITSELF.

The following commands let you specify a field for the operation: Clear, Copy, Cut, Paste, `Insert Calculated Result`, `Insert from Index`, `Insert from Last Record`, and `Insert Current Date/Time/User`.

GOTCHA #39 FROM FILEMAKER TECH INFO: FORGETTING TO HANDLE ERRORS.

You can't always assume that your script ran properly. For example, if your script does a Perform Find, you might want to check if the script found anything. If not, you may want to branch to some activity that's different from what you would do if some records were found. Use the `Set Error Capture on` early in the script and insert a little code dealing with the errors.

GOTCHA #40 FROM FILEMAKER TECH INFO: APPLYING THE SCRIPT TO MORE RECORDS THAN YOU INTENDED.

Sometimes, you need to run a script only on the current record, so you want to make it the entire found set at the beginning of the script. Do a Find All, then omit this record, and, triumphantly, find the omitted records. Now your current record is the found set. (Rich suggests new syntax: Find All Now, then Show All Records.)

GOTCHA #41: SORTING BEFORE FINDING.

If you have both a Find and a Sort in the script, put them in that order. If you Sort, then Find, you lose all the results of your sort.

Gotcha #42: Trying to include more than one setting per script for Find, Sort, Import, Export, Page Setup, Print Setup.

Within a single script, you can perform a Find 10 times, but each step will do the same find. So if you try to create two different finds in the same script, the settings from the second one will triumph over the settings for the first one, and so on. You can have only one set of settings for each of these commands per script.

Gotcha #43 from Marc Norman: Placing duplicated scripts in the wrong spot.

In ScriptMaker, you can select multiple steps, including ones that are not contiguous, and then use Duplicate to dupe the group. This new group of script steps shows up immediately after the bottommost step you selected for that group. If you don't want the duplicate group to appear in that position, include a step further down, where you want the group to appear, as the last item in the duplicate group. Duplicate, and the group lands where you want it. Then you can delete that unnecessary step from the duplicate group because you only selected it for the sake of the positioning.

PART IV

REACHING OUT

16 Integrating FileMaker, Expanding Its Reach   497

17 FileMaker Pro Multiuser Design and Deployment Considerations   519

FileMaker is everywhere. In this part, we'll explore the myriad ways your database can exchange data with various devices and applications by using industry standards and taking advantage of many interconnecting networks.

CHAPTER 16

INTEGRATING FILEMAKER, EXPANDING ITS REACH

In this chapter

FileMaker at the Center   498

Examples of the New Connectivity   499

How FileMaker Connects   500

Different Ways of Connecting with FileMaker   501

Taking Advantage of Industry Standards for Data Exchange   505

Using ODBC, JDBC, and Java   506

Going from HTML to XML and WML   517

And Don't Forget Reports   518

FileMaker at the Center

In the beginning, FileMaker ran only on the Mac. Then came FileMaker Pro 2, which ran on both Mac and Windows computers. Then with FileMaker Pro 4, we saw cross-platform Web capabilities. With 4.1 we got new import capabilities, following the Open Database Connectivity (ODBC) specs for receiving data. FileMaker Pro 5 adds support for the eXtensible Markup Language (XML), and acts as an ODBC source as well, so other programs can now swap info with FileMaker following the ODBC specs. Through the serial port, FileMaker can trigger scientific instruments to collect information, or, in a small business, open a cash drawer. FileMaker can communicate with pagers, cell phones, PDAs, wireless PDA, and old-fashioned email. The FileMaker world has expanded far beyond the desktop, and as developers, we need to collect information and distribute it among many different platforms, programs, and devices, relying on industry standards, as shown in Figure 16.1. We can now connect with all these other technologies to solve business problems more effectively than before.

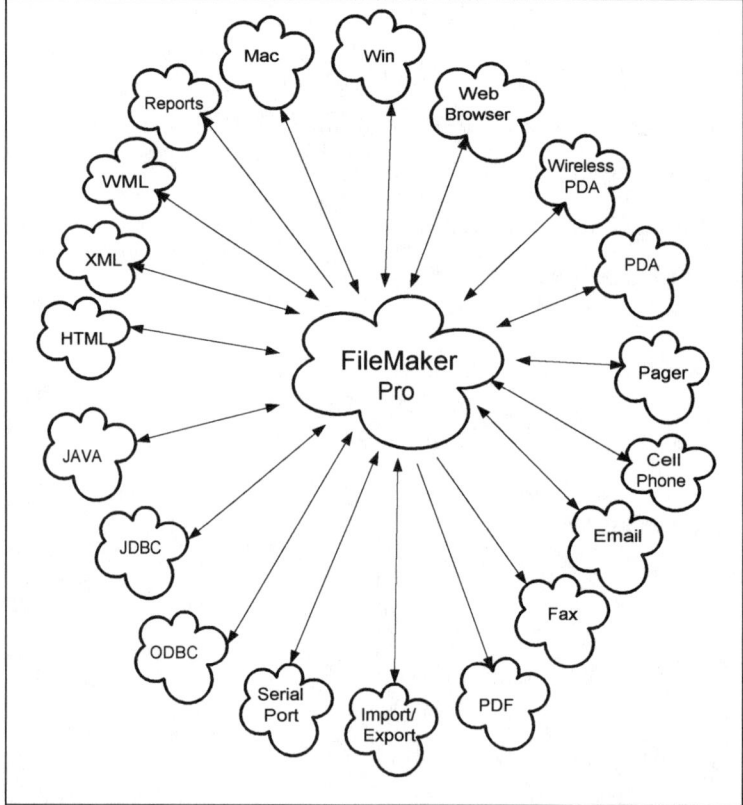

Figure 16.1
FileMaker sits at the center, orchestrating the flow of data.

When you put FileMaker at the center of the universe like this, it can integrate with each of these technologies, holding them all together. For example, a client can enter a contact on a wireless PDA, submit that record to a FileMaker database, and, on creation of the new record, FileMaker can dispatch an email welcoming that person as a customer, attaching files that describe relevant products.

Examples of the New Connectivity

To give you a snapshot of the ways FileMaker can draw together information from many different technologies and send that info back out to other ones, here are some anecdotes from our experiences with clients.

Salespeople on the Road

There is a sales organization living inside a financial institution. The salespeople run around the country doing deals, and for cost and efficiency, a single salesperson tries to line up a series of meetings with various current and potential customers during each trip. Of course, the salesperson may be on the road meeting with folks, making a few scribbled notes during those meetings, then coming back home for the weekend, and finally coming into the office on Monday, but by then, many details have grown fuzzy. The boss wanted to help the salesperson capture the information soon after the moment of contact, because the accuracy and depth of detail would be better. The solution relied on the Palm VII access to a FileMaker database. Right after a meeting, the salesperson can now search for the organization's record, and add comments and insights, while sitting in the rental car out on the lot. The improved information on each customer gave the team a competitive advantage. Wireless connectivity was only one of the possible avenues, but our client went down this route because he felt that the Palm VII fitted into his salespeople's way of life best.

Furniture Inventories on the Hoof

When we are consumers looking at the way businesses operate, we see ways that this new FileMaker technology could help. We recently visited a furniture store that takes up a few acres. Each salesperson walked around the floor with a thick bundle of green-and-white–striped computer printouts of the inventory as of that morning. We pointed to one item after another, and asked, "Is this available?" The salesperson had to flip through the paper and say, "Yes," or "No," or "It will be available soon." We thought: If the salespeople only had a Palm, they could walk over to the cradle, which has a cable connected to the computer, press the HotSync button, causing the synchronizing operation to come alive. In a few seconds, then, the salesperson could check the inventory, live. The snapshot of the whole database would come down to their PDA, and now, walking around the warehouse, the salespeople could do a search on the database, for various items, as the customers ask.

You might wonder whether we'd recommend allowing salespeople to place orders via the PDAs. Perhaps. But the biggest bang for the buck would be displaying the up-to-the-moment inventory. Think of how much paper they would save—and how much back pain they could avoid. Also, we find it helpful to move development forward one step at a time. The initial stages, although less glamorous, often turn out to give the client the biggest return on the investment.

Upscale Furnishings

A fancy furniture store's online presence depends on data from an Oracle database, but the managers have to do lots of ad hoc reporting. The team members like having FileMaker pull data from the Oracle database via ODBC so they can make up reports any way they want without struggling with the query tools for Oracle or turning to an IT person to write up a new report.

Press Office

A major university's press office used to generate a press release on paper, distributing that by email, snail mail, and fax. They had a database of press contacts, which they would print out. A manager would circle each contact to which a particular story should be sent. Then someone else would determine that contact's preferred way of receiving the releases. That staffer, then, would sit by the fax machine and send out the faxes; go to the email program and copy and paste the story, emailing each story individually; and finally, photocopy the story, handprint addresses on envelopes, and mail those out. You can imagine how much time it took the staff person to send out a big story to hundreds of contacts. (Minor or very local stories just went to a few contacts).

We created a FileMaker database for their contacts, categorized in groups such as technology editors, theater critics, or Rich's special list. The body of the press release went into the database as a story (essentially a record). Then they could create a distribution list for the story, and that list might include individuals or whole groups. (We double-check to make sure nobody gets the same release twice). Then the staffer can press a button saying, "Distribute this story." For each contact who wants to receive an email, FileMaker composes and sends the email story, using its own Send Email command. For each person who prefers faxes, FileMaker makes up and sends the fax, using an add-on called FaxTool (http://www.datadesigns.com). And finally, for the old folks who like paper, FileMaker generates letters and envelopes for snail mail. In this way, FileMaker goes beyond its own desktop to solve business problems. The office staff could measure the benefits in time spent, speed of delivery, accuracy, and that intangible, a higher level of professionalism.

How FileMaker Connects

Historically, FileMaker lived on its own desktop computer. You could retrieve and manipulate information living on the hard disk. With FileMaker Pro 4, though, we could reach out to the Web using the Web Companion. And with its new plug-in architecture, third parties could add little utilities written outside of FileMaker to handle functions such as file handling (as with the TROI File plug in) and making charts based on your numbers (0azium Charts). And, therefore, as other programs get the ability to communicate with FileMaker, you can pull in their data and manipulate it in FileMaker in many different ways.

There are two main external interfaces to FileMaker. Plug-ins use a published spec called the Plug-In Architecture, which is accessible by developers via the Calculation engine. Then there is a Companion Interface, a confidential, internal Application Programming Interface

(API), which is used by the Web Companion. The specs for the Companion Interface are not available outside of FileMaker, but the existing companions already written using that interface will allow you to do more with FileMaker than you could do with some of the plug-ins, such as choosing and using custom interfaces developed by FileMaker or its own developers.

Increasingly, because the Companion Interface is not public, clever programmers are relying on the Web Companion itself as an API to FileMaker. Here are some plug-in vendors with whom we have had great success:

- Troi Automatisering — http://www.troi.com
- Professional Data Management — http://www.profdata.nl
- Protolight Software — http://www.geocities.com/siliconvalley/network/9327/home.html
- e4Marketing — http://www.e4marketing.com
- Waves In Motion — http://www.wmotion.com
- New Millennium Communications — http://www.newmillennium.com

You can also find lists of plug-ins available with descriptions at the FileMaker Web site.

Different Ways of Connecting with FileMaker

In the old days, if we wanted to get data out of the database, we might print out or display a report or a set of records. But today we can send those records and reports to many different platforms on an incredible array of different physical devices, using industry standards for data exchange. FileMaker Pro can make much of this data exchange possible, and thanks to its plug-in architecture (a stroke of genius on the part of someone at FileMaker), we can turn to plug-ins for additional outreach.

Platforms

We're all familiar with FileMaker Pro's two operating-system platforms—the Mac and Windows—and the more-or-less cross-platform Web browser. Long ago, users could only get data on the desktop (or at the printer on the next desk). The Web browser is the most dramatic way that data has been freed from the constraints of a user's operating system. Now anyone who's on the Web can access the FileMaker Pro data, even, horrors, when using a Web browser on a UNIX or Linux system, a mainframe, or some obscure lingering mini-computer in a university. One reason why IT folks are migrating to Web delivery is because they do not have to worry as much about deployment, updates, installations, and troubleshooting for multiple applications and drivers on multiple platforms.

The pendulum is swinging back. Years ago, the VT100 and VT220 were industry standards from Digital, describing how we ought to paint a screen. The terminal was dumb, because it could collect and display information, but not process it. The pendulum, nudged by Apple, swung back, leading consumers and businesses in a rush to personal computers on the desktop, so we struggled to create client-server setups, where a lot of processing went on right on the desktop. The hassles of maintenance, updating, and control have driven the pendulum back the other way, although not all the way, so that now we have a desktop device with a lot of processing power, using the Web browser, which is another industry standard for painting the screen with data from a whole network of remote servers. Handheld devices extend this model, because they have enough processing power to get, manipulate, and send information, while depending on much larger computers out there on the network for mass storage, high-speed processing, and routing. The latest trend means we can communicate with many forms of smart "terminals," that is, the gizmos at the end of the line. And now that "line" is wireless, too.

The FileMaker Server often sits at the center of a local area network, but communicates anywhere the network reaches, including across the Internet. The desktop version of FileMaker can communicate with the server, so FileMaker itself becomes a mechanism for displaying, manipulating, and sending data, even though the data is maintained by the server software. The server is ideally suited to managing a network of FileMaker Pro users, particularly when you have a lot of users and data. But the server itself is fairly thin, as software goes, because it does not display the data or publish to the Web, or integrate with ODBC or XML. (There is no interface to the data.) It is just a supercharged database engine, communicating with FileMaker Macintosh and Windows clients.

WIRELESS PDAS, PDAS, PAGERS, AND CELL PHONES

Personal Digital Assistants (PDAs) are used by many of our customers, to get their lives organized. Eventually, folks realize that these devices can carry database information around, such as contact info, product specs, price lists, and catalogs. For instance, there are many database products developed specifically for the Palm series, such as Jfile (http://www.land-j.com/jfile.html), HanDBase (http://www.handbase.com), and Satellite Forms (http://www.pumatech.com). You can use a utility to synchronize Jfile with FileMaker on the Mac desktop (http://www.fmsync.com). HanDBase syncs up with a desktop version of FileMaker on Windows, using the HanDBase desktop software, which we can control with custom batch files to send data back and forth to FileMaker and the HanDBase software on the Palm. Satellite Forms requires some customizing to sync with FileMaker Pro.

Because these devices are disconnected, you have to ponder where the data is being changed (on one side, the other, or both sides). If data is only updated on one side, then the synchronization process always flows from master to slave, an arrangement that keeps things simple. If data is being changed on both sides, though, you face the gnarly issue of performing true synchronization. If the same piece of information can be changed on both sides, then whose changes do you keep? This synchronization process depends on the business rules for coping with the different ways that data may be modified in your environment.

Being able to carry data with you in such a convenient device is very appealing, and will become ever more popular. Letting users add records, delete data, and run calculations—you are offering data to go. That's exciting. But synchronization is not simple.

A wireless PDA connects the user, live, to the data, avoiding these problems of synchronization. Data is never out-of-date. Data is hot, fresh, and steaming in the user's hand.

For instance, we've done wireless connections using the Palm VII. We developed custom Palm Query Applications (PQAs), which combine HTML and graphic files to display on the Palm VII, with hypertext links to a FileMaker database with the Web Companion enabled. FileMaker has no idea that a Palm VII is out there. FileMaker just knows that some Internet browser is sending a request for an action, such as deleting a record, adding a record, searching, or sorting. For information on PQAs go to http://www.palm.net and go to the Development Zone.

When developing for a Palm device, you have to think about the small screen size. You can't show as much at once as on a computer screen. Also, the throughput is slower so you need to minimize the amount of information you draw down or send through the pipeline, moment to moment. You can't build a complex layout as you would for someone with a desktop monitor. And, yes, each wireless device costs more than a regular PDA with cradle, and your customer faces a monthly fee for connectivity. But going wireless is definitely cool because your users can get at data no matter where they are. The gizmo's perfect for small amounts of data that the users have to look up or enter on-the-fly. They don't have to wait for the operating system to come on; it is instantly on. And the device is right there in a pocket in their cargo pants.

Tip from
Rich

> As PDAs become more prevalent, fashions are going to change, adding more pockets. Sure, an average shirt has one pocket where you can put glasses, pens. But now it has a Palm. We predict that shirts will have more pockets. We particularly recommend cargo pants, with half a dozen pockets, perfect for your pager, your wireless PDA, your glasses, your pens, your GPS locator, your CD player, and your jewelry boxes.

CASE STUDY: GET US TO THE STAGE DELI

Rich was in New York with a group of relatives, huddled together in Times Square. Rich likes the Stage Deli, and he wanted to find out how to get there. He flipped open the Palm VII, went to the yellow pages, did a search on the Stage Deli, found the address and phone number. He pulled out the cell phone, dialed the deli, and asked how to get there from Times Square. Meanwhile, the relatives were staring in bewilderment, and asking his wife, "Is he always like this?" She said, "Yeah, basically."

> **CASE STUDY: THE LIGHT BULB GOES ON**
>
> Rich's business partner was half an hour early for a meeting with a customer. While sitting in the car, he thought that he'd like to buy a bulb for his projector, but he didn't know the area well. He flipped open the Palm VII, did a search for audio-visual stores in the area, came up with one a mile away, called them on the cell phone to check if the item was in stock, drove down, and picked it up. He made it back in plenty of time for the meeting with the customer. That's the kind of instant access that makes the wireless PDA such a convenience.

At a recent Seybold Conference, Rich was giving a talk to an audience of developers, managers, and marketeers. Back on his office desktop computer, he had a database open and running under FileMaker Pro 5 Unlimited, with Web publishing turned on. He asked for a volunteer to give a name, address, and phone number. Through a Web browser on a desktop machine on the podium, Rich added that record to the database back in his office. Then, flipping open the Palm VII, Rich activated a custom PQA he had written, which connected to the same database going through the air to a cell, and from that cell back to the Palm site, and from there over the Internet to the office, which routed it to the proper desktop computer. He ran a query for that person's record, which brought the record back to the Palm site, and through one of the cells back to the Palm VII, displaying the results in Rich's hand. He pressed a hypertext link on the results page, to drill down to the full details of the contact information about the audience member. In a few seconds, the Palm VII displayed a record with a few buttons at the bottom.

Using the first button, Rich emailed the person with a custom message using the person's name and sales info (along with a PDF attachment). At the same time, email went out to a salesperson, saying that the message had gone out to the potential customer, along with the name of the attachment. Finally, a note was added to a log field on the customer record, saying that this info had been sent to this contact on this date at this time.

Then on the desktop computer on the podium, Rich logged into his America Online account to show the email sent to him as the designated salesperson. The audience volunteer also had email waiting for him. Rich now pressed the other button on the form on the Palm VII, which paged the sales contact (who, in this case, was Rich), telling him to call the contact. An email was sent out to a pager from Rich's office, and ten or fifteen seconds later Rich's cell phone rang with a message saying to call this customer. His cell phone interprets the phone number within the text, so all he had to do was press Talk to dial the number. So he pressed Talk, and the cell phone dialed the customer's phone number. Because this razzamatazz was still rare, the audience applauded. But within a few years, folks will take for granted this capability to move freely among different devices and sources of data.

In this new world, FileMaker is a lot more than a pile of data; it is now a manager of the flow of information into and out of these different technologies. You are doing more than manage data; you are managing its circulation. Imagine how many permutations of communication become possible when you integrate pagers, cell phones, regular PDAs, wireless PDAs, desktop computers, and servers.

Taking Advantage of Industry Standards for Data Exchange

FileMaker can take advantage of a wide range of industry standards to allow you to exchange data with many other devices, applications, and computers all over the place—with users in cars, checkout counters, supermarket aisles, or on the beach. In many cases, you can even manipulate the data at a distance.

FileMaker can, for instance, send and receive emails, piggybacking on a user's email software. The scripting language contains a SendEmail command, compatible with certain email programs such as Outlook on Windows and Eudora on the Mac. If your users have those email programs, the script can identify the subject line, message, and email addresses. These can be hardcoded, or you can use values from fields, so that you can customize the field content in order to send out personalized emails. You can also enclose an attached file.

> **Tip from**
> *Rich*
>
> If your users do not have one of the compatible email programs, consider a plug-in that gives FileMaker the ability to work with other email programs. Go to the FileMaker site, click the Solutions tab, click Find Plug-Ins, and search for email. (On Mac OS, this can be done with any of a series of AppleScripts.)

FileMaker can also dispatch faxes, relying on a cross-platform tool such as FaxTool, available at http://www.datadesigns.com. You need to have some faxing software loaded. On a Mac that would be FaxSTF, and on Windows, WinFax Pro. You use steps in a script to communicate with FaxTool, a stand-alone application, which in turn translates data and instructions and passes those along to those fax applications, initiating the faxing process. (We have found FaxTool very reliable.)

Acrobat's Portable Document Format (PDF) offers users the ability to send a fully formatted report to someone who lacks the application it was created in, the fonts, or the graphic files. The whole shebang goes out in the PDF file, and, as long as the recipients have the free Acrobat Reader, they can see and print the document just as it would look if printed on paper back at your user's office. In fact, when your user has the full Acrobat application, it acts like a printer, coming up in the list of printers. If a user wants to distribute a report company-wide and some people do not have FileMaker, printing to a PDF and emailing that (or posting it on a server) gets the information out to everyone. Distant salespeople can download the PDF and use the Acrobat Reader to view it on their laptop screens in the hotel, rather than hoping to get a fax through the luggage room downstairs. Your user needs to choose the Acrobat driver in the list of printers, give the file a name, and specify a location for the file, such as an Intranet server for all employees. Or your user can send that file as an attachment to an email.

Importing and exporting also follow industry standards, so you can move data in and out of FileMaker, sending and receiving the data to and from applications that adhere to the same standards. For instance, you could export a SYLK file with spreadsheet information, and, potentially, email that to people. This might be an interesting way to communicate information to many customers or employees in a form that they could quickly manipulate and reuse.

→If you want to export information to create Web pages, **see** "Exporting Data as HTML Pages with the Results of Calculations," **p. 267**, or if you want to export RTF text **see** "Creating a Fully Formatted Document for Database Publishing," **p. 313**.

Serial communication, another industry standard, allows FileMaker to receive or send information through the serial port, hooking up to devices such as point-of-sale terminals and scientific instruments. You need to use a plug-in such as the TROI Serial Plug-in to allow FileMaker this direct connection to a lot of devices. For instance, you can have FileMaker connect to a modem, do custom switchboard dialing, capture incoming caller ID information, collect credit card information, scan products with a barcode reader, send and gather data to and from control units, or open a cash drawer.

Using ODBC, JDBC, and Java

Originally, the desktop database vendors offered an easy-to-use graphic interface for users, but had to write their own drivers to query every other data source their customers wanted to connect to. For instance, Omnis had to write drivers to query Oracle, Sybase, and Informix databases. So did Fourth Dimension. Eventually, the industry agreed that standards would save everyone a lot of work. If every desktop database supported the standard, and if every backend data source also supported the standard, then a database vendor could rely on a single piece of connectivity software to carry out all exchanges. ODBC is a documented Application Programming Interface (API)—that is, a spec defining a standard way for database applications to talk to one another and to exchange data. FileMaker 4.1 could import data from an ODBC source such as Oracle, SQL Server, an Excel spreadsheet, or a text file; with FileMaker 5.0 the new ODBC driver allows FileMaker to act as an ODBC source for other applications looking for data, handling queries from other databases, query tools, Web sites, or Microsoft Office applications.

Now FileMaker Pro 5 can communicate with any other database that supports the ODBC standard. It can import from an ODBC source and act as an ODBC source for another application seeking information or sending information into FileMaker. So far, FileMaker Pro 5 cannot put data back into an ODBC source. But there is a plug-in to handle this task. A Dutch company called Professional Data Management (http://www.profdata.nl) offers an ODBC plug-in that lets FileMaker import and then put data back into an ODBC source. Of course, with the new possibilities come heavier responsibilities for you as a developer. For instance, strangers can now read your field names, so the text needs to articulate the purpose and perhaps the type of each field.

Making FileMaker Pro a Data Source for ODBC Applications

You add FileMaker Pro as a data source in this way:

1. In FileMaker Pro, go into the Application Preferences, shown in Figure 16.2, and on the Plug-Ins tab turn on either the Local or Remote Data Access Companions. Choose the Local Data Access Companion if you want to use a local query tool to get at the data. Choose the Remote Data Access Companion if you want to use a different query tool on a remote computer to query via TCP/IP.

Figure 16.2
Application Preferences lets you turn on a data access companion.

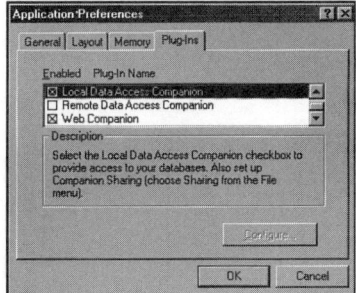

2. Having enabled the access companion, go to the database you want to become a data source and choose File, Sharing. You see the File Sharing dialog, shown in Figure 16.3.

Figure 16.3
The File Sharing dialog lets you identify the access companion.

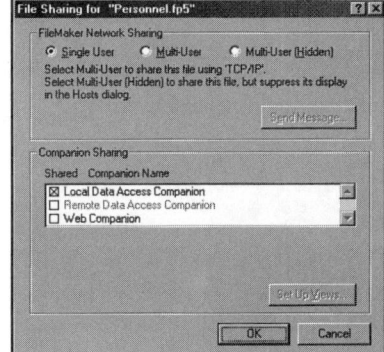

3. In the File Sharing dialog, enable the same access companion you set before. That's all you need to do within FileMaker. Now you have to turn to the operating system.
4. To create a Data Source Name (DSN), open the ODBC control panel called ODBC Data Sources (32-bit). You see the panel shown in Figure 16.4.

Figure 16.4
You are creating a Data Source Name (DSN).

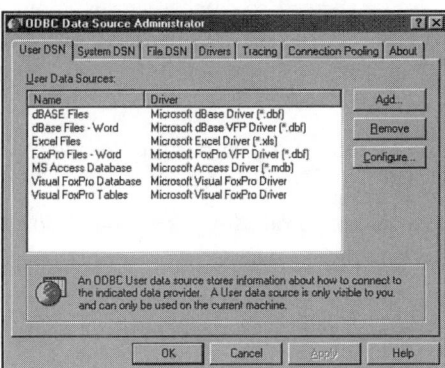

5. If your database file is not in the list of data sources, click Add. You see the dialog called Create New Data Source, with a list of all current ODBC drivers as shown in Figure 16.5.

Figure 16.5
You see a list of all current ODBC drivers.

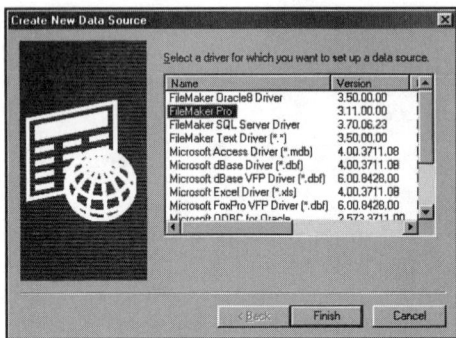

6. Select FileMaker Pro from the list of drivers, and click Finish. You're brought back to the ODBC FileMaker Pro Driver Setup dialog (see Figure 16.6).

Figure 16.6
The ODBC FileMaker Pro Driver Setup dialog lets you identify your Data Source Name.

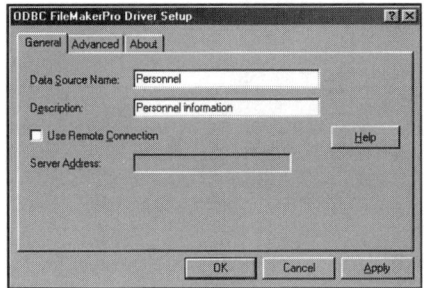

7. Fill in the Data Source Name (the file name, which in this example is *Personnel*) and description.

8. If you are going to be using a FileMaker Pro database across a network, or as a database behind a Web application for Peer Web Services or Internet Information Service, click Use Remote Connection and fill in the IP address. (We're not doing this in this example.)

9. To fine-tune the exchanges, click the Advanced tab and do one or more of the following:

    - Establish a maximum text length for all the text columns, so the driver does not allocate more space than it really needs.
    - Determine the number of files you want kept open, even when the tables are apparently closed, to speed up queries using File OpenCache.
    - Define the Fetch Chunk Size, stating the number of rows you want FileMaker Pro to bring back each time it processes a request to fetch some data (too high, and you lose speed; too low, and you have to go back for more pretty often).

- If you don't like a regular ASCII sort (lowercase letters before uppercase letters), and prefer to have the driver itself perform an International Sort as defined by your operating system, check International Sort.
- If you are using Active Server Pages and don't mind taking a hit on performance in exchange for making your own life easier, choose Number, Date, and Time as Text, because you won't have to worry about the exact SQL escape sequences for date and time values.

10. Make sure that FileMaker Pro is running when you want to share data.

GETTING ODBC DATA OUT OF FILEMAKER

The process of getting data out of FileMaker as an ODBC source is similar to the process you go through to pull data into FileMaker from an ODBC source (in some other application). Here we'll walk you through the process of getting data from FileMaker and putting that into a brand new Excel file.

1. Go into Excel.
2. Choose Data, Get External Data, New Database Query. You see the Choose Data Source dialog (see Figure 16.7).

Figure 16.7
Here you can choose the data source.

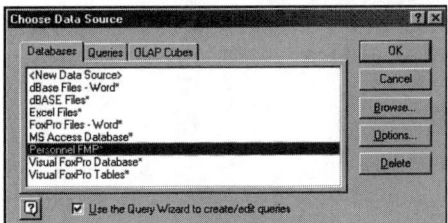

3. Choose the data source from the list and click OK, leaving the Data Query Wizard checked, to see a methodical progression of decisions. (When you know what you're doing, you won't need the wizard, so you could uncheck it and start creating your own SQL.) You now see the dialog shown in Figure 16.8. (This screen is the equivalent of the Select tab in the FileMaker ODBC Import dialog.)

Figure 16.8
Now you get to identify the fields you want and the order in which you want them.

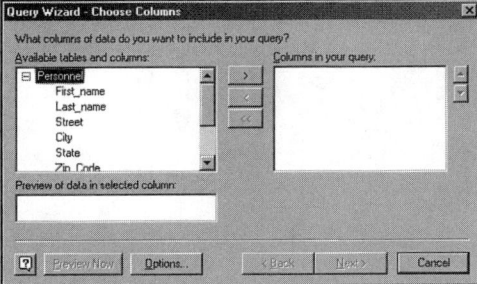

4. Choose the fields (known here as columns) and arrange them in the order you want. When you have made selections, the Next button comes alive.
5. Click Next to go to the Filter Data dialog, shown in Figure 16.9, and specify which records you want. This is the equivalent of the Where tab in the FileMaker ODBC Import dialog.

Figure 16.9
The Filter Data dialog lets you specify which records you want.

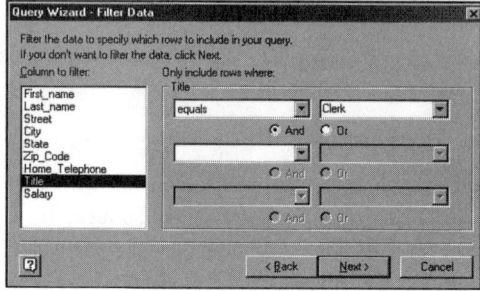

6. Click Next, to go to the Sort Order dialog (see Figure 16.10), and specify a sort order. This is the equivalent of the Order By tab in the FileMaker ODBC Import dialog.

Figure 16.10
Here you specify the sort order.

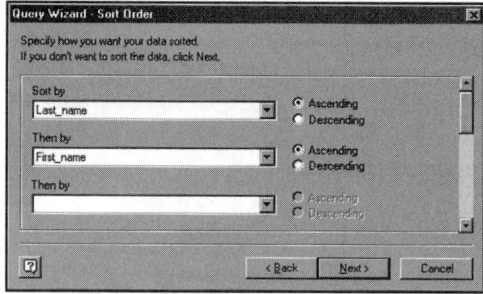

7. Click Next to go to the Finish dialog, shown in Figure 16.11.

Figure 16.11
The process is almost complete.

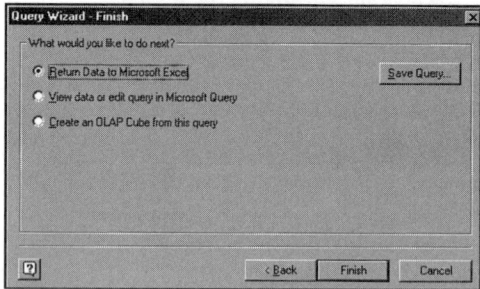

8. In the Finish dialog, choose Return Data to Microsoft Excel and click Finish. You see another dialog asking how you want the data returned (see Figure 16.12).

Figure 16.12
You're asked how you want your data returned.

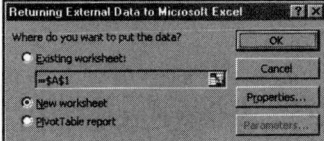

9. Choose New Worksheet to get a brand new Excel file and click OK. You see the data in an Excel worksheet, as shown in Figure 16.13.

Figure 16.13
The new Excel worksheet displays your data, brought in from FileMaker.

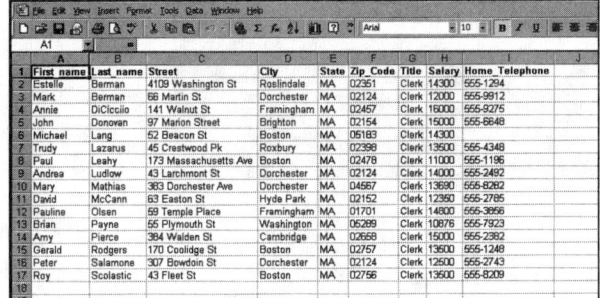

10. Go back to your FileMaker file, to confirm that the query in fact generated a found set, as shown in Figure 16.14.

Figure 16.14
Your original FileMaker file shows that you now have generated a new found set.

FileMaker Inc.'s decision to connect to other applications through these industry standards was a major leap forward, because it meant our data became accessible to many more people, and IT and IS groups could now use their standard tools to get data in and out of FileMaker. IT and IS groups can now feel more secure because FileMaker offers them so many ways to access the FileMaker data.

IMPORTING ODBC DATA

Here's how to set up FileMaker Pro to import ODBC data, using the Windows version. (The Mac version works similarly, with mild variations in the look of the setup dialogs.)

1. Create a Data Source Name (DSN) by going into the Control Panel for setting ODBC Data Source, shown in Figure 16.15

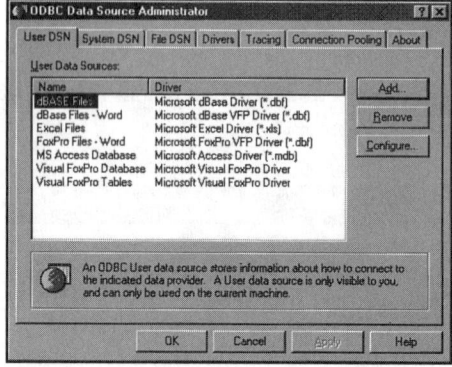

Figure 16.15
First you create a Data Source Name (DSN).

2. Click Add and choose a driver in the Create New Data Source dialog shown in Figure 16.16. (In this case we choose the FileMaker Pro Text Driver.) Then click Finish. In this case, we choose the Text Driver, because the target file is a text file.

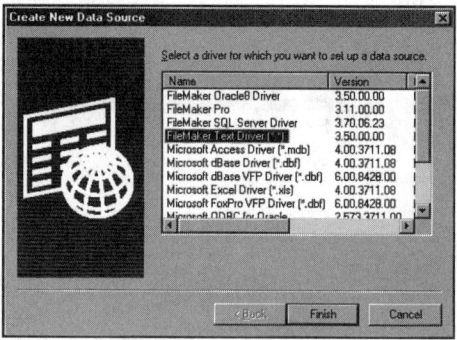

Figure 16.16
You are identifying a new data source.

3. In the ODBC Text Driver Setup dialog, give your new DSN a name, a description, and a path to the text file you want to be the data source (see Figure 16.17). Click OK. You have set up that file as an ODBC source so FileMaker can use that DSN configuration to import data from that text file, using a SQL statement within FileMaker.
4. To get the data out of the text file, open the FileMaker Pro database you want to import the data into and choose File, Import.
5. At the bottom of the Import dialog, use the pop-up menu of File of Type to see places from which you can import data and choose ODBC Data Sources. That brings up the Select ODBC Data Source dialog, shown in Figure 16.18.

Figure 16.17
You must describe your new Data Source Name.

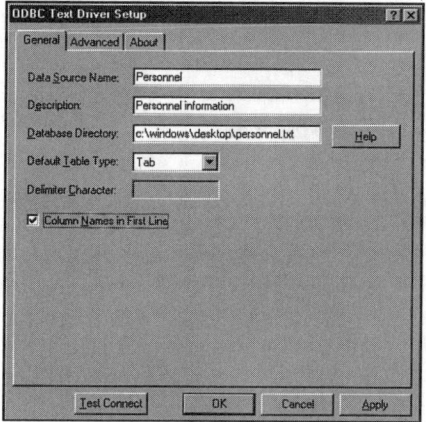

Figure 16.18
The Select ODBC Data Source dialog lets you identify the DSN from which you want to draw data.

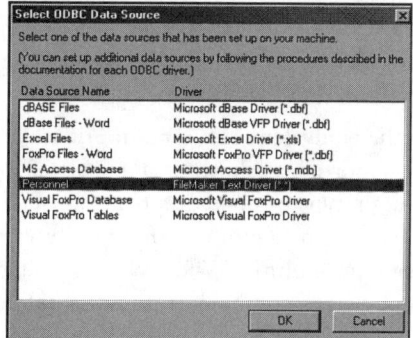

6. Pick the DSN you want to import from and click OK. You are asked for your user name and password as shown in Figure 16.19

Figure 16.19
You are asked for your user name and password.

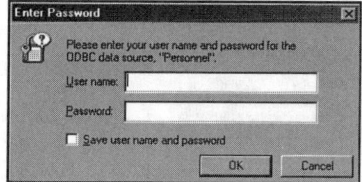

7. Enter your user name and password, if any, and click OK. The SQL query builder appears (see Figure 16.20), so you can build a SQL query to run against the data source.

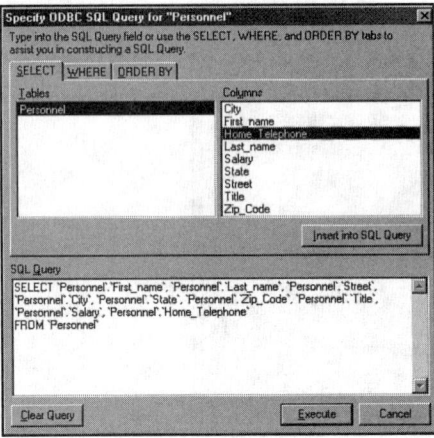

Figure 16.20
The dialog called Specify ODBC SQL Query lets you build your query.

8. In the dialog called Specify ODBC SQL Query, choose Select tab and identify which files (called tables in SQL) and which fields (called columns) contain the information you want to import. Select the file and the fields; then click Insert into SQL Query.

9. Click the Where tab, which is the equivalent of a Find in FileMaker, and specify which records (called rows) you want imported, as shown in Figure 16.21. Use the drop-down menus to specify the table, column, type of operation (such as exact match, contains), and what you would like to search against (another column or a value). Then click Insert into SQL Query. (You can put multiple Where clauses, using AND, OR, or NOT, to show how the different clauses combine or do not combine with each other.)

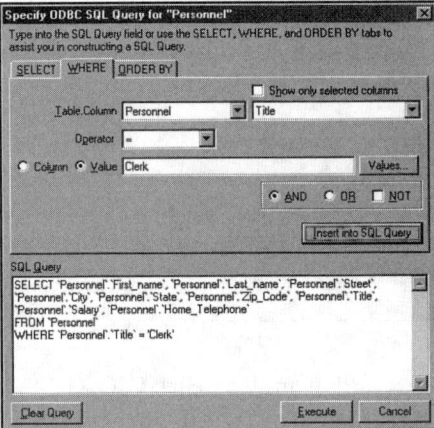

Figure 16.21
The Where tab is equivalent to a Find in FileMaker.

> **Caution**
>
> Remember, it is not enough to make all these choices. You must click Insert into SQL Query to have those choices included in your query.

10. Move to the Order By tab, shown in Figure 16.22, to specify the columns by which you want the records sorted (such as last name, then first name). Click Insert into SQL Query.

Figure 16.22
The Order By tab lets you identify the fields you want the records sorted by.

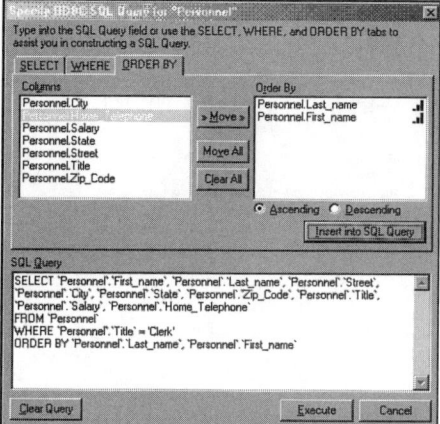

11. Click Execute. You see the standard Import Field Mapping dialog (see Figure 16.23).

Figure 16.23
This is the standard Import Field Mapping dialog.

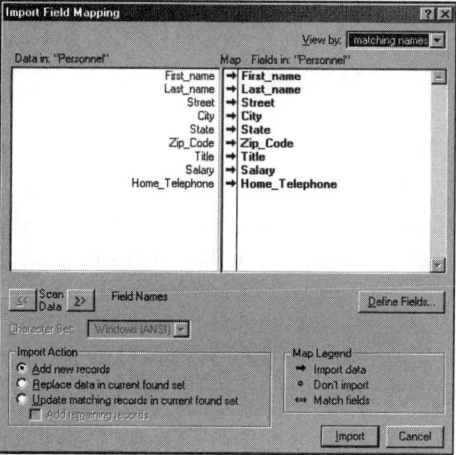

12. Drag fields up or down to align them with the data from the ODBC source. Click the arrow to enable importing (or click again to turn the arrow off, if you do not want to bring that data in). Click Import. You get your data, as shown in Figure 16.24.

Figure 16.24
At last your data appears.

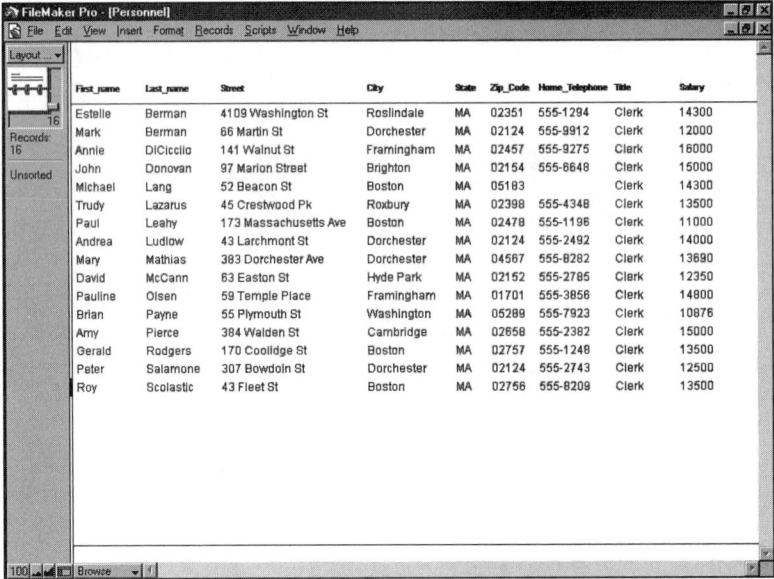

> **Note**
>
> If you do need to import data over and over using the same SQL statement, you can save the SQL import in the Import Records script step so you do not have to recreate the choices every time.

JDBC AND JAVA

JDBC is another industry standard designed to let you issue SQL statements to a database from within Java. The process for setting up JDBC is very similar to that for ODBC, and the interface uses the standard SQL language. The Java API that comes with FileMaker Pro 5 Developer, though, offers a different, less-standard approach. The Java API approach allows a Java programmer to send requests to the FileMaker Web Companion and get results back. The Java class library of the API also gives the Java programmer the ability to retrieve some metadata about what is going on inside FileMaker.

Basically, with the Java API, you are communicating with the Web Companion using the proprietary Claris Dynamic Markup Language (CDML) language, which many Java programmers will not be familiar with. JDBC and SQL, by contrast, are well-known standards, which more Java programmers will feel comfortable with.

> **Tip from**
> *Rich*
>
> Using the FMP ODBC driver, Casahl is about to release ecKnowledge® (pronounced e-c-knowledge), a tool for managing FileMaker's communication with other environments, such as database management systems, enterprise resource planning software, ancient legacy applications, groupware applications, directories, Web portals, and, yes, even desktop applications.

Going from HTML to XML and WML

Historically, we have presented information to a Web browser using the Hypertext Markup Language to describe the way the page ought to look. HTML tags, though, contained little information about the content or the structure of the information. You might have a first name, last name, and job title, but as far as the browser was concerned, that text was just a paragraph. Standard HTML has no way of spotting a first name or distinguishing a first name from a last name.

The eXtensible Markup Language, a subset of the Standard General Markup Language (SGML), lets you create a vocabulary and syntax for identifying the content elements that will appear on a Web page. XML allows you to define a piece of information such as a City or Part Number, so that your Web page contains a sequence of name-and-value pairs. Basically, an opening tag defines the element, then comes the data, and finally a closing tag concludes the element. You have seen this tagging operation in HyperText Markup Language, another derivative of SGML, but XML focuses on content and structure.

XML does not describe the look of an element, because it is not focused on formatting. That's the big difference between HTML and XML.

To take care of formatting, you use a style sheet in Cascading Stylesheets(CSS) or the eXtensible Style Language(xSL), sending the style sheet out along with the XML-tagged data. A style sheet created in the eXtensible Style Language (XSL) also lets you transform one set of tags into another to match an industry standard, for instance, or a vocabulary that the receiving company prefers. Basically, a style sheet lists the format you want to apply to each content element. Similarly, you can offer the user the ability to switch presentations simply by switching to another style sheet. In this way, the browser does all the hard work of formatting. Of course, not all browsers support CSS, XSL, or XML; if you are working on an Intranet, where the company issues an XML-compatible browser, you can be sure that every user can see your XML pages with style sheets. Over the Internet, you cannot be confident that every user has the right browser.

Because the elements are identified by content tags (essentially identifying records and fields, using identifiers for individual rows and columns), you can also have the server dispatch a JavaScript or VBscript applet to manipulate the data down on the client's computer, avoiding further trips back to the server. Unlike static HTML pages, the XML data can be sliced and diced locally, as a user carries out additional searches and sorts on his or her desktop computer. You could even download hundreds of records and offer a button allowing the user to look at the next ten, and the next ten, pulling them off the user's computer rather than going out over the Internet to fetch more records.

Because the elements are identified by content tags, which will probably correspond to the field names, you can also use XML to trade data with other companies, as long as both companies agree on the tags. If they do not agree, then an XSL style sheet can translate one set of tags to another. XML, then, offers a convenient way of exchanging data between businesses, and because it takes so much less programming than Electronic Data Interchange, XML is rapidly becoming an important standard for business-to-business commerce.

FileMaker handles XML through the Web Companion, using a CDML link syntax similar to what you would use when doing custom Web publishing. With custom Web publishing, of course, there is a -format page syntax that specifies the name of a format page located inside the Web folder, which lives inside the FileMaker folder. When working with XML, the format portion of the parameter says that XML is in use, and it specifies which XML grammar to use, of the three that FileMaker currently offers:

- If you want to use the field names as element names, use the FMPDSORESULT grammar. The problem is that you must create a style for each field (now an element), in your style sheet, and as a result the style sheet only applies to material coming out of this particular database.
- If you do not care to style individual fields, use FMPXMLRESULT, which uses a fixed set of elements. The same style sheet, then, can be used for all database material using this grammar. You specify a style for the generic field element, rather than individual fields.
- If you want to focus on the layout of the field, use FMPXMLLAYOUT, which describes a particular layout.

Deploying XML works best when all your users, without exception, have browsers that can read XML. Right now, Internet Explorer 5 and Mozilla can do that, and with them you can get all the benefits of XML because you ship XML files to the client, which then does a lot of the processing for you, using the style sheet and any applets or Javascripts you send along with the file. (Your mileage may vary. Browsers only follow standards so far.)

If some or most users don't have browsers that can read XML, you're forced to manipulate the XML file on the server, dispatching HTML pages to the users' browsers. Now the server is back in the business of manipulating all that data whenever the user wants to sort, search, or update records. Why bother, then? Well, FileMaker does a quicker job of offering up XML than making up HTML pages, so you are offloading the conversion into HTML to another server which would interpret the XML using the style sheet and kick out the HTML pages.

And Don't Forget Reports

A report contains more than just the details of the data, because it may involve creative combinations of the data and summaries, as well as a well-thought-out layout and labels. In these ways, a FileMaker report goes beyond what you can normally achieve using standards such as ODBC. You have more control over the way the data is presented. So whether you are just sending a report to a printer, displaying it on-screen, pouring it into a PDF file, or sending it by fax, your report offers a great value to your users.

Remember that a report is more than data thrown against a page. You are arranging that data in a way that helps people absorb it and understand it. Ask people what they think about the report, because they will suggest little changes that make a big difference to their ability to soak up the meaning of the data from your report. Yes, reports are as old as FileMaker, but they're still an excellent way of communicating the meaning within your data, in many media.

CHAPTER 17

FILEMAKER PRO MULTIUSER DESIGN AND DEPLOYMENT CONSIDERATIONS

In this chapter

Written by Steven Blackwell

- The Idea of Multiple Users   520
- Designing Multiuser Files   521
- Deploying Multiuser Files   523
- FileMaker Server   524
- Multiuser Deployment, Design, and Networking Tips and Pitfalls Checklist   528

The Idea of Multiple Users

FileMaker Pro's greatest strength has always been its capacity to share information among users. Each subsequent version of FileMaker Pro and its companion application, FileMaker Server, has improved on that core capacity.

What exactly do we mean by multiuser file design and deployment? Basically this: While many FileMaker Pro databases designed for one person can easily be converted without change to permit use by multiple users simultaneously, there are also many instances where such multiple user files require different design criteria than does a one-person file. Such files can also require some deployment rules as well.

First, in order to be shared among multiple users, the files require connection to some sort of a network environment. In most instances in enterprise environments, this is an Ethernet-based network. This network consists of multiple computers, the cabling and switches needed to connect them, and a management system to oversee the network.

Second, each user desiring to connect to the shared, multiuser files must have a copy of FileMaker Pro on the local hard drive. Part of the installation process for FileMaker Pro includes networking protocol options. FileMaker Pro 5 supports these networking protocols, one of which must be present for multiple users to connect to the files.

As you can see from Table 17.1, TCP/IP is the only cross-platform protocol for FileMaker Pro 5; indeed, it is the preferred protocol. If you have a browser such as Netscape or Internet Explorer installed on your machine, you already have the TCP/IP protocol present.

TABLE 17.1 SUPPORTED NETWORKING PROTOCOLS

Operating System	Supported Network Protocols
Macintosh OS	AppleTalk, TCP/IP
Windows 98, Windows NT4, Windows 2000PE	IPX/SPX, TCP/IP

Third, the files must be hosted either by FileMaker Pro itself in what is called peer-to-peer mode or by FileMaker Server. For a variety of reasons, some of which we will elaborate on later in this chapter, we recommend the peer-to-peer mode only for a small set of files and a small number of users. Five files and five users are good limits for real-world, peer-to-peer sharing. Otherwise, we recommend the use of FileMaker Server.

Tip from
Steven

> Always access files using FileMaker Pro's built-in capacity, through the Hosts button in the Open dialog. This means, for example, that you should avoid the use of shortcuts or aliases especially to files mounted on remote volumes. It also means not accessing files through mapped volumes, through the Network Neighborhood, or through the Chooser. Do not attempt to use the operating system's networking features to access multiuser files. It can wreak severe and irreversible damage on the files.

Designing Multiuser Files

When designing files that will be accessed by more than one user, developers must consider a number of additional implications. These considerations center on the prevention of unintended and erroneous results of scripted actions when multiple users are accessing a file and on unexpected and potentially confusing dialogs appearing while users are navigating through the files.

FileMaker Pro employs a technique called *record locking* to prevent two users from simultaneously accessing the same record in a given file. This is done to protect the record, to protect its data, and to prevent conflicting overwriting of data. The more people who are using a shared multi-user database, the more likely some of them will simultaneously attempt to access the same record. When you attempt to put the cursor in a field on a record that is being used by someone else, FileMaker Pro presents a message saying, in effect, "You cannot make changes in this record right now because Rich Coulombre is modifying it." This alerts you to the fact that the record is locked.

However, if you happen to be running a scripted routine that requires writing to a group of records, one of which is locked by another user, the scripted routine can fail without any warning. The locked record or records will not have their values replaced or updated. This bump in the road can lead to erroneous and incomplete results. Error trapping routines can help overcome these problems.

The error code for a locked record is Error 301. Using the following ScriptMaker steps, you can trap for the presence of this error in a batch-driven process, such as a "Replace," that irreversibly replaces the value in a given field with some other literal or calculated value, in the current found set of records:

```
Set Error Capture On
Allow User Abort Off
Replace [with appropriate parameters]
If StatusCurrentError= 301
       —take some appropriate action
End If
```

Extremely important: You must place the Capture Step (If StatusCurrentError=301) *immediately after* the action that could cause the error to occur. Or, if you want to retain the error value for subsequent review, set it into a Global field.

If using a looping script to go from record to record to do this, the steps would be a little different:

```
Set Error Capture On
Allow User Abort Off
Go to Record [first]
Loop
Set field [with appropriate parameters]
If StatusCurrentError= 301
        —take some appropriate action
End If
Go to record [next, exit after last]
End loop
```

> **Caution**
>
> If you turn on Set Error Capture, you absolutely must handle the errors. Otherwise, the script will fail without any warning at all, because you have captured and eliminated from display FileMaker Pro's built-in, generic error message.

> **Tip from Steven**
>
> If setting more than one field in a record, add a step to go to one of the fields first, locking the record. Then set all the fields, followed by an exit record step. This approach results in much faster performance, and it protects the record while the process is happening.

The purpose of these error-handling routines is to alert you to the fact that a particular record has been skipped, thus possibly affecting the accuracy or completeness of a routine's results. You can then find the skipped records and make adjustments to them.

Other actions can also lock records. There are many different circumstances that can induce a lock on a given record; here are a few of them.

A FileMaker Pro developer can make extensive use of Global fields. These fields can be Text, Number, Date, Time, or Container fields. *Global fields are local to each user.* Each user can have a different value in a particular global field than each and every other user has. This is a powerful feature, permitting a wide variety of design options. However, even though global fields are local to a user, *if one user clicks into a Global field displayed in a particular record, it locks other users out of nonglobal fields in that same record.* When a user first connects to a hosted file, the values in the Globals are taken from the host. But while a user can change those Globals locally, their value on the hosted file in the machine doing the hosting is not changed. And when users quit FileMaker Pro and then reconnect later, the Global values are set to match the host's values.

Additionally, a fairly wide range of other ScriptMaker steps whose successful execution depends on "write-access" to a record can create issues if a record is locked. These include the following:

- Clear
- Copy
- Cut
- Delete all records
- Delete portal row
- Delete record
- Import
- Insert (in its various forms)
- Paste
- Relookup
- Replace

- Save A Copy
- Select All
- Set Field

Certain portal actions can lock records, and certain record actions can lock portals as well.

- If User #1 is in a field in Record #1 that also has a portal displaying related records, that record is of course locked. However, if User #2 is accessing any *other* record in the file, and if the first record displayed in the portal in User #2's record is the *same* first record displayed in User #1's record's portal, then User #2 will get a record locked message merely by scrolling the portal. The most immediate workaround is for User #2 to click into a row other than the first row. Then the portal can be scrolled successfully.
- Conversely, if a user has clicked into a field in a portal, the user has also locked the "parent" record that displays the portal.
- If two users are looking at the same parent record and neither of them has clicked into a field, when one user scrolls the portal with the scroll bar, the entire record plus the portal is locked from other users.

Now, if that's not complex enough, we should also note that the behavior can be different depending on whether the files are hosted by FileMaker Server or by FileMaker Pro itself. The key point is the same however: Certain actions taken by one user can lock a record and prevent it from being accessed or used by another, with erroneous or unexpected results when multiple record transactions are processed.

Deploying Multiuser Files

By far the best way to deploy numerous multi-user files to multiple users is through FileMaker Server. FileMaker Server 5 can host up to 125 files for up to 250 guests simultaneously. Guests can be running either Windows or Macintosh versions of FileMaker Pro 5, or both simultaneously.

FileMaker Server offers the advantages of speed, safety, and a vastly increased number of users and files over peer-to-peer networking schemes. Peer-to-peer is limited by the number of available network connections or sockets. Here are some formulas to assist in calculating sockets.

> Sockets available= $\{\{2^8\}-2\}$ (or 254 total) {That's 2 to the 8th power, or 256, minus 2, equaling 254}
>
> Number of sockets consumed= Number of files × number of users × 2

Calculating the Sharing

Suppose that you have 10 users and 5 files, and you want to share the files peer-to-peer.

First, subtract 7 sockets that FileMaker Pro retains for its own internal use. Now there are 247 left for use (254−7=247). Each file opened by the host requires two sockets. So if there are 5 files opened by the host, the host consumes 10 sockets (2×5=10), leaving 237 sockets available for guests (247−10=237). If there are 10 guests of these 5 files, each will use 10 sockets (2×5=10) for a total of 100 sockets consumed by guests (10×10=100). This leaves 137 sockets free (237−100=137). So far, so good.

Now, let's try 10 files for 10 guests.

The host retains 7 sockets, leaving 247 for use, (254−7=247).

The host needs 20 sockets to host 10 files (10×2=20), leaving 227 available for guests (247−20=227).

Each guest needs 20 sockets (10×2=20), and there are 10 guests consuming a total of 200 sockets (20×10=200), leaving only 27 sockets free.

Whoops, you can see the beginning of a problem here. Plus, FileMaker Pro creates temporary files during activities such as sorts and Sub-summaries, and these files can rapidly exceed the total available.

Here's another scenario: Where there are 50 files opened, the maximum number a copy of FileMaker Pro 5 can open.

The host retains 7, leaving 247 available.

The host needs 100 sockets to host 50 files (50×2=20), leaving 147 available for guests (247−100=147).

Two guests then try to connect. The first one needs 100 sockets to connect to all 50 files (2×50=100), leaving 47 available! (147−100=47). Whoops! The second guest then lacks enough sockets to be able to connect to all the files.

So using peer-to-peer, two guests cannot connect to 50 files. A safer set of calculations to use when estimating whether FileMaker Pro is capable of serving peer-to-peer are these :

Sockets available = 254

Sockets consumed by host= (4× number of files) + 7

Sockets consumed by guests= 4× number of files × number of guests

In total, sockets consumed by host + sockets consumed by guests must be fewer than 254. That, plus performance and safety issues, is why FileMaker Server is the better bet.

FileMaker Server

FileMaker Server is a specialized piece of software designed to host files for guest access across both Local Area Networks (LANs) and Wide Area Networks (WANs). The WAN can be a leased line connection, a Virtual Private Network, the public Internet, or a dial-up connection.

FileMaker Server is the core of the modern distributed information system using FileMaker Pro. It hosts files that are simultaneously accessible in a variety of methods and fashions:

- Over the LAN to users running FileMaker Pro 5
- Over a WAN, either private or public, to users running FileMaker Pro 5
- Over a remote dial-up PPP type connection using either Apple Remote Access 3 or Windows DialUp Networking at speeds up to dual-channel ISDN levels
- To a corporate Intranet using FileMaker Pro 5 Unlimited to broadcast to users accessing information via web browsers or via JAVA applets

- To the public Internet using FileMaker Pro 5 Unlimited to broadcast to users accessing information via web browsers or via JAVA applets
- To the public Internet using multiple copies of FileMaker Pro 5 Unlimited running on a RAIC (Redundant Array of Inexpensive Computers) in conjunction with popular Web Server programs such as Apache, IIS, WebStar, and so on. This configuration provides for Secure Sockets, for load balancing, and for fault tolerance.
- To users of Wireless Application Protocol devices such as PDAs or cellular telephones in conjunction with Wireless MarkUp Language (WML) and WMLScript
- To browsers, microbrowsers, or other applications capable of receiving XML/XSL formatted data using FileMaker Pro 5 Unlimited

FileMaker Server is a "thin-server," and as such it does not directly serve data via such items as ODBC, XML, JDBC, Apple Events (other than its own suites that are basically metadata), or the Web Companion. Files that are guests of FileMaker Server can serve data via these alternative APIs, however.

FileMaker Server 5 comes on a hybrid installation CD. It requires a CPU running Macintosh OS 8.6 or higher, Windows NT4 Server, or Windows 2000. It also has some hardware requirements worthy of note. Microsoft notes that not all Intel-based CPUs are certified for use with Windows NT or Windows 2000. Their official Hardware Compatibility List (HCL) notes those CPUs on which their software is certified.

A server is not just a workstation that someone has decided to convert and rename. The drives that are installed in many desktop computers are not suitable for use as a database server's drives. And frequently the amount of RAM and the chips installed are not adequate, either. For best performance, installed RAM should be between 128MB to 256MB, and the drives should be UltraWide SCSI or better. FileMaker Server makes intensive use of cache-to-disk activity, and the higher performance drives produce better results.

Generally speaking, fast servers and fast workstations are the optimal combination. However, the clock speed and chip set of the workstation is more a determinant in shared FileMaker Pro file performance than the speed of the server.

On the Macintosh OS, FileMaker Server runs as an application, whereas on Windows its runs as a service. Therefore, we recommend you follow the installation instructions carefully and read the specifications accompanying the product to assure its optimal use.

FileMaker Server 5 comes with many new configuration features. On the Macintosh OS these can be accessed locally directly on the server through three windows called from the menu bar. On the Windows side, these same features are called from the Server management console run by the Microsoft Management Console, available through the Start Menu at the desktop (see Figure 17.1).

Figure 17.1
The Properties Tab offers information about the FileMaker Server 5 for Windows NT4 and Windows 2000SE.

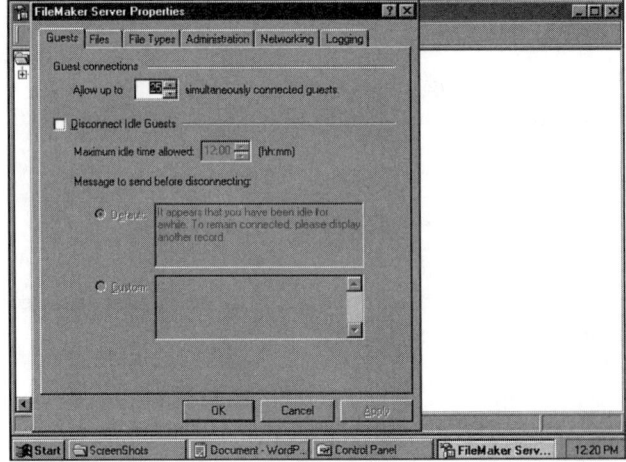

Some of the configuration features include

- Setting the maximum number of guests (up to 250 via TCP/IP)
- Setting the maximum number of hosted files (up to 125)
- Selecting networking protocols (Mac: AppleTalk or TCP/IP or both), (Windows: IPX/SPX, TCP/IP, or both)
- Permitting FileMaker Server to host single-user files
- Disconnecting idle guests after a specified interval (minimum 30 minutes)
- Permitting remote administration of the files and the FileMaker Server program
- Reserving a specific part of the memory for cache
- Flushing cache at specified intervals
- Specifying a custom name for host
- Maximizing CPU performance (Mac OS)
- Automatic opening of files with custom extensions (Windows, up to 16 total)

Here are some specific ways to enhance the performance of FileMaker Server:

- Never turn on file sharing on the CPU hosting the files. FileMaker Server doesn't need it; and flipping this switch can degrade performance, often dramatically.
- On the Mac OS, always check the Maximize Performance box and run FileMaker Server as the frontmost application.
- Set an amount of RAM (Mac OS via the Get Info box) or memory (Windows via preferences) to produce cache hits of 95 or greater consistently in normal use. Hits can be monitored via the local Usage Statistics Windows (Mac OS) or via the Remote Admin Usage Statistics windows (Mac OS or Windows).

- Select only one networking protocol unless you absolutely need to use two. The preferred protocol is TCP/IP. TCP/IP is the only protocol for cross-platform networks.
- Be sure that the server has a fixed IP address, not a dynamically assigned one.
- Set the maximum number of guests and the maximum number of hosted files to be only slightly more than what you expect will be needed.
- Always access the files hosted by FileMaker Server through FileMaker Pro's built-in capacity, *never* through the OS networking capacity or such things as aliases, short-cuts, mapped volumes, shared or mounted drives, and so on. Failure to follow this prescription is the main cause of multiuser deployment problems. You can make a local "Opener file" or "Launcher file" whose sole purpose is to connect to files hosted by FileMaker Server across the LAN or WAN. Users can double-click on this file on their local hard drive or "C" drive to access the hosted files. On the Mac OS, you can also open such files through Apple Events if you are acquainted with that API. (But you should not do so through program linking. Use the local copy of FileMaker Pro on your hard drive.)

Defining Fields as Sole Guest

A new feature in FileMaker 5 for versions starting with 5.0v3 is the ability to define fields while the sole guest of a hosted file using FileMaker Server 5. *Sole guest* means expressly and exclusively that—the only guest. To utilize this feature, the file must be hosted by FileMaker Server. Access the "Define Fields" option by the menu or keyboard command. If you are the sole guest, you will be able to define fields. This change is designed primarily to enable developers to define additional fields while a file is being hosted. Its use should be confined to circumstances where no other guests are likely to try to connect to the server's files. Use it with extreme caution.

Safe Hosting

FileMaker Server also allows for the safe hosting of files. One of the key reasons why FileMaker Server should always be run on a dedicated machine is to avoid some other program misbehaving, causing that machine to hang or to crash. Such a crash would necessitate a forced restart, which damages the files. If FileMaker Pro or FileMaker Server is hosting files running on a workstation in use by other programs, performance will also suffer dramatically, and the propensity and likelihood of crashes and corruption is significant.

FileMaker Server 5 also has the capacity to generate automatic backups using its own built-in backup routine. Or, on the Macintosh OS version, that backup can also be run with Apple Events. Good deployment practice regarding frequency of backups will vary depending on specific business circumstances. However, databases should be backed up regularly, and a copy of those backups should be removed from the premises. Should an accident or disaster occur, it is of little consolation or usefulness to have backups if the backups are simultaneously damaged or destroyed by the same calamity.

FileMaker Server 5 can be administered remotely from any machine on the network running FileMaker Pro 5 that can connect to that server. Remote Administration is the principal method of administration for FileMaker Pro Windows users. Remote Administration has several requirements:

- It must be enabled in FileMaker Server Preferences.
- It can require the use of a password (recommended), but it can be used without a password if you so choose.
- Full features require the use of a special FileMaker Pro plug-in that ships on the FileMaker Server install CD. It must be installed properly in the FileMaker Extensions Folder (Macintosh OS) or the FileMaker System Folder (Windows), and it must be enabled in the FileMaker Pro preferences related to plug-ins, similar to other plug-ins.
- Without the plug-in, if Remote Administration is enabled a user or administrator can
    - View a list of folders that contain database files hosted by FileMaker Server 5.
    - View a list of database files hosted by FileMaker Server and the number of guests connected to each.
    - View a list of all guests and the database files to which they are connected.
    - View usage statistics for FileMaker Server 5.

With the plug-in installed, a user or administrator can do all those elements, plus

- Open FileMaker PRO 5 files for access by FileMaker PRO 5 guests through FileMaker Server 5.
- Close files hosted by FileMaker Server 5.
- Disconnect a selected FileMaker PRO 5 guest from one or all hosted files.
- Send messages to guests of hosted files.

These features are selected through three special FileMaker Pro 5 databases created by FileMaker Server 5. They are called "Usage," "Admin," and "Data," and they are accessible through the Hosts dialog box, as are other FileMaker Pro files. These temporary files are cleared on quitting FileMaker Server or on turning off Remote Administration in the Preferences section of FileMaker Server 5.

Multiuser Deployment, Design, and Networking Tips and Pitfalls Checklist

Here are some pitfalls to watch out for when designing and setting up a multiuser environment.

1. Servers need fixed IP addresses; otherwise networking may fail.
2. If you are using network address translation (NAT) with FileMaker Server 5, Port 5003 must be enabled for TCP, but filtered (off) for UDP. This is different than was the case

in FileMaker Pro Server 3. If you are not using network address translation, Port 5003 should be enabled for both TCP and UDP. Failure to do this will prevent users from seeing a list of hosted files if they connect from outside the firewall.

3. When making a dialup connection for remote access with either Apple Remote Access 3 or Windows DialUp Networking, the connection inside the LAN should be made to the network, not to a specific CPU on the network. This is accomplished through the use of some sort of a PPP Server box, and it permits simultaneous multiple remote dial-up access by both Windows and Macintosh FileMaker Pro clients to files hosted by FileMaker Server, either Macintosh OS or Windows. Dialup can range from 33.6Kbps up to compressed 256Kbps dual channel ISDN.

4. If you plan to use TimBukTu to administer remotely a server CPU located inside a firewall that is running FileMaker Server, and if you plan to connect via TCP (as through the Internet), then Port 1417 for TCP and Port 407 for UDP must be enabled or the TimBukTu scheme will not work.

5. If you have a script that depends on a specific platform (Macintosh OS or Windows) such as Perform AppleScript or Send DDE, and FileMaker Pro is running on the opposite platform, the step will be skipped with possible negative consequences. You can use `StatusCurrentPlatform` to trap for the operating System. 1 is Macintosh, 2 is Windows, -2 is Windows NT—all in FileMaker Pro 5. A similar situation exists for various operating systems—for example, Macintosh OS 8.6 versus 9 or Windows 98 versus Windows 2000 PE. These can be trapped by use of the StatusCurrentSystemVersion function. A specific version of FileMaker Pro 5 can be trapped for with the `StatusCurrentAppVersion` function. These distinctions are important as features are changed from version to version or from one operating system to another.

6. If connecting remotely to a large FileMaker Pro 5 file hosted by FileMaker Server 5, script the connection to go to an empty found set and a blank layout. This way only the record IDs will download to the remote users, not all the metadata about the layouts. This can significantly speed up connection time. Avoid complex graphics and colors in this same scenario.

7. Avoid having *any* files on drives with the same names as files hosted by the FileMaker Server, because FileMaker Pro may very well attempt to access them instead of the hosted files. Put such files on removable media—and remove them—or zip or stuff them. Do not ignore this form of housecleaning.

8. Open files hosted on the server only through use of the Hosts dialog box, through an "Opener file" or "Launcher file," or through Apple Events on the Macintosh OS. Do not use the operating system's networking capability to open the files, for example, aliases, shortcuts, mounted drives, mapped volumes, network neighborhood, the Chooser, and so on. You will damage your files if you do not open them properly.

9. Do not run file sharing on the CPU where FileMaker Server is running. File sharing will degrade performance and possibly damage the files. Neither FileMaker Server 5 nor FileMaker Pro 5 needs file sharing enabled.

10. Do not back up files by any method while they are open and running because you may get unhealthy backups. Best to use the built-in FileMaker Server backup routine, which pauses the files and writes the backups to the hard drive, then reactivates them. Alternatively, you may script the closing of the files, and then back up the closed files to removable media or a networked volume.

11. Placing FileMaker Pro files into the same folder (or one level down) as the FileMaker Server application will cause the files automatically to be hosted when FileMaker Server is started.

12. When installing FileMaker Server 5 on the Windows NT 4 or Windows 2000 SE platforms, Internet Explorer 4 or greater is required to make the Microsoft Management Console function correctly. The MMC is used to configure FileMaker Server's features and options on the Windows NT 4 and Windows 2000 SE platforms.

13. When installing FileMaker Server 5 on the Windows NT 4 or Windows 2000 SE platforms, if you want the installation to occur somewhere other than on the "C" drive, you must select your own built-in backup routine. Then you can navigate through the available volumes of your drives and select a customized location (see Figure 17.2).

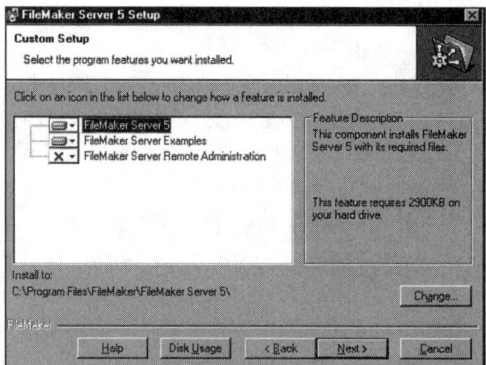

Figure 17.2
The Custom Install option lets you put the program on a specific U drive.

14. When you are using the TCP/IP protocol on a local area network, choose File, Open, Hosts, and you will generally see the names of all hosted files that live within the same subnet. If the files live on a different subnet, you will have to enter the IP address of their server. Various OS upgrades, hot fixes, and Service Packs may affect the way this works. Always utilize the latest update available for FileMaker Server 5, found on the FileMaker, Inc. Web site at http://www.filemaker.com.

15. FileMaker Server 5 can host up to 125 files; however, any guest can open a maximum of 50 files, including any temporary ones that FileMaker Pro needs to create on a local hard drive. Close files not needed for immediate use by a local guest via a script if there is a danger of hitting the 50 file limit.

16. If a file ever crashes or is forced quit, it will likely need to be recovered. The *only purpose* of the FileMaker Pro "Recover" function is to get the file into sufficiently good condition so that the data can be extracted and then imported into a clean clone of that

file. Therefore, (1) always have clean clones of the most current version of all files, (2) do not continue to use "Recovered" files, and (3) do not run the "Recover" function as part of "routine" maintenance. This is distinguished from compression of the files, a process achieved by using the FileMaker Pro option to save a compressed copy. Save that copy to a folder or directory other than the one where the active database is stored, using exactly the same name as the active database. Then close the active database, remove it from the computer, and replace it with the compressed copy of the same name.

17. If you can not see files hosted by FileMaker Server 5 over the network, check the following items as a first start:
    - File is set to multiuser, *not* set to multiuser *hidden*.
    - Networking protocol in FileMaker Pro 5 is correctly selected.
    - Server and workstation are both connected to the network.
    - You are using FileMaker Pro 5 to attempt the connection, not an earlier version. FileMaker Pro 5 files are hosted by FileMaker Server 5, and FileMaker Pro 5 can only see hosted files emanating from FileMaker Server 5, not from other versions.
    - You have entered the correct IP address if the server is outside the current subnet.
    - You are running the most current versions of both FileMaker Pro 5 and FileMaker Server 5.

18. Speed of access across a LAN, and especially across a WAN, and more especially for remote access dial-up (even at higher bandwidths) depends on file architecture questions, network architecture, and latency of connection more than on any other factors. Optimize all these factors for better speed and performance. It is also important to give the FileMaker Pro 5 application sufficient memory in the Preferences (Windows) or through the Get Info box setting (Macintosh OS). 8192 KB is a good starting place.

19. FileMaker Server 5 can utilize up to 40 MB of memory. Anything above that is not used, and even that amount is rarely needed. FileMaker Pro 5 for Windows can utilize up to 9999 KB of memory. FileMaker Pro 5 for Macintosh can utilize more, but diminishing returns set in at approximately 20 MB. These settings do affect multiuser, network performance. Remember that the objective, as far as FileMaker Server is concerned, is to achieve cache hits of 95 or higher consistently during normal operations. Hits are monitored in the usage statistics window, either locally (Macintosh OS) or remotely (Windows and Macintosh OS).

20. Graphics inserted into container fields by reference are *not* available over the network through FileMaker Pro. There are workarounds, the most obvious of which is to insert the actual graphic, rather than a reference to it. This can cause file size to increase, but those issues can be met with file architecture. On the Macintosh OS, sound files are available over the network, but QuickTime movies are not. One way of accessing such files is to put them into a shared folder on a file server—*not on the database server*

running FileMaker Server—that all users can access. That way they will be available through the database over the network. The reference in the database container field must point to the shared volume.

21. Insure that any screen savers other than a totally blank screen are disabled on the CPU running FileMaker Server. Screen savers are highly processor intensive, and you don't need to run them. Just turn the monitor off if need be. Also be sure that the hard drive is not set to spin down or to "sleep" at all. Otherwise, connections will be lost.

22. On the Macintosh OS 8.6 and 9, turn Virtual Memory off on the CPU hosting FileMaker Server 5. FileMaker Server 5 makes extensive and intensive use of cache to disk writing. Virtual memory can slow this process and interfere with it.

INDEX

Symbols

& (ampersand), 279, 283, 314
$ (dollar sign), 71
// (slashes, double), 322

A

access files, 417-420
Acrobat Reader, exporting to, 505
Active Server Pages, 509
addresses in calculations, 283-284
Admin database, 528
aggregate functions, 338-339
aging invoices, 288
aligning objects, 233-237
Allow User Abort [Off], 119, 371, 434
ampersand (&), 279, 283, 314
Analyzer tool, 80, 483
AND, 204, 310
Apple events, 487
AppleTalk, 520
Application Preferences dialog, 255
archives, deleting records to, 161-162
arrow keys, aligning objects with, 235
attributes. *See also* fields
   conversion to fields, 56
   naming, 42, 51
   planning, 40-41, 85
automatic backups, 527
automatic data entry, 185-191
   calculated values, 187-188
   lookup fields, 189-191
   serial numbers, 186
   text, 187

B

backups, 527, 530
bad data, 174-176. *See also* data entry
Bar Graphs, 329-330
Beep steps, 483
blocking entry to fields, 118-119
Blue World Communications, 253. *See also* Lasso
bodies, 345, 351, 363
boilerplate text, 71
break fields, 349
Browse mode, 459, 491
   reports in, 381-382
   scripts to enter, 371
   Summary fields, 382, 384
browsers, 250
   color schemes, 258
   FileMaker Pro Server, 259
   forms, 262
   JavaScript, 265
   limitations, 265-266
   platform independence, 501-502
   vs. FileMaker layouts, 250
   Web Companion, interacting with, 250-251, 253
   XML, 517-518
business rules, 57
buttons
   Custom Web Publishing, 262
   default choices, 467
   Exit, 476, 478
   Halt, 476, 478
   hiding, 415
   interfaces, designing for, 238-240
   invisible, 240
   for listing files, 109
   numbering, 467
   omitting printing, 240
   Pause, 476
   Resume, 476, 478
   scripts with, 476-479
   showing, 239

C

calculated key fields, conditional value lists, 183-184

Calculation fields, 63, 69, 74-75, 196-197
Allow Entry into Field option, 285
blocking entry with, 119
for Radio Buttons, 310
found sets, 326
GetSummary function, 358
in reports, 379
naming, 112
Options dialog, 274
overlapping, 284-289
Storage Option button, 196
to protect from user entry, 196-197

calculations, 187-188, 274. *See also* **Calculation fields**
& (ampersand), 314
aggregate functions, 338-339
Bar Graphs, 329-330
carriage returns in, 203
Case statement, 295-296, 307-308
check boxes, 316-320
Choose function, 300, 307-308
complex, 301
conditional, 307-312
Container results, 312-313
dates, 294-304
DayOfWeek function, 278, 300-301
delimiters, 333
editing, 330
functions, 274
graphics as flags, 312-313
IF, 307-312
Int function, 277
mail merges, 321-323
Mod function, 277, 298
operators, 274
order of, 292
PatternCount function, 311
percentages, 311
Position function, 336
random numbers, 326, 328-329
Replace function, 329
rounding, 275-276 328-329
RTF, 313-316
search and replace, 323-326
Sylk format, 316
text, 279-293
time, 305-306
Trim function, 334
unstored, 288, 295

Cancel buttons, 368

carriage returns, 210-211, 425

Casahl, 516

cascading deletes, 153-155

Cascading Stylesheets (CSS), 517

cascading updates, 136

Case statement, 295-296, 307-308, 360-361

CDML (Claris Dynamic Markup Language), 253-254, 272, 516

CGIs (common gateway interfaces), 251-253

characters, reserved, 60-61

check boxes, 179-181
borders, 181
calculations, 316-320
comma-separated lists from, 319-320
display of data, 181
distinguishing values, 181
exporting data, 180
fields, searching and sorting on, 180
sorting multiple responses, 317-318

children
creating from parent, 123, 144-145
deleting from scripts, 466
Foreign keys, 134
grandchildren, 128-130
lists of related, 424
multiple parents, 149, 151-152
orphans, 137
records disappearing, 124
self-joins, 422
sorting within parents, 123-124

Choose function, 300, 307-308

Cinco Group's Theme Creator, 342

Claris Dynamic Markup Language (CDML), 253-254, 272, 516

Clear, 522

close boxes, 370

code tables, 131

commands
Allow User Abort [Off], 119, 371, 434
Edit menu
Preferences, 255
File menu
Define Fields, 185, 189, 461
Define Value Lists, 138
Import, 512
Relationships, 115, 120
Format menu
Field Format, 140, 194
Sliding & Printing, 240, 347

Layout menu
  Part Setup, 349
  Set Layouts Order, 217
Records menu
  Delete Record, 159
Scripts menu
  Reset Values, 477
View menu
  Page Margins, 346
  Show, 239

comments, 488

comments in scripts, 450

common gateway interfaces (CGIs), 251-253

Companion Interface, 500

compression of files, 531

concatenation symbol, 279, 283, 314

conditional text, 287-289

conditional calculations, 307-312

conditional validation, 206-208

conditional value lists, 181-185

configuration of multiuser systems, 526

constant fields, 130

constant files, 130-131

Constants files, 457

constraints, 57

consulting, 38-39

Container fields, 67, 73-74
  Global, 401
  reports, 379
  results of calculations, 312-313
  size limitations, 74
  storage of objects, 73-74

Continue buttons, 368

coordinates of objects, 234

Copy step, 492, 522

creating
  fields, 110
  files, 108
  portals, 124-126
  records, 170
  relationships, 112-117, 120, 122
  tables, 108

cross-platform environments, 253

CSS (Cascading Stylesheets), 517

cultures, company, 24-25

currency
  division operations with, 358
  rounding, 275-276

CurrentDate, 294

CurrentError, 368

custom delimiters. *See* **delimiters**

Custom Web Publishing, 254, 260-264

Cut step, 522

D

data, health of. *See* **bad data**

data entry, 176
  Allow Entry into the Field option, 194-195
  automatic, 185-191
  bad data, 174-176
  Calculation fields. *See* Calculation fields
  carriage returns, 210-211
  check boxes, 179-181
  checking by calculation, 199-200, 202-203
  conditional validation, 206-208
  conditional value lists, 181-185
  create only, 208
  current user, 193
  duplicated records, 188
  editing privileges, 192-193, 208
  empty fields, 198-199
  existing values option, 199
  Global fields, 205-206
  human validation, 176
  in a range option, 199
  list format, 176, 228
  lookup fields, 189-191
  Merge fields, 192-194
  messages, 205
  planning, 237-238
  pop-up lists, 176-177
  pop-up menus, 177-178
  protecting fields, 192-197
  radio buttons, 178-181
  required fields, 238
  scripted permission, 195
  Social Security numbers, 202-203
  soft validation, 204
  strictness options, 204
  tab order, 209-210
  task sequences, 238
  type checking, 198
  unique data option, 198
  validity checking, 176, 197-203
  value list membership option, 199

data types. *See* **fields, types**

DataBasix, 454

Date function, 297, 302-303

dates, 62-65
  appointment calculations, 295-297
  automatic entry, 186

business days, 298
calculations, 294-304
completion of tasks, 298-300
CurrentDate, 294
Date function, 297, 302-303
DateToText function, 280
DayOfWeek function, 278, 300-301
days in month, 303
days in quarter, 304
days of week, 297-299
empty fields, 296
fields, 71-72
finding, 475
first in quarter, 303
first of month, 301-302
formats, 66
last day of month, 302-303
last in quarter, 303
months, lengths of, 297
parsing, 301-304
quarters, 304
in reports, 379
separators, 304
Status function, 294-295
subtotalling on, 354-355
subtracting, 69, 294
type checking, 198
unstored calculations, 295

DateToText function, 280

DayOfWeek function, 278, 300-301

Define Fields command (File menu), 185, 189, 461

Define Fields dialog, 59
field order, 76
Foreign key validity check, 138
Summary fields, 348

Define Relationships dialog, 115-116, 120-122, 126

Define Scripts dialog, 444

Define Value Lists command (File menu), 138

Delete all records, 522

Delete portal row, 522

Delete Record command (Records menu), 159, 522

deleting
cascading, 153-155
children to deleted table, 161-162
Delete Record command, 159, 522
fields, 77-78
restricted, 159-160
with scripts, 465-468

delimiters, 332, 335-336

design, planning, 22-24

Developer layouts, 356

Developer's Notes script, 450

diagram creation, 58

DialogMagic
password changes, 193
resetting auto-entered fields, 111

dialup connections, 529

division, money, 358

dollar ($) signs in Number fields, 71

drilling down, 398-400

drivers, ODBC, 508

DSN (Data Source Name), 507-508, 512

duplicated records
auto-entry data, 188
checking for, 468
eliminating, 437

duplicating layouts, 232

duplicating records, 476

E

e4Marketing, 501

ecKnowledge ®, 516

Edit menu commands
Edit Relationship dialog, 116, 121
Preferences, 255

Edit Relationship dialog box, 116

email, 500, 505

empty values, 41

endless loops, Mac, escaping, 434

Enter Find Mode, 447

EnterFindMode function, 371

entities. *See also* **Entity Relationship Diagrams**
conversion to files, 56
naming, 42, 51
planning, 39-40

Entity Relationship Diagrams, 24, 39, 85, 94-98
attributes, 40-42, 46
bottom up method, 43
candidate lists, 42-43
classes of entities, 43
crowsfoot lines, 49
defining relationships, 44-47
entities, 42, 46-47
finalizing, 51
formalizing, 49-51
naming conventions, 51
one-to-one relationships, 47
portals, dumb tricks, 396
reports, 40
singleton, 47
software for, 49
starting at heart of, 43-44

system requirements, 48-49
top down method, 42
user interfaces, 215-217
ERDs. *See* **Entity Relationship Diagrams**
error handling, 492
creating error messages, 369
ErrorCapture, 372
ranges of errors, 370
scripts, 368-371
error messages, 401, 371
CurrentError, 368
invalid Foreign key, 139
error pages, 263
Error step 301, 521-522
error trapping
Error 301, 521-522
text calculations, 282
ErrorCapture, 372
Exact function, 279
Excel, importing ODBC data from Filemaker, 509-511
Exit Script function, 410
Export step, 447
exporting, 498
carriage returns, 211
check box data, 180
email, 505
faxing, 505
ODBC, 509-511
PDF files, 505
reports, 518
SYLK files, 505
to Web pages, 267-269
to word-processing, 313-316
eXtensible Style Language(XSL), 517

F

faxing, 505
FaxSTF, 505
FaxTool, 500, 505
Fetch Chunk Size, 508
Field Definition Tables, 24
Field Format command (Format menu), 140, 194
Field Specification Lists, 56-59
fields. *See also* **data entry**
Allow Entry into Field option, 285
Analyzer tool, 80
from attributes, 56
automatic entry, 185-188
blocking entry to, 118-119
boilerplate text, 71
break, 349
Calculation. *See* Calculation fields
changing names, 79
changing types of, 78-79
constant, 130
constraints, 56
Container. *See* Container fields
copying formatting, 232
creating, 110
Custom Web Publishing, 261-262
dates, 62-66, 71-72
Define Fields dialog box, 59
defining, 98
deleting, 77-78
displaying related, 117-120
finding in, 65
formatting, 62, 65-69, 401
Global, 75, 456-457
graphic. *See* Container fields
graphic formatting, 401

hiding, 415
importing, 81
indexes to, 62, 64
keys, 56
Merge, 192-194
naming, 59-62, 79, 112
Number, 64-66, 71
numbers in text fields, 63
numeric IDs of, 79
one-to-many relationships, 57
options, 56
order of listing, 76
phone numbers. *See* telephone numbers
planning, 24, 52, 90, 98
prefixes, 62
printing list of, 80
question marks in, 68
QuickTime format, 74
Repeating, 338
restrictions on, 114
RTF, 314
searching and replacing, 323-326
selecting for relationships, 116
serial number, 110-111
Set Fields, 457
sole guests, 527
sound. *See* Container fields
specifying, 56-57, 59
Summary, 69, 75, 348-352, 354
Text, 64, 68, 70-71, 379
text in number fields, 65
time, 67, 72-73. *See also* dates
types, 56, 62-64, 78-79
validating dates, 65
View Only, 118
without layouts, 403
zip codes, 70

Fields command (Define menu), 189

File menu commands
Define Fields, 185
Define Value Lists, 138
Import, 512
Relationships, 115, 120

file sharing, 529
ODBC, 507
Web Companion, 257-259

File Sharing dialog, 257-259

File Structure Diagrams, 24, 52-54, 58

File Toolbox, 211

FileMaker Pro 5 Unlimited, 524-525

FileMaker Server, 502, 524
access methods, 527
backups, 530
configuration features, 525-526
copies only publishing, 259
file service, 523, 529
files per client limitation, 530
hardware requirements, 525
hosting methods, 524
installation, 525, 530
IP addresses, 527-528
memory requirements, 531
performance options, 526
publishing to Web, 259
remote administration, 528
safe hosting, 527
screen savers, 532
service method, 525
sole guests, 527
troubleshooting, 531
Virtual Memory, 532

files
access, 417-420
closing all, 459
compression, 531
constant, 130-131
creating, 108
designing for multiuser systems, 521
extensions, 109
field creation, 110
handling of missing by FileMaker, 110
hosted, maximum, 526
joins between. *See* joins
listing with button, 109
maximum number of, 220, 530
naming, 108-110, 529
networks, 110
opening in multiuser systems, 529
planning, 86
QuickTime format, 74
recovering, 530
relationships between. *See* relationships
safe hosting, 527
scripts, 445
self-joins, 97, 422-431
startup, 455

filtering records in portals, 418

Find mode, 459, 474

finding
by example for scripts, 447
dates, 475
multiple criteria, 127
relationships, 127
scripts for, 474-475
within portals, 127

fixed values, 76

fixed-length records, 331-335

folders, multiuser environments, 530

Footers
editable, 366
field types in, 379

Foreign keys
cascading updates, 136
compound, 169-171
defined, 134
empty, 140
Field Specification Lists, 57
multiple, 149, 151-152
naming, 112
populating methods, 140-149, 152
portals for creation of, 142, 144-147
relationships, creating, 122
scripts for assignment, 147-148, 150, 152
scripts for creating, 143-144
validity, 134, 137-149, 152

Format menu commands
Field Format, 140, 194
Sliding & Printing, 240, 347

format pages, 252-253, 263

formatting
copying, 232, 343
fields, 62, 65-68
numbers vs. rounding, 328
setting defaults, 230-231, 343
telephone numbers, 284

forms, Custom Web Publishing, 261-263

found sets
capturing ID's of, 471
copying to clipboard, 471
current record only, 492
importing, 334
Omit Record, 475
reports from, 363
Status function, 356

.fp5, 109

functions, 274. *See also* calculations

G

Get method, 261

GetSummary function, 358-361

Global fields, 75
 Container fields with, 401
 in reports, 379
 initialization, 456-457
 naming, 112
 record locking with, 522
 relationships, 401
 scripts, 475
 text fields for editable parts, 366
 validating, 205-206

Go Away layout, 456

Go to Field command, 286, 404

Go to Portal Row command, 486

goalpost characters, 329

Grand Totals, 348

Grand Summaries. *See* Leading Grand Summaries; Trailing Grand Summaries

grandchildren, 128-130

grandparents, 128-130

graphics. *See also* Container fields
 flags for calculations, 312-313
 multiuser systems, 531
 object movement, 234

groups, 192-193, 208

H

Halt Script, 410, 482

hand-held computers, 499, 502-503

HanDBase, 502

Headers, 344
 editable, 366
 field types in, 379

Hosts button, 520

Hour function, 306

HTML, 268, 517
 CDML, 253-254
 editors, 254
 format pages, 252-253
 forms, 261-263

HTTP protocols, 253

I

IF, 307-312, 486

Import command (File menu), 512

Import step, 447, 522

importing, 498
 custom delimiters, 335-336
 fixed-length records, 333-335
 found sets, 334
 Import Order option, 335
 JDBC, 516
 ODBC data, 512, 514-515
 parent records, 168
 referential integrity, 167-169, 172
 scripts, 451-452
 serial numbers, 111, 153

indexes, 62, 64
 calculated key fields, 184
 paragraph identification, 405
 relationships, 129

inner joins, 435

Insert Calculated Result, 492

Insert step, 522

installation, FileMaker Server, 530

Instant Web Publishing, 254-257, 259

Int function, 277

interface prototyper, 245-248

interfaces, 214. *See also* layouts
 aligning objects, 233-235
 bolding text, 231
 buttons, 221, 224-225, 238-240, 246
 colors, using in, 224, 229
 consistency in, 226-227, 230
 copying formats, 232
 cross platform font, 232
 data entry, 228, 237-238
 default formatting, 230-231
 default views, 220
 deleting records, 229
 drawing programs, copying from, 232
 duplicating layouts, 232
 Entity Relationship Diagrams, 215-217
 external, 500
 font selection, 231
 found sets, 222
 grouping by function, 224-225, 240
 hidden layouts, 217
 italic text, 231
 key fields, 237-238
 key rules for, 221-222
 labels and headings, 226
 layout schemas, 230

layouts, 217
limiting choices, 227
lists, 228, 240
menus, 218-220, 247
minor information in, 224
navigation, 216-220, 240
parent-child navigation, 216
peer reviews of, 228
planning, 214-215
prototype testing, 243-248
required fields, 238
screen sizes, 223
scrolling, 222-223
search buttons, 240
selecting from lists, 225-226, 228
single record view, 222
sizing, 222-223, 230
sorting in, 222, 228
tabs, 217-221, 224, 246-247
task lists, 215
task sequences, 238
user mindsets, 221
views, button for switching, 224
welcome screens, 220

Internet access, 266

Intranets, 524

IP addresses, 527-528

IP guest limit, 257

IPX/SPX, 520

IsEmpty function, 284

IsValid function, 461

J

Java
API, 516
applets, 524
JavaScript, 265, 271
JDBC, 516

JDBC, 516

Jfile, 502

join files
for reports, 365-366
parent-to-parent navigation script, 464
planning, 94, 97-98
referential integrity, 169-171

joins. *See also* **relationships**
inner, 435
outer, 435-438
self-joins, 97, 422-431

K

keys
calculated, 403, 405-406, 414
Foreign. *See* Foreign keys
ID history, 425
Primary. *See* Primary keys
self-joins, 428

L

Landscape setting, 452

Lasso, 251-252, 271-272

Last function, 339

Layout menu commands, Set Layouts Order, 217

Layout Setup dialog, 346

Layout view
Portal tool, 124
specifying related fields, 117

layouts. *See also* **interfaces**
aligning objects, 233-235
copying formats, 232
default formatting, 230-231
Developer, 356
displaying related fields, 117-120

duplicating, 232
Fixed Paper Margins option, 373-374
for reports. *See* reports, 342
Go Away, 456
locking out users, 456
maximum length, 363
navigation scripts, 459-461
object's coordinates, 234
parts. *See* parts
preventing access to, 165
scripts for returning to same, 370
SecureFM, 456
selection with scripts, 372, 455-456, 460
single record view, 222
Size palette, 230
sizing, 222-223
Summary fields, 348
Web, 259

Layouts menu commands, Part Setup, 349

Leading Grand Summaries, 344
Browse mode, 382
field types in, 379

Leading Sub-summaries, 345
Browse mode, 381
field types in, 379

Left function, 279, 281-282, 337

legacy data, 175

Length function, 279, 282

links, 260-261

literal text
Local Data Access Companion, 506
maximum number of characters, 315

logging scripts, 483

lookup fields, 130, 189-191

loops, exiting, 485

M

Macs and PCs, mixed systems, 250
mail merges, 321-325
many-to-many-to-many relationships, 431-435
margins, 373
measurement units, changing, 230
medians, 374-378
menus. *See also* **commands**
   for user navigation, 218-220
   locking users out of, 456-457
   referential integrity, 164-165
Merge fields, 192-194
merges, 321-325
Microsoft Excel, 509-511
Microsoft Management Console Server management, 525, 530
Middle function, 279, 281-282, 336-337
MiddleWords function, 292
Minute function, 306
Mod function, 277, 298
modes
   selecting with scripts, 459
   troubleshooting, 491
modules, script, 450-452
modulo. *See* **Mod function**
money. *See* **currency**
multiuser systems
   cache hits, 531
   clients, maximum number of, 526
   configuration, 526
   dialup connections, 529
   file design, 521
   file service, 523
   FileMaker Pro 5 Unlimited, 524
   FileMaker Server. *See* **FileMaker Server**
   files, maximum, 526, 530
   files, opening in, 529
   folders, 530
   graphics, 531
   Hosts button, 520
   IP addresses, 528
   network protocols for, 520
   peer-to-peer mode, 520, 523-524
   performance options, 526
   platform specific scripts, 529
   problems, 110
   program linking, 527
   record locking, 521-523
   remote administration, 526, 528
   remote connection scripts, 529
   Replace command, 488
   safe hosting, 527
   sole guests, 527
   troubleshooting, 527, 531
   unintended results, 521

N

names (of persons)
   calculations, 290-293
   revising, 378
naming
   fields, 59-62, 112
   files, 108-110
   prefixes, 62
   Primary keys, 111, 168
   relationships, 112-113
   reserved characters, 60-61
   scripts, 448-449
   serial numbers, 111

NAT (network address translation), 528
network access, 266
network address translation (NAT), 528
networks. *See also* multiuser systems
   AppleTalk, 520
   dialup connections, 529
   Intranets, 524
   IPX/SPX, 520
   Macintosh OS, 520
   mixed systems (Mac and Windows), 250
   NAT, 528
   peer-to-peer mode, 520
   ports, 528-529
   protocols, 520
   RAIC, 525
   remote access, 529
   remote dial-up, 524
   socket availability formula, 523-524
   speed of access, 531
   subnets, 530
   TCP/IP, 520, 528
   TimBukTu, 529
   UDP, 528
   WANs, 524
   Web Server programs, 525
   Windows, 520
   Wireless Application Protocol, 525
New Millennium Communications, 456, 501
nonprintable areas, 346, 373-374
Number fields, 64-65, 71
   dollar ($) sign in, 71
   in reports, 379
   type checking, 198
   validity checking, 202
Number Format dialog box, 65-66

O

ODBC (Open Database Connectivity), 498, 506
  adding FileMaker as data source, 506
  advanced options, 508-509
  drivers, 508
  DSN (Data Source Name), 507-508, 512
  exporting, 509-511
  Fetch Chunk Size, 508
  file sharing, 507
  Import Field Mapping dialog, 515
  importing data, 512, 514
  Local Data Access Companion, 506
  querying via TCP/IP, 506
  Remote Data Access Companion, 506
  Select ODBC Data Source dialog, 512
  SQL query builder, 513, 515
  support for, 272
  Use Remote Connection option, 508

Omit Record, 475

Open Database Connectivity. *See* **ODBC**

operators, 274

OR, 204

outer joins, 435-438

overlapping fields, 284-285, 287-289

P

Page Margins command (View Menu), 346

page numbers as break fields, 355

Page Setup command, 452

Page Setup step, 447

Paint Bucket tool, 288

Palm computers, 499, 502-503

Palm Query Applications (PQAs), 503-504

paragraphs, 405

parents
  cascading deletes, 153-155
  creating records from within children, 166-167
  deleting from scripts, 465
  displaying child data, 127-128
  grandparents, 128-130
  lists of related, 425-426
  restricted deletes, 123, 159-160
  self-joins, 422
  sorting children within, 123-124
  viewing all in portal, 396-397

Part Definition dialog, 349

Part Setup command (Layouts menu), 349

Part Setup dialog, 346

parts, 343
  Bodies, 345, 351, 363
  breaking at page boundaries, 346
  footers, 366
  Global text fields with, 366
  headers, 344, 366
  kinds of, 343
  Leading Grand Summaries, 344, 379, 382
  Leading Sub-summaries, 345, 379, 381
  limit per layout, 343
  Part Definition dialog, 349

  Part Setup dialog, 346
  printing, 346-347
  Sub-summaries, 344, 354
    by page, 355-356
    dates, 355
    leading, 345, 379, 381
    leading or trailing options, 350
    many-to-many-to-many relationships, 432, 434-435
    missing, 379
    reports from children, 363
    scripting, 372
    subtotals, 351
    Summary fields in, 348, 380
    Trailing, 345, 352
    without Summary fields, 357
  Title Footers, 345
  Title Headers, 344
  Trailing Grand Summaries, 345, 351-352, 379, 382
  Trailing Sub-summaries, 345, 352, 379, 381

passwords
  create only, 208
  DialogMagic, 193
  groups, 192-193
  referential integrity, 165
  remote administration, 528
  scripts needing, 490

Paste step, 492, 522

PatternCount function, 289-291, 311

PDAs (Personal Digital Assistants), 499, 502-504, 525

PDF (Portable Document Format), 505

peer-to-peer mode, 520, 523-524

percentage calculations, 311

Perform Find, 447

Perform Script step, 445, 449

phone numbers. *See* telephone numbers

pipelining, 128-129, 430

planning, 22-24
   attributes, 40-41, 54, 85
   automation, 35
   benchmarks, 27
   budgets, 35-38, 48
   business problem to be solved, 35
   business rules, 88
   consulting, 38-39
   current system, 27
   data entry, 29-30, 35-36
   database structures, 39
   documentation, 34, 38
   entities, 39-40
   Entity Relationship Diagrams. *See* Entity Relationship Diagrams
   Field Definition Tables, 24
   fields, 52, 90, 98
   File Structure Diagrams, 24, 52-54
   files, 86
   filing systems, 35-36, 54
   forms, 28
   functionality, 36
   goals, 35-36
   join files, 94, 97-98
   manager interviews, 26-28
   many-to-many relationships, 85
   naming conventions, 51
   organizational goals, 27
   PQAs, 503-504
   proposals, 30, 34, 37
   purpose of system, 36
   records, 87-90
   relationships, 97
   reports, 27-28, 35, 241-243
   security, 35
   special automation, 28
   staff interviews, 28-30
   studying customers' needs, 24-25
   tables, 52
   time to completion, 37-38
   user interfaces, 214-215
   Web access, 35
   Web delivery, 264-266

platform independence, 501-502

Plug-In Architecture, 500

plug-ins, 500
   email, 505
   ODBC, 506
   remote administration, 528
   vendors, 501
   Web Companion, 255

Plug Ins tab, Web Companion, 255

pop-up lists, 176-177, 181-182

pop-up menus, 177-178

Portable Document Format. *See* **PDF**

portals, 396, 420
   access files with, 417-420
   all parent records, viewing, 396-397
   borders and fills, 416
   children, 123, 144-147
   conditional value lists with, 398-400
   creating, 124-126
   deleting records, 125
   disappearing, 414-416
   displaying data, 127-128
   drilling down in, 398-400
   editing in, 419-420
   filtering, 405-406, 418
   find within, 127
   forced updates, 414
   Foreign keys, populating, 142, 144-147
   highlighting selections, 401-402
   inserting records, 409-410
   many-to-many-to-many relationships, 432
   match fields, 397
   multiple, moving records between, 403-404
   options, 125
   parent/child model, 396
   Primary keys, 396
   printing from, 361-363
   record locking, 523
   record subsets, viewing, 405-406
   relationships, 124-126, 400
   as reporting mechanisms, 436-437
   rows, special ordering of, 406-412
   self-joins, 423-426, 428-431
   size limits when printing, 362
   sorted by users, 412, 414
   sorting within, 126
   value lists, 184

ports, 257, 260, 528-529

Position function, 280, 319, 336

Post method, 261

preferences, locking layout tools, 232

Preferences command (Edit menu), 255

prefixes for field names, 112

Preview mode, 379-381, 385
Primary keys
  auto-entry of, 137
  changed, 135-136
  defined, 134
  editing, 136, 152-153
  Field Specification Lists, 57
  naming, 111-112, 168
  non-unique, 134-135
  pipelining, 129
  portals, 396
  relationships, creating, 122
  reusing, 136
  uniqueness, 134, 136-137
Print Setup, 447, 452
printing. *See also* reports
  current record only, 489
  from scripts, 447, 472-474
  nonprintable areas, 373-374
  orientation, 372
  parts, 346-347
  reports, 241-243, 346-347, 373-374
  scripts, 484
  startup scripts for, 457-458
privileges
  editing fields, 192-193, 208
  Web, 264
Professional Data Management, 501, 506
program linking, 527
Protolight Software, 211, 501
prototyper, 245-248

Q-R

QuickTime movies, 74, 531

radio buttons, 178-181, 310-312
RAIC (Redundant Array of Inexpensive Computers), 525
Random function, 326-329
ranges, testing for, 310
record locking, 521-523
records. *See also* rows
  creating, 170, 468
  disappearing children, 124
  duplicating, 476
  ordering of, 407
  planning, 87-90
  relationships, 116
Records menu commands, Delete Record, 159
recovering files, 530
Redundant Array of Inexpensive Computers (RAIC), 525
references, revising, 378
referential integrity, 134
  children with multiple parents, 149, 151-152
  compound Foreign keys, 169-171
  Delete Record command, 159
  deleted records tables, 161-162
  deletion of parents, 153-156, 158
  Foreign keys, 134-135, 137-149, 152
  imported records, 167-169
  incomplete parent records, 166-167
  join files, 169-171
  layouts, 165-166
  menus, 164-165
  need for, 134
  passwords, 165

Primary keys, 134-137, 152-153
  reassigning children, 155-156, 158
  restricted deletes, 159-160
  rules of, 134, 136-140
  script access, 166
  testing for, 172
  threats and countermeasures, 152-169
refreshing in scripts, 485
relationships
  allow creation of related records option, 117, 122-123, 144
  blocking field entry, 118-119
  calculated key fields, 183-184
  cascading deletes, 153-155
  chains of, 128-130
  changed file names, 113
  child-to-parent, 114-120
  conditional value lists, 181-185
  constant, 130-131
  Constant value, 397
  creating, 112-117, 120-122
  creation of related records option, 397
  Define dialog, 115-116, 120-122
  deletion option, 117, 122, 153-155
  displaying, 117-120
  Edit Relationship dialog, 116, 121
  fields, selecting, 116
  finds, 119, 127
  flow of information, 113-114

global values, 401
golden rule of, 112
indexing, 129
joins. *See* joins
lookup fields, 189
lookups, 130
many-to-many self-joins, 426-431
many-to-many-to-many, 431-435
naming, 112-113
one-to-many, 113
options, 117, 122-124
parent-to-child, 120-131
pipelining, 128-129
planning, 97
portals, 124-126, 400
primary keys, 129
for pushing data, 404
records, 116
replicating data, 130
Restricted Delete, 123
restrictions on fields, 114
self-joins. *See* joins, self-joins
sorting, 117, 123-124, 126
viewing rules, 113

Relationships command (File menu, Define submenu), 115, 120

Relookup, 522

remote access, 529

remote administration, 256, 526, 528

Remote Data Access Companion, 506

remote dial-up, 524

Repeating fields, 338

Replace command, 488, 522

Replace function, 319-320, 324-326, 329, 356, 434

replicating data, 130

Report Wizard, 342-343

reports
bodies, 345, 351, 363
break fields, 349
broken lines, 347
Browse mode, 381-382
Case function in, 360-361
from children, 363-365
columns, number of, 351-352
copying formatting to objects, 343
editable headers and footers, 366
exporting, 518
Fixed Paper Margins option, 373-374
Footers, 366
found sets of children, 363
Grand Totals, 348
Headers, 344, 366
join files for, 365
layouts for, 342-343
Leading Grand Summaries. *See* Leading Grand Summaries
Leading Sub-summaries. *See* Leading Sub-summaries
margins, 346
maximum length, 363
medians, 374-378
methods of generation, 242
nonprintable areas, 346, 373-374
of search results, 367-373
orientation, 372
page breaks, 346, 355
from parents, 361-363, 365
parent vs. children files, 361
parts. *See* parts
placeholders for calculations, 360

planning, 27-28, 35, 241-243
portals as, 436-437
Preview mode, 379-381, 385
previews, 372
Print mode, 379-381
printing, 241-243, 346-347, 373-374
samples, 350-351
scripts for, 371, 470-474
sliding data, 347
source options, 361
Sub-summaries, 344, 354
  by page, 355-356
  dates, 355
  leading or trailing options, 350
  many-to-many-to-many relationships, 432, 434-435
  missing, 379
  reports from children, 363
  scripting, 372
  subtotals, 351
  Summary fields in, 348, 380
  Trailing, 345, 352
  without Summary fields, 357
subtotals, 348-350
  by time periods, 354-355
  multiple levels of, 353, 363
  in portals, 362
summary, 242
Summary fields in, 348-354, 379-381
Title Footers, 345
Title Headers, 344
Trailing Grand Summaries, 345, 351-352
Trailing Sub-summaries, 345, 352
types of, 350

variation from view modes, 378-386
Web Companion, 265
with portals, 361-363
wizard, 342-343

reserved characters, 60-61

Reset Values command (Scripts menu), 477

Restore, 474, 485

restricted deletes, 155, 159-160

Right function, 281-282, 337

Round function, 328-329

rounding calculations, 275-276

rows. *See also* **records**
identification, 110-111
inserting in portals, 407
portals, 125
tracking, 244

RTF files, 313-314

S

safe hosting, 527

Satellite Forms, 502

Save A Copy, 523

screen savers, 532

screen sizes, effects on layouts, 223

Script Definition dialog, 445-446

ScriptMaker, 444, 449, 493

scripts
access rights, 490
Allow User Abort (Off), 371
Analyzer, 483
Apple events, 487
Beep steps, 483

Browse Mode, 371
button launching, 476-479
Cancel buttons, 368
capturing ID's of found sets, 471
category selection, 400
child-to-parent navigation, 461-462
clearing forms, 370
close boxes, 370
closing all files, 459
combining keys from multiple files, 433-435
commenting out steps, 482
comments, 450, 488
comparisons, 490
Constants files, 457
Continue buttons, 368
Copy, 492
creating from steps, 446
data entry permission, 195
dates, finding, 475
Define Scripts dialog, 444
defined, 444
deleting records, 159-164, 465-468
Developer's Notes, 450
duplicated, 493
duplicates, eliminating, 438, 468
duplicating records, 476
editable report parts, 367
editing with keyboard controls, 446
Error 301, 521-522
error handling, 368-371, 492
ErrorCapture, 372
Exit Script function, 410
files, 445
filtering in portals, 418
Find All, 462
Find Mode, 474
finding by example, 447
finds, canned, 474-475

fixed-length record importing, 333
Foreign key assignment, 147-148, 150, 152
found sets, 222
freezing the screen, 486
Global fields, 475
Go to Portal Row command, 486
Halt Script function, 410, 482
hung, stopping, 372
Ifs, 486
importing, 451-452
importing records with, 164, 337
initializing variables, 456-457, 460
insert operations, 489
inserting Calculated Result, 492
inserting records in portals, 409-410
Landscape setting, 452
layout selection, 370, 372, 455-456, 459-462, 487
logging, 458, 483
loops, exiting, 485
maximizing windows at startup, 454-455
medians, 375-378
mode choice, 459, 461
modules, 450-452
moving records in portal, 407-410
name-dependent, 413
naming, 448-449
new child records with keys, 143-144
Omit Record, 475
opening existing, 445
outer joins, 436
page orientation, 372
Page Setup command, 452
parent-child navigation, 461-465
parent-to-parent navigation, 464-465

parents, checking for valid, 461-462
Paste, 492
pausing, 482
Perform Script step, 445
platform specific, 529
posting messages to users, 487
previews of reports, 372
printing, 484
printing from, 472-474
processor speed, 486
protecting from users, 452
random numbers, 326
ranges of dates, 489
reassigning children, 158
record locking, 521-522
records, creating new, 468
recursive calls to, 488
referencing external, 491
referential integrity, 166
refreshing in, 485
remote connection, 529
Replace command, 488
reports, 371, 470-474
Restore, 474, 485
restoring windows, 454
returning to original file, 489
returning to original record, 469
running, methods of, 453
Script Definition dialog, 445-446
ScriptMaker. *See* ScriptMaker
search and replace, 323-326
searches for reports, 367-373
Set Error Capture, 492, 521-522
SetField, 293, 457, 486, 488-489, 492
settings, 446-447, 490, 493
Show Message, 482
show_selected_customer, 462
show_selected_payment, 463
showing all records, 456
shutdown, 458-459
skipped records, 488
sorting with, 411-413, 447, 468-470
Speak, 487
square brackets in, 446
startup, 453-458, 490
Status Area, 455
Status functions, 491, 521, 529
steps. *See* steps
subscript option, 473
troubleshooting, 482-492
unsorting, 456
users cancelling, 371
validity checks, 175
View menu, 446
Web, 251
Web detail reports, 269-271
welcome screens, 457
windows, sizing, 454, 462

Scripts menu commands, Reset Values, 477

Scrolling user interfaces, 222-223

searching. *See also* **finding**
check box fields, 180
replacing within a field, 323-326
reports from, 367-373

Seconds function, 306

SecureFM, 456

security
planning, 35
Web, 264

Select All, 523

Select ODBC Data Source dialog, 512

self-joins. *See* joins, self-joins

SendEmail command, 500, 505

serial communication, 506

serial numbers
automatic entry, 186
creating, 110-111
importing, 111, 153

server services. *See* FileMaker Server

Set Alignment dialog, 234

Set Error Capture, 492, 521-522

Set Field step, 446, 457, 523

Set Layouts Order command (Layout menu), 217

SetField function, 293, 370, 486, 488-489, 492

Shift key, 235-237

shortcuts, field formatting, 69

Show command (View menu), 239

Show Message function, 370, 482

show_selected_customer, 462

show_selected_payment script, 463

shutdown scripts, 458-459

simulating typing in Calculation fields, 284-285, 287

single user setting, 438

size limitations of databases, 74

slashes, double (//), 322

Sliding & Printing command (Format menu), 240, 347

Social Security numbers, 202-203, 281

sockets availability formula, 523-524

soft validation, 204

sole guests, 527

Sort step, 447

sorting
  check box fields, 180
  example for scripts, 447
  followed by Find, 492
  GetSummary function, 359
  interfaces, 222, 228
  page number, 356
  parent fields, 120
  portals, 126, 412-413
  relationships, 123-126
  reports from children, 363
  scripts for, 372, 411, 468-470

sound files, 531

Speak, 487

Specify Calculation dialog, Storage Options dialog, 295

SQL query builder, 513, 515

startup files, 455

startup scripts, 453-458, 490

Status (CurrentError) function, 368

Status Area scripts, 455

Status function, 356
  CurrentError, 491
  CurrentGroups, 193
  CurrentMessageChoice, 370
  dates, 294-295

StatusCurrentError, 521

StatusCurrentPlatform, 529

steps, 446-447, 522

Storage Options dialog, 295

style sheets (XML), 517-518

Sub-summaries, 344, 354
  by page, 355-356
  dates, 355
  leading or trailing options, 350
  many-to-many-to-many relationships, 432, 434-435
  missing, 379
  reports from children, 363
  scripting, 372
  subtotals, 351
  Summary fields in, 348, 380
  Trailing, 345, 352
  without Summary fields, 357

subnets, 530

subscript option, 473

Substitute function, 320, 322, 325

subtotals, 348-350, 358
  by time periods, 354-355
  in portals, 362
  multiple levels of, 353, 363

Summary fields, 69, 75, 348-352, 354
  Browse mode, 382, 384
  fractions in, 380
  GetSummary function, 358-361
  Grand Totals, 348
  in reports, 379-380
  reusing, 349
  running counts, 380
  statistical, 380
  in Sub-summaries, 380
  subtotals. *See* subtotals

Sylk format, 316, 505

System 8 sound files, 74

T

T-Square, 233

Tab Interface tool, 245-248

tab order, 174, 209-210

tables
  creating, 108
  fields in. *See* fields
  planning, 52
  row identification, 110-111

tabs, 217-221

task lists interfaces, 215

TCP/IP, 528
  access, 266
  multiuser systems, 520
  querying ODBC through, 506
  subnets, 530

telephone numbers, 70, 281-287

text
  & (ampersand), 279, 283, 314
  addresses, 283-284
  aligning baselines, 235
  calculations, 279-285, 287-293, 313-314
  conditional, 287-289
  DateToText function, 280
  editing calculations, 330
  error trapping, 282
  Exact function, 279
  fields. *See* Text fields

Left function, 279, 281-282, 337
Length function, 279, 282
literal, maximum number of characters, 315
mail merges, 321-323
Middle function, 279-282, 336-337
MiddleWords function, 292
names, 290-293
parsing names, 290-293
parsing numbers, 281-282
PatternCount function, 289-291
Position function, 280, 319, 336
Replace function, 319-320, 324-326
returns, 284
Right function, 281-282, 337
search and replace, 323-326
searching for strings, 289
spaces, 284
Substitute function, 320, 322, 325
telephone numbers, 284-285, 287
TimeToText function, 280
Trim function, 334

Text fields, 64, 68, 70-71, 379

Text Format dialog box, 68

Theme Creator, 342

themes, 342-343

TimBukTu, 529

time. *See also* **dates**
automatic entry, 186
calculations, 305-306
Hour function, 306
Minute function, 306
Seconds function, 306
subtracting, 305
TimeToText function, 280

Time fields, 72-73, 379

Time Format dialog box, 67

TimeToText function, 280

Title Footers, 345
Browse mode, 381
field types in, 379

Title Headers, 344
Browse mode, 381
field types in, 379

tools, reusing, 232

Trailing Grand Summaries, 345, 351-352
Browse mode, 382
field types in, 379

Trailing Sub-summaries, 345, 352
Browse mode, 381
field types in, 379

Trim function, 334

TROI plug-in, 267, 269-271, 316, 501, 506

troubleshooting
access rights for scripts, 490
Analyzer, 483
Apple events, 487
comparisons, 490
data problems, 174-176
error handling, 492
FileMaker Server, 531
Go to Portal Row command, 486
Ifs, 486
imported scripts, 491
insert operations, 489
interrupting scripts, 482
layout selection failures, 487
logging, 483
Mac/Windows incompatibility, 491
modes, 491
multiuser systems, 527, 531
Preview, 489
processor speed, 486
ranges of dates, 489
Replace command, 488
Restore, 485
row mismatches, 490
scripts, 482-492
SetField, 486
skipped records, 488
slow conditional execution, 486
startup scripts, 453, 490
Status [CurrentError], 491
validation messages, 205
variables, 485
version specific bugs, 488

types of fields. *See* **fields, types**

typos in data, 174

U

UDP, 528

underscore characters, 448

UNIX, posting HTML files to, 267

Usage database, 528

Use Remote Connection option, 508

user access, referential integrity, 164

user interfaces. *See* **interfaces**

user navigation, 217-220

V

validity checking, 57, 197
by calculation, 199-200, 202-203
conditional, 206-208
compound Foreign keys, 169-171

empty fields, 198-199
existing values option, 199
Global fields, 205-206
in a range option, 199
messages, 205
Number fields, 202
scripts for, 175
Social Security numbers, 202-203
soft validation, 204
strictness options, 204
type checking, 198
unique data option, 198
users circumventing, 174
validate only if field has been modified option, 207
value list membership option, 199

value lists
conditional value lists, 181-185
indexes, 182
portals, 184
Use Value List from Another File option, 184
validity checking, 199
ValueListItems function, 424

ValueListItems function, 424

variables, initializing in scripts, 456-457, 460

versions, compatibility, 531

versions, trapping, 529

View menu commands
Page Margins, 346
Show, 239

View Only fields, formatting, 118

Virtual Memory, 532

Visio Professional, 58

W

Waves in Motion, 80, 483, 501

Web, 250
browsers. *See* browsers
calculating pages, 267-269
CGIs, 251-253
color schemes, 258
Companion. *See* Web Companion
Custom Web Publishing, 254, 260-263
detail records, 269-271
exporting data to Web pages, 267-269
FileMaker legacy, 251-253
FileMaker Pro 5 Unlimited version, 257
FileMaker Pro Server, 259
format pages, 252-253
HTML editors, 254
HTTP protocols, 253
Instant Web Publishing, 254-257, 259
IP guest limit, 257
JavaScript, 271
Lasso, 251-252, 271-272
layouts, 259
limitations, 265-266
operations available, 266
permissions to publish to, 258
planning, 264-266
port option, 257
RAIC, 525
scripts, 251
security, 256-257, 264
Style tab, 258
TROI plug-in, 267, 269-271, 316, 501, 506
turning on sharing, 255
UNIX, 267

Web Companion, 250, 253
as an API to FileMaker, 501
CDML, 253-254, 272
changes in records, 251
color schemes, 258
Companion Interface, 500
configuring, 255-257
connection to databases, 250-251
copies only publishing, 259
Custom Web Publishing, 260-264
file sharing, 257-259
format pages, 253
Get method, 261
Instant Web Publishing, 255-257, 259
Java API with, 516
limitations, 265-266
operations available, 266
planning, 264-266
Plug Ins tab, 255
Post method, 261
reports, 265
search settings, 259
security options, 256-257
sort settings, 259
XML, 518

Web Security Database, 256

Web Server programs, 525

Web servers, FileMaker as, 254

Web Style tab, 258

welcome screens, 220, 457

windows, 454

Windows NT/2000, 530

WinFax Pro, 505

Wireless Application Protocol, 525

Wireless MarkUp Language (WML), 525

World Wide Web. *See* Web

X-Z

XML (eXtensible Markup Language), 517-518, 525

zip codes, 70
zoom levels, 236

Read This Before Opening the Software

License Agreement

By opening this package, you are agreeing to be bound by the following agreement:

You may not copy or redistribute the entire CD-ROM as a whole. Copying and redistribution of individual software programs on the CD-ROM is governed by terms set by the licensors or individual copyright holders.

The installer and code from the author(s) are copyrighted by the publisher and the author(s).

This software is sold as-is, without warranty of any kind, either expressed or implied, including but not limited to the implied warranties of merchantability and fitness for a particular purpose. Neither the publisher nor its dealers or distributors assumes any liability for any alleged or actual damages arising from the use of this program. (Some states do not allow for the exclusion of implied warranties, so the exclusion may not apply to you.)

NOTE: **This CD-ROM uses long and mixed-case filenames requiring the use of a protected-mode CD-ROM Driver.**